D0921967

GED® TEST

Related Titles

GED® Test Power Practice
GED® Test Mathematical Reasoning Flash Review
GED® Test RLA Flash Review
GED® Test Science Flash Review
GED® Test Social Studies Flash Review

GED® TEST

LEARNINGEXPRESS®

NEW YORK

Cataloging-in-Publication Data is on file with the Library of Congress.

Printed in the United States of America

9 8 7 6 5 4 3 2 1

ISBN 978-1-61103-016-7

For more information on LearningExpress, other LearningExpress products, or bulk sales,
please write to us at:
    80 Broad Street
    4th Floor
    New York, NY 10004

Or visit us at:
    www.learningexpressllc.com

CONTENTS ▶

CONTENTS

GED® TEST

INTRODUCTION TO THE GED® TEST ▶

If you're ready to start preparing for the GED® test, earn your high school equivalency credential, and open new doors for academic and career success, then you've come to the right place!

You should choose to take the GED® test if you would like to receive a high school credential but you are unable to complete the graduation requirements at a traditional high school. The GED® test measures how well you understand and analyze high school–level math, reading, writing, science, and social studies. Passing the GED® test, and earning a high school equivalency credential, shows that you have high school–level academic skills. It can help open the door to a better job, a college education, and wonderful new life opportunities.

How to Use This Book

This helpful guide will teach you exactly what you need to know to succeed on this high-stakes exam—what the GED® test is like, how to prepare for test day, and what it will take to earn your best possible scores on each section of the exam. It includes important test information and lots of helpful practice and review. We recommend that you go through each section of the book carefully, giving extra attention to the test areas that you need the most help with. It's our goal to make sure that you are confident and well prepared when you decide to take the official GED® test.

After you are done reviewing all the topics covered on the exam, take the full-length practice tests in Chapters 15 through 18. These exams look a lot like the actual GED® test. Because the tests in this book are on paper—and not on a computer screen—some of the questions can't look exactly like those you will see on test day, but we have made these questions look as close to the computerized version as they can.

You will have a chance to work with a computerized GED® test and all its interactive question types on the free online test you have access to via this book. Visit page 579 to find out how to take this computerized exam.

Good luck with your preparation and on the test!

All about the GED® Test

The GED® test measures how well you can apply problem solving, analytical reasoning, and critical thinking alongside your understanding of high school–level math, reading, writing, science, and social studies. Passing the GED® test proves you have a high school–level education. If you pass, you will be awarded a GED® test credential, the equivalent of a high school diploma.

Four separate tests make up the GED® test:

1. Mathematical Reasoning
2. Reasoning through Language Arts (RLA)
3. Social Studies
4. Science

To score your best on each test, not only will you need to know the basics of each subject, but you'll also need to use critical thinking, writing, and problem-solving skills.

If this sounds like a lot to handle, don't worry—this book is designed to help you overcome any test anxiety or fear you're experiencing, through careful and effective preparation alongside proven strategies for maximizing your test time and earning your best possible scores.

How Is the Test Taken?

You will take the GED® test on a computer. Although you absolutely do not need to be a computer expert to take the GED® test, you should be comfortable using a mouse and typing on a keyboard.

Test Length

You can choose to take all four GED® tests at once, or you can take each test separately. The entire exam will take about seven hours to complete. The timing for each subject area is as follows:

- Mathematical Reasoning—115 minutes
- Reasoning through Language Arts—150 minutes (including a 10-minute break)
- Science—90 minutes
- Social Studies—90 minutes

When Can You Take the GED® Test?

There are a variety of scheduling options for taking the GED® test, depending on your state and area. Please check with the official GED® Testing Service® for scheduling options available to you:

http://www.gedtestingscrvice.com/
ged-testing-service

Where Can You Take the GED® Test?

To find a GED® testing center that's convenient for you, go online to the following link, choose your location, and enter your zip code:

www.gedtestingservice.com/testers/
locate-a-testing-center

How Do You Sign Up for the Test?

You can sign up for any or all of the GED® tests online at the official GED® Testing Service website and get more information on options in your area.

How Much Will the Test Cost?

Each of the four GED® tests costs $30 to take, for a total of $120 for all four tests.

You can pay for any or all parts of the test you are ready to take. There might also be additional fees, depending on which state you will take the test in. You may be eligible for a fee waiver to help cover the cost; you can contact the official GED® Testing Service for available options for paying for the tests.

How Are the Tests Scored?

A minimum score of 150 is required to pass each test. Each question on the GED® test is assigned a different point value depending on its difficulty. You will find out your score or scores on the same day you take each test.

Question Types

Most of the questions on the GED® test are multiple choice, where you pick the best answer out of four given choices: **a**, **b**, **c**, or **d**. Because you'll take the test on a computer, you'll also see some other kinds of questions, which will ask you to use your mouse to move images around, use the keyboard to type in your answer, and other types of interactivity.

These other question types are called:

- Drag and drop
- Drop-down
- Fill in the blank
- Hot spot
- Short answer and extended response

If you have never used a computer or a mouse before, it may take some getting used to. The key is to practice, practice, practice! Read on to get the information you need to be comfortable with how the GED® test works and what you'll need to do in order to make your way through the test. Here we review each question type carefully, so you'll know exactly what to expect on test day.

Drag and Drop

For these questions, you will need to click on the correct object, hold down the mouse, and drag the object to the appropriate place in the problem, diagram, chart, or graph that you're given. Drag-and-drop questions have two areas; one area shows all of the possible answer choices, and the other area is where you will move the correct answer(s). You will need to drag one or more answers from the first area to the second area.

To answer a drag-and-drop question, you will click and hold the mouse on an answer and move it (drag it) to the correct area of the screen. Then let go of the mouse (drop it). You can remove an answer and switch it with another answer at any time.

You'll see a question similar to this on the test screen:

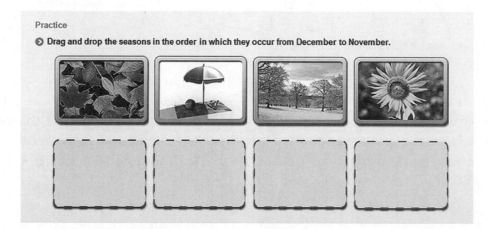

Practice

⊙ **Drag and drop the seasons in the order in which they occur from December to November.**

Of course, within this book you can't drag and drop items. For the purposes of this book, you will choose from a list of items, as you would on a typical drag-and-drop question, and write the correct answer(s) in the appropriate spot.

Drop-Down

In drop-down questions, you will need to select the answer or phrase to complete a sentence or problem from a menu that drops down with the click of a button. Drop-down questions are very similar to multiple-choice questions. To answer the question, click your mouse on the arrow to show all of the answer choices. Then click on your chosen answer to complete the sentence, paragraph, or equation.

You'll see a question similar to this on the test screen:

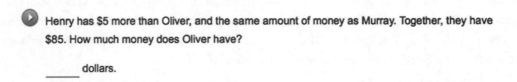

Fill in the Blank

These questions ask you to manually type in answer(s) to a problem rather than selecting from several choices. The fill-in-the-blank questions in this book look almost exactly like the ones you'll encounter in the online test, but here you will of course have to write in your answer instead of typing it.

> Henry has $5 more than Oliver, and the same amount of money as Murray. Together, they have $85. How much money does Oliver have?
>
> _____ dollars.

Hot Spot

For hot-spot questions, you will be asked to click on an area of the screen to indicate where the correct answer is located. For instance, you may be asked to plot a point by clicking on the corresponding online graph or may be asked to click on a certain area of a map.

To answer the question, click on the correct spot of the image provided. You can change your answer by simply clicking on another area.

You'll see a question similar to this on the test screen:

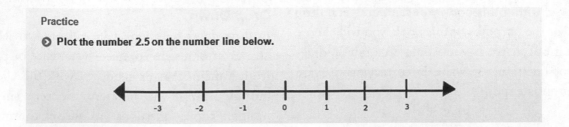

In this book, you may be asked to draw a dot on a specific point or to circle a certain part of a diagram to simulate practicing this type of question.

Short Answer and Extended Response

These types of questions are similar to fill-in-the-blank questions—you must type your response in the provided text box. You should feel comfortable typing on a keyboard in order to answer these questions, since there is a time limit for each test. Therefore, it is essential to practice before the day of the test.

- **Short answer questions** require you to write a paragraph instead of a word or two, usually in response to a passage or an image. These questions can usually be answered with just a few sentences and will probably take about 10 minutes to complete.
- **Extended response questions** require you to write an essay. You will be given 45 minutes to read one or two informational articles (a total of 550 to 650 words) and type an essay response (on the computer, using a simple word processing program) that contains evidence and examples.

When using this book, you can choose to either handwrite your short answers and extended responses or type them on a computer or typewriter.

On test day, the text box you'll see on your screen will look similar to this:

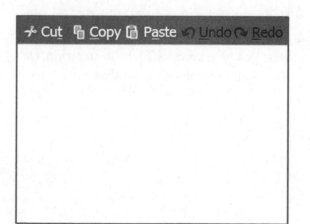

Notice that at the top of the box you will find tools to help you edit your answer if necessary. You can do the following:

- **Select your words:** Before you can copy or cut words or sentences (explained next), you first need to know how to highlight the exact text you want to work with. Highlight text by dragging your mouse across it while holding down the left mouse button.

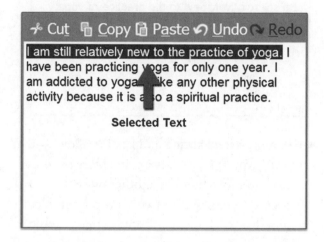

Selected Text

- **Copy and paste:** Copying and pasting allows you to repeat a word or words in another place in your essay.
  - **Step 1**—Highlight the words you want to copy, and then click the "Copy" option on the toolbar.

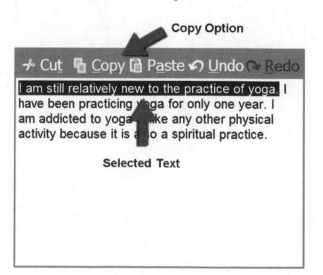

Copy Option

Selected Text

○ **Step 2**—Next, click your mouse where you want to paste the words, and then click the "Paste" option.

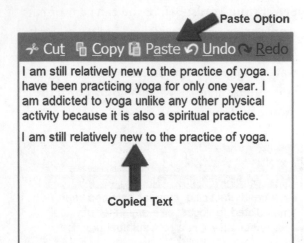

Paste Option

Copied Text

■ **Cut and paste:** Cutting and pasting allows you to select a word or words from one place in your essay and move them to another place.

○ **Step 1**—Highlight the words you want to cut, and then click the "Cut" option on the toolbar.

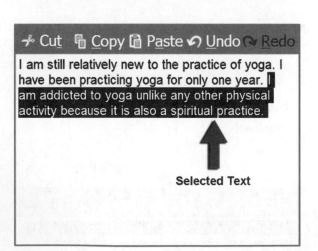

Selected Text

Cut Option

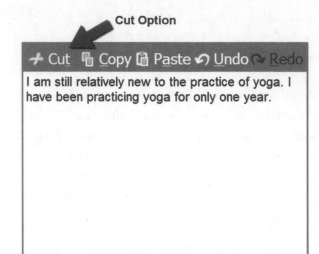

○ **Step 2**—Next, click your mouse where you want to paste the words, and then click the "Paste" option.

Paste Option

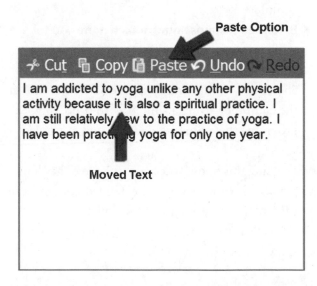

Moved Text

■ **Undo and redo:** If you've accidentally typed in wrong words, you can quickly and easily undo what you have entered. To undo an action, click the "Undo" option on the toolbar.

Undo Option

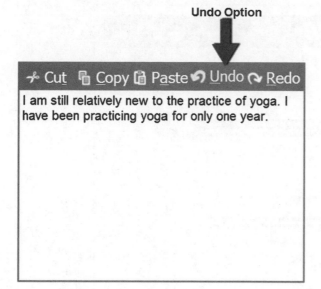

Maybe you've decided *not* to undo your original answer, and you want to go back to what you originally wrote. This is when you redo an action. To reverse an undo action, click the "Redo" option on the toolbar.

Redo Option

Getting Comfortable with the GED® Test

When you're ready to take the GED® test, you'll want to save all your energy for answering questions. You don't want to waste time being unsure of how to use the computer correctly. Use the following information to help you get prepared.

Basic Clicking and Navigation

When you take the GED® test, you'll see different buttons on each screen.

You will need to know how to **point** and **click** these buttons to move through the different pages of the test, find important information, and choose an answer.

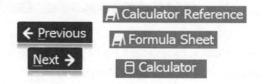

To point and click, move your mouse over the button, image, or text you want to choose and then click the left side of the mouse. (Your cursor will change to a hand when the mouse is over your selected item.)

Single and Split Screen

During the test, you will need to read a passage or look at a graph or other information in order to answer a question. The GED® test will show you this kind of information in one of two ways:

- If it is short, the information or image and its question(s) will be on a single page for you to read and answer.

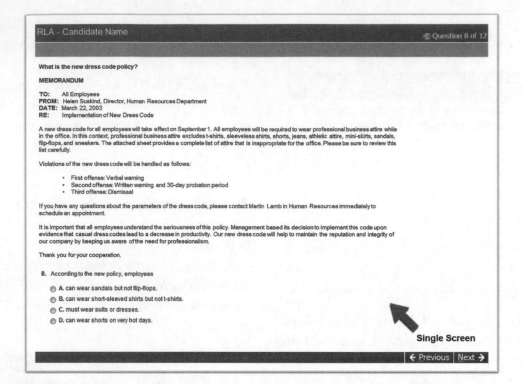

Single Screen

Sometimes there will be a lot of information—for example, a long reading passage. You may see all the information in a **split screen**. In this case, your computer screen will be split into two columns, with the stimulus on one side and the question(s) on the other.

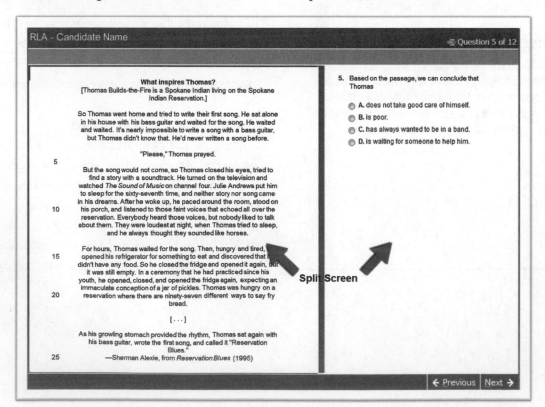

Split Screen

- Sometimes, all of the information will not completely show up on a screen because it is too long. You will need to use the mouse to scroll to see all of the information or a test question. You can use the **scroll bar** to move up or down a document to see the parts that do not show up in the main area of the screen.

- **Vertical scroll bars** will show up on the right side of the window if what you need to read is too long to fit within the window. This lets you move it up and down.
- **Horizontal scroll bars** will show up across the bottom of the window if what you need to read is too wide to fit within the window. This lets you move it left and right.

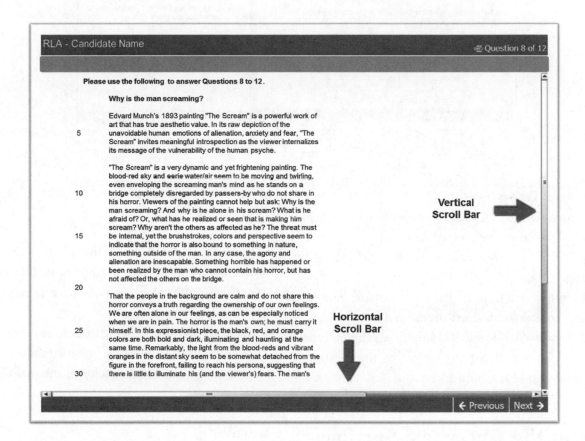

To use the scroll bar, place the mouse pointer over the scroll bar. Hold down the mouse button and drag the scroll bar up or down, or right or left, without letting go of the button.

Page Tabs

Sometimes you will see **page tabs** at the top of a document you are asked to read. Each tab stands for a different page that you must read to answer the questions. You will need to click on each tab to see and read each page in order to answer your questions.

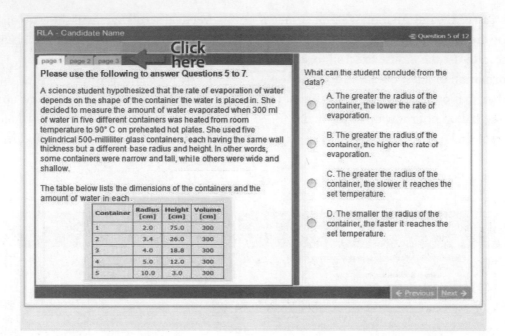

Click and Drag

Sometimes, you will have to move windows that appear on the computer screen in order to answer a question. You can move windows by **clicking and dragging**.

To move a window, place the cursor over it, press and hold down the left mouse button, and then move the mouse while still holding down the button. When you have dragged the object to the location you want, let go of the button.

About the GED® Test Sections

Before you make your way through the rest of the book, let's briefly explore each of the four GED® test sections. The more information you have before test day, the more confident and prepared you'll be for success!

Mathematical Reasoning

On the GED® Mathematical Reasoning test, you will have 115 minutes (just under two hours) to answer 45 questions. These questions will fall into two areas:

quantitative problem solving and algebraic problem solving.

- **Quantitative problem solving** questions cover basic math concepts like multiples, factors, exponents, absolute value, ratios, averages, and probability.
- **Algebraic problem solving** questions cover basic topics in algebra, including linear equations, quadratic equations, functions, linear inequalities, and more.

Calculator

An online calculator, called the **TI-30XS Multi-View™**, will be available to you for most of the questions within the Mathematical Reasoning section. You'll also be able to bring your own TI-30XS Multi-View calculator to the exam for use during the test.

Your first five questions will be non-calculator questions, but the rest of the test will have this on-screen calculator available for you to use. If you have never used the TI-30XS MultiView or another scientific calculator before, be sure to practice using it before you take the actual test.

The GED® Testing Service has created a calculator reference sheet and tutorial videos on its website to help you practice. The reference sheet will also be available for you to use during the test. However, you should be comfortable with the functions of the calculator *before* taking the test. You will not want to take extra time to read through the directions while trying to complete the problems on test day.

The reference sheet can be found at www.ged testingservice.com.

Formulas

A list of formulas will be available for you to use during the test. However, the list will *not* include basic formulas such as the area of a rectangle or triangle, circumference of a circle, or perimeter of geometric figures. You will be expected to know these already.

Review the Appendix at the end of the book to see the list of formulas you will be given on test day.

Reasoning through Language Arts

The GED® Reasoning through Language Arts (RLA) exam tests your reading, writing, and English-language skills. Questions in this section will ask you to do things like identify the main idea or theme in a reading passage or determine the meanings of words within a passage. The RLA section also tests your knowledge of grammar, sentence structure, and the mechanics of language. Sharpening your reading and writing skills is important for the GED® test, and not only for the RLA section; the GED® Social Studies test and the GED® Science test also measure your ability to understand and communicate ideas through writing.

There are 48 questions and one extended response question on the RLA test. You will have 150 minutes to complete the entire exam, with one 10-minute scheduled break. For most of the questions on the RLA test, you will be given a reading passage, followed by six to eight questions that test your ability to understand and analyze what you have read.

Drop-down items are mostly used on the GED® RLA exam to test grammar and English-language mechanics. Drop-down questions are inserted in the middle of paragraphs. You will be asked to "drop down" a menu with several sentence choices and choose the one that fits best grammatically in the sentence.

Passage Types for Reading Questions

Of the reading passages on the RLA test, 25% will be literature. This includes historical and modern fiction, as well as nonfiction like biographies or essays. You might generally think of literature as fiction (invented stories), but literary texts can also be nonfiction (true stories). The other 75% of the reading passages will be from informational texts, including workplace documents (like memos or letters). These passages will often cover topics in social studies and science.

The RLA test also features historical passages that are considered part of the "Great American Conversation." These include documents, essays, and speeches that have helped shape American history. There are no poetry or drama passages on the RLA test.

Extended Response Questions

As you learned earlier in the chapter, the extended response item requires you to find and use information from the reading passage (or passages) to answer the question in a well-thought-out essay. You will be asked to analyze an issue and likely also asked to provide an opinion on what you have read. You will have 45 minutes of your total RLA time to complete this essay—that includes brainstorming, writing a draft, writing a final version, and proofreading your work.

Science

The GED® Science test focuses on scientific reasoning and tests how well you understand and can apply science principles in real-world situations. It is made up of 35 questions, which you will have 90 minutes to complete.

The test will include reading passages, graphs, and charts. The majority of the information you need to answer questions will be within the exam itself, whether in a diagram or in a passage. The test does *not* ask you to memorize science facts beforehand.

The science topics covered on the GED® Science test are:

- **Physical science**—40% of the questions
- **Life science**—40% of the questions
- **Earth and space science**—20% of the questions

On the GED® Science test, physical science includes high school physics and chemistry and covers the structure of atoms, the structure of matter, the properties of matter, chemical reactions, conservation of mass and energy, increase in disorder, the laws of motion, forces, and the interactions of energy and matter.

Life science deals with subjects covered in high school biology classes, including cell structure, heredity, biological evolution, behavior, and interdependence of organisms.

Earth and space questions will test your knowledge of Earth and the solar system, the geochemical cycles, the origin and evolution of the Earth and the universe, and energy in the Earth system.

Social Studies

The GED® Social Studies test is made up of 35 questions and one extended response item. You will have 65 minutes to answer the questions and 25 minutes to write your essay. The questions on this test are based on information provided to you, such as brief texts, excerpts from speeches, maps, graphics, and tables. As on the GED® Science exam, the information you'll need to answer questions on the GED® Social Studies test will be contained in the passages, political cartoons, maps, and other information presented on the test. You do not have to memorize names, dates, places, and facts beforehand.

As on the GED® RLA test, many of the brief texts featured will be drawn from materials reflecting the "Great American Conversation," which includes documents like the Declaration of Independence and other notable historical texts from U.S. history.

The Social Studies exam focuses on four areas:

1. **Civics and government**—50% of the questions
2. **United States history**—20% of the questions
3. **Economics**—15% of the questions
4. **Geography and the world**—15% of the questions

Summary

Now that you're more familiar with the GED® test, we can begin reviewing each GED® test section in greater depth and tackle some helpful test practice. The practice questions in this book are designed to be as close as possible to the actual questions you'll see on test day. Each practice question in this book is accompanied by a very detailed answer explanation—so you'll be able to see not only why the correct answer is right but also why each of the other choices is incorrect. Use the information, review, and practice provided in this book to develop a solid study plan between now and test day.

Best of luck on your GED® test study journey—and on your test-taking experience!

I ▶ GED®
MATHEMATICAL
REASONING TEST

This section of the GED® test review focuses on the GED® Mathematical Reasoning test. The purpose of the Mathematical Reasoning test is to assess your *depth* of math knowledge. In addition to being able to demonstrate your ability to perform computations correctly, this test assesses your ability to reason mathematically: to build solution pathways and to evaluate the lines of reasoning as you solve problems. In other words, are you able to identify how to start a problem? Can you change your course of action when your original solution pathway is not working? Can you recognize flaws in your reasoning or that of others? Do you understand what you are doing, or are you simply following a memorized procedure?

Building your conceptual understanding of math will not only help you pass this test but will also aid you in furthering your education and in securing and maintaining future jobs.

You will be given 115 minutes to complete the Mathematical Reasoning test. There will be 46 questions, but the scoring is done on a scaled basis, so that each question may be worth more than one point. You will need to get a scaled score of 150 to pass the Mathematical Reasoning module.

Mathematical Reasoning Test Structure

More than half of this test contains problems for which you have to use algebraic thinking. Don't let this scare you! Think of algebra as being able to reason through math in a sometimes abstract, yet logical way. Algebraic thinking is ingrained in everyday life; you are already using this way of thinking without even realizing it! Do you ever calculate how much more money you need to pay your rent and bills based on what you already have in your bank account? That's one example of algebraic thinking.

The types of items you will encounter on the actual test are discussed next. We also explain ways that you can practice for the online test with this print book.

Multiple-Choice Questions (More than 50%)

Multiple-choice questions on the GED® Mathematical Reasoning test ask you to select the best answer from four choices. To select an answer, you will click your mouse in the circle next to that answer choice. To change your answer, click the circle of another answer choice. In this book, you can practice by circling the correct response to a multiple-choice question.

Fill-in-the-Blank Questions

For fill-in-the-blank questions, you will need to type in an answer or answers, rather than being presented with a selection of possible answers from which to choose. In this book, you can practice by writing in the correct answer on the given line or lines.

Hot-Spot Questions

For hot-spot questions, you will need to click on an area of the screen to indicate where the correct answer is located. For instance, you may be asked to plot a point by clicking on an empty graph. In this book, you can practice by identifying where the correct answer is located and marking the location on paper in the appropriate spot.

Drag-and-Drop Questions

To answer drag-and-drop questions, you will need to click on the correct object, hold down the mouse, and drag the object to the appropriate place in the problem, diagram, chart, or graph. In this book, you can practice by identifying which object will complete the problem, diagram, chart, or graph and writing it in instead of dragging it.

Drop-Down Questions

For drop-down questions, you will need to select the correct numerical answer or phrase to complete a sentence or problem. You will click your mouse on the arrow to show all of the answer choices. Then, you will click on your chosen answer to complete the sentence, paragraph, or equation. This type of question is similar to a multiple-choice item.

Calculator Use

An online calculator, called TI-30XS MultiView, will be available for most of the questions. The first five questions on the test will be non-calculator questions. These questions may deal with ordering fractions and decimals, using the least common multiple (LCM) and the greatest common factor (GCF), using the distributive property, simplifying or solving problems using the rules of exponents, or identifying absolute value, among other skills and concepts. The rest of the test will have the on-screen calculator available for you to use.

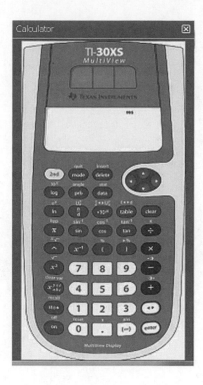

If you have never used the TI-30XS MultiView calculator, you should practice using it before you take the actual test.

The GED® Testing Service has created a calculator reference sheet and tutorial videos on its website to help you practice. The reference sheet will also be available for you to use during the test. However, you should be comfortable with the functions of the calculator *before* taking the test. You will not want to take extra time to read through the directions while trying to complete the problems. The reference sheet can be found at www.gedtestingservice.com.

Formulas

A list of formulas will be available for you to use during the test. However, it will *not* include basic formulas such as the area of a rectangle or triangle, the circumference of a circle, and the perimeters of geometric figures. You will be expected to know these already. If you do not know these formulas off the top of your head, you will find them in Chapter 4 of this book.

The formulas available to you on the GED® test are in the Appendix at the end of this book.

Mathematical Reasoning Review Chapters

The following review chapters will help you brush up on concepts and skills. The math content has been broken into the following chapters:

- Numbers and Quantities (Chapter 1)
- Algebra and Functions (Chapter 2)
- Graphs and Tables (Chapter 3)
- Geometry Basics (Chapter 4)
- Statistics and Probability (Chapter 5)

If you practice a little bit of math every day, not only will you see an improvement in your test scores, but you will also notice that you are retaining information better and longer.

1 ▶ NUMBERS AND QUANTITIES

Working with numbers and quantities allows you to deal with many problems you may encounter throughout your daily routine. Knowing what a percent is, for instance, and how to calculate it, gives you the tools you need to figure out how much an item on sale costs or what amount of interest you would pay on a student loan.

This chapter reviews types and properties of numbers and how to manipulate them, such as number lines, simplest forms, least common multiples (LCMs), and square and cube roots, as well as rates, percents, and proportions. Included throughout are practice exercises that will help reinforce the concepts discussed. The answers and explanations for all practice questions can be found at the end of the chapter.

Rules of Numbers

There are certain rules you must master before you move on to more complicated mathematics. Once you are comfortable with these skills, you can feel confident when tackling problems that have multiple steps.

The Distributive Property

The **distributive property** does exactly what it sounds like it does—distributes a number or term to other numbers or terms. Whenever you see a number outside parentheses that has another function inside, at some point you will want to use the distributive property, which means you will multiply everything inside the parentheses by that number.

For instance, if we needed to expand the problem $5(3 + 2)$, we would distribute the 5 to the 3 by multiplying 5×3 and then distribute the 5 to the 2 by multiplying 5×2. The result would be $15 + 10 = 25$.

The distributive property will help you when simplifying long problems. The next concept is better for figuring out division.

Least Common Multiple

The **least common multiple** (LCM) is the lowest multiple shared by two numbers. To understand what a multiple is, think of it this way: if one number can be divided by a second number evenly, then the first number is a multiple of the second number. For instance, 4 is a multiple of 2, 6 is a multiple of 2, and 8 is a multiple of 2. You'll see later, when we discuss the greatest common factor (GCF), that finding the LCM requires us to go in the direction opposite the one we use when finding the GCF.

An easier way to think about this is to picture the multiplication table. Multiples are numbers that result when multiplying one number by whole numbers: 1, 2, 3, 4, 5, and so forth. For example, if we wanted to find the multiples of 6, we would start by asking ourselves "What's 6×1? What's 6×2? What's 6×3?" In reality, a number has an infinite number of multiples. However, for the purposes here, we will just list some of them:

Multiples of 6: 6, 12, 18, 24, 30, 36, 42, 48, 54, 60. . . .

LCMs are necessary when finding common denominators, and common denominators are necessary when adding, subtracting, or comparing fractions.

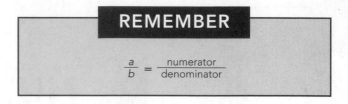

REMEMBER

$$\frac{a}{b} = \frac{\text{numerator}}{\text{denominator}}$$

For example, if we wanted to order the following fractions from least to greatest,

$$\frac{1}{2}, \frac{7}{8}, \frac{3}{4}$$

we would first need to find a common denominator among 2, 8, and 4. Let's break this down into steps.

First let's list the multiples of each number.

2: 2, 4, 6, 8, 10. . . .
8: 8, 16, 24, 32. . . .
4: 4, 8, 12, 16, 20. . . .

Then, let's find the smallest number they all share—that they have in common. This is the LCM. In this case, it is 8.

2: 2, 4, 6, **8**, 10. . . .
8: **8**, 16, 24, 32. . . .
4: 4, **8**, 12, 16, 20. . . .

Next, let's write equivalent fractions with the least common multiple as the new denominator. Remember, whatever number you multiply the original denominator by to get the new denominator, you have to multiply the original numerator by that same number to get the new numerator. Keep in mind that in this way you're really just multiplying the fraction by 1 and not actually changing it.

$$\frac{1}{2} \times \frac{4}{4} = \frac{4}{8}$$

$$\frac{7}{8} \times \frac{1}{1} = \frac{7}{8}$$

$$\frac{3}{4} \times \frac{2}{2} = \frac{6}{8}$$

So, we can easily see from the new, equivalent fractions that the order of these fractions from least to greatest is $\frac{1}{2}, \frac{3}{4}, \frac{6}{8}$.

This also works if we wanted to subtract $\frac{1}{2}$ from $\frac{7}{8}$. We would use the same equivalent fractions as previously:

$$\frac{7}{8} - \frac{4}{8} = \frac{3}{8}$$

See how the LCM is useful? As mentioned before, we also will need to find the greatest common factor when working with numbers.

Greatest Common Factor

A number that divides evenly into a second number is referred to as a *factor* of the second number. For instance, 2 is a factor of 4, 6, 8, and so on. The **greatest common factor** (GCF) of two or more numbers is the largest number that is a factor of the two or more numbers you are considering.

Finding the GCF between two or more numbers is necessary to reduce fractions (i.e., to put fractions in their **lowest terms**). This is often necessary for answering questions and is also really useful for simplifying complex questions and being able to answer them faster.

For instance, if you need to put $\frac{6}{10}$ in lowest terms, first you need to find the GCF of 6 and 10. An easy way to do this is to list the factors of each number and see which number is the largest factor the two numbers share:

6: 1, 2, 3, 6
10: 1, 2, 5, 10

The biggest factor that both 6 and 10 share is 2. Therefore, let's divide both 6 and 10, the numerator and denominator, respectively, by 2:

$$\frac{6}{10} \div \frac{2}{2} = \frac{3}{5}$$

Because you are dividing by the same number—in this case, $\frac{2}{2}$—you are essentially dividing by 1. As you know, any number divided by 1 yields the original number. Therefore, even though the answer of $\frac{3}{5}$ looks different, it is equivalent to $\frac{6}{10}$ and is in lowest terms.

If a question asks you to rewrite an expression using the distributive property, find the GCF of the two numbers and then divide each number by the GCF.

Practice

1. Write the following expression in lowest terms using the distributive property.
   64 − 8. _____

> ## SIMPLEST FORM
>
> **Simplest form** refers to the most simplified version of an answer. For instance, even though $\frac{6}{10}$ and $\frac{3}{5}$ are equivalent (as illustrated in the previous section), the fraction $\frac{3}{5}$ is in simplest form because it cannot be reduced any further. The reason this is so important is that, unless instructed otherwise, you should *always* give the answer in simplest form on the test.

Number Lines

On the GED® test, you may be asked to put fractions, decimals, and rational numbers in order. Likely, you will need to be able to order specified numbers on a number line. There are a few things to keep in mind when arranging numbers on a number line from least to greatest.

Watch Out for the Negatives!

As you go further to the left on the number line, the absolute values of the numbers get BIGGER (an explanation of absolute value is included later in this chapter). If negative numbers scare you, just think about them in terms of money. If you keep spending more money than you have in your bank account, you go deeper and deeper into debt. If you have only $3 in your bank account and you buy a sandwich for $5, you will be $2 in the hole. That number is located two spaces to the left of 0 on this number line:

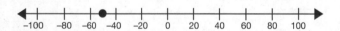

This is true for bigger numbers as well. If you have $100 in your checking account and you spend $150, you owe $50. So your bank account—before overdraft fees of course—is negative $50. On a number line like the next one, –50 would be 50 spaces to the left of 0.

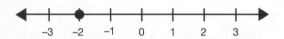

Find Common Denominators to Order Fractions

The surest way to be certain that you are ordering fractions correctly is to rewrite the fractions so they share a common denominator. Review the least common multiple section for a more detailed explanation of rewriting equivalent fractions. Let's practice this skill with the following question.

Practice

2. Order the following fractions on the number line: $\frac{1}{2}, \frac{7}{8}, \frac{3}{4}$.

Ordering Decimals

Place values to the right of the decimal point represent parts of a whole. The names of the place values look similar to those of numbers to the left of the decimal point. However, note the -*ths* at the end of each name in the chart.

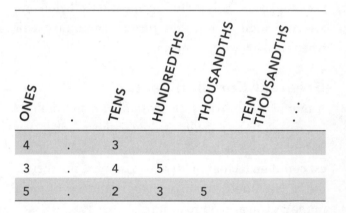

ONES	.	TENS	HUNDREDTHS	THOUSANDTHS	TEN THOUSANDTHS	...
4	.	3				
3	.	4	5			
5	.	2	3	5		

The first number listed in the table is read, "Four and three tenths." To illustrate this as a mixed number (a whole number and a fraction), it is written like it sounds: $4\frac{3}{10}$.

The second number listed is read as "three and forty-five hundredths." As a mixed number, it is written $3\frac{45}{100}$.

The third number listed above is read as "five and two hundred thirty-five thousandths." It is written $5\frac{235}{1,000}$.

To order decimals on the number line, you can use the previous strategy of writing decimals as fractions with a power of 10 (10, 100, 1,000, 10,000, and so forth).

For example, let's order the following decimals from least to greatest:

1.2, 1.40, 1.15, 1.67, and 1.53.

Each of these decimals has two digits to the right of the decimal point except the number 1.2. However, adding zeros at the end of a decimal number does not change the value: 1.2 is equivalent to 1.20, which is also equivalent to 1.200. The pattern continues.

To make the comparison easier, simply add a zero to 1.2 so that each number has the same amount of digits to the right of the decimal point. Then, note that each denominator will be 100 since there are two digits to the right of each decimal point (the hundredths place).

$$1.20 = 1\frac{20}{100}$$
$$1.40 = 1\frac{40}{100}$$
$$1.15 = 1\frac{15}{100}$$
$$1.67 = 1\frac{67}{100}$$
$$1.53 = 1\frac{53}{100}$$

Since each fraction has the same denominator, it is easy to determine the order of the numbers: 1.15, 1.2, 1.4, 1.53, and 1.67.

It is also helpful to think about decimals in terms of money. For instance, 1.2 is like $1.20. We all know that this amount is a little more than $1. Another example: 3.76 is like $3.76—it is about $\frac{3}{4}$ of the way between $3 and $4. The following number line illustrates this concept.

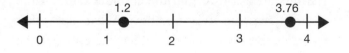

Laws of Exponents

An exponent—written as a small number to the upper right of a number—indicates how many times a number should be multiplied by itself. For instance, 10^2 (read as 10 to the second power) means 10×10, or 100; and 10^3 (read as 10 to the third power) means $10 \times 10 \times 10$, or 1,000.

There are six laws of exponents:

1. $x^0 = 1$
   Examples: $2^0 = 1$; $6^0 = 1$

2. $x^1 = x$
   Examples: $7^1 = 7$; $100^1 = 100$

3. $x^{-1} = \frac{1}{x^1}$
   Examples: $5^{-2} = \frac{1}{5^2}$; $8^{-3} = \frac{1}{8^3}$

4. $x^m x^n = x^{m+n}$
   Example: $2^2 \cdot 2^3 = 2^{2+3} = 2^5$

5. $\frac{x^m}{x^n} = x^{m-n}$
   Example: $\frac{3^5}{3^2} = 3^{5-2} = 3^3$

6. $(x^m)^n = x^{mn}$
   Example: $(4^2)^3 = 4^{(2)(3)} = 4^6$

Squares and Cubes

Squaring and cubing numbers uses the exponents 2 and 3. When you square a number, you multiply a number by itself:

$$4^2 = 4 \times 4 = 16$$

Notice that this is *different* from multiplying by 2. If we multiply 4×2, we get 8—not 16.

When you cube a number, you multiply a number by itself, using the number three times:

$$4^3 = 4 \times 4 \times 4 = 64$$

Notice that this is *different* from multiplying by 3. If we multiply 4×3, we get 12—not 64.

To square or cube a number means you are raising that number to the second or third power. The 2 and the 3 are exponents. You'll notice that when you raise a number to a power, the number grows quickly. You may have heard people say things like "The population has grown exponentially." That just means it increased very quickly.

Square Roots and Cube Roots

Roots undo exponents. Square rooting and cube rooting involve backwards thinking. For instance, if a problem states, "What is the square root of 16?" it is asking you for the number that equals 16 when multiplied by itself. Mathematically, it is written

$$\sqrt{16} = ?$$

So, what number, when multiplied by itself (i.e., when squared), yields 16? Four!

$$4 \times 4 = 16$$
$$4^2 = 16$$

So, $\sqrt{16} = 4$.

Cube roots function in the same way. To find a cube root of a number, ask yourself, "What number used three times in multiplication gives me this number?" Mathematically, cube roots are written like the following: $\sqrt[3]{27}$.

So, what is the $\sqrt[3]{27}$? What number multiplied by itself three times yields 27? Three!

$$3 \times 3 \times 3 = 27$$
$$3^3 = 27$$

So, $\sqrt[3]{27} = 3$

It is also important to understand how to simplify expressions that contain roots. We will review this process with two forms—whole numbers and fractions.

Whole Numbers

$$\sqrt{a \cdot b} = \sqrt{a} \cdot \sqrt{b}$$

Example: Simplify $\sqrt{27}$.
$$\sqrt{27} = \sqrt{3 \cdot 9} = \sqrt{3} \cdot \sqrt{9} = 3\sqrt{3}$$

Practice

3. Simplify $\sqrt{20} \cdot \sqrt{12}$. _____

Fractions

$$\sqrt{\frac{a}{b}} = \frac{\sqrt{a}}{\sqrt{b}}$$

Example: Simplify $\sqrt{\frac{4}{9}}$.

$$\sqrt{\frac{4}{9}} = \frac{\sqrt{4}}{\sqrt{9}} = \frac{2}{3}$$

Absolute Value

The absolute value of a number tells us how far away it is from zero. For instance, the number 8 is a distance of 8 from zero. The number 400 is a distance of 400 from zero. What about the number −10? Think about it. Even though it is a negative number, it is still a distance of 10 from zero—just to the left of zero instead of to the right.

The absolute value is written mathematically like the following examples:

- $|8| = 8$ (Read: the absolute value of 8 is 8)
- $|-10| = 10$ (Read: the absolute value of −10 is 10)

You may be asked to find the absolute value of the distance between two numbers. What does that mean? It means to find the difference between the numbers (subtract) and then record the absolute value of the answer.

Practice

4. Find $|x - y|$ when $x = 3$ and $y = 8$. _____

5. Find the absolute value of the difference between 5 and 3. _____

Scientific Notation

What does it mean to write a number in scientific notation? The general format for a number written in scientific notation is $a \times 10^b$. An example of a number written in scientific notation is 2.6×10^4.

Scientific notation is a way to write really big or really small numbers in shorthand. There are two rules when it comes to writing numbers in scientific notation:

1. The number should always be between 0 and 10.
2. The exponent is dictated by the number of spaces the decimal point moves to the left or to the right.

For instance, say we want to write the number 9,800,000 in scientific notation. Since the number needs to be between 0 and 10, our decimal point is going to be moved from the right of the last zero to the right of 9. Thus, the number becomes 9.8. However, we need this number to be equivalent to 9,800,000, so we can't stop at 9.8. This is where the second rule comes in. We need to multiply by a power of 10. Count how many spaces you moved the decimal point to the *left*. Did you get six? Good. So, we write the number as 9.8×10^6.

Suppose we have a really small number—say, 0.000047—that needs to be written in scientific notation. We are going to approach this the same way. First, we need to write a number that is between 0 and 10: 4.7. Next, we need to multiply by a power of 10 to make this notation represent the original number. To get to 4.7, we moved the decimal point five spaces to the *right*. We reflect this in the power of 10 by writing a negative exponent: 4.7×10^{-5}.

To convert a number in scientific notation to a standard number, simply reverse the steps.

9.8×10^6 indicates that we need to move the decimal point six spaces to the *right* to get a large number: 9,800,000.

4.7×10^{-5} indicates that we need to move the decimal point five spaces to the *left* to get a really small number: 0.000047.

So, how does scientific notation play out in the real world? Suppose you were measuring a planet's distance from the sun in kilometers (km). That would end up being a pretty large number! Instead of writing a number with a bunch of place values, you can simply and concisely write it using scientific notation. Or suppose you needed to give a pipe's width in terms of meters (m). Instead of writing a long number, you could concisely write it in scientific notation.

Practice

6. Which of the following is the number 316.72 written in scientific notation?
   a. 3.1672×10^{-2}
   b. 3.1672×10^2
   c. 3.1672×10^3
   d. 3.1672×10^1

7. Pluto is 5,914,000,000 km from the sun. This distance can be written in scientific notation as:
   a. 59.14×10^8
   b. 5.914×10^9
   c. 0.5914×10^{10}
   d. 5.914×10^6

Percentages

When you break down the word *percent* into two parts—*per* and *cent*—it means "for every hundred." A percentage conveys a number that is a part of, or a fraction of, 100. For instance, 37% means 37 out of 100. Thus, it could also be written as $\frac{37}{100}$.

Let's not stop there! Not only can we write 37% as a fraction, but we can also write is as a decimal. Remember, to have a denominator of 100, there must be two digits to the right of the decimal point. So $\frac{37}{100}$ is read as "thirty-seven hundredths." As a decimal, it is written as 0.37. Simply take the original percentage of 37 and then move the decimal point two spaces to the left to get 0.37. Not three spaces. Not one space. Always two. Why? It is representative of hundredths, or per hundred. So, 37% is equivalent to 0.37. (This is important to remember, because when we use percentages in real-world problems, we will be converting them into decimals.)

Fractions, decimals, and percentages are equivalent:

$$\frac{37}{100} = 0.37 = 37\%$$

How does this make sense? Well, they all express values that are parts, or fractions, of 100.

The following are some problems that deal with percentages in real-life situations.

Simple Interest

Suppose you took out a five-year car loan for $12,000, with an interest rate of 6.5% per year. You might want to figure out how much money you will be paying in interest.

To solve this problem, we need to use the simple interest formula: $I = prt$, where p = the principal balance, r = the interest rate, and t = the duration or time.

Before we start substituting numbers to solve this problem, we need to convert the percentage to a decimal. Remember, we just move the decimal point two spaces to the left. So 6.5% becomes 0.065.

When we substitute values into the formula, we get the following equation:

$$I = (12,000)(0.065)(5)$$
$$I = 3,900$$

Therefore, you will be paying a total amount of $3,900 in interest over the course of the five-year loan.

Practice

8. If Veronica deposits $5,000 in her savings account with a yearly interest rate of 9% and leaves the money in the account for eight years, how much interest will her money earn?
   a. $360,000
   b. $45,000
   c. $3,600
   d. $450

Tax

If you go to the store to purchase household items, you take into account the tax in your total, right? How do you do that? Let's say that you spend $46.98 on household items before tax. If you are taxed 7%, what is your total bill?

Like the previous problem, you need to convert the 7% to a decimal. Move the decimal point two spaces to the left to get 0.07. This is the number to be used in the problem.

To find how much tax you pay, multiply the total cost before tax, $46.98, by 0.07:

$$46.98 \times 0.07 = 3.2886$$

Since we are talking about money, let's round that to $3.29. We are not done yet, though! The question asks for the total bill, so we need to add $3.29 to $46.98. When we do that, we end up with $50.27.

Markups/Markdowns

Every month you budget for fun money. You are able to put aside $30 each month. You see a pair of shoes that you really want for $90, but you have only $65 saved. The next week the shoes go on sale for 25% off. Do you have enough money to buy them?

To solve this problem, we need to figure out the sale price of the shoes. The first step is to convert the percentage to a decimal. So 25% becomes 0.25 when we move the decimal point two spaces to the left. Multiply 0.25 by 90, the price of the shoes, to figure out how much they are marked down to:

$$90 \times 0.25 = 22.5$$

Remember, $22.50 is not the sale price of the shoes, but the amount taken off the original $90. So, you need to subtract $22.50 from $90, which results in $67.50. If you have only $65, unfortunately you do not have enough money.

Practice

9. Mr. Jordan is planning to buy a treadmill. The treadmill he wants is on sale at 10% off the retail price of $700. Mr. Jordan has an additional coupon for 5% off after the discount has been applied. What is the final cost of the treadmill, not including any taxes or assembly fees?

    a. $587.50
    b. $598.50
    c. $630.00
    d. $668.50

Percentage Increase/Decrease

Your rent went from $800 a month to $875 per month. To consider whether the increase is fair, thinking about it in terms of a percentage is helpful.

To find the percentage increase, we first have to figure out how much more the current price is than the original price. By doing a simple subtraction problem, we find that $875 – $800 = $75. To figure out the percentage increase, we divide 75 by the total original amount (remember, percentages convey parts of wholes):

$$\frac{75}{800} = 0.09375$$

To figure out the percentage increase from this decimal, we need to use backwards thinking. To convert percentages to decimals, we move the decimal two spaces to the left. So to convert decimals to percentages, we move the decimal two spaces to the *right*.

$$0.09375 = 9.375\%$$

Let's round our answer to the nearest tenth, 9.4%.

Rates

We use rates every day without even realizing it. What are rates? Miles per hour (mph), price per pound, and persons per square mile are all examples of rates. They are written most often as fractions, with the numerator as the first unit listed and the denominator as the second unit listed. Let's look at some applications of the concept.

Speed

It took Denise 1 hour and 45 minutes to walk a four-mile trail. How many miles per hour did she walk, rounded to the nearest tenth of a mile?

To find how many miles per hour, we write our fraction with the number of miles as the numerator and the number of hours as the denominator: $\frac{4 \text{ miles}}{1.75 \text{ hours}}$. This is now a simple division problem: $4 \div 1.75 = 2.28$. Rounded to the nearest tenth, Denise walked 2.3 miles per hour.

Practice

10. Suppose a jet can fly a distance of 5,100 miles in three hours. If the jet travels at the same average speed throughout its flight, how many hours will it take the jet to travel 22,950 miles?

a. 4.5 hours

b. 13.5 hours

c. 15.3 hours

d. 18 hours

Prices

Rick's Market is selling 12-pound turkeys for $19.50 each, and Mike's Meats is selling 15-pound turkeys for $23.85. Which store offers the better price per pound of turkey?

To find the better price per pound of turkey, we need to calculate the rate for each turkey. The price per pound at Rick's Market is $\frac{\$19.50}{12\text{ lbs}}$, or $1.63/lb. The price per pound at Mike's Meats is $\frac{\$23.85}{15\text{ lbs}}$, or $1.59/lb. Even though a turkey costs more at Mike's Meats, it offers a better price per pound of turkey.

Practice

11. Joe made $90 babysitting for 12 hours. At this rate, how long will it take him to make an additional $300?

a. 25 hours

b. 7.5 hours

c. 40 hours

d. 28 hours

Density

An estimated 392,880 people live within 58 square miles in Minneapolis, MN. Approximately 3.82 million people live within 503 square miles in Los Angeles, CA. What is the difference of people per square mile between these two cities?

To find the persons per square mile in Minneapolis, we need to first write our fraction: $\frac{392,880\text{ people}}{58\text{ square miles}}$. There are 6,774 people per square mile in Minneapolis (rounded from 6,773.79).

To find the people per square mile in Los Angeles, we write another fraction: $\frac{3,820,000\text{ people}}{503\text{ square miles}}$. There are 7,594 people per square mile in Los Angeles (rounded from 7,594.43).

To find the difference of people per square mile between Minneapolis and Los Angeles, we subtract 6,774 from 7,594.

$$7,594 - 6,774 = 820 \text{ people per square mile}$$

Proportions

Proportions are two equivalent ratios or fractions. For instance, if two fractions are proportional, one can be obtained from the other by multiplying the numerator and denominator by the same number. Let's look at an example to illustrate this concept.

The fractions $\frac{12}{3}$ and $\frac{60}{15}$ are proportional. Why? The numerator and denominator both increase by a factor of 5:

$$\frac{12}{3} \times \frac{5}{5} = \frac{60}{15}$$

We could also find that these two are proportional by cross multiplication. What does that mean? In general, if $\frac{a}{b} = \frac{c}{d}$, then $a \times d = b \times c$. Let's check if this holds true for the previous problem:

$$12 \times 15 = 180 \text{ and } 60 \times 3 = 180$$

It works!

Practice

12. If K.P. can read 1,000 words in 5 minutes, how many words could he read in 12 minutes?

———

13. Sandy's Treasures sells used books in bundles at a great discount. According to the table, how much would it cost to buy nine used books?

_____

BUNDLES OF BOOKS	PRICE
3	$15
6	$30
9	x
12	$60
15	$75

Undefined Numerical Expressions

Fractions are division problems. For instance, $\frac{5}{6}$ is the same as $5 \div 6$, and $\frac{4}{3}$ is the same as $4 \div 3$. When we talk about undefined numerical expressions, we are talking about the impossibility of 0 being in the denominator—the impossibility of dividing something into 0 parts. When simplifying numerical expressions, it is considered undefined if 0 is in the denominator because it is not possible—there is no such quantity.

Consider simplifying this expression:

$\frac{5 - xy}{x + 9}$ when $x = -9$ and $y = 2$.

Simplified, it looks like this:

$$\frac{5 - (-9)(2)}{-9 + 9} = \frac{5 - (-18)}{-9 + 9} = \frac{5 + 18}{0} = \frac{23}{0}$$

Therefore, this numerical expression is undefined because it is impossible to divide 23 into 0 parts.

CAUTION

Don't confuse $\frac{0}{23}$ with $\frac{23}{0}$.

$\frac{0}{23} = 0$

It is possible to have 0 out of 23 total pieces. However, it is impossible to have 23 pieces and divide them into 0 groups.

Practice

14. For what two values of x is the following numerical expression undefined? $\frac{12x}{x^2 - 25}$.

_____

Summary

Now that you have a solid foundation of numbers and quantity basics, it's time to build on your knowledge and move on to the next chapter on algebra and functions. Practice the skills you've learned with the following review questions, and go back to any sections that are giving you trouble at any point during your mathematics studies. Practice and review are the keys to success on the GED® Mathematics test. You're on your way to mastering the skills you need to pass!

Numbers and Quantities Review

1. Put the following numbers in order from least to greatest:
15, 1.0005, $\frac{3}{2}$, 1.005. _____

2. Which absolute value expression illustrates the distance between point *A* and point *B* on the following number line?

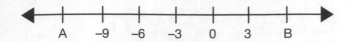

    A   −9   −6   −3   0   3   B

  a. $|12 - 6|$

  b. $|-12 + 6|$

  c. $|-12 - 6|$

  d. $|6 - 12|$

3. Simplify the following problem: $\sqrt{\frac{75}{72}}$.

  a. $\dfrac{5\sqrt{3}}{3\sqrt{8}}$

  b. $\dfrac{3\sqrt{5}}{8\sqrt{3}}$

  c. $\dfrac{25 \cdot 3}{8 \cdot 9}$

  d. $\sqrt{\dfrac{75}{72}}$

4. The table shows Ms. Kayla's GED® students' results from a keyboarding quiz. What is the difference in words per minute (wpm) between the fastest- and the slowest-typing student?

_____

NAME	WORDS TYPED	MINUTES
Percy	90	2
Derrick	67	2
Toneshia	84	2
Connie	70	2
Frank	59	2

5. Samantha went to a local restaurant to celebrate her birthday with a friend. The charge for the meal was $15. Samantha paid with a $20 bill and tipped the waiter 15% of the cost of the meal. How much change did she have left?

  a. $2.25

  b. $2.75

  c. $3.50

  d. $3.75

6. Jeremy purchased six cans of tomatoes for $5.34. At this rate, how much would he pay for 11 cans of tomatoes?

  a. $10.68

  b. $9.79

  c. $9.90

  d. $11.00

7. The scale on a state map is 1 inch:24 miles. How many miles apart are two cities if they are 3 inches apart on the map?

  a. 32 miles

  b. 72 miles

  c. 80 miles

  d. 96 miles

8. What is 0.00231 written in scientific notation?

  a. 231×10^{-3}

  b. 231×10^{-5}

  c. 2.31×10^{-3}

  d. 2.31×10^{3}

9. What is the sum of 12.03 and 4.5?

  a. 7.53

  b. 12.48

  c. 16.53

  d. 57.03

10. Solve for *x*: $\frac{8}{10} = \frac{x}{100}$. _____

Answers and Explanations

Chapter Practice

1. **8(8 − 1).** Since 64 can be divided by 8, and 8 can be divided by 8, 8 is the GCF. If we then divide both 64 and 8 by 8, we can create the new expression 8(8 − 1), which has that whole parentheses look of the distributive property we looked at before.

2.

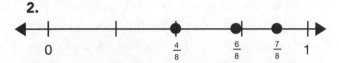

First, rewrite the fractions so that the denominator (the bottom number) of each fraction is the same. To do this, look for what number all three numbers—2, 8, and 4—can go into. The answer is 8. One of the fractions already has a denominator of 8, so that fraction is good to go. Changing the denominator of the other two fractions, $\frac{1}{2}$ becomes $\frac{4}{8}$, and $\frac{3}{4}$ becomes $\frac{6}{8}$. Now it is easy to see that $\frac{4}{8}$ is smaller than $\frac{6}{8}$, which is smaller than $\frac{7}{8}$.

3. **$4\sqrt{15}$.** Both of these numbers, 20 and 12, have a factor of 4, which is a perfect square. Therefore, these square roots can be simplified.
$$\sqrt{20} = \sqrt{4 \cdot 5} = \sqrt{4} \cdot \sqrt{5} = 2\sqrt{5}$$
$$\sqrt{12} = \sqrt{4 \cdot 3} = \sqrt{4} \cdot \sqrt{3} = 2\sqrt{3}$$
So, $\sqrt{20} \cdot \sqrt{12} = 2\sqrt{5} \cdot 2\sqrt{3}$. When simplified further, the answer is $4\sqrt{15}$.

4. $|3 - 8| = |-5| = \mathbf{5}$

5. **2.** $|5 - 3| = |2| = 2$. If the numbers were reversed, the absolute value of the difference would be $|3 - 5| = |-2| = 2$. Either way you write the numbers, as long as you are taking the absolute value of the difference between the two numbers, you will always get the same answer.

6. **b.** Scientific notation expresses a number as the product of a number between 1 and 10, including 1 but excluding 10, and a power of 10. If the number is greater than 1, then the exponent of 10 is non-negative. So, to write 316.72 in scientific notation, move the decimal point two places to the left to get a number between 1 and 10, and write the power of 10 as 2 because you moved the decimal point two places to the left.

7. **b.** A number in scientific notation is written as a number that is at least 1 but less than 10, multiplied by a power of 10. The power of 10 is the number of places that the decimal is moved to transform the number into decimal notation (regular numbers). If the decimal point in the number 5.914 is moved nine places to the right, the number becomes 5,914,000,000.

8. **c.** In the formula $I = prt$, the amount of money deposited is called the principal, p. The interest rate per year is represented by r, and t represents the number of years. The interest rate must be written as a decimal. Here, $p = 5,000$, $r = 9\% = 0.09$, and $t = 8$. Substitute these numbers for the respective variables and multiply: $I = 5,000 \times 0.09 \times 8 = \$3,600$.

9. **b.** This question requires taking your time and making sure you do all the required steps. Do one step at a time to arrive at the correct answer.
   First, find the sale price after the 10% has been deducted (remember, 10% is the same as 0.10):
$$\$700 - 0.10(\$700) = \$700 - \$70$$
$$= \$630$$
   Now, apply the 5% coupon to the discounted price of $630. Remember, 5% is the same as 0.05. Be sure to subtract from $630, not from the original price of $700.
$$\$630 - 0.05(\$630) = \$630 - \$31.50$$
$$= \$598.50$$

10. b. Dividing 5,100 miles by three hours gives you the speed of the jet in miles per hour:

$\frac{5,100}{3} = 1,700$ miles per hour

Therefore, to fly a distance of 22,950 miles, divide the distance 22,950 miles by 1,700 miles per hour, which equals $\frac{22,950}{1,700} = 13.5$ hours.

11. c. Find how much Joe makes per hour:

$\$90 \div 12 = \$7.50$

Joe makes $7.50 per hour.

To find how many hours he will need to babysit to earn $300, divide $300 by $7.50:

$\$300 \div 7.50 = 40$

It will take Joe 40 hours to earn an additional $300.

12. 2,400 words. Let's set up a proportional relationship by writing two fractions. Let's use x to represent the number of words per 12 minutes:

$\frac{1,000}{5} = \frac{x}{12}$

Cross multiply to solve for x:

$1,000 \times 12 = 5x$

$12,000 = 5x$

$\frac{12,000}{5} = 2,400$

13. $45. One way to find the cost of nine used books is to figure out the relationship between the number of books and the price of the other bundles. Do you notice a pattern? Do you see that each time the number of books is multiplied by 5 to get the price of each bundle? If we multiply 9 by 5, the answer is $45.

Another way to find the cost of the bundle of 9 books is to set up two equivalent fractions and solve for x:

$\frac{6}{30} = \frac{9}{x}$

$6x = 30 \times 9$

$6x = 270$

$x = \frac{270}{6}$

$x = 45$

14. −5 and 5. We are only concerned with the denominator when talking about undefined expressions. We need to find the two values of x that make the denominator equal to zero. Let's set up an equation and solve for x:

$x^2 - 25 = 0$

$x^2 = 25$

$\sqrt{x^2} = \sqrt{25}$

$x = 5$ and -5

Remember, a square root is the number that, when multiplied by itself, gives you the number you start with. In this problem, we are looking for the number that when multiplied by itself yields 25, which is 5. Also, when you square a negative number, you get a positive answer. So, -5×-5 *also* equals 25. Therefore, the two values of x that make the equation undefined are 5 and −5.

Numbers and Quantities Review

1. 1.0005, 1.005, $\frac{3}{2}$, 15. All of these numbers, when rewritten, contain the digits 1 and 5. The number $1.005 = 1\frac{5}{1,000}$, the number $1.0005 = 1\frac{5}{10,000}$, and $\frac{3}{2} = 1\frac{1}{2} = 1.5$. Therefore, 1.0005 is less than 1.005, which, in turn, is less than 1.5. The greatest number is 15.

2. c. To answer this question, it is helpful to remember that the absolute value of the number is the distance between that number and 0. The scale of the number line is 3-unit increments. Thus, point A is −12 and point B is 6. To find the difference between these two numbers, simply make a subtraction problem and take the absolute value. Choice **a** includes +12, not −12. Choice **b** reflects the sum, not the difference. For choice **d** to be correct, it should read $|6 - (-12)|$.

3. **a.** To simplify this expression, knowledge of the laws of roots is needed. The square root of a fraction is equivalent to the square root of the numerator and the square root of the denominator: $\frac{\sqrt{75}}{\sqrt{72}}$. It is also important to recognize that if we rewrite each term as a product of two factors, we may be able further simplify. $\frac{\sqrt{75}}{\sqrt{72}}$ can be written as $\frac{\sqrt{25} \cdot \sqrt{3}}{\sqrt{9} \cdot \sqrt{8}}$. This can be further simplified because 25 and 9 are both perfect squares. $\frac{\sqrt{25} \cdot \sqrt{3}}{\sqrt{9} \cdot \sqrt{8}} = \frac{5\sqrt{3}}{3\sqrt{8}}$. Choice **b** has the square root signs assigned to the wrong numbers. Option **c** reflects a factorization of 75 and 72 but lost the square root. Choice **d** suggests that this problem cannot be simplified, when in fact it can.

4. **15.5 wpm.** To answer this question, it is helpful to recall that words per minute is a rate. First, notice that the quiz results were for 2 minutes, not 1 minute. We need to find words per minute. To do this, simply divide each number of words typed by 2 to find the words per minute for each person. Since each number is being divided by the same number, we only need to do this for the greatest and the smallest number of words typed. $\frac{90 \text{ words}}{2 \text{ minutes}} = 45$ wpm. $\frac{59 \text{ words}}{2 \text{ minutes}} = 29.5$ wpm. To find the difference, simply subtract 29.5 from 45 to get 15.5 wpm. Alternatively, subtract the smallest number of words typed from the largest number and divide the difference by 2.

5. **b.** A 15% tip on a charge of $15 equals $2.25. Therefore, the total amount that Samantha paid was $15.00 + $2.25 = $17.25. The difference equals $20.00 − $17.25 = $2.75.

6. **b.** To find the cost of one can of tomatoes, divide the cost of six cans ($5.34) by 6:
   $$\$5.34 \div 6 = \$0.89$$
   Each can of tomatoes costs $0.89.
   Next, to find the cost of 11 cans, multiply $0.89 by 11:
   $$\$0.89 \times 11 = \$9.79$$
   The cost of 11 cans of tomatoes is $9.79.

7. **b.** Because 1 inch on the map represents 24 miles, 3 inches on the map represent 3 × 24, or 72 miles.

8. **c.** A number can be written in scientific notation as the product of a number between 1 and 10, including 1 and excluding 10, and a power of 10. If a number is less than 1, the power of 10 is negative. So, to write 0.00231 in scientific notation, start at the decimal point and move it to the right until you have one non-zero digit to the left of it. You must move the decimal point three places to get 2.31, so you multiply that number by 10 to the power of −3 because the number 0.00231 is smaller than 1 and you moved the decimal point three places to the right. So, in scientific notation:
   $$0.00231 = 2.31 \times 10^{-3}$$

9. c. *Sum* is a key word that means add. You need to add the numbers 12.03 and 4.5. Place the numbers one over the other and line up the decimal points.

12.03

+4.5

Because 4.5 does not show as many decimal places as 12.03, add a zero on the end of 4.5 to make 4.50. Then each number will show the same number of places to the right of the decimal. These will be easier to add.

12.03

+4.50

Now add each column one at a time starting on the right.

12.03

+4.50

16.53

10. 80. First, divide the denominator on the left into the new denominator on the right: $100 \div 10 = 10$. Then, multiply 10 by the numerator on the left to solve for x: $8 \times 10 = 80$.

2 ▶ ALGEBRA AND FUNCTIONS

In this chapter, we're reviewing the basic principles associated with algebra and functions. Understanding these principles will lead you to being able to recognize and work through these problems as you go.

Algebra is an organized system of rules that help solve problems for **unknowns**. This organized system of rules is similar to rules for a board game. To be successful at algebra, like any game, you must learn the rules of play. As you work through this chapter, be sure to pay special attention to any new words you may encounter. Once you understand what is being asked of you, it will be much easier to grasp algebraic concepts.

The answers and explanations for all practice questions are at the end of the chapter.

Signed Numbers

Let's start with rules for signed numbers. When solving problems, there are a few rules to remember about signed numbers (i.e., + and − numbers).

Multiplication and Division

Multiplication and division have straightforward rules. The product involving an odd number of negatives is negative, and the product involving an even number of negatives is positive, assuming that none of the numbers is zero.

Rule 1: $(+)(+) = +$ and $+/+ = +$
Example: $5 \cdot 5 = 25$

Rule 2: $(-)(-) = +$ and $-/- = +$
Example: $-5 \cdot -5 = 25$

Rule 3: $(-)(+) = -$ and $-/+ = -$
Example: $-5 \cdot 5 = -25$

Practice

1. If n is a positive number, will the solution to the following problem be positive or negative? $\frac{(-n)^3}{n} \cdot$ _____

Adding and subtracting with negative numbers can be a bit trickier. However, there are rules to help you with this as well.

Addition

Rule 1: When you add a positive to a positive, the answer is positive.
$60 + 34 = 94$

Rule 2: When you add a negative number to a negative number, the answer is negative.
$-20 + -31 = -51$

If you start with $20 of debt and pick up $31 more of debt, you have a total of $51 of debt. If you think about it as it is on the number line, both numbers are going in the same direction—to the left.

Rule 3: When you add a positive and a negative number, you simply need to find the difference between the two numbers. To determine the sign of the answer, use the sign of the number with the larger absolute value.

Let's look at $60 - 84$.

On the number line, the two numbers are going in opposite directions. In this problem, even though 60 is written first, it is smaller. To find the absolute value of the answer, switch the numbers around: $84 - 60$. This equals 24. Now, which number has the greater absolute value? -84. So the answer is negative. $60 - 84 = -24$. If this is confusing, think about it in terms of money. If you have $60 and spend $84, you are in debt $24.

Subtraction

Rule 1: Adding a negative is the same as subtracting a positive.
$60 + -9$ is the same as $60 - 9$.

Rule 2: Subtracting a negative number is the same as adding a positive.
$70 - -31$ is the same as $70 + 31$

Order of Operations

The order of operations helps you to correctly solve complex problems that include more than one operation. These are rules as well, and ensure that everyone follows the same steps to solve a given problem.

The rules of order are:

1. **P**arentheses
2. **E**xponents and roots
3. **M**ultiplication and **d**ivision
4. **A**ddition and **s**ubtraction

The operations in rules 2, 3, and 4 are performed as they arise from left to right in a problem.

You can remember them easily by this acronym: PEMDAS. You can also remember the acronym by reciting, "Purple Elephants Marching Down a Street" or "Please Excuse My Dear Aunt Sally." However you remember it, remember it! It will guide your steps when solving problems.

Example

Solve $4x^2 + 3(1 - x)$, when $x = -2$.

a. 21
b. 25
c. 73
d. 77

First, let's substitute -2 for every x and rewrite the expression:

$$4(-2)^2 + 3(1 - -2)$$

While it may be tempting to go from left to right, we need to be careful. We cannot multiply -2×4 and then square the answer because **Exponents** come before **Multiplication** in the order of operations. Plus, we also have **Parentheses** in the second half of the problem, and the order of operations indicates we do them *first*. Always.

So let's go through the steps one by one:

1. We have **Parentheses**: $(1 - -2)$. When subtracting a negative number, the negatives turn into addition. Thus, $(1 - -2)$ really is $(1 + 2)$, which equals 3. Our problem now reads:
   $$4(-2)^2 + 3(3)$$
2. We have **Exponents**: $(-2)^2$. This is 4. Our problem now reads:
   $$4(4) + 3(3)$$
3. We have **Multiplication**: $4(4)$ and $3(3)$. $4(4) = 16$ and $3(3) = 9$. Our problem now reads:
   $$16 + 9$$
4. We have **Addition**: $16 + 9$, which equals 25.

Therefore, the answer is choice **b**, 25!

You get choice **a**, 21, if you don't do the parentheses first and just multiply 3×1 and then subtract -2. You get choice **c**, 73, if you multiply 4×-2 and then square it, along with not computing the parentheses first. You get choice **d**, 78, if you multiply 4×-2 and then square it but still compute the second half correctly.

Practice

2. Solve $(52 + \sqrt{64}) \div 10$. _____

3. Evaluate the following expression:
$$(5 - 3) \times (4 + 4 \div 2)$$

a. 6
b. 8
c. 10
d. 12

Performing Operations on Expressions

Keeping in the theme of operations, let's look at the rules and methods used to perform operations on expressions. (An expression is a combination of numbers and/or symbols that indicate a specific value.)

Distributive Property with Linear Expressions

We looked at the distributive property in the previous chapter. Remember, it does exactly what it sounds like it does—distributes a number or term to other numbers or terms. Parentheses and multiplication are always involved.

For instance, if we needed to expand the problem $5(3 + y)$, we would distribute the 5 to the 3 by multiplying 5×3, and then distribute the 5 to the y by multiplying $5 \times y$. The result would be $15 + 5y$.

Adding and Subtracting Polynomial Expressions

When adding and subtracting terms in polynomial expressions, we can only add and subtract *like* terms. Numbers can be added to numbers, x^2's can be added to x^2's, $y3$'s can be added to y^3's, xyz's can be added to xyz's, and so forth.

Example

Simplify $(6x^2 + 2xy - 9) - (4x^3 + 2x^2 - 5xy + 8)$.

This looks complicated, but really it is just adding and subtracting coefficients—the numbers in front of the variables—of like terms. One thing important to note in this problem is that we are subtracting a *quantity*. This means that the minus sign needs to be distributed to each of the terms in parentheses after it. The minus sign will make each of the terms in parentheses its opposite. The first step in simplifying this problem is to rewrite it with the distributed negative:

$$6x^2 + 2xy - 9 - 4x^3 - 2x^2 + 5xy - 8$$

The second step in simplifying is to combine *like* terms.

$$6x^2 - 2x^2 = 4x^2$$
$$2xy + 5xy = 7xy$$
$$-9 - 8 = -17$$

$-4x^3$ has no other term like it, so it stays the same.

The last step is to rewrite the expression with the combined terms:

$$-4x^3 + 4x^2 + 7xy - 17$$

(*Note:* It's helpful to write the terms so that the value of the exponents goes from greatest to least as you read from left to right. Also, remember that positive numbers will have a plus sign in front while negative numbers will have a minus sign.)

Multiplying Polynomial Expressions

When multiplying polynomial expressions, we don't have to worry about combining like terms. To multiply two expressions, simply multiply the like terms together to yield an answer that is a combination of the two terms. Here are some examples:

$(5x)(6x) = 30x^2$: $5 \times 6 = 30$ and $x \cdot x = x^2$.
$(4xy)(3x) = 12x^2y$: $4 \times 3 = 12$, $x \cdot x = x^2$, and y stays the same.

Dividing Polynomial Expressions

When dividing polynomial expressions, we are looking for ways to reduce and/or cancel values to yield a simplified answer. For example, let's say we were asked to simplify the following expression:

$$\frac{4y^3x^2}{2yx}$$

We need to call to mind our knowledge about reducing fractions as well as our knowledge about dividing exponents. To simplify this expression, let's look at the numbers first. Can we reduce at all? Yes! We can divide 4 by 2, and then we are left with a 2 in the numerator only:

$$\frac{4y^3x^2}{2yx} = \frac{2y^3x^2}{yx}$$

Is there anything else we can simplify? There are x's and y's in both the numerator and the denominator, so we can divide the denominator into the numerator. Let's take the terms one at a time:

$$\frac{y^3}{y} = y^2$$

> ### NOTE
> When dividing exponents, we subtract their values. Thus, $3 - 1 = 2$, which is why we are still left with y^2 in the example.

$$\frac{x^2}{x} = x$$

Our complete answer is $2y^2x$.

Practice
4. Simplify the following expression: $\frac{7x^4y^5}{x^5y^6}$.

Multiplying Binomials (FOIL)

We FOIL when we are multiplying two binomials, or two expressions with two terms each. For example, take $(x + 2)(x - 4)$. To solve this problem, apply FOIL: multiply **f**irsts, **o**utsides, **i**nsides, **l**asts.

Multiply Firsts:
$(\underline{x} + 2)(\underline{x} - 4) = \underline{x^2}$

Multiply Outsides:
$(\underline{x} + 2)(x \underline{- 4}) = x^2 \underline{- 4x}$

Multiply Insides:
$(x + \underline{2})(\underline{x} - 4) = x^2 - 4x + \underline{2x}$

Multiply Lasts:
$(x + \underline{2})(x \underline{- 4}) = x^2 - 4x + 2x \underline{- 8}$

We get the final answer after combining the two like terms, $-4x$ and $2x$:

$$x^2 - 2x - 8$$

Practice

5. Apply FOIL to the following multiplication problem: $(y + 2)(y - 2)$. _____

Factoring

When factoring, we are going backwards from FOIL. Let's look at an example to illustrate this concept.

Factor the polynomial expression $x^2 - 3x + 2$.

To do this, we must keep FOIL in mind. Remember, when we were multiplying two binomials, we multiplied the <u>first</u> two terms together to get the first term of our answer. Thus, the first terms of our binomials need to equal x^2 when multiplied together. So far, we know the following:

$$(x \quad)(x \quad)$$

The next step of FOIL was to multiply the <u>outsides</u> and the <u>insides</u> to get two different products. To obtain the final answer, we combined these two products to get our middle term. Thus, when factoring, we must find a combination that when adding the products of the outsides and the insides, we get a sum of $-3x$.

However, before proceeding, we need to also keep in mind that the last term of the answer when applying FOIL is the result of the product of the <u>last</u> terms of the binomials. So, not only do the products of the outsides and the insides need to combine to equal $-3x$, but the lasts need to yield a product of $+2$.

$$x^2 - 3x + 2 = (x + ?)(x + ?)$$

What two numbers when added equal -3, but when multiplied equal $+2$? What about -2 and -1?

$$-2 + -1 = -3$$
$$-2 \times -1 = 2$$

Let's plug these numbers in!

When factored, $x^2 - 3x + 2 = (x - 2)(x - 1)$.

To check, we can FOIL our answer to make sure we factored correctly.

Multiply Firsts:
$(\underline{x} - 2)(\underline{x} - 1) = \underline{x^2}$

Multiply Outsides:
$(\underline{x} - 2)(x \underline{- 1}) = x^2 \underline{- 1x}$

Multiply Insides:
$(x \underline{- 2})(\underline{x} - 1) = x^2 - 1x \underline{- 2x}$

Multiply Lasts:
$(x \underline{- 2})(x \underline{- 1}) = x^2 - 1x - 2x + \underline{2}$

Combine the two like terms to get the final answer: $x^2 - 3x + 2$.

Practice

6. Factor $y^4 - 25$. _____

7. For what values of x is the function $f(x)$ undefined?
$f(x) = \frac{3}{x^2 - 3x + 2}$. _____

Substitution

The principle of substitution applies to any variable expression—linear, rational, or polynomial—where values are given to replace the variable(s). Once the variables are replaced by the given values, the order of operations is used to solve or simplify the problem.

Example

Given the equation $V = s^3$, solve for V if $s = \frac{1}{4}$.

To solve for V, we first need to replace every s from the original equation with the given value of $\frac{1}{4}$. So, the equation now reads:

$$V = \left(\frac{1}{4}\right)^3$$

When we solve for s, we get $\frac{1}{64}$:

$$\frac{1}{4} \times \frac{1}{4} \times \frac{1}{4} = \frac{1}{64}$$

Practice

8. What is $2x^2 + x - 4$ when $x = -3$? _____

Solving Problems and Equations

Your GED® test will expand on basic math concepts to test them via more complex problems and equations. This section introduces the question types you will face on the exam.

Word-to-Symbol Translations

There are several key words to remember when translating word problems into mathematical sentences.

Sum: A sum of two or more numbers is the answer to an <u>addition</u> problem.

- **Example:** The sum of 3 and 5 is 8 (i.e., $3 + 5 = 8$).

Difference: A difference between two numbers is the answer to a <u>subtraction</u> problem.

- **Example:** The difference of 5 and 4 is 1 (i.e., $5 - 4 = 1$).

Quotient: A quotient is the answer to a <u>division</u> problem.

- **Example:** The quotient of 18 and 6 is 3 (i.e., $18 \div 6 = 3$).

Product: A product is the answer to a <u>multiplication</u> problem.

- **Example:** The product of 8 and 9 is 72 (i.e., $8 \times 9 = 72$).

Coefficient: A coefficient is the number or symbol multiplied by a variable in an algebraic expression.

- **Example:** $4x^2 + 3x - 2$; 4 and 3 are coefficients.
- **Example:** y has a coefficient of 9 (i.e., $9y$).

Quantity of: "The quantity of" indicates that there are two or more terms combined to make one term. This combination of multiple terms into one is illustrated with parentheses.

- **Example:** Six times the quantity of 5 plus x^2; $6(5 + x^2)$.

Also, pay attention to the wording and the order of the terms stated. For instance, where is the word *from* placed in phrases that indicate subtraction?

"Subtract y from 5" is translated as "$5 - y$" and *not* "$y - 5$." This is because the phrase states that y is the term being subtracted, and not 5.

Another phrase to keep in mind is *less than*. Which number is less than which? It is very important to pay close attention.

- "Two less than x" is translated "$x - 2$" because the phrase indicates that we are talking about a number that is 2 less than the value of x (i.e., x is greater).
- "14 less than $2y$" is translated as "$2y - 14$." The phrase indicates that we are starting with a value

of $2y$ and then subtracting 14. Whatever the answer is, we know it is 14 less than the value of $2y$.

Now, what if the problem said, "14 is less than $2y$"? That one word "is" changes everything. It is now a mathematical inequality with the words "*is* less than." Translated, this is $14 < 2y$. (Remember, the open part of the inequality sign opens toward the bigger number and points to the smaller number.)

What about "7 is greater than or equal to $4z$"? How would this be written mathematically? Remember, the open part of the inequality sign opens toward the bigger number. This would be written: $7 \geq 4z$.

You may also need to use word-to-symbol translations when using variables to represent relationships between numbers in word problems. For instance, say that Sally is twice as old as Jim. To represent their ages algebraically without knowing their actual ages, we could use j to represent Jim's age and $2j$ to represent Sally's age.

REMEMBER

When translating words into symbols, it is important to read the problem critically, pay attention to the exact wording, and keep these key words and phrases in mind. These tips are essential to solving algebraic word problems.

Practice

9. Richard has a T-shirt company. He needs to make at least $2,500 this month to meet his sales goal. If each T-shirt costs $16.50, what is the minimum number of T-shirts Richard needs to sell to reach his goal?

Solving Linear Equations

A linear equation is an equation with one or more variables to the first power. Examples include:

$$3x + 7 = -5$$
$$y = mx + b$$
$$4z - 3 + n = 2$$

To solve linear equations with one variable, we need to get the variable by itself on one side of the equation. For instance, to find what x is in the equation $3x + 7 = -5$, we need to get x by itself. The goal is to get a mathematical sentence that reads "$x =$ a number."

How do we do this? By stripping away the other numbers through performing opposite operations. In the following example, what is on the same side of the equation as x?

$$3x + 7 = -5$$

3 and 7: x is being multiplied by 3 and then added to 7. To undo these operations, we need to do the opposite.

REMEMBER

Some opposites, or inverses, to keep in mind are:
- Addition and subtraction are opposites.
- Multiplication and division are opposites.
- Exponents and roots are opposites (squares and square roots, cubes and cube roots, etc.).

One other *very* important thing to keep in mind when solving linear equations: whatever you do to one side of the equation, you *must* do to the other. This is so that you maintain a balance on each side of the equal sign.

So, looking at $3x + 7 = -5$, let's perform opposite operations to get x by itself. Start from the number furthest from x on the same side and work your way to x.

$$3x + 7 = -5$$
$$\underline{-7 \qquad -7}$$
$$3x + 0 = -12$$
$$\frac{3x}{3} = \frac{-12}{3}$$
$$x = -4$$

Practice
10. Solve for y in the equation $2y - 4 = 21$.

Systems of Linear Equations

What is a system of linear equations? It is two equations, each with an x term and a y term. What do we do with systems of equations? The goal is to find the solution to the system, meaning the point (x,y) where the two linear equations (lines) intersect. Here is an example of a system of linear equations:

$$y = 2x - 4$$
$$4y = 6x + 2$$

There are three ways to find the solution to these two equations: substitution, linear combination, and graphing.

Substitution

In order to find the solution for this system of equations using substitution, we first need to isolate one of the variables in one of the equations in order to substitute an equivalent value in the other equation. Luckily, one of the equations already has isolated y: $y = 2x - 4$. So, the next step is to use $2x - 4$ in place of y in the second equation so we can solve for x:

$$4(2x - 4) = 6x + 2$$

Distribute the 4 to each of the terms in the quantity $2x - 4$:

$$8x - 16 = 6x + 2$$

Next, get all the numbers on one side of the equation and the x quantity on the other. Add 16 to both sides and subtract $6x$ from both sides:

$$8x - 16 = 6x + \ 2$$
$$+16 \qquad +16$$
$$8x = 6x + 18$$
$$-6x \quad -6x$$
$$2x = 18$$

To isolate x, we need to divide each side of the equation by 2.

$$\frac{2x}{2} = \frac{18}{2}$$
$$x = 9$$

So, if $x = 9$, what is the y-coordinate that corresponds with that x-coordinate? To find y, we substitute 9 for x into one of the original equations.

$$y = 2x - 4$$
$$y = 2(9) - 4$$
$$y = 18 - 4$$
$$y = 14$$

The solution to this system of equations is (9,14). Always write the x-coordinate first.

Linear Combination

The method of linear combination is just what it sounds like: we are going to combine the two linear equations.

$$y = 2x - 4$$
$$4y = 6x + 2$$

The goal of combining the two equations is to eliminate one of the variables. We do this by adding the equations together. However, sometimes just adding the equations together as they are written will not cancel either variable out. Can we add y and $4y$ to get zero? No. Can we add $2x$ and $6x$ to get zero? No. So we need to do some manipulation.

Let's focus on eliminating the x's. If we have $6x$ in one equation, then we need $-6x$ in the other equation so that we get a sum of zero when they are added together. Is there a way to make the $2x$ into a $-6x$? Could we multiply by -3? Yes! If we multiply $2x$ by -3, then we *must* multiply the rest of the terms in that equation by -3:

$$(-3)y = -3(2x - 4)$$

Once the -3 is distributed to, or multiplied by, each term, we have

$$-3y = -6x + 12$$

How does this help us? Well, let's put the two equations on top of each other again, this time using the new, manipulated equation:

$$-3y = -6x + 12$$
$$\underline{+4y = 6x + 2}$$

Notice that when we proceed to add each term together, we add $6x$ and $-6x$, which equals zero. That is what we want! Then, we can solve for y since it will be the only variable:

$$\begin{aligned} -3y &= -6x\ +\ 12 \\ \underline{+4y} &= \underline{6x\ +\ 2} \\ y &= 0\ +\ 14 \\ y &= 14 \end{aligned}$$

Now that we know that $y = 14$, we can solve for x by substituting 14 for y into one of the original equations:

$$y = 2x - 4$$
$$14 = 2x - 4$$

Add 4 to each side to get all the numbers on one side and all the x's on the other.

$$\begin{aligned} 14 &= 2x - 4 \\ \underline{+4} & \underline{+4} \\ 18 &= 2x \end{aligned}$$

Divide each side of the equation by 2 to isolate x.

$$\frac{18}{2} = \frac{2x}{2}$$
$$9 = x$$

The solution to this system of equations is $(9,14)$. Again, we always write the x-coordinate first.

Practice

11. Edward's school is having a raffle contest. People can buy a red ticket for $10 for a chance to win a new TV or a blue ticket for $5 for a chance to win a brand-new bicycle. Edward sold a record high of 130 tickets for a total of $1,100. How many of each color ticket did Edward sell? _____

Graphing

$$y = 2x - 4$$
$$4y = 6x + 2$$

To solve this system of equations by graphing, we need to graph each of these lines. The point where these two lines intersect is the solution.

How do we plot these lines? First, we need each line to be in **slope-intercept form**. That is, we need each line to mirror the format $y = mx + b$.

USEFUL TERMS IN UNDERSTANDING AND CONSTRUCTING GRAPHS

- *m* is the slope of the line
- *b* is the *y*-intercept (i.e., where the line intercepts the *y*-axis).
- *x* and *y* are the values that make up the coordinates on the line. There are infinite values of *x* that yield corresponding values of *y* on the line.

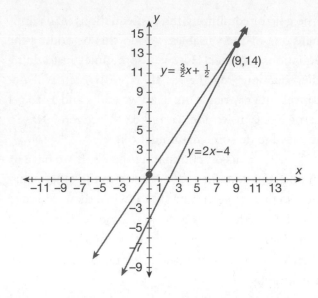

The first equation is already in slope-intercept form, so we do not need to change it. However, we need to isolate *y* in the second equation to get it into slope-intercept form.

$$4y = 6x + 2$$

To get rid of the coefficient of 4, we need to divide each side of the equation by 4.

$$\frac{4y}{4} = \frac{6x + 2}{4}$$
$$y = \frac{6}{4}x + \frac{2}{4}$$

Notice that both of the fractions are not in lowest form. We can reduce both of them by taking a factor of 2 out of each equation:

$$y = \frac{3}{2}x + \frac{1}{2}$$

This is now in slope-intercept form and can be graphed. When you graph the two lines, you see that the one solution that works for both is (9,14)—this is the one place where the lines cross.

Linear Inequalities

Solving linear inequalities is almost exactly the same as solving linear equations. The only difference is that there is not an equal sign. Instead, there is an inequality sign ($<, >, \leq, \geq$). This changes the *meaning* of the number sentence but not the method of isolating the variable on one side of the inequality.

Example
Solve $2x + 4 \leq 0$.

Just like when solving linear equations (i.e., $2x + 4 = 0$) we isolate *x* on one side of the equation:

$$
\begin{array}{rl}
2x + 4 \leq & 0 \\
\underline{-4 \qquad} & \underline{-4} \\
2x \leq & -4 \\
\frac{2x}{2} \leq & \frac{-4}{2} \\
x \leq & -2
\end{array}
$$

What does this number sentence mean? It means that to keep $2x + 4 \leq 0$ a true statement, we can substitute *any* value of *x* that is *less than or equal to –2*.

Practice

12. Solve $y + 4 > 7.$ _____

Graphing the Solution on a Number Line

You may be asked to graph the solution to an inequality on a number line. Let's use the previous two examples to illustrate how this is done.

$$x \leq -2$$

We need to show on the number line that for the inequality $2x + 4 \leq 0$, we can have a value of x that is *less than or equal to* –2. To do this, we plot a point at –2 and then shade in the rest of the number line to the left of –2. We represent that the number line goes on forever—to infinity—by putting an arrow at the end.

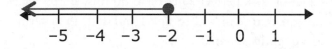

Practice

13. Graph the following inequality on the number line: $y > 3$.

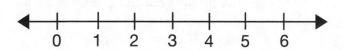

Using Inequalities to Represent Real-World Situations

There are times when we need to use inequality statements in real-world contexts. For instance, let's say that you are making a monthly budget based on a new job you just got, and you are trying to figure out how much spending money you will have each month. You make $1,500 a month after taxes. You have $1,000 of expenses, including rent, utilities, and food. You want to put at least $325 in savings each month. How much spending money could you potentially have each month?

We can use an inequality to represent this scenario. We know how much money you are starting with: $1,500. We also know the amounts of money you will be subtracting each month: $1,000 + $325. To find how much money is left over, we simply subtract:

$$1,500 - 1,000 - 325 = 175$$

How do we write this inequality? The scenario indicates that you want to save *at least* $325 per month. That means you could potentially save more. You don't need to spend the remaining money. This is what indicates that we are going to have a statement of inequality—it will show the limit of your monthly spending money even if you do not use it all.

So, can you spend more than $175 if you want to save at least $325? No! You have only $175 left after expenses and savings, so whatever you spend has to be equal to or less than $175. Represented in a number sentence, it looks like this: 1,500 − 1,000 − 325 ≥ x; or, when simplified further, 175 ≥ x. The variable x is the amount of spending money.

Quadratic Equations

A quadratic equation has a form where a, b, and c are coefficients. The square of x in the first term is what makes this equation a quadratic equation:

$$ax^2 + bx + c = 0$$

The goal of solving a quadratic equation is to find what values of x make the quadratic equation equal to 0. There are several ways to solve a quadratic equation to find these x values.

Quadratic Formula

Let's say we needed to solve the equation $x^2 + 2x = 15$. First, we need to convert this into the quadratic form so that we have the equation set equal to 0:

$$x^2 + 2x - 15 = 0$$

Next, we need to follow the quadratic formula. *This formula will be available to you during the test:*

$$x = \frac{-b \pm \sqrt{b^2 - 4ac}}{2a}$$

Look at the form of the quadratic equation and compare it to our problem:

$$ax^2 + bx + c = 0$$
$$x^2 + 2x - 15 = 0$$

We see that $a = 1$, $b = 2$, and $c = -15$. Let's substitute those values into the quadratic formula:

$$x = \frac{-2 \pm \sqrt{2^2 - 4(1)(-15)}}{2(1)}$$

$$x = \frac{-2 \pm \sqrt{4 - -60}}{2}$$

$$x = \frac{-2 \pm \sqrt{4 + 60}}{2}$$

$$x = \frac{-2 \pm \sqrt{64}}{2}$$

$$x = \frac{-2 \pm 8}{2}$$

Because of the $\pm$ sign, we have two different equations that will yield two different solutions:

$$x = \frac{-2+8}{2} = \frac{6}{2} = 3$$
$$x = \frac{-2-8}{2} = \frac{-10}{2} = -5$$

Therefore, the two solutions of the quadratic equation $x^2 + 2x - 15 = 0$ are $x = 3$ and $x = -5$. If you substitute either of these values into the equation, the answer will be 0.

Completing the Square

The key to completing the square is to focus on the x^2 and x terms—in this case, $x^2 + 2x$.

Step 1: Get the numbers on one side of the equation and the x^2 and x terms on the other:

$$\begin{array}{r} x^2 + 2x - 15 = 0 \\ +15 \quad\quad +15 \\ \hline x^2 + 2x \quad = 15 \end{array}$$

Step 2: Look at the x term: $2x$. The coefficient of this term is 2. Divide this number in half and then square it:

$$\frac{2}{2} = 1$$
$$1^2 = 1$$

Step 3: Add this squared number to both sides of the equation.

$$x^2 + 2x + 1 = 15 + 1$$

Step 4: Now, we want to write the left side of the equation as a perfect square. To do this, simply take the square root of both x^2 and 1 and write these terms as a quantity squared:

$$(x + 1)^2 = 16$$

Step 5: Take the square root of both sides of the equation. Remember, when square rooting a number, we need to take into account that we could have squared not only a positive number but also a negative number to get the value. So,

$$\sqrt{(x + 1)^2} = \pm\sqrt{16}$$
$$x + 1 = \pm 4$$

Just like when we used the quadratic formula to solve for the values of x, we have two equations that will yield two solutions to this quadratic equation:

$$\begin{array}{r} x + 1 = 4 \\ -1 \quad\quad -1 \\ \hline x \quad\quad = 3 \end{array}$$

$$\begin{array}{r} x + 1 = -4 \\ -1 \quad\quad -1 \\ \hline x \quad\quad = -5 \end{array}$$

The solutions for this quadratic equation (the values of x that make this equation equal to 0) are $x = 3$ and $x = -5$. Look familiar? Good! We should get the same answers no matter which method we use.

Factoring

Factoring quadratic equations is easy when we understand how binomials are multiplied in the first place. A binomial is an expression with two terms. To multiply binomials, simply FOIL: multiply the first terms, outside terms, inside terms, and last terms.

> **Example**
> Expand $(x - 7)(x + 4)$.

Multiply Firsts:
$(\underline{x} - 7)(\underline{x} + 4) = \underline{x^2}$

Multiply Outsides:
$(\underline{x} - 7)(x + \underline{4}) = x^2 + \underline{4x}$

Multiply Insides:
$(x - \underline{7})(\underline{x} + 4) = x^2 + 4x \underline{- 7x}$

Multiply Lasts:
$(x \underline{- 7})(x + \underline{4}) = x^2 + 4x - 7x \underline{- 28}$

Combine the x terms to simplify:

$$x^2 + 4x - 7x - 28 = x^2 - 3x - 28$$

Therefore, when factoring, we need to work backwards.

The equation $x^2 - 3x - 28$, when factored, is $(x - 7)(x + 4)$. The equation is equal to 0 when $x = 7$ and/or when $x = -4$.

Let's look at the equation we have been working with in the other methods of solving quadratic equations.

$$x^2 + 2x - 15 = 0$$

We want to factor this so that we have a product of two binomials:

$$(\quad)(\quad)$$

How do we decide what the terms of these binomials are? Let's think about how we expanded the previous example. We first multiplied the first terms of each. So, if we have x^2, we must have multiplied x times x:

$$(x \quad)(x \quad)$$

Next, we need to find numbers that when combined (outsides and insides) equal $+2$ and when multiplied (lasts) equal -15.

What are the factors of 15? 1, 3, 5, 15. Right away, we see that 3 and 5 are two units apart. We need to find a combination of these numbers that when added together yield $+2$ and when multiplied yield -15.

> $(+3)(-5) = -15$; this requirement is fulfilled!
> $+3 - 5 = -2$; but we need $+2$, not -2.

Let's switch the signs on the numbers:

> $(-3)(5) = -15$
> $-3 + 5 = +2$

This works! So let's plug our values into the binomials:

$$(x - 3)(x + 5)$$

When we factor, we see that for this product to equal 0, x equals 3 and/or -5. These are the solutions that we got when we used the quadratic formula and completed the square!

Square Root Technique (Inspection)

The square root technique, or **inspection**, is used only when we do not have an x term. For instance, for the quadratic equation we have been working with, $x^2 + 2x - 15 = 0$, we would not use inspection to solve for the values of x, due to the $2x$ term.

However, if we had $x^2 = 36$ or $x^2 - 64 = 0$, we could use the method of inspection.

Example

Solve $x^2 = 36$.

To use inspection, we simply inspect the equation to look for perfect squares. We can easily get x by itself by square rooting both sides of the equation. Remember, we have to account for a potential negative value of x, so don't forget the $\pm$ sign!

$$\sqrt{x^2} = \pm\sqrt{36}$$
$$x = \pm 6$$

$x = 6$ and $x = -6$ are the two solutions to this equation.

Practice

14. Solve $x^2 - 64 = 0$. _____

15. Solve $x^2 + 40 = 45$. _____

Negative Numbers

Last, consider the following equation.

Solve $x^2 = -25$.

Can a number, when squared, ever be negative? No. A negative number when multiplied by a negative number is always positive. So, for this equation, there are *no* solutions.

Real-World Context

There are times when knowing how to solve quadratic equations helps us figure out real-life situations. For instance, as a landscaper, if you were given instructions to lay stone tiles where the length would be twice as long as the width and your budget would pay for 72 square feet of tile, how would you figure out the dimensions of the tiled area?

Let's draw a picture:

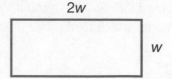

We know that when we find the area of a rectangle, we get square units. Quadratic equations involve square units, so that is our clue that we can use the quadratic equation to find w.

$$(2w)(w) = 72$$
$$2w^2 = 72$$

We now have to figure out which method to use to solve this equation: quadratic formula, completing the square, factoring, or inspection. Since we do not have a w term, completing the square and factoring can be ruled out. Do you notice that if we divided each side of the equation by 2, we would get a situation where we have perfect squares?

$$\frac{2w^2}{2} = \frac{72}{2}$$
$$w^2 = 36$$

We are perfectly set up to use the method of inspection.

$$\sqrt{w^2} = \pm\sqrt{36}$$
$$w = \pm 6$$

$w = 6$ and $w = -6$ are solutions to this equation. However, we are talking about dimensions of a tiled area, so it does not make sense to have negative numbers. Therefore, $w = 6$.

If the width is 6, we simply multiply that by 2 to get the length.

Thus, the dimensions of the stone tiled area are going to be 12 feet by 6 feet.

Functions

A function is a mathematical expression that states the relationship between an input and an output. Where do we see functions in real life? Everywhere! Any equation that allows you to substitute an input to get a corresponding output is a function. For instance, determining a distance when given a rate and a time is a function. How the area of a triangle changes as the base length changes is a function. Calculating your pay rate is a function. Even if the function notation $f(x)$ is not explicitly used, whenever we plug a value in to get a different value out, we are working with functions.

Comparing Proportional Relationships

When comparing proportional relationships, we look at the rate of change of each. The rate of change is simply the change in y values divided by the change in x values, $\frac{\Delta y}{\Delta x}$.

For the equation of a line $y = mx$, m is the slope, or rate of change. To identify the rate of change for an equation of a line is easy: simply look at the value of m in the equation.

For instance, for the equation $y = \frac{1}{2}x$, the rate of change is $\frac{1}{2}$. For the following table of values, we can find the rate of change by using the formula $\frac{\Delta y}{\Delta x}$.

x	y
3	6
4	8
5	10
6	12

Divide the difference of any two y values by the difference of their corresponding x values:

$$\frac{8-6}{4-3} = \frac{2}{1} = 2$$

Therefore, the rate of change, or the slope of the line if we were to graph it, is 2: $y = 2x$.

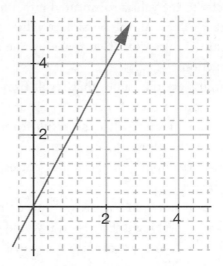

To find the rate of change of a graph, we keep the same formula in mind: $\frac{\Delta y}{\Delta x}$.

We see that the line passes through the origin (0,0) as well as the point (2,4). We can use these two points to determine the slope, or rate of change, by calculating $\frac{\Delta y}{\Delta x}$:

$$\frac{4-0}{2-0} = \frac{4}{2} = 2$$

The rate of change of this line is 2.

Practice

16. What function represents the information in the following table?

x	f(x)
–3	–23
0	4
3	–23
6	–104

a. $3x^2 - 4$
b. $-2x^2 - 4$
c. $2x^2 - 4$
d. $-3x^2 + 4$

Evaluating Functions: Inputs and Outputs

Inputs refer to the values substituted into a function. These are x values. All the possible x values that can be substituted into a function make up the **domain** of the function.

Outputs are the values that result from substituting an input into the function. These are y values. All the possible y values that can result from a function make up the **range** of a function.

For every input (x), there is a corresponding output (y).

Function notation for the output, or range, is $f(x)$. Instead of writing it $y = x^2 - 1$, it would be written $f(x) = x^2 - 1$. The $f(x)$ means that we will be substituting x values into the function f to get output values, or the range.

Example
$f(x) = 2x + 4$

Find $f(x)$, when $x = -9$. This can also be written "Find $f(-9)$."

Substitute -9 for x into the equation:

$f(x) = 2(-9) + 4$
$f(x) = -18 + 4$
$f(x) = -14$

Practice
17. Given the following equation, fill in the chart for all values of $f(x)$.
$f(x) = 3x^3 - 12$

x	f(x)
1	
3	
5	
7	

18. Find the domain of the following function:
$\frac{3 + x^2}{9 - x^2} = f(x).$ _____

19. Evaluate the function $f(x) = 2x^2 + 3x$ when $x = 2a.$ _____

20. Write a function to represent the following situation:

Greg is paid an hourly rate as well as a commission for the number of refrigerators he sells in one day. He gets $13 per hour and works 8-hour days. For every refrigerator he sells, he gets $40. What function represents the amount of money Greg earns on a given day?

_____

Comparing Properties of Functions

To compare properties of quadratic equations, it is first important to know that quadratic equations, when graphed, are in the shape of a parabola.

As you can see, it is a U-shaped curve. The parabola can be either facing up or facing down. If the parabola is facing up, as in Figure 1, there is a minimum y-coordinate. In this case, the minimum is 0. The function does not have a y value below that point. If the parabola is facing down, as in Figure 2, there is a maximum y-coordinate. In this case, the maximum is 4. The function does not have a y-coordinate above that point.

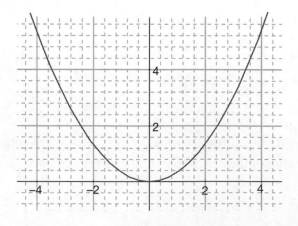

Figure 1

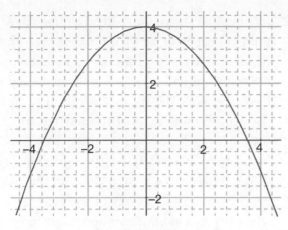

Figure 2

Suppose we were given an algebraic expression of a quadratic equation and were asked to find the maximum or minimum of that function. How would we do that?

1. Remember that the generic quadratic equation is $ax^2 + bx + c = 0$.
2. If the value of $a < 0$, the function will yield a maximum value for y. The parabola will be facing down.

For example, $f(x) = -4x^2 + x - 3$ has $a = -4$, which is less than 0. The parabola has a shape similar to the one in Figure 2. So, it has a maximum y-coordinate.

How do we find what the maximum y-coordinate is? Luckily, there is a procedure we can follow. The important thing to remember is that to find where there is a maximum or a minimum, we need to find $\frac{-b}{2a}$ and then plug that value back into the equation. That might sound confusing, so let's walk through a couple of examples.

Example
$$f(x) = -4x^2 + x - 3$$
$$\frac{-b}{2a} = \frac{-1}{2(-4)} = \frac{-1}{-8} = \frac{1}{8}$$

Plug $\frac{1}{8}$ back into $f(x)$ to find the maximum value of y:

$$f = -4(\tfrac{1}{8})^2 + (\tfrac{1}{8}) - 3$$
$$= -4(\tfrac{1}{16}) + (\tfrac{1}{8}) - 3$$
$$= (-\tfrac{1}{4}) + (\tfrac{1}{8}) - 3$$
$$= \tfrac{-2}{8} + \tfrac{1}{8} - 3$$
$$= \tfrac{-1}{8} - 3$$
$$= -3\tfrac{1}{8}$$

$f(x) = \frac{-25}{8}$ is the maximum value of this function.

3. If the value of $a > 0$, the function will yield a minimum value for y. The parabola will be facing up.

For example, $f(x) = 2x^2 - 3x + 4$ has a value of $a = 2$, which is greater than 0. The parabola has a shape similar to the one in Figure 1. So, it has a minimum y-coordinate. How do we find what the minimum y-coordinate is? Follow the same procedure as in the previous example. Again, the important thing to remember is that to find where there is a maximum or a minimum, we need to find $\frac{-b}{2a}$ and then plug that value back into the equation:

$$f(x) = 2x^2 - 3x + 4$$
$$\frac{-b}{2a} = \frac{3}{2(2)} = \frac{3}{4}$$

Plug $\frac{3}{4}$ back into $f(x)$ to find the maximum value of y:

$$f(\tfrac{3}{4}) = 2(\tfrac{3}{4})^2 - 3(\tfrac{3}{4}) + 4$$
$$= 2(\tfrac{9}{16}) - (\tfrac{9}{4}) + 4$$

cross out the 2 by dividing the 16 by 2 in the first term. This will avoid having to simplify it in the next step:

$$= \left(\tfrac{9}{8}\right) - \left(\tfrac{9}{4}\right) + 4$$
$$= \left(\tfrac{9}{8}\right) - \left(\tfrac{18}{8}\right) + 4$$
$$= -\left(\tfrac{9}{8}\right) + 4$$
$$= -\left(\tfrac{9}{8}\right) + \tfrac{32}{8}$$

$f(x) = \frac{23}{8}$ is the minimum value of this function.

Practice

21. Look at these two functions and determine which function has the greater maximum.

a.

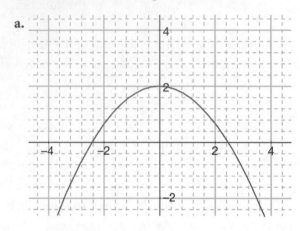

b. $f(x) = -x^2 + 5x$

Algebra and Functions Review

1. Expand and simplify the following expression:
$7(x + 2y - 3) - 3(2x - 4y + 1)$
a. $x + 2y - 18$
b. $13x - 2y - 2$
c. $x + 26y - 24$
d. $x + 6y - 4$

2. Johanna and Paolo just finished a three-day promotional event for their new business. They distributed flyers to businesses and homes in the neighborhood to let the public know about their new shop. They printed a total of 1,000 flyers for this promotional effort and distributed them over the course of three days. They have x flyers left over. If they are expecting a 15% response rate—meaning that, of the flyers handed out, 15% will bring in one person—which expression illustrates how many more customers they are expecting in the near future as a result of this promotional effort?
a. $15(1,000 - x)$
b. $15(1,000x)$
c. $15 + 1,000 - x$
d. $0.15(1,000 - x)$

3. Which of the following is an equivalent expression of $2y^2 - yp - p^2$?
a. $(2y + p)(y - p)$
b. $(y + p)(y - p)$
c. $2(y^2 - yp - p^2)$
d. $(2y - p)(y + p)$

4. Aaron owns a pretzel stand. After observing sales patterns for a few months, he realizes that he needs to have three times as much cheese as he does ranch dressing to fulfill customers' orders. For every 48 ounces of cheese Aaron buys, how much ranch dressing should he buy?
a. 144 oz.
b. 24 oz.
c. 12 oz.
d. 16 oz.

5. Farhiyo and Jen sold T-shirts for a campus club last Saturday. The club made $550 from selling these T-shirts. After donating some of the money to a local shelter, the club made $100 more than it donated. How much money did the club donate? _____

6. Richard wants to start a waterless car wash business. He has $2,000 to buy start-up materials. If the bottled product costs $24.50 per bottle, which expression represents how many bottles of product (p) he can purchase?

a. $2,000 \leq 24.5p$

b. $24.5 + p < 2,000$

c. $24.5p \leq 2,000$

d. $\frac{24.5}{p} \leq 2,000$

7. Find the two solutions to the equation $x^2 - 5x = -6$.

a. 2, −3

b. 2, 3

c. −2, −3

d. −2, 3

8. A host for a party decides to buy three balloons for every guest, plus 20 balloons to decorate the hall. If g represents the number of guests invited to the party and b represents the total number of balloons to be purchased, which equation shows the relationship between the number of balloons (b) and the number of guests (g)?

a. $b = 3(g + 20)$

b. $b = 3g + 20$

c. $b = 60g$

d. $b = 23g$

9. Which expression is the equivalent of $32x^2 + 4x - 8$?

a. $32(x^2 + 4x - 8)$

b. $4x(x + x - 8)$

c. $4(x^2 + x - 2)$

d. $4(8x^2 + x - 2)$

10. Evaluate: $5 \times (10 - 2) \div 2^2$. _____

11. Which of the following is equivalent to $2x(3xy + y)$?

a. $6x^2y + 2xy$

b. $6xy + 2xy$

c. $5x^2y + 2x + y$

d. $3xy + 2x + y$

12. If the sum of two polynomials is $8p^2 + 4p + 1$ and one of the polynomials is $8p^2 - 2p + 6$, what is the other polynomial?

a. $6p - 5$

b. $2p + 7$

c. $16p^2 - 2p + 7$

d. $16p^2 + 2p + 7$

13. Which of the following is a factored form of $10x^4y^6 - 5x^3y$?

a. $5xy^5$

b. $5x^3y$

c. $5x^3y(2xy^5 - y)$

d. $5x^3y(2xy^5 - 1)$

14. The product of 16 and one-half of a number is 136. Find the number. _____

15. Which answer choice represents the solution for the following systems of equations?

$$4x - 5y = 5$$
$$5y = 20 - x$$

a.

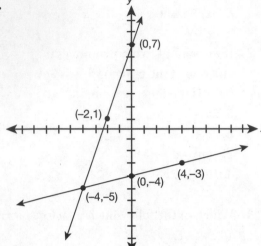

b.

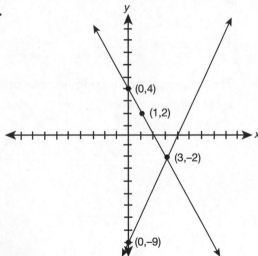

c.

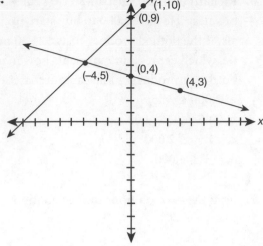

d.

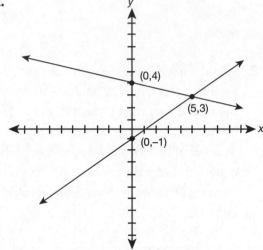

16. Carla's dance squad organizes a car wash in the municipal parking lot. It costs them $250 to rent the lot, and they pay $35 for cleansers. If they charge $5 per car, how many cars must they wash to raise more money than expenses?
   a. 50 cars
   b. 51 cars
   c. 57 cars
   d. 58 cars

17. Janet offered to pick up doughnuts and coffee for her employees with the expectation of being reimbursed for at least half of the cost of the doughnuts. If she spent twice as much on doughnuts as she did on coffee, what expression shows the minimum cost, C, she is expecting to pay out of her own pocket?

   a. $C \geq (0.5)(x) + 2x$
   b. $C \geq (0.5)(2x) + x$
   c. $C \geq (0.5)(2x)$
   d. $C \geq (0.5)(2x + x)$

18. Find the roots of the following equation:
$-2(x^2 - 10x - 24) = 0$

   a. $\{-11, 14\}$
   b. $\{2, -12\}$
   c. $\{-2, -11, 14\}$
   d. $\{-2, 12\}$

19. Solve for x: $x^2 + 5x + 2x + 10 = 0$. _____

20. Write the algebraic expression that represents the phrase *three less than six times a number*.

   _____

Answers and Explanations

Chapter Practice

1. negative. How many negative numbers are multiplied in the numerator? Three. How many negative numbers are in the denominator? None. Since there is an odd number of negative signs, the answer will be negative.

2. 6. Taking the steps one by one:
We have parentheses, $(52 + \sqrt{64})$. In the parentheses we have a square root, so we need to solve that in order to add it to 52. The $\sqrt{64} = 8$.
$52 + 8 = 60$.
We have division: $60 \div 10$, which equals 6, so $(52 + \sqrt{64}) \div 10 = 6$.
It is important that the order of operations is followed to find the right answer.

3. d. Order of operations says that you should first perform any operations in parentheses, and then perform all multiplication and division, moving from left to right; then perform all addition and subtraction, again moving from left to right.
Start by simplifying the expressions inside both sets of parentheses, and in the second expression, be sure to divide 4 by 2 before adding 4:

$(5 - 3) \times (4 + 4 \div 2)$
$= 2 \times (4 + 2)$
$= 2 \times 6$
$= 12$

4. $\frac{7}{xy}$. There are x's and y's in both the numerator and denominator, so we can simplify. Again, we need to keep in mind our rule of dividing exponents. When simplifying $\frac{x^4}{x^5}$, subtract the exponent in the denominator from the exponent in the numerator to find the remaining power of x:

$$4 - 5 = -1$$

So, we are left with x^{-1}. Since it is a negative exponent, the x will be in the denominator. When simplifying $\frac{y^5}{y^6}$, subtract the exponent in the denominator from the exponent in the numerator to find the remaining power of y:

$$5 - 6 = -1$$

So, we are left with y^{-1}, which means we also still have a y in the denominator. Our answer, then, is $\frac{7}{xy}$.

5. $y^2 - 4$.

Multiply Firsts:

$(\underline{y} + 2)(\underline{y} - 2) = \underline{y^2}$

Multiply Outsides:

$(\underline{y} + 2)(y \underline{- 2}) = y^2 \underline{- 2y}$

Multiply Insides:

$(y + \underline{2})(\underline{y} - 2) = y^2 - 2y + \underline{2y}$

Multiply Lasts:

$(y + \underline{2})(y \underline{- 2}) = y^2 - 2y + 2y \underline{- 4}$

When simplified, this expression is $y^2 - 4$. Do you see how this is a difference of squares? Both y^2 and 4 are squares of numbers.

6. $(y^2 + 5)(y^2 - 5)$. Notice that there are only two terms, not three. Ask yourself, could this be a difference of squares?

Is y^4 the square of a number? Yes. $(y^2)(y^2) = y^4$

Is 25 the square of a number? Yes. $(5)(5) = 25$

So, to write this expression in factored form, we write two binomials using the square roots, which we just found. One will be addition and one will be subtraction.

The factored answer of $y^4 - 25 = (y^2 + 5)(y^2 - 5)$. Again, let's check our answer by FOILing.

Multiply Firsts:

$(\underline{y^2} + 5)(\underline{y^2} - 5) = \underline{y^4}$

Multiply Outsides:

$(\underline{y^2} + 5)(y^2 \underline{- 5}) = y^4 \underline{- 5y^2}$

Multiply Insides:

$(y^2 + \underline{5})(\underline{y^2} - 5) = y^4 - 5y^2 + \underline{5y^2}$

Multiply Lasts:

$(y^2 + \underline{5})(y^2 \underline{- 5}) = y^4 - 5y^2 + 5y^2 \underline{- 25}$

Combine the like terms, $-5y^2 + 5y^2$, and we get zero. Thus, we are left with $y^4 - 25$. It worked!

7. $x = 2$ and $x = 1$. For an expression or function to be undefined, the denominator must equal zero. In this case, we have a polynomial expression in the denominator. To find the values of x where $f(x)$ is undefined, we must first factor the polynomial. Refer to the first example for step-by-step instructions of how to factor it. When factored, $x^2 - 3x + 2 = (x - 2)(x - 1)$.

So, $f(x) = \frac{3}{(x - 2)(x - 1)}$.

What would make the denominator zero? If we multiply any number by zero the answer is zero. So, let's look at what would make each factor in our denominator zero.

When would $x - 2 = 0$? When $x = 2$.

When would $x - 1 = 0$? When $x = 1$.

So, the two values of x where the function $f(x)$ is undefined are $x = 2$ and $x = 1$.

8. 11. Again, wherever we see an *x*, we need to replace it with the given value of –3. After substituting, the equation reads:

$$2(-3)^2 + -3 - 4$$

Remember, PEMDAS. Exponents come first. Which number is being squared? The parentheses indicate that it is just the –3. What is $(-3)^2$? $(-3)(-3) = +9$.

$$2(9) + -3 - 4$$

Multiplication comes next in the order of operations. What is being multiplied? $2(9) = 18$.

$$18 + -3 - 4$$

We have only addition and subtraction left, so we now just solve the problem left to right.

$$18 + -3 - 4$$
$$15 - 4 = 11$$

9. 152. To translate these words into symbols so we can solve the problem, we first need to identify the unknown. What is it that we are trying to find out? The number of T-shirts. This is what then becomes represented by a variable. So, let's say *t* is the number of T-shirts.

We know that Richard needs to make at least $2,500. What do the words *at least* sound like? Could he make more? We're sure he'd love to! So, the words "at least" indicate that we have an inequality on our hands. The total amount Richard makes should be equal to *or* greater than $2,500.

How do we calculate how much money Richard will make? He gets $16.50 per T-shirt sold. So, we are going to be multiplying $16.50 by our variable *t*, which represents the number of T-shirts, to get a product of $16.50*t*.

Putting everything together, we now get the mathematical statement $2,500 \leq 16.50t$. The inequality sign is pointing to 2,500 because Richard wants more than $2,500 if he can sell that many shirts!

We solve this inequality just like we would if there were an equal sign. Divide both sides by 16.50 to undo the multiplication of 16.50*t*.

$$\frac{2,500}{16.50} \leq \frac{16.50t}{16.50}$$

Now, $\frac{16.50}{16.50} = 1$, so we now have *t* by itself on one side of the inequality. On the other side of the inequality, we can simplify and get 151.5. This number represents the number of T-shirts, so we need to round up to get a whole number, 152. Therefore, Richard needs to sell at least 152 T-shirts to make his goal of $2,500. Mathematically, this is written $152 \leq t$, as we hope the number of T-shirts, *t*, is greater than 152. However, *t* needs to be *at least* equal to 152 for Richard to make $2,500.

10. **12.5 or $12\frac{1}{2}$.** Remember, start with the farthest number from the variable on the same side of the equation. In this case, it is a –4. To undo it, we must add 4 to each side of the equation.

$$2y - 4 = 21$$
$$\underline{+4 \quad +4}$$
$$2y + 0 = 25$$

Next, divide each side of the equation by 2 to isolate y.

$$\frac{2y}{2} = \frac{25}{2}$$
$$y = 12.5 \text{ or } 12\frac{1}{2}.$$

11. **Edward sold 40 $5 blue tickets and 90 $10 red tickets.** We need to use a system of equations to solve this problem. We know that Edward sold 130 red and blue tickets combined. Let's use r for the red tickets and b for the blue tickets. Our first equation is $r + b = 130$. We also know the prices of each ticket and the total cost. Our second equation is $10r + 5b = 1,100$. Our system of equations, then, is

$$r + b = 130$$
$$10r + 5b = 1,100$$

Remember, to solve this problem, we have three possible methods. However, let's use the method of substitution.

If we use the first equation to isolate r, we need to subtract b from both sides of the equation:

$$r + b = 130$$
$$\underline{-b \quad -b}$$
$$r = 130 - b$$

Now, we can substitute $130 - b$ for r in the second equation.

$$10r + 5b = 1,100$$
$$10(130 - b) + 5b = 1,100$$

Distribute 10 to each of the terms in parentheses.

$$1,300 - 10b + 5b = 1,100$$

Combine the b's and the numbers, each on one side of the equation.

$$1,300 - 10b + 5b = 1,100$$
$$\underline{-1,300 \qquad\qquad -1,300}$$
$$-5b = -200$$

Divide each side by –5 now to isolate b.

$$\frac{-5b}{-5} = \frac{-200}{-5}$$
$$b = 40$$

What was b representing again? The number of blue $5 tickets sold. How are we going to find the number of red tickets? Substitute 40 for b in the equation $r + b = 130$:

$$r + b = 130$$
$$r + 40 = 130$$

Subtract 40 from each side to get r by itself.

$$r + 40 = 130$$
$$\underline{-40 \qquad -40}$$
$$r \qquad = \quad 90$$

Therefore, 40 $5 blue tickets were sold and 90 $10 red tickets were sold.

12. **$y > 3$.** Again, isolate the variable on one side of the inequality.

$$y + 4 > 7$$
$$\underline{-4 \quad -4}$$
$$y \qquad > 3$$

What does this number sentence mean? It means that to keep $y + 4 > 7$ a true statement, we can substitute *any* value of y that is *greater than 3*.

13.

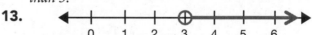

We need to show that for the inequality $y + 4 > 7$, we can have a value of y that is greater than 3. To do this, we plot an open circle at 3 (y cannot equal 3 according to this number statement) and then draw an arrow extending to the right of 3.

14. **$x = 8$ and -8.** First, let's get all the numbers on one side of the equation:

$$x^2 - 64 = 0$$
$$\underline{+64 \quad +64}$$
$$x^2 \quad\ = 64$$

Next, solve for the values of x by taking the square root of both sides:

$$\sqrt{x^2} = \pm\sqrt{64}$$
$$x = \pm 8$$

$x = 8$ and $x = -8$ are the two solutions to this equation.

15. **$x = +\sqrt{5}$ and $-\sqrt{5}$**

$$x^2 + 40 = 45$$
$$\underline{-40 \ -40}$$
$$x^2 \quad\ = 5$$
$$\sqrt{x^2} \ = \pm\sqrt{5}$$

$x = +\sqrt{5}$ and $x = -\sqrt{5}$ are the two solutions to this equation.

16. **d.** By plugging the values from the table into each of the equations, it is clear that $-3x^2 + 4$ is the only equation that satisfies the relationships between the inputs and outputs. Without even substituting all of the inputs to check the outputs, the input 0 makes it obvious that **d** is the only function that satisfies the relationship.

17.

x	f(x)
1	–9
3	69
5	363
7	1,017

To find the output values, we need to substitute our inputs into the function $f(x)$.

$$f(x) = 3x^3 - 12$$
$$f(1) = 3(1)^3 - 12$$
$$= 3 - 12$$
$$= -9$$
$$f(3) = 3(3)^3 - 12$$
$$= 3(27) - 12$$
$$= 81 - 12$$
$$= 69$$
$$f(5) = 3(5)^3 - 12$$
$$= 3(125) - 12$$
$$= 375 - 12$$
$$= 363$$
$$f(7) = 3(7)x^3 - 12$$
$$= 3(343) - 12$$
$$= 1,029 - 12$$
$$= 1,017$$

Notice that $f(x)$ is the y-coordinate. These points could be plotted on a graph to see this portion of the function.

18. $x \neq 3, -3$. What is the domain again? The set of inputs. The x values. We need to know what x values can be substituted into this equation to yield an output of $f(x)$.

For many functions, there are no restrictions. For instance, for $f(x) = x^2$, we can plug in any value we want and we will get an output for $f(x)$. However, for the function in this problem, we have to pay special attention to the fact that it is a fraction.

What do we know about fractions? The denominator can *never* be 0. So, we need to find which value(s) of x will result in 0 in the denominator. To do this, set the current denominator equal to 0.

$$9 - x^2 = 0$$

Solve for x by first moving the x^2 to the other side of the equation.

$$\begin{array}{r} 9 - x^2 = 0 \\ + x^2 + x^2 \\ \hline 9 \quad = x^2 \end{array}$$

Now, take the square root of both sides:

$$\sqrt{9} = \sqrt{x^2}$$
$$\pm 3 = x$$

Therefore, the function $f(x) = \frac{3 + x^2}{9 - x^2}$ has a domain where $x \neq 3, -3$.

19. $2(4a^2 + 3a)$. Just like the previous problems, we substitute the x value, or input, to get the value of $f(x)$, or the output:

$$f(x) = 2x^2 + 3x$$
$$f(2a) = 2(2a)^2 + 3(2a)$$
$$= 2(4a^2) + 6a$$
$$= 8a^2 + 6a$$
$$= 2(4a^2 + 3a)$$

The last step of the solution reflects the un-distribution of a 2.

20. $M = 104 + 40n$ **(variables will vary).** Let's use M for the total amount of money Greg earns on a given day. We know for sure that he gets paid $13 per hour and that he works 8 hours per day. So far,

$$M = (13)(8)$$

In addition, though, Greg gets a $40 commission for every refrigerator he sells. Let's let n stand for the number of refrigerators Greg sells. This probably changes from day to day. When we put this into the equation, we multiply it by $40, since Greg gets $40 for each refrigerator he sells.

$$M = (13)(8) + 40n$$

Simplified, the function is

$$M = 104 + 40n$$

This is a function because the value M will change depending on the value, n, that is substituted into the equation. Each input n will yield a different output, M.

21. b. For function A, we can see that the maximum value is $f(x) = 2$.

For function B, we need to do a little more work. Remember, to find the value of x where $f(x)$ has a maximum value, we need to use the equation $\frac{-b}{2a}$.

$$f(x) = -x^2 + 5x$$
$$\frac{-b}{2a} = \frac{-5}{2(-1)} = \frac{-5}{-2} = \frac{5}{2}$$

Plug $\frac{5}{2}$ back into the function $f(x) = -x^2 + 5x$.

$$f\left(\tfrac{5}{2}\right) = -\left(\tfrac{5}{2}\right)^2 + 5\left(\tfrac{5}{2}\right)$$
$$= -\left(\tfrac{25}{4}\right) + \left(\tfrac{25}{2}\right)$$
$$= -\left(\tfrac{25}{4}\right) + \left(\tfrac{50}{4}\right)$$
$$= \left(\tfrac{25}{4}\right) = 6\tfrac{1}{4}$$

The maximum value of $f(x) = -x^2 + 5x$ is $6\tfrac{1}{4}$. Therefore, function B has the greater maximum value.

Algebra and Functions Review

1. **c.** This problem requires us to use the distributive property for two parts of the expression. First, we need to distribute 7 to each of the factors in the quantity after it: x, $2y$, and -3. This gives us $7x + 14y - 21$. Next, we need to distribute the -3 to each of the terms in the quantity after it: $2x$, $-4y$, and 1. This gives us $-6x + 12y - 3$. Now, we need to combine like terms to simplify the expression: $7x + 14y - 21 - 6x + 12y - 3 = x + 26y - 24$. Choice **a** did not distribute the negative with the 3 in the second half of the problem. Choice **b** reflects incorrectly distributing the coefficients and negatives to the other terms. Choice **d** did not distribute the coefficient to each term.

2. **d.** In order to find out how many flyers Johanna and Paolo passed out, we need to subtract x, the amount left over, from the total, 1,000. Once we get that value, we multiply by 15% by changing 15% to a decimal, 0.15. Multiply 0.15 by $(1,000 - x)$ to get the number of new customers they will anticipate. Choices **a** and **b** do not convert the percentage to an equivalent decimal before multiplying. In addition, choice **b** multiplies the total number of flyers by the amount left over instead of subtracting it. Choice **c** reflects a lack of understanding of how to calculate the anticipated response rate.

3. **a.** Looking at the answer options, we can deduce that we need to factor $2y^2 - yp - p^2$. Keeping in mind how to FOIL backwards, we get the two factors $(2y + p)(y - p)$. When these two binomials are multiplied, or FOILed, we get the original expression. Choice **b** does not have the necessary factor of 2 to get $2y^2$. Choice **c** incorrectly factors out a 2 from the first term only. Choice **c** has the addition and subtraction signs incorrectly placed. The way **d** is written, we would get $+yp$ instead of $-yp$ when multiplied out.

4. **d.** Since we know that Aaron needs three times as much cheese as ranch dressing, we know that the 48 ounces of cheese are three times the needed ranch dressing. Either multiply 48 by $\frac{1}{3}$ or divide 48 by 3. They are essentially doing the same thing. The answer is 16 ounces of ranch. Choice **a** multiplies 48 by 3 instead of dividing 48 by 3. Choices **b** and **c** are factors of 48 and demonstrate a lack of understanding of how to calculate the answer to the problem.

5. **$225.** A system of equations is needed to solve this problem. If C = the amount of money the club profits and D = the amount of money donated, the following two equations are true:

$$C + D = 550$$
$$C - 100 = D$$

When $C - 100$ is substituted into the first equation for D, the equation reads $C + C - 100 = 550$.

$$2C - 100 = 550$$
$$2C = 650$$
$$C = 325$$

When this value is substituted for C in the second equation, the equation reads $325 - 100 = 225$.

6. c. The number of bottles of product purchased is multiplied by the cost of the each bottle. This product is set less than or equal to $2,000, which is the total amount Richard is able to spend. Solving for p will yield the number of bottles that can be purchased without going over his $2,000 budget. Choice **a** is incorrect because it indicates that Richard would be able to spend any amount equal to or greater than $2,000. Choice **b** is incorrect because it does not take into account that (1) the cost needs to be multiplied by the number of bottles purchased and (2) the amount Richard is able to spend can equal $2,000. Choice **d** is incorrect because it indicates that the cost of one of the bottles of product should be divided by the number of bottles; however, the cost should be multiplied by the number of bottles of product to yield the price of the total purchase.

7. b. This is a quadratic equation and can be solved in several ways: factoring, completing the square, or using the quadratic formula. However, looking at the terms $-5x$ and -6, it is apparent that factors of 6 can add to 5, so we will factor this quadratic to get the solutions. First, we set the equation equal to 0: $x^2 - 5x + 6 = 0$. We want to find the two values of x where the equation is equal to 0. By factoring, we get $(x - 2)(x - 3)$. Multiply it out if necessary to check that it in fact yields the original equation. Anything multiplied by 0 is 0, so for what values of x would we get an answer of 0? When $x = 2$ and when $x = 3$. Choices **a**, **c**, and **d** have incorrectly placed positive and negative signs.

8. b. The party host must buy three balloons for each guest, so $3g$ represents the correct number of balloons for all the guests. The host must also buy 20 more balloons for the hall, so the total number of balloons is the number needed for the guests plus 20 more. This is the equation $b = 3g + 20$.

9. d. This answer is equivalent to the original because each of the terms was divided by 4, and then accurately written as a product of 4 and the quantity $8x^2 + x - 2$. This, in effect, is the un-distribution of a 4 from each term. Choices **a** and **b** incorrectly factor out 32 and $4x$, respectively, which leaves the remaining terms incorrect. Choice **c** looks very similar to choice **d**, but the 4 is not correctly factored out of the term $32x^2$.

10. Rewrite the expression and then use the order of operations to simplify the expression:
$$5 \times (10 - 2) \div 2^2$$
$$= 5 \times \frac{(10 - 2)}{2^2}$$
$$= 5 \times \frac{8}{4}$$
$$= 5 \times 2$$
$$= 10$$

11. a. $2x(3xy + y) = 2x(3xy) + 2x(y) = 6x^2y + 2xy$.

12. a. Deciding whether to add or subtract is the trick to answering this question.

Sum = first polynomial + second polynomial Since the sum is already given, do not add. Instead, subtract the polynomial given from the sum to find the other polynomial. Be sure to combine like terms, distribute the subtraction, and be careful with negatives.
$$(8p^2 + 4p + 1) - (8p^2 - 2p + 6)$$
$$= (8p^2 - 8p^2) + (4p - (-2p)) + (1 - 6)$$
$$= 0 + (4p + 2p) + (-5)$$
$$= 6p - 5$$

13. d. To factor means to divide out the largest factor that all of the terms have in common.
First, consider the coefficients: 5 is a factor of both coefficients, so divide the 5 out.
Next, consider the variable x: x^3 is a factor of both terms, so divide out the x^3.
Finally, consider the variable y: The second term has y raised to only the first power, so y is the largest factor.
After determining the largest factor, rewrite the expression by dividing each term by the factor:
$$5x^3y(2xy^5 - 1)$$

14. 17. Let x equal the number sought. The word *product* tells us to multiply 16 by one-half x, or $(16)(0.5x)$, which we set equal to 136. Therefore, $(16)(0.5x) = 136$, which reduces to $8x = 136$, resulting in $x = 17$.

15. d. Transform one of the equations into slope/ y-intercept form:
$$4x - 5y = 5$$
Subtract $4x$ from both sides:
$$4x - 4x - 5y = 5 - 4x$$
Simplify:
$$-5y = 5 - 4x$$
Commutative property:
$$-5y = -4x + 5$$
Divide both sides by -5:
$$y = \frac{4}{5}x - 1$$
The equation is in the proper slope/y-intercept form:
$$m = \frac{4}{5}$$
$$b = -1$$
The y-intercept is at the point $(0,-1)$.
The slope tells you to go up 4 spaces and right 5 for $(5,3)$.

16. d. The amount of money Carla's dance squad raises from washing cars must be greater than the amount of money it costs to hold the car wash. First, find the total expenses. Renting the lot costs $250 and the cleansers cost $35. Add those figures to find the total expenses:
$$\$250 + \$35 = \$285$$
Carla's dance squad must collect more than $285. If the number of cars washed is represented by c, then the inequality $5c > 285$ can be used to determine how many cars must be washed for the dance squad to raise more money than expenses.
The dance squad earns $5 per car. Divide $285 by $5 to find the number of cars the squad must wash to meet its expenses:
$$\$285 \div \$5 = 57$$
$$c > 57$$
Only 58 cars is greater than 57.

17. b. Since Janet spent twice as much on doughnuts as she did on coffee, the same variable can be used. The amount spent on doughnuts is $2x$ and the amount spent on coffee is x. She is expecting to get repaid for at least half of the cost of the doughnuts, $2x$. The inequality that represents the total cost for her, then, is $C \geq (0.5)(2x) + x$.

18. d. Given $-2(x^2 - 10x - 24) = 0$, first factor the equation:
$$-2(x^2 - 10x - 24) = 0$$
$$-2(x - 12)(x + 2) = 0$$
Next, set each of the pairs of parentheses equal to zero:
$$x - 12 = 0$$
$$x + 2 = 0$$
For these equations, $x - 12 = 0$ yields $x = 12$, and $x + 2 = 0$ yields $x = -2$.
Thus, $\{-2,12\}$ is the correct answer.

19. $x = -5$ **and** $x = -2$. Combine like terms:

$$x^2 + 7x + 10 = 0$$

Factor:

$(x + 5)(x + 2) = 0$, so $x + 5 = 0$ and $x + 2 = 0$

$x = -5$ and $x = -2$

Now check the answers:

$-5 + 5 = 0$ and $-2 + 2 = 0$

Therefore, x is equal to both -5 and -2.

20. $6x - 3$. Let *a number* be represented by x. *Less than* indicates subtraction, and *times* indicates multiplication.

Although *less than* comes before *times* in the written phrase, it comes after it in the algebraic expression. To help you understand this, think of how you would find 4 less than 10. You would compute $10 - 4$.

Thus, the phrase *three less than six times a number* is represented by $6x - 3$.

CHAPTER

3 ▶ GRAPHS AND TABLES

Tables and graphs (sometimes referred to as charts) allow us to present information visually on a wide range of subjects: the rising cost of healthcare, for instance, or the number and types of people who live in a community. Graphic information is everywhere—television commercials, newspaper reports, web pages, and elsewhere.

This chapter shows you how to understand and manipulate data so that you can create graphs that accurately portray information as well as understand graphs to answer questions. Answers and explanations for all practice questions are at the end of the chapter.

Representing Data with Different Types of Graphs

One set of data can be represented in many different graphical formats. The GED® test will ask you to answer questions based on information presented in bar graphs, circle graphs/pie charts, dot plots, box plots, histograms, and scatter plots.

Bar Graphs

Bar graphs are used to represent and display data with differing values for each category. The differing heights of the bars offer a quick-glance comparison of data. There are two types of bar graphs: vertical and horizontal.

Vertical bar graphs display the categories along the *x*-axis and the values along the *y*-axis.

For example, the following bar graph shows the average number of children per household for Carolyn Dexter's family. The data includes the past four generations in addition to the current generation of the Dexter clan.

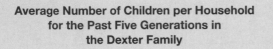

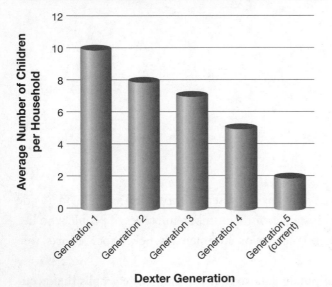

Dexter Generation

As you can see, the categories—Generation 1, Generation 2, Generation 3, Generation 4, and Generation 5 (current)—are placed along the *x*-axis. The data values—the average number of children per household—are placed along the *y*-axis. At a quick glance, you can see that the average number of children per household has decreased from generation to generation.

Horizontal bar graphs display the categories along the *y*-axis and the data values along the *x*-axis. Using the same data as before, we can also make a horizontal bar graph. It would look like the following:

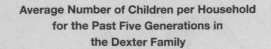

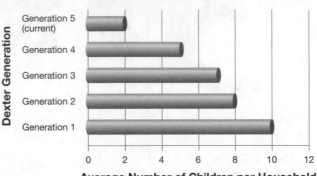

Average Number of Children per Household

Here, you can see, the categories—Generation 1, Generation 2, Generation 3, Generation 4, and Generation 5 (current)—are now placed along the *y*-axis. The data values—the average number of children per household—are now placed along the *x*-axis. Still, it is easy to see at a quick glance that the average number of children per household has decreased from generation to generation.

On the GED® test, you may be asked to interpret information presented in bar graphs or finish constructing a bar graph by dragging and dropping the correct bar height to complete the graph according to a given set of data.

Practice

1. On average, how many more children did households have in the first generation than the current Dexter generation, according to the graphs? _____

2. There are five different types of books at the Everdale Library. The numbers of the various types of books are shown in this bar graph:

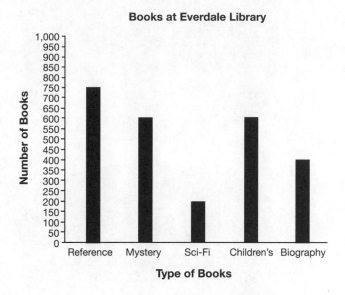

Books at Everdale Library

Everdale Library has as many mystery books as it has _____ books.

Circle Graphs/Pie Charts

Circle graphs, or **pie charts**, are used to express data that collectively makes a whole. This is best used when looking at percentages out of 100%. It's good for getting a comparison of a particular piece of information against the whole. For instance, if 80% of all children in developing countries under the age of five are malnourished, a circle graph could easily display this data.

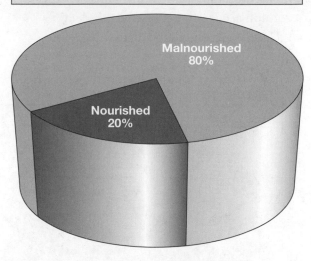

Percentage of Malnourished Children under Five Years in Developing Countries

The 80% of malnourished children under five years old in developing countries plus the 20% of nourished children under five years old in developing countries equals a whole 100% of children under five years old in developing countries. The circle graph provides a visual representation of the statistics.

On the test, you may have to identify the correct piece of the circle to complete a graph, similar to the bar graph example. Or you may have to find percentages of data to correctly construct the circle graph, or at least recognize the correct graph.

Practice

3. Based on the values in the table, which circle graph accurately represents this data?
U.S. Census Bureau Statistics, 2012

SINGLE MOTHERS WITH CHILDREN UNDER 18	SINGLE FATHERS WITH CHILDREN UNDER 18
10.322 million	1.956 million

a.

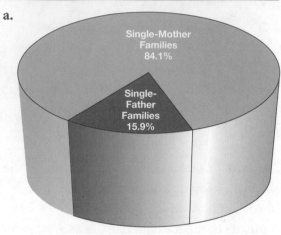

b.

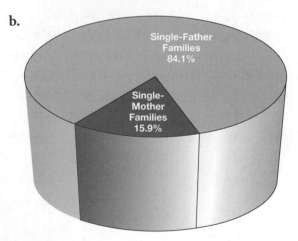

c.

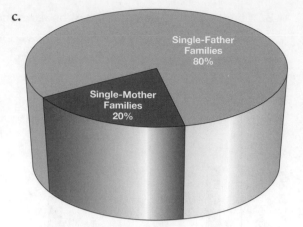

d.

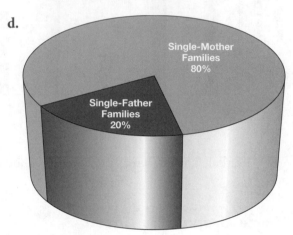

Dot Plots

Dot plots are used to display categorical data on a number line. They are what they sound like: plotted dots on a number line. However, frequency of each number plotted is taken into account, and it will look like the examples that follow where higher frequency means more X's or dots above the number line.

Example

Miss Betty gave her students a test that was worth 100 points. She knows that a good way to visualize this data and see a snapshot of the whole class's test scores

is to make a dot plot. She takes the information from the table and creates a dot plot.

STUDENT	SCORE
Devon	92
Jorge	84
Janice	79
Travonda	92
Gwen	84
Ronald	94
Shirley	92

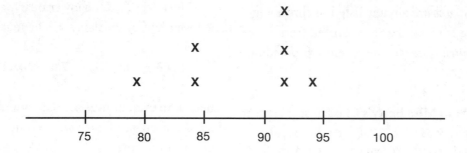

As you can see, one test score was a 79, so one X is plotted at 79. Two scores were 84, so two X's stacked on top of each other are plotted at 84. Three scores were 92, so three X's are plotted at 92. Last, one score was 94, so one X is plotted at 94.

This visualization of data allows Miss Betty to quickly see the range of test scores: 79 to 94. It also gives her a visualization of how well her students are doing as a whole. On the GED® test, you will be asked to interpret information of dot plots as well as use them to find missing information.

Practice

4. Suppose Miss Betty has eight students, not seven, and that the eighth student's score is between 84 and 92. The median of all eight scores is 90.5. Plot the missing score on the following dot plot. Draw an X where the missing score would land on the plot.

STUDENT	SCORE
Devon	92
Jorge	84
Janice	79
Travonda	92
Gwen	84
Ronald	94
Shirley	92
8th student	X

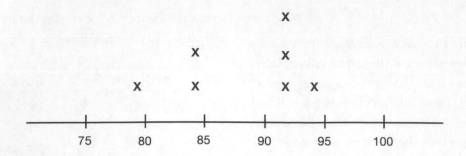

Box Plots

Box plots are similar to dot plots; however, box plots allow us to summarize a large amount of data. For instance, suppose Miss Betty has 25 students, and she wants a good way to summarize the score data of the recent test. The scores are already listed in chronological order. If data is given that is *not* listed from least to greatest, you *must* order the data before proceeding with the box plot.

25 Scores from Miss Betty's Class Test
55, 65, 67, 69, 75, 76, 78, 79, 82, 83, 84, 85, 86, 87, 87, 89, 90, 91, 91, 91, 92, 93, 93, 93, 100

Even though there are 25 numbers in the data set, because a box plot offers a summary of the data, only five numbers will be plotted:

1. Median of the entire data set
2. Lower quartile (i.e., the median of the lower half of the data set)
3. Upper quartile (i.e., the median of the upper half of the data set)
4. Lower extreme (i.e., the lowest point of the data set)
5. Upper extreme (i.e., the highest point of the data set)

So, how do we find these five numbers? Let's start with the median of the entire data set. Look at the chronological list of data. What is the very middle number (i.e., the median)?

55, 65, 67, 69, 75, 76, 78, 79, 82, 83, 84, 85, **86**, 87, 87, 89, 90, 91, 91, 91, 92, 93, 93, 93, 100

The number 86 is the median because there is an even 12 numbers on each side of it in the data set.

Next, let's find the lower quartile, the median of the lower half of the data set. The first 12 values are:

55, 65, 67, 69, 75, **76, 78**, 79, 82, 83, 84, 85. . . .

There is an even number of data points, so we need to find the average of the two middle numbers to get our lower quartile:

$$\frac{76 + 78}{} = 77$$

The number 77 is the lower quartile, the median of the lower half of the data set.

To find the upper quartile, find the median of the upper half of the data set:

. . . 87, 87, 89, 90, 91, **91, 91**, 92, 93, 93, 93, 100

Again, there are 12 numbers, but the two middle numbers are the same, so it is easy to take the average of them to get the upper quartile:

$$\frac{91 + 91}{2} = 91$$

The number 91 is the upper quartile, the median of the upper half of the data set.

The lower and upper extremes are easy to find. They are simply the lowest number and the highest number in the data set—in this case, 55 and 100.

Now that we have our five points, let's plot them on the number line.

Lower extreme: 55
Lower quartile: 77

Median: 86
Upper quartile: 91
Upper extreme: 100

The bolded numbers are going to become lines to make a box. The extremes are simply going to be dots.

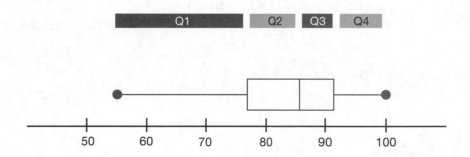

Do you see how the box contains three vertical lines? These represent the values of 77, 86, and 91. The box lets Miss Betty see that the majority of her students fall within the range of the boxed values. The points let Miss Betty see the outliers of data—how far above and below her students scored with respect to the box. Remember, the box has been made according to three median values of the data set. Looking at the box plot, Miss Betty can also see that the lower half of her class's scores are more spread out and the upper half of her class's scores are more bunched.

The last terminology you should know for box plots involves quartiles. The data is split up into four quartiles, as shown:

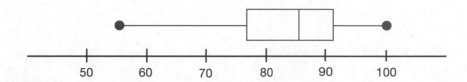

Practice

5. Which destination has more consistent temperature in the fall: Minnesota or Alaska? _____

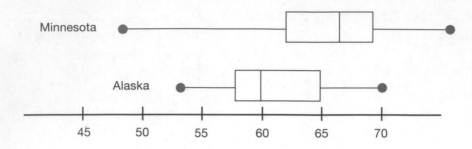

6. What is the median of the data displayed here? _____

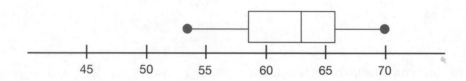

Histograms

Histograms are graphs that allow ranges of data to be displayed. These ranges are plotted with side-by-side bars.

The following example shows the number of students in each age range enrolled in Mr. Duvall's college class.

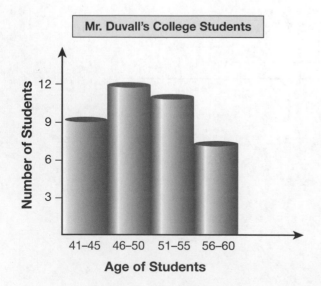

On the GED® test, you may be asked to drag and drop the appropriate bar to complete a set of data, or you may be asked to provide answers based on reading the histogram.

Example

How many students are in Mr. Duvall's class?

    A. 50
    B. 44
    C. 39
    D. 35

The correct answer is choice **c.** Add up how many students are in each of the age ranges:

    9 41- to 45-year-olds
    12 46- to 50-year-olds
    11 51- to 55-year-olds
    +7 56- to 60-year-olds
    39 students

Practice

7. According to the graph, what percentage of students are ages 46 to 50? _____

8. According to the graph, what is the percentage difference between the age group with the highest number of students and the age group with the lowest number of students? _____

Scatter Plots

Scatter plots of bivariate data—data with two variables—allow us to assess the relationship between the two variables and make predictions about data not contained in the graph.

Here are some terms to know with respect to scatter plots:

Cluster: A cluster of points is where most of the plotted points are located. It can also refer to the direction of the plotted points as a whole.

Outlier: This is a point that is not with the cluster. It is either significantly larger or smaller or a point that does not correlate with the rest of the data.

Linear association: A graph has linear association if the plotted points resemble a line.

Nonlinear association: A graph has nonlinear association if the plotted points resemble a curve.

Positive association: Positive association of bivariate data means that as one variable increases, the other increases as well.

Negative association: Negative association of bivariate data means that as one variable increases, the other decreases.

Creating a Scatter Plot

Here is a table of bivariate data: the number of hours each student studied each week compared to the number of weeks it took each to pass his or her GED® test.

HOURS OF STUDYING	NUMBER OF WEEKS TO PASS GED
1	30
3	25
4	24
6	21
8	19
10	27
11	17
12	16
14	14
17	13
20	10

To graph this data, treat one variable as the x-coordinate and the other variable as the y-coordinate. There are 11 (x,y) coordinates for this collected data. When plotting points, there are six things to keep in mind:

1. The x-axis is horizontal.
2. The y-axis is vertical.
3. The x-coordinate is always the first term listed in the parentheses (x,y).
4. The y-coordinate is always the second term listed in the parentheses (x,y).
5. The point of intersection between the x- and y-axis is called the **origin**. It has an x value of 0 and a y value of 0. It is written $(0,0)$.
6. There are four different quadrants that make up the coordinate plane. As you can see from the following graph, any y value below the x-axis is negative. Any x value to the left of the y-axis is also negative.

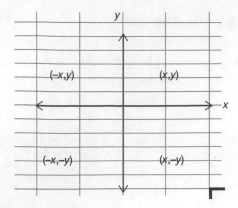

To plot the point (−3,6), you would start at the origin and move three spaces to the *left* and six spaces *up*.

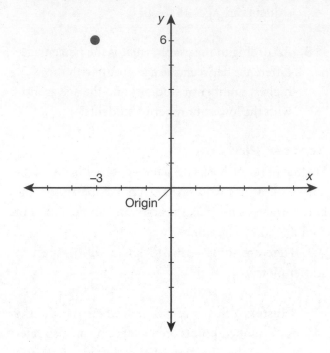

To plot the point (4,−5), you would start at the origin and move four spaces to the *right* and five spaces *down*.

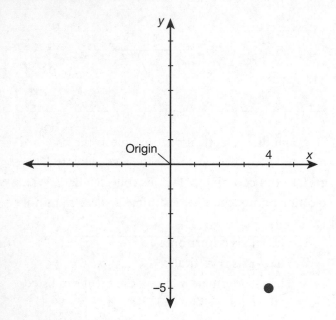

If we refer back to the data just listed and plot these points as (*x,y*) coordinates, the result would look like this:

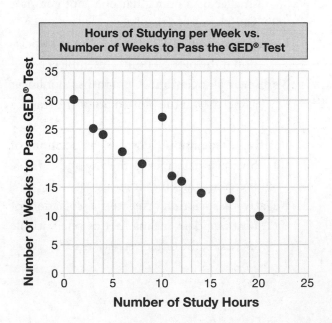

It might be helpful at this point for you to return to Chapter 2 on algebra and functions to reread the information on slope: what it is, how to find it, and what it represents. Understanding the concept of slope will help you determine trends in information when reading scatter plots.

Practice

Use the preceding data to answer questions 9 through 11.

9. Does this data show a positive or negative association? _____

10. Which point would be considered an outlier?
  a. (14,14)
  b. (3,25)
  c. (10,27)
  d. (17,13)

11. Which statement is NOT true about this graph?
  a. The data shows negative linear association.
  b. The data shows that more hours one studies each week, the more quickly one passes the GED® test.
  c. The data shows negative nonlinear association.
  d. One can quite confidently predict that a student who studies 19 hours a week will pass the GED® test in roughly 11 weeks.

Graphs in the Real World

In addition to knowing how to answer questions on the GED® test, understanding how graphs are constructed and convey meaning is extremely important for job skills and in further education. Displaying data graphically can offer powerful evidence to support claims. For instance, one could use the data from the bar graph to support the claim that changes in society over the past 100 years have resulted in a decrease in the number of children per family. The

data represented in the circle graph could be used to argue that single mothers need more financial and educational support. The data from the box plot shows Miss Betty that the majority of her students are succeeding as well as illustrates that there are a few students who may need extra help. Mr. Duvall can use the histogram to recruit other middle-aged adults who may be wary of starting college at their age. The scatter plot can encourage students to study more so that they pass their GED® test faster.

Parallel and Perpendicular Lines

Two lines are **parallel** if they have the *same* slope. For instance, $y = 7x + 5$ and $y = 7x - 34$ are parallel. The slope of each line is 7.

Two lines are **perpendicular** if their slopes are *opposite reciprocals*. For instance, if the slope of a line A is 2, then the slope of its perpendicular line B is $-\frac{1}{2}$.

An infinite number of lines could be parallel and perpendicular to a given line when you look only at the slope as the determining factor. The only thing that changes with each of these lines is the y-intercept—where it crosses the y-axis.

However, what if we wanted to find a *particular* line that is parallel or perpendicular to a given line? As long as we know the slope and a point through which the line passes, we can find a particular parallel or perpendicular line.

Example

Find the equation of the line that is parallel to $3y - 6 = 18x$ and passes through the point $(0,-3)$.

First, we need to get the given line into slope-intercept form: $y = mx + b$:

$$3y - 6 = 18x$$
$$\underline{+6 \qquad +6}$$
$$3y = 18x + 6$$
$$\frac{3y}{3} = \frac{18x}{3} + 6$$
$$y = 6x + 2$$

Our slope is 6, so the slope of the parallel line is also 6. Since we know an x and a y value for this parallel line, we can substitute these values into the slope-intercept form to find b, the y-intercept.

$$y = mx + b$$
$$-3 = 6(0) + b$$
$$-3 = b$$

So, the equation of the parallel line to $3y - 6 = 18x$ that passes through $(0,-3)$ is:

$$y = mx + b$$
$$y = 6x - 3$$

Practice

12. What line is parallel to the line $y - 2 = 3x$?
   a. $y = 2x - 1$
   b. $y = 3x + 3$
   c. $y = -2x - 6$
   d. $y = \frac{-1}{3}x + 9$

13. What is the slope of a line perpendicular to $y + \frac{3}{4}x = 1$?
   a. $\frac{-4}{3}$
   b. -1
   c. 1
   d. $\frac{4}{3}$

14. Find the equation of the line that is perpendicular to $y = \frac{1}{4}x + 6$ that passes through the point $(-2,8)$. _____

Key Features of Graphs

There are many features of graphs that are used to describe and identify functions.

Intercepts

There are **x-intercepts** and **y-intercepts**, which are points at which the graph line intersects an axis. As you would imagine, x-intercepts intercept, or cross over, the x-axis, and y-intercepts intercept, or cross over, the y-axis.

Look at the following graph of $y = x + 4$.

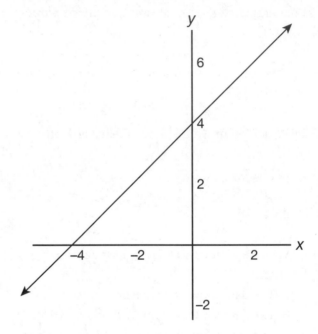

At which point does the line cross the x-axis?

$(-4,0)$

The x-intercept of this function is -4. What do you notice about the y value? It is 0. Does this make sense? If a function crosses the x-axis, then at that exact point there is no height—upward or downward movement—of the function. Therefore, the y value must be 0.

At which point does the line cross the y-axis?

$(0,4)$

The y-intercept is 4. What do you notice about the x value? It is 0. Does this make sense? If a function crosses the *y*-axis at that exact point, there is no width—left or right movement—of the function. Therefore, the value of *x* must be 0.

Sometimes functions have more than one *x*-intercept and/or *y*-intercept. Look at the following graph.

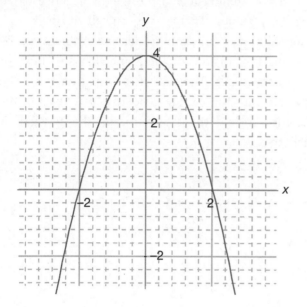

How many *y*-intercepts does this parabola have?

One: When $x = 0$, $y = 4$.

How many *x*-intercepts does this parabola have?

Two: When $y = 0$, $x = 2$ and -2.

If you did not have a graph to look at, could you find values of the *x*- and/or *y*-intercept(s)? Since we know that at the point of intersection the other coordinate value is 0, we can determine what the intercept values are when we have an equation. We have already started practicing this concept with the equation of a line, $y = mx + b$, where *b* is the *y*-intercept.

Practice

15. What is the *y*-intercept of the function $f(x) = 3x + 4$? _____

16. Where does the function $f(x) = 5x^2 - 25$ intersect the *x*-axis? _____

Increasing and Decreasing

A way to think about the concept of increasing and decreasing intervals is to observe whether the graph is rising or falling from left to right. A function is said to be **increasing** during intervals over which the graph rises from left to right. Conversely, a function is said to be **decreasing** during intervals over which the graph falls from left to right. The points at which a function changes from increasing to decreasing or from decreasing to increasing are points on the graph where the function is said to be *neither* increasing *nor* decreasing.

Intervals during which the function increases are described as having a non-negative slope. Intervals during which the function decreases are described as having a non-positive slope. For instance, the function graphed next is increasing from before we even see the graph (from negative *x* values) all the way to the *y* value of 4. Since it appears this graph goes on forever, we use the symbol to represent infinity. So, the interval over which this function increases and has a non-negative slope is $(-\infty, 0)$.

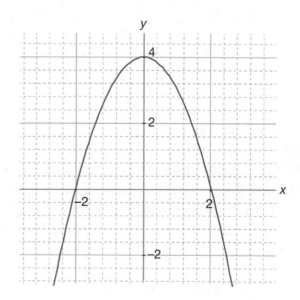

Where does this same function decrease? From 0 to what appears to be infinity. The interval over which the function is decreasing and has a non-positive slope is written (0,∞). It is very important to use parentheses ( ) instead of brackets [ ] because 0 is *not* included in either the increasing or decreasing—it is simply the *x* value at which the function switches direction—and infinity is not a finite amount. Brackets indicate that the value is included in the interval.

Let's look at another function to illustrate the increasing and decreasing of functions.

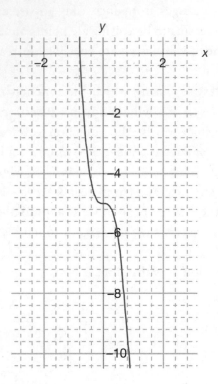

Over which interval(s) is the *f*(*x*) increasing? Over which interval(s) is the *f*(*x*) decreasing?

There are no intervals where *f*(*x*) is increasing. There is a point when the function intersects the *y*-axis where it is neither increasing nor decreasing: (0,–5). With the exception of this point where the graph is neither rising nor falling, the graph maintains a non-positive slope (i.e., the graph falls from left to right). Since we have an interval where the function decreases, and then the point (0,–5), and

then another interval where the function decreases, we write the two decreasing intervals joined with a ∪ to illustrate this concept.

The function *f*(*x*) decreases (–∞,0) ∪ (0,∞).

Positive and Negative

Functions are considered positive or negative based on the *y* values. That is, we can tell during which interval(s) the function is positive or negative by looking for portions of the graph that are above or below the *x*-axis. Any part of the function above the *x*-axis means the *y* value is **positive**. Any part of the function below the *x*-axis means the *y* value is **negative**.

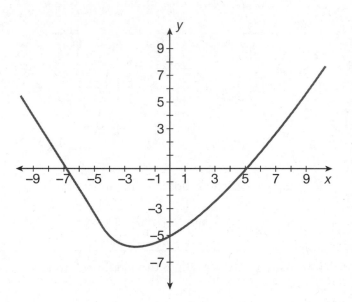

This function is positive on the intervals (∞,–7) ∪ (5,∞) and is *negative* on the interval (–7,5).

Relative Maximums and Minimums

Maximums are heights of the function, and **minimums** are lows of the function. Maximums and minimums occur where there are changes in the direction of the graph. When a function increases and then decreases, a maximum occurs. When a function decreases and then increases, a minimum occurs. There may be several maximums and minimums of a function—thus, the term *relative*, which refers to the region of the graph where a given maximum or minimum is located. Take a look at this graph:

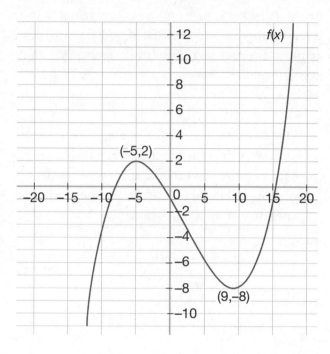

At what point does the function $f(x)$ have a maximum?

The graph switches from decreasing to increasing at the point $(9,-8)$, making it a relative minimum value.

At what point does the function $f(x)$ have a maximum?

The graph switches from increasing to decreasing at the point $(-5,2)$, making it a relative maximum value.

Symmetries

Some graphs are **symmetrical** about the x-axis or y-axis. Creating symmetry is like looking in a mirror. If you were given half of the information of a symmetrical function, you would be able to complete the graph. For instance, look at this graph:

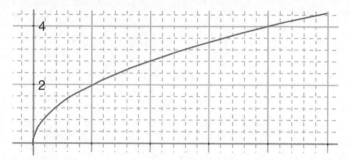

If this function is symmetrical about the x-axis, you can mirror the relationship and sketch the rest of the graph.

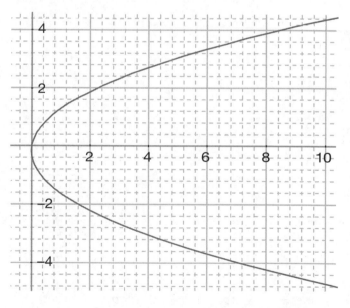

Consider this next graph:

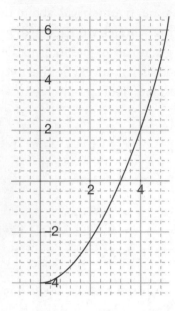

If you were told it is symmetrical about the *y*-axis, how would you complete the graph?

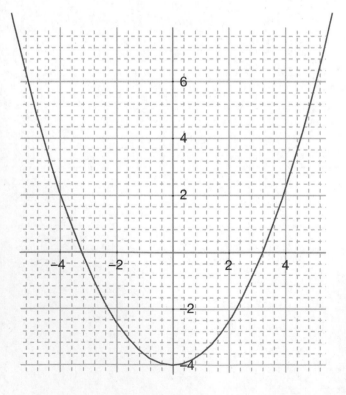

End Behavior

End behavior refers to what the function is doing as the *y* values approach ±∞. If you look at a graph, it is easy to tell what is happening to the *y* values as the *x* values change. However, what if you do not have a graph in front of you, but rather have only a functional formula? There are a few things to keep in mind:

- If the function has an even leading power (i.e., x^2, x^4, x^6, etc.), then the function will have a *parabolic shape*. If the leading coefficient is positive, the parabola will be face up; if the leading coefficient is negative, it will be face down.

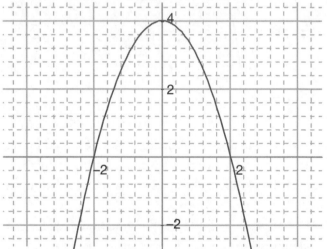

NOTE

When there is a positive leading coefficient, as *x* approaches negative infinity (written *x* → −∞), *y* approaches positive infinity (written $f(x) → ∞$). In addition, as *x* → +∞ +, $f(x) → ∞$.

When there is a negative leading coefficient, as *x* → ∞, $f(x) → ∞$. In addition, as *x* → +∞, $f(x) → −∞$.

■ If the function has an odd leading power (i.e., x^3, x^5, x^7, etc.), then the function will have a *cubic shape*. If the leading coefficient is positive, the function will start from the bottom left of the graph; if the leading coefficient is negative, the function will start from the upper left of the graph.

> **NOTE**
>
> When there is a positive leading coefficient, as $x \to -\infty$, $f(x) \to -\infty$. In addition, as $x \to +\infty$, $f(x) \to +\infty$.
>
> When there is a negative leading coefficient, as $x \to -\infty$, $f(x) \to +\infty$. In addition, as $x \to +\infty$, $f(x) \to -\infty$.

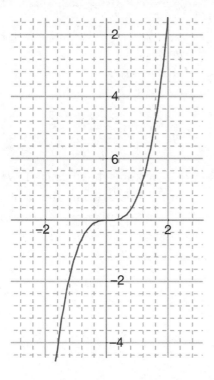

Practice

17. What is the end behavior of the function $x^4 + 3x^3 - 2x$ as $x \to -\infty$? _____

18. What is the end behavior of the function $-2x^5 + 3x^3 + x^2$ as $x \to +\infty$? _____

Equation of a Line

As we've covered before, the equation of any line is $y = mx + b$. The variables x and y represent any (x,y) coordinate on the line. The variable m represents the slope, and the variable b represents the y-intercept.

Imagine drawing a line. You could go on forever if you didn't have walls, doors, street signs, trees, and so forth in the way. Lines are infinite. Thus, they have an infinite number of points on them. The equation of a distinct line will have a definite slope and a definite y-intercept named in the equation, but the variables x and y will remain in the general equation. The following are examples of equations of distinct lines. Any (x,y) coordinates that satisfy this relationship are located on the given line.

$$y = 8x + 6$$
$$y = -3x + 2$$
$$y = \frac{1}{2}x - 3$$

However, what if we don't know the equation of a certain line, but we have other information about it? Can we still figure out what line it is? Yes! As long as we have either a given point and a given slope or two distinct points, we can identify a specific line.

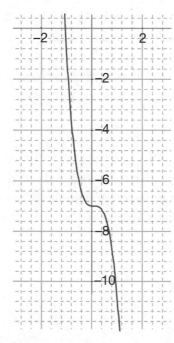

Given Slope, Given Point

If we know the slope and a point (x,y), that takes care of three of the four variables in the equation $y = mx + b$. We can solve for the unknown, b, and then rewrite the equation with the value of b.

Example

Find the equation of the line that has a slope of 4 and passes through the point $(-1,7)$.

Substitute the known values into the equation $y = mx + b$ and solve for b:

$$y = mx + b$$
$$7 = 4(-1) + b$$
$$7 = -4 + b$$
$$\underline{+4 \quad +4}$$
$$11 = b$$

Now, include the value of b in the equation and write it so that x and y are back in the equation:

$$y = 4x + 11$$

Practice

19. Find the equation of the line that passes through $(9,-5)$ and has a slope of 0.5.

_____

Two Given Points

We can also find the equation of a specific line if we have two distinct points on the line, even if we don't have the slope. This method has several steps to remember.

Let's say we want to know the equation of the line that passes through $(2,0)$ and $(-3,5)$.

Step 1: Use the equation $y - y_1 = m(x - x_1)$ to find the slope.

If it helps to keep the points straight, you can label the points (it doesn't matter which point you

choose to have a subscript, as long as you are consistent):

$$(2,0) \qquad (-3,5)$$
$$(x,y) \qquad (x_1,y_1)$$

Now, plug these values into the equation and solve for slope, m.

$$y - y_1 = m(x - x_1)$$
$$0 - 5 = m(2 - (-3))$$
$$-5 = m(2 + 3)$$
$$\frac{-5}{5} = \frac{m(5)}{5}$$
$$-1 = m$$

Step 2: Now that we know the slope is -1, we can find the equation of the line by using the same equation and *one* of the points—either one—to substitute for (x_1,y_1).

$$y - 5 = -1(x - (-3))$$
$$y - 5 = -1(x + 3)$$
$$y - 5 = -x - 3$$
$$\underline{+5 \qquad\qquad +5}$$
$$y = -x + 2$$

Practice

20. What is the equation of the line that passes through $(-6,3)$ and $(-1,11)$? _____

Graphing a Linear Equation

Graphing a linear equation is quite simple.

1. If you are given two distinct points, simply plot both points and draw a line through them.
2. If you are given the slope and one distinct point, plot the given point and then use the knowledge of slope $= \frac{\text{rise}}{\text{run}}$ to draw the line.

For instance, you are asked to graph the line that has a slope of $\frac{4}{3}$ and passes through the point (2,0). First, plot the point (2,0):

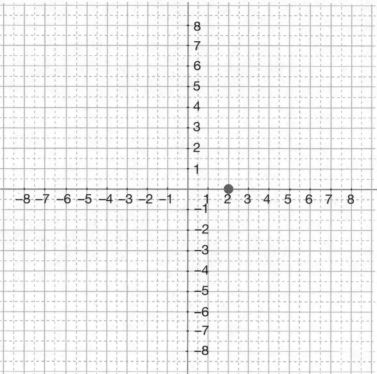

Now that the point is graphed, we need to find another point to draw a line. Since we know the slope is $\frac{4}{3}$, start at the plotted point (2,0) and go up 4 and to the right 3:

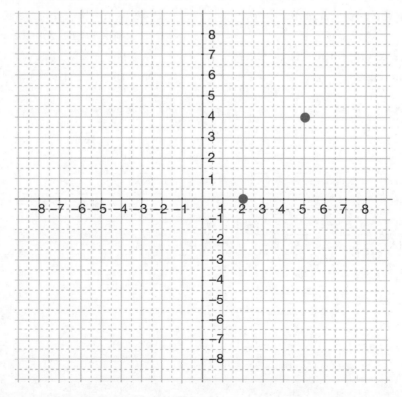

Last, draw a line that goes through both points:

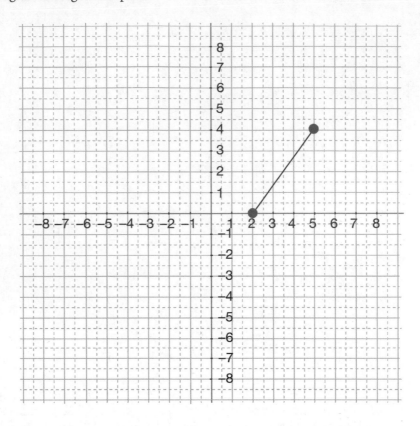

3. If you are given the equation of a line, you can graph it by using the *y*-intercept and slope values.

For instance, to graph the line $y = 2x - 1$, first plot the *y*-intercept:

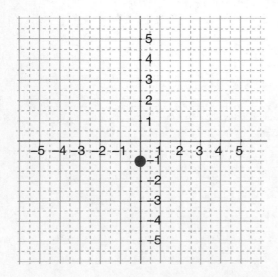

Since we know the slope is 2, we can follow the same procedure as in the previous example to graph the line: start at $(0,-1)$ and go up 2 and over 1:

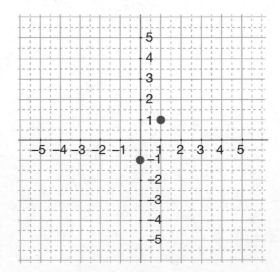

Last, draw a line that goes through both points:

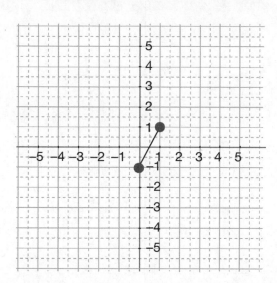

Graphs and Tables Review

1. What is an equation of the line that passes through (–4,3) and has a slope of $\frac{1}{2}$?
   a. $x - 2y + 10 = 0$
   b. $2x - 4y - 6 = 0$
   c. $-4x - 3y - 7 = 0$
   d. $-4x + 3y + \frac{1}{2} = 0$

2. Which graph has a y-intercept at –5 and increases during the interval $(-\infty,-5) \cup (-5,\infty)$?

   a.

   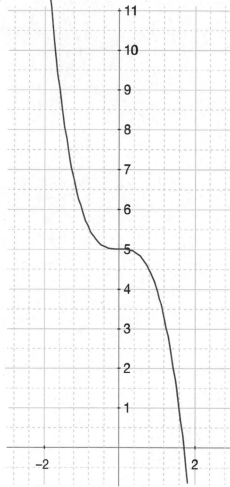

b.

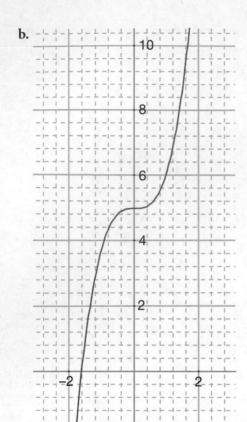

c.

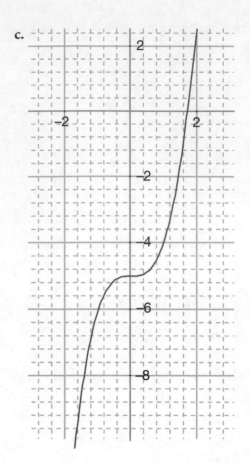

d.

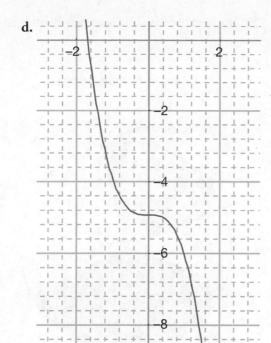

3. Cecilia plots on a bar graph the cost of her cell phone bill for each month from January through September. How much did Cecilia spend on her cell phone in April and May combined? _____

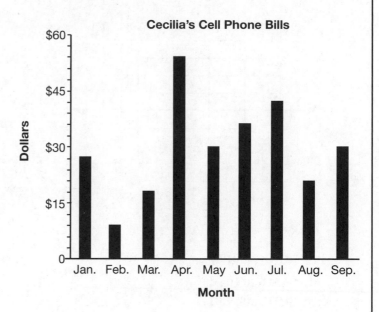

4. This box-and-whisker plot shows the prices of textbooks at a local high school. What range describes the middle 50% of the prices (p) of the textbooks?

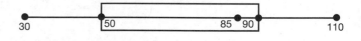

a. $30 < p < $85
b. $50 < p < $85
c. $50 < p < $90
d. $85 < p < $90

5. The figure shown is a rectangle. If connected, which of the following pairs of points would produce a line of symmetry?

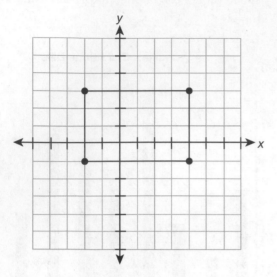

a. (−2,−1) and (4,−1)
b. (0,3) and (0,−1)
c. (4,3) and (4,−1)
d. (4,3) and (−2,−1)

6. The graph shows the Johnson family budget for one month.

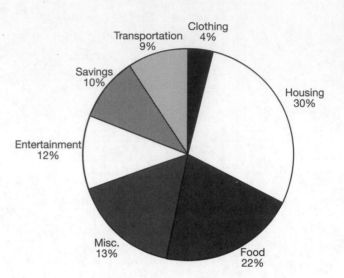

In percentage of overall expenses, how much more money is spent on food than on transportation and clothing combined?

_____

7. Which of the following statements best describes the relationship between the data points shown on the scatter plot?

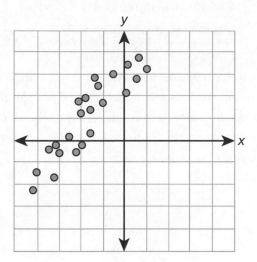

a. There is a positive correlation.
b. There is a negative correlation.
c. There does not appear to be any correlation.
d. It cannot be determined without knowing the values of the data points.

Answers and Explanations

Chapter Practice

1. 8. The first generation displayed is Generation 1. The height of the bar for Generation 1 is 10, which means each household had an average of 10 children. The height of the bar for the current generation, Generation 5, is 2, which means that each household in the Dexter family today has an average of 2 children. On average, the difference between the first generation displayed and the current Dexter generation is 8 children per household.

2. children's. The bars on the graph represent each type of book in Everdale Library. If two bars are the same height, that means they represent the same quantity, or number, of books. The bar labeled "Mystery" represents 600 books. The only other bar that is the same height as the "Mystery" bar is the "Children's" bar, which also represents 600 books. Everdale Library has as many mystery books as it has children's books.

3. **a.** To represent information in a circle graph, we have to first find the percentage of the whole for each statistic, since the circle represents a whole. First, we need to find the total number of single parents by adding 10.322 million and 1.956 million:

$$\begin{array}{r} 10.322 \text{ million} \\ +\ 1.956 \text{ million} \\ \hline 12.278 \text{ million} \end{array}$$

Now that we know the total number of families, we can find the percentage of single-mother families and single-father families by doing division problems:

$$\frac{\text{\# of single-mother families}}{\text{Total number of families}} = \frac{10.322 \text{ million}}{12.278 \text{ million}} = 0.8406$$
= 84.1% (when rounded)

$$\frac{\text{\# of single-father families}}{\text{Total number of families}} = \frac{1.956 \text{ million}}{12.278 \text{ million}} = 0.1593 =$$
15.9% (when rounded)

Choice **b** has the statistics for single fathers and single mothers reversed. Choice **d** is a rounded answer, but with choice **a** available, choice **d** is not as accurate. Choice **c** is similar to choice **d**, but the statistics are reversed.

4.

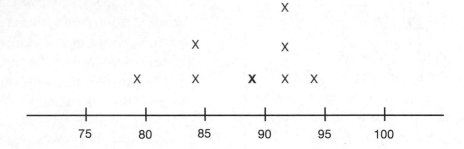

The median of a data set is always the very middle number when they are arranged chronologically. With an odd number of data points, finding the median is easy. However, when you have an even number of data points, there are two middle numbers. The median is then the average of those two middle numbers.

To find the missing score, we first need to order the data points from least to greatest:

79, 84, 84, 92, 92, 92, 94

The problem states that the missing point in the data set is between 84 and 92. So, let's let x represent the missing score and add it to our chronological list:

79, 84, 84, x, 92, 92, 92, 94

The middle two numbers are x and 92.

The problem also states that the average of these two numbers is 90.5. Let's set up an equation and then solve for x:

$$\begin{array}{rcl} \frac{x+92}{2} & = & 90.5 \\ 2(\frac{x+92}{2}) & = & (90.5)2 \\ x+92 & = & 181 \\ \underline{-92} & & \underline{-92} \\ x & = & 89 \end{array}$$

The missing point is 89. Place an X on the dot plot to represent this value.

5. **Alaska.** The span of the extreme temperatures is not quite as long in Alaska as the span of the extreme temperatures in Minnesota. Therefore, if you were trying to decide where to go for vacation in the fall and you wanted to pack rather lightly, you would want to go to Alaska since you would not need to bring as many clothes to allow for changing weather.

6. **63.** To find the median of the data displayed, look for the value of the central line in the box.

7. **31%.** To find the percentage of students ages 46 to 50, you first have to find the total number of students. In the first example, we calculated 39 total students. Reading the graph, we can see that the number of students ages 46 to 50 is 12. To find the percentage, we simply divide 12 by 39 and then move the decimal point two spaces to the right.

$\frac{12}{39} = 0.307 = 30.7 = 31\%$ (when rounded)

So, 31% of Mr. Duvall's students are ages 46 to 50.

8. **13%.** We found the percentage of the age group with the highest number of students in the second example. Next, we need to find the percentage of students in the age group with the lowest number of students. The lowest number of students in an age group is 7, in the 56 to 60 age range. Find the percentage by dividing 7 by the total number of students, and then move the decimal place.

$\frac{7}{39} = 0.179 = 17.9 = 18\%$ (when rounded)

The percentage difference is then

$$\begin{array}{r} 31\% \\ -18\% \\ \hline 13\% \end{array}$$

So, the percentage difference between the age groups with the highest number of students and the lowest number of students in Mr. Duvall's class is 13%.

9. **negative association.** Look back at the six terms defined earlier. Negative association means that as one variable increases, the other decreases. In this graph, as the number of hours of studying increases, the amount of time it takes to pass the GED® test decreases.

10. **c.** This point on the graph is located away from the cluster that is trending downward. There must be other reasons that this student did not pass his or her GED® test in fewer weeks, because it does not follow the trend.

11. **c.** The graph does show a linear association, so choice **c** is not true. The graph has a negative association: as the number of hours of studying increases, the number of weeks it takes to pass the GED® test decreases. Since the graph does have a linear association, one can predict values not plotted that follow the linear progression.

12. **b.** The slope of the given line is 3, and the slope of the line in option **b** is also 3. Parallel lines have the same slope. Choices **a** and **c** mistakenly use the *y*-intercept value of 2, and choice **d** has a slope that renders it perpendicular to the given line.

13. d. To accurately identify the slope of a line perpendicular to the given one when the x term is on the other side of the equation, manipulate the equation to put it in $y = mx + b$ form.

$$y + \frac{3}{4}x = 1$$
$$\underline{-\frac{3}{4}x \qquad -\frac{3}{4}x}$$
$$y \qquad = \frac{-3}{4}x + 1$$

The slope is $\frac{-3}{4}$, so the perpendicular slope must be the opposite reciprocal—a positive $\frac{4}{3}$. Choices **b** and **c** confuse the y-intercept term for the slope. Choice **a** has the wrong sign because the x term was not moved to the other side of the equation before identifying the slope.

An infinite number of lines could be parallel and perpendicular to a given line when we look only at the slope as the determining factor. The only thing that changes with each of these lines is the y-intercept—where it crosses the y-axis.

14. $y = -4x$. If the slope of the given line is $\frac{1}{4}$, what is the slope of any line perpendicular to it? The opposite reciprocal: -4. Now that we have identified the slope, let's substitute the given x and y values into the slope-intercept equation to find the y-intercept of this particular line:

$$y = mx + b$$
$$8 = -4(-2) + b$$
$$8 = 8 + b$$
$$\underline{-8 \quad -8}$$
$$0 = b$$

The equation of the line perpendicular to $y = \frac{1}{4}x + 6$ that passes through $(-2,8)$ is $y = -4x + 0$, or just $y = -4x$.

15. 4. Since we know that the y-intercept is located on the y-axis (and therefore $x = 0$), let's substitute 0 in for x and see what y value we get. Remember, $f(x)$ and y represent the same thing.

$$f(x) = 3x + 4$$
$$f(x) = 3(0) + 4$$
$$f(x) = 4$$

16. $x = \sqrt{5}$. Since we know that the x-intercept is located on the x-axis, and therefore $y = 0$, let's substitute 0 for y and see what x value we get.

$$f(x) = 5x^2 - 25$$
$$0 = 5x^2 - 25$$
$$\underline{+25 \qquad +25}$$
$$25 = 5x^2$$
$$\frac{25}{5} = \frac{5x^2}{5}$$
$$5 = x^2$$
$$\sqrt{5} = \sqrt{x^2}$$
$$\pm\sqrt{5} = x$$

Since we have to take into account values when square rooting, there are two places where the function $f(x) = 5x^2 - 25$ intercepts the x-axis.

17. as $x \to -\infty$, $f(x) \to +\infty$. We are concerned about only the first term. It has an even power of x and a positive coefficient. Therefore, it will behave like a parabola with a positive coefficient, like the example shown. The parabolic shape will be upright, so as $x \to -\infty$, $f(x) \to +\infty$.

18. as $x \to +\infty$, $f(x) \to -\infty$. Again, we are concerned with only the first term. It has an odd power of x and a negative coefficient. Therefore, it will behave like a cubic function with a negative coefficient, like the example shown above. The function will generally decrease from the left of the graph to the right of the graph. As $x \to +\infty$, $f(x) \to -\infty$.

19. $y = 0.5x - 9.5$. Substitute the known values into the equation $y = mx + b$ and solve for b.

$$y = mx + b$$
$$-5 = 0.5(9) + b$$
$$-5 = 4.5 + b$$
$$\underline{-4.5 \quad -4.5}$$
$$-9.5 = b$$

The equation of this line, then, is $y = 0.5x - 9.5$.

20. $y = \frac{8}{5}x + \frac{63}{5}$. Use the equation $y - y_1 = m(x - x_1)$ to first find the slope, and then find the equation of the line.

Step 1:

$$y - y_1 = m(x - x_1)$$
$$3 - 11 = m(-6 - (-1))$$
$$-8 = m(-6 + 1)$$
$$\frac{-8}{-5} = \frac{m - 5}{-5}$$
$$\frac{8}{5} = m$$

Step 2:

$$y - 11 = \frac{8}{5}(x - (-1))$$
$$y - 11 = \frac{8}{5}(x + 1)$$
$$y - 11 = \frac{8}{5}x + \frac{8}{5}$$
$$\underline{+11 \qquad\qquad +11}$$
$$y = \frac{8}{5}x + \frac{63}{5}$$

Graphs and Tables Review

1. a. Use the point-slope form of an equation and the information given to answer the question: $y - y_1 = m(x - x_1)$.

Given:

$$x_1 = -4$$
$$y_1 = 3$$
$$m = \frac{1}{2}$$

Equation: $y - y_1 = m(x - x_1)$

Substitute: $y - 3 = \frac{1}{2}[x - (-4)]$

Simplify: $y - 3 = \frac{1}{2}(x + 4)$

Multiply by 2 to clear fractions: $2y - 6 = x + 4$

Add 6 to both sides: $2y = x + 10$

Rearrange terms to look like choices: $0 = x - 2y + 10$

2. c. This graph intercepts the y-axis at -5. It also increases from $(-\infty, -5) \cup (-5, \infty)$.

3. $84. Use the bar graph to find how much Cecilia spent on her cell phone in April and how much she spent on her cell phone in May. Then add those two values to find how much she spent in the two months combined.

Each tick mark on the vertical axis of the graph represents $3. Cecilia spent $54 in April and $30 in May.

$$\$54 + \$30 = \$84$$

Cecilia spent $84 on her cell phone in April and May combined.

4. c. Each point on a box-and-whisker plot represents the beginning and/or end of a quartile. The leftmost point represents the beginning of the first quartile, the next point represents the end of the first quartile and the beginning of the second quartile, and so on. Each quartile accounts for 25% of the data. Since there are four quartiles in a data set, the middle two quartiles (the second and third quartiles) represent the middle 50% of the data.

For this data set, the beginning of the second quartile is $50 and the end of the third quartile is $90. So, the middle 50% of the data is between $50 and $90.

5. d. When drawn through a figure, a line of symmetry divides the figure in half and produces two new figures that are mirror images of each other.

On the diagram, label each of the points given in the choices. Then, draw a line connecting each pair of points.

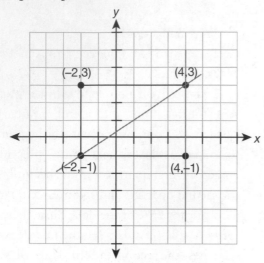

Consider the line. Does the line cut the rectangle in half and form two mirror images?

Yes; this line divides the rectangle into two triangles that are mirror images of each other.

6. 9%. To find the difference between food and the combined total of transportation and clothing expenses, look at the numbers on the graph. Food expense is 22%, transportation is 9%, and clothing is 4%; $22 - (9 + 4) = 9\%$.

7. a. When looking at a scatter plot of data points, a correlation exists if there is a relationship between x and y that holds true for the majority of the points. For example, if the y values get larger as the x values get larger, there is a positive correlation. In other words, if the points seem to rise as you move from left to right on the graph, there is a positive correlation. Similarly, if the y values get smaller as the x values get larger, there is a negative correlation; the values are behaving in an opposite way to each other.

According to this scatter plot, there is a distinct relationship. As the x values get larger, so do the y values. Therefore, there is a positive correlation.

4 ▶ GEOMETRY BASICS

Geometry is the branch of mathematics concerned with spatial relationships. The building blocks of geometry are points, lines, angles, surfaces, and solids. Understanding the properties of these elements, the relationships between them, and how to measure and manipulate them will not just allow you to succeed on the GED® test; it will also offer you tools to understand the world around you.

Answers and explanations for all practice questions are at the end of the chapter.

NOTE

The formulas for perimeter, area, and circumference will *not* be available to you during the test. Make sure to take note of and memorize these formulas.

Perimeter

Peri means "around" and *meter* means "measure." So, the **perimeter** of any figure is simply the measure around the figure.

Rectangles and Squares

To find the perimeter of a rectangle or square, simply find the sum of the measurements of each side of the figure.

> **Perimeter of a rectangle** = $l + l + w + w = 2l + 2w$ (l = length and w = width)

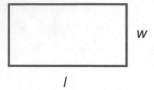

> **Perimeter of a square** = $s + s + s + s = 4s$ (s = side length)

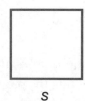

Practice

1. Find the perimeter of the following rectangle:

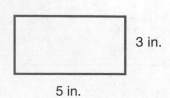

3 in.

5 in.

2. Find the perimeter of the following square:

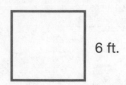

6 ft.

Triangles

To find the perimeter of a **triangle**, simply sum the measurements of the three sides.

For example, let's find the perimeter of the following triangle:

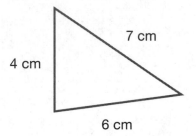

7 cm

4 cm

6 cm

Perimeter = 4 cm + 6 cm + 7 cm = 17 cm

Pythagorean Theorem

The Pythagorean theorem is used to find a missing side of a *right* triangle.

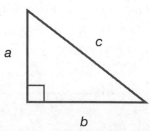

The theorem that shows the relationship between these three sides is

$$a^2 + b^2 = c^2$$

When using this formula for right triangles, sides a and b are interchangeable, but c is always the longest side. This is called the **hypotenuse**.

Example

What is the length of side b?

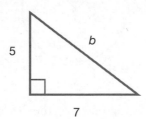

Use the Pythagorean theorem to find side b. Substitute the given values into the equation:

$$a^2 + b^2 = c^2$$
$$5^2 + 7^2 = b^2$$
$$25 + 49 = b^2$$
$$74 = b^2$$
$$\sqrt{74} = \sqrt{b^2}$$
$$8.60 = b$$

Practice

3. What is the missing side length of the following triangle? _____

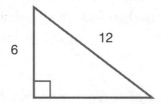

4. Reggie bikes to work every day, going 10 miles north from his house on Robert Street and then going 8 miles east on Dodd Road. He can bike 18 mph. How much time would Reggie save if he used the bike path that cuts straight through the park? _____

Polygons

To find the perimeter of a **polygon**, find the sum of the measurements of all the sides. For example, let's find the perimeter of the following figure:

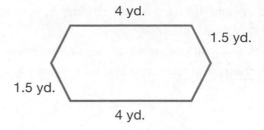

Perimeter = 4 yd. + 4 yd. + 1.5 yd. + 1.5 yd. +
      1.5 yd. + 1.5 yd.
      = 2(4 yd.) + 4(1.5 yd.)
      = 8 yd. + 6 yd.
      = 14 yd.

Practice

5. One side of a regular octagon has a length of 4 cm. What is the perimeter of the octagon?
  a. 8 cm
  b. 24 cm
  c. 36 cm
  d. 32 cm

6. Rusty needs to order enough wood to fence in the community garden grounds, which are in the shape of a regular pentagon—a pentagon with five congruent sides. If the fencing costs $12.50 per foot, how much will it cost to fence in the community garden? _____

15 ft.

Circumference

The **circumference** of a circle measures the distance around the circle. This concept is similar to finding the perimeter of a straight-sided figure. However, since a circle does not have any straight sides, the distance around the circle—the circumference—needs to be calculated differently.

Before you can calculate the circumference of a circle, there are a few terms you need to know.

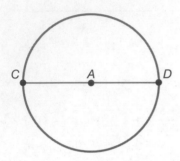

Center: In the figure, the center is at point A.

Radius: Any line that is drawn from the center, A, to the outside of the circle is called a radius. Thus, the line from A to D, $\overline{AD}$, is a radius, and the distance from A to C, $\overline{CA}$, is a radius. Therefore, $\overline{AD} = \overline{CA}$.

Diameter: Any line that is drawn from one end of the circle to the other end *and* passes through the center of the circle is called a diameter. Thus, the line is a diameter because it passes through the center of the circle, A.

Notice that $\overline{CA} + \overline{AD} = \overline{CD}$. The length of the diameter of a circle is equivalent to two times the radius: $d = 2r$.

π (pi—sounds like "pie") = 3.14159265359 . . .

For the purposes of equations involving circles, you can round to 3.14.

REMEMBER

The formula for finding the circumference of a circle is **$2\pi r$** or **$2d$**.

Example

What is the circumference of the following circle if $\overline{AB} = 4$ cm?

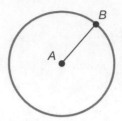

To find the circumference of the circle, use the formula $2\pi r$. In this problem, the radius, r, is 4 cm:

$$C = 2\pi r$$
$$= 2\pi(4 \text{ cm})$$
$$= 8(3.14) \text{ cm}$$
$$= 25.12 \text{ cm}$$

Practice

7. If the circumference of the circle is 62.8 mm, what is the diameter of $\overline{CD}$? _____

Area

Whereas the perimeter refers to the measurement *around* a figure, **area** refers to the measurement *inside* a figure. In general, to find the area of figures such as rectangles, squares, triangles, and circles, you will use multiplication.

Rectangles and Squares

The formula for the area of a rectangle is:

Area = base × height, or $A = bh$

The formula for the area of a square is:

Area = side × side, or $A = s^2$

Example
What is the area of this figure?

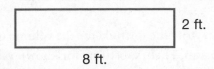

8 ft.

2 ft.

Remember, area = base × height.

$A = bh$
$= (8 \text{ ft.})(2 \text{ ft.})$
$= 16 \text{ ft.}^2$

Notice that the units are squared since we are multiplying feet by feet.

Practice
8. If the area of a square is 52 in.^{2}, what is its perimeter to the nearest tenth of an inch?

_____

Triangles
The area of a triangle is $\frac{1}{2} \times$ base × height, or $A = \frac{1}{2}bh$. This formula looks similar to the area of a rectangle, except the formula for the area of a triangle includes multiplying by $\frac{1}{2}$. Why is that? Notice in the following figure that a triangle is half of a rectangle.

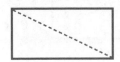

Example
What is the area of the following triangle?

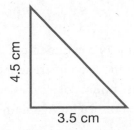

4.5 cm

3.5 cm

$A = \frac{1}{2}bh$
$= (\frac{1}{2})(3.5 \text{ cm})(4.5 \text{ cm})$
$= (\frac{1}{2})(15.75 \text{ cm}^2)$
$= 7.875 \text{ cm}^2 \approx 7.88 \text{ cm}^2$

Circles
The equation for the area of a circle is $A = \pi r^2$.

Example
Find the area of the following circle if line AB measures 2.75 inches.

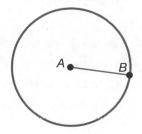

$A = \pi r^2$
$A = \pi(2.75 \text{ in.})^2$
$= 7.5625 \text{ in.}^2$
$= 23.74625 \text{ in.}^2 \approx 23.75 \text{ in.}^2$

Practice
9. What is the area of this circle? _____

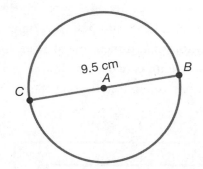

9.5 cm

10. Brenda has hired a landscaper to turn her soil-covered backyard into a unique hangout spot. She would like to have a circular deck with a diameter of 10 feet built in the middle of her rectangular backyard, which is 25 feet by 18 feet. Since the yard is soil right now, she is going to purchase sod to go around the deck. If the contractor charges $1.20 per square foot of sod installed, how much will the purchase of the sod cost Brenda? _____

Volume

Volume refers to the entire amount of space enclosed within a three-dimensional figure. The formulas for calculating the volume of a rectangular prism, right prism, cylinder, right pyramid, cone, and sphere will be available to you during the GED® test. You do not need to memorize the formulas; just become comfortable with using them.

Rectangular/Right Prisms

To find the volume of a **rectangular prism**, or **right prism**, use the following formula: $V = Bh$, where B is the area of the base (length × width) and h is the height.

Notice that the only difference between the area of a rectangle and the volume of a rectangular prism is the addition of a dimension of height. Pay close attention to the units of volume in this section. They are cubed, not squared, reflecting the addition of a dimension.

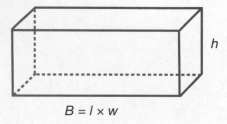

$B = l \times w$

Example

If the height of the prism is 3 cm and the length of the prism is 8 cm, what is the width in cm if the volume is 96 cm³?

First, write the formula for the volume of a rectangular prism. Then, substitute for known values.

$$V = Bh$$
$$96 \text{ cm}^3 = (8 \text{ cm})(3 \text{ cm})w$$
$$\frac{96 \text{ cm}^3}{24 \text{ cm}^2} = \frac{(24 \text{ cm}^2)w}{24 \text{ cm}^2}$$
$$4 \text{ cm} = w$$

Practice

11. These two boxes have the same volume ($V = l \times w \times h$). Find the length of the missing side on box *B*.

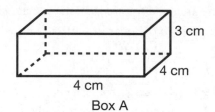

3 cm

4 cm

4 cm

Box A

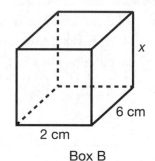

x

6 cm

2 cm

Box B

    a. 3
    b. 4
    c. 5
    d. 6

Cylinders

To find the volume of a **cylinder**, use the formula $V = \pi r^2 h$. Notice that the only difference between the area of a circle and the volume of a cylinder is the addition of the dimension of height. Again, this addition of a term to multiply in the equation will change the units from squared units to cubic units.

Practice

12. Find the volume of the cylinder shown here.

_____

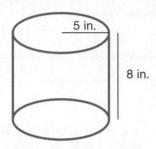

5 in.

8 in.

13. An empty cylindrical can has a height of 4 inches and a base with a radius of 1.5 inches. Melanie fills the can with water. What is the volume of the water Melanie pours into the can?

   a. 5.5π cubic inches

   b. 6π cubic inches

   c. 6.5π cubic inches

   d. 9π cubic inches

Right Pyramids

To find the volume of a **right pyramid**, use the formula $V = \frac{1}{3}Bh$, where B is the area of the base and h is the height of the prism from the center of the base to the point of the pyramid.

Example

Let's find the height of this pyramid if the volume is 54 mm³.

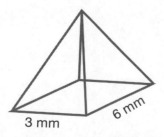

3 mm   6 mm

We know the volume is 54 mm³. We can find B by multiplying the length × width of the rectangular base:

$$B = (6 \text{ mm})(3 \text{ mm})$$
$$= 18 \text{ mm}^2$$

Return to the formula and substitute the known values to find the height:

$$V = \frac{1}{3}Bh$$
$$54 \text{ mm}^3 = \frac{1}{3}(18 \text{ mm}^2)(h)$$
$$(3)(54 \text{ mm}^3) = (3)\frac{1}{3}(18 \text{ mm}^2)(h)$$
$$162 \text{ mm}^3 = (18 \text{ mm}^2)h$$
$$9 \text{ mm} = h$$

Right Circular Cones

To find the volume of a **right circular cone**, use the formula $V = \frac{1}{3}\pi r^2 h$. Notice that it is similar to the volume of a cylinder except for the factor of $\frac{1}{3}$.

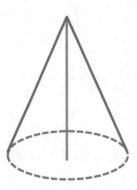

Practice

14. Find the radius of the cone if the volume is 148 cm³ and the height is 7 cm. Round your answer to the nearest tenth of a centimeter.

_____

Spheres

To find the volume of a **sphere**, use the formula $V = \frac{4}{3}\pi r^3$.

Example

Let's find the volume of this sphere if the diameter is 11 inches.

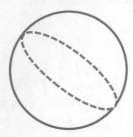

The diameter of 11 inches informs us that the radius is half of 11 inches; the radius is, therefore, 5.5 inches. Substitute this value back into the formula to find the volume of the sphere:

$$V = \frac{4}{3}\pi r^3$$
$$V = \frac{4}{3}\pi(5.5 \text{ in.})^3$$
$$V = \frac{4}{3}\pi(166.375 \text{ in.}^3)$$
$$V = \frac{4}{3}(522.4175 \text{ in.}^3)$$
$$= 696.5566 \text{ in.}^3$$

Surface Area

Surface area refers to the area of the entire *outside* of a three-dimensional figure. The formulas for calculating the surface area of a rectangular prism, right prism, cylinder, right pyramid, cone, and sphere will be available to you during the test. You do not need to memorize the formulas; just become comfortable with using them.

Rectangular/Right Prisms

The formula for calculating the surface area of a rectangular, or right, prism is

$$SA = ph + 2B$$

where B is the area of the base, p is the perimeter of base B, and h is the height.

Example

Let's calculate the surface area of this figure.

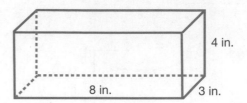

There are three unknown values you need to find in order to solve for the surface area: p, h, and B.

p = the perimeter of the base = 8 in. + 8 in. + 3 in. + 3 in. = 22 in.
h = the height of the prism = 4 in.
B = the area of the base = (8 in.)(3 in.) = 24 in.^{2}

Substitute these values into the formula to get

$$SA = (22 \text{ in.})(4 \text{ in.}) + 2(24 \text{ in.}^2)$$
$$= 88 \text{ in.}^2 + 48 \text{ in.}^2$$
$$= 136 \text{ in.}^2$$

So, the surface area of the figure is 136 square inches.

Right Circular Cylinders

The formula for the surface area of a cylinder is

$$SA = 2\pi rh + 2\pi r^2$$

where r is the radius and h is the height of the cylinder.

Practice

15. Find the surface area of a cylinder that has a diameter of 12 cm and a height of 20 cm. _____

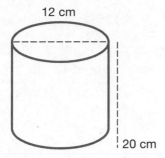

12 cm

20 cm

Right Pyramids

The formula for the surface area of a right pyramid is

$$SA = \frac{1}{2}ps + B$$

where B is the area of the base, p is the perimeter of base B, and s is the slant length.

Since it is a right pyramid, the highest point is directly above the center of the base. Thus, all four slant lengths are the same.

Example

For example, let's find the surface area of the right pyramid pictured:

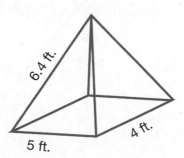

6.4 ft.

5 ft.

4 ft.

We can see that the slant length, s, is 6.4 ft. To find p and B, we need to do a few calculations.

p = the perimeter of base B = 5 ft. + 5 ft. + 4 ft. + 4 ft. = 18 ft.

B = the area of the base = (5 ft.)(4 ft.) = 20 ft.²

Substitute these values into the formula:

$$SA = \frac{1}{2}ps + B$$
$$SA = \frac{1}{2}(18 \text{ ft.})(6.4 \text{ ft.}) + 20 \text{ ft.}^2$$
$$= 57.6 \text{ ft.}^2 + 20 \text{ ft.}^2$$
$$= 77.6 \text{ ft.}^2$$

So, the surface area of the pyramid is 77.6 square feet.

Right Circular Cones

The formula for the surface area of a cone is

$$SA = \pi rs + \pi r^2$$

where r is the radius and s is the slant length.

Practice

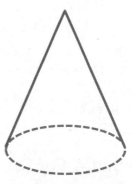

16. Find the surface area of the right circular cone that has a radius of 10 mm and a slant length of 25 mm. _____

Spheres

The formula for the surface area of a sphere is

$$SA = 4r^2$$

where r is the radius.

Notice that this formula is the area of one circle, πr^2, multiplied by 4.

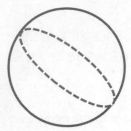

Let's calculate the radius of a sphere if its surface area is 113.04 square inches.

In this problem, the surface area is given, and we need to solve for the radius. Substitute the value of the surface area into the formula and solve for r.

$SA = 4\pi r^2$

$113.04 \text{ in.}^2 = 4\pi r^2$

$\dfrac{113.04 \text{ in.}^2}{4(3.14)} = \dfrac{4(3.14)r^2}{4(3.14)}$

$9 \text{ in.}^2 = r^2$

$\sqrt{9 \text{ in.}^2} = \sqrt{r^2}$

$3 \text{ in.} = r$

So, the radius of the sphere is 3 in.

Scale Factor

A scale factor is a factor that multiplies a term to change the value at a constant rate. For example, if 4 is multiplied by a scale factor of 3, the value is now 12.

Scale factors can be used in a variety of settings: maps, floor plans, blueprints, and other geometric drawings. For example, to reproduce the floor plan of an office building on a size of paper that is manageable, scale factors are necessary. If every shape and dimension of the floor plan is reduced by the same factor, the drawing will be an accurate reproduction of the spatial dimensions.

Example

What are the new dimensions of this triangle if it is increased by a scale factor of 4?

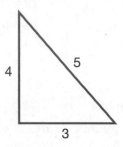

Multiply each side length by 4 to get the new dimensions:

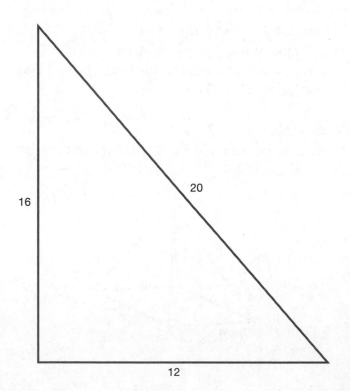

Geometry Basics Review

1. The length of a side of square *A* is twice as long as a side of square *B*. How much larger is the area of square *A*?
   a. 4 times larger
   b. 2 times larger
   c. 8 times larger
   d. 0.5 times larger

2. The perimeter of a square is 24 inches. What is its area?
   a. 144 in.^{2}
   b. 576 in.^{2}
   c. 16 in.^{2}
   d. 36 in.^{2}

3. Find the area of the shaded region in this figure. Remember that the formula for the area of a circle is $A = \pi r^2$.

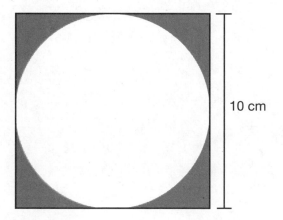

10 cm

   a. 100 cm^2
   b. 78.5 cm^2
   c. 21.5 cm^2
   d. 178.5 cm^2

4. The surface area of a cube is given by the expression $6s^2$, where *s* is the length of an edge. If a cube has a surface area of 54 square centimeters, what is the length of its edges?
   a. 3 cm
   b. 6 cm
   c. 9 cm
   d. 81 cm

5. If the edge of a cube is 10 cm and the edge of a second cube is 8 cm, what is the difference in the surface areas of the two cubes?
   a. 216 cm^2
   b. 384 cm^2
   c. 488 cm^2
   d. 600 cm^2

6. Find the area of the following shape.

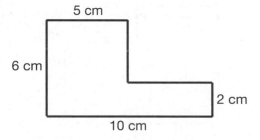

   a. 60 cm^2
   b. 23 cm^2
   c. 50 cm^2
   d. 40 cm^2

7. The distance between Hamden and Milford is 1.75 cm on a map. In real life, Hamden is 105 km from Milford. On the same map, Cheshire is 2 cm from Mystic. How far is Cheshire from Mystic in real life?
   a. 210 km
   b. 3.5 km
   c. 120 km
   d. 107 km

8. The following figure is a regular octagon. What is the perimeter of the figure? _____

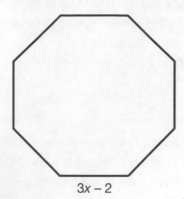

$3x - 2$

9. Jim works for a carpeting company. His next job is to recarpet an office space. According to the diagram, how many square feet of carpet does he need to complete this job?

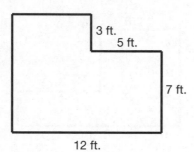

3 ft.
5 ft.
7 ft.
12 ft.

  a. 44 ft.^{2}
  b. 105 ft.^{2}
  c. 120 ft.^{2}
  d. 144 ft.^{2}

10. The perimeter of a rectangle is 64. The length of one of the sides of the rectangle is 8. Find the lengths of the other three sides.
  a. 10, 23, 23
  b. 8, 22, 22
  c. 8, 24, 24
  d. 12, 22, 22

Answers and Explanations

Chapter Practice

1. 16 in.

$$\text{Perimeter} = 2l + 2w$$
$$= 2(5 \text{ in.}) + 2(3 \text{ in.})$$
$$= 10 \text{ in.} + 6 \text{ in.}$$
$$= 16 \text{ in.}$$

2. 24 ft.

$$\text{Perimeter} = 4(6 \text{ ft.})$$
$$= 24 \text{ ft.}$$

3. 10.4. Again, substitute the given values into the Pythagorean theorem. Note that the missing side is *not* the hypotenuse, so let's use a as the missing side length.

$$a^2 + 62 = 122$$
$$a^2 + 36 = 144$$
$$a^2 + 36 = 144$$
$$\underline{\; -36 \quad -36}$$
$$\sqrt{a^2} = \sqrt{108}$$
$$a \approx 10.4$$

4. 17 minutes. First, let's find how long it takes Reggie to get to work using his normal route. He bikes 10 miles north and then 8 miles east for a total of 18 miles. If he bikes 18 mph, how long does it take him to get to work? Use the *distance = rate × time* formula and solve for time:

$$d = rt$$
$$18 = 18t$$
$$\frac{18}{18} = \frac{18t}{18}$$
$$1 \text{ hour} = t$$

It takes Reggie 1 hour to get to work using his normal route. To find how long it would take him to get to work using the bike path, we need to find its distance using the Pythagorean theorem.

$$a^2 + b^2 = c^2$$
$$10^2 + 8^2 = c^2$$
$$100 + 64 = c^2$$
$$164 = c^2$$
$$\sqrt{164} = \sqrt{c^2}$$
$$12.8 = c$$

The distance from Reggie's house to work using the bike path is 12.8 miles. Use the distance formula to find how long it will take Reggie to get to work using the bike path:

$$d = rt$$
$$12.8 = 18t$$
$$0.71 \text{ hours} = t$$

To find how much faster Reggie would get to work using the bike path versus his normal route, subtract the two times.

0.71 of an hour = (0.71)(60) = 42.6 ≈ 43 minutes

60 minutes – 43 minutes = 17 minutes

So, if Reggie uses the bike path to get to work, he will get to work 17 minutes faster than by taking his normal route.

5. d. A regular octagon has eight sides, all of which are the same length. The perimeter is the length around the outside of a figure. If all eight sides of 4 cm each are added up, the perimeter is 32 cm.

6. $937.50. Since the garden is in the shape of a regular pentagon, the side lengths are equivalent. Therefore, the perimeter is

$$p = 5(15 \text{ ft.})$$
$$= 75 \text{ ft.}$$

The cost of the fencing is $12.50 per foot, so the total cost to fence in the community garden is

$$C = (75 \text{ ft.})(\$12.50)$$
$$= \$937.50$$

7. 20 mm. Remember, the equation for circumference is $C = 2\pi r$ or $C = \pi d$. Since we need to find the diameter to solve this problem, let's use $C = \pi d$.

$$C = \pi d$$
$$62.8 \text{ mm} = (3.14)d$$
$$20 \text{ mm} = d$$

8. 28.8 in. First, you need to find the side length of the square by solving for s using the equation for area:

$$A = s^2$$
$$52 \text{ in.}^2 = s^2$$
$$\sqrt{52 \text{ in.}^2} = \sqrt{s^2}$$
$$7.2 \text{ in.} = s$$

Now that we know what s is, we can find the perimeter:

$$P = 4(7.2 \text{ in.})$$
$$= 28.8 \text{ in.}$$

9. 70.85 cm². The equation for the area of a circle requires the value of the radius, r. However, in this problem we have been given the diameter. Remember, $d = 2r$, so $\frac{d}{2} = r$.

$$\frac{9.5 \text{ cm}}{2} = 4.75 \text{ cm} = r$$

Now, use the equation for area:

$$A = \pi r^2$$
$$= \pi (4.75 \text{ cm})^2$$
$$= 22.5626\pi \text{ cm}^2$$
$$= 70.84625 \text{ cm}^2 \approx 70.85 \text{ cm}^2$$

10. $445.80. To find the cost of the sod, we need to find the area of the rectangular yard and then subtract the area of the circular deck.

$$A_{yard} = \text{length} \times \text{width}$$
$$= (25 \text{ ft.})(18 \text{ ft.})$$
$$= 450 \text{ ft.}^2$$
$$A_{deck} = \pi r^2$$
$$= (3.14)(5 \text{ ft.})^2$$
$$= 78.5 \text{ ft.}^2$$
$$A_{sod} = 450 \text{ ft.}^2 - 78.5 \text{ ft.}^2$$
$$= 371.5 \text{ ft.}^2$$

Last, multiply the sodded area by the cost per square foot to get the total cost of installation of sod.

$$\text{Cost} = (371.5)(\$1.20)$$
$$= \$445.80$$

11. b. The volume of box A is 48 cm^3 ($4 \times 4 \times 3 = 48$). The volume of box B must also be 48 cm^3, so the three dimensions of box B will multiply to 48. Solve the equation for x:

$$2 \times 6 \times x = 48$$
$$12x = 48$$
$$x = 4$$

12. 628 in^3. The formula for the volume of a cylinder is $V = \pi r^2 h$. From the diagram, we can see that the height of the cylinder is 8 inches and the radius is 5 inches. Substitute these values into the formula to solve for the volume.

$$V = \pi r^2 h$$
$$= \pi(5 \text{ in.})^2(8 \text{ in.})$$
$$= \pi(25 \text{ in.}^2)(8 \text{ in.})$$
$$= (3.14)(200 \text{ in.}^3)$$
$$= 628 \text{ in.}^3$$

13. d. Use the formula $V = \pi r^2 h$, where r is the radius of the base and h is the height of the cylinder: $\pi(1.52)4 = \pi \times 2.25 \times 4$, which equals 9π.

14. 4.49 cm. The formula for the volume of a cone is $V = \frac{1}{3}r^2 h$. We have values for V and h:

$$V = 148 \text{ cm}^3$$
$$h = 7 \text{ cm}$$

We then substitute these values into the formula, giving us the following equation with r as the only unknown:

$$V = \frac{1}{3}r^2 h$$
$$148 \text{ cm}^3 = \frac{1}{3}r^2(7 \text{ cm})$$
$$(3)148 \text{ cm}^3 = (3)\frac{1}{3}r^2(7 \text{ cm})$$
$$444 \text{ cm}^3 = (3.14)(7 \text{ cm})r^2$$
$$\frac{444 \text{ cm}^3}{(3.14)(7 \text{ cm})} = \frac{(3.14)(7 \text{ cm})r^2}{(3.14)(7 \text{ cm})}$$
$$20.2 \text{ cm}^2 = r^2$$
$$\sqrt{20.2 \text{ cm}^2} = \sqrt{r^2}$$
$$4.49 \text{ cm} = r$$

Rounded to the nearest tenth of a centimeter, the volume is 4.5 cm.

15. 979.68 cm^3. To substitute values into the formula $SA = 2\pi rh + 2\pi r^2$, we first need to identify the radius. The problem states that the diameter is 12 cm. The radius is half of the diameter, so the radius = 6 cm.

Now, substitute values into the formula for the surface area of a cylinder:

$$SA = 2\pi rh + 2\pi r^2$$
$$= 2\pi(6 \text{ cm})(20 \text{ cm}) + 2\pi(6 \text{ cm})^2$$
$$= 2\pi(120 \text{ cm}^2) + 2\pi(36 \text{ cm}^2)$$
$$= 2(3.14)(120 \text{ cm}^2) + 2(3.14)(36 \text{ cm}^2)$$
$$= 753.6 \text{ cm}^2 + 226.08 \text{ cm}^2$$
$$= 979.68 \text{ cm}^2$$

So, the surface area of the cylinder is 979.68 cm^2.

16. 1,099 mm^2. Since the values for s and r are given in the question, we can substitute them into the formula and solve for surface area:

$$SA = \pi rs + \pi r^2$$
$$= (3.14)(10 \text{ mm})(25 \text{ mm}) +$$
$$(3.14)(10 \text{ mm})^2$$
$$= 785 \text{ mm}^2 + 314 \text{ mm}^2$$
$$= 1,099 \text{ mm}^2$$

Geometry Basics Review

1. a. *Method 1:*

Choose a few examples of the given situation and analyze the results.

Example: If square A has sides of length 10, square B will have sides of length 5.

Then, the area of A is 100, and the area of B is 25.

The area of square A is 4 times the area of square B.

Example: If square A has sides of length 6, square B will have sides of length 3.

Then, the area of A is 36, and the area of B is 9.

The area of square A is 4 times the area of square B.

If you continue to try other situations, the results will be the same. The area of the larger square is always 4 times the area of the smaller square.

Method 2:

The situation can be analyzed algebraically.

Length of side of square $B = x$

Length of side of square $A = 2x$

Area of square $B = x^2$

Area of square $A = (2x)^2 = 4x^2$

$4x^2$ is 4 times x^2.

2. d. All sides of a square are the same length. The perimeter is the distance around the outside of a figure. You can divide the perimeter of a square by 4 to determine the length of a side: $24 \div 4 = 6$. Therefore, the length of a side of the square is 6 inches. To find the area, multiply the length by the width. In a square, the length and the width are the same. In this case, they are both 6 inches, and $6 \times 6 = 36$. The area of the square is 36 square inches.

3. c. To find the area of the shaded region, subtract the area of the circle from the area of the square. Notice that the radius of the circle is half the length of one side of the square. Therefore, the radius is 5 cm.

Area of square: $10 \times 10 = 100$ cm^2

Area of circle: $3.14 \times 5^2 = 3.14 \times 25 = 78.5$ cm^2

Area of shaded region: square – circle

$100 - 78.5 = 21.5$ cm^2

The area of the shaded region is 21.5 cm^2.

4. a. The surface area of the cube is the product of 6 and a number squared. So, you can write the equation $6s^2 = 54$ and solve it for s:

$6s^2 = 54$

$s^2 = 9$

Because $s^2 = 9$, each edge measures 3 cm.

5. a. Since each edge of a cube has the same length, the area of each face is s^2. There are six faces on every cube, so the surface area of a cube is $6s^2$.

The surface area of the first cube is:

$6(10^2) = 6(100) = 600$

The surface area of the second cube is:

$6(8^2) = 6(64) = 384$

The difference between the two surface areas is:

$600 - 384 = 216$

6. d. Find the lengths of the two missing sides. The horizontal missing side can be found by subtracting the 5 cm side from the 10 cm side. Therefore, the horizontal missing side is 5 cm. The vertical missing side can be found by subtracting the 2 cm side from the 6 cm side across from it. Therefore, the vertical missing side is 4 cm.

The following drawing shows all of the sides.

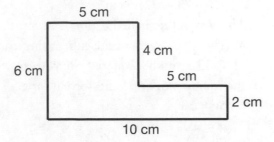

The shape can be broken into two rectangles (two possible ways are shown).

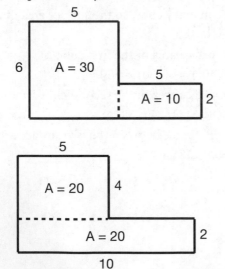

In the first figure, the area of the larger rectangle is 30 cm², and the smaller rectangle is 10 cm². The total area is 40 cm² (30 + 10). In the second figure, the area of the top rectangle is 20 cm², and the area of the bottom rectangle is 20 cm². The total area is 40 cm² (20 + 20).

7. c.

Method 1:

Set up a proportion comparing the distance in real life and the distance on the map:

$$\frac{\text{map Hamden to Milford}}{\text{real-life Hamden to Milford}} = \frac{\text{map Cheshire to Mystic}}{\text{real-life Cheshire to Mystic}}$$

$$\frac{1.75x}{105} = \frac{2}{x}$$

$$1.75x = 210$$

$$x = 120$$

The distance between Cheshire and Mystic is 120 km.

Method 2:

Determine the number of kilometers represented by 1 cm on the map: $105 \div 1.75 = 60$. Each centimeter on the map is 60 km in real life.

The distance from Cheshire to Mystic on the map is 2 cm. Since $2 \times 60 = 120$, the distance from Cheshire to Mystic in real life is 120 km.

8. $24x - 16$. The perimeter of a figure is the distance around it. For a regular octagon (whose sides all have equal lengths), the perimeter can be found by multiplying the length of one side times the total number of sides. According to the diagram, the length of each side of the octagon is $3x - 2$, so the perimeter is $8(3x - 2)$. Be sure to distribute the 8 to both terms inside the parentheses so as not to arrive at $24x - 2$, which is incorrect.

When the 8 is distributed correctly,

$$P = 8(3x) - 8(2)$$
$$= 24x - 16$$

9. b. There are two ways to solve this problem. The first is to divide the room into two rectangles, calculate the area of each, and add the areas together. There are two ways to divide the room into two rectangles:

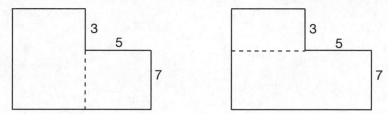

In the diagram on the left, one rectangle has a length of 5 feet and a width of 7 feet and the other has a length of 10 feet, resulting from 7 + 3, and a width of 7, resulting from 12 − 5. To find the area of the room, set up the following equation: (5 ft.)(7 ft.) + (10 ft.)(7 ft.). This yields 105 ft.² as the area of the room.

In the diagram on the right, one rectangle has a length of 12 feet and a width of 7 feet and the other has a length of 7 feet, resulting from 12 − 5, and a width of 3 feet. To find the area of the room, set up the following equation: (12 ft.)(7 ft.) + (7 ft.)(3 ft.). This also yields 105 ft.² as the area of the room.

The second method is to calculate the area of the big rectangle—(12 ft.)(10 ft.)—and subtract the area of the part of the room that is missing—(5 ft.)(3 ft.). This equation reads 120 ft.² − 15 ft.² = 105 square feet.

10. c. The perimeter of a figure is the distance around the figure. Since the opposite sides of a rectangle are equal, and one side of this rectangle has a length of 8, another side also has a length of 8. The set of numbers whose sum is 64 when added to 8 is 8 + 8 + 24 + 24 = 64.

5 ▶ STATISTICS AND PROBABILITY

T he field of statistics revolves around data—how it is collected, organized, manipulated, and presented. Probability is a specific application of statistics that aims to arrive at conclusions based on current tendencies. This chapter reviews some basic concepts in statistics, such as the mean (average) and median of a data set.

Measures of Central Tendencies

Measures of central tendencies are a way to talk about a data set using one number to summarize the data. As you will see throughout this book, many sections of the GED® test will require you to understand how to both find and interpret these measurements in order to understand data presented, whether it be something like scientific experiment data, information in a social studies population table, or a straightforward math problem. There are four different measures of central tendencies that you will need to know how to calculate: mean, median, mode, and weighted average.

Mean

The **mean** is the same as the *average* of a data set. To find the mean, add up all the numbers in the data set and then divide by the total number of data values. For instance, if there are five numbers in a set of data, add up the five numbers and then divide by 5. If there are 12 numbers in a set of data, add up the 12 numbers and then divide by 12.

$$\frac{\text{sum of data values}}{\text{total \# of data values}} = \text{average (mean)}$$

Take the following scenario as an example.

Example

Bobbi buys groceries every two weeks. Her last four grocery bills were $75.30, $59.65, $72.92, and $67.20. What is the average amount of money Bobbi spends every two weeks on groceries?

To find the average amount Bobbi spends on groceries, add up the four grocery bills and then divide by 4:

$75.30 + $59.65 + $72.92 + $67.20 = $275.07

$$\frac{\$275.07}{4} \approx \$68.77$$

Let's work through a more complicated example.

Ms. Reba keeps track of how many students drop in Monday through Thursday to study for their GED® test. Usually, students come in groups. Here is a chart of last week's numbers:

	3	4	
	4	—	
2	3	—	4
5			2
Monday	Tuesday	Wednesday	Thursday

Ms. Reba forgot to write down two numbers for Wednesday. If the average number of students per group was 3.2, and one of the unknown groups had one more student than the other unknown group, what is the average number of students who came to see Ms. Reba each day?

First, interpret the words into math. We know that one of the Wednesday groups had one more student than the other. Assign x to one of the groups and $x + 1$ to the other.

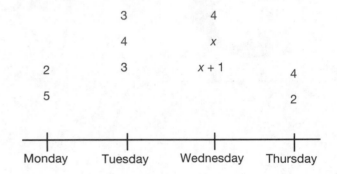

	3	4	
	4	x	
2	3	$x + 1$	4
5			2
Monday	Tuesday	Wednesday	Thursday

Next, add up all the numbers, divide by 10, and set it equal to the known average of 3.2:

$$\frac{2+5+3+4+3+4+x+x+1+4+2}{10} = 3.2$$

$$\frac{28+2x}{10} = 3.2$$

$$\frac{10(28+2x)}{10} = (3.2)10$$

$$28 + 2x = 32$$

$$\underline{-28 \qquad -28}$$

$$2x = 4$$

$$\frac{2x}{2} = \frac{4}{2}$$

$$x = 2$$

So now we know that one of the Wednesday groups had 2 students (x) and the other had 3 students ($x + 1$).

Finally, we can calculate the average number of students Ms. Reba saw per day:

Monday: $2 + 5 = 7$
Tuesday: $3 + 4 + 3 = 10$
Wednesday: $4 + 2 + 3 = 9$
Thursday: $4 + 2 = 6$

$$\frac{7+10+9+6}{4} = 8 \text{ students per day}$$

Practice

1. Mr. Carlo's class is learning about frogs. He took his class to the pond to observe them in their environment. One of the assignments was for each of the 14 students to measure one frog in order to calculate an average length. The average length was 2.35 inches. Using the following data, calculate the length of the 14th frog.

FROG	LENGTH (IN.)
1	2.3
2	1.9
3	2.0
4	2.4
5	2.5
6	3.0
7	2.7
8	2.6
9	2.5
10	2.4
11	2.3
12	2.1
13	2.4
14	x

Median

The **median** of a data set is the middle value of a chronological set of data. To understand the concept, consider this question:

What is the median of the following data values?
63, 72, 54, 69, 66

To find the median, first rewrite the numbers in chronological order:

54, 63, 66, 69, 72

The median is 66 because there are two numbers to the left and two numbers to the right of it.

54, 63, $\boxed{66}$, 69, 72

Finding the median is very simple when there is an odd number of values. However, what if there is an even number of values? In that case, take the average of the middle two numbers.

What is the median of the following data values?

23, 10, 31, 5, 39, 33

First, rewrite the values in chronological order:

5, 10, 23, 31, 33, 39

The two middle numbers are 23 and 31:

5, 10, $\boxed{23, 31,}$ 33, 39

The median of this data set is the average of 23 and 31:

$$\frac{23 + 31}{2} = 27$$

Mode

The **mode** of a data set is the number that appears most often.

Example

What is the mode of the following data set?

3, 4, 2, 9, 8, 9, 2, 9, 9, 4

The mode of the data set is 9, as it appears more than any other number in the data set.

A set of numbers can have one mode (if one number appears more often than the others, as just shown), no modes (if there is not any number that appears more than once), or multiple modes (if more than one number appears the most times).

Practice

Identify the modes of the following data sets.

2. 45, 56, 23, 45, 12, 56, 38 _____

3. 100, 96, 94, 101, 106 _____

Weighted Average

A **weighted average** is able to account for terms within a situation that have different values or relevance. To explain this concept, let's look at a few examples.

Example

Suppose Shirley owns a bakery and is ordering supplies to make her famous pies. If she orders a shipment of 20 cans of peaches for $32.50 and a shipment of 24 cans of cherries for $34.00, what is the average price Shirley pays per can of fruit?

The price of the peaches is different from the price of the cherries. Therefore, the prices have different relevance when calculating the average.

To find the answer to this question, you need to find the sum of the total cost of fruit and divide by the number of cans:

$$\frac{\$32.50 + \$34}{44 \text{ cans}} = \frac{\$66.50}{44 \text{ cans}} \approx \$1.50 \text{ per can of fruit}$$

Let's work through another example:

Five-year-old Larry made up a card game using four tens, three jacks, two queens, and one king. He assigned a point value to each of the cards, which is shown in this table:

CARD	FREQUENCY	POINT VALUE
Tens	4	5
Jacks	3	10
Queens	2	15
Kings	1	20

What is the average point value of each card?

Since each card is assigned a different value, we will need to calculate a weighted average. To do so, we must first multiply the number of each card by its point value and then add up the total value of all the cards.

$$(4)(5) = 20$$
$$(3)(10) = 30$$
$$2(15) = 30$$
$$1(20) = 20$$
$$20 + 30 + 30 + 20 = 100$$

Next, we'll divide the total value of all the cards by the total number of cards used in the game. There are 10 cards used in the game $(4 + 3 + 2 + 1)$.

So, the (weighted) average value of each card is:

$$100 \div 10 = 10 \text{ points}$$

Practice

4. Myrna teaches at a university. When assigning final grades, she gives each type of assignment a different level of importance. The collection of Myrna's assignments are worth a total of 100 points.

ASSIGNMENT	NUMBER	PERCENTAGE
Tests	4	70%
Homework	6	10%
Final exam	1	20%

Chad's scores are shown in the next table. What is his final grade for the course? _____

ASSIGNMENT	SCORES
Tests	78, 85, 88, 90
Homework	87, 90, 83, 93, 91, 90
Final exam	82

5. Mr. Gallespie is a high school science teacher. The weight he gives each assignment is listed in the following table.

ASSIGNMENT	NUMBER	PERCENTAGE
Tests	5	60%
Homework	5	15%
Experiments	4	25%

Looking at Katie's scores, calculate her final grade for the semester to the nearest hundredth of a percentage point. _____

ASSIGNMENT	SCORES (OUT OF 100)
Tests	93, 97, 88, 91, 95
Homework	90, 99, 100, 95, 96
Experiments	89, 90, 85, 92

Probability

There are two types of probability: simple and compound. Simple probability refers to a single event, whereas compound probability refers to multiple events with more than one condition.

Simple Probability

Simple probability is calculated by finding the likelihood of getting the number of outcomes that fit a specific criterion versus the number of *total* outcomes. This is usually represented by a fraction or a percentage.

$$\frac{\text{\# of outcomes that fit the specified criterion}}{\text{\# of total possible outcomes}}$$

A very common example of probability is a coin toss. *What is the probability that a coin will land on heads when tossed into the air?*

To find the answer, write a fraction that follows the guidelines just mentioned. First, figure out how many possible outcomes there are when a coin is tossed into the air.

2: heads and tails.

Then, figure out how many outcomes fit the criterion laid out in the problem:

1: only heads

Assuming that the two outcomes are equally likely, the probability that the coin will land on heads when tossed into the air is $\frac{1}{2}$, or 50%.

Practice

6. What is the probability of grabbing a blue candy out of a bag with the following contents? _____

Green	6
Yellow	5
Brown	10
Red	8
Blue	7
Orange	6

Compound Probability

Compound probability refers to events with more than one condition. For instance, consider the following question.

What is the probability of getting heads twice in a row?

An extra step is required to solve compound probability problems.

First, calculate the probability of getting heads once: $\frac{1}{2}$.

Then, calculate the probability of getting heads a second time. The result is the same: $\frac{1}{2}$.

To find the probability of both of these events *together*, you multiply:

$$\frac{1}{2} \times \frac{1}{2} = \frac{1}{4}$$

The compound probability, then, of both of these events occurring is $\frac{1}{4}$, or 25%.

Example

Suppose there are eight tennis balls in a container: five green and three red. What is the probability of pulling out a green ball on the first try and then a red ball on the second try, without adding the first green ball back into the container?

To find the answer to this problem, let's first find the probability of pulling a green tennis ball out of the container. There are five green tennis balls and eight total tennis balls. Therefore, the probability of pulling out a green tennis ball on the first try is $\frac{5}{8}$.

Now you have to consider how the problem changes after this first step, as you calculate the probability of pulling a red ball the second time. After taking the green tennis ball out of the container, there are only seven balls left—the total has changed from eight to seven. There are three red tennis balls. Therefore, the probability of pulling out a red tennis ball after the green tennis ball is $\frac{3}{7}$.

Find the compound probability of these events by multiplying:

$$\frac{5}{8} \times \frac{3}{7} = \frac{15}{56}$$

Practice

7. Refer to the table with the number of candies, reprinted here:

Green	6
Yellow	5
Brown	10
Red	8
Blue	7
Orange	6

What is the percentage probability of grabbing a blue candy the first time and then another blue candy the next time, without replacing the first blue candy? _____

Counting Techniques

The counting techniques featured on the GED® test are permutations and combinations.

Permutations

Permutations are combinations where the order matters. For instance, a question might ask for the number of ways first, second, third, and fourth place trophies could be awarded to 15 different teams. This is an example of a permutation because you're not just finding four teams, you're being asked to find four teams in a defined and ranked order.

Let's work out this example to illustrate this concept.

There are 15 different teams and only four trophies.

How many teams could win first place?

15

After the first place trophy is given out, how many teams are left to win second place?

14

After second place is handed out, how many teams are left to win third place?

13

After third place is handed out, how many teams are left to win fourth place?

12

Therefore, the number of possible combinations for the 15 teams to win the four trophies is:

$$15 \times 14 \times 13 \times 12 = 32{,}760.$$

Permutations Formula

There is a formula that can be applied to any problem regarding permutation:

$P(n,k) = \dfrac{n!}{}$, where n is the number of options and k is the number of choices made.

Using the preceding problem to illustrate this formula, $n = 15$ and $k = 4$:

$$P(15,4) = \frac{15!}{(15-4)!}$$

$$= \frac{15 \times 14 \times 13 \times 12 \times 11 \times 10 \times 9 \times 8 \times 7 \times 6 \times 5 \times 4 \times 3 \times 2 \times 1}{11 \times 10 \times 9 \times 8 \times 7 \times 6 \times 5 \times 4 \times 3 \times 2 \times 1}$$

$$= \frac{15 \times 14 \times 13 \times 12 \times \cancel{11 \times 10 \times 9 \times 8 \times 7 \times 6 \times 5 \times 4 \times 3 \times 2 \times 1}}{\cancel{11 \times 10 \times 9 \times 8 \times 7 \times 6 \times 5 \times 4 \times 3 \times 2 \times 1}}$$

$$= 15 \times 14 \times 13 \times 12 = 32,760.$$

Practice

8. There are 20 athletes competing in a swim meet for first, second, and third places. How many different ways could the trophies be awarded? _____

Combinations

Order does not matter with **combinations**. For instance, the number of combinations of three different appetizers a group could order at a restaurant is an example of a combination. It does not matter what order the chosen appetizers are listed in: salad, soup, and flatbread is the same as soup, flatbread, and salad.

The formula for combinations is similar to the one for permutations; however, another factor is added to the denominator to reduce the number of possibilities. Again, if order does not matter, then 1, 2, 3 is the same as 3, 2, 1; thus, the combination is counted only once.

Combinations Formula

$C(n,k) = \dfrac{P(n,k)}{k!} = \dfrac{n!}{k!(n-k)!}$, where n is the number of options and k is the number of choices made.

Notice that the only difference between the formula for permutation and combination is the $k!$ in the denominator of the combination formula. Again, this is to eliminate repetitive combinations in the answer, since order does not matter.

Example

Let's say there are 13 different appetizers to choose from at a restaurant. There is a special where you can order three appetizers for $12.99. How many different combinations of three appetizers could you order?

Using the combinations formula, $n = 13$ and $k = 3$.

$$C(13,3) = \frac{13 \times 12 \times 11 \times 10 \times 9 \times 8 \times 7 \times 6 \times 5 \times 4 \times 3 \times 2 \times 1}{3 \times 2 \times 1\,(10 \times 9 \times 8 \times 7 \times 6 \times 5 \times 4 \times 3 \times 2 \times 1)}$$

$$= \frac{13 \times 12 \times 11 \times \cancel{10 \times 9 \times 8 \times 7 \times 6 \times 5 \times 4 \times 3 \times 2 \times 1}}{3 \times 2 \times 1\,(\cancel{10 \times 9 \times 8 \times 7 \times 6 \times 5 \times 4 \times 3 \times 2 \times 1})}$$

$$= \frac{1,716}{6}$$

$$= 286$$

Thus, there are 286 different combinations of three different appetizers when there are 13 options to choose from.

Practice

9. There are 10 different colors of sticky notes in the supply closet at Zachary's office. Employees can choose four different colors to organize their materials. How many different color combinations could Zachary select when choosing four sticky notes? _____

Statistics and Probability Review

1. Ethan writes down the sale of every ice cream cone by flavor during his shift at Ice Cream Heaven: vanilla, chocolate, strawberry, strawberry, coffee, chocolate, pistachio, strawberry, mint, vanilla, mint, chocolate, butter pecan, chocolate, coffee, pistachio, chocolate. Which ice cream flavor is the mode during Ethan's shift?
   a. chocolate
   b. butter pecan
   c. strawberry
   d. vanilla

2. Phoebe works part-time at the movie theater. Her schedule for the next three weeks, shown here, lists the number of hours Phoebe will work each day.

SUNDAY	MONDAY	TUESDAY	WEDNESDAY	THURSDAY	FRIDAY	SATURDAY
0	7	0	4	4	5	0
0	4	6	5	3	2	0
0	5	4	3	6	5	0

   What is the median number of hours Phoebe will work in one day over the next three weeks?
   a. 0 hours
   b. 3 hours
   c. 4 hours
   d. 5 hours

3. Pat spends Friday night at the bowling alley. In his first four games, he bowls scores of 123, 165, 127, and 144. If the mean of Pat's five games is 146, what does Pat bowl in his fifth game?
   a. 140
   b. 141
   c. 146
   d. 171

4. Jackie plays a ring-finding game in her swimming pool. She has 30 seconds to retrieve as many rings as she can from the bottom of the pool. She plays the game nine times, and her scores are shown in the table. What is Jackie's median score?

GAME NUMBER	RING SCORE
1	4
2	3
3	5
4	8
5	6
6	3
7	9
8	3
9	4

   a. 3
   b. 4
   c. 5
   d. 6

5. A spinner is divided into ten equal sections, numbered 1 through 10. If the spinner is spun once, what is the probability that the spinner will land on a number less than 5?

a. $\frac{1}{5}$

b. $\frac{2}{5}$

c. $\frac{1}{2}$

d. $\frac{1}{10}$

6. A piggy bank contains three quarters, five pennies, two nickels, and six dimes. Evander picks a coin at random from the bank and pulls out a quarter. This quarter is NOT replaced. If Evander selects another coin, what is the probability that it will be a quarter?

a. $\frac{2}{15}$

b. $\frac{3}{15}$

c. $\frac{2}{16}$

d. $\frac{3}{16}$

7. Yolanda is playing a matching game with her niece. To start the game, 28 cards are face down on the table. Each player gets a turn to flip over two cards and hope they are a match. Each card has exactly one match. If Yolanda goes first, what is the probability that she will get a matching pair during her first turn?

a. $\frac{2}{28}$

b. $\frac{1}{378}$

c. $\frac{1}{14}$

d. $\frac{3}{378}$

8. How many different ways could the first-, second-, and third-place trophies be awarded to the Little League teams in the end-of-season tournament?

| Panthers |
| Cougars |
| Sharks |
| Lions |
| Tigers |
| Blue Devils |
| Mariners |

a. 5,040

b. 7

c. 210

d. 3

9. Joan has seven CDs she wants to pack in her suitcase, but only four will fit. How many different combinations of CDs could be packed in Joan's suitcase?

a. 28

b. 35

c. 210

d. 840

10. The graph shows how much homework Michael has done each night. What is the mean number of hours Michael has spent doing homework on the nights shown? _____

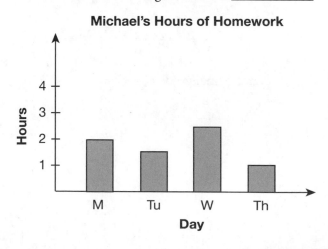

Michael's Hours of Homework

Answers and Explanations

Chapter Practice

1. **1.8 in.** Assign a variable to the missing length, x. Write an equation of the average, and then solve for x:

   $$\text{average/mean} = \frac{\text{sum of data values}}{\text{\# of data values}}$$

   $$2.35 =$$
   $$\frac{2.3 + 1.9 + 2.0 + 2.4 + 2.5 + 3.0 + 2.7 + 2.6 + 2.5 + 2.4 + 2.3 + 2.1 + 2.4 + x}{14}$$

   $$2.35 = \frac{31.1 + x}{14}$$
   $$2.35(14) = \frac{14(31.1 + x)}{14}$$
   $$32.9 = 31.1 + x$$
   $$\underline{-31.1 \quad\quad -31.1}$$
   $$1.8 = x$$

   The length of the 14th frog is 1.8 inches.

2. **45 and 56.** There are two modes in this data set, as both 45 and 56 appear twice.

3. **None.** Since no numbers appear more than once in this data set, we can say that there is no mode for this set of data.

4. **85%.** To find Chad's final grade, each assignment needs to be weighted differently. First, find the average of each type of assignment and then multiply by the percentage Myrna assigns to it. Then, add the percentages together to find Chad's final grade:

   $$\text{Final grade} = 0.70\left(\frac{78 + 85 + 88 + 90}{4}\right)$$
   $$+ 0.10\left(\frac{87 + 90 + 83 + 93 + 91 + 90}{6}\right) + 0.20(82)$$
   $$= 0.70(85.25) + 0.10(89)$$
   $$+ 0.20(82)$$
   $$= 59.675 + 8.9 + 16.4$$
   $$= 84.975$$

   Chad's final grade is $\approx 85\%$.

5. **92.33%.** To find Katie's final grade, a weighted average must be calculated since Mr. Gallespie weights each type of assignment differently. Find the average score of each type of assignment, multiply it by its percentage weight, then add the percentages together to get Katie's final grade.

   $$\text{Final grade} = 0.60\left(\frac{93 + 97 + 88 + 91 + 95}{5}\right)$$
   $$+ 0.15\left(\frac{90 + 99 + 100 + 95 + 96}{5}\right)$$
   $$+ 0.25\left(\frac{89 + 90 + 85 + 92}{4}\right)$$
   $$= 0.60(92.8) + 0.15(96) +$$
   $$0.25(89)$$
   $$= 55.68 + 14.4 + 22.25$$
   $$= 92.33$$

6. $\frac{1}{6}$. There are seven blue candies in the bag. To find the probability that a blue one is selected, add up the total number of candies in the bag and divide 7 by it.

   $$\text{Probability}_{\text{blue}} = \frac{7}{6 + 5 + 10 + 8 + 7 + 6}$$
   $$= \frac{7}{42} = \frac{1}{6}$$

   The probability of getting a blue candy out of the bag is $\frac{1}{6}$.

7. **2.4%.** The probability of grabbing a blue candy the first time is $\frac{7}{42}$. What is the probability of getting a blue candy the next time? After one piece is taken out, there are six blue candies left and 41 candies left overall. So, the compound probability of getting two blue candies the first two times is found by multiplying the probability of the two events together:

   $$\frac{7}{42} \times \frac{6}{41} = \frac{42}{1,722} = 0.024 = 2.4\%$$

8. 6,840. This is a problem of permutation (i.e., the order matters). Just by thinking about it, how many athletes can win first place? 20. How many can win second place after first place has been awarded? 19. How many can win third place after first and second places have been awarded? 18. So, the number of combinations the trophies could be awarded is $20 \times 19 \times 18 = 6,840$.

Using the formula, we will get the same answer:
$$P(20,3) = \frac{n!}{k!(n-k)!} = \frac{20!}{(20-3)!}$$

$$= \frac{20 \times 19 \times 18 \times 17 \times 16 \times 15 \times 14 \times 13 \times 12 \times 11 \times 10 \times 9 \times 8 \times 7 \times 6 \times 5 \times 4 \times 3 \times 2 \times 1}{17 \times 16 \times 15 \times 14 \times 13 \times 12 \times 11 \times 10 \times 9 \times 8 \times 7 \times 6 \times 5 \times 4 \times 3 \times 2 \times 1}$$

$$= \frac{20 \times 19 \times 18 \times \cancel{17 \times 16 \times 15 \times 14 \times 13 \times 12 \times 11 \times 10 \times 9 \times 8 \times 7 \times 6 \times 5 \times 4 \times 3 \times 2 \times 1}}{\cancel{17 \times 16 \times 15 \times 14 \times 13 \times 12 \times 11 \times 10 \times 9 \times 8 \times 7 \times 6 \times 5 \times 4 \times 3 \times 2 \times 1}}$$

$$= 20 \times 19 \times 18 = 6,840$$

9. 210. This is an example of combination, where the order does not matter. Use the formula for combinations to find how many color combinations of four sticky notes can result from ten different colors.
$$C(10,4) = \frac{10!}{4!(10-4)!}$$
$$= \frac{10 \times 9 \times 8 \times 7 \times 6 \times 5 \times 4 \times 3 \times 2 \times 1}{4 \times 3 \times 2 \times 1(6 \times 5 \times 4 \times 3 \times 2 \times 1)}$$
$$= \frac{10 \times 9 \times 8 \times 7 \times \cancel{6 \times 5 \times 4 \times 3 \times 2 \times 1}}{4 \times 3 \times 2 \times 1(\cancel{6 \times 5 \times 4 \times 3 \times 2 \times 1})} = \frac{10 \times 9 \times 8 \times 7}{4 \times 3 \times 2 \times 1}$$
$$= \frac{5,040}{24} = 210$$

Statistics and Probability Review

1. a. The mode of a data set is the piece of data that occurs the most often. To find the ice cream flavor that is the mode during Ethan's shift, find the ice cream flavor that was sold more than any other flavor. Add up the number of ice cream cone sales by flavor:

butter pecan: 1

chocolate: 5

coffee: 2

mint: 2

pistachio: 2

strawberry: 3

vanilla: 2

The ice cream flavor that was sold the most during Ethan's shift was chocolate, so it is the mode.

2. c. The median of a data set is the piece of data that occurs right in the middle after the data is put in order. To find the median number of hours Phoebe will work in one day over the next three weeks, put the number of hours she works each day in order and choose the number in the middle:

0, 0, 0, 0, 0, 0, 0, 2, 3, 3, **4**, 4, 4, 4, 5, 5, 5, 5, 6, 6, 7

There are 21 days on the schedule, so the middle number is the eleventh number shown above, 4. The median number of hours Phoebe will work is 4.

3. d. The mean, or average score, of Pat's five games is 146. That means that Pat scores a total of 5×146, or 730, over five games. Let x represent Pat's score in the fifth game. His total score over five games is equal to:

$123 + 165 + 127 + 144 + x = 559 + x$

Now, set that total equal to Pat's total score, 730:

$559 + x = 730$

Subtract 559 from both sides:

$x = 171$

Pat scores 171 in his fifth game.

To check your answer, add Pat's score in each of the five games and divide the sum by 5:

$123 + 165 + 127 + 144 + 171 = 730$

The dividend should be equal to Pat's mean, 146:

$730 \div 5 = 146$

4. b. Put the nine ring scores in order from least to greatest. The middle value (the fifth value) is the median score:

3, 3, 3, 4, **4**, 5, 6, 8, 9

The median score is 4.

5. b. The spinner has ten equal sections, so the probability of the spinner landing on any one number is $\frac{1}{10}$. There are four numbers on the spinner that are less than 5 (1, 2, 3, and 4). The probability of the spinner landing on a number less than 5 is $\frac{1}{10}$, or $\frac{2}{5}$.

6. a. Before Evander removes a coin, there are 16 coins in the bank:

> 3 quarters + 5 pennies + 2 nickels +
> 6 dimes = 16 coins

After Evander removes the first quarter, there are:

> 2 quarters + 5 pennies + 2 nickels +
> 6 dimes = 15 coins

There are only 15 coins in the bank now, and only two of them are quarters. If Evander selects another coin, the probability that it will be a quarter is $\frac{2}{15}$.

7. b. This is a situation of probability with dependent events (i.e., the first event is dependent on the second event). Therefore, we need to multiply the two separate probabilities together to get the compound probability. For the first card, there are two possibilities out of a total of 28 cards. For the second card, there is only one chance that Yolanda will pick the matching card out of a remaining 27 cards. Multiply these two fractions together to get the answer:

$$\frac{2}{28} \times \frac{1}{27} = \frac{2}{756} = \frac{1}{378}$$

8. c. This is a problem involving permutation, which requires the following formula: $\frac{n!}{(n-r)!}$, where n = the total number of options and r = the number of options chosen. Since there are seven teams that could win a trophy, $n = 7$. Only three teams will get trophies, so $r = 3$. When these values are substituted into the equation, we get $\frac{n!}{(n-r)!} = \frac{7!}{(7-3)!} = \frac{7 \cdot 6 \cdot 5 \cdot 4 \cdot 3 \cdot 2 \cdot 1}{4 \cdot 3 \cdot 2 \cdot 1}$ $= 7 \cdot 6 \cdot 5 = 210$.

9. b. Joan can fit four of her seven CDs in her suitcase. It is important to understand that the order in which she chooses the CDs does not matter. The group of CDs A, B, C, and D is the same as the group A, B, D, and C, or D, C, A, and B.

This is a combination problem, so you must use the combination formula to find the answer:
$C(n,k) = \frac{n!}{k!(n-k)!}$, where n is the number of options and k is the number of choices made.

Joan has seven CDs and chooses four. Divide by 4! to ensure that you do not count the same group of four CDs more than once:

$$\frac{7 \times 6 \times 5 \times 4 \times 3 \times 2 \times 1}{(4 \times 3 \times 2 \times 1)(3 \times 2 \times 1)} = \frac{7 \times 6 \times 5 \times \cancel{4 \times 3 \times 2 \times 1}}{(\cancel{4 \times 3 \times 2 \times 1})(3 \times 2 \times 1)}$$
$$= \frac{7 \times 6 \times 5}{3 \times 2 \times 1} = \frac{210}{6} = 35$$

10. 1.75 hours. The mean is the average. To find the average of four numbers, find the sum of the numbers and divide by 4. Michael spent 2 hours doing homework on Monday, 1.5 hours on Tuesday, 2.5 hours on Wednesday, and 1 hour on Thursday. The sum of this time is 7 hours $(2 + 1.5 + 2.5 + 1 = 7)$. Next, divide 7 by 4 $(7 \div 4 = 1.75)$. The mean is 1.75 hours.

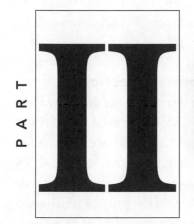

II ▶ GED® REASONING THROUGH LANGUAGE ARTS TEST

The GED® Reasoning through Language Arts (RLA) test measures how well you can apply problem solving, analytical reasoning, and critical thinking skills alongside your understanding of high school–level language arts.

RLA SKILL AREAS

The GED® RLA test concentrates on the following skill areas:
- The ability to read closely
- The ability to write clearly
- The ability to edit effectively and use standard written English appropriately

You will have 150 minutes to complete the entire exam, with one ten-minute scheduled break. Each question on the GED® RLA test is assigned a different point value depending on its difficulty, and a minimum score of 150 is required for passing the test. Use your time effectively and wisely to ensure you earn your best possible test score.

RLA Test Structure

The GED® RLA test is delivered on a computer and consists of approximately 50 multiple-choice, fill-in-the-blank, drop-down, drag-and-drop, and hot-spot questions, including an extended response question.

Multiple-Choice Questions

Multiple-choice questions on the GED® RLA test ask you to select the best answer from four choices. To select an answer, click the mouse in the circle next to that answer choice. To change your answer, click the circle of another answer choice.

Fill-in-the-Blank Questions

Fill-in-the-blank questions on the GED® RLA test ask you to type information into one or more blank space(s). There are no answer choices given to you— you must come up with what you think is the correct word or phrase and type it in the blank.

Drop-Down Questions

Drop-down questions on the GED® RLA test ask you to choose an answer from a single drop-down list or a group of drop-down lists within a sentence or paragraph. To answer the question, click your mouse on the arrow to show all of the answer choices and then click on your chosen answer to complete the sentence or paragraph.

Drag-and-Drop Questions

Drag-and-drop questions on the GED® RLA test have two areas: one area shows all of the answer choices, and the other area is where you will move the correct answers. You will need to drag one or more answers from the first area to the second area. To answer a drag-and-drop question, click and hold the mouse on an answer and move it (drag the answer) to the correct area of the screen. Then let go of the mouse (drop the answer). You can remove an answer and switch it with another answer at any time.

Hot-Spot Questions

Hot-spot questions on the GED® RLA test ask you to choose a certain place on an image. To answer the question, click on the correct spot of the image. You can change your answer by simply clicking on another area.

Extended Response Question

The extended response test item—the one essay question—is placed in the middle of the GED® RLA test. You will be given 45 minutes to read one or two informational passages (ranging between 450 and 900 words) and type a response on the computer. This question requires you to read the prompt (the passage or passages provided), create an argument based on it, and write a strong essay with evidence and examples.

You should feel comfortable typing on a keyboard in order to answer this kind of question, since there is a time limit of 45 minutes to read the material provided and construct your response.

RLA Review Chapters

The following review chapters will help you brush up on concepts, skills, and the format and scoring of the GED® RLA test. The RLA content has been broken into the following chapters:

- Reading Comprehension (Chapter 6)
- Language and Grammar (Chapter 7)
- The Extended Response Essay (Chapter 8)

Practice each skill a little every day, and you are sure to see an improvement in your comprehension, language, and writing skills. Good luck!

6 ▶ READING COMPREHENSION

Many of the questions on the GED® RLA test are designed to uncover how well you understand and think about what you read. Each of these questions will be tied to a reading passage—for instance, a newspaper article, part of a novel, or a president's speech. You'll need to read the passage carefully in order to answer the question correctly. In some cases, the answer will be obvious to you; in other cases, you'll have to do a little detective work to figure out the correct choice.

Answers and explanations for all practice questions are at the end of the chapter.

Main Ideas and Supporting Details

In this section, we'll walk you step-by-step through many of the tools you'll need to become a good detective and improve your score on the GED® RLA test. One of the most important skills to have when you read a passage on the GED® test (or in everyday life, for that matter) is the ability to identify the main idea of the passage and to see how the writer supports that idea.

Subject versus Main Idea

There's a difference between the **subject** of a piece of writing and its **main idea**. To see the difference, read through the following short passage:

PROMPT

Today's postal service is more efficient and reliable than ever before. Mail that used to take months to move by horse and by foot now moves around the country in days or hours by truck, train, and plane. First-class mail usually moves from New York City to Los Angeles in three days or less. If your letter or package is urgent, the U.S. Postal Service offers Priority Mail and Express Mail services. Priority Mail is guaranteed to go anywhere in the United States in two days or less. Express Mail will get your package there overnight.

Say someone asked you, "What is the main idea of this reading?" You might be tempted to answer, "The post office." But you'd be wrong. This passage is about the post office, yes—but the post office is not the main idea of the passage. The post office is merely the subject of the passage (who or what the passage is about). The main idea must say something about this subject.

The main idea of a text is usually an assertion about the subject. An assertion is a statement that requires evidence (proof) to be accepted as true. The main idea is also something more: it is the idea that holds together or controls the passage. The other sentences and ideas in the passage will relate to that main idea and serve as evidence that the assertion is true. You might think of the main idea as a net that is cast over the other sentences. The main idea must be general enough to hold all of these sentences together.

Let's take another look at the postal service paragraph, this time to identify the main idea. Look for the idea that makes an assertion about the postal service and holds together or controls the whole paragraph.

Which of the following three statements best summarizes the main idea?

A. Express Mail is a good way to send urgent mail.
B. Mail service today is more effective and dependable than it was in the past.
C. First-class mail usually takes three days or less.

Because choice **A** is specific—it tells us only about Express Mail—it cannot be the main idea. It does not encompass the rest of the sentences in the paragraph (for instance, it doesn't cover Priority Mail or first-class mail). Choice **C** is also too specific. It tells us only about first-class mail. Choice **B** is the correct answer. It is general enough to encompass the whole passage, and each of the other sentences in the paragraph offers proof that the idea is true.

Topic Sentences

You'll notice that in the paragraph about the postal service, the main idea is expressed clearly in the first sentence: *Today's postal service is more efficient and reliable than ever before.* A sentence that clearly states the main idea of a paragraph or passage is called a **topic sentence**.

In most cases, as in the postal service paragraph, the topic sentence is located at (or near) the beginning of the passage. Sometimes, however, it is located at the end—the writer gives his or her supporting evidence up front and then reveals at the end what all of that evidence adds up to. Less often, but on occasion, the topic sentence can be found in the middle of the passage.

Whatever the case, the topic sentence—like *Today's postal service is more efficient and reliable than ever before*—is an assertion, and it needs proof. In a well-written passage, the writer will supply facts and ideas throughout the text as proof that his or her main idea is right.

Supporting Evidence

Supporting evidence is the set of specific facts and ideas that explain and support the main idea. These details provide you with a more complete picture of what the author is trying to say.

Supporting evidence can be factual information, reasoning, examples, and descriptions that relate to the main idea.

Let's go back briefly to that paragraph on the postal service:

PROMPT

Today's postal service is more efficient and reliable than ever before. Mail that used to take months to move by horse and by foot now moves around the country in days or hours by truck, train, and plane. First-class mail usually moves from New York City to Los Angeles in three days or less. If your letter or package is urgent, the U.S. Postal Service offers Priority Mail and Express Mail services. Priority Mail is guaranteed to go anywhere in the United States in two days or less. Express Mail will get your package there overnight.

In this case, the paragraph is chock-full of evidence that supports the main idea (which is *Today's postal service is more efficient and reliable than ever before*). For example, look at the second sentence:

> *Mail that used to take months to move by horse and by foot now moves around the country in days or hours by truck, train, and plane.*

The fact that the postal service can move mail around the country in days or hours provides evidence that it has improved its efficiency since the time when this process took months.

The other sentences provide even more evidence of efficiency—explaining that mail can get to its destination in three days, in two days, or overnight (all much quicker than months!).

In addition, the next to last sentence in the paragraph offers support for the topic sentence's assertion that the postal service is more reliable:

> *Priority Mail is guaranteed to go anywhere in the United States in two days or less.*

The last sentence also helps to bolster that claim:

> *Express Mail will get your package there overnight.*

Practice

Read the next passage and answer the questions that follow.

DON'T LET LIGHTNING STRIKE YOU

Have you heard the saying "When thunder roars, go indoors"? Each year in the United States, more than 400 people are struck by lightning. On average, between 55 and 60 people are killed; hundreds of others suffer permanent neurological disabilities. Most of these tragedies can be avoided with a few simple precautions.

The National Oceanic and Atmospheric Administration (NOAA) collects information on weather-related deaths to learn how to prevent these tragedies. Many lightning victims say they were caught outside in the storm and couldn't get to a safe place. Other victims waited too long before seeking shelter; by heading to a safe place five to ten minutes sooner, they could have avoided being struck by lightning. Some people were struck because they went back outside too soon. Finally, some victims were struck inside homes or buildings while they were using electrical equipment or corded phones or were in contact with plumbing, a metal door, or a window frame.

There are a few things you might not know about lightning. First, all thunderstorms produce lightning and are dangerous. In the United States, in an average year, lightning kills about the same number of people as tornadoes do and causes more deaths than hurricanes do. Lightning often strikes outside the area of heavy rain and may strike as far as ten miles from any rainfall. Many lightning deaths occur ahead of storms or after storms have seemingly passed.

What should you do if you are caught outside near a thunderstorm? Keep in mind that there is no safe place outside in a thunderstorm. If you're outside and hear thunder, the only way to significantly reduce your risk of becoming a lightning casualty is to get inside a substantial building or hard-topped metal vehicle as fast as you can. In addition, you should avoid open areas, isolated tall trees, towers, or utility poles. Stay away from metal conductors such as wires or fences. Metal does not attract lightning, but lightning can travel long distances through it. If you are with a group of people, spread out. While this actually increases the chances that someone might get struck, it tends to prevent multiple casualties and increases the chances that someone could help if a person is struck.

Remember, if you can hear thunder, you are in danger. Don't be fooled by blue skies. If there is thunder, lightning is close enough to pose an immediate danger. Stay inside a safe building or vehicle for at least 30 minutes after you hear the last thunder clap.

—*Adapted from an article by the Federal Citizens Information Center (publications.USA.gov).*

1. Which excerpt from the article provides the least supporting evidence for the main idea?

   a. *Other victims waited too long before seeking shelter; by heading to a safe place five to ten minutes sooner, they could have avoided being struck by lightning.*

   b. *Lightning often strikes outside the area of heavy rain and may strike as far as ten miles from any rainfall.*

   c. *Stay away from metal conductors such as wires or fences. Metal does not attract lightning, but lightning can travel long distances through it.*

   d. *If you are with a group of people, spread out. While this actually increases the chances that someone might get struck, it tends to prevent multiple casualties and increases the chances that someone could help if a person is struck.*

2. Which sentence from the article best serves as the topic sentence of the article?

   a. *Have you heard the saying "When thunder roars, go indoors"?*

   b. *Each year in the United States, more than 400 people are struck by lightning.*

   c. *Most of these tragedies can be avoided with a few simple precautions.*

   d. *The National Oceanic and Atmospheric Administration (NOAA) collects information on weather-related deaths to learn how to prevent these tragedies.*

Facts versus Opinions

A **fact** is a statement of truth. It is based on direct evidence, actual experience, or observation. An **opinion** is a statement of belief, judgment, or feeling. It shows someone's personal thoughts about a subject. Some opinions are *based on* facts, but they are still someone's personal feelings about a subject, not facts themselves. Opinions are debatable; facts are not.

As an example of fact versus opinion, look at these two sentences, which discuss the same event:

> *Today, the president of North American Airlines, Maria Delgado, announced that she is lowering employee pay by 50%, discontinuing health insurance, and reducing vacation time by 30%.*

> *In her announcement today, the president of North American Airlines, Maria Delgado, showed that she cares more about money than her employees' welfare by slashing pay and vacation time and axing health insurance.*

Both sentences describe Maria Delgado's announcement, but there is a big difference in how they do so.

The first sentence is completely *factual*—it communicates only the facts of the day. The second sentence is highly *opinionated*. It communicates certain facts—that Maria Delgado is the president of North American Airlines, that she made an announcement today, and that she will be cutting pay, health coverage, and vacation time—but mixed in with those facts is a lot of opinion: that her plans show that she cares more about money than about the employees.

The writer also communicates his or her opinion by using words such as *slashing* and *axing*—they have a negative implication. By using these words instead of neutral words like *reducing*, *lowering*, or *ending*, the writer emphasizes the belief that Ms. Delgado's plans are violent and harmful to employees.

Another important difference between the sentences is that the first sentence contains facts that are either right or wrong, while the second sentence is open to conversation and debate.

Others might have a completely different opinion of Ms. Delgado and her actions at North American Airlines. For example, they may say that Ms. Delgado is really a nice woman who is doing all she can to help her employees during a difficult time. Even though the company has less money this year, she is not laying off any workers, but she has to reduce pay and benefits to keep them on.

Still others might have yet another opinion of Ms. Delgado and her plan.

Observations and Inferences

Making **observations** means looking carefully at the text and noticing specific things about *how it is written*. You may notice, for example, the point of view that the author has chosen. You may also notice:

- Particular words and phrases the writer uses
- The way those words and phrases are arranged in sentences and paragraphs
- Repeated word patterns or sentence patterns

- Important details about people, places, and things

If you make good observations, you can then make valid **inferences**. Inferences are conclusions that you make based on reasons, facts, or evidence. You are constantly making inferences based on your observations, even when you're not reading. For example, if you notice that the sky is full of dark, heavy clouds, you might infer that it is going to rain; if you notice that your coworker has a stack of gardening books on her desk, you might infer that she likes to garden. On the GED® RLA test, you may be asked to make an inference about a character, setting, or situation based on the information that is provided in a passage.

If you make an incorrect inference, it is probably because you haven't looked closely enough at the passage. As a result, you may base your inferences on your own ideas and experiences, not on what's actually written in the passage. If that's the case, it means you are forcing your own ideas on the author rather than listening to what the author has to say. It's critical, then, to pay close attention to what the writer is saying and how he or she says it.

Practice

Read the passage and answer the questions that follow.

FDA WIDENS LOOK AT ARSENIC IN APPLE JUICE

Some consumers are understandably surprised to learn that arsenic is present in water, air, and soil, and as a result, it can be found in certain foods and beverages, including apple juice and juice concentrates. Arsenic is present in the environment as a naturally occurring substance and also as a result of contamination from human activity, such as past use of fertilizers and arsenic-based pesticides, which may still be in the soil, explains Donald Zink, PhD, senior science adviser at the U.S. Food and Drug Administration (FDA)'s Center for Food Safety and Applied Nutrition. "While environmental contaminants like arsenic are unavoidable in food," says Zink, "the goal is to keep the levels of arsenic that people consume over the course of their lives as low as possible."

That's where the FDA and the U.S. Environmental Protection Agency (EPA) come in. Their job is to monitor food and the environment and take action when needed to protect the American public. The FDA has been testing and monitoring fruit juices, including apple juice, for arsenic content for more than 20 years, says Michael R. Taylor, the FDA's deputy commissioner for foods. "We are confident in the overall safety of apple juice consumed in this country because we continue to find that apple juice, on average, contains low amounts of arsenic."

In fact, the FDA's most recent tests done in 2010 and 2011 show on average about three parts of arsenic in every one billion parts of apple juice. That is lower than the 10 parts per billion (ppb) set by the EPA as the maximum level allowed in public drinking water.

"Our test results over many years support the overall safety of apple juice," says Taylor, "but we see a small percentage of individual samples tested that contain higher levels of arsenic. We want to minimize the public's exposure to arsenic in foods as much as we can." For that reason, the FDA plans to consider all the relevant evidence, and based on this work, it may set a guidance or other maximum level to further reduce arsenic in apple juice and juice products.

To further protect the public's health, the FDA is also taking the following actions:

- Enhancing its surveillance of arsenic in apple juice and juice concentrate. The agency will shortly have results for an additional 90 samples of apple juice and juice concentrate and soon after will sample additional types of juice and juice concentrates.
- Continuing to test samples of apple juice imported into the United States from China. The most recent results included more than 70 samples from China, and 95% of these contained less than the 10 ppb level used for drinking water.
- Working with the EPA to coordinate the review of the risk assessment being prepared and discussing other steps the two agencies can take to reduce the overall levels of arsenic in the environment and in foods.

The bottom line is that the FDA is working hard to ensure the safety of the foods people consume and to do so based on the best science. And the best thing families can do is to consume a variety of foods and beverages and follow a well-balanced diet consistent with the Dietary Guidelines for Americans.

3. Which of the following statements can be inferred from the recommendation at the very end: *the best thing families can do is to consume a variety of foods and beverages?*

   a. If you don't focus too much of your diet on one food or beverage—such as apple juice—to begin with, you will have a lower risk of exposure to any contaminants found in that food or beverage.

   b. Apple juice is one of many beverages available to consumers in the United States.

   c. One way of reducing obesity in the United States is for people to consume a variety of fruits and vegetables, including apple products.

   d. It can be difficult to encourage children to try other types of juices, but parents should make the effort.

4. Which of the following statements is the most logical inference based on the purpose of the article and the information it contains?

   a. Apple juice is being monitored for arsenic because more juice products are being imported from sources outside the United States, such as China.

   b. Apple juice is being monitored for arsenic because the FDA recently discovered high levels of arsenic in other types of juice.

   c. Apple juice is being monitored for arsenic because it is a popular beverage.

   d. Apple juice is being monitored for arsenic because it has surpassed orange juice in consumer preference.

Theme

We've already discussed ways of finding the main idea in nonfiction passages (newspaper articles, documents, and other kinds of writing that contain facts and/or opinions). You'll find many reading passages of this type on the GED® RLA test. You'll also find another type of passage: fiction. These will be excerpts from novels or short stories—writing that tells a story that is either completely or partially imaginary.

Every work of fiction contains a **theme**: the idea that lies beneath the story. The theme can be a lesson or message of the story, a question that the author is asking through the story, or a general concept. Themes are similar to main ideas, but there is one big difference: Unlike in nonfiction writing, where writers often summarize their main idea in a topic sentence or a paragraph, the theme of a work of fiction is rarely spelled out so clearly. To find it, you will need to read closely and consider not just *what* the story is about but *how* the writer tells that story. In other words, look past the action (or plot), and ask yourself what it all may mean.

As an example, say you're reading a novel about a poor woman's journey from Korea to the United States in the 1940s. It may describe the details of the character's childhood on a farm in Korea, the boat trip that she took as a young adult to San Francisco, the elderly man who swindled her out of her life savings because she didn't speak English, the difficulties she had finding a job, and the satisfaction she ultimately felt as she worked hard to make a living. These are the facts of the plot, but the theme of the novel is something very different. Here are some possible themes:

- The theme could be a *message or lesson*. For instance: *You can reach your goals more easily if you block out your problems and focus only on your goal.*

- The theme could be *a question*. For instance: *Do you lose part of yourself when you leave your culture? Is it better to stay where you are and face the difficulties there, or do you become more of your real self when you leave your culture and make your own way in the world?*

- The theme could be *a specific idea about life or people.* For instance: *Desperation brings out the very worst in people and the very best.*
- The theme could also be *a simpler, more general concept.* For instance, perhaps the novel is an exploration of the theme of youth and aging.

Note that more than one theme may be valid for a work of fiction, and other readers may come to a different conclusion than you do. This is part of the reward of reading fiction—seeing the ideas behind what you read and discussing those ideas with other people. (Often these are ideas about life, which will be interesting to you as you make your own way in the world.)

> ### NOTE
>
> Although a work of fiction may have more than one possible theme, don't worry that this will cause confusion on the GED® RLA test. Every question about theme on the GED® RLA test will have only one, clearly correct answer. There are no "trick" questions on the exam.

Finding the Theme

As you read a work of fiction closely, pay attention to the following elements in order to find the theme:

- **Repetition:** Note whether the author repeats certain words, phrases, symbols, actions, or ideas, or whether certain characters reappear throughout a story. This is often a clue that those words, phrases, characters, and so on have a special importance in the story—and to the theme.

- **Connections:** In many stories, one specific thing may not be repeated, but if you look closely, you'll find that the writer uses repetition in a more complicated way. For example, let's say the first chapter of a book takes place in a house by a river, which is flooding after a bad storm. The climax of the book takes place on a train that's traveling through the dusty plains of Texas. The end of the book takes place on a street in New York City, where children have uncapped a fire hydrant and are playing in the water. While a river, a plain, and a fire hydrant are very different things, there is a pattern running through the book: water—either too much or too little. Ask yourself if this pattern helps to reveal the theme.

- **Timing:** Consider when events occur in a story and whether there is a pattern. For example, let's say in one short story, whenever the main character, a firefighter, puts on his firefighting uniform in the morning, a mouse—a common symbol for cowardice and weakness—peeks its head out of a hole in the wall. Is this pattern a reminder that we all have to battle our weaknesses? Or that even when someone acts bravely, he or she is still vulnerable? Patterns are usually connected to the theme and can help us understand it.

- **Omission:** Often it's what a writer *doesn't* write about that's most important. Is there a detail or event that's glaringly left out of the story? This may be directly tied to the theme.

Practice

Read the passage and answer the questions that follow.

FOUR SIMPLE TIPS TO HELP YOU LAND A GREAT JOB

Whether you're just graduating and entering the job market for the first time or you're changing careers, searching for a job is never easy. In today's high-tech society, many potential employers are turning to social media to learn more about you.

"Before you even walk through the door for your first interview, it is highly likely the person waiting on the other side has seen more than just your resume," says Lauren Berger, CEO of InternQueen.com. "The way you present yourself online speaks volumes to hiring managers about your tech savvy and comfort level with social media—both critical skills demanded by virtually every employer."

With technology playing an established role in our lives and social networks easily accessible to potential employers, establishing a strong digital footprint and personal brand is crucial to success. So how can you use technology to land that first job and make the best first impression?

Here are four top tech tools and social media tips for landing your dream job:

1. Get organized. While it may seem like a minor detail, one of the first things you should do is get a professional e-mail address. The college e-mail or cutesy address you created back in high school won't impress a job recruiter.

2. Leverage your networks and set informational interviews. Make a target list of employers you'd like to work for and do some research about them, identifying one person from each company whom you'd like to meet. Reach out to that person and explain that you're really interested in the company and what his or her department does. Then ask if he or she will take five minutes to sit down and tell you how he or she got started and give you some advice.

3. Put your best "digital foot" forward. You have one chance to make a first impression, so make sure it's a good one. This means not only dressing professionally but also using your style (both online and off) to demonstrate your personal interests. Building your personal brand and establishing relationships within the industry will help open doors to opportunities you may not have discovered otherwise. Make sure that your online presence is up to date and also reflects your best attributes. This includes maintaining a consistent resume and work experience information across your networks to build familiarity among possible recruiters.

4. Lead with your strengths. Ask your friends and previous employers what your strengths are, and use specific examples during your interview to highlight them. You can also use this opportunity to demonstrate your experience with technology. If you are consistently told how well organized you are, share a previous work experience that demonstrates how you used technology and what value this brings to the employer. If you have a laptop or a tablet computer, consider bringing it to the interview to show off your portfolio of work. This instantly demonstrates you're on the cutting edge of new technology—a value for any employer.

These seemingly simple tips can help you stand out from the crowd and boost your chances of finding that great job.

5. Of the following choices, which skills does the author emphasize as being important to potential employers?

a. leadership and the ability to resolve conflict

b. digital literacy and expertise with Internet communications

c. loyalty and a strong work ethic

d. creativity and knowledge of computer hardware

6. Based on the passage, which of the following statements would the author most likely make when advising someone who was recently laid off and is in the process of applying for jobs?

a. Update your career wardrobe and hire a professional to revise your resume.

b. Consider getting retrained in a field that is growing in career opportunities.

c. Evaluate how your job qualifications can be demonstrated through the use of technology.

d. Schedule as many informational interviews as you can at each company you are interested in, and attend a weekly job-support group.

Relationships and Structure

Understanding how different elements develop in a passage is a crucial part of reading comprehension. In this section, we discuss some of the building blocks of writing and see how they interrelate.

Descriptive Elements

Authors use **descriptive elements** and details to help readers create a mental picture. Descriptive details in writing let you more easily visualize a person, place, object, or event. In this excerpt from the short story "A Rose for Emily" by William Faulkner, do you see how detailed Faulkner gets when describing the character?

EXCERPT

They rose when she entered—a small, fat woman in black, with a thin gold chain descending to her waist and vanishing into her belt, leaning on an ebony cane with a tarnished gold head. Her skeleton was small and spare; perhaps that was why what would have been merely plumpness in another was obesity in her. She looked bloated, like a body long submerged in motionless water, and of that pallid hue. Her eyes, lost in the fatty ridges of her face, looked like two small pieces of coal pressed into a lump of dough as they moved from one face to another while the visitors stated their errand.

As you can see, the writer uses many specific details to help you create a picture in your mind of what Miss Emily looks like and how she acts. Look at how richly he describes the character in just the first sentence:

- *a small, fat woman in black*
- *a thin gold chain descending to her waist and vanishing into her belt*
- *leaning on an ebony cane with a tarnished gold head*

These elaborate descriptions add to your understanding of the character. They help you better understand the events in the story—the portrait of Miss Emily grows with every detail and sets you up for her meeting with her visitors.

Interpreting Relationships

When you see a passage on the GED® test, pay special attention to how different people or characters relate to one another. Thinking about why the author puts each person, place, and thing into a passage will help you better understand it.

Here is another excerpt from "A Rose for Emily":

EXCERPT

[Miss Emily's] voice was dry and cold. "I have no taxes in Jefferson. Colonel Sartoris explained it to me. Perhaps one of you can gain access to the city records and satisfy yourselves."

"But we have. We are the city authorities, Miss Emily. Didn't you get a notice from the sheriff, signed by him?"

"I received a paper, yes," Miss Emily said. "Perhaps he considers himself the sheriff. . . . I have no taxes in Jefferson."

"But there is nothing on the books to show that, you see. We must go by the—"

"See Colonel Sartoris. I have no taxes in Jefferson."

"But Miss Emily—"

"See Colonel Sartoris." (Colonel Sartoris had been dead almost ten years.) "I have no taxes in Jefferson. Tobe! . . . Show these gentlemen out."

Based on the dialogue between Miss Emily and the town authorities, the reader understands that Miss Emily is not intimidated by them. The town authorities, on the other hand, are confused by Miss Emily's unwillingness to bow to their power. Furthermore, do you see how your understanding of this conversation is affected by the colorful description of Miss Emily that you read earlier? Without that detailed description, you might have had a very different interpretation of the conversation.

Structure

Readers also need to understand how an author organizes his or her writing and how this affects its overall meaning. You may be asked to identify these features of a passage:

- cause and effect
- sequence of events or time order of events
- compare and contrast

Cause and Effect

In a **cause-and-effect** relationship, one action or event (the cause) creates another action or event (the effect). Consider the following examples:

Because she'd studied for the GED® every morning during her commute to work, Maria felt ready to take the test.

Here, the cause is Maria's studying every morning during her commute. The effect is the fact that she feels ready to take the test.

If it rains too hard, we'll have to cancel the picnic.

Here, heavy rain would cause the cancellation of the picnic (the effect).

Sequence

Sequence is the order in which events happen over time. Some passages describe events **chronologically**: in the same order that they occurred in real life or in the make-believe world of a novel or a short story. For instance, in a novel about a doomed love affair, if the writer chooses to tell the story in chronological order, the book may begin with the couple meeting for the first time, then describe moments in their relationship, and end with their breakup.

That same love affair could also be described in a completely different order: for example, the writer could start the story with their breakup, and then piece together why that breakup happened by describing moments in the couple's relationship through memories or flashbacks. When you read passages on the GED® test, pay close attention to the sequence of events—if the sequence is tricky, you are sure to see questions asking about it!

Compare and Contrast

We spend a good deal of our lives comparing and contrasting things. When we want to explain something, for example, we often **compare** it to something else (showing how two or more things are similar). We might say, for example, that mint chocolate chip ice cream tastes just like a peppermint-filled chocolate, or that our new boss looks a lot like Will Smith. When we want to show how things are different or not alike, we **contrast** them. We might say that our friend Sam looks nothing like his brother Pat, or that Italian is a much harder language to learn than Spanish.

Comparing and contrasting are common techniques in writing, too. They can be used for many reasons—for example, to describe a character more colorfully or to provide support for an argument that the writer is making.

Transitions Used to Compare and Contrast

As you read the next passage, about gardeners and parents, notice the transitional words and phrases that indicate when the writer is comparing (showing similarity) and when the writer is contrasting (showing difference). There are several transitional words and phrases writers use to show comparison and contrast.

Here are some words and phrases that can be used to show *similarity*:

- similarly
- likewise
- like
- just as
- in the same way
- and
- also

These words and phrases can be used to show *difference*:

- on the other hand
- on the contrary
- however
- nevertheless
- conversely
- yet
- but

Practice

Read the passage and answer the questions that follow.

GARDENERS AND PARENTS

Planting a garden is a lot like having a family. Both require a great deal of work, especially as they grow and as the seasons change. As summer days lengthen, your plants become dependent on you for sustenance, much like your children depend on you for food and drink. Like a thirsty child asking for a drink of water, your plants do the same. Their bent, wilted "body" language, translated, issues a demand much the way your child requests milk or juice. When their collective thirsts are quenched, you see the way they both thrive in your care. The fussy child becomes satisfied, and the plant reaches toward the sun in a showy display. You might also find that you have to clean the space around your plants much like you would pick up toys and clothes that have been left helter-skelter in your toddler's room. Similarly, plants shed spent petals, roses need to be pruned, and weeds need to be pulled. To keep children healthy, parents protect their children against disease with medicine, and gardeners do the same with insect repellent. To nourish them, parents give children vitamins, and gardeners use fertilizer, as both promote healthy growth. As children grow and become adults, they need less and less care. However, here's where the similarity ends. While plants die or become dormant during winter, children still maintain a vital role in the family unit.

7. In this passage, the writer compares being a parent to being a _____.

8. Which of the following pairs shows a **contrast**, not a comparison, between being a parent and being a gardener?
   a. Parents give vitamins to children to keep them healthy; gardeners give fertilizer to their plants to keep them healthy.
   b. Parents pick up toys and clothes in their children's room; gardeners pull up weeds around their plants.
   c. Children remain an important part of the family after they grow up; plants die or become dormant after the growing season ends.
   d. Children ask parents for milk or juice when they are thirsty; plants bend or wilt when they need water, showing gardeners that they are thirsty.

Reading More Closely

As you practice more and more with reading passages, you will begin to notice how specific sentences or paragraphs relate to each other and to the passage as a whole. When you are aware of how an author has structured his or her writing, it will help you understand the writer's meaning even better. Structure, word choice, description, and detail all give shape to a text and affect its meaning.

The following excerpt is from the speech that John F. Kennedy gave when he was sworn in as president in 1961.

EXCERPT

The world is very different now. For man holds in his mortal hands the power to abolish all forms of human poverty and all forms of human life. And yet the same revolutionary beliefs for which our forebears fought are still at issue around the globe—the belief that the rights of man come not from the generosity of the state, but from the hand of God.

As you read this passage closely, you should pay attention to certain words or phrases and how they build on each other.

The phrase *mortal hands* has a more powerful meaning than if the word *mortal* was not included. Words such as *revolutionary beliefs* and *forebears* reinforce Kennedy's appeal to the audience to make a connection with the birth of the nation.

The structure and word choice of the passage affect its tone and meaning and support Kennedy's purpose to inspire his audience. Later on in the speech are six paragraphs that all begin with the same pattern:

> *To those old allies whose cultural and spiritual origins we share. . . .*
>
> *To those new States whom we welcome to the ranks of the free. . . .*
>
> *To those peoples in the huts and villages across the globe struggling to break the bonds of mass misery. . . .*
>
> *To our sister republics south of our border. . . .*
>
> *To that world assembly of sovereign states. . . .*
>
> *Finally, to those nations who would make themselves our adversary. . . .*

This is a great example of the use of **repetition** and **parallel structure** to strengthen meaning and focus the listener's attention.

Practice

Read the passage and answer the questions that follow.

"THE MAGNOLIA TREE," FROM THE MEMOIR *CROSS CREEK* (1942), BY MARJORIE KINNAN RAWLINGS

I do not know the irreducible minimum of happiness for any other spirit than my own. It is impossible to be certain even of mine. Yet I believe that I know my tangible desideratum. It is a tree-top against a patch of sky. If I should lie crippled or long ill, or should have the quite conceivable misfortune to be clapped in jail, I could survive, I think, given this one token of the physical world. I know that I lived on one such in my first days at the Creek.

The tree was a magnolia, taller than the tallest orange trees around it. There is no such thing in the world as an ugly tree, but the magnolia grandiflora has a unique perfection. No matter how crowded it may be, no matter how thickly holly and live oak and sweet gum may grow up around it, it develops with complete symmetry, so that one wonders whether character in all things, human as well as vegetable, may not be implicit. Neither is its development ruthless, achieved at the expense of its neighbors, for it is one of the few trees that may be allowed to stand in an orange grove, seeming to steal nothing from the expensively nourished citrus. The young of the tree is courteous, waiting for the parent to be done with life before presuming to take it over. There are never seedling magnolias under or near an old magnolia. When the tree at last dies, the young glossy sprouts appear from nowhere, exulting in the sun and air for which they may have waited a long hundred years.

The tree is beautiful the year around. It need not wait for a brief burst of blooming to justify itself, like the wild plum and the hawthorn. It is handsomer than most dressed only in its broad leaves, shining like dark polished jade, so that when I am desperate for decoration, I break a few sprays for the house and find them an ornament of which a Japanese artist would approve. The tree sheds some of its leaves just before it blooms, as though it shook off old garments to be cleansed and ready for the new. There is a dry pattering to earth of the hard leaves and for a brief time the tree is parched and drawn, the rosy-lichened trunk gray and anxious. Then pale green spires cover the boughs, unfolding into freshly lacquered leaves, and at their tips the blooms appear. When, in late April or early May, the pale buds unfold into great white waxy blossoms, sometimes eight or ten inches across, and the perfume is a delirious thing on the spring air, I would not trade one tree for a conservatory filled with orchids. The blooms, for all their size and thickness, are as delicate as orchids in that they reject the touch of human hands. They must be cut or broken carefully and placed in a jar of water without brushing the edges, or the creamy petals will turn in an hour to brown velvet. Properly handled, they open in the house as on the tree, the cupped buds bursting open suddenly, the full-blown flowers shedding the red-tipped stamens in a shower, so that in a quiet room you hear them sifting onto the table top. The red seed cones are as fine as candles. They mature slowly from the top of the tree down, as a Christmas tree is lighted.

9. To what does the author compare magnolia
blooms?
   a. orchids
   b. candles
   c. Christmas trees
   d. jade

10. The passage describes the yearly cycle of a
magnolia tree. Select the answer that puts the
following statements in chronological order:
   1. The tree is covered in flower buds.
   2. The tree grows fresh green leaves.
   3. The air around the tree is perfumed.
   4. Leaves fall off the tree.
   a. 3, 2, 4, 1
   b. 2, 3, 4, 1
   c. 1, 2, 4, 3
   d. 4, 2, 1, 3

Interpreting What You Read

As we touched on, your job as a reader is not only to
understand the literal meaning of a word, paragraph,
article, or book, but to read between the lines in order
to discover the full meaning of the text. Just as in spoken conversation, where you have many ways to communicate what you are thinking—through a joke, a
story, even a facial expression—writers have many
techniques to communicate with their readers.

Text with layers of meaning is often more colorful, more convincing, more emotional, or more
meaningful than text that simply spells out what the
author is trying to say in a clear, factual way.

It's important to try to pick up on a writer's
clues, just as, for example, you would pick up on a
look of disappointment when a friend says, "That's
fine." You immediately recognize that your friend
does not really think that whatever happened is fine.
This section describes the techniques that writers
use—many of which you probably have already
picked up on—and how to identify them.

Interpreting Specific Words

On the GED® RLA test, you may be asked to figure
out the definition of vocabulary words by looking at
their **context**—the words and meanings that surround the vocabulary words.

For an example of how to do this, read the following paragraph about one of the nation's favorite
pastimes.

REALITY TV

Most reality TV shows center on two common motivators: fame and money. The
shows transform waitresses, hairdressers,
investment bankers, counselors, and teachers, to name a few, from obscure figures to
household names. A lucky few successfully
parlay their 15 minutes of fame into celebrity. Even if you are not interested in fame,
you can probably understand the desire for
lots of money. Watching people eat large
insects, reveal their innermost thoughts to
millions of people, and allow themselves to
be filmed 24 hours a day for a huge financial reward seems to have mass appeal for
viewers. Whatever their attraction, these
shows are among the most popular on television, and every season, they proliferate
like weeds in an untended garden. The networks are quickly replacing more traditional
dramas and comedies with reality TV programs, which earn millions of dollars in
advertising revenue. Whether you love it or
hate it, one thing is for sure—reality TV is
here to stay!

One of the more difficult words in the paragraph is
obscure. With a little detective work, we can determine the definition of that word by looking at how it

is used in the paragraph. Let's look at the context in which it appears:

The shows transform waitresses, hairdressers, investment bankers, counselors, and teachers, to name a few, from obscure figures to household names.

Given the sentence, what can we tell about *obscure*? Well, since the shows transform waitresses, hairdressers, investment bankers, counselors, and teachers from one position—*obscure* figures—to another position—household names—that immediately tells us that an obscure figure and a household name are two different things.

Furthermore, we know from the sentence that the people in question are involved in typical, everyday jobs (waitresses, hairdressers, bankers, etc.) and that from this position, they are transformed into household names, which means they achieve some level of fame and notoriety. Now you can take a pretty good guess at the meaning of *obscure*.

Before they become household names, the waitresses, hairdressers, investment bankers, counselors, and teachers are

A. famous and notorious.
B. unknown and undistinguished.
C. unique and distinctive.

The correct answer, of course, is **B**. It certainly can't be **A**, because we know that these people are not yet famous. The reality shows will make them famous, but until that happens, they remain *obscure*. Answer **C** doesn't really make sense because we know from the passage that these people are waitresses, hairdressers, investment bankers, counselors, and teachers. Now, these are all very respectable jobs, but they are fairly common, so they wouldn't be described as unique or distinctive. Furthermore, we can tell that **B** is the correct answer because we can substitute the

word *obscure* with the word *unknown* or *undistinguished* in the sentence and both would make sense.

How Much Context Do You Need?

In the previous example, you would still be able to understand the main message of the passage even if you didn't know—or couldn't figure out—the meaning of *obscure*. In some cases, however, your understanding of a passage depends on your understanding of a particular word or phrase. Can you understand the following sentence, for example, without knowing what *adversely* means?

Reality TV shows will adversely affect traditional dramas and comedies.

What does *adversely* mean in this sentence? Is it something good or bad? As good a detective as you may be, there simply aren't enough clues in this sentence to tell you what this word means. But a passage with more information will give you what you need to determine meaning from context.

Reality TV shows will adversely affect traditional dramas and comedies. As reality TV increases in popularity, network executives will begin canceling more traditional dramas and comedies and replacing them with the latest in reality TV.

In the passage, *adversely* most nearly means

A. mildly, slightly.
B. kindly, gently.
C. negatively, unfavorably.
D. immediately, swiftly.

The correct answer is **C**, negatively, unfavorably. The passage provides clues that allow you to determine the meaning of *adversely*. It tells you that as reality TV becomes more popular, network executives will cancel more traditional dramas and comedies and replace them with reality TV programming. So the meaning of *adversely* is neither **A**, mildly, slightly, nor **B**, kindly, gently. And based on the passage, you can't really tell if these changes will be immediate or swift (**D**) because the sentence doesn't say anything about the exact time frame in which these changes will occur. Remember, good detectives don't make assumptions they can't support with facts; and there are no facts in this sentence to support the assumption that changes will occur immediately. Thus, **C** is the best answer choice.

You may also have noticed that *adversely* is very similar to *adversary*. And if you know that an *adversary* is a hostile opponent or enemy, then you know that *adversely* cannot be something positive. Or if you know the word *adversity*—hardship or misfortune—then you know that *adversely* must mean something negative or difficult. All these words share the same root, *advers-*. Only the endings change.

Connotative Meaning

Authors use words in certain ways to help them describe characters or events and create a particular mood or tone.

The **connotative** meaning of a word is its suggested meaning, as opposed to the literal or exact definition. For instance, if you are angry with someone and refer to him or her as a "rat," you are suggesting that the person is mean or disgraceful, not an actual rodent.

Writers use **figurative** language to create images with words and express ideas in creative ways. Figurative devices include metaphors and similes.

Metaphors

Before we explain what it is, look at this example of a metaphor:

> *Janie was <u>the heart</u> of the organization: all ideas came from her and circulated back to her for her feedback.*

Here *the heart* is a metaphor—Janie was not literally a human heart, but she acted as a heart at the organization. All ideas flowed through her, just as blood is pumped out from and flows back to the heart in the human body.

A **metaphor** is a word or phrase for one thing that the writer uses to refer to another thing, showing that they are similar.

Here is another example:

> *His smile is <u>a ray of sunshine</u> that makes people feel happy, no matter how down they are.*

Of course, the smile is not literally made of sunshine. The writer is using the metaphor *ray of sunshine* to express the positive effect of the person's smile on the people around him.

Similes

Similes are similar to metaphors, but they use the words *like* or *as*. For example:

> *His smile is <u>like a ray of sunshine</u>.*
> *My puppy Waldo is <u>as sweet as a teddy bear</u>.*
> *Running errands for my boss is <u>as much fun as going to the dentist</u>.*

Here's a fourth example, which you may have even noticed when you read the very descriptive paragraph from the short story "A Rose for Emily," earlier in the course:

> *Her eyes, lost in the fatty ridges of her face, <u>looked like two small pieces of coal pressed into a lump of dough</u> as they moved from one face to another while the visitors stated their errand.*

A Closer Look at Figurative Language

In some passages, the use of figurative language can be much more complicated than in the sentences in the preceding section, but if you break it down, you'll see the hidden meaning.

This passage from John F. Kennedy's 1961 inaugural address uses figurative language to discuss sophisticated ideas with the audience. In the second paragraph, reprinted here, you can see several examples.

EXCERPT

We dare not forget today that we are the heirs of that first revolution. Let the word go forth from this time and place, to friend and foe alike, that the torch has been passed to a new generation of Americans—born in this century, tempered by war, disciplined by a hard and bitter peace, proud of our ancient heritage—and unwilling to witness or permit the slow undoing of those human rights to which this nation has always been committed, and to which we are committed today at home and around the world.

Let's look at the first sentence:

We dare not forget today that we are the heirs of that first revolution.

By using the word *heirs*, President Kennedy communicates a deep sense of obligation to the American public listening to him. Hearing that word makes an audience think of family history and connection.

Now, let's look at the second sentence:

Let the word go forth from this time and place, to friend and foe alike, that the torch has been passed to a new generation of Americans—born in this century, tempered by war, disciplined by a hard and bitter peace, proud of our ancient heritage—and unwilling to witness or permit the

slow undoing of those human rights to which this nation has always been committed, and to which we are committed today at home and around the world.

In this (very long) sentence, the image of a flame in the torch suggests the power and intensity of Kennedy's call to action. The metaphor gains even more intensity and atmosphere from the image of an Olympic marathon—the torch has been passed—in which a runner literally passes a lighted torch to the next runner in the relay team.

Tone

Tone is the mood or attitude conveyed in writing. Even in passages that may seem very straightforward, good writers are very careful about the exact words they choose and the style of their language.

Consider another excerpt from the earlier article "Four Simple Tips to Help You Land a Great Job."

EXCERPT

If you're among the more than 1.5 million college grads looking for work this year, you will need to work smarter to stand above the crowd and land that dream job or internship.

As you probably picked up, the language is direct and simple. The author speaks directly to you, the reader. The writing is informal, but it grabs you right away with action and purpose (note the phrase *land a great job* in the title, for example). In the sentence, the phrase *stand above the crowd* is an example of figurative language—the writer is not telling you to literally stand taller than other people in a crowd. But even though it is figurative, it is not poetic or emotional, as the figurative language in President Kennedy's inaugural speech is.

As you can see from these two excerpts, good writers use a tone that is appropriate to their purpose. The inaugural speech uses language to inspire listeners to action in the name of higher goals, while the guide for job seekers uses a more personal and direct style to offer advice for finding work.

Point of View and Purpose

Figuring out an author's **point of view** and **purpose** is important to understanding the meaning of a passage. The author's point of view can be described as his or her attitude toward a subject. An author's purpose is the reason for writing about a specific topic.

Sometimes a writer chooses to tell a story through the eyes of someone completely outside the action of the story. Other times, a character within the story is telling it.

You can identify an author's viewpoint based on passage details, vocabulary, and word choice, as well as the author's background. This last element can be challenging because it may require not only knowledge about the author but also some background information about the time period in which the passage was written and what important events happened then.

EXCERPTED FROM MARJORIE KINNAN RAWLINGS'S *CROSS CREEK*, A MEMOIR ABOUT LIFE ON A FLORIDA ORANGE GROVE (1942)

I see no reason for denying so fundamental an urge, ruin or no. It is more important to live the life one wishes to live, and to go down with it if necessary, quite contentedly, than to live more profitably but less happily. Yet to achieve content under sometimes adverse circumstances requires first an adjustment within oneself, and this I had already made, and after that, a recognition that one is not unique in being obliged to toil and struggle and suffer. This is the simplest of all facts and the most difficult for the individual ego to accept.

A close reading of this passage requires that you first pay attention to the year in which it was published—1942. What significant events happened in the United States around this time? The nation was recovering from the Great Depression and had just entered World War II. Rawlings is writing about the years before this, but it is important to know that these events were happening because they may shape the viewpoint of the author.

In this excerpt, Rawlings talks about living the life one wants to live, even if it means suffering diffi-culties, instead of having more money but being less happy. She acknowledges that the struggle she faced was not really unique—everyone experiences difficulties. Rawlings implies that complaining about one's lot in life is a waste of time. This summarizes her point of view, which may have been shaped not only by her personal experiences but by what was happening in society at this time.

What might be Rawlings's purpose for writing *Cross Creek*? Based on her style and viewpoint, the reader can conclude that she wanted to provide readers with a glimpse of life in a Southern community, including its challenges and imperfections. In reading this memoir, a person might connect on some level with the struggles that Rawlings faced.

Practice

Read the passage and answer the questions that follow.

EXCERPTED FROM THE MEMOIR *CROSS CREEK* (1942), BY MARJORIE KINNAN RAWLINGS

It is always bewildering to change one's complete way of life. I was fitted by temperament and by inheritance for farm and country living, yet to take it up after some thirty years of urban life was not too easy. I had known my maternal grandfather's Michigan farm, but there I was both guest and child, and the only duties were to gather the eggs from the sweet-smelling hayloft. I had known my father's Maryland farm, but that farm was his love, his escape from Washington governmental routine, and we lived there only in the too few summers. I had no duties there at all. There was only delight; the flowering locust grove; the gentle cows in pasture; Rock Creek, which ran, ten miles away from its Washington park, at the foot of the hill of the locusts, where my brother and I learned to swim and to fish for tiny and almost untakable fishes; long walks with my father through the woods where he hoped someday to build a home; jaunts with him behind Old Dan in the carriage, to the county seat of Rockville, or to buy mules at Frederick. These things got in the blood but were no preparation for running a farm oneself.

When I bought the Florida orange grove with my inheritance that represented my share of the Maryland farm, my father's sister Madeline wrote me in lament. "You have in you," she said, "that fatal drop of Pearce blood, clamoring for change and adventure, and above all, for a farm. I never knew a Pearce who didn't secretly long for a farm. Mother had one, Uncle Pierman was ruined by one, there was your father's tragic experience. I had one, once." I see no reason for denying so fundamental an urge, ruin or no. It is more important to live the life one wishes to live, and to go down with it if necessary, quite contentedly, than to live more profitably but less happily. Yet to achieve content under sometimes adverse circumstances requires first an adjustment within oneself, and this I had already made, and after that, a recognition that one is not unique in being obliged to toil and struggle and suffer. This is the simplest of all facts and the most difficult for the individual ego to accept. As I look back on those first difficult times at the Creek, when it seemed as though the actual labor was more than I could bear, and the making of a living on the grove impossible, it was Martha who drew aside a curtain and led me in to the company of all those who had loved the Creek and been tormented by it.

11. Madeline's attitude toward the writer's decision to purchase the farm could best be described as
a. nostalgic for days gone by.
b. enthusiastic but concerned.
c. understanding but foreboding.
d. indifferent.

12. The passage suggests which of the following about the writer's decision to purchase the farm in Cross Creek?
a. She deeply regretted her decision because of the amount of work required to run the farm.
b. She was ready to separate from her domineering family and live on her own on the farm.
c. She was enthusiastic about owning the farm and appreciated the experiences that prepared her for this endeavor.
d. She had a deep desire for rural life and knew she must fulfill this longing to be truly happy.

13. In the last sentence, *the Creek* refers to
a. a farm in Michigan.
b. an orange grove in Florida.
c. Rock Creek, ten miles from Washington, DC.
d. a farm in Maryland.

14. The phrase *it was Martha who drew aside a curtain* is a metaphor that could be best interpreted as
a. Martha opened the curtains of the author's house, filling it with sunlight.
b. Martha gave the author clarity by offering an inside perspective.
c. Martha alleviated some of the author's burden at the Creek by opening the curtains and doing other household tasks.
d. none of the above.

Summary

The reading questions on the GED® RLA test will evaluate your ability to read complex passages closely. You will be asked questions requiring several steps of critical thinking to arrive at the correct answer. Before you take the GED® test, practice reading informational and historical texts, as well as various types of literature. Engage in active reading, ask yourself questions, and notice the different ways that writers make their points or tell their stories.

The more you practice the strategies presented in this chapter, the more successful you will be on the GED® RLA test.

Reading Comprehension Review

Use the following passage to answer questions 1 and 2.

FDA WIDENS LOOK AT ARSENIC IN APPLE JUICE

Some consumers are understandably surprised to learn that arsenic is present in water, air, and soil, and as a result, it can be found in certain foods and beverages, including apple juice and juice concentrates. Arsenic is present in the environment as a naturally occurring substance and also as a result of contamination from human activity, such as past use of fertilizers and arsenic-based pesticides, which may still be in the soil, explains Donald Zink, PhD, senior science adviser at the U.S. Food and Drug Administration's (FDA's) Center for Food Safety and Applied Nutrition. "While environmental contaminants like arsenic are unavoidable in food," says Zink, "the goal is to keep the levels of arsenic that people consume over the course of their lives as low as possible."

That's where the FDA and the U.S. Environmental Protection Agency (EPA) come in. Their job is to monitor food and the environment and take action when needed to protect the American public. The FDA has been testing and monitoring fruit juices, including apple juice, for arsenic content for more than 20 years, says Michael R. Taylor, the FDA's deputy commissioner for foods. "We are confident in the overall safety of apple juice consumed in this country because we continue to find that apple juice, on average, contains low amounts of arsenic."

In fact, the FDA's most recent tests done in 2010 and 2011 show on average about three parts of arsenic in every one billion parts of apple juice. That is lower than the 10 parts per billion (ppb) set by the EPA as the maximum level allowed in public drinking water.

"Our test results over many years support the overall safety of apple juice," says Taylor, "but we see a small percentage of individual samples tested that contain higher levels of arsenic. We want to minimize the public's exposure to arsenic in foods as much as we can." For that reason, the FDA plans to consider all the relevant evidence, and based on this work, it may set a guidance or other maximum level to further reduce arsenic in apple juice and juice products.

To further protect the public's health, the FDA is also taking the following actions:

- Enhancing its surveillance of arsenic in apple juice and juice concentrate. The agency will shortly have results for an additional 90 samples of apple juice and juice concentrate and soon after will sample additional types of juice and juice concentrates.

- Continuing to test samples of apple juice imported into the United States from China. The most recent results included more than 70 samples from China, and 95% of these contained less than the 10 ppb level used for drinking water.

- Working with the EPA to coordinate the review of the risk assessment being prepared and discussing other steps the two agencies can take to reduce the overall levels of arsenic in the environment and in foods.

The bottom line is that the FDA is working hard to ensure the safety of the foods people consume and to do so based on the best science. And the best thing families can do is to consume a variety of foods and beverages and follow a well-balanced diet consistent with the Dietary Guidelines for Americans.

1. What is *arsenic*?
   a. It is a preservative added to apple juice and other fruit juices to increase their shelf life.
   b. It is a naturally occurring element that can be hazardous to your health if you consume too much of it.
   c. It is a vitamin found in apple juice and other fruit juices that can be hazardous to your health if you consume too much of it.
   d. It is an artificial sweetener used in beverages to reduce calorie levels.

2. In the following sentence, what does *10 ppb* mean? *The most recent results included more than 70 samples from China, and 95% of these contained less than the 10 ppb level used for drinking water.*
   a. 10 percent per beverage
   b. 10 parts of pesticides in beverages
   c. 10 parts per billion
   d. none of the above

Use the following passage to answer questions 3 and 4.

EXCERPTED FROM *ARMY LETTERS FROM AN OFFICER'S WIFE, 1871–1888,* BY FRANCES M.A. ROE

Fort Lyon, Colorado Territory, October 1871.

After months of anticipation and days of weary travel we have at last got to our army home! As you know, Fort Lyon is fifty miles from Kit Carson, and we came all that distance in a funny looking stage coach called a "jerkey," and a good name for it, too, for at times it seesawed back and forth and then sideways, in an awful breakneck way. The day was glorious, and the atmosphere so clear, we could see miles and miles in every direction. But there was not one object to be seen on the vast rolling plains—not a tree or a house, except the wretched ranch and stockade where we got fresh horses and a perfectly uneatable dinner.

It was dark when we reached the post, so of course we could see nothing that night. General and Mrs. Phillips gave us a most cordial welcome—just as though they had known us always. Dinner was served soon after we arrived, and the cheerful dining room, and the table with its dainty china and bright silver, was such a surprise—so much nicer than anything we had expected to find here, and all so different from the terrible places we had seen since reaching the plains. General Phillips is not a real general—only so by brevet, for gallant service during the war. I was so disappointed when I was told this, but Faye says that he is very much afraid that I will have cause, sooner or later, to think that the grade of captain is quite high enough. He thinks this way because, having graduated at West Point this year, he is only a second lieutenant just now, and General Phillips is his captain and company commander.

It seems that in the Army, lieutenants are called "Mister" always, but all other officers must be addressed by their rank. At least that is what they tell me. But in Faye's company, the captain is called general, and the first lieutenant is called major, and as this is most confusing, I get things mixed sometimes. Most girls would. A soldier in uniform waited upon us at dinner, and that seemed so funny. I wanted to watch him all the time, which distracted me, I suppose, for once I called General Phillips "Mister"! It so happened, too, that just that instant there was not a sound in the room, so everyone heard the blunder. General Phillips straightened back in his chair, and his little son gave a smothered giggle—for which he should have been sent to bed at once. But that was not all! That soldier, who had been so dignified and stiff, put his hand over his mouth and fairly rushed from the room so he could laugh outright. And how I longed to run some place, too—but not to laugh, oh, no!

These soldiers are not nearly as nice as one would suppose them to be, when one sees them dressed up in their blue uniforms with bright brass buttons. And they can make mistakes, too, for yesterday, when I asked that same man a question, he answered, "Yes, Sorr!" Then I smiled, of course, but he did not seem to have enough sense to see why. When I told Faye about it, he looked vexed and said I must never laugh at an enlisted man—that it was not dignified in the wife of an officer to do so. And then I told him that an officer should teach an enlisted man not to snicker at his wife, and not to call her "Sorr," which was disrespectful. I wanted to say more, but Faye suddenly left the room.

(continues)

Yesterday morning, directly after guard-mounting, Faye put on his full-dress uniform—epaulets, beautiful scarlet sash, and sword—and went over to the office of the commanding officer to report officially. The officer in command of the post is lieutenant colonel of the regiment, but he, also, is a general by brevet, and one can see by his very walk that he expects this to be remembered always. So it is apparent to me that the safest thing to do is to call everyone general—there seem to be so many here. If I make a mistake, it will be on the right side, at least.

3. Who is Faye?
  a. the person to whom Frances Roe is writing
  b. the general's wife
  c. Francis Roe's husband
  d. a soldier whom Frances Roe gets to know at Fort Lyon

4. In general, what seems to be Frances's attitude toward army protocol?
  a. disinterested and bored
  b. interested but furious
  c. devoted and serious
  d. curious but questioning

Use the following passage to answer questions 5 and 6.

EXCERPTED FROM THE TRUE SHORT STORY "TO BUILD A FIRE" (1908), BY JACK LONDON

Day had broken cold and grey, exceedingly cold and grey, when the man turned aside from the main Yukon trail and climbed the high earth bank, where a dim and little traveled trail led eastward through the fat spruce timberland. It was a steep bank, and he paused for breath at the top, excusing the act to himself by looking at his watch. It was nine o'clock. There was no sun nor hint of sun, though there was not a cloud in the sky. It was a clear day, and yet there seemed an intangible pall over the face of things, a subtle gloom that made the day dark, and that was due to the absence of sun. This fact did not worry the man. He was used to the lack of sun. It had been days since he had seen the sun, and he knew that a few more days must pass before that cheerful orb, due south, would just peep above the sky line and dip immediately from view.

The man flung a look back along the way he had come. The Yukon lay a mile wide and hidden under three feet of ice. On top of this ice were as many feet of snow. It was all pure white, rolling in gentle undulations where the ice jams of the freeze-up had formed. North and south, as far as his eye could see, it was unbroken white, save for a dark hair-line that curved and twisted from around the spruce-covered island to the south, and that curved and twisted away into the north, where it disappeared behind another spruce-covered island. This dark hair-line was the trail—the main trail—that led south five hundred miles to the Chilcoot Pass, Dyea, and salt water; and that led north seventy miles to Dawson, and still on to the north a thousand miles to Nulato, and finally to St. Michael on Bering Sea, a thousand miles and half a thousand more.

(continues)

But all this—the mysterious, far-reaching hair-line trail, the absence of sun from the sky, the tremendous cold, and the strangeness and weirdness of it all—made no impression on the man. It was not because he was long used to it. He was a newcomer in the land, a *chechaquo*, and this was his first winter.

The trouble with him was that he was without imagination. He was quick and alert in the things of life, but only in the things, and not in the significances. Fifty degrees below zero meant eighty-odd degrees of frost. Such fact impressed him as being cold and uncomfortable, and that was all. It did not lead him to meditate upon his frailty as a creature of temperature, and upon man's frailty in general, able only to live within certain narrow limits of heat and cold; and from there on it did not lead him to the conjectural field of immortality and man's place in the universe. Fifty degrees below zero stood for a bite of frost that hurt and that must be guarded against by the use of mittens, ear flaps, warm moccasins, and thick socks. Fifty degrees below zero was to him just precisely fifty degrees below zero. That there should be anything more to it than that was a thought that never entered his head.

5. Which of the following best expresses the theme of the passage?
   a. A person must have rigorous training to face the harsh elements of nature.
   b. It is extremely foolish to travel alone in unknown terrain.
   c. A person must learn to see beyond the facts to understand the meaning of life.
   d. With hard work and perseverance, a person can triumph over any adversity.

6. Which words describe the man as he appears in the passage?
   a. innocent, heroic
   b. knowledgeable, matter-of-fact
   c. rebellious, observant
   d. religious, young

Use the following passage to answer questions 7–9.

Imani P. Jones
421 Carroll Street
Franklin, NY 10821
(512) 555-4390

May 22, 2014

Shanice Childress-Harris
Owner
Luxalot Florists, Inc.
80 River Street
Franklin, NY 10821

Dear Ms. Childress-Harris:

I am writing to register a complaint about the floral displays that were prepared and delivered by Luxalot Florists for my son DeAndre Jones's wedding on May 18. After consulting with your assistant, Maurice Thomas, on February 13 and again on March 1, we thought that our desires were understood and that Maurice and the rest of the team had a clear plan for the wedding's floral designs.

We asked for Luxalot to deliver two standing bouquets for the entrance to the chapel, one larger standing bouquet for the altar, and 18 centerpieces for the tables at the reception. Maurice asked us what colors we preferred, and we told him that the wedding's color scheme was white, yellow, and fuchsia. He suggested that a beautiful combination in these colors would be First Snow tulips, Sunray roses, and Hot Pink ranunculus. He also wanted to add a few stems of filler flowers, such as baby's breath and Queen Anne's lace, which I thought was a good idea to reduce the overall cost.

I was shocked to see a completely different combination of flowers than the one we had discussed on the day of the wedding. The bouquets consisted primarily of baby's breath and Queen Anne's lace, and the other flowers were carnations, lilies, and irises. At the reception, we saw that the centerpieces had the same combination and also learned that only 14 centerpieces had been sent, so four tables were not adorned with flowers.

I am writing to you to request a refund of half ($2,700) of the amount I paid for the flower displays ($5,400). I would ask for a full refund, but the flowers that did arrive were very fresh and in the correct color scheme.

I await your prompt response to this matter.
Sincerely,

Imani P. Jones

7. In the first sentence of the letter, the word *register* means
   a. a machine that calculates and holds money at a store.
   b. registrar.
   c. formally submit.
   d. withdraw.

8. Based on the information in the second paragraph of the letter, we can infer that the definition of *fuchsia* is
   a. the color white.
   b. bright pink.
   c. a type of flower.
   d. none of the above.

9. Based on the letter, which is NOT a reason why the writer wants a refund?
   a. The flower displays contained too many inexpensive flowers.
   b. The flower displays contained the incorrect types of flowers.
   c. Luxalot did not send the correct number of flower displays.
   d. The flower displays were in the wrong colors.

Use the following passage to answer questions 10–13.

IS YOUR DROWSINESS DANGEROUS?

Despite common misconceptions, anyone—regardless of gender, weight, or fitness level—can develop obstructive sleep apnea, a life-threatening condition characterized by episodes of complete or partial airway obstruction during sleep. As many as 12 million to 18 million American adults have untreated sleep apnea, and the experts at the American Academy of Sleep Medicine are recommending the following steps for diagnosis and treatment to significantly improve overall health, mood, and productivity.

First, be aware of the risk factors. Your risk of sleep apnea increases between middle and older age and with the amount of excess body weight you carry. In general, men have a greater likelihood of developing the disease. However, menopause is a risk factor for sleep apnea in women. Your risk is also higher if family members have been diagnosed with sleep apnea. Smoking is another significant risk factor, as well as being a detriment to your overall health.

In addition to these more commonly known risk factors, many people don't realize that they're in greater danger of developing sleep apnea if they already suffer from other common diseases. "Seven in ten type 2 diabetics and 30% to 40% of adults with hypertension also have obstructive sleep apnea," says Dr. M. Safwan Badr, president of the American Academy of Sleep Medicine. "As a result, patients with these conditions should pay close attention for potential symptoms and then seek necessary treatment."

(continues)

It's important to watch for symptoms. While the symptom most commonly associated with sleep apnea is snoring, not everyone who snores has the disease. However, when snoring is paired with choking, gasping, or pauses in breathing during sleep, it's a more likely indicator of sleep apnea. Sleep apnea symptoms also may appear during the daytime and include morning headaches, excessive sleepiness, trouble concentrating, memory or learning problems, and general moodiness, irritability, or depression.

"Sleep apnea can make you wake up in the morning feeling tired, even though you believe you've had a full night of sleep," says Badr. "During the day, you may feel incredibly fatigued because you're actually waking up numerous times throughout the night and your body isn't getting the rest it needs."

If you suspect that you have the risk factors and symptoms of sleep apnea, it's important that you are evaluated by a board-certified sleep-medicine physician right away. Left untreated, sleep apnea may have a serious impact on your overall health, even increasing your risk of death. The sleep-medicine physician will have the training and expertise to diagnose your condition. He or she will conduct a thorough physical examination and sleep evaluation, asking questions like whether symptoms began when you gained weight or stopped exercising, and whether your partner or roommate has complained that you snore or make choking noises in your sleep. If the sleep physician determines that you are at risk for obstructive sleep apnea, then you will be scheduled for a sleep study.

Once diagnosed, the recommended treatment for sleep apnea is continuous positive airway pressure (CPAP) therapy, which provides a steady stream of air through a mask to gently keep the patient's airway open throughout the night, making it easier to breathe. In patients with moderate or severe sleep apnea, it's estimated that CPAP therapy reduces the ten-year risk of heart attack by 49% and stroke by 31%.

"Treating sleep apnea provides all the benefits of improved sleep, including increased alertness during the day and improved memory and cognitive function," says Badr. "Clinical evidence also shows that sleep apnea treatment lowers blood pressure, thus decreasing your risk of cardiovascular disease, and improves nighttime glucose levels and insulin sensitivity among type 2 diabetics."

—Adapted from an article published on Brandpoint.com.

10. According to the passage, what are some of the symptoms of sleep apnea?
   a. heartburn, nausea, and upper abdominal pain when awake
   b. migraines, excessive eating, and chest pain at night
   c. choking, gasping, and pauses while breathing during sleep
   d. type 2 diabetes, menopause, and hypertension

11. Which statement best expresses the main idea of the passage?
   a. Sleep apnea primarily affects people with hypertension and diabetes.
   b. Everyone should be aware of the risk factors and signs of sleep apnea and get tested if there is reason for concern.
   c. As many as 12 million to 18 million American adults are living with sleep apnea but have not been treated.
   d. Sleep apnea is a condition that can be successfully treated with continuous positive airway pressure (CPAP) therapy.

12. How does the author present and develop the key ideas of this passage?
   a. by listing facts and advice related to sleep apnea
   b. by presenting a chronological order of the development of sleep apnea as a person ages
   c. by describing the differences between people who have sleep apnea and those who don't
   d. by giving examples of patients who have been treated successfully for sleep apnea

13. Based on the passage, we can infer that the author has which of the following viewpoints?
   a. To accurately identify and treat sleep apnea, it's better to see a board-certified sleep-medicine doctor than to see another type of doctor.
   b. The medical profession overdiagnoses sleep apnea, causing increased anxiety and irritability in patients.
   c. It's a shame that sleep apnea is so difficult to diagnose, leaving many Americans untreated.
   d. Screening for sleep apnea must be part of a person's annual checkup with one's primary-care physician.

Answers and Explanations

Chapter Practice

1. **b.** The main idea of the article is that many lightning-related tragedies can be avoided through simple precautions. This choice is a fact about lightning that does not directly relate to the idea of precautions.

2. **c.** This sentence best summarizes the main idea of the article. The article goes on to explain why people were struck in the past and the precautions that people can take to prevent the same tragedies from happening in the future.

3. **a.** One of the ideas presented in the article is that it is better if people's exposure to arsenic over their lifetime is as small as possible. Although it's usually present in very small amounts, arsenic is commonly found in apple juice. You can reduce your risk altogether simply by not overloading on apple juice—or any one food or beverage, for that matter.

4. **c.** This is a general statement that can be inferred from the article. The government wants to reduce the American public's exposure to arsenic, and monitoring and lowering arsenic levels in a popular drink is one way to accomplish this.

5. **b.** The main idea of the article is that employers are increasingly using social media, so using social media and other tech tools can improve your chances of finding a job. In the third paragraph, the author states, *With technology playing an established role in our lives and social networks easily accessible to potential employers, establishing a strong digital footprint and personal brand is crucial to success.* The writer then goes on to suggest tips for improving the way readers use e-mail and other Internet communications.

6. **c.** The underlying premise of the article is that having strong computer-literacy skills is important during job searches. More specifically, the author advises readers, *Make sure that your online presence is up to date and also reflects your best attributes.*

7. In this passage, the writer compares being a parent to being a **gardener**. Throughout the passage, the writer lists the many ways that he or she thinks being a parent is similar to being a gardener.

8. **c.** The last sentence of the passage points out one difference between being a parent and being a gardener: after parents raise their children, the children still maintain an important role in the family, but after gardeners raise plants, the plants die or go dormant in the garden.

9. **a.** The author states, *The blooms, for all their size and thickness, are as delicate as orchids in that they reject the touch of human hands.*

10. **d.** According to the author, on magnolia trees, *there is a dry pattering to earth of the hard leaves and for a brief time the tree is parched and drawn, the rosy-lichened trunk gray and anxious. Then pale green spires cover the boughs, unfolding into freshly lacquered leaves, and at their tips the blooms appear. When, in late April or early May, the pale buds unfold into great white waxy blossoms, . . . the perfume is a delirious thing on the spring air.*

11. **c.** Madeline recognizes the family instinct to own a farm, but she calls it "fatal" and mentions other family members' bad experiences.

12. d. There are several lines in the passage that support this choice. The narrator says that she was *fitted by temperament . . . for farm and country living* and that her experiences on farms as a child *got in the blood.* Her father's sister made a similar observation: *You have in you that fatal drop of Pearce blood, clamoring for change and adventure, and above all, for a farm.* The narrator adds that *I see no reason for denying so fundamental an urge, ruin or no. It is more important to live the life one wishes to live, and to go down with it if necessary, quite contentedly, than to live more profitably but less happily.*

13. b. The second paragraph starts off with a reference to the Florida orange grove that the narrator purchases. She doesn't mention it by name at first, but she does in the last sentence. You can also assume that *the Creek* is short for *Cross Creek,* which is the name of the book.

14. b. In the sentence before this line, the author says that she was troubled by the hard work at the Creek and the difficulty of making a living on the grove. Relief came when someone named Martha *drew aside a curtain* and welcomed her into the group of people who had a history with the farm. This implies that by pulling back the curtain, Martha was clearing up some of the writer's confusion or angst by sharing information about the grove in the past.

Reading Comprehension Review

1. b. The first paragraph states that *arsenic is present in the environment as a naturally occurring substance.* We can infer that it is hazardous—or hurtful—to people's health because it is referred to as a *contaminant.* Another important reason is because officials are trying to keep apple juice safe by making sure that arsenic levels are very low; that implies that arsenic at higher levels makes food unsafe.

2. c. The term *parts per billion (ppb)* is mentioned in the third paragraph in the same context—discussing the amount of arsenic found in drinks.

3. c. There are several clues throughout the letter that Faye is Frances's husband, but the biggest one appears in the fourth paragraph: *When I told Faye about it, he looked vexed and said I must never laugh at an enlisted man—that it was not dignified in the wife of an officer to do so. And then I told him that an officer should teach an enlisted man not to snicker at his wife, and not to call her "Sorr," which was disrespectful. I wanted to say more, but Faye suddenly left the room.* We can infer that this was a private disagreement between a husband and a wife. Faye thought that Frances had not acted like a dignified wife, but Frances said that Faye should have stood up for her: *I told him that an officer should teach an enlisted man not to snicker at his wife, and not to call her "Sorr," which was disrespectful.* Faye may have taken this comment personally, because he suddenly left the room.

4. d. She seems interested in the ins and outs of army protocol—she describes details and tries to figure out the rules of rank—but she also questions why things are as they are.

5. c. The writer hints at this point when he notes that *all this—the mysterious, far-reaching hairline trail, the absence of sun from the sky, the tremendous cold, and the strangeness and weirdness of it all—made no impression on the man.* The ideas presented in the last paragraph also support this theme.

6. b. Although the writer criticizes the man for not thinking deeply about his circumstances and about life in general, the man does seem knowledgeable. He knows about the path of the sun, he knows the exact temperature, and it's suggested that he knows the exact path of the trail he is on. *Matter-of-fact* is also a good description for the man. There are many reasons to think that the man focuses on the world around him in a straightforward way. For example, the writer notes that *He was quick and alert in the things of life, but only in the things, and not in the significances.* The last three sentences of the passage offer further evidence that he is matter-of-fact.

7. c. The letter writer is indeed submitting her complaint to the owner of Luxalot and writing it in a formal way. The word *register* has many meanings. One of them is a machine that calculates and holds money at a store (*cash register*), but that doesn't make sense in this sentence. We are looking for a different meaning of the word *register*. Also note that in the sentence, *register* is used as a verb, whereas a machine that calculates and holds money at a store is a noun. *Registrar* means an official record keeper (for instance, the person at a school or college who keeps records and helps to sign up students for classes). Finally, the letter writer is presenting her complaint to the owner of Luxalot and wants the owner to take action. She is not withdrawing, or removing, her complaint.

8. b. The word is used in the statement that *the wedding's color scheme was white, yellow, and fuchsia.* Then, in the next sentence, the writer mentions the types of flowers that would fit that combination of colors: *First Snow tulips, Sunray roses, and Hot Pink ranunculus.* We can deduce that First Snow tulips are white flowers (because snow is white), that Sunray roses are yellow flowers (because the sun is yellow), and that Hot Pink ranunculus are fuchsia-colored flowers. *Fuchsia* probably means hot—or bright—pink.

9. d. This is not a reason why the writer is dissatisfied. At the end of the letter, she explains, *I would ask for a full refund, but the flowers that did arrive were . . . in the correct color scheme.* Choice **a** is a reason why the writer is dissatisfied. She mentions that the original plan was to use *a few stems of filler flowers, such as baby's breath and Queen Anne's lace, which I thought was a good idea to reduce the overall cost.* We can assume that baby's breath and Queen Anne's lace are inexpensive flowers because Mrs. Jones calls them *filler flowers* and because if they are used, the cost goes down. Then, on the day of the wedding, *The bouquets consisted primarily of baby's breath and Queen Anne's lace—not a few stems,* as had been discussed. This all adds up to mean that the displays contained too many inexpensive flowers. Choice **b** is an incorrect choice because the writer says that the plan was to use mainly tulips, roses, and ranunculus. Instead, the company delivered mainly *baby's breath and Queen Anne's lace, and the other flowers were carnations, lilies, and irises.* Choice **c** is an incorrect choice because she says that she ordered 18 centerpieces, but only 14 were delivered.

10. c. All three of these symptoms are listed in the article as possible signs that a person suffers from sleep apnea. Migraines are a type of headache, and the article does mention that headaches could be a symptom, but it specifies *morning* headaches. Also, the article does not mention excessive eating or chest pains as signs of sleep apnea. (Sleep apnea may cause heart attacks—which can cause a person to feel chest pain—but that does not mean that chest pain is a sign of sleep apnea.) Choice **d** is incorrect because each of these is mentioned as a *risk factor* for developing sleep apnea—people who have type 2 diabetes or hypertension or who are going through menopause may be more likely to develop sleep apnea, but this doesn't mean that these conditions are *symptoms* of having sleep apnea. (If you don't quite understand this point, consider this everyday example: Standing outside in the freezing rain would be a *risk factor* for getting a cold. The *symptoms* of having indeed come down with a cold would be coughing, sneezing, and a runny nose.)

11. b. The writer starts off by saying that *anyone—regardless of gender, weight, or fitness level—can develop obstructive sleep apnea*, which suggests that everyone should be knowledgeable about the condition. At different points in the article, the author also states: *First, be aware of the risk factors*; *It's important to watch for symptoms*; and *If you suspect that you have the risk factors and symptoms of sleep apnea, it's important that you are evaluated by a board-certified sleep-medicine physician right away*. Choice **a** is incorrect because although, according to the article, a large portion of people who have hypertension and type 2 also have sleep apnea, that does not mean that sleep apnea primarily affects people with those conditions. In fact, the first paragraph of the article stresses that *anyone* can develop sleep apnea. Choices **c** and **d** are not main ideas of the passage.

12. a. The author presents facts about the symptoms, diagnosis, and treatment of sleep apnea, and advises readers to pay attention to risk factors and symptoms and to get tested if they think they may have sleep apnea. *Chronological* means ordered by time from start to finish, as in a time line. The author does not discuss the development of sleep apnea over time. The author also does not discuss specific people who have sleep apnea.

13. a. This choice is supported by these sentences in the article: *If you suspect that you have the risk factors and symptoms of sleep apnea, it's important that you are evaluated by a board-certified sleep-medicine physician right away. . . . The sleep-medicine physician will have the training and expertise to diagnose your condition. He or she will conduct a thorough physical examination . . .* The author emphasizes the skill of board-certified sleep-medicine doctors when it comes to sleep apnea, never mentions other types of doctors (here or elsewhere in the article), and encourages readers to visit a board-certified sleep-medicine doctor if they think they may have sleep apnea. All of this suggests that when it comes to sleep apnea, the author probably thinks that it is better to see a board-certified sleep-medicine doctor than to see another type of doctor. Choice **b** is incorrect because overdiagnosis is not mentioned or implied in the article. Instead, the author discusses sleep-medicine doctors' ability to diagnose sleep apnea accurately. Choice **c** is incorrect because the author does not say or imply that sleep apnea is difficult to diagnose. Instead, one of the big messages of the article is that many people with sleep apnea are going untreated simply because they've never asked to be screened in the first place. The author does not imply choice **d** in the article.

7 ▶ LANGUAGE AND GRAMMAR

Many of the questions on the GED® RLA exam are designed to test your knowledge of grammar, word usage, and language mechanics. Make sure you are prepared by carefully reviewing this chapter and answering the practice questions. Answers and explanations for all practice questions are at the end of the chapter.

Frequently Confused Words and Homonyms

Quick—what's the difference between *it's* and *its*? *Know* and *no*? *To* and *too*?

Like many words in the English language, these words often confuse people because they sound the same but have very different meanings. Other frequently confused words have the same *spelling* but different meanings. All of these are called **homonyms**.

To help avoid confusion on the GED® test—and in everyday life—familiarize yourself with the following homonyms and other words (such as *affect* and *effect*) that people often mix up.

Words to Remember

affect/effect

Here are the two definitions of *affect* and *effect* that people often confuse:

> to *affect* (verb): to influence
>> Eric's childhood in rural Arkansas *affected* how he viewed the world.
>
> *effect* (noun): the result of influence
>> Eric's childhood in rural Arkansas had an *effect* on how he viewed the world.

Both words also have other meanings, which you should try not to confuse:

> to *effect* (verb): to cause something to happen, accomplish
>> Over time, the union's efforts effected change at the factory.
>
> to *affect* (verb): to pretend or make a display of
>> The designer sometimes *affected* a British accent when he went to parties, which was ridiculous because he had been born and raised in New Jersey.
>
> *affect* (noun): a feeling or emotion, or the way that a feeling or emotion is expressed physically
>> He had a calm, cool *affect*, which was disturbing because his son had just gone missing.

its/it's

> *its*: belonging to a certain animal or thing
>> The dog wants *its* bone.
>
> *it's*: the contraction of *it is*
>> *It's* too hot to go outside.

lie/lay

> *lie*: to make an untrue statement (verb); an untrue statement (noun)

> Never *lie* on a job application, because if they detect *the lie*, you probably won't get hired.
>
> *lie, lay*: the present and past tenses of the verb *to lie*, meaning to recline or rest in a horizontal position
>> Every Sunday afternoon, I *lie* on the couch and watch movies.
>> Last Sunday afternoon, I *lay* on the couch and watched movies.
>
> *lay, laid*: the present and past tenses of the verb *to lay*, meaning to put something down
>> You can *lay* the baby down in Sarah's old crib.
>> He *laid* the baby down in Sarah's old crib.

know/no; knew/new

> *know*: to be well informed, to recognize
>> I *know* a lot about growing tomatoes.
>
> *no*: zero, none
>> I have *no* idea how to grow tomatoes.
>
> *knew*: past tense of the verb *to know*
>> I *knew* how to grow tomatoes when I was younger.
>
> *new*: appearing or made for the first time
>> I will need to buy *new* tomatoes.

through/threw

> *through*: a preposition meaning into one side and out the other
>> Don't worry—I know you will make it *through* this difficult period.
>
> *threw*: past tense of the verb *to throw*
>> He *threw* out his house keys by mistake!

then/than

then: after something has happened, next
> First I will do my laundry, and *then* I will wash the kitchen floor.

than: a word used when comparing two things
> I would rather go to Florida this winter *than* stay in Wisconsin.

Practice

Select the word that best fits each sentence.

1. Jill, go rest while I _____ out the silver and get the table ready for the party.
a. lie
b. lay

2. Mira _____ the congregation in song at the memorial service yesterday.
a. lead
b. led

3. I plan to pick up my paycheck this afternoon and _____ cash it at the bank on the corner.
a. than
b. then

4. It's a shame that Tim and Jean and _____ children won't be at the reunion on Saturday.
a. their
b. there

Verbs

Verbs are the heart of a sentence. They express the action or state of being of the subject, telling us what the subject is doing, thinking, or feeling. They also tell us when that action or state of being occurs—in the past, present, or future—and they can communicate more complicated ideas, for instance whether something happens often or whether there is a possibility that something will happen in the future.

Infinitive and Simple Present Tense

An **infinitive** is the base form of the verb plus the word *to*, such as *to go*, *to dream*, and *to eat*. The infinitive form can be used in many ways in a sentence.

Here are some examples:

> *Tong promises* to return *by noon*.
> To walk *was the most logical decision*.

One of the most common mistakes in English involves the infinitive. People often say *try and* do something rather than the correct *try to* do something. For example:

Incorrect: Try and *come to work on time tomorrow*.
Correct: Try *to come to work on time tomorrow*.

Incorrect: I'll try and *buy the tickets at the box office rather than online*.
Correct: I'll try *to buy the tickets at the box office rather than online*.

This may be tested on the GED® test, so make sure you know the difference.

Simple present tense is the verb form that communicates facts or indicates that something occurs on a regular basis. For example:

> *The assistants* commute *to work on the subway, but their boss takes a limo*.

I commute *to work every morning on the subway.*

She speaks *English.*

I am from Philadelphia.

Dogs bark, *and cats* meow.

In the Caribbean, the water is *aqua blue.*

Marissa runs *five miles every weekend.*

The simple present tense of regular verbs is formed as follows, using the verb *to drive* as an example:

	SINGULAR	PLURAL
First person (I/we)	Base form (drive)	Base form (drive)
Second person (you)	Base form (drive)	Base form (drive)
Third person (he/she/they)	Base form plus -s or -es (drives)	Base form (drive)

Present Continuous Tense

Present continuous tense is the verb form that describes what is happening now, at this exact moment. It ends in *-ing* and is accompanied by one of the following helping verbs: *am*, *is*, or *are* (the present tense of the verb *to be*). For instance:

Adam is driving *to the fair.*

They are driving *to the picnic.*

Gerunds

Words that end in *-ing* don't always function as verbs. Sometimes they act as nouns and are called **gerunds**. They can also function as adjectives.

Examples:

Tracy enjoys running *on the beach.*

Here, *running* serves as a noun—it is the thing that Tracy enjoys.

The loading *dock is outside the back door.*

Here, *loading* serves as an adjective—it describes the dock.

Here is an example of how the same word can have three different functions:

verb:	*He is* screaming *loudly.*
gerund (noun):	*That* screaming *is driving me crazy.*
adjective:	*The* screaming *boy finally stopped.*

When correcting sentences on the GED® RLA test, do not assume that a word that ends in *-ing* is a verb. You will need to read closely to determine how the word functions in the sentence. Here are a few guidelines for identifying and using gerunds:

1. Gerunds are often used after a preposition.
   Keza thought that by taking *the train she would* save money and time.
   Noriel was afraid of offending *her host, but she couldn't eat dinner.*

2. Gerunds frequently follow these verbs:

admit	dislike	practice
avoid	enjoy	put off
appreciate	escape	quit
can't help	finish	recall
consider	imagine	resist
delay	keep	risk
deny	miss	suggest
discuss	postpone	tolerate

We should discuss buying *a new computer.*

I quit smoking.

Past Tense

Simple past tense is the verb form that expresses what happened at a specific moment in the past.

It rained *for three hours yesterday.*

She opened *the door and* welcomed *the guests.*

Past Continuous Tense

The **past continuous tense** indicates that an action happened in the past and continued for some time. It's used with the helping verb *was* or *were*.

> *She* was walking *when the rain started.*
> *While they* were singing, *the phone rang.*

Past Perfect Tense

Used with the helping verb *had*, the **past perfect tense** indicates that an action happened in the past before another action happened in the past. This may sound confusing, but it's a tense that you probably often use in everyday speech. Look at these examples:

> *Yesterday, Theresa told me that she thought Harry* had played *too much golf during their honeymoon.*

Notice that the sentence places us at one point in time—when Theresa was talking and thinking—and it uses the past perfect to look back at an earlier point in time, when something may have happened during her honeymoon.

> *Jack's vacation was cut short when he broke his ankle in London, but he* had had *the time of his life in Paris.*

In this sentence, we're placed at the time when Jack's vacation was cut short, and we're looking back at the time when he enjoyed himself in Paris.

> *Aisling's parents* had *always* wanted *her to become a doctor, but in college she decided to become an English major.*

The time that Aisling's parents wanted her to become a doctor happened before the time that she decided to become an English major.

Past Perfect and the Conditional

On the GED® test, you may be asked to use the past perfect in another situation: **conditional sentences** set in the past.

You probably use the conditional all the time in everyday life without knowing it. It follows this general pattern: *If this happens, then that happens.* Look at these examples:

> *I will go inside* if *you tell me to.*
> *If* you don't know where those cookies came from, *you shouldn't eat them.*

Now look at these examples of conditional sentences set in the past. They all include the past perfect:

> *I would have brought sunscreen if I had known it was going to be so hot and sunny.*
> *If you had really wanted to keep that job, you would have gotten to work on time.*
> *If someone had called to tell me that the doctor's office was closed, I would have stayed in bed.*

NOTE

Conditional sentences in the past often include the words *would have*.

Regular versus Irregular Verbs

Most English verbs are regular—they follow a standard set of rules for forming the simple past tense. Usually, add *-ed*.

> *He interrupted me when I was typing.*

If the verb ends with the letter *e*, just add *-d*.

> *The prisoners* escaped.

If the verb ends with the letter *y*, change the *y* to an *i* and add -*ed*.

> *I carried the water pitcher to the table.*

Irregular Verbs

About 150 English verbs are irregular—they don't follow the standard rules for changing tense.

Many irregular verbs form the past tense by changing the vowel to *a*. For example:

Present	Simple Past
begin	began
sing	sang
spring	sprang
come	came
overcome	overcame
run	ran

Other irregular verbs are more "irregular," such as these below:

Present	Simple Past
bite	bit
bring	brought
dig	dug
hear	heard
leave	left
plead	pled
send	sent

In English, as in many other languages, the essential verb, *to be*, is highly irregular:

Subject	Present	Simple Past
I	am	was
you	are	were
he, she, it	is	was
we	are	were
they	are	were

Using a Consistent Tense

A common writing mistake is to jump between verb tenses when it is not necessary or correct to do so. You may be asked to spot this mistake on the GED® RLA test.

If a writer indicates that a certain action takes place at a certain time, he or she should be consistent in the use of verb tense when writing about that action elsewhere in the sentence (or paragraph or story). Review the following examples:

> **Incorrect:** *She* left *the house and* forgets *her keys in the kitchen.*
> **Correct:** *She* left *the house and* forgot *her keys in the kitchen.*

> **Incorrect:** *Jon* signed up *to run the marathon, but after talking to his doctor, he* decides *it would be too strenuous.*
> **Correct:** *Jon* signed up *to run the marathon, but after talking to his doctor, he* decided *it would be too strenuous.*

Subject–Verb Agreement

In grammar, agreement means that verbs should agree with their subjects. If the subject is singular, the verb should be singular. If the subject is plural, the verb should be plural. Because we often use incorrect grammar when we speak, identifying correct subject–verb agreement can be challenging.

Read the following examples, which highlight common agreement errors:

> **Incorrect:** The president, *along with his wife and two daughters,* are *going to Hawaii on vacation.*
> **Correct:** The president, *along with his wife and two daughters,* is *going to Hawaii on vacation.*

Although we know that four people are going on vacation—the president, his wife, and their two daughters—the sentence really has only one subject:

the president. The phrase *along with his wife and two daughters* is just a side point; it is set off with commas and is not essential to the grammar of the sentence. Since the real subject, *the president*, is singular, the verb should be singular too: *is*.

> ## NOTE
>
> It's easy to read sentences such as the first example and think that they are correct. That is because a plural word—in this case, *daughters*—is the word that comes right before the verb. The phrase *two daughters are* sounds natural, even though in this sentence it is not correct. Make sure to keep in mind what the real subject of a sentence is, so you know what verb form is necessary.

Incorrect: *The jury* have *left the courtroom to make* their *decision.*

Correct: *The* jury has *left the courtroom to make* its *decision.*

Although *jury* refers to a group of people, the actual word *jury* is a singular noun—it means all of the jury members taken as a whole.

Here are examples of other nouns that may seem plural at first but are usually treated as singular and take a singular verb: *team, family, group, band, committee, tribe, audience,* and *flock.*

Incorrect: *That* boxer don't *have a chance against Carl.*

Correct: *That* boxer doesn't *have a chance against Carl.*

Although the first sentence may sound correct in casual speech, the word *boxer* is singular, so it should be followed by a singular verb form. *Don't* is a plural form.

How to Get Subject–Verb Agreement Right

Your main challenge when deciding if a sentence has correct subject–verb agreement will probably be determining who or what serves as the subject of the sentence.

In most cases, this should be simple and will come naturally to you. But as you saw in the previous examples, sometimes the real subject is not immediately obvious.

Here is another example. Can you identify the subject of the sentence?

Only one of the students was officially registered for class.

In this sentence, the subject is *one*, not *students*. Although it may seem as if the students are performing the action, the true subject of the sentence is the *one* student—whoever that person may be—meaning that the sentence requires the singular verb *was*.

Here's another example:

Vanessa and Erin are going to join the committee.

It's easy to see that there are two subjects in this sentence: *Vanessa* and *Erin*. The verb is correctly plural: *are*.

Now review these similar sentences:

Either Vanessa or Erin is going to join the committee.

Neither Vanessa nor Erin is going to join the committee.

In both cases, even though there are still two names—*Vanessa* and *Erin*—the subject is singular. In the first case, only one of them is going to join the committee (we don't know who, but it will be only one of them). In the second case, neither one will; *neither* also requires a singular verb.

NOTE

If one plural and one singular subject are connected by *or* or *nor*, the verb form must agree with the closer subject. For instance:

> Neither Vanessa nor the teachers want
> to join the committee.
> Neither the teachers nor Vanessa wants
> to join the committee.

Let's go back to our original example:

> Vanessa and Erin are going to join the committee.

There are two nouns at the start of the sentence, and it is clear that there are two subjects: *Vanessa* and *Erin*.

Now take a look at this example:

> Peanut butter and jelly is my favorite type of sandwich.

Although the phrase *peanut butter and jelly* is made up of two nouns, we know that the term *peanut butter and jelly* refers to one thing: a particular type of sandwich filling. In this case, you'd treat the whole phrase as one subject, so you would use a singular verb form (*is*).

Here are other examples of subjects that may look plural at first glance but are really singular:

> Spaghetti and meatballs *was my grandmother's favorite dish.*
> The New York Times *is delivered to my door every morning.*
> The United States *has never won the Olympic gold in that sport.*

Here is one last type of sentence that often causes subject–verb agreement problems: sentences that start with words such as *There's*, *Here's*, and *What's*.

Note that in these sentences, the subject comes *after* the verb. For example:

> There's my dog, playing by the park bench.

The subject of the sentence is *my dog*.

> **Incorrect:** There's *still three empty seats.*
> **Correct:** There are *still three empty seats.*

Don't forget that *There's* is really a shorthand (or contraction) of the phrase *There is*. Since the subject of this sentence—*seats*—is plural, the sentence requires a plural introduction: *There are*.

> **Incorrect:** What's *the side effects of this medication?*
> **Correct:** What are *the side effects of this medication?*

Similarly, *What's* is a contraction of *What is*, which is incorrect here because the subject of this sentence is plural: *side effects*.

Practice

For each sentence, fill in the blank with either *is* or *are*.

5. Red Rocks _____ their favorite concert venue in Colorado.

6. Julio, as well as the rest of the band, _____ excited about performing at Red Rocks.

7. Two members of the band _____ still back at the hotel.

8. Everyone _____ supposed to be onstage right now!

9. Where _____ Julio and the guitar player?

For the following three questions, select the best revision of the underlined part of the sentence.

10. Catherine is gone to the store later today.
   a. go
   b. will go
   c. went
   d. has gone

11. Gerald and Yolanda have visited me yesterday.
   a. visited
   b. are visiting
   c. visits
   d. had visited

12. Neither you nor your cousins appearing in the photograph.
   a. appears
   b. is appearing
   c. appear
   d. to appear

Pronouns

In order to understand the correct use of pronouns, you must first have a clear understanding of what a noun is. **Nouns** are words that identify objects.

> **People:** students, brother, David, neighbor
> **Places:** New York City, ocean, university, Jupiter
> **Things:** books, Saturday, bathing suit, the U.S. Navy
> **Ideas and qualities:** beauty, faith, anger, justice

A **pronoun** is a word that replaces or refers to a noun. Consider the following examples:

> Sheldon *prefers cereal to toast and jam.*

This can be rewritten with a pronoun as:

> He *prefers cereal to toast and jam.*
> *Last Friday,* Josh *drove to* Kathy *and* Tina's *cabin.*

This can be rewritten with pronouns as:

> *Last Friday,* he *drove to their cabin.*
> Jackson *doesn't care about anyone except* Jackson.

This can be rewritten with pronouns as:

> He *doesn't care about anyone except* himself.

There are many pronouns in the English language, depending on what type of noun the pronoun is replacing and how the pronoun functions in a sentence. Here are some examples of pronouns: *I, you, she, he, we, they, it, this, that, myself, ourselves, whoever, whomever, mine, yours.*

Pronouns and Antecedents

When a pronoun is used in a sentence, it should be clear what noun(s) it is substituting for or referring to. That noun is called an **antecedent**. For example:

> Adam *had fun while* he *was on vacation in Puerto Rico.*

The pronoun *he* is another way of saying the word *Adam. Adam* is the antecedent of *he.*

Here is another:

> My grandparents *first met when* they *were in college.*

The plural pronoun *they* stands in for the plural noun *grandparents,* which is the antecedent.

This may seem simple enough, but confusion over pronouns and antecedents can arise in more complicated sentences. You may be asked to spot or correct this type of problem on the GED® RLA test.

Consider this incorrect sentence:

Despite what the president told the reporters, they are not going to authorize military action.

The sentence may sound correct to the ear, but if we give it some thought, do we really know what is meant by the pronoun *they*? (To put it another way: Do we know what the antecedent is of *they*?)

They is a plural pronoun, so it can't refer to *the president*, which is a singular noun. It could refer to *the reporters*, which is a plural noun, but that doesn't make sense logically—reporters are not in charge of the military.

Does *they* mean some other group of people (members of a committee or army generals)? Or should it be changed to *he*, to mean *the president*?

As you can see, when there is no obvious antecedent to a pronoun, the meaning of an entire sentence can be unclear.

Beware of *They*

Another common pronoun problem arises when the writer is discussing a person (singular) but isn't sure what gender to use—*she/her/her* or *he/him/his*—so tries to keep things vague by using a plural pronoun (*they/them/their*) instead. Consider this example:

If a student is late to class three times, they will be reported to the principal.

The pronoun *they* doesn't work here because it's plural but its antecedent is the singular noun *student*. Here is a correct way to rewrite the sentence:

If a student is late to class three times, he or she will be reported to the principal.

Or you could rephrase the sentence this way:

If students are late to class three times, they will be reported to the principal.

Subject Pronouns and Object Pronouns

When editing sentences for correct pronoun use, you will need to determine whether the pronoun is the subject or the object of the sentence. Consider the following sentence:

Jane brought Jack to the dentist.

Jane is the subject of the sentence—the person who is acting out the verb *brought*. *Jack* is the object—the person who is receiving the action of the verb.

If we wanted to swap out the words *Jane* and *Jack* with pronouns, we would need to use a subjective pronoun for *Jane* and an objective pronoun for *Jack*. Note the correct sentence, after a couple of incorrect tries:

Incorrect: She *brought* he *to the dentist.*
Incorrect: Her *brought* him *to the dentist.*
Correct: She *brought* him *to the dentist.*

Here is a list of subject and object pronouns. Make sure you know the difference:

Subject	Object
I	me
you	you
he	him
she	her
it	it
we	us
who	whom
they	them

Who versus Whom

This brings us to one of the most common grammar problems in the English language: using the word *who* (a subjective pronoun) when the word *whom* (an objective pronoun) is called for. This error could appear on the GED® RLA test, so make sure you know how to spot it.

Consider the following examples:

Who *made dinner last night?*

Who is the subject of this sentence. Whoever that mysterious meal-preparing person is, he or she performed the action of the sentence (making dinner).

Whom *should John invite to your party?*

Here, *John* is the subject of the sentence. John is going to perform the action of the sentence (inviting one or more guests). *Whom* is the object of the sentence: it refers to one or more persons who will receive the action of the sentence (John's invitation).

An easy way to test whether you should use *who* or *whom* in a sentence is to swap it for another pronoun that you're more familiar with and check to see if that makes sense.

Let's try out this trick on the following sentence:

[Who/Whom] *is Jake going to marry?*

First, let's try to answer the question with the word *she*. It is a subjective pronoun, so it will test whether the subjective pronoun *who* would work in the sentence.

[Who/Whom] *is Jake going to marry? Jake is going to marry* she.

That is clearly not grammatical. Now let's try an objective pronoun, *her*:

[Who/Whom] *is Jake going to marry? Jake is going to marry* her.

That makes sense, so we know that we need another objective pronoun—*whom*—for the question:

Whom *is Jake going to marry?*

Here is another example:

Incorrect: *Ms. Dee is the teacher* who *I always ask for advice.*
Correct: *Ms. Dee is the teacher* whom *I always ask for advice.*

When deciding whether to use *who* or *whom*, look at the core phrase: *I ask* _____.

I ask her would be grammatical, not *I ask she*. Therefore, in our sentence, we need to use the same type of pronoun as *her* (objective). That means we need to use *whom*.

Incorrect: *Gordon is the man* whom *lives down the street.*
Correct: *Gordon is the man* who *lives down the street.*

To determine *who* versus *whom*, the core phrase is: _____ *lives down the street.*

Let's test it:

Him *lives down the street.*
He *lives down the street.*

The second sentence, with the subjective pronoun *he*, is correct, so we should use *who* in our sentence.

Now take a look at these more advanced examples to prepare for the GED® RLA test.

The same rules for *who* and *whom* apply to *whoever* and *whomever*.

Incorrect: *I'll play chess with* whoever.
Correct: *I'll play chess with* whomever.

The core phrase here is: *I'll play with* _____. The missing word is an object of the preposition *with*, so we need to use the objective pronoun *whomever*.

Let's do that test again, just to be sure. Let's try the sentence with a subjective pronoun, *she*:

I'll play chess with she.

That is clearly not correct. The subjective pronoun *whoever* is therefore not correct. Now let's try the objective pronoun *her*:

I'll play chess with her.

That's a perfect fit, so the objective pronoun *whomever* must be right.

Practice

For each of the following questions, fill in the blank with *who*, *whom*, *whoever*, or *whomever*.

13. _____ are you taking to the dance?

14. _____ is making that noise had better quiet down!

15. That man over there is the customer _____ complained about me to my boss.

16. _____ is taking you to the dance?

Possessive Pronouns

Like possessive nouns (such as *Carla's*, *the house's*, *the three players'*), possessive pronouns show ownership. However, possessive pronouns do *not* use apostrophes.

Incorrect: *The purple and green balloons were their's.*
Correct: *The purple and green balloons were theirs.*

Incorrect: It's *tail was long and furry.*
Correct: Its *tail was long and furry.*

Note that some possessive pronouns function as adjectives and are used to describe a noun. For instance: *my* car (*my* describes the noun *car*), *her* tennis shoes (*her* describes the noun *tennis shoes*), and *your* strawberries (*your* describes the noun *strawberries*).

Other possessive pronouns function as nouns themselves, for instance:

The blue car is mine.
Those tennis shoes are hers.
Yours *are sweeter than* ours.

Make sure you are familiar with the spelling of both types of possessive pronouns:

Possessive (adjective)	Possessive (noun)
my	mine
your	yours
his	his
her	hers
its	its
our	ours
whose	whose
their	theirs

Read the following sentence. Then replace the underlined words with the correct pronouns:

When Lisa and Jim's friend Tony arrived home from Iraq, <u>Lisa and Jim</u> took <u>Tony</u> to <u>Tony's</u> favorite restaurant and told <u>Tony</u> to order whatever <u>Tony</u> liked.

When Lisa and Jim's friend Tony arrived home from Iraq, *they* took *him* to *his* favorite restaurant and told *him* to order whatever *he* liked.

Lisa and Jim translates to *they* because *Lisa and Jim* serves as a subject of the sentence (Lisa and Jim are the people who are performing the main action—taking Tony to dinner).

Tony's is a possessive noun, which translates to the possessive pronoun *his*.

To figure out the rest of the answers—pronouns that replace the word *Tony*—ask yourself whether *Tony* is a subject (performing an action) or an object (receiving an action). If he's the subject, make it *he*. If he's the object, make it *him*.

Pronouns Combined with Other Nouns

Often pronouns are combined with other subjects or objects in a sentence. For instance, in the following sentence, there is one subject (*Ruth*) and two objects (*Peter* and _____):

> *Ruth drove Peter and _____ to the football game.*

Do you know which pronoun should fill in the blank?

> Ruth drove Peter and *me* to the football game.
> Ruth drove Peter and *I* to the football game.

Although the second sentence may sound correct, it is not. (It may sound correct to you because we hear this type of phrasing all the time. Many people use it because they think it sounds more proper or formal, but in reality it is poor grammar.)

The first sentence is right. The word *me* is an objective pronoun, which is what is needed in the grammar of this sentence. *I* is a subjective pronoun, which is incorrect here.

There's an easy trick for finding the correct pronoun in situations such as this (when a pronoun is combined with another noun and you want to know what type of pronoun to use): **Cross out the other phrase**—here, *Peter and*—**and then see what pronoun you need**. Here it would be:

> *Ruth drove* me *to the football game.*

You would never say:

> *Ruth drove* I *to the football game.*

Practice

For each of the following questions, choose the pronoun that fits best.

17. Joe had _____ temperature taken at the doctor's office on Tuesday.
  a. its
  b. his
  c. him
  d. none of the above

18. Someone forgot to lock up _____ shoes and gym bag.
  a. his or her
  b. his or hers
  c. their
  d. there

19. The closet is so dark! I can't tell which coat is _____ and which is _____.
  a. your, my
  b. yours, mine
  c. our, their
  d. our, they're

Dangling and Misplaced Modifiers

A **dangling modifier** is a misplaced word or phrase. If a word or a phrase is placed incorrectly in a sentence, the meaning of the sentence can be misinterpreted.

How to Spot Dangling Modifiers

Incorrect: *Running for the bus, my backpack fell in the street.*

This suggests that the subject of the sentence—*my backpack*—was running for the bus, which we know is not correct!

The phrase *Running for the bus* is a **dangling modifier** because it describes the action of the person speaking, but that person is not mentioned in the sentence.

Here is the sentence written correctly:

Correct: *As I was running for the bus, my backpack fell in the street.*

When editing sentences for dangling modifiers, pay attention to words that end in *-ing* and appear at the beginning of the sentence. This can signal a sentence that has a dangling modifier. For example:

Incorrect: *Searching the entire house, the key was under the table.*

This sentence says that the key searched the entire house, which doesn't make sense.

Correct: *After searching the entire house, he found the key under the table.*

> ### NOTE
> Most dangling modifiers occur at the beginnings of sentences, but they can appear at the ends of sentences, too.

How to Spot Misplaced Modifiers

Now let's look at a similar type of error: **misplaced modifiers**. These are phrases or clauses that appear in the wrong spot in a sentence, so it seems as if they describe one thing when they really are intended to describe something else.

For example:

Incorrect: *Ten minutes later, a sad-looking man in a dirty suit with yellow teeth entered the room.*

Correct: *Ten minutes later, a sad-looking man who wore a dirty suit and had yellow teeth entered the room.*

The suit didn't have yellow teeth—the man did.

Incorrect: *She gave homemade treats to the kids wrapped in tinfoil.*

Correct: *She gave the kids homemade treats wrapped in tinfoil.*

The kids weren't wrapped in tinfoil—the treats were.

Only, Just, Barely, and Nearly

The words *only*, *barely*, *just*, and *almost* should appear right before the noun or verb being modified. Their placement determines the message of the sentence.

Only Peter ran to the store. (No one else but Peter went.)

Peter only ran to the store. (He didn't walk.)

Peter ran only to the store. (He didn't go anywhere else.)

Peter ran to the only store. (There was no other
store around but that one.)

Peter ran to the store only. (He ran to the store
and did nothing else.)

Practice

For each of the following sentences, select the best
revision.

20. Moving to Nevada, Shira's truck broke down.
   a. While Shira was moving to Nevada, her
   truck broke down.
   b. Shira's truck, moving to Nevada, broke
   down.
   c. Shira's truck broke down while moving to
   Nevada.
   d. The sentence is correct as is.

21. Exhausted after a long day at the office, Tom
only used the treadmill for ten minutes before
heading home from the gym.
   a. After Tom's exhausting day at the office, he
   only used the treadmill for ten minutes
   before heading home from the gym.
   b. Exhausted after a long day at the office, Tom
   headed home from the gym after only using
   the treadmill for ten minutes.
   c. Exhausted after a long day at the office, Tom
   used the treadmill for only ten minutes
   before heading home from the gym.
   d. The sentence is correct as is.

22. Historians have wondered whether General
Thomas Herald was really a woman in disguise
for more than 200 years.
   a. For more than 200 years, historians have
   wondered whether General Thomas Herald
   was really a woman in disguise.
   b. Historians have wondered, Was General
   Thomas Herald really a woman in disguise
   for more than 200 years?
   c. Historians have wondered whether General
   Thomas Herald, in disguise, was really a
   woman for more than 200 years.
   d. The sentence is correct as is.

Sentence Construction

Sentence construction refers to the way sentences are
created: how we join together subjects, verbs, objects,
and other elements to express a complete thought.

Complete Sentences

You can't just string words together to create a sentence. To form a complete sentence, you need to have
three basic elements:

1. A **subject**: This is who or what the sentence is
   about.
2. A **predicate**: This states what the subject is or
   does.
3. The sentence must express a **complete thought**.

Look at this example:

The phone is ringing.

This is a short but complete sentence. Why? It satisfies the three requirements:

1. It has a subject: *the phone.*
2. It has a predicate: *is ringing.* It explains what the subject is doing.
3. It expresses a complete thought. We know what happened and what was involved.

Now look at these examples:

> *Sit down.*
> *Don't run.*
> *Give me a break.*

Are they complete sentences? Yes. These are very short, complete sentences that command, or tell, someone to do something. You can see that each has a predicate, but where is the subject? When it comes to commands, grammar experts think of the subject as being built into the command—the subject is the person being spoken to. What's important to remember is that commands can stand on their own as real sentences.

If a string of words doesn't have a subject or a predicate, it is a **sentence fragment**. Sentence fragments cannot stand on their own.

Practice

Identify the subject and the predicate of the following sentences.

23. The woman in the lobby is waiting for Mr. Williams.
Subject: _____
Predicate: _____

24. Mr. Williams went downstairs.
Subject: _____
Predicate: _____

Independent and Dependent Clauses

One of the building blocks of writing is the **clause**: a string of words that includes a subject and a predicate. Some clauses express a complete thought and can stand on their own as sentences. These are called **independent clauses**.

Other clauses, however, express an incomplete thought and cannot stand on their own. These are called **dependent clauses**. They need to be attached to an independent clause in order to fully make sense.

Here are some examples of both types:

> **Independent clause:** *It started snowing.*
> **Dependent clause:** *After Emily won the contest.*

Notice that the first clause expresses a complete idea (it began to snow) and that it is a grammatically correct sentence on its own.

But the dependent clause is incomplete—it's begging for a resolution. (After Emily won the contest, *what happened?*). As is, this clause is not a sentence; it's a sentence fragment. To create a grammatically correct sentence in this case, you can do two things:

- Simply remove the word *after*:
  Emily won the contest.
- Attach the dependent clause to an independent clause using a comma:

After Emily won the contest,	*she jumped up and down in excitement.*
dependent clause	independent clause

Here's another example:

> **Dependent clause:** *That you should avoid eating in order to lose weight.*

As is, it's not a real sentence. To create a real sentence in this case, you can:

- Remove the word *that*:
  You should avoid eating in order to lose weight.
- Attach the dependent clause to an independent clause; for instance:

Potato chips and cookies are two foods	*that you should avoid eating in order to lose weight.*
independent clause	dependent clause

Coordinating Conjunctions

You probably use **coordinating conjunctions** all the time without realizing that they have a name; they are words that are used to connect independent clauses together to create one longer sentence. There are seven coordinating conjunctions: *for, and, nor, but, or, yet,* and *so.* You can use the acronym FANBOYS to remember them.

Here's an example of how they're used:

Independent clause: *It's going to rain this afternoon.*
Independent clause: *I still want to go to the game.*

We can use the coordinating conjunction *but* (plus a comma) to join them together:

It's going to rain this afternoon, but *I still want to go to the game.*

Subordinating Conjunctions

Another way to connect clauses is to use a **subordinating conjunction**—words such as *after, because,* and *unless.*

As an example, let's join together these two independent clauses:

Independent clause: *No one takes out the garbage.*
Independent clause: *It smells horrible in the garage.*

Depending on which conjunction we choose, we'll communicate additional information about the situation in the garage. For example:

It smells horrible in the garage because *no one takes out the garbage.*

By using *because,* we're making the point that the odor is caused by the fact that no one takes out the garbage. If we choose a different conjunction, we'll describe a different scenario and make a different point. For instance:

Even though *it smells horrible in the garage, no one takes out the garbage.*

Here's another example of two independent clauses and ways to connect them:

Independent clause: *Jonathan quit.*
Independent clause: *I had to work overtime.*
I had to work overtime after *Jonathan quit.*
Because *Jonathan quit, I had to work overtime.*

You may have noticed that when you add a subordinating conjunction to an independent clause, you create a **dependent clause.** For example, in the example just given, *Jonathan quit* is an independent clause. Even though it's just two words, it can function as a real sentence all by itself. But if you add a subordinating conjunction, it no longer can stand on its own as a real sentence. For example, *Because Jonathan quit* is not a complete thought. It prompts the reader to ask, *Because what?*

Here's a list of common subordinating conjunctions:

SUBORDINATING CONJUNCTION	USE	EXAMPLE
because since so that in order that	to show cause and effect or purpose	• We are attending class *because* we want to pass our GED® test. • *Since* I no longer work at Cost Club, I can't receive an employee discount. • I lived next to Beekman Junior College *so that* I could walk to school every day.
before after while when whenever until once as soon as as long as	to show time or time sequence	• *Before* I lived in Mason City, I lived in Des Moines. • I break out in hives *whenever* I eat strawberries. • I can handle the stress at work *as long as* I exercise daily.
though although even though whereas	to show contrast	• Peter passed the test *even though* he was very nervous. • Wendy loves to read books for school, *although* she gets distracted easily. • Jake was horrible at keeping a budget, *whereas* Bob always had his money in order.
if unless whether	to show a condition	• *If* you study hard and come to class, you will succeed. • You cannot take the exam *unless* you have proper identification.
as though as if as much as	to show similarity	• She looked *as though* she had seen a ghost. • *As much as* I want to visit my daughter, I don't think I'll be able to until next year.
where wherever	to show place	• The children want to know *where* their parents used to live.

Practice

Read the two clauses, and then choose which sentence does NOT combine them correctly.

25. **Independent clause:** *I moved to Paris.*
    Independent clause: *I learned how to speak French.*
    a. I moved to Paris, so I learned how to speak French.
    b. After I moved to Paris, I learned how to speak French.
    c. I learned how to speak French after I moved to Paris.
    d. I moved to Paris, wherever I learned how to speak French.

Run-On Sentences

A **run-on sentence** occurs when one independent clause runs right into another independent clause without proper punctuation. Sometimes no punctuation is used at all, while other times there is just a comma between the two thoughts.

Here are some examples of run-on sentences:

Terri wants to leave now, she's tired.
Whether or not you believe me it's true I did not lie to you.

There are several ways to correct this type of error. You can:

■ Add a *period*, a *question mark*, or an *exclamation point* to create separate sentences.

- Add a *conjunction* (and a comma, if needed) to join the clauses together.
- Add a *semicolon*, *colon*, or *dash* to join the clauses together.
- *Rewrite* one or more of the clauses.

Here are a few ways to correct the earlier examples:

> *Terri wants to leave now—she's tired.*
> *Terri wants to leave now because she's tired.*
> *Whether or not you believe me, it's true. I did not lie to you!*
> *Whether or not you believe me, it's true; I did not lie to you.*
> *Whether or not you believe me, it's true—I did not lie to you.*

Practice

Select the revision that is NOT a good way to correct the run-on sentence.

26. Greenville is in the middle of nowhere, it's a really boring place to grow up.
    a. Greenville is in the middle of nowhere. It's a really boring place to grow up.
    b. Greenville is a really boring place to grow up; in the middle of nowhere.
    c. Greenville is a really boring place to grow up because it's in the middle of nowhere.
    d. Greenville is a really boring place to grow up—it's in the middle of nowhere.

Complex Sentences

As you learned before, many sentences contain both a dependent clause and an independent clause (they're joined together by the subordinating conjunction that's built into the dependent clause). This type of sentence is called a **complex sentence**. A complex sentence can begin with either the independent clause or the dependent clause. Comma placement depends on how the sentence is constructed.

> *While you were sleeping / , / the thunderstorm came through the city.*

Dependent clause / comma / independent clause

> *The thunderstorm came through the city / while you were sleeping.*

Independent clause / no comma / dependent clause

> *Because the city received so much snow / , / school will be canceled today.*

Dependent clause / comma / independent clause

> *School will be canceled today / because the city received so much snow.*

Independent clause / no comma / dependent clause

Did you notice a pattern with the commas? When the dependent clause is tacked onto the beginning of the independent clause, a comma is needed between the two clauses. When the dependent clause is tacked onto the end of the independent clause, no comma is needed.

You can use this rule when correcting sentences on the GED® test. Be careful to understand what is being said in the sentence you are correcting, however; sometimes the meaning of the sentence or other grammar rules will affect whether you should use a comma.

Which of the following sentences is NOT correctly punctuated?
a. Even though I ate a huge dinner, I still want to try your macaroni and cheese.
b. I know it will be really delicious because the chef used so much cheese and cream.
c. Please don't finish it, before I get to try a spoonful.
d. If you don't want me to have any, just tell me.

Choice **c** is the correct answer. Here, the sentence starts off with an *independent* clause. There should not be a comma.

Parallel Construction

Before we explain this idea, look at the following example:

> *When Jim was dieting, he would usually eat just brown rice, grilled chicken, salad, and treat himself to nonfat ice cream for dessert.*

Did you notice a problem with this sentence? The problem is that the elements are not all parallel. **Parallelism** is a grammar rule that says that similar elements in a sentence should be written in a similar way.

Here, the similar elements are the four things that Jim WOULD eat when he was dieting. Let's look at them:

1. brown rice
2. grilled chicken
3. salad
4. treat himself to nonfat ice cream for dessert

You may have noticed that the first three items are parallel—they're all nouns—but the fourth item is different—it's a long phrase that starts off with a verb (*treat*).

There's another problem, too. Look at the words that introduce those four items:

> *When Jim was dieting, he would usually eat just . . .*

Each of the items needs to make sense after that introduction. To test this, just plug in each of the items after the introduction.

For example, the first item makes sense:

> *When Jim was dieting, he would usually eat just brown rice.*

The second item is grammatical, too:

> *When Jim was dieting, he would usually eat just grilled chicken.*

The third item is also grammatical:

> *When Jim was dieting, he would usually eat just salad.*

But the fourth item doesn't make sense after the introduction:

> *When Jim was dieting, he would usually eat just treat himself to nonfat ice cream for dessert.*

There are many ways to fix the original sentence, but here is the most obvious way:

> *When Jim was dieting, he would usually eat just brown rice, grilled chicken, salad,* and nonfat ice cream for dessert.

We deleted *treat himself to*. Now all four items are parallel—they're all nouns.

Practice

27. Select the best revision of this sentence:

> After Tina got her GED, she had to decide whether she was going to apply to colleges, look for a better job, or staying in her current job.

  a. After Tina got her GED, she had to decide whether she was going to apply to colleges, looking for a better job, or staying in her current job.

  b. After Tina got her GED, she had to decide whether she was going to apply to colleges, look for a better job, or in her current job.

  c. After Tina got her GED, she had to decide whether she was going to apply to colleges, look for a better job, or stay in her current job.

  d. The sentence is correct as is.

28. Identify the subject of the following sentence:

> They intend to buy the company this year.

  a. company
  b. this year
  c. They
  d. intend

29. Identify the dependent clause in the following sentence:

> If you think it is a good team, go see the Heat.

  a. if you think it is a good team
  b. go see the Heat
  c. a good team
  d. This sentence has no dependent clause.

30. Identify which of the following is a sentence fragment:

  a. I went.
  b. Who wrote this?
  c. Not going to happen today.
  d. Go away.

31. Select the best revision of the following run-on sentence:

> I'm going away on business, could you please watch the house, I'll be gone this weekend and I'd be most grateful.

  a. I'm going away on business this weekend. Could you please watch the house? I'd be most grateful.

  b. I'm going away on business, could you please watch the house? I'll be gone this weekend, and I'd be most grateful.

  c. I'm going away on business. Could you please watch the house. I'll be gone this weekend. I'd be most grateful.

  d. Could you please watch the house this weekend? I'm going away on business, I'd be most grateful.

32. Select the sentence that is NOT correctly punctuated.

  a. Since I started my new job last year, my life has changed dramatically.

  b. As long as I've been working, I've never really enjoyed what I was doing until now.

  c. It's less about the pay than it is about the people—I get along great with my coworkers.

  d. I'm going to try to keep this job, until I'm old and gray.

Capitalization

After you read certain passages on the GED® test, you'll be asked to fix grammar errors contained in some of the sentences. One of the things you may need to correct is capitalization, so it's important that you learn the rules of when to use capital letters and when to use lowercase letters.

You probably already know that the first letter of the first word of every sentence must be capitalized and that the pronoun *I* should always be a capital letter, but there are many other times when you should use uppercase letters, too.

Titles and Names

Titles such as *Ms., Mrs., Miss, Mr.,* and *Dr.* are always capitalized.

Many other words in the English language—nouns such as *mayor, judge, princess,* and *chairperson*—can serve as a title when placed in front of a person's name. When they are used this way, these words should be capitalized. For example:

> *Secretary of State* John Kerry
> *President* Barack Obama
> *Aunt* Jane
> *Uncle* Tim
> *Queen* Elizabeth
> *Prince* Harry
> *Pope* Francis
> *Judge* Judy
> *Ambassador* Jackson
> *General* Jack Kurutz
> *Private* Benjamin

These words do double duty in the English language. As you can see in the list, they can serve as titles when placed in front of a person's name. But they also often serve as plain old nouns. On the GED® test, don't automatically capitalize words like *president, general,* or *king* when you see them. In many cases, they are simply being used as common nouns and should be lowercase. Look at these examples:

> **Used as a title:** *President* Barack Obama
> **Used as a noun:** The *president* of the United States is Barack Obama.
> **Used as a title:** *General* Jack Kurutz
> **Used as a noun:** Jack Kurutz was a heroic *general* in World War II.
> **Used as a noun and as a title:** My favorite *aunt* is *Aunt* Jane.

Proper Nouns

A **proper noun** is a specific person, place, or thing. The names of these people, places, and things should always be capitalized.

Here are some examples of proper nouns and how they should be capitalized:

People	Places	Things/Events/Etc.
Eleanor Roosevelt	United States of America	Philadelphia Eagles
Lady Gaga	China	United Airlines
John F. Kennedy	Los Angeles	Crest
George Bush Sr.	North Fourth Street	Oscar Mayer
Uncle Tim	Central Park	ESPN
Mayor Ed Koch	Union Station	NASA
Queen Elizabeth	Eiffel Tower	Saturn
	Woodside Hospital	Battle of Bunker Hill
		St. Patrick's Day
		Fourth of July
		Car and Driver (the magazine)
		Modern Family (the TV show)
		In the Name of the Father (the movie)
		"Livin' on a Prayer" (the song)

You may have noticed that some of the words in these names—such as *the* and *of*—are *not* capitalized, although we stated earlier that proper nouns should always be capitalized. Why is this?

The rules of capitalization are very detailed—and sometimes the experts differ on what they should be—but in general, in proper names the following words should be lowercase unless they are the first word of the name.

- *the*, *a*, *an* (articles)
- *to*, *from*, *on*, *in*, *of*, *with*, and other prepositions (some experts capitalize prepositions that have four or more letters)
- *and*, *but*, *or*, *yet* (conjunctions)

Remember that when these words start off the proper noun, they are capitalized, not lowercase. For example: *In Touch* (the magazine), *A Beautiful Mind* (the movie), *For Whom the Bell Tolls* (the book).

Geographical Words

As with other proper names, the names of countries, states, cities, regions, and the like—and the words that are based on them—should be capitalized. For example:

> *Asia, Asian*
> *Portugal, Portuguese*
> *France, French, Frenchwoman, Frenchman*
> *Great Britain, British*
> *Middle East, Middle Eastern*
> *the South, Southern* (referring to those states in the United States)
> *Antarctica*
> *Rome, Roman*
> *New York City, New Yorker*
> *Morris County*

Movies, Books, Songs, and So On

The names of books, movies, plays, TV shows, songs, albums, and the like are another type of proper noun and should be capitalized. The same goes for newspaper headlines, the titles of magazine articles, the titles of essays you write, and more. For example:

> *Romeo and Juliet* (play)
> *Back to the Future* (movie)
> *The Big Bang Theory* (TV show)
> *The Wind in the Willows* (book)
> "Mayor Vows: City Will Bounce Back from Hurricane Sandy" (newspaper headline)
> "Why Violence Is Never the Answer" (magazine article)

Events and Time Periods

As with other proper nouns, specific historical periods and events should be capitalized. Centuries should not be capitalized when used as a regular noun in a sentence, though. Look at these examples:

> the Revolutionary War
> the Great Depression
> the Middle Ages
> The twentieth century marked a turning point in technology.

Directions

Directions on the compass (*west*, *south*, *northeast*, etc.) are considered to be common nouns and are not capitalized.

Directions also sometimes serve as proper names of specific places, however. When used in this way, they should be capitalized, as all proper nouns should be.

For example:

> *The Grand Canyon is one of the biggest tourist attractions in the* Southwest.

Here, *Southwest* means a specific region of the United States—the southwest corner of the country that includes Arizona and New Mexico.

> *The school is five miles* southwest *of Santa Fe.*

Here, *southwest* means the compass direction, so it should be lowercase.

Calendar Items

The days of the week, the months of the year, and holidays all need to be capitalized. (Do not capitalize the seasons unless they are used in a proper name, in a title, or in another way that would require a noun to have an uppercase letter.) Examples:

> *Monday*
> *January*
> *Easter*
> *Fourth of July*
> *summer, fall, winter, spring*

Note this example:

> *The club's Tenth Annual* Winter *Showcase will be held in January.*

In this case, *Winter* is capitalized because it is part of a proper name—the name of a specific event—not because it's a season. The name of the event could just as easily be *Tenth Annual* Talent *Showcase*.

Proper Nouns versus Common Nouns

Here is one more important thing to think about with proper nouns: You'll often find them blended with common nouns—for example, *Crest toothpaste* or *Oscar Mayer hot dogs*.

Notice that *toothpaste* and *hot dogs* are lowercase. Why?

The word *Crest* is a proper noun—it's a brand name—but *toothpaste* is a regular old noun. It should stay lowercase. Similarly, *Oscar Mayer* is a brand name, but *hot dogs* is a common noun, so it should be lowercase.

What if you encounter an example like *United Airlines*? Should *Airlines* be capitalized? Well, this depends on whether or not it is part of the official name of the company. In this case, it is—*United Airlines* is the full, proper name of the business, so *Airlines* should be capitalized.

Just remember: if you know (or can figure out from the passage you're reading) that a word is part of a proper name, it should be capitalized. If it is just a common noun, it should be lowercase.

Now look at these examples of proper nouns blended with common nouns. Note which words are capitalized (the proper noun) and which are lowercase (the common noun):

> *The* Supreme Court *justice gave a speech at the school.*
> *I have a coupon for a free* McDonald's *hamburger.*
> *The* NASA *space shuttle will blast off on Sunday.*

Capitalization in Quotations

When a direct quote is included in a sentence and it's paired with a phrase like *she said*, *they shouted*, *he replied*, or *I wrote* to explain who is doing the talking (or the shouting, replying, or writing), the first word of the quotation should be capitalized.

Here are some examples:

Incorrect: *After dessert, he said quietly, "this was the worst meal of my life."*

Correct: *After dessert, he said quietly, "This was the worst meal of my life."*

Incorrect: *The chef told his assistant, "when you learn how to bake wedding cakes, you will get a raise."*

Correct: *The chef told his assistant, "When you learn how to bake wedding cakes, you will get a raise."*

Incorrect: *When I asked what her costume was, Erica replied, "a scary clown."*

Correct: *When I asked what her costume was, Erica replied, "A scary clown."*

While *A scary clown* is not a complete sentence, it is a complete quote, and it is introduced by the phrase *Erica replied*. Therefore, the first word of the quote should be capitalized.

> ### NOTE
>
> When a quote is split in two in a sentence, do not capitalize the first word of the second part, unless there is another reason to do so.

To explain this point, let's go back to one of the previous examples:

> *The chef told his assistant, "When you learn how to bake wedding cakes, you will get a raise."*

The sentence can be reworked by splitting the quote in two:

> *"When you learn how to bake wedding cakes," the chef told his assistant, "you will get a raise."*

Note that *you* should still be lowercase. This is because it is a word that is a continuation of a quoted sentence ("*When you learn how to bake wedding cakes, you will get a raise*"); it is not the first word of the quoted sentence.

Here are two more correct examples that make the same point:

> *"When you go on the boat," Carlos told us, "do not feed the sharks."*
> *Carlos told us, "Do not feed the sharks."*

Now look at this final example, to avoid confusion on the GED® test:

> *"Mia is on her way," Mike said. "She just arrived at the bus station."*

Why should *She* be capitalized? Because this is not a case of a quoted sentence being split up. Instead, there are two complete, separate sentences:

Note that the first sentence ends in a period.

> *"Mia is on her way," Mike said.*

and

> *"She just arrived at the bus station."*

She should be capitalized because it's the first word of a sentence, even though that sentence happens to be a quote.

Using Apostrophes to Create Possessive Nouns and Contractions

In English, apostrophes are an important tool that can help you create possessive words (*the dog's house, Aunt Jane's car*) as well as contractions (*they're, it's*). This lesson explains how and when to use apostrophes.

Possessive Nouns

A **possessive noun** shows the ownership that the noun has over something else. To make a noun possessive, add the following to the end of the word:

- **For most singular nouns:** Add an apostrophe and the letter *s*.
- **For most plural nouns:** Add just an apostrophe.

Look at these examples:

> Anthony's office
> the child's blanket
> the two brothers' toys
> the ladies' room
> the dog's bones [one dog has bones]
> the dogs' bones [two or more dogs have bones]

NOTE

Some plural nouns do not end in s, such as *children*, *women*, *mice*, and *deer*. In these cases, add an apostrophe and an s:
> the children's books
> the mice's cheese

When you are editing a sentence that contains a possessive noun, you will need to decide if it is singular or plural. The best way to do this is to read the entire sentence for clues.

A Mistake to Avoid

Here are some examples of a basic grammar mistake that many people make and that may be tested on the GED® test:

> **Incorrect:** *The* boy's *are building a treehouse.*
> **Incorrect:** *I just adopted two* puppy's.

What's the problem with these sentences? In each, the writer tried to make a plural word by using an apostrophe and the letter *s*. Look at the correct versions:

> **Correct:** *The* boys *are building a treehouse.*
> **Correct:** *I just adopted two* puppies.

There is no need for an apostrophe when a noun is plural. Use apostrophes when you make nouns possessive (for instance, *the* boys' *treehouse*, *the* puppies' *adoption*), not when you simply make nouns plural (*the* boys *have a treehouse*, *the* puppies *were adopted*).

Contractions

A **contraction** refers to the process of joining together two words to create one shorter word. An apostrophe replaces the letter(s) removed in the process.

The following is a list of common contractions:

aren't = are not	let's = let us	weren't = were not
can't = cannot	mightn't = might not	what'll = what will; what shall
couldn't = could not	mustn't = must not	what're = what are
didn't = did not	shan't = shall not	what's = what is; what has
doesn't = does not	she'd = she had; she would	what've = what have
don't = do not	she'll = she will; she shall	where's = where is; where has
hadn't = had not	she's = she is; she has	who'd = who had; who would
hasn't = has not	shouldn't = should not	who'll = who will; who shall
haven't = have not	that's = that is; that has	who's = who is; who has
he'd = he had; he would	there's = there is; there has	who've = who have
he'll = he will; he shall	they'd = they had; they would	won't = will not
he's = he is; he has	they'll = they will; they shall	wouldn't = would not
I'd = I had; I would	they're = they are	you'd = you had; you would
I'll = I will; I shall	they've = they have	you'll = you will; you shall
I'm = I am	we'd = we had; we would	you're = you are
I've = I have	we're = we are	you've = you have
isn't = is not	we've = we have	

For practice, replace the underlined words with the correct contractions.

> <u>Do not</u> forget that <u>we are</u> right around the corner if you <u>cannot</u> find the keys.

> **Answer:** *Don't* forget that *we're* right around the corner if you *can't* find the keys.

The contraction of *do not* is *don't*, the contraction of *we are* is *we're* (NOT *were*!), and the contraction of *cannot* is *can't*.

Contractions versus Possessive Pronouns

In English, there are a few contractions that are pronounced the same as a few possessive pronouns, and many people mistake these words. You may see questions on the GED® test that assess whether you know the difference.

Here's an example:

Correct: *The dog hurt its paw.*
Incorrect: *The dog hurt it's paw.*

The second sentence is incorrect because *it's* is a contraction of *it is*. That means that the sentence really says *The dog hurts it is paw*, which does not make any sense.

Here are some words that people commonly confuse:

Contraction	Possessive Pronoun
it's (it is)	its
you're (you are)	your
they're (they are)	their
who's (who is)	whose

An easy way to remember this is to think about what a contraction really is: in casual speech, we sometimes slide two words together, making one word. (*You are* becomes *you're*; *would not* becomes *wouldn't*; and so on.) In the process of sliding the words together, we drop out one or two of the letters. The apostrophe replaces the letter(s) that dropped out. (When we contract *you are* to make *you're*, we drop the *a*. The apostrophe replaces that *a*.)

Practice

33. Select the grammatically correct sentence.
   a. We're going to stay at my familys house.
   b. We're going to stay at my family's house.
   c. We're going to stay at my families house.
   d. Were going to stay at my family's house.

34. Select the grammatically correct sentence.
   a. Toms sister wasn't planning to come to his childrens' graduation.
   b. Tom's sister wasnt planning to come to his childrens' graduation.
   c. Tom's sister wasn't planning to come to his children's graduation.
   d. none of the above

35. Select the grammatically correct sentence.
   a. You're not going to fix that cars problems without the proper tools.
   b. Your not going to fix that cars problem's without the proper tools.
   c. You're not going to fix that cars' problems without the proper tools.
   d. none of the above

Sentence Punctuation

Proper punctuation marks are necessary when writing complete and correct sentences.

End Marks

A complete sentence must end with correct punctuation. The punctuation at the end of the sentence depends on what type of sentence it is.

   1. A statement ends with a period.
      Minnesota is known for its cold winters.
   2. A question ends with a question mark.
      Do you think it will snow tonight?
   3. An exclamation—that is, a sentence with strong emotion—ends with an exclamation point.
      Call the police!

Commas

Commas are used to indicate breaks in different parts of a sentence. People are often confused about when to use a comma—it is common to place too many commas in a sentence. The following list outlines comma rules for standard English:

   1. Use commas to separate three or more items in a series that includes the word *and* or *or*.
      I lost my wallet, my gloves, and my car keys all on one day.
      Add ketchup, mayonnaise, or mustard to the sandwich.
      Bring the paperwork, three forms of ID, and a photo to the office.
   Note that the comma is placed **before** *and* or *or*, not after it.
   Do not use a comma when only two items are joined by *and* or *or*. That is not a series, so it doesn't need a comma.

   Incorrect: *Bring the paperwork, and three forms of ID to the office.*

Correct: *Bring the paperwork and three forms of ID to the office.*

2. Use a comma after an introductory phrase. An **introductory phrase** can be a prepositional phrase that begins a sentence.

    In the end, Jamie was glad she had worked all weekend painting her room.
    After hearing the weather report, the boss moved the company picnic indoors.

3. Use a comma before a coordinating conjunction that joins two independent clauses. An **independent clause** contains a subject and a verb and would function as a grammatically correct sentence if it stood alone. Examples of coordinating conjunctions that join independent clauses are *and*, *but*, *nor*, *or*, *so*, and *yet*.

    I wanted to go to the movies, but I didn't have enough money to pay for the ticket.
    William completed the computer training, so he decided to apply for a new job.

4. Use commas to separate an appositive from the rest of the sentence if it is a nonrestrictive **appositive** that gives information about something mentioned in the sentence but it is not essential to the core meaning or grammar of the sentence. Do not use commas with restrictive appositives (e.g., *the poet Robert Burns*).

    Renita, the tall girl down the hall, will pick up my mail while I am on vacation.
    The office will be closed on Friday, the last day of the month.

5. Use a comma when a dependent clause comes before the independent clause.

    After I complete my degree, I plan to move to Los Angeles.
    If you are sick, you must contact your supervisor.

6. Use a comma to separate the year in a date.
    March 14, 2008, is my daughter's birthday.

7. Use commas to separate a state name from a city name (or a country name from a city name, etc.).

    Kansas City, Kansas, is my birthplace.
    I'd love to visit my friends in Alberta, Canada, next year.
    The flight began in Beijing, China, stopped in Osaka, Japan, and arrived 12 hours later in San Francisco, California.

Practice

36. Select the best revision of the sentence below: Larry my friend since high school lives next door.
    a. Larry, my friend from high school lives next door.
    b. Larry, my friend from high school lives, next door.
    c. Larry, my friend from high school, lives next door.
    d. Correct as is.

Semicolons and Colons

A **semicolon** (;) can be used to join two independent clauses. Joining two independent clauses this way suggests that the two clauses are related in meaning and of equal importance.

Every Friday we go out for dinner and see a movie; it is our reward for a long week at work.

There are several instances when a **colon** (:) can be used in a sentence.

1. Use a colon after an independent clause to introduce a list.
    Travis requested his favorite meal for his birthday: pizza, cheese bread, and ice cream.

2. Use a colon after an independent clause to introduce a quotation.

> *Emily explained her reason for leaving the magazine: "It's a dead-end job, no matter how hard I work."*

3. Use a colon between two independent clauses when you want to emphasize the second clause.

> *The result of the poll was clear: Obama would probably win the election.*

Quotation Marks

Quotation marks are used around direct quotes—that is, the words a person or character says. For example:

> *Uncle John said, "It has been years since I have seen my sister's children."*
>
> *"I refuse to pay for this meal," Laura shouted, "because there is a bug in my salad!"*

Put punctuation marks before the first quotation mark and inside of the final quotation mark.

Quotation marks are also used around the names of poems, song titles, short stories, magazine or newspaper articles, essays, speeches, chapter titles, and other short works. (Titles of movies, books, TV series, etc. are usually set in italics.)

> *Her daughter would not stop singing "Row, Row, Row Your Boat" as they drove to the lake.*
>
> *My favorite poem is "Wild Geese," by Mary Oliver.*

Practice

Select the best revision of the following sentences.

37. Do you think Ted remembered his book, pen, and paper?
    a. Do you think Ted remembered his: book, pen, and paper?
    b. Do you think Ted remembered his book, pen and paper?
    c. Do you think Ted remembered his book; pen; and paper?
    d. The sentence is correct as is.

38. He was born in February 1994 at the main hospital in Duluth Minnesota.
    a. He was born in February 1994 at the main hospital in Duluth, Minnesota.
    b. He was born in February, 1994, at the main hospital in Duluth Minnesota.
    c. He was born in February, 1994 at the main hospital in Duluth, Minnesota.
    d. The sentence is correct as is.

39. My mother said, "I like vacationing in three states: Texas New Mexico and Arizona."
    a. My mother said, "I like vacationing in three states, Texas, New Mexico, and Arizona.
    b. My mother said, I like vacationing in three states: Texas, New Mexico, and Arizona.
    c. My mother said, "I like vacationing in three states: Texas, New Mexico, and Arizona."
    d. The sentence is correct as is.

Summary

Language and grammar questions on the GED® RLA test will test your knowledge of grammar, word usage, and language mechanics. You will be asked questions that will require critical thinking to arrive at the correct answer.

Before you take the GED® test, practice your grammar skills by building sentences and reviewing how the parts fit together. Engage in active reading, ask yourself questions, and review the language mechanics present in the passages you read. The more you review the information presented in this section, the more successful you will be on the GED® RLA test.

Language and Grammar Review

For questions 1–5, select the correct version of the underlined sentence or portion of a sentence in the passage.

Millennials Take New Approach to Work-Life Balance

—Adapted from an article published on Brandpoint.com

1. More and more, Millennials are on the road for work. In an average month, one in four business-traveling Millennials travels overnight for work at least once per week. As the line between "personal" and "business" grows thinner and thinner for this generation, <u>Millennials are increasingly finding adventure thru business.</u>
   a. Millennials are increasingly finding adventure threw business.
   b. Millennials are increasingly finding adventure through business.
   c. Millennials are increasingly found to have adventure through business.
   d. This is correct as is.

2. More than any other group, Millennial business travelers are likely to add on extra days to their work-related trips for leisure travel (84%), according to the Hilton Garden Inn Discovery and Connection Survey.
   <u>As the economy improves business travel across the nation is on the rise.</u> According to the Global Business Travel Association, U.S. business travel is expected to grow 5.1% in 2013.
   a. As the economy improves, business travel across the nation is on the rise.
   b. As the economy improves business travel, the nation is on the rise.
   c. As the economy improves, business travel across the nation rose.
   d. The sentence is correct as is.

3. As more Millennials hit the road for work, they are keeping top of mind a few simple business travel perks to fulfill their appetite for personal adventure and discovery:
   Fly for free. <u>Those flying for business can earn airline miles in they're name.</u> These business miles quickly add up, allowing travelers to upgrade seats or add another destination without accruing additional cost. Business travelers can then use these miles to bring a friend or loved one on the trip with them—quickly transitioning from business to family vacation or romantic getaway once the weekend hits.
   a. Those flying for business can earn airline miles in there name.
   b. Those flying for business can earn airline miles in your name.
   c. Those flying for business can earn airline miles in their name.
   d. The sentence is correct as is.

4. Earn hotel perks. Frequent stays in hotels offering rewards programs can grant business travelers <u>benefits such as free overnight stays late checkout and complimentary breakfast</u>. These extras turn a business trip into much more, especially when additional nights are used to extend a business trip into a vacation.
   a. benefits such as free overnight stays, late checkout and complimentary breakfast.
   b. benefits such as free overnight stays, late checkout, and complimentary breakfast.
   c. benefits such as free, overnight stays, late checkout, and complimentary, breakfast.
   d. This is correct as is.

5. Millennials continue to be at the forefront of achieving work-life balance <u>by using business travel to discover new cities, taste authentic cuisines, explore different cultures, and connecting with new people across the globe</u>.
   a. by using business travel to discover new cities, taste authentic cuisines, explore different cultures, and connect with new people across the globe.
   b. by using business travel to discover new cities, taste authentic cuisines, explore different cultures, while connecting with new people across the globe.
   c. by using business travel to discovering new cities, tasting authentic cuisines, exploring different cultures, and connecting with new people across the globe.
   d. This is correct as is.

6. Choose the sentence that contains correct capitalization.
   a. She and i are really hoping the Brooklyn Nets do well this year.
   b. She and I are really hoping the Brooklyn Nets do well this Year.
   c. She and I are really hoping the Brooklyn nets do well this year.
   d. She and I are really hoping the Brooklyn Nets do well this year.

7. Select the answer choice that contains correct punctuation.
   a. "I married him because I thought he was a gentleman. I thought he knew something about breeding, but he wasn't fit to lick my shoe." Says Catherine, a character in *The Great Gatsby*.
   b. "I married him because I thought he was a gentleman," Catherine, a character in *The Great Gatsby*, says, "I thought he knew something about breeding, but he wasn't fit to lick my shoe."
   c. "I married him because I thought he was a gentleman," Catherine, a character in *The Great Gatsby*, says. "I thought he knew something about breeding, but he wasn't fit to lick my shoe."
   d. None of the above is correct.

For questions 8 and 9, select the word that best completes the sentence.

8. Melissa's friend asked _____ for a ride home.
   a. they
   b. hers
   c. she
   d. none of the above

9. To _____ are you speaking?
   a. who
   b. whom
   c. when
   d. none of the above

Answers and Explanations

Chapter Practice

1. b. Jill, go lie down while I **lay** out the silver and get the table ready for the party.

2. b. Mira **led** the congregation in song at the memorial service yesterday.

3. b. I plan to pick up my paycheck this afternoon and **then** cash it at the bank on the corner.

4. b. It's a shame that Tim and Jean and their children won't be **there** on Saturday.

5. Red Rocks **is** their favorite concert venue in Colorado. By itself, the word *rocks* is plural, of course, but *Red Rocks* is a proper noun—it's the name of one specific place in Colorado. Since *Red Rocks* is a singular noun, we need to use *is*.

6. Julio, as well as the rest of the band, is excited about performing at Red Rocks. The subject of this sentence is *Julio*, not *Julio, as well as the rest of the band*. Why? The phrase *the rest of the band* is set off with commas as a side point. Since the subject of the sentence, *Julio*, is a singular noun—one person—we need to use *is* (the singular form of the verb *to be*).

7. Two members of the band **are** still back at the hotel. What is the subject of this sentence—*Two members* or *the band*? It is *two members*. As a result, we need to use the verb *are*.

8. Everyone **is** supposed to be onstage right now! The word *everyone* may refer to a lot of people, but the word itself is singular. Therefore we need to use *is*.

9. Where **are** Julio and the guitar player? There are two subjects in this sentence: *Julio* and *the guitar player*. Therefore we need to use *are* (the plural form of the verb *to be*).

10. b. Because the sentence includes the phrase *later today*, we know that we need a future verb form. The sentence should read: *Catherine will go to the store later today.*

11. a. *Visited* is the simple past tense form of the verb *to visit*, which makes sense in this sentence because we know this happened yesterday, not last week or right now.

12. c. When a singular subject and a plural subject are connected by *nor*, the verb must agree with the closer subject—in this case, the plural *cousins*. This choice, *appear*, is the correct verb form for a plural subject.

13. Whom are you taking to the dance? Here, the mystery person will be taken to a dance—an action will be performed on him or her. Therefore the mystery person is an object, and we need to use a pronoun that works with objects: *whom*.

14. Whoever is making that noise had better quiet down! When deciding whether to use *who/whoever* or *whom/whomever*, you need to ask if the person in question is the subject of the sentence (performing the action) or the object (receiving the action). Here, the mystery person being yelled at is the subject of the sentence—he or she is making the noise—so we need to use *whoever*, a pronoun for subjects. If the person were the object, we'd need to use *whomever*, a pronoun for objects.

15. That man over there is the customer **who** complained about me to my boss. In the second part of the sentence, the customer performs the action—*complaining*—so he or she is the subject. We need to use *who*, a pronoun for subjects.

16. Who is taking you to the dance? The mystery person here is performing the action—taking you to the dance. Therefore, he or she is the subject. We need to use a pronoun that works with subjects: *who*.

17. b. We need a possessive pronoun that fits with *Joe*—a singular male noun. That is *his*.

18. a. We don't know the gender of the person who forgot to lock up the shoes and gym bag, but we know it is one person (*someone* is singular). As a result, we need to use *his or her* (singular possessive pronouns).

19. b. These possessive pronouns are used correctly and make sense in this sentence.

20. a. *Moving to Nevada* is a dangling modifier. We all know that it was *Shira* who moved to Nevada—the truck didn't move to Nevada. But based on the structure of this sentence, *moving to Nevada* modifies *Shira's truck*. The revision in this choice corrects that problem.

21. c. In the original sentence, the word *only* is in the wrong spot, and this choice moves it to where it belongs, right before *ten minutes*. What's wrong with the original sentence? The word *only* modifies the wrong thing; the sentence says that Tom *only used the treadmill* at the gym. We know that this is not correct, of course. Tom surely did many things at the gym: he must have opened the front door, walked over to the machines, and selected a treadmill; maybe he changed into his gym clothes, drank some water, and said hello to a friend, too.

22. a. The problem with the original sentence is that the phrase *for more than 200 years* modifies the wrong thing—it suggests that the general may have been in disguise for 200 years. This doesn't make any sense—people don't live for 200 years! This choice correctly places *for more than 200 years* right before *historians have wondered*—it's the wondering that's been happening for 200 years.

23. Subject: *the woman*; **Predicate:** *is waiting for Mr. Williams.* This is a complete sentence: it expresses a complete idea and includes a subject and a predicate. Note that the subject is *the woman*, not *the lobby*—the lobby isn't waiting for Mr. Williams.

24. Subject: *Mr. Williams*; **Predicate:** *went down-stairs.* This is a complete sentence: It expresses a complete idea and includes a subject and a predicate.

25. d. This sentence uses a subordinating conjunction—*wherever*—but *wherever* doesn't make sense here. Here is a better use of *wherever* to combine two clauses: *Wherever I go with Andy, he always seems to know someone.*

26. b. This revision tries to blend the clauses together with a semicolon, but in the process it chops out some key words. By itself, *in the middle of nowhere* is not a clause and it doesn't make sense tacked on at the end with a semicolon.

27. c. The problem with the original sentence is that it contains a series (*apply to colleges, look for a better job, or staying in her current job*), but the series is not parallel. The third item (*staying in her current job*) doesn't fit with the first two, and it also doesn't make sense with the phrase that introduces the series (*she had to decide whether she was going to . . .*). This revision is correct because the third item has been fixed—it is now similar to the other two items (it starts off with the correct verb form, *stay*), and it makes sense logically in the sentence.

28. c. In this sentence, *They* identifies who or what is performing the action. It is therefore the subject of the sentence.

29. a. The first part of this sentence, *If you think it is a good team*, would be a fragment if it stood alone. It makes us wonder, okay, if we think the Heat is a good team, *then what?* It needs an additional thought to form a complete sentence.

30. c. *Not going to happen today* is a sentence fragment because it's missing a subject and a proper verb. If we add these elements, we can turn it into a complete sentence. For example: *The meeting is not going to happen today.*

31. a. This revision combines the first clause (*I'm going away on business*) and the third clause (*I'll be gone this weekend*) into one complete sentence. This is a good idea, because these clauses communicate related ideas—they provide the background information that the speaker wants the listener to know before he or she asks for a favor. This choice also turns *could you please watch the house* into its own sentence by capitalizing *could* and adding a question mark (all questions should end with a question mark). The last sentence is now its own sentence, too.

32. d. This sentence starts off with an independent clause and ends with a dependent clause. There is no reason for the comma.

33. b. Both *We're* (meaning *We are*) and the possessive *family's* are spelled correctly.

34. c. The possessives *Tom's* and the possessive *children's* are spelled correctly, as is *wasn't* (a contraction meaning *was not*).

35. d. The sentence should read: *You're not going to fix that car's problems without the proper tools.*

36. c. In this sentence, the phrase *my friend from high school* is an appositive: it gives additional information about the subject, Larry, but is not essential to the meaning of the sentence (that he lives next door). Commas are always used to set off appositives from the rest of the sentence.

37. d. The sentence is correctly punctuated as is.

38. a. There is no reason for commas in the date *February 1994* (a month and year), but there should be a comma between the city and state (*Duluth, Minnesota*).

39. c. This sentence requires a comma to set off the quote, quotation marks to surround the quote, a colon to introduce the list of three states (because it comes after an independent clause, *I like vacationing in three states*), and commas after the words *Texas* and *New Mexico*.

Language and Grammar Review

1. b. This sentence correctly changes *thru* to *through*, which is the proper spelling.

2. a. It is hard to tell because the underlined sentence is not punctuated properly, but there are really two clauses here. The first clause (*As the economy improves*) is a dependent clause, so it should be joined with a comma to the independent clause that follows (*business travel across the nation is on the rise*).

3. c. The word *they're* should be changed to the possessive pronoun *their*. *They're* is a contraction meaning *they are*.

4. b. This sentence includes a list of three things: (1) *free overnight stays*, (2) *late checkout*, and (3) *complimentary breakfast*. In a series, there should be commas (or semicolons, in special situations) after every item except for the last one. This revision follows that rule.

5. a. The problem with the sentence in the passage is that it contains a series that is not parallel. There is a list of four items, and the first three items are worded in a similar way (*discover . . . , taste . . . , explore . . .*), but the fourth item is different (*connecting . . .*). This revision corrects the problem. It changes the fourth item, *connecting with new people*, to *connect with new people*, which matches the verb form in the other items. The phrase *connect with new people* also fits grammatically with the first part of the sentence. The phrase *connecting with new people* didn't work. Why? Remove the first three items of the series to see what we were really saying with *connecting*. The sentence would read: *Millennials continue to be at the forefront of achieving work-life balance by using business travel to . . . connecting with new people across the globe*, but this doesn't make any sense.

6. d. The pronoun *I* and the proper noun *Brooklyn Nets* are both correctly capitalized.

7. c. This is correct punctuation and organization of a quote.

8. d. This sentence calls for an object pronoun, explaining whom Melissa's friend asked for a ride. None of the choices are appropriate pronouns.

9. b. Let's rewrite this sentence: *You are speaking to _____*. The speaker (*you*) is the subject—he or she is performing the action of the sentence (talking to someone). What we need here is an object pronoun, for the person being spoken to. *Whom* is an object pronoun and makes sense in this sentence.

8 ▶ THE EXTENDED RESPONSE ESSAY

The Extended Response section of the GED® Reasoning through Language Arts (RLA) test is an essay question. You will be asked to read one or two passages and then answer a question, also called a prompt. The prompt will ask you to write an essay that takes a position on what you've read. Examples of topics include the pros and cons of all-day kindergarten or food choices in school cafeterias. You will be prompted to analyze both positions, determine which position is best supported, and include evidence from the readings to support your written position. You will have 45 minutes to read the given passage(s) and then write and edit your essay on the computer.

Before you take the GED® RLA test, practice your typing skills. On exam day, you will have a lot to say, and you don't want to waste part of your 45 minutes hunting for letters on the keyboard. A good goal for taking the GED® RLA test is to be comfortable typing sentences on a computer. When you practice essay writing, set a timer for yourself so you can see what it feels like to type with the clock ticking.

Before You Write Your Essay

Producing a great essay for the GED® test requires a step-by-step process, and many of those steps take place *before* you write it. Take the time to work through this lesson, and you'll have a good foundation for writing your best essay on test day.

ERASABLE WHITEBOARDS

When you take the GED® test, you will be provided with an erasable whiteboard to jot down notes. These are especially useful during the extended response question, as you prepare to write your essay. If you need additional whiteboards during testing, you can request a fresh one and turn in the one that you've already used. You are allowed to have only one whiteboard at a time.

Understanding the Prompt

Writing an extended response essay requires you not only to analyze the passage(s) but also to respond to a specific prompt. Take a look at this sample prompt:

PROMPT

In the following article, the pros and cons of wearing school uniforms are discussed. In your response, analyze both positions to determine which view is best supported. Use relevant and specific evidence from the passage to support your response.

Type your response in the box; you will have approximately 45 minutes to complete it.

To understand exactly what you're being asked to write about, carefully read the prompt and identify:

- **The issue** (*pros and cons of wearing school uniforms*)
- **The description of what you are asked to do** (*analyze both positions; determine which view is best supported; use relevant and specific evidence from the passage to support your response*)
- **Instructions for completing the task** (*type your response in the box; you will have approximately 45 minutes to complete it*)

Reading the Passage(s)

There's a natural tendency to want to rush into writing the essay—that's what you are being tested on, after all—and to skimp on reading the passage(s). Avoid doing this. The only way to produce a good essay is to read the passage(s) carefully, understand it/them, and pull out what you will need when you write.

Follow these **five steps** as you read the passage(s). At the end of the process, you will have good information and ideas to use as you write your essay.

1. Before you start to read, **scan the passage(s)** to get a sense of what the passage(s) is/are about and note how the information is organized.
2. **Read the passage(s).** Because you know you will definitely have to respond, as you read try to relate the information in the passage(s) to your own life experiences.
3. As you read, use your whiteboard to **write down questions** that you have about the content.
4. **Determine the author's main argument**, and write that down. Then quickly outline the main points that the author makes to support that argument and restate them in your own words.

5. **Evaluate the author's argument.** Did he or she provide good support or enough evidence for it? Why or why not? Does the way the author writes affect you emotionally? Why or why not?

Writing a Thesis Statement

The extended response requires you to take a stance on a topic and then back up this stance with specific evidence. To do this, start off your essay with a strong, clear claim—also called a **thesis statement**—and follow it with facts and ideas that support that claim. The goal of your essay is to convince the reader that your thesis statement is true through the evidence you provide.

> ### TAKE NOTE
>
> Your thesis statement must be based on information that you read in the passage(s). (The supporting points that you use to back it up should also include information that you read in the passage(s), but they may be based on your own opinions and life experiences, too.)

Read through these two examples of thesis statements:

- *Public schools need to support healthy nutrition; therefore, vending machines that sell candy and soda to students should be forbidden.*
- *To protect the health and well-being of cats and dogs, pet owners have a responsibility to neuter their pets.*

Collecting Details from Passages

To support your thesis, gather information from the passage(s) that will allow you to express a strong opinion. A good essay will include specific details that will help the reader understand your position.

> ### TAKE NOTE
>
> On the GED® test, you must include evidence from the passage(s) that supports your thesis statement and also analyze evidence in the passage(s) that *does not* support your position.

As you jot down details from the passage(s) to use in your essay, ask the following questions:

1. Does this information support my thesis statement?
2. Does this evidence persuade the reader to believe or agree with my position?

The following is an example of a passage that presents an issue (the pros and cons of school uniforms). We will analyze this passage in the next section. Write down notes, important details, and a thesis statement as you read.

THE PROS AND CONS OF SCHOOL UNIFORMS FOR YOUR CHILD

Although uniforms have been a mainstay of private schools, public schools jumped on the bandwagon in 1994, when the California school district of Long Beach implemented school uniforms. According to the Long Beach school district, within one year after the implementation of uniforms, the fights and muggings at school decreased by 50%, while committed sexual offenses were reduced by 74%. Across the country, similar statistics abound; for example, at Ruffner Middle School in Norfolk, Virginia, the number of discipline referrals decreased by 42% once uniforms were enforced. Subsequently, fueled by these statistics, more schools across the country are implementing uniforms in public schools. Nonetheless, there are other statistics that argue that uniforms are not as beneficial as school administrators believe. Thus, the question still remains: Are public school uniforms good for your child?

There are fundamentally two benefits associated with school uniforms: a focus on learning, as well as a reduction of violence on campus. Many school administrators and parents believe that uniforms create a better learning environment at school. First and foremost, students are not distracted by how they look and therefore pay more attention to learning at school. The peer pressures of stylish dressing with the best brands are alleviated, and students can focus more on their schoolwork, rather than on social appearances. In fact, the socioeconomic differences present among students are equalized with school uniforms, minimizing the pressure to fit in with the right clothing choices.

According to the publication *School Administrator*, the mandate of uniforms on campuses has reduced tardiness, skipped classes, suspensions, and discipline referrals. In addition, with the visual uniformity present across all students, school pride has increased. Similar to athletic team uniforms, dressing cohesively increases pride, unity, and a renewed commitment to the school. With uniforms, a more professional tone is set in school, encouraging students to take their studies more seriously. Uniforms are more expensive up front, as the parent must invest in all of the staples; however, as the school year progresses, there are fewer purchases that need to be made. Last, uniforms at school reduce the prevalence of violence, which is a major concern for many public schools. Outsiders who do not belong on campus are easily identified and thus do not pose a great threat to the students. Uniforms also reduce the cliques and gangs on school campuses. When it is not easy to identify members of gangs, the fights and violence decrease. Students can no longer be distracted by who is wearing which gang color, and therefore, the campus is kept safer with less incidence of fighting.

The opponents of public school uniforms, as outlined by the ACLU's argument for the First Amendment, argue that uniforms stifle a student's need for self-expression. Students need to be encouraged to embrace their individualism, and uniforms deny that self-expression. According to opponents of uniforms, even preschoolers should have input into their wardrobes, and the need to encourage personality, confidence, and independence grows more important as the student becomes older. Without the outlet of expression in their clothing choices, students may turn to inappropriate hairstyles, jewelry, or makeup. Denying students their ability to express individualism and belief in a subculture, whether preppy, hip-hop, punk, or jock, could stymie their transition from childhood into adulthood. Controlling the socialization process could harm them as

(*continues*)

adults; they may not be prepared for the real world, where people are indeed judged by their appearances. In addition, others argue that uniforms may not be comfortable for all students. As it is important to ensure that the student is comfortable in order to maximize learning outcomes, uniforms may stymie academic focus. Students cannot wear their uniforms outside of school, and thus, there is the double cost of both uniforms and a casual wardrobe.

—Adapted from "Public School Uniforms: The Pros and Cons for Your Child," by Grace Chen, April 23, 2008, publicschoolreview.com.

Organization of Your Essay

A good GED® test essay starts with an introductory paragraph that presents the main idea, follows with body paragraphs that contain support for the main idea, and closes with a concluding paragraph.

Writing Your Introduction

Keep in mind these two goals as you write your introduction:

1. **Clearly state your main point or thesis statement.**

    As you write the body paragraphs, you can refer to your introduction to make sure your evidence supports the thesis.

2. **Present your plan to support your main point.** For example, if you are going to refer to three points of evidence from the passage(s), briefly mention them in the introduction. This will give your essay some structure—helpful for your readers, because they will know what to expect, and helpful for you, because you will have a built-in guide as you write the rest of the piece.

    It's also a good way to make sure up front that you will be able to defend your argument with evidence. If you can't find evidence to support your claim, then you need to rethink your thesis statement.

Problems to Avoid in Introductions

1. **Don't mention how you plan to write your essay.** Your position and supporting evidence should speak for themselves.

    Incorrect: *I am going to tell you why students in public schools should wear uniforms. I will present the best argument for this position that shows why this is a good thing to do. I will also explain why the information against school uniforms does not present a good argument.*

    Correct: *There are many benefits that result from mandating student uniforms in public schools. These benefits include an overall lower cost, the sense of school harmony they promote, and the respect that is associated with them. Evidence from school administrators, students, and parents supports these advantages, which outweigh the negatives of mandating school uniforms.*

2. **Don't use meaningless or empty words to sound clever or repeat the same point using synonyms.** Consider the following example:

    School uniforms are critical to student success. They are essential for helping students accomplish their best in school. Uniforms play a significant role in helping students have a positive experience in school.

    These three sentences all say the same thing!

3. **Don't make excuses for your writing.** You want to convey a clear, confident position to the reader. Don't start your essay with something like the following:

Although I'm not familiar with the debate over school uniforms, I think I would probably say that it's a good idea for students to wear them.

Building Your Argument

To write the body of your essay, you will need to provide support for your claim or thesis statement. Return to your notes to see what evidence you highlighted as you read the passage(s). On the extended response, it is okay to use evidence from your personal experiences, but much of the essay should be based on evidence found in the reading passage(s) and on your analysis of this evidence.

If the writer of the passage makes his or her own argument, you should also include an analysis of the author's argument, or arguments, in your essay. To earn the highest score possible, you should discuss whether you think the writer is making a good case, and why or why not.

NOTE

Don't try to argue a claim if you can't fully support it. If you cannot find enough evidence from the passage(s) to back up your thesis, then you will have to develop a new one.

A good way to arrange your evidence is in the order of strength: start with the weakest evidence and end with the strongest. In addition to listing details that support your thesis, you should also list details that go *against* your thesis and then talk about why you disagree with them. Arguments like this help strengthen your point.

After you have grouped your supporting evidence using the erasable whiteboard, you will be ready to construct a simple outline to draft your essay.

Constructing a Draft

One method of constructing a draft, or the first version of your essay, is to create a simple outline. You can do this on the computer in the space provided for the essay and then erase it after you finish writing the essay. You might also want to create the outline on your personal whiteboard, which has the advantage of saving space on the computer screen.

Begin by thinking about your thesis. Decide the stance you want to take, and write your thoughts into one complete sentence. For example, what thesis statement would you make for an essay about the school uniform passage?

Every extended response essay should follow this basic structure:

1. **Introduction** (states thesis)
2. **Body** (explains and supports thesis with evidence from the passage and your insights)
3. **Conclusion** (brings closure and restates thesis)

Here is an example, using the passage about school uniforms:

> **Thesis statement:** *There are many benefits that result from mandating student uniforms in public schools.*
>
> **Body paragraph(s):** Make sure these include evidence from the text, not only your opinion:

1. *Decrease in negative behavior*
   Evidence from the passage: *School administrators report a reduction in fighting, tardiness, and other discipline problems.*

2. *Increase in learning*
    Evidence from the passage: *School administrators and parents report a better focus on learning because students are not distracted by the pressure to fit in.*
3. *Professional, respectful atmosphere at school*
    Evidence from the passage: *Schools report an increase in school pride and commitment to school.*

Conclusion: *Evidence from school administrators and other experts supports these advantages, which outweigh the negatives of mandating school uniforms.*

Sometimes three paragraphs—an introductory paragraph, a body paragraph, and a concluding paragraph—are enough to make your point, but you may need more (usually extra body paragraphs).

NOTE

For an essay to be effective, each paragraph must be effective, too. This means that each paragraph must be well developed. Each paragraph should have a minimum of three sentences, but it's usually necessary to write five to eight sentences to explain your thoughts adequately.

Once you have a clear, detailed outline, you can begin to write your essay. As noted earlier, your introduction should include your claim or thesis statement. Here is an example of an introductory paragraph:

There are many benefits that result from mandating student uniforms in public schools. These benefits include an overall lower cost, the sense of school harmony they promote, and the respect that is associated with them. Evidence from school administrators, students, and parents

supports these advantages, which outweigh the negatives of mandating school uniforms.

After you have composed your introduction, write the body of the essay to support your claim, and then add a conclusion paragraph that makes a final comment and restates your thesis.

WARNING!

You *cannot* copy and paste exact text from the passage(s) into the body of your essay without using quotation marks. If you do make this mistake, your essay will receive a score of 0! You are required either to include quotation marks or to paraphrase the points (put what the author says into your own words).

Example of an Extended Response Essay

Now take a look at this great example of a high-scoring essay, which follows the structure we've discussed. The writer is responding to the prompt for the school uniform passage.

PROMPT

In the following article, the pros and cons of wearing school uniforms are discussed. In your response, analyze both positions to determine which view is best supported. Use relevant and specific evidence from the passage to support your response.

Type your response in the box; you will have approimately 45 minutes to complete it.

THE EXTENDED RESPONSE ESSAY

PROS AND CONS OF SCHOOL UNIFORMS

There are many benefits that result from mandating student uniforms in public schools. These benefits include an overall lower cost, the sense of harmony they promote, and the respect that is associated with them. Evidence from school administrators, students, and parents supports these advantages, which outweigh the negatives of mandating school uniforms.

As noted in the article by Grace Chen, evidence from schools in California and elsewhere revealed that when students were required to wear uniforms, there was a significant drop in negative behaviors on campus. For example, one school district reported that after one year of students wearing uniforms, the number of fights and muggings went down by 50%. The publication *School Administrator* had similar findings: when students wore uniforms, there was a decrease in tardiness, skipping school, and even suspensions.

School administrators and parents also report that when students are not focused on how they look or succumbing to pressure from their classmates to dress in a certain way, more attention can be paid to the task of learning in the school environment. While Chen cites the opinion that uniforms repress individual style, students have opportunities to express their style outside the school setting. Opponents also claim that there could be a greater financial cost to families if uniforms are required; however, in my experience, this is a weak argument. For example, in my school district, there is financial aid available to every family in need to help with the cost of uniforms, and in some schools, uniforms are free to qualifying families.

In addition, Chen notes that uniforms create "a more professional tone . . . in school," saying that this practice encourages students to take pride in their school and creates a sense of community. These are skills that young people need in adulthood whether they go on to college or enter the workforce. If wearing school uniforms helps students at a young age to increase their awareness of some of the things that are important for college and career readiness, then this is something school districts need to consider. A young person's ability to transition successfully to adulthood requires far more than attentiveness to his or her individual style. Many workplaces have employee dress codes, and those who do not follow the company policy for appropriate dress may face termination. Therefore, school uniforms may actually help young people develop the mind-set they need to be effective team players in the workplace.

Although some students may complain about the requirement of school uniforms, the evidence presented in this article strongly suggests that the benefits outweigh the disadvantages. Chen notes that school officials have data that prove the positive effects of uniforms: fewer behavior problems, an increase in school pride, and greater attention to learning. Based on this evidence, more districts should consider implementing uniforms in their schools.

Notice that the fourth paragraph includes a phrase from the passage, and it's correctly enclosed by quotation marks. What are the three dots in the quote? They are an ellipsis, which indicates that the essay writer removed one or more words from the original phrase. The original line in the passage is *a more professional tone is set in school*. This doesn't work grammatically in the sentence in the essay, so the essay writer removed *is set* and replaced those two words with an ellipsis.

Also note that the writing style is formal and that the word choice is precise in order to convey specific ideas.

The Final Steps

The sample essay you just read is the final, submitted version of the essay. When you write *your* essay, you will probably need to revise your first draft before you get to this stage. You'll want to read it over carefully and make changes to improve it. Focus on improving the text (what you say) and style (how you say it), as well as fixing grammar and language errors that you may not have noticed when you were writing.

Evaluating Your Work

Use this checklist to help you evaluate your first draft to make revisions. Your response should:

- Introduce a clear point of view, distinguishing it from an opposing point of view as necessary.
- Develop the point of view and an opposing point of view fairly, give evidence for each, and point out the strengths and weaknesses of both.
- Provide a conclusion that supports the argument presented.
- Follow the rules of standard written English.

Managing Your Time

You will have 45 minutes to complete your extended response for the GED® RLA test. This requires careful planning and time management to read the passage(s) and then write your essay.

In general, you should organize your time by spending:

- **10–12 minutes** reading the passage(s) and establishing your thesis
- **20–25 minutes** creating a quick outline and writing your response
- **10–15 minutes** reviewing and revising your response

When you answer the practice question at the end of this section, set a timer to make sure that you are on track.

How Your Essay Will Be Scored

Your extended response essay will be scored based on three traits, or elements:

- **Trait 1:** Creation of arguments and use of evidence
- **Trait 2:** Development of ideas and organizational structure
- **Trait 3:** Clarity and command of standard English conventions

Your essay will be scored on a scale where each trait is worth up to 2 points, for a possible total of 6 points. The total is then doubled, so the maximum number of possible points you can earn is 12.

Creation of Arguments and Use of Evidence

Trait 1 tests your ability to write an essay that takes a stance based on the information in the reading passage(s). To earn the highest score possible, you must carefully read the information and express a clear opinion about what you've read. You will be scored on how well you use the information from the passage(s) to support your argument.

NOTE

To earn the highest score possible, you must reference and restate information from the passage(s), not just mention information from your own personal experiences.

Your score will also be based on how well you analyze the author's argument in the passage(s), if he or she makes one. To earn the highest score possible, discuss whether you think the author is making a good argument, and why or why not.

For your reference, here is a table that the GED® test scorers will use when determining if your essay should get a score of 2, 1, or 0 for Trait 1.

TO ATTAIN A SCORE OF:	DESCRIPTION
2	■ Generates text-based argument(s) and establishes a purpose that is connected to the prompt ■ Cites relevant and specific evidence from the source text(s) to support argument(s) ■ Analyzes the issue and/or evaluates the validity of the argumentation within the source texts (e.g., distinguishes between supported and unsupported claims, makes reasonable inferences about underlying premises or assumptions, identifies fallacious reasoning, evaluates the credibility of sources, etc.)
1	■ Generates an argument and demonstrates some connection to the prompt ■ Cites some evidence from the source text(s) to support argument(s) (may include a mix of relevant and irrelevant citations or a mix of textual and non-textual references) ■ Partially analyzes the issue and/or evaluates the validity of the argumentation within the source texts; may be simplistic, limited, or inaccurate
0	■ May attempt to create an argument OR lacks purpose or connection to the prompt OR does neither ■ Cites minimal or no evidence from source text(s) (sections of text may be copied from source) ■ Minimally analyzes the issue and/or evaluates the validity of the argumentation within the source texts; may completely lack analysis or demonstrate minimal or no understanding of the given argument(s)

Development of Ideas and Organization Structure

Trait 2 tests whether you respond to the writing prompt with a well-structured essay. Support of your thesis must come from evidence in the passage(s), as well as personal opinions and experiences that build on your central idea. Your ideas must be fully explained and include specific details.

Your essay should use words and phrases that allow your details and ideas to flow naturally.

Here is a table that the GED® test scorers will use when determining if your essay should get a score of 2, 1, or 0 for Trait 2.

TO ATTAIN A SCORE OF:	DESCRIPTION
2	■ Contains ideas that are well developed and generally logical; most ideas are elaborated upon ■ Contains a sensible progression of ideas with clear connections between details and main points ■ Establishes an organizational structure that conveys the message and purpose of the response; applies transitional devices appropriately ■ Establishes and maintains a formal style and appropriate tone that demonstrate awareness of the audience and purpose of the task ■ Chooses specific words to express ideas clearly
1	■ Contains ideas that are inconsistently developed and/or may reflect simplistic or vague reasoning; some ideas are elaborated ■ Demonstrates some evidence of a progression of ideas but details may be disjointed or lacking connection to main idea ■ Establishes an organization structure that may inconsistently group ideas or is partially effective at conveying the message of the task; uses transitional devices inconsistently ■ May inconsistently maintain a formal style and appropriate tone to demonstrate an awareness of the audience and purpose of the task ■ May occasionally misuse words and/or choose words that express ideas in vague terms
0	■ Contains ideas that are insufficiently or illogically developed with minimal or no elaboration of main ideas ■ Contains an unclear or no progression of ideas; details may be absent or irrelevant to the main idea ■ Establishes an ineffective or no discernible organizational structure; does not apply transitional devices or does so inappropriately ■ Uses an informal style and/or inappropriate tone that demonstrates limited or no awareness of audience and purpose ■ May frequently misuse words, overuse slang, or express ideas in a vague or rapturous manner

Clarity and Command of Standard English Conventions

Trait 3 tests how well you create the sentences that make up your essay. To earn a high score, you will need to write sentences with variety—some short, some long, some simple, some complex. You will also need to prove that you have a good handle on standard English, including correct word choice, grammar, and sentence structure.

If you need to review any topics in grammar, usage, or mechanics, revisit Chapter 7 of this book.

Here is a table that the GED® test scorers will use when determining if your essay should get a score of 2, 1, or 0 for Trait 3.

TO ATTAIN A SCORE OF:	DESCRIPTION
2	<ul><li>Demonstrates largely correct sentence structure and a general fluency that enhances clarity with specific regard to the following skills:<ul><li>varied sentence structure within a paragraph or paragraphs</li><li>correct subordination, coordination, and parallelism</li><li>avoidance of wordiness and awkward sentence structures</li><li>usage of transitional words, conjunctive adverbs, and other words that support logic and clarity</li><li>avoidance of run-on sentences, fused sentences, or sentence fragments</li></ul></li><li>Demonstrates competent application of the conventions of English usage with specific regard to the following skills:</li><li>frequently confused words and homonyms, including contractions<ul><li>subject-verb agreement</li><li>pronoun usage, including pronoun antecedent agreement, unclear pronoun references, and pronoun case</li><li>placement of modifiers and correct word order</li><li>capitalization (e.g., proper nouns, titles, and beginnings of sentences)</li><li>use of apostrophes, with possessive nouns</li><li>use of punctuation (e.g., commas in a series or in appositives and other nonessential elements, end marks, and appropriate punctuation for clause separation)</li></ul></li><li>Response may contain some errors in mechanics and conventions but they do not interfere with comprehension; overall, standard usage is at a level appropriate for on-demand draft writing</li></ul>
1	<ul><li>Demonstrates inconsistent sentence structure; may contain some repetitive, choppy, rambling, or awkward sentences that may detract from clarity; demonstrates inconsistent control over skills listed in the first bullet under Trait 3, score of 2</li><li>Demonstrates inconsistent control of basic conventions with specific regard to skills listed in the second bullet under Trait 3, score of 2</li><li>May contain frequent errors in mechanics and conventions that occasionally interfere with comprehension; standard usage is at a minimally acceptable level of appropriateness for on-demand draft writing</li></ul>
0	<ul><li>Demonstrates consistently flawed sentence structure so that meaning may be obscured; demonstrates minimal control over skills listed in the first bullet of Trait 3, score of 2</li><li>Demonstrates minimal control of basic conventions with specific regard to skills listed in the second bullet under Trait 3, score of 2</li><li>Contains severe and frequent errors in mechanics and conventions that interfere with comprehension; overall standard usage is at an unacceptable level for appropriateness for on-demand draft writing OR</li><li>Response is insufficient to demonstrate level of mastery over conventions and usage</li></ul>

Avoid an Automatic Zero Score

If your essay has any of the following problems, it will *automatically* receive a score of 0:

- The entire essay is made up of text copied from the passage(s) or the prompt.
- The essay shows no evidence that the test taker has read the prompt.
- The essay is on the wrong topic.
- The essay is incomprehensible (cannot be understood).
- The essay is not in English.
- The essay section is blank.

Extended Response Practice

Use the following prompt to answer this sample extended response question. As you write your essay, be sure to:

- Decide which position presented in the passage(s) is better supported by evidence.
- Explain why your chosen position has better support.

- Recognize that the position with better support may not be the position you agree with.
- Present multiple pieces of evidence from the passage(s) to defend your assertions.
- Thoroughly construct your main points, organizing them logically, with strong supporting details.
- Connect your sentences, paragraphs, and ideas with transitional words and phrases.
- Express your ideas clearly and choose your words carefully.
- Use varied sentence structures to increase the clarity of your response.
- Reread and revise your response.

PROMPT

The following passage discusses the debate over violent video games and their effect on young people. Take no more than 45 minutes to read the passage, write your essay, and then revise it.

VIOLENT VIDEO GAMES— ARE THEY HARMFUL TO YOUNG PEOPLE?

The debate over the effects of video games on the behavior of youths continues today with reports of school shootings and violent acts in urban neighborhoods. Violent video games are often cited as the culprit for increased violent behavior in youths. Some people contend that these games desensitize players to violence and teach children that violence is an acceptable way to resolve conflicts. Video game supporters state that research on the topic is unsound and that no direct relationship has been found between video games and violent behavior. In fact, some argue that violent video games may reduce violence by providing a safe outlet for aggressive and angry feelings.

In testimony presented at a 2012 federal hearing addressing the regulation of the video game rating system, Cindy Marrix, a psychologist and researcher at the Media and Mind Institute at Wollash University, in Wollash, Idaho, stated there is overwhelming evidence that supports the link between violent video games and aggressive behavior in young people. Dr. Marrix stated that research shows that violent video games are more likely than other media to lead to aggressive behavior because of the repetitive nature of game activities and players' identification with violent characters.

Dr. Marrix also noted that the practice of being rewarded for many acts of violence may intensify a game player's learning of violent acts. She believes that electronic media play a significant role in the emotional and social development of youth. While there are many video games that promote learning and cooperative behavior, studies suggest that the video games that include aggression, violence, and sexualized violence may have a negative impact on children.

Research results reveal that violent video games do increase feelings of hostility and thoughts about aggression. Dr. Marrix contends that the entertainment industry must recognize the link between violent behaviors and violent video games, and that these games should depict the realistic consequences of violence to show children that violence is not an effective means of resolving conflict.

While the concerns about the effects of violent video games are understandable, there are also a number of experts who claim there is no link between video games and violence. After examination of the research evidence, several authorities have concluded that these studies do not scientifically validate the hypothesis that the games increase violence. In fact, millions of children and adults play these games without any ill effects.

Researchers Dr. Erica Trounce and Dr. Jacob Smith state that concerns about current video games are really no different than those of previous generations regarding the new media of earlier times. Drs. Trounce and Smith state that research findings that claim violent video games create violent behaviors come from poorly conducted studies and sensational news reports.

The findings of two recent studies were reported in 2014 in the scientific journal *Behind the Brain*. Participants of the first study were assigned to play either a violent or a nonviolent video game for two hours per day for 20 days. Although male participants were observed to have greater aggression during the time they played the violent game than female participants, the

(continues)

results of this study revealed no increase of real-life aggression in players of the violent games. Results of the second study indicated that a predisposition to respond to certain situations with acts of aggression, family violence, and male gender were predictive of violent crime, but exposure to violent video games was not. These results suggest that playing violent video games does not demonstrate a significant risk for future violent acts.

Worldwide video game sales are predicted to reach $73.5 billion in 2013. As games get more complex and lifelike, the discussion over whether children should be allowed to be exposed to violent video games will continue.

Read the passage and construct an essay that addresses the following question: *Do violent video games promote violent behavior in youths?* In your response, analyze both positions to determine which is better supported. Use relevant and specific evidence to support your response.

_____

_____

_____

_____

_____

_____

_____

_____

_____

_____

Extended Response Practice Sample Essays

Sample Score 2 Response

There is strong reason to believe that violent video games help create a culture of violence among America's youths. The playing of violent video games can cause players to blur the line between fantasy and reality and make them believe there are no consequences for violent actions. Evidence from a variety of sources such as psychologists and scientific researchers shows that we must take steps to curb children's exposure to violent video games.

As the testimony of Dr. Cindy Marrix makes clear, violent video games have a much greater impact on the behavior of players than other forms of media. Beyond the "repetitive nature of game activities and players' identification with violent characters" that she mentions, I would also argue that the interactive component of video games makes them more dangerous than violent movies or television. This is because players actively contribute to the games' violent story lines, whereas movies and television are passive viewing experiences. Additionally, as Dr. Marrix contends, the system of rewarding game players for violent actions both desensitizes players to violence and lends positive associations to violent acts.

While the passage contains evidence against the link between violent video games and violent behavior, I do not believe it is as strong as the argument represented by Dr. Marrix. Most significantly, the study published in *Behind the Brain* does not seem to take into consideration the long-term effects of playing violent video games over a sustained amount of time. Perhaps players' levels of aggression do not rise after a few days' or weeks' worth of play, but what about over the course of 10 or 15 years? Most game players I know, whether they play violent or nonviolent games, have been doing so since early childhood. Even if many years spent playing such games does not result in violent behavior, at the very least these games

remove the danger from violent behavior and make it appear almost normal. This can't be good for players' abilities to empathize with victims of violence or fully grasp the problem of violence in the world today.

Dr. Marrix is right to call for increased vigilance on the part of both the game makers and the general public when it comes to violence in video games. As the passage predicts, these games will only get more lifelike with time, raising further questions about the relationship between simulated and real violence. Factors such as a player's psychological health and family background definitely play a part in his or her tendencies toward violence, but the influence of interactive media on a child's emotional development cannot be ignored.

About This Essay

This extended response is a Score 2 because it contains an argument that is clearly connected to the prompt. The author does this by using evidence from the passage and attributing it correctly (this means that the writer explained who or what is the source of the evidence). The writer makes reasonable inferences, makes reasonable claims, and organizes his or her points in a logical way. He or she looks at both sides of the debate with fairness and objectivity, adding personal observations only when they are relevant to the response. The language, style, and tone of the essay remain formal throughout. Sentence structure is clear and precise, and the writer has a varied vocabulary. He or she follows basic grammar rules, including proper capitalization and punctuation.

Sample Score 1 Response

This essay discusses violence and video games. In my opinion violence is a problem today but video games don't make it any worse. Video games can even help with hand eye coordination and reflexes.

The first source, Dr. Marrix, discusses why she thinks that video games lead to violence. She says that people who play video games are more aggressive than people who don't and that they have a hard time telling the difference between what's real and what isn't. Maybe there is some truth to this but I know people who have played video games for years and they are not violent. I think it depends on people's families, if their families are good and teach them not to be aggressive and violent then they should be able to play video games without resulting in social violence. Dr. Marrix believes that players "identify" with violent characters and that this makes them want to act like the characters in real life, but I think it's more like the second source, Doctor Trounce, says: "violent behaviors come from poorly conducted studies and sensational news reports." What she means is that the news media is responsible for blowing up the problem of violent video games to sensationalize a story. It really has no grounding in reality. I also agree with the study in Behind the Brain magazine, that states that there is no increase in real-life aggression when people play video games. This refutes Dr. Marrix's point that there is a link between the two. The study also backs up what I said about the importance of family in raising nonviolent children.

The article states that people are going to spend "73.5 billion" dollars on games by the end of 2013. This alone is enough to show that games are not going away and that they are very difficult to regulate because they take up such a large part of the economy. Dr. Marrix suggests they change the content of the games, but that will be difficult because so many people buy them. Instead they should let the consumers decide if they can handle the content of the games. Games like Grand theft Auto can even help people's driving abilities and even pilots sometimes train on simulators so it is proven that simulated electronic media can have positive value in society. Plus the magazine study shows that it is usually only males that have the problem with violence and video games, not the entire population. In conclusion I do not see an established link between violence and video games, at least not enough so that we have to change

our national policy toward games, like Dr. Marrix suggests.

About This Essay

This extended response is a Score 1 because the argument has some connection to the prompt, but the author wanders in making his or her point. He or she does not follow a logical progression to explain his or her argument. The writer does not analyze the evidence from the text in depth, and little is done to show how it connects to the author's thesis. The essay writer makes similar points repeatedly, using a tone that wavers between formal and casual. There are run-on sentences, some errors in punctuation and capitalization, inaccurate quotes, and awkward transitions between parts of the essay.

Sample Score 0 Response

The article says video games lead to violence I agree cuz video games r violent & lotsa people play em that r violent. i'd say ban all the video games cuz they lead to violence! The game Call of Duty's very violent, I know ppl who play it n the graffix r super real looking. Not good for society to have ppl playin these games. in the article it sez ppl get aggressive when they play too many games. I would agree wit this, they have trouble telling whats real and whats fake. The dr. in the article sez these games have "negative impact" which is true if you've ever seen how violent the games can b. other parts in the article talk bout how the games arent that violent that ppl can play them w/o being violent but I dont know, I think they raise aggression in players. games once were simpler, not so violent, but now theyre super violent, the doctors in the article even think so. ppl are gonna spend "7.53 billion" on games the article states, so its a bigger problem then really anyone can handle at this point . . . its one of the biggest parts of the media and ppl will find ways to get their games. its to bad b/c I think its bad for society to have all these people playing so many games not thinking about real problems in society like war etc. but I dunno I dont think theres a solution rite now . . . sad that ppl become so violent with games.

About This Essay

This extended response is a Score 0 because it has little or no connection to the prompt, follows no logical progression, and includes little evidence from the passage. There is very little analysis of the issue or of the studies mentioned in the passage; while there is a very general thesis, it is not fully explained. The author uses slang and shorthand spellings (for instance, "sez" and "dunno") and writes in a tone that is too casual. There are many errors in spelling, capitalization, punctuation, and basic grammar rules, and the dollar amount is quoted inaccurately. These prevent the reader from fully understanding what the writer is trying to say.

PART III

GED® SCIENCE TEST

The GED® Science test focuses on using critical thinking and reasoning skills along with the fundamentals of scientific reasoning and application of science practices in real-world scenarios. This may sound overwhelming, but the following chapters will give you the information and strategies for tackling this test.

The test includes reading passages, analyzing graphs and charts, problem solving, and answering questions, all containing science content. There are also some question sets (i.e., more than one question asked about a particular graphic or passage). You will have 90 minutes to complete the test.

The GED® Science test assesses important science ideas in two ways:

1. Every question tests a science practice skill and measures critical thinking and reasoning skills that are key to understanding scientific information.
2. Additionally, each question is drawn from one of the three main content areas in science—life science, physical science, and earth and space science.

Understanding the science practice skills and reviewing the information covered within the three main content areas will help when preparing for the test.

GED Science Test Structure

The GED® Science test consists of 35 questions based on a variety of materials, including brief texts, graphics, and tables.

Multiple-Choice Questions

This is the main question type on the GED® Science test, and it is designed to evaluate your ability to apply general science concepts to various problem-solving and critical-thinking questions. Each multiple-choice question is followed by four answer choices labeled **a** through **d.** You will be instructed to select the best answer to the question. There is no penalty for guessing.

Fill-in-the-Blank Questions

For fill-in-the-blank questions, you will be given a sentence or paragraph that includes a blank. You must manually type your answer into this blank. There will be no choices from which to select your answer.

Drag-and-Drop Questions

For drag-and-drop items, you will need to click on the correct object, hold down the mouse, and drag the object to the appropriate place in the problem, diagram, chart, or graph.

Hot-Spot Questions

Hot-spot questions require you to click on an area of the screen to indicate where the correct answer is located. For instance, you may be asked to plot a point by clicking on a corresponding online graph. You can change your answer by simply clicking on another area.

Drop-Down Questions

These questions will have one or more drop-down menus with options that you can select to complete a sentence or problem. To answer the question, click your mouse on the arrow to show all of the answer choices. Then click on your chosen answer to complete the sentence or paragraph.

Short Answer Questions

The GED® Science test includes short answer questions. In these, you will be asked to respond with a short paragraph to information presented in a passage or graphic. Short answer questions are not timed separately, so you will need to watch your time when writing your response. It is recommended that you spend approximately 10 minutes on each short answer question.

Answering GED® Science Test Questions

As noted before, the test items may include a scenario that has one question or multiple questions associated with it. For example, you may read a passage about predator-prey population dynamics and review a graph that shows the numbers of rabbits and lynx over time. You then may be asked several questions about the passage and the data in the graph. Other prompts will include charts, diagrams, tables, and brief text passages.

Problem-solving questions will ask you to *apply* your understanding of information presented as part of the question. Questions of this type could require you to:

- interpret results or draw conclusions based on results
- analyze experimental flaws or logical fallacies in arguments
- make a prediction based on information provided in the question
- select the best procedure or method to accomplish a scientific goal
- select a diagram that best illustrates a principle
- apply scientific knowledge to everyday life
- use the work of renowned scientists to explain everyday global issues

Test Topics

The science topics covered on the GED® Science test are:

- Physical science—40% of the questions
- Life science—40% of the questions
- Earth and space science—20% of the questions

On the GED® Science test, physical science includes high school physics and chemistry, life science deals with subjects covered in high school biology classes, and earth and space science questions cover high school earth science and astronomy. You should be familiar with the concepts listed and use the content review chapters following to help you refresh your knowledge of them.

NOTE

All the information you will need to answer the questions on the GED® Science test is actually within the passages themselves. The GED® test questions test your ability to read and comprehend scientific information; they do *not* test your memory or knowledge of science.

The review chapters in this book will give you a solid background of the sciences you must know to succeed on the exam, so you can read the passages with ease and clarity. The science review chapters in this book will also give you practice reading scientific language, and the practice questions throughout will test your ability to comprehend what you have read, just as the GED® test asks you to do.

Science Practices and Review Chapters

In the next chapter, we will review the science practice skills in more detail. These skills, as noted previously, are used in each question to measure the critical thinking and reasoning ability necessary for scientific inquiry. These skills include comprehending scientific presentations, designing investigations or experiments, reasoning from data, and using probability and statistics in a scientific context. Reviewing these skills is key to doing well on the GED® Science test.

The other chapters in this section of the book include a basic review of the three science areas covered on the GED® Science test: life science, physical science, and earth and space science.

Let's get started with reviewing what you need to do well on the GED® Science test!

9 ▶ SCIENCE PRACTICES

S cience practices can be best described as the skills necessary for understanding scientific concepts using critical thinking and reasoning, as well as reading comprehension and quantitative analysis, or mathematical comprehension. In short, you can think of them as comprehension, analysis, and solving skills.

While it's relatively easy to simply describe these skills, it is also still necessary for you to review them in preparation for the test in the same way that runners train their muscles in preparation for a marathon. So let's start doing some laps, or reviewing some of these specific skills! All answers and explanations for the practice questions throughout are at the end of the chapter.

Comprehending Scientific Presentations

Scientific data and presentations are encountered every day in life, as well as on the GED® Science test. You might find scientific concepts and data in a newspaper or magazine article, a TV program, or an advertisement. Regardless, there are several important things that you must be able to do so that you can understand what is being presented:

- *Understand the textual information being presented.* What is the presenter trying to say by his or her words or language? Do you know the meaning of the scientific terms (jargon) being used?
- *Understand any symbolic or mathematical representations.* Scientists often use symbols or abbreviations to represent scientific quantities (e.g., forces, chemical formulas, biological quantities). In many presentations, they use mathematical equations that represent the relationships between scientific phenomena.
- *Understand visual information.* Do you remember the saying that "a picture is worth a thousand words"? Scientists often present information visually in the form of graphs, tables, and diagrams. Visual representations shorten the amount of text or spoken words necessary to convey information and can clearly show relationships between scientific phenomena.

These three skills encompass comprehending a scientific presentation as a whole and are necessary for understanding the questions you may be asked in the GED® Science test.

Let's look at these in detail.

Understand the Textual Information Being Presented

In life and on the GED® Science test, scientific information is often presented in written form. On the test, you will be asked to read short passages full of scientific information. Within these passages, there will be a wealth of important ideas that you must be able to recognize. There may be obstacles to recognizing the ideas (such as unfamiliar vocabulary terms); however, there will also often be clues to help you navigate around these obstacles.

As an example, read the following passage and consider how you would analyze the information in it.

ANATOMY OF MUSCLES

Muscles are made of bundles of cells wrapped in connective tissue called *fascicles*. Each bundle contains many cylindrical muscle cells or muscle fibers. Like other cells, muscle fibers have mitochondria that provide energy, a plasma membrane that separates the inside and outside of the cell, and endoplasmic reticulum, where proteins are made. However, muscle cells are different from other cells in several ways. First, muscle cells have more than one nucleus. Second, the muscle cell's plasma membrane surrounds bundles of cylindrical myofibrils that contain protein filaments and regularly folds into the deep parts of the fiber to form a transverse tubule or T-tubule. Third, the muscle cell's endoplasmic reticulum is called sarcoplasmic reticulum; it is regularly structured, envelops the myofibrils, and ends near the T-tubule in sacs called *terminal cisternae*.

Here are some tips to help you with analyzing this information:

1. **Look at the title.**
   The title tells us that the passage is going to be about the *structure or anatomy of muscles*.
2. **Look at patterns in the information, such as patterns in the subjects.**
   The subjects of the sentences all have *muscle* in common. The pattern of *muscle* as the subject of each sentence also provides a clue as to the subject of the entire passage. So, what do you think is the main purpose of this passage? The main purpose of this passage is to *describe the structure of muscles*.

3. **Look for details in the sentences and note them on scratch paper.**

   One detail is that the second sentence mentions that bundles contain many *cylindrical* cells.

4. **Look for similarities and differences in the information.**

   The fifth sentence of the passage states, *First, muscle cells have more than one nucleus.* This sentence shows one of the differences between muscle cells and other cells.

5. **Use context clues (*called, or*) to define unfamiliar terms.**

   ... bundles of cells wrapped in connective tissue called fascicles. The word *called* connects the term with its definition.

   ... many cylindrical muscle cells or muscle fibers. The word *or* connects the term *fibers* with another more familiar term, *cells*.

6. **Note information set off by commas and by *that* clauses.**

   For example, *a plasma membrane that separates the inside and outside of the cell* reveals that the function of the plasma membrane is to separate the inside from the outside of the cell.

Note that each sentence provides more details about the subject. You may need to write details down on scratch paper, especially for long reading passages. By looking at details in each sentence, you can gather important information. GED® test questions often focus on details to assess your comprehension of the passage.

Practice

1. According to the passage, what is the shape of a muscle cell?
   a. sphere
   b. cylinder
   c. disc
   d. cube

Notice that the passage also describes both how muscle cells are like other cells and how they are different from other cells. There are clues in the sentences:

- *Like other cells, muscle fibers have mitochondria . . . , plasma membrane . . . , and endoplasmic reticulum.*
- *However, muscle cells are different from other cells in several ways.* (The next sentences detail the ways that muscle cells are different.)

Looking at how the information is similar and how it is different can help you interpret the main ideas of the information presented. The GED® Science test often assesses whether you can distinguish differences stated in scientific presentations.

Practice

2. Which is a difference between a muscle cell and another type of cell?
   a. Only muscle cells have mitochondria.
   b. The plasma membrane separates the inside from the outside of the cell.
   c. Muscle cells have more than one nucleus.
   d. Muscle cells do not have endoplasmic reticulum.

Understand Symbols, Terms, and Phrases in Scientific Presentations

The GED® Science test also uses symbols (scientific and mathematical), chemical formulas, and equations (mathematical, chemical) to present information. Since you won't be supplied with a science formula sheet on test day, any mathematical equations will have to be defined in context. Let's look at an example.

LIGHT WAVES AND THEIR PROPERTIES

In the late seventeenth century, Isaac Newton explained light as consisting of particles. But in the early twentieth century, physicists began explaining light not as a particle, but rather as a wave. A wave is a periodic oscillation. The shape of a wave starts from a zero level and increases to the highest point or crest. Then it decreases past zero to its lowest level or trough. From the trough, it rises again to zero and another crest. This wave pattern repeats itself over time.

The wave has three properties that describe it: amplitude, wavelength, and frequency.

Amplitude (A) is the distance from the zero point to the crest of the wave and has the SI unit of meters (m). Wavelength (λ) is the distance from the peak of one wave to the peak of the next wave or the trough of one wave to the trough of the next wave; λ has the International System of Units (SI) unit of meters (m). The frequency (ν) is the number of wave cycles per unit time; the SI unit of frequency is the hertz (Hz). The speed of a wave is the product of the wavelength and the frequency. In the case of a light wave, the speed of light (c) is a constant (3×10^8 m/s) and is described by this formula: $c = \lambda\nu$. The wavelengths of light vary from extremely short gamma rays ($\lambda < 10^{-12}$ m) to very long radio waves ($\lambda > 1$ m).

This passage is loaded with many concepts, terms, and symbols, and an equation:

- **New terms:** *wave, periodic, oscillation, crest, trough, amplitude, wavelength, frequency*
- **Symbols:** A, λ, ν, c
- **Units:** m, Hz, m/s
- **Equation:** $c = \lambda\nu$

Most of the terms are clearly defined in sentences of the passage. For example, we are told the specific meanings of *wave, amplitude, wavelength,* and *frequency*. The terms *crest* and *trough* we can get by the word *or*, which relates the term to its meaning—for example, *to the highest point or crest* and *to its lowest level or trough*. The terms *periodic* and *oscillation* you will either know or have to think about or deduce from the reading and the sentence that states, *This wave pattern repeats itself over time.*

Symbols and units are often shown in parentheses after their first mention.

Notice that the formula is stated in words (*The speed of a wave is the product of the wavelength and the frequency*) and in mathematical symbols ($c = \lambda\nu$).

Let's look at another example.

COMBINATION REACTION

Oxygen is a very corrosive substance and will combine with many other substances or oxidize other substances. A common example is that of a piece of iron left out in the air. Over time, the iron rusts. The rust is a chemical change and can be described by a chemical reaction. Four atoms of solid iron (Fe) combine with three molecules of gaseous oxygen (O_2) from the air to form two molecules of solid iron oxide (Fe_2O_3). The chemical reaction can be written by this chemical equation:

$$4Fe(s) + 3O_2(g) \rightarrow 2Fe_2O_3(s)$$

This class of chemical reaction is called a *combination reaction.*

The terms *oxidize* and *combination reaction* may be unfamiliar. You can get the meaning of *oxidize* from the first sentence, *Oxygen is a very corrosive substance and will combine with many other substances or oxidize other substances.* *Oxidize* thus means to combine with oxygen, and the two words sound similar.

Similarly, a *combination reaction* is one where molecules combine together. You can get this from the word *combine* in the fifth sentence, where the chemical reaction is described.

Practice

3. Using the information presented in the passage, write each substance's symbol below its name in the table.

- Fe_2O_3
- Fe
- O_2

IRON	OXYGEN	IRON OXIDE

Understand and Explain Visual Scientific Presentations

Humans are visual animals, and many of us learn difficult concepts more easily by visual means. Visual scientific presentations often take the form of charts and graphs. On the GED® Science test, you may be required to understand a graphic like a diagram or table and put its meaning into words. You need to be able to restate or translate information into different formats. When you see this type of presentation, first determine the purpose. What is it trying to illustrate or convey?

Graphs

Simply put, a **graph** is a diagram that shows a relationship between two or more things. For example:

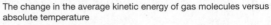
The change in the average kinetic energy of gas molecules versus absolute temperature

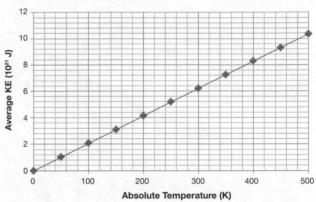

Using the title and headings, you should be able to identify that this graph represents the relationship between the *average kinetic energy (KE) of gas molecules* and *absolute temperature*. What do you think the numbers on the graph represent?

In this graph, the numbers on the horizontal (right-to-left) axis, or ***x*-axis**, represent the temperature in degrees Kelvin (K), and the numbers on the vertical (down-to-up) axis, or ***y*-axis**, represent the average kinetic energy (KE) of gas molecules.

It's important to note the axis labels. Looking at the vertical or *y*-axis, for example, you see that the numbers are labeled 2, 4, 6, 8, 10, and 12. But if you look at the axis label, each number represents 10^{21} joules (J), not whole numbers. This distinction could be very important if you were asked to answer questions based on the graph. The points are plotted on the graph and connected by a line to show the linear, or direct, relationship between these two factors.

The graph in this example correlates just two things. However, a graph can correlate more than two things at a time. When this happens, the additional data sets are usually graphed in another color or pattern to avoid confusion. If there is more than one data set or more than one variable, a **legend** will help you interpret the graph. It will list the symbols, colors, or patterns used to label a particular data set.

For example, in the following graph the legend lists atmospheric CO_2, seawater pCO_2, and seawater pH.

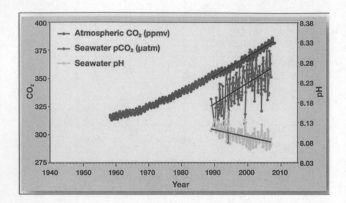

A look at the vertical axes and the legend tells you that this graph shows the correlation between the changes in carbon dioxide (CO_2) levels in the atmosphere and the ocean over time, as well as the pH of seawater over time.

Tables and Charts

Tables have horizontal rows and vertical columns. The data entries in a single row of a table or chart usually have something in common. The same is true for the data entries in a single column. **Charts** are often used to show trends. Look for changes in numerical values to spot those trends.

The following chart detailing the pH scale uses images and numbers to demonstrate what the different pH numbers actually mean. The chart has an arrow that describes a continuum of conditions from acidic through neutral to basic, and there is a color scale that shows this continuum. There are three columns of numbers. One shows the pH of a substance. The other two show the concentrations of hydrogen ions (H^+), one with numbers in scientific notation and the other in actual decimal numbers. Note that

the symbol for hydrogen ions (H^+) is used but not defined. Some abbreviations, like chemical symbols, are often assumed.

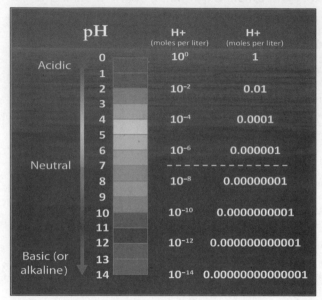

Practice

4. Look at the pH scale. What is its range?

_____

5. Notice that the concentrations of hydrogen ions correspond to values of pH. If a chemist measures a solution with a pH value of 9, what is the hydrogen ion concentration?
   a. 10^{-9} moles per liter
   b. 10^9 moles per liter
   c. $\frac{1}{9}$ mole per liter
   d. 9.0 moles per liter

6. From the arrow on the left, notice that acidic substances have pH values less than 7, while basic substances have pH values greater than 7. If a chemist measures that a solution has a pH value of 5.5, this indicates the solution is

- acidic.
- alkaline.
- neutral.

Diagrams

Diagrams are often used to show processes on the GED® Science test. In the following diagram of the water cycle, you can see that there are three main places for water to be exchanged among the oceans and rivers, the atmosphere, and the ground. Pay attention to any labeled features and arrows. Generally, arrows connect processes. In this case, arrows show the direction of water flow, and the terms name the processes.

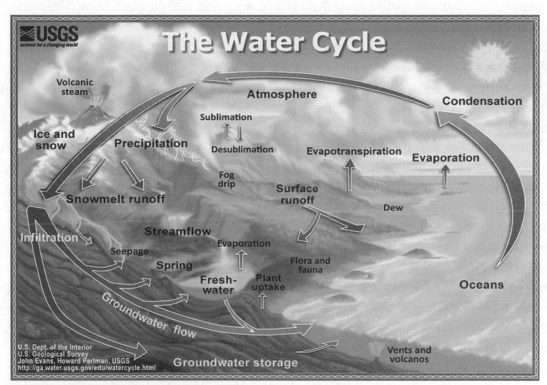

Source: http://water.usgs.gov/edu/watercycle.html.

Practice

7. In this diagram, what is the name of the process that moves water directly from bodies of water into the atmosphere? _____

8. Which way does water move during infiltration?
   a. from air into the ground
   b. from ground up to the surface
   c. from surface down into the ground
   d. from surface into the air

The key to understanding any type of scientific presentation is reading and looking carefully and critically. This type of careful evaluation will allow you to interpret which pieces of information go together, to determine relationships, and to clarify explanations.

Designing Investigations

Good scientific investigations begin with a question that often asks *What if?*, *How?*, or *What effect will something have?* The question should be one that can be investigated through experimentation and will then yield data. The experiment should also be repeatable. This allows other people to replicate the experiment to verify that the results stay the same.

On the GED® Science test, you will be provided descriptions of an experiment in a reading passage and the results in a table or in graph form. From the description, you will be asked to evaluate the design of the experiment. You will also be asked about the results and conclusions from the experiment based on the results. So, it is important that you know how scientific investigations work.

Scientific investigations are hypothesis driven. A **hypothesis** is a predictive answer to a question. It is an explanation on trial, one that can be tested. Deductive reasoning is used to test a hypotheses. The test is accomplished by designing and conducting an experiment. The experiment yields results (data). If the experiment was designed and conducted correctly and the data fit what was predicted by the hypothesis, then the experimenter must conclude that the hypothesis was correct. Otherwise, the experimenter must reject the current hypothesis and change it or form a new one. This scientific method is the basis of science. No hypothesis is accepted just because the scientist or others believe it is true; it must be testable and withstand experimental trial by many experiments conducted by different scientists before it is accepted.

To evaluate these scientific investigations, ask these questions:

- What was the hypothesis?
- What was the independent variable?
- What was/were the dependent variable(s)?
- What were the other variables, and were they controlled?
- Were the measurement methods appropriate to what was being measured?
- Was the number of samples adequate?
- Overall, was the experimental design appropriate to test the hypothesis?

Let's look at the scientific method as it applies to experiments and experimental design topics on the GED® Science test.

Identify Possible Sources of Error and Change an Investigation to Remove the Error

In science, the word *error* doesn't always mean *mistake*; it might mean that there is uncertainty in the design. A source of error is any factor that could affect the outcome of the investigation. There are numerous possibilities for error in any experiment, so you will want to focus on the factors that matter the most.

When evaluating the design of an experiment for errors, ask yourself these questions:

- *Is the hypothesis of the experiment testable?* For example, a teenage student wants to assess a claim that a new acne product improves the condition of the skin. If the student merely takes the word of celebrity endorsers, does that mean the product works well? If the student conducts an experiment to measure the incidence of acne upon treatment with the product, then that is a way to test the hypothesis.

- *Does what the experimenter measured reflect what is predicted by the hypothesis?* For example, if the hypothesis predicts that a treatment for acne reduces the incidence of blemishes, then does the investigator measure the number of blemishes over an area of the skin with time or the rate at which blemishes disappear?

- *Does the experiment have a control group?* A control is an experimental treatment where all the variables that affect the experimental group are the same except one—the one that is testing the hypothesis. For example, in an experiment to test acne medication, there might be a group of people who do not receive the acne medication but who are studied for the same amount of time, eat the same type of foods, are the same age and sex, and so on. The results from the experimental group are compared to those of the control group to test the hypothesis.

- *Is the experimental method specified in enough detail so that another investigator could repeat the experiment?* Remember that experiments must be able to be repeated by others and must produce the same results so that the hypothesis can be evaluated. In the example of acne medication, does the experimental procedure specify how much medication should be applied to the skin and how often? Does the procedure mention anything about how often the subjects should wash their faces?

- *Are there enough subjects or samples in each group to represent a more general population?* For example, if the acne medication study looks at only four people (one teenage male and three teenage girls), are these groups sufficient to represent the larger population of teenagers?

- *Is the data gathered accurately and precisely?* For example, in the acne study, does the investigator count the number of blemishes, note their size, note the area over which they occurred, or measure the length of time that they remained visible?

Practice

Read the following experimental design carefully. Critically review it to identify possible sources of error. Then, explain how that source of error would have affected the results. Think about specific things that can change the end result of the experiment.

MEAT TENDERIZER EXPERIMENT

A group of students wants to know what effect meat tenderizer will have on starches, fats, and proteins.

The group hypothesizes that meat tenderizer will break down proteins but not starches or fats.

They formulate the following experimental design:

1. Add water to six jars.
2. Add 9 grams of meat tenderizer to three of the jars of water, and stir until dissolved.
3. Place one sample of starch, of fat, and of protein in each of the three jars that contain meat tenderizer.
4. Place one sample of starch, of fat, and of protein in the three remaining jars.
5. Put lids on all six jars.
6. Observe changes after 24 hours.

9. What possible sources of errors do you see in this design? Is the hypothesis stated adequately to make a predictable result? Write your response on the lines below.

_____

_____

_____

10. Look at the first step of the experimental design. Is there something not specified?

_____

_____

_____

11. What about step 2? Is there something not specified?

_____

_____

_____

12. What is unclear about steps 3 and 4?

_____

_____

_____

13. What is unclear about step 6?

_____

_____

_____

Consider this example:

SLEEPINESS EXPERIMENT

Ruby and Mary are identical twins. They are often sleepy at noontime while attending their science class. They want to know why they frequently fall asleep at this time of day. Possible explanations might include:

- Eating a big lunch right before science class every day makes the twins sleepy.
- The classroom is too warm.
- The twins are less engaged in this class because they sit at the back of the room, instead of at the front as in the rest of their classes.
- The science teacher has a monotonous voice that Mary and Ruby find boring.
- Ruby and Mary become tired at noontime every day.

Identify and Refine Hypotheses for Investigation

Asking questions and defining problems are essential to the investigative process. Once those questions have been asked, the next step is trying to find and investigate the answer.

A **hypothesis** is a prediction, an attempted answer to the question being investigated. A hypothesis attempts to predict the outcome of the experiment and suggests one or more possible reasons for the results. A good hypothesis should be based on observations and prior knowledge.

Each of these possible explanations for the twins falling asleep in class is a potential hypothesis. A hypothesis should be stated in a way that allows you to make a prediction that can be investigated by experiments or more observation. Proposing more than one hypothesis can be a good scientific practice.

Last, hypotheses can be eliminated—but not confirmed—with 100% certainty.

Let's rephrase two of the possible explanations into questions to show how they might be tested.

Possible Explanation: *Eating a big lunch right before science class every day makes the twins sleepy.*

Question 1:	Does eating a big lunch before science class make them sleepy?
Hypothesis 1:	If the twins become sleepy because they eat a big lunch before the noon class, then postponing lunch should make them less sleepy.
Suggested Experiment:	Ruby postpones lunch until science is over at 1 P.M., whereas Mary still eats lunch at 11 A.M.
Predicted Result:	Ruby should be less tired and Mary should still be sleepy in science class.

Possible Explanation: *The twins are less engaged in this class because they sit at the back of the room, instead of at the front as in the rest of their classes.*

Question 2:	Are Mary and Ruby less engaged in this class because they sit at the back of the room, instead of at the front as in the rest of their classes?
Hypothesis 2:	If the twins become sleepy in the noon class because they sit in the back of the room, then moving to the front of the room should make them less sleepy.
Suggested Experiment:	Ruby moves to the front of the room, while Mary remains in the back.
Predicted Result:	Ruby should be less tired and more alert than Mary, and Mary should be sleepy during the science class.

Notice the *If . . . then . . .* format of the two hypotheses. It is not required that you format a hypothesis this way. However, it can provide you with a simple way to make sure that your hypothesis fits the criteria of a testable prediction.

Practice
Try this example.

DOG FOOD EXPERIMENT

Jim has two overweight dachshunds. He sees an advertisement for a new reduced-calorie dog food that claims to allow the dogs to eat normally but still lose weight.

14. Propose a hypothesis to test the claim in the advertisement. What is the hypothesis, suggested experiment, and predicted result?
Hypothesis:

_____

_____

_____

Suggested experiment:

_____

Predicted result:

_____

_____

Identify and Interpret Variables in Investigations
On the GED® Science test you might be asked to identify the different variables in an investigation, so understanding and being able to spot these variables are an important skill. **Variables** are factors in an

experiment that can be *changed*, *measured*, or *controlled*:

- **Independent variables** are the manipulated variables. They are the factors that will be intentionally changed during the investigation to find out what effect they have on something else. Usually, time is an independent variable because the investigator can always decide how long to look at something.
- **Dependent variables** are the responding variables. These are the factors that are observed and measured to see if they are affected by the change made in the independent variable.
- **Controls** are variables that must be kept exactly the same to make sure that they do not affect the dependent variable.

WEED KILLER EXPERIMENT

James wants to know how effective a weed killer is in preventing the growth of dandelions. James sets up an experiment with the following procedures to test the effectiveness of the weed killer.

1. Take two identical areas of grass and label them 1 and 2.
2. Apply the weed killer to area 2.
3. Seed both areas with the same number of dandelion seeds.
4. Water the areas daily with the same amount of water.
5. Expose the areas to the same amount of sunlight and temperature.
6. Once they bloom, count the number of dandelions in each area once a day for one week.
7. Record the results.

In this experiment:

- The **independent variable** is the weed killer. It is the manipulated factor that is being tested because James wants to find out what effect it has on something else.
- The **dependent variable** is the number of dandelions growing in the areas of grass. The number of dandelions is the responding variable, the factor that is observed and measured to see if it is affected by the changes made by the presence or absence of the weed killer.
- There are six **controlled variables**—the identical areas of grass, amounts of dandelions seeded, amounts of water used daily, lighting and temperature, and time of investigation.

Identify Strengths and Weaknesses of Investigation Designs

Experimental designs are not just about a list of procedures. It is important to understand the weaknesses and the strengths of a design. While a well-written list of procedures can be a strength of a scientific investigation, there are more factors at work. For example:

- Does the investigation have a clear purpose?
- Can the stated problem really be investigated using the designed procedures?
- Are the objectives measurable?
- Are the planned procedures appropriate to the project?
- Can the data be analyzed in a meaningful way?
- What are the financial and time costs involved in the experiment and analysis?
- Is there any potential harm to the subjects?
- Is the investigation repeatable by others?
- Are there safeguards to minimize bias and invalidity?

Here is a description of a student's scientific investigation. Read it to identify the strengths and weaknesses of the design. Look at each sentence and try to analyze what might help or hurt the investigation.

VITAMINS AND GROWTH EXPERIMENT

Andrew is studying the effect of vitamins on the growth of mice. His hypothesis is that mice receiving a daily vitamin will grow faster than those not receiving the vitamin. To test his hypothesis, he follows these procedures. He obtains two identical mice and places them in the same cage. He feeds them the same food and the same amount of water. One mouse gets 5 milligrams of vitamin powder sprinkled on its food every day, while the other does not. He weighs the mice daily, giving them an edible treat if they cooperate during the handling and weighing.

First, the strengths of this experimental design:

- The hypothesis is measurable and testable.
- The independent variable is clearly identified as the vitamin. The dependent variable is identified as the growth of the mice as measured by changes in weight.

Now, some of the weaknesses:

- Are only two mice (one control, one experimental) sufficient to represent a larger population?
- The mice are identical, but there is no mention of a way to identify which mouse gets the vitamin and which does not.

- The mice are placed in the same cage, meaning that they both have access to the food sprinkled with the vitamin. This may invalidate the data.
- Has the vitamin been approved for use in mice? Can the mice be harmed by ingesting the vitamin?
- Giving the mice an edible treat at unspecified intervals introduces another independent variable.

Practice

Use the passage to answer the questions that follow.

PAINT DURABILITY EXPERIMENT

A paint company has developed a new brand of outdoor latex paint (Brand X) that it thinks might be more durable than another company's brand (Brand Y). To save money, the company paints boards of different scrap wood with Brand X and Brand Y paints. Employees paint boards with the same number of coats of paint and measure the paint thickness of each board. They place matched boards painted with Brand X and Brand Y in different environments (desert, temperate forest, arctic tundra) for 12 months. After 12 months, they measure the paint thickness of each board again. They find that the boards painted with Brand Y have thinner coats of paint than those painted with Brand X. They conclude that Brand X is more durable than Brand Y.

15. What is the hypothesis of this experiment?

_____

_____

_____

16. Is this hypothesis testable? _____

17. Identify the controlled and uncontrolled factors in the experiment. Write each of the experiment factors in the correct table column.

Controlled	Uncontrolled

- The boards were painted with the same number of coats to the same paint thickness.
- The boards were matched in size.
- Weather conditions varied.
- The boards were made of different woods.
- The boards were exposed to the same weather conditions for the same amount of time.

Design a Scientific Investigation

Planning and designing scientific investigations requires the ability to test a hypothesis that has been formed. As you've learned, the investigator needs to identify the important variables and determine how they might be observed, measured, and controlled. In fact, being able to control factors in the experiment is critical to the investigation. In many instances, especially investigations that take place outside of the laboratory, there are often conditions that are outside the control of the investigator.

The investigator must also make decisions about what measurements will be taken and what instruments are best suited to making those measurements. Because precision is a key issue, it is important to measure the variable as accurately as possible. This will reduce sources of error in the experimental design.

An important part of the investigation is the data that is produced. Selecting an appropriate format in which to record data is also part of good experimental design.

Now let's design an experiment. Here's the question:

> **Does Fertilizer A help plants grow faster than Fertilizer B?**

First, identify what variables will be tested and what variables should be controlled. Fertilizers A and B should be applied to the same type of plant. This makes the type of plant one of your controls.

Should all the plants be fertilized?
No, there should be a control that has no fertilizer for comparison to make sure that both types of fertilizer are working. For the plants that are being fertilized, the amount of fertilizer being applied should be the same.

Should one plant get more sunlight or water or be exposed to different temperatures than the other experimental plant?
No. Water, temperature, and amount of light should also be controls, as well as the length of the experiment (time).

What will be the independent variable?
The type of fertilizer

What will be the dependent variable?
The plant growth

Now that these decisions have been made, writing a set of procedures for the investigative design will allow you to follow the guidelines and carry out the experiment.

The scientific investigative procedures might look something like this when you are finished:

FERTILIZERS AND GROWTH EXPERIMENT

1. Take 30 bean sprouts of equal height and weight, potted in identical containers with identical types and amounts of soil. Label the bean sprouts: Plant 1, Plant 2, Plant 3, . . . Plant 30.
2. Place each of the plants on the windowsill of a room with controlled temperature.
3. Treat Plants 1–10 with 4 grams of Fertilizer A every day at 7:30 A.M.
4. Treat Plants 11–20 with 4 grams of Fertilizer B every day at 7:30 A.M.
5. Do not fertilize Plants 21–30.
6. Water each plant at 8 A.M. daily. Give each plant 20 milliliters of water.
7. Measure the height of each plant with a metric ruler daily at 5 P.M.
8. Record the measurements.

Reasoning from Data

On the GED® Science test you will be expected to evaluate and verify various sources of data to form a hypothesis, come to a conclusion, or answer a question. You should be prepared to make sense of information from a variety of texts, data sets, and models. Applying scientific reasoning to this process will help you link evidence to claims and assess how data supports conclusions. You may also be asked to use statistical data in mathematical ways to determine probabilities or statistical variance. For each of these expectations, you should be able to interpret tables, diagrams, charts, and other texts; to explain and predict causal relationships; and to arrive at conclusions. This lesson will help you review and practice these important skills.

Use Evidence to Support a Finding or Conclusion

On test day you may be asked to gather information to support a finding or conclusion. In these cases, you will be provided with a written source—some sort of scientific literature or technical information. Now, what do you do with it?

First, critically read the source to determine the central, or main, ideas. Look for any conclusions the author may have made based on evidence presented in the source. Compare and evaluate the sources of information to see if they support the finding or conclusion with which you have been presented.

What specifically are you looking for? Here are some suggestions:

- Look for valid and reliable claims that are verified with data.
- Examine the method or design of the investigation that produced the data. Remember that if the investigation that produced the data is flawed, then the data itself is flawed.
- Evaluate the reliability of the sources of information. Reliable sources may include government institutions, universities, and some non-profit institutions.
- When possible, combine information from a variety of sources to establish evidence and resolve any conflicting information.

Read the following excerpt.

ARE BIOFUELS THE ANSWER?

As the world searches for alternatives to petroleum, corn-based ethanol and other biofuels derived from organic material have been considered as the perfect answer to transportation fuel problems. In fact, a U.S. government energy bill mandates that over 30 billion gallons of biofuels a year be used by the year 2020. However, separate studies released by the Nature Conservancy and Ivy League institutions reveal that ethanol may not be the best answer in the fight against global warming. They say using biofuels could make things worse.

Biofuel crops, such as corn and sugar cane, remove carbon from Earth's atmosphere while they are growing. When biofuels are burned, they emit fewer greenhouse gases than fossil fuels like coal or oil. This makes biofuels almost carbon-neutral. However, studies are showing that ethanol could be even more dangerous for the environment than fossil fuels. The Ivy League study noted that clearing previously untouched land to grow biofuel crops releases long-contained carbon into the atmosphere. While planting biofuel crops in already tilled land is all right, the problem arises when farmers disturb new land to grow more sugar cane or corn. Additionally, food and feed crops are being displaced by biofuel crops. The Nature Conservancy warns that "converting rainforests, peat lands, savannas, or grasslands to produce biofuels in Brazil, Southeast Asia, and the United States creates a 'biofuel carbon debt' by releasing 17 to 420 times more carbon dioxide than the fossil fuels they replace." Other negative effects include the extreme amounts of water needed for irrigation, runoffs from pesticides and fertilizers, and the natural gas used to make the fertilizers that adds to the carbon deficit.

Your task is to gather information that supports the conclusion that corn-based ethanol is not a sustainable source of transportation fuel for the future. Let's look at information in the passage and address the points mentioned earlier.

Are the claims in the article from reliable sources?

The article mentions studies released by the Nature Conservancy and Ivy League institutions. These institutions generally count as reliable and valid sources.

Are they verified with supporting data?

This article excerpt does not include copies of the data from the studies it mentions. However, the quote from the Nature Conservancy does provide some supporting data for the answer: "converting rainforests, peat lands, savannas, or grasslands to produce biofuels in Brazil, Southeast Asia, and the United States creates a 'biofuel carbon debt' by releasing 17 to 420 times more carbon dioxide than the fossil fuels they replace."

Are there various sources to help establish evidence and resolve conflicting information?

Yes, the article cites reports from the Nature Conservancy, Ivy League institutions, and a U.S. government energy bill.

Let's combine the evidence supporting the claims that ethanol is not a sustainable source of transportation fuel:

- Clearing previously untouched land to grow bio-fuel crops releases long-contained carbon into the atmosphere.
- Growing biofuel crops displaces food and feed crops.
- Biofuel crops need extreme amounts of water for irrigation.
- Treating fields of biofuel crops with pesticides and fertilizers creates pollution when these chemicals run off into waterways.
- Making fertilizers for growing biofuel crops requires natural gas, which adds to the carbon deficit.

Taken together, all of these points support the idea that growing biofuel crops for transportation is not sustainable and may be worse than burning the fossil fuels that they are intended to replace.

Use Data to Arrive at a Conclusion

Another important scientific practice skill is that of using data or evidence to arrive at a conclusion. To do this well on the GED® Science test, you need to synthesize information from the sources with which you are provided. The sources might include texts, experimental results, models, or data sets. Critically read the information provided to you. You will need to interpret the tables, diagrams, charts, and any coordinating information. Then, apply scientific reasoning to arrive at a conclusion. Take a look at the following example.

AVOIDING VITAMIN D DEFICIENCY

Approximately one billion people worldwide have vitamin D deficiency. This deficiency is thought to be largely due to insufficient exposure to the sun. In some cases, poor diet can also play a role. There is increasing evidence that vitamin D deficiency also increases a person's susceptibility to autoimmune conditions. Additionally, a lack of vitamin D can impact bone development.

The main source of vitamin D in the body comes from exposing the skin to sunlight. Just 10 minutes of exposure to ultraviolet B radiation wavelengths between 280 and 315 nm, five days a week, will give most people enough vitamin D. However, extended exposure to ultraviolet radiation from the sun is known to increase the risk of skin cancer. Widespread campaigns for the use of sunscreen and sun avoidance have reduced the incidences of skin cancers. However, sunscreens with sun protection factors of 15 or higher also decrease the body's ability to synthesize vitamin D by 99%.

RADIATION TYPE	UVA	UVB	UVC
linked to	aging	burning	
wavelength	400 nm to 315 nm	315 nm to 280 nm	280 nm to 100 nm
% reaching Earth at noon	0.95	0.05	0%—absorbed by ozone, molecular oxygen, and water vapor in the upper atmosphere
% reaching Earth before 10 a.m. and after 2 p.m.	0.99	0.01	0
% reaching Earth (average)	0.97	0.03	0

What are the consequences of vitamin D deficiency?

Poor bone development and autoimmune disease

How do we make vitamin D?

Exposure to ultraviolet radiation

What type of radiation is necessary to make vitamin D?

UVB radiation (315 to 289 nm)

How much daily sunlight exposure is necessary to make vitamin D?

10 minutes

From information in the passage, what are the apparent contradictions regarding vitamin D deficiency and sunlight exposure?

While exposure to ultraviolet radiation is important for your body to make vitamin D, it also puts you at risk for cancer.

So, how can we resolve this contradiction and come to a conclusion? Let's look at the information further.

When does the amount of UVA reaching the Earth peak?

Before 10 A.M. and after 2 P.M.

When does the amount of UVB reaching the Earth peak?

Noon

Does wearing sunscreen reduce UV exposure?

Yes, when the SPF value is greater than 15.

Now, let's put all the information together to draw a conclusion about how we can safely expose our skin to ultraviolet radiation to make vitamin D but minimally risk skin cancer:

SYNTHESIZING VITAMIN D SAFELY

A daily exposure of ten minutes of UVB sunlight therapy at noon has been shown to reduce risks of autoimmune disease and improve bone health. UVB peaks at noon, while UVA peaks before 10 A.M. and after 2 P.M. So, by going outside for 10 minutes around noon and wearing a sunscreen with an SPF factor less than 15, we can have beneficial sunlight therapy for vitamin D synthesis with a relatively low risk of skin cancer associated with exposure to ultraviolet radiation.

Note that we used multiple pieces of scientific information in the passage and the data table to come to a conclusion regarding the risks and benefits of exposure to sunlight for vitamin D therapy.

Practice

Use the following information to answer questions 18 and 19.

WOLVES AND MOOSE POPULATIONS

Wolves originally crossed an ice bridge from Canada to Isle Royale, MI, and the wolf population was established. Moose were native to the island. Since the 1950s, ecologists have studied the moose and wolf populations on the island. The population data are shown in the graph.

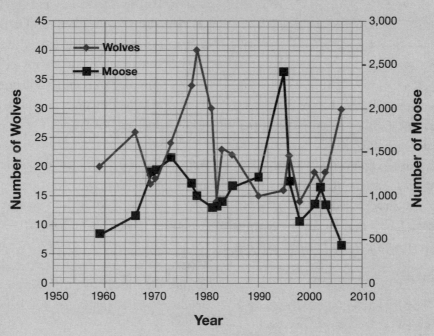

Ecologists noted several events, which are summarized in the table:

YEAR	EVENT
1964–1972	Mild winters
1972–1980	Severe winters
1981–1984	Humans' inadvertent introduction of canine parvovirus to the island
1997	Severe winter, outbreak of moose ticks, new world emigration from Canada

18. Does a stable relationship hold after 1995? Why or why not?

_____

_____

19. Based on the information, what can you conclude about the relationship between moose (prey) and wolves (predator) between 1959 and 1995?

_____

_____

_____

_____

_____

Formulating a hypothesis—a testable prediction—involves asking questions about data and claims that are made. You can ask a question about data that will lead you to analyze more evidence and make interpretations about that evidence. On the GED® Science test, you may be asked to make a prediction based on a given data set or textual evidence. As always, reading and analyzing the information critically and carefully are key.

Use Sampling Techniques to Answer Scientific Questions

Scientific questions involving sampling techniques often use statistics and probability to explain concepts such as variation and distribution in populations. To be well prepared to answer questions using this science practice, you should become familiar with the following types of statistical and probability concepts:

- **Mean** ($\overline{X}$)—the average, computed as the sum of all the observed outcomes from the sample divided by the total number of events.

- **Mode**—the number of a set of data with the highest frequency (i.e., that occurs more often than any of the other numbers in the set).
- **Median**—the middle value or score. If you have an even number of values in a set, take the average of the two middle values. The median is better for describing the typical value and is often used for income or home prices.
- **Variance** (σ^2)—a measure of how far the data is spread apart.
- **Standard deviation** (σ)—the square root of the variance, which can be thought of as measuring how far the data values lie from the mean.
- **Probability**—the likelihood of one or more events happening divided by the number of possible outcomes. If you have ever used percentages, fractions, or ratios to describe or predict the likelihood of an outcome, you have measured probability.

Here's how you'd find the mean, median, and mode for a list of values:

12, 17, 12, 13, 12, 15, 13, 20, 12

Mean

To find the mean, take the values, add them up, and divide by how many values you have.

1. Add the values. The sum is 126 (12 + 17 + 12 + 13 + 12 + 15 + 13 + 20 + 12 = 126).
2. Count up how many items or values you have added: 9.
3. Divide the sum of the values (126) by the number of values (9), and you get 14 (126 ÷ 9 = 14).

The mean, or average, is 14.

Median

To find the median, reorder the values from lowest to highest. The median will be the number in the middle. If you have an even number of values, the median will be the average of the two numbers in the middle.

1. First, put the values in order from smallest to largest: 12, 12, 12, 12, 13, 13, 15, 17, 20.
2. Then, find the number in the middle of this list. There are nine numbers in the list, so the middle one will be the fifth number: 12, 12, 12, 12, **13**, 13, 15, 17, 20.

The median is 13.

Mode

The mode refers to the value that occurs most frequently in the list. If you have a list of three numbers and one occurs twice, that will be the mode. In longer lists, it will again help to put the values in order. From then on, it's simple! Just look for the number that occurs most often:

1. Put in order from smallest to largest: 12, 12, 12, 12, 13, 13, 15, 17, 20.
2. Look for the number that occurs most often: **12, 12, 12, 12**, 13, 13, 15, 17, 20.

There are four 12s, more than any other number. The mode is 12.

Here's another example.

A restaurant owner wants to know how much customers spend at the establishment. She randomly selects 10 receipts from groups of four diners and records the following data: 44, 50, 38, 96, 42, 47, 40, 39, 46, 50

What is the average amount of money that a group of four spends at the restaurant? You learned previously that to calculate the mean, add all the numbers and divide by the number of values, in this case 10. The mean (or average) of the values is 49.2 or $49.20.

To get the variance and standard deviation of this data, you must perform the following steps:

1. First, find the mean of your given values. This step is complete—49.2. Now that you know this number, set up a table that subtracts the mean from each observed value.

Value	–	Mean	=
44	–	49.2	−5.2
50	–	49.2	0.8
38	–	49.2	−11.2
96	–	49.2	46.8
42	–	49.2	−7.2
47	–	49.2	−2.2
40	–	49.2	−9.2
39	–	49.2	−10.2
46	–	49.2	−3.2
50	–	49.2	0.8

2. Square each of the differences, and then add up all those values.

Value	–	Mean	=	x^2	=
44	–	49.2	–5.2	-5.2×-5.2	27.04
50	–	49.2	0.8	0.8×0.8	0.64
38	–	49.2	–11.2	-11.2×-11.2	125.44
96	–	49.2	46.8	46.8×46.8	2,190.24
42	–	49.2	–7.2	-7.2×-7.2	51.84
47	–	49.2	–2.2	-2.2×-2.2	4.84
40	–	49.2	–9.2	-9.2×-9.2	84.64
39	–	49.2	–10.2	-10.2×-10.2	104.04
46	–	49.2	–3.2	-3.2×-3.2	10.24
50	–	49.2	0.8	0.8×0.8	0.64
				Total:	**2,599.60**

3. Divide by $n - 1$, where n is the number of items in the sample (10). This is the variance.

$$\sigma^2_x = \frac{2,599.60}{n-1}$$

$$\sigma^2_x = \frac{2,599.60}{10-1}$$

$$\sigma^2_x = \frac{2,599.60}{9}$$

$$\sigma^2_x = 288.8 \text{ or } 289 \text{ rounded}$$

4. To get the standard deviation, take the square root of the variance:

$$\sigma_x = \sqrt{289}$$

$$\sigma_x = 17$$

The standard deviation can be thought of as measuring how far the data values lie from the mean, so take the mean and move one standard deviation in either direction.

The mean of the values was 49.2 and the standard deviation is 17.

- $49.2 - 17 = 32.2$
- $49.2 + 17 = 66.2$

Therefore, most groups of four customers spend between $32.20 and $66.20.

Now, let's look at an example of probability:

The seven days of the week are written on scraps of paper and placed into a hat. What is the probability of picking a weekend day out of the hat?

The event is choosing a day that falls on the weekend. This is what you want to answer:

1. The number of outcomes is the total number of days in a week, 7.
2. There are 2 weekend days.
3. $2 \div 7 = 0.2857$

Practice

Use a calculator for the following questions, if needed.

In an experiment, Jan records the heights in centimeters of five plants:

10.1, 9.8, 10.0, 10.1, 9.9

20. The mean height of the plants is _____ cm.

21. The median height of the plants is _____ cm.

22. The mode height of the plants is _____ cm.

Whether you are using data to form a hypothesis or a conclusion, or to support findings or probabilities, critically reading and analyzing the information is important. Take the time to identify the main idea and logically interpret the data. Do not be intimidated by large sets of data or wordy texts. Look for coordinating information. Then, evaluate how that information supports your task and use it to answer the necessary questions.

Evaluating Conclusions and Evidence

On the GED® Science test, as in life, you will have to evaluate theories, conclusions, and claims. For example, as you are viewing some page on the Internet, an advertisement might pop up and make a claim such as this: "Revolutionary new fruit lets you shed pounds!" Accompanying the claim, there may be a testimonial from some man or woman who claims to have lost 40 pounds while eating this fruit; before-and-after photos are often included. There may even be an endorsement by some celebrity as to the fruit's effectiveness for losing weight. The advertisement might link to another web page for you to buy the fruit or some extract from it. So, you must then draw some conclusion or make a judgment based on the information presented. Is there enough information? Is the information scientifically valid? Is it worth spending money on the product? Is it safe?

Evaluating scientific findings, drawing conclusions, and making judgments are what scientists do. They evaluate experiments, analyze scientific data (data obtained by themselves and others), draw conclusions, and make judgments. The conclusions and judgments help them accept or reject hypotheses and modify theories. In this section, we examine and practice such skills.

Making Judgments about Whether Theories or Conclusions are Supported or Challenged by Data or Evidence

In any scientific experiment, the hypothesis makes some sort of testable prediction. The investigator designs an experiment to test the hypothesis and gathers data. The investigator must then examine the data to determine whether the data supports or refutes the prediction made by the hypothesis. The data must be scrutinized thoroughly with a skeptical eye. As you learned previously, critical questions must be asked about the methods used in the investigation. For example, was the experimental design adequate to test the hypothesis? Were the technologies used appropriate? Were all the variables identified and properly controlled, except for the independent and dependent variables? Was the control group appropriate? Were there enough samples taken? Once such questions have been answered satisfactorily, then we have confidence about the data obtained and whether it can support or refute the hypothesis.

Let's look at an example.

BRAND X VERSUS BRAND Y FERTILIZER EXPERIMENT

A company claims that its new fertilizer, Brand X, will make plants, such as tomato plants, grow faster and produce more fruit than a leading brand by another company, Brand Y. The directions for each fertilizer indicate that they are used at the same concentration (50 g/kg soil). A scientist uses 150 tomato plant seedlings. He divides the seedlings into three groups of 50 plants. Each seedling is 10 to 12 cm high at the start of the study and is planted in a pot containing 1 kg of potting soil; the soil is identical for all groups. To one group (control), nothing is added to the soil. To a second group, 50 g of Brand Y is added to the soil of each plant. To a third group, 50 g of Brand X is added to the soil. All of the plants are grouped together in the same greenhouse at a constant temperature of 25°C. The light in the greenhouse is uniformly illuminated and all plants are exposed to a 12-hour on/off cycle. The plants are carefully watered each day with 200 mL of water each. The height of each plant is measured and recorded weekly for 20 weeks. In addition, the number of tomatoes produced by each plant is noted at the end of the experiment (week 20).

Before we examine the data, review the experimental design:

What was the hypothesis?

If tomato plants are treated with Brand X, then they should grow faster and produce more tomatoes than those treated with Brand Y or untreated.

What was the independent variable?

The amount of time that growth was measured (weeks).

What was/were the dependent variable(s)?

The average height of the tomato plants and the number of tomatoes produced per plant.

What were the other variables, and were they controlled?

Other variables were the temperature of the greenhouse as well as the amounts of soil, water, and sunlight. All of these variables were controlled.

Was the number of samples adequate?

Yes, 50 samples in each group were adequate.

Overall, was the experimental design appropriate to test the hypothesis?

Yes, the experimental design was adequate and appropriate.

Look at the data obtained from the experiment. The average height of the plants in each group is shown in the graph.

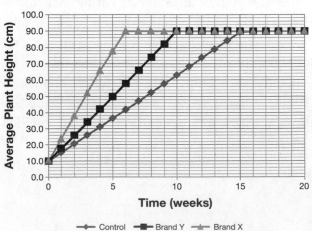

Effects of Fertilizer Treatment on Tomato Plant Growth

Here are some questions to consider when looking at the graph:

What was the maximum height of tomato plants in each group?
The maximum height was 90 cm in each group.

How long did it take each group to reach the maximum height?
The control plants took 15 weeks to reach the maximum height, while plants treated with Brand Y and Brand X took 10 weeks and 6 weeks, respectively.

Which plants grew the fastest?
Brand X grew fastest (about 13.3 cm/week). Brand Y grew the next fastest (about 8 cm/week). The control plants grew the slowest (about 5.3 cm/week).

Consider the hypothesis. Did the growth results support the prediction made in the hypothesis?
Yes, as predicted, the plants treated with Brand X fertilizer grew faster than the control plants and the Brand Y–treated plants.

Now, look at the number of tomatoes produced by the plants, as shown in the table.

EFFECT OF FERTILIZER ON TOMATO PLANT PRODUCTION	
TREATMENT	**AVERAGE NUMBER OF TOMATOES PER PLANT**
Control	3.5
Brand Y	7.2
Brand X	6.1

Use this data to answer the following questions.

Practice

23. Did treating the plants with fertilizers increase the fruit production?
    a. Yes
    b. No

24. Consider the hypothesis. Did the plants treated with Brand X produce more tomatoes than those treated with Brand Y?
    a. Yes
    b. No

25. Now that you have all this data, what would you conclude about the company's claims regarding Brand X? Remember that the company claimed Brand X would cause plants to grow faster *and* produce more fruit.

    _____

    _____

    _____

In this example, we were able to use data to evaluate a claim (hypothesis or theory) by examining the experimental procedure and then the data obtained from that experiment. Once we were convinced that the experiment was sound, we were confident that the data could be used. In this case, there were multiple findings; the data supported one claim (faster growth) but challenged another (increased tomato production).

Often, the details of the experimental design and procedures may not be available, so you must look at the data only. Always keep in mind what predictions are made by the hypothesis, claim, or theory. Does the data address those predictions? What can you conclude from the data? How does the data relate to the predictions? Does the data support the hypothesis? Does the data refute the hypothesis? If the data refutes the hypothesis, then how should the hypothesis be modified?

Bring Together and Make Sense of Multiple Findings, Conclusions, or Theories

On the GED® Science test you will be asked to examine multiple pieces of information to come to conclusions and make judgments. Consider the following example.

EFFECTS OF TEMPERATURE AND PRESSURE

The Haber process is a chemical reaction where nitrogen and hydrogen gases are combined to form ammonia gas. The reaction is represented by this chemical equation:

$$N_2\,(g) + 3\,H_2\,(g) \underset{\text{endothermic}}{\overset{\text{exothermic}}{\rightleftharpoons}} 2\,NH_3\,(g)$$

Chemists studied the effects of increasing pressure on the gases in the reaction. The same amounts of nitrogen and hydrogen gases were combined in a fixed chamber. They increased the pressure of the chamber from 0 to 400 atmospheres. They repeated the experiment at several fixed temperatures from 350°C to 550°C. In each case, they measured the percent yield of ammonia produced in the reaction. The data are shown in the graph:

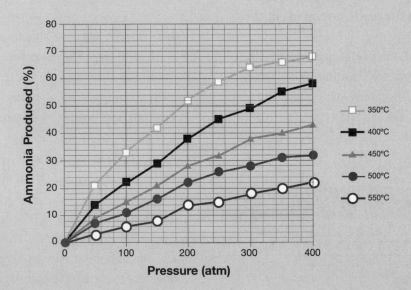

As you can see, the results contain more than one piece of information. Don't get confused by the multiple lines. Let's look at each individually:

- How does the percent yield of ammonia change with increasing pressure at 350°C?
- How does the percent yield of ammonia change with increasing pressure at 400°C?
- How does the percent yield of ammonia change with increasing pressure at 450°C?
- How does the percent yield of ammonia change with increasing pressure at 500°C?
- How does the percent yield of ammonia change with increasing pressure at 550°C?

The answer to all these questions is—*it increases*. So, generally, if you increase the pressure of the reaction at a fixed temperature, you will increase the production of ammonia.

Now, let's look at the effects of temperature by examining the graph:

- How does the percent yield of ammonia change with increasing temperature at a pressure of 50 atm?
- How does the percent yield of ammonia change with increasing temperature at a pressure of 100 atm?
- How does the percent yield of ammonia change with increasing temperature at a pressure of 200 atm?
- How does the percent yield of ammonia change with increasing temperature at a pressure of 300 atm?
- How does the percent yield of ammonia change with increasing temperature at a pressure of 400 atm?

The answer to all these questions is—*it decreases*. So, generally, if you increase the temperature of the

reaction at a fixed pressure, you will decrease the production of ammonia.

From a practical industrial standpoint, there are costs associated with building an apparatus that can increase pressures and temperatures. The changes in costs of increasing pressure and temperature are shown in the graphs:

Cost Increases Associated with Increasing Pressure

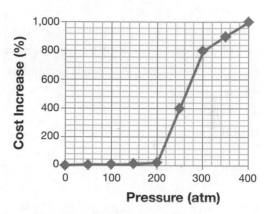

Cost Increases Associated with Increasing Temperature

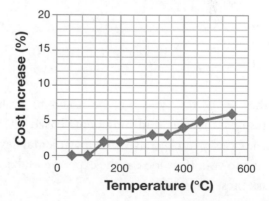

By this example, you can see how decision makers (e.g., scientists, engineers, project managers, etc.) can integrate multiple pieces of information to make conclusions and judgments.

Use this information to answer the following questions.

Practice

26. Suppose that you are a chemical engineer and must make a facility that will produce large amounts of ammonia using the Haber process. The best conditions to produce the greatest percent yield of ammonia would be:

_____ atm at _____°C.

27. Which is the highest pressure that the reaction can be run at without significantly increasing the costs (significant increase is defined as greater than 25%)?
   a. 100 atm
   b. 200 atm
   c. 300 atm
   d. 400 atm

28. Which is the highest temperature that the reaction can be run at without significantly increasing the costs (significant increase is defined as greater than 25%)?
   a. 350°C
   b. 400°C
   c. 500°C
   d. 550°C

On the GED® test, you will be asked to evaluate conclusions, theories, and judgments based on data. In some cases, you may have the experimental designs available to you. If so, look at the experimental design and ask these questions:

- What was the hypothesis?
- What was the independent variable?
- What was/were the dependent variable(s)?
- What were the other variables, and were they controlled?
- Were the measurement methods appropriate to what was being measured?

- Was the number of samples adequate?
- Overall, was the experimental design appropriate to test the hypothesis?

If you are satisfied with the answers to these questions, then you can be confident that the data is appropriate to address the hypothesis. You can then draw conclusions from the data. In doing so, you may look at the patterns in the data. Once you have drawn conclusions, you can then ask, "Do the conclusions from the data support or refute the hypothesis?"

In many cases, you may not have details of the experimental design available. So, you need to assess whether the data are appropriate to evaluate the hypothesis. For example, a hypothesis dealing with growth of an organism might be appropriately assessed with height or weight data, but not temperature measurements.

In some instances, you may have multiple pieces of information available and must integrate them into conclusions, judgments, or theories. For example, what is the most cost-effective way to produce ammonia?

Expressing Scientific Information

When carrying out experiments, scientists gather data. The data can be **qualitative data**. For example, the color of the solution changes from clear to dark purple as the chemical reaction proceeds. Most often, the data is **quantitative data**—the data are numbers. The numbers may be described verbally, as in a sentence. Numerical data is most often expressed in graphs, tables, or other charts, where it can easily be analyzed for patterns. This section examines various ways of expressing scientific data.

Express Scientific Information or Findings Visually

Numerical data can be either categorical data or continuous data. **Categorical data** has the numbers broken up into groups or categories. **Continuous data** has numbers expressed on a continuous number line. Both categorical and continuous data can be expressed visually in tables, charts, or graphs. Let's look at some examples.

RATING A CEREAL

A survey asks 100 respondents to rate how well they like a particular brand of cereal on a scale of 1 to 4. The number 1 represented "Did not like at all," 2 represented "Did not like or dislike," 3 represented "Liked," and 4 represented "Liked very much." The responses were 10, 25, 30, and 35 for responses 1, 2, 3, and 4, respectively. You see that the responses are grouped into distinct categories (1, 2, 3, or 4), so this is categorical data. One way to express this data visually is to organize it into a table. The first column contains the categories of responses. This column is usually the independent variable. In contrast, the second column contains the total number of respondents in each category, which is the dependent variable. The table would look like this:

CONSUMER OPINION OF CEREAL BRAND X	
RESPONSE	**NUMBER**
1. Did not like at all	10
2. Did not like or dislike	25
3. Liked	30
4. Liked very much	35

Another way to express categorical data is by using a **pie chart**. Here, the number of each category is converted to a percentage. Each category is represented by a "slice" that corresponds to that category's percentage of the whole.

Here, you can more easily see that more respondents had a favorable opinion (*Liked very much* and *Liked*):

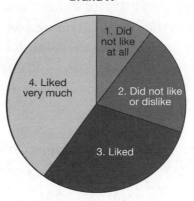

Consumer Opinion of Cereal Brand X

A third way to visualize this data is by using a **bar graph**. In this type of graph, the categories are plotted on the *x*-axis, while the number of respondents in each category is plotted on the *y*-axis. The bar graph of this data looks like this:

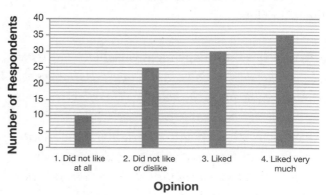

Consumer Opinion of Cereal Brand X

Consider an example of continuous data. Jamie is doing an experiment in physics class. In the experiment, he is trying to answer the question "How does the velocity of a ball rolling down a ramp change with time?"

Distances along the ramp are marked at 0.1, 0.2, 0.3, 0.4, and 0.5 m. He rolls a ball down the ramp. He starts a stopwatch when he releases the ball at the top of the ramp and stops it when the ball passes the first mark. He repeats this four times and records the average time. He repeats the experiment again, but this time he stops the watch at the second mark and records the time. He continues with the procedure until he records the average time to the last mark. He then calculates the velocities. The data are shown in the table.

DISTANCE (M)	TIME (S)	VELOCITY (M/S)
0	0	0
0.1	0.20	0.50
0.2	0.28	0.70
0.3	0.35	0.88
0.4	0.40	1.00
0.5	0.45	1.13

To visualize how the velocity changes, Jamie decides to make a graph. The variables are time and velocity. First, he must determine the dependent and independent variables.

- **Which is the independent variable?** *Time is the independent variable. Ask yourself: Is time changed by the velocity of the ball? No. Therefore, time must be the independent variable.*
- **Which is the dependent variable?** *If the velocity of the ball does not change time, then time may change the velocity of the ball. Therefore, the velocity of the ball is the dependent variable.*

In a graph, the independent variable gets plotted on the horizontal axis, or x-axis. The dependent variable gets plotted on the vertical axis or y-axis. In this example, time gets plotted on the x-axis and velocity gets plotted on the y-axis. We choose a scale on each axis that will include all the values and is divided evenly. The x-axis and the y-axis do not need to have the same values.

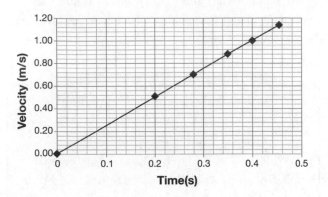

This graph is an example of a **linear line graph**; it is perhaps the most common type of line graph that you will see. Other types of line graphs may be **nonlinear**. For example, if Jamie plotted the distance versus time, he would get a graph like this:

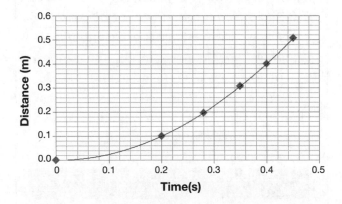

This is an example of a non-linear line graph. Note that the distance that the ball rolls down the ramp increases with time, but not at a constant rate.

Express Scientific Information or Findings Using Numbers or Symbols

Scientific data can be **quantitative** (expressed with numbers) or **qualitative** (expressed verbally or with symbols). Such data may be organized into a table. Let's look at an example.

Cindy is conducting an experiment on human hearing and musical notes. She blindfolds a subject and plays a reference note like middle C (C_4). Next, she plays another note and asks the subject whether the note was higher or lower relative to the reference note. She indicates a higher pitch with one or more "+" signs and a lower note with one or more "−" signs. She organizes her subject's responses in a table like this:

MUSICAL NOTE	RELATIVE PITCH
G_3	− −
A_3	−
Middle C (C_4)	0
D_4	+
E_4	+ +

Suppose that Cindy had a microphone hooked up to an oscilloscope where she could measure the frequency of each musical note. She could then add quantitative data (frequencies) to her table:

MUSICAL NOTE	RELATIVE PITCH	FREQUENCY (HZ)
G_3	− −	196
A_3	−	220
Middle C (C_4)	0	262
D_4	+	294
E_4	+ +	330

Note that the quantitative data still shows the notes in the same order from lowest to highest as the qualitative data does. However, Cindy can now answer the question that an E_4 musical note is 134 Hz higher than a G_3 musical note.

Practice

Jill is watching the development of red color in a solution with time during a chemical reaction. She notes the time and rates the color on a scale of 1 to 10 with 1 being light red (almost pink) and 10 being dark red (almost purple). She expresses her data in a table:

TIME (MINUTES)	RELATIVE RED COLOR
1	1
2	3
3	5
4	6
5	6

29. After 1 minute, what color is the solution?

_____

30. What color does the solution finally develop?

_____

Express Scientific Information or Findings in Words

When publishing scientific papers or reports, space may be limited. Producing graphs or tables may be expensive. Therefore, some data may need to be summarized verbally. In addition, some information may be noteworthy but not important enough to justify its own table, graph, or chart. Consider this example:

DROPPED BALL EXPERIMENT

A student drops a ball from a tall building, while another student videotapes the ball's path. They repeat the experiment 10 times. From the videotape, they measure the distance and calculate the velocities and accelerations with time. They average the values and plot them on graphs:

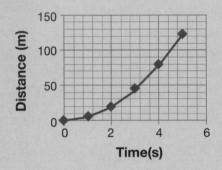

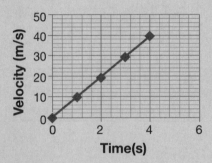

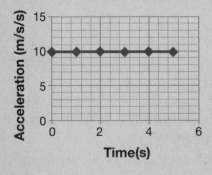

How could we simplify the description of these results? First, look at the graph of acceleration. Note that acceleration does not change; it is constant at 10 m/s/s. So, one way to simplify the presentation might be to eliminate that graph and verbally state the result:

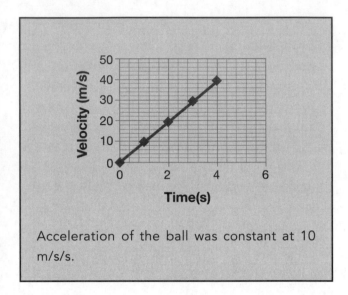

Acceleration of the ball was constant at 10 m/s/s.

How might the students simplify the presentation of the results even further?

The velocity graph could also be described verbally. For example, the velocity of the ball *increased linearly from zero at a constant rate of 10 m/s.* (Note: The rate of a linear graph is the slope of the line.) Pick any two points on the line and use the slope formula. For example, use (4,40) and (0,0). The slope becomes:

$$m = \frac{(y_2 - y_1)}{(x_2 - x_1)}$$

$$m = \frac{(40 - 0)}{(4 - 0)}$$

$$m = \frac{40}{4}$$

$$m = 10$$

Plus, we already know that the acceleration of the ball was constant at 10 m/s/s. So, the only graph that needs to be displayed is the graph of distance versus time.

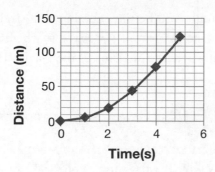

You will learn more about calculating acceleration and velocity later on in this chapter.

Practice

A biochemist conducts an experiment in which she measures the rate of a reaction as a function of temperature. The reaction is conducted in the presence and in the absence of an enzyme. She also monitors the pH of the reaction. Here are the data:

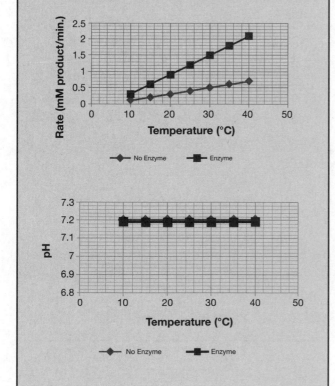

31. Which data is the most important?
    a. rate versus temperature
    b. pH versus temperature

32. How would you simplify this presentation?

Scientific Theories and Probabilities and Statistics

We've learned that scientists and others must often present information and data, and that the information may be qualitative data or quantitative data. Most often, qualitative data may be expressed verbally or in tables using symbols or numbers. Quantitative data is best presented visually so that one can see the patterns in the data to draw conclusions.

To understand the world around us, scientists carry out experiments, gather data, draw conclusions, and form theories and models. The theories and models lead to new predictions that can be tested by experiments. Thus, the cycle continues as new discoveries are made and old ideas are either discarded or modified into new ones that better explain natural phenomena.

One important aspect of analyzing experimental data, especially quantitative data, is determining whether a finding is significant or due to some random error. Often, scientists describe sets of data statistically and perform statistical (i.e., mathematical) tests on the data to determine its significance. Let's examine various ways of examining data statistically in the context of scientific investigations.

Understand and Apply Scientific Models, Theories, and Processes

Theories and models are ways that scientists formulate and express ideas to explain the world around them. Models and theories not only explain but also make predictions that can be tested with experiments. Models may be physical or mathematical.

The most common mathematical model that you will encounter will be the equation of a straight line relating a y-variable to an x-variable. This equation often has the general form of $\boldsymbol{y = mx + b}$, where m is the slope of the line and b is the y-intercept (the y-coordinate of a point where the line crosses the y-axis). Here's an example of a linear model:

LINEAR EXAMPLE

Starting 2.0 m away from you, a man walks in a straight line farther from you at a constant velocity. His position with time is shown in the table and the graph. What was the man's velocity?

Time (s)	Position (m)
0	2.00
1	3.50
2	5.00
3	6.50
4	8.00
5	9.50
6	11.00
7	12.50
8	14.00
9	15.50
10	17.00

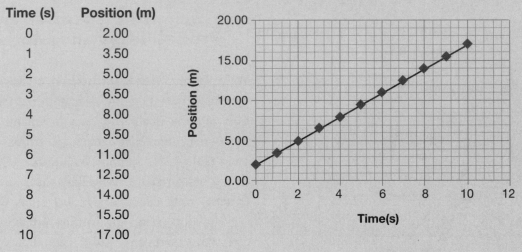

By definition, **velocity** is the rate of change of position with time or the slope of the straight line on a position-time graph. It's a straight line because the man is walking at constant velocity. So, to find the equation of the line, we must first calculate the slope of the line:

1. Pick any two points on the line. We'll use (2,5) and (4,8).
2. Use the slope equation:

$$m = \frac{(y_2 - y_1)}{(x_2 - y_1)}$$

$$m = \frac{(8\ m - 5\ m)}{(4\ s - 2\ s)}$$

$$m = \frac{(3\ m)}{(2\ s)}$$

$$m = 1.5\frac{m}{s}$$

So, the man's velocity is 1.5 m/s.

3. Now, let's find the y-intercept. At time zero, the man started from 2 m away. Therefore, the y-intercept is 2 m. You can see this on the graph as well. It's the point where the line crosses the y-axis (vertical axis).
4. So, the equation of the line in the form $y = mx + b$ becomes: $y = 1.5x + 2$.

Here are some examples of other mathematical models that you may encounter in science. Don't worry about the math, but just pay attention to the shapes of the curves.

Power Function

$y = ax^n$ where a is a coefficient, x is the base, and n is a whole number exponent. For example, if you had a penny and each day it was doubled, how much would you have on the 30th day? Here are the equation and graph:

$y = ax^n$, where $a = 0.01$, $x = 2$, $n = 30$

$y = (0.01)(2^{30})$

$y = (0.01)(1,073,741,824)$

$y = 10,737,418.24$

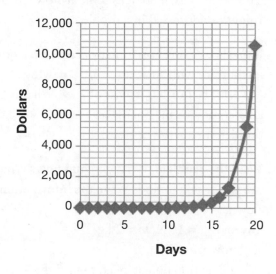

Exponential Function

$y = ce^x$, where c is a constant, e is the base of a natural logarithm, and x is a whole number exponent. Often population growth and decay of radioactive substances follow these functions. For example, radioactive phosphorus-32 has a half-life of 14.26 days. Here is the graph of the decay of 2 g of radioactive phosphorus-32 over time (don't worry about the math; just recognize the shape of the graph).

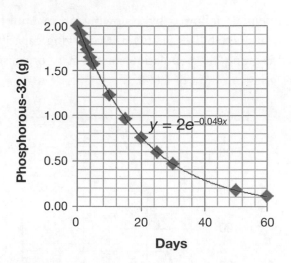

Exponential growth curves have the same shape but increase instead of decrease. Here's one for a population that starts with 10 organisms and grows exponentially.

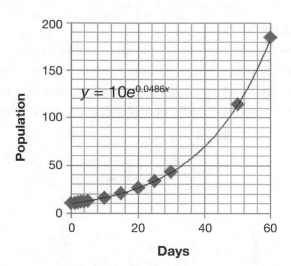

Sigmoidal Curve

Often called an S-curve, this function describes the growth of populations where there is a limit to growth or carrying capacity of the environment. (Again, don't worry about the math; just recognize the shape of the curve.) In a population growth curve like this, there is a rapid phase of growth (almost exponential) followed by a slowing phase until the population stabilizes at its limit (carrying capacity). In this graph, the population started at 10 organisms and grew to a limit of 1,000.

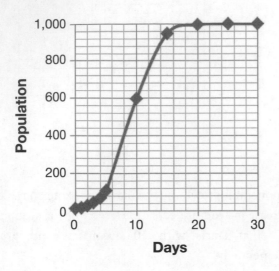

Parabolic Function

This type of curve has the form $y = ax^2 + bx + c$. This equation describes the path of a projectile, like a football kicked at an angle. Here is the graph of a ball thrown with a velocity of 4.47 m/s at an angle of 66°.

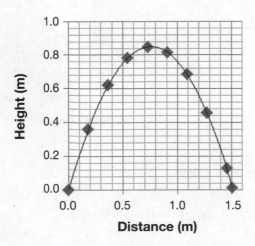

Apply Formulas from Scientific Theories

Equations in science are a guide to thinking. They show how variables relate to each other. For example, Newton's second law of motion relates the net force on an object (F_{net}), the mass of the object (m), and the object's acceleration (a).

$$a = \frac{F_{net}}{m}$$

The law combines two ideas in one equation. First, the greater the force on an object, the greater the acceleration of the object (i.e., acceleration is proportional to the net force). Second, when given the same net force applied to objects, the greater the mass, the slower the acceleration (i.e., acceleration is inversely proportional to mass). So, let's look at how this formula might be addressed in a problem:

> John slides a box horizontally across a frictionless surface with a net force of 10 newtons (10 N). The box has a mass of 2 kg. What is the acceleration of the box? Here's how to solve the problem in a series of steps:

1. **Read the problem.** What do you know? What are you trying to find? Write the information down.
   Given: F_{net} = 10 N, m = 2 kg
   Unknown: a = ?
2. What equation do you need to find the unknown information?
   $$a = \frac{F_{net}}{m}$$
3. **Is the equation in the form that you need to solve for the unknown?** If not, rearrange the equation algebraically to find the unknown. In this case, the equation is in the correct form to solve for a.
4. **Substitute the known values into the equation and solve for the unknown:**
   $$a = \frac{F_{net}}{m}$$
   $$a = \frac{10\,\text{N}}{2\,\text{kg}}$$
   $$a = 5\ \text{m/s}^2$$

5. Check your answer. Does it make sense? Are the units correct? In this case, yes, m/s^2 is the unit of acceleration.

Use Counting Techniques to Solve Scientific Problems

There are certain types of scientific investigations where the scientist must determine all possible outcomes of some event. Let's look at an example.

KINDS OF DACHSHUNDS

A breeder of dachshunds knows that the dog comes in three coats (long-haired, short-haired, wire-haired), three possible colors (red, brown, black), and two patterns (solid, dappled). Hhow many kinds of dachshunds could there be?

To solve this, we will use the **fundamental rule of counting**, which states:

> In a sequence of n events, in which the first one has k_1 possibilities, the second one has k_2 possibilities, on to the nth one, which has k_n possibilities, the total number of sequences will be: $k_1 \cdot k_2 \cdot k_3 \cdots k_n$

So, for the dachshunds: coat (k_1) = 3, color (k_2) = 3, and pattern (k_3) = 2. Therefore, by the fundamental rule of counting, the total number of outcomes = 3 · 3 · 2 = 18.

Practice

CODONS

Inside each cell of your body, ribonucleic acid (RNA) contains information to build proteins. A molecule of ribonucleic acid has four nitrogen bases: adenine (A), guanine (G), cytosine (C), and uracil (U). A sequence of three nitrogen bases makes up a codon, which is a unit that codes for one amino acid.

33. How many distinct codons can be made from the nitrogen bases of RNA? _____

Now, suppose a molecular biologist wants to make an artificial RNA codon of three nitrogen bases without repeating any single base. How many possibilities are there? In this type of problem, the scientist is using a permutation. A **permutation** is an ordered arrangement of r objects, which are chosen from n different objects, and the order is important. So, let's look at it this way:

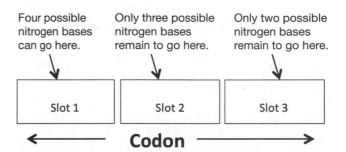

The number of possible permutations is 4 × 3 × 2 = 24.

Permutations are denoted in this manner: $_nP_r$. So, for this example, the permutation can be denoted as $_4P_3$.

We can calculate any permutation according to this formula: $_nP_r = \frac{n!}{(n-4)!}$, where $n!$ means n factorial, which is $n! = n \cdot (n-1) \cdot (n-2) \cdot (n-3) \ldots 1$. (Many calculators with statistical functions have factorial keys on them.) Now let's see how we use the formula for our scientist's example from the previous practice:

$$_nP_r = \frac{n!}{(n-r)!}$$

$$_4P_3 = \frac{4!}{(4-3)!}$$

$$_4P_3 = \frac{4 \cdot 3 \cdot 2 \cdot 1}{1!} = \frac{24}{1} = 24$$

There are 24 possible permutations of nitrogen bases.

Determine the Probability of Events

Sometimes in science, we must make predictions on the outcomes of events. These predictions are called probabilities. The **probability** of an event is the likelihood that that event will occur. Probability is a number between 0 and 1. It can be expressed as a fraction, decimal, or percent. For example, a school organization sells 100 raffle tickets for a prize. Only one ticket will get drawn to win the prize (outcome A). So, the theoretical probability of the event happening is represented by $P(A)$, which can be calculated as follows:

$$P(A) = \frac{\text{number of outcomes of } A}{\text{total number of possible outcomes}}$$

If you buy one ticket, what is the probability that you have the winning ticket?

$$P(A) = \frac{\text{number of outcomes of } A}{\text{total number of possible outcomes}}$$

$$P(A) = \frac{1}{100} = 0.01 = 1\%$$

The probability of having the winning ticket is 1%.

Sometimes, it is not possible to measure all the possible outcomes. So, you must find the **experimental probability**. To do so, you must conduct multiple trials and measure the number of trials where the outcome A occurs.

$$P(A) = \frac{\text{number of trials of } A \text{ occurs}}{\text{total number of trials}}$$

When tall pea plants are mated or crossed, there is a chance that some of the offspring will be short. A scientist conducts 100 crosses. Of these 100 crosses, six produce short pea plants. What is the experimental probability of producing a short pea plant in any one cross?

$$P(A) = \frac{\text{number of trials of } A \text{ occurs}}{\text{total number of trials}}$$

$$P(A) = \frac{6}{100} = 0.06 = 6\%$$

If the height of the pea plant and whether it produces round or wrinkled seeds are independent events, then what will the probability be of producing a plant that is short and has wrinkled seeds? For independent events (A, B), the probability of both of them occurring [$P(A \text{ and } B)$] is the product of the probabilities of each individual event: $P(A \text{ and } B) = P(A) \cdot P(B)$. So, we can calculate the probability of producing an offspring that is short and will produce wrinkled seeds:

$$P(A \text{ and } B) = P(A) \cdot P(B)$$

$$P(A \text{ and } B) = 0.06 \cdot 0.025$$

$$P(A \text{ and } B) = 0.0015 \cdot 0.15\%$$

Practice

34. An agricultural scientist conducts 800 trials in crossing pea plants that produce seeds with round seed coats. In these trials, 20 produce seeds with wrinkled seed coats. What is the probability of producing a plant that will yield wrinkled seeds? _____

Summary

This chapter has given you a solid foundation of how to approach scientific information with an analytic and critical eye. The ability to understand science data, passages, and experiments is the main skill you need to score well on the GED® Science test. Remember, all the information you need to answer science questions is presented to you on the test. What the GED® test asks you to do is analyze this information with a scientific mind. The skills in this chapter will help you approach science questions with confidence on test day.

Now, let's apply what was reviewed here to the science knowledge itself in the next three chapters, starting with life science.

Science Practices Review

Use the following information to answer question 1.

REDUCING OBESITY IN CHILDREN

Today, about 30% of the children in the United States are overweight or obese. This puts them at increased risk for diseases such as diabetes (measured by fasting glucose levels) and heart disease (due to high cholesterol levels). The local county health department wants to improve the health of the young children in the community. Most research indicates that changing diet and exercise is the best way to reduce obesity in children, but the health department suspects that children may not be willing to change both diet and exercise.

The county health department undertakes a new program to encourage children to eat better and exercise. They enroll 200 children in a six-month program and plan to set up three groups:

- Group 1: diet and exercise
- Group 2: diet only
- Group 3: exercise only

The county health department hypothesizes that the children in the diet and exercise group will have the best outcomes.

1. Design a controlled experiment that the county health department can use to determine the effectiveness of the program. Include descriptions of data collection and how the health department will determine if their hypothesis is correct. Write your experiment plan on the lines.

_____

_____

_____

_____

_____

_____

_____

_____

_____

_____

_____

_____

_____

Use the following information to answer questions 2–6.

ARE PRESERVATIVES EFFECTIVE?

Katy always buys bread with preservatives so that it will last longer. She wants to know if the preservatives really do make a difference in slowing the growth of mold on bread. She conducts the following experiment:

1. Obtains one slice of bread containing preservatives and one slice of bread without any preservatives.
2. Dampens two paper towels.
3. Places each paper towel inside a separate zip-top plastic bag.
4. Places one slice of bread in each bag, seals the bags, and labels the bags.
5. Puts the bags in a dark, temperature-controlled environment for one week.
6. Records the mold growth once a day for one week.

2. What is the most likely hypothesis for Katy's experiment?
   a. If bread is damp, then it will grow mold faster than dry bread.
   b. If bread is placed in a cool, dark environment, then it will stay preserved longer.
   c. If bread with preservatives is placed in plastic, then it will resist mold for more than one week
   d. If bread has preservatives, it will grow mold more slowly than bread without preservatives.

3. Which is the dependent variable in Katy's experiment?
   a. time
   b. moisture
   c. mold growth
   d. bread with preservatives

4. Which is the independent variable in Katy's experiment?
   a. time
   b. moisture
   c. mold growth
   d. bread with preservatives

5. Which is a controlled variable in Katy's experiment?
   a. bread without preservatives
   b. moisture
   c. mold growth
   d. bread with preservatives

6. Which is a weakness in Katy's experiment?
   a. the use of damp paper towels
   b. the use of plastic bags
   c. not specifying how mold growth is measured
   d. placing one slice of bread in each bag

Use the following information to answer questions 7–9.

When the brakes are applied in a moving car, the force of friction between the road surface and the vehicle's tires is what stops the car. The force of friction depends on the coefficient of friction, which varies with the road conditions (dry, wet, icy) and seasons (summer, winter). In a collision, a police officer can measure the braking distance by the skid marks, note the road conditions, and determine the initial velocity of the car. The data are shown in the graph.

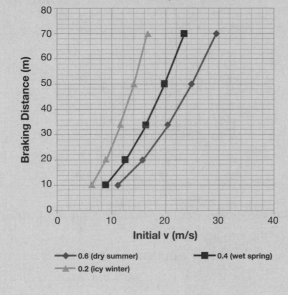

7. On a road under icy winter conditions, a car is traveling at 10 m/s initially when it brakes. The car will travel _____ m before it stops.

8. On a road under wet summer conditions, a car has a braking distance of 60 m. How fast was the car going initially?
   a. less than 15 m/s
   b. 15 to 22 m/s
   c. 22 to 27 m/s
   d. greater than 27 m/s

9. On a road under wet, spring conditions, a car has a braking distance of 40 m. The initial speed of the car was _____ m/s.

10. Jenny does an experiment with her friend to test her friend's ability to hear loud (indicated by positives) or soft (indicated by negatives) sounds relative to a reference sound. The data are shown in the table.

SOUND	RELATIVE INTENSITY
A	+ +
B	− −
C	−
D	+ + +
E	− − −

Which sound was closest to the reference sound?
   a. Sound C
   b. Sound B
   c. Sound A
   d. Sound D

11. A forecast shows the chance of rain on Friday is 10%, 30%, 70%, and 50% for Miami, Los Angeles, Seattle, and Chicago, respectively. What is the probability that it will rain in all four cities on Friday? _____

12. In a physics experiment, a student makes several measurements of the velocity of a sound wave from a tuning fork. The measurements (in m/s) are:
   341, 343, 330, 335, 338, 345, 341
   Which is the mean of the data?
   a. 339
   b. 341
   c. 345
   d. 2,373

13. The probability of having a male offspring is 50%, while the probability of having type O+ blood is 37.4%. The two outcomes are independent of each other. What is the probability of having a baby boy with type O+ blood?

a. 18.7%

b. 12.6%

c. 87.4%

d. 50%

14. A student observes a chemical reaction in a series of tubes. After 5 minutes of reaction time, she rates the development of blue color on a scale of 1 to 5 (1 = pale blue, 5 = navy blue). The results are shown in the table:

TUBE NUMBER	RELATIVE COLOR
A	3
B	5
C	1
D	4
E	2

Which represents the series of tubes in order from least color development to most color development?

a. A < B < C < D < E

b. C < E < A < D < B

c. E < D < A < B < C

d. E < D < C < B < A

15. A chemistry student conducts an experiment in which he keeps the temperature and volume of a gas constant. He increases the amount of the gas and measures the pressure. The data are shown in the table. He creates a graph in his lab report and the teacher marks it wrong.

AMOUNT (mol)	P (kPA)
0	0
1	101
2	203
3	304
4	406
5	506

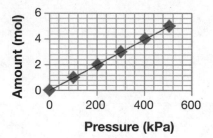

Which error did the student commit in making the graph?

a. The *x*-axis is not graded in even increments.

b. The *y*-axis is not graded in even increments.

c. There should be no line through the data points.

d. The variables are plotted on the wrong axes.

Answers and Explanations

Chapter Practice

1. b. The second sentence mentions that bundles contain many *cylindrical* muscle cells.

2. c. The fifth sentence of the passage states, *First, muscle cells have more than one nucleus.*

3.

IRON	OXYGEN	IRON OXIDE
Fe	O_2	Fe_2O_3

4. The pH scale in this chart has values from **0 to 14**.

5. a. Note that each number on the pH scale corresponds to a negative exponent when the hydrogen ion concentration is expressed in scientific notation. pH 2 = 10^{-2} moles per liter, pH 4 = 10^{-4} moles per liter, and pH 6 = 10^{-6} moles per liter. So, pH 9 = 10^{-9} moles per liter.

6. acidic. Any pH value below 7.0 indicates an acidic substance.

7. evaporation. The bodies of water in the diagram are the ocean and freshwater. From both you will see an upward arrow labeled "Evaporation." So, evaporation is the process by which water moves from bodies of water into the atmosphere.

8. c. On the left-hand side of the diagram you can see that melting ice and snow on the surface penetrate or infiltrate into the ground.

9. *Answers will vary:*
In this case, the hypothesis predicts that the meat tenderizer will break down proteins but not starches or fats. However, what is meant exactly by *break down* is not specified.

10. *Answers will vary:*
Yes, the size of the jars, as well as the amount of water added, is not specified. Also, were the jars glass or plastic?

11. *Answers will vary:*
Although the amount of meat tenderizer is specified, no brand or type of meat tenderizer is specified. This might be important.

12. *Answers will vary:*
Although the directions say to place one sample of starch, fat, and protein in each jar, the amounts and types of the samples are not specified. What is the source of the starch: bread flour, cornmeal, or something else? What is the source of the fat: butter, lard, vegetable oil, or something else? What is the source of the protein: ground beef, pork, chicken, fish, soybeans, or something else?

13. *Answers will vary:*
What types of changes should you look for: changes in size, weight, color, and so on? Under what conditions were the jars kept? Temperature, humidity, and the amount of light are critical variables in many experiments.

14. *Answers will vary. The following are examples of high-scoring responses.*
Hypothesis:
If Jim places one dog on the new dog food, then that dog should lose weight compared to the other.
Suggested experiment:
Feed both dogs at the same time with the same amount of dog food. Substitute the new reduced-calorie dog food for the normal dog food for one of the dogs. Separate the dogs when they are eating so that one dog does not eat the other's food. Measure the weight of both dogs weekly over the course of six weeks.
Predicted result:
The dog on the reduced-calorie dog food should lose weight compared to the dog on the regular dog food.

15. *Answers will vary:*

If Brand X is more durable than Brand Y under outside conditions, then the paint coatings on boards painted with Brand X will be thicker than Brand Y.

16. Yes. The hypothesis is testable.

17.

CONTROLLED	UNCONTROLLED
The boards were painted with the same number of coats to the same paint thickness.	Weather conditions varied.
The boards were matched in size.	The boards were made of different woods.
The boards were exposed to the same weather conditions for the same amount of time.	

18. *Answers may vary:*

No. After 1995, the moose population crashed and remained low due to the severe winter and disease, but the wolf population increased.

19. *Answers may vary:*

The increase in the moose population (1964–1972) induced increased predation by wolves and a subsequent increase in the wolf population. Once the wolf population crashed from disease (1981–1990), the moose population recovered and increased through 1995.

20. The mean height of the plants is **9.98 cm.** First arrange the heights in ascending order:

9.8, 9.9, 10.0, 10.1, 10.1

$$\text{mean} = \frac{9.8 + 9.9 + 10.0 + 10.1 + 10.1}{5}$$

$$\text{mean} = \frac{49.9}{5}$$

$$\text{mean} = 9.98$$

21. The median height of the plants is **10.0 cm.** First arrange the heights in ascending order:

9.8, 9.9, 10.0, 10.1, 10.1

The median is the middle value, which is 10.0 cm.

22. The mode height of the plants is **10.1 cm.** The mode is the most frequent value, which is 10.1 cm: 9.8, 9.9, 10.0, 10.1, 10.1.

23. a. Yes. The fertilizer-treated plants produced almost twice as many tomatoes as the control plants.

24. b. No. The plants treated with Brand X produced slightly fewer tomatoes than those treated with Brand Y.

25. *Answers will vary:*

The results of this study show that while the company's claim that plants treated with Brand X grow faster is true, their claim that the plants will produce more fruit is not true.

26. 400 atm at **350°C.** The best conditions to produce the greatest percent yield of ammonia would be 400 atm at 350°C. These conditions have the highest yield of ammonia (68%).

27. b. Achieving a 200-atm pressure is the highest that can be done without the cost significantly increasing.

28. d. Temperatures up to 550°C can be achieved with only a 6% increase in cost (not significant by definition).

29. pink. After looking at the table and the timing, you would probably determine that the solution is almost pink.

30. red. The solution develops a red, perhaps a slightly dark red color, as indicated by 6 being slightly above the middle of the scale.

31. a. The biochemist would want to show the rate versus temperature data, as that is what is changing.

32. *Answers may vary:*

The pH of the reaction does not significantly change with temperature and could be easily stated verbally as *The pH of the reaction mixture was constant at approximately 7.20.*

33. 64. There are three nitrogen bases in each codon. Each position can be filled with one of four nitrogen bases. So, using the fundamental rule of counting, we get:

$$k_1 \cdot k_2 \cdot k_3 = 4 \cdot 4 \cdot 4 = 64.$$

34. $\frac{1}{40}$ **or 0.025 or 2.5%.**

$$P(A) = \frac{\text{number of trials of } A \text{ occurs}}{\text{total number of trials}}$$

$$P(A) = \frac{20}{800} = \frac{1}{40} = 0.025 = 2.5\%$$

Science Practices Review

1. *Answers will vary:*

The county health department should randomly assign the 200 children to one of three experimental groups, as well as a control group, as follows:

- Group 1: diet and exercise (50 children)
- Group 2: diet only (50 children)
- Group 3: exercise only (50 children)
- Control group: no change in daily routine (50 children)

The health department employees would have to take measurements on all of the children before the intervention begins, at two months, and at six months to measure the change over time. They would take height, weight, cholesterol level, and fasting blood glucose level. They would also need to ask questions about the diet of the children and the amount of exercise they do on a daily basis.

The children in Group 1 (diet and exercise) would be on a diet lower in fat and sugar (weekly menus provided by the health department) and would be asked to double the amount of exercise they do in a week (e.g., if they normally exercise 20 minutes per week, then they will be asked to exercise 40 minutes per week). Parents would be asked to keep a food log and record the exercise on a daily basis. The children in Group 2 (diet change only) would be on the same reduced-fat and lower-sugar diet as the children in Group 1 but would not change their exercise routines. Parents would be asked to keep a food log and record the exercise on a daily basis.

The children in Group 3 (exercise change only) would not be asked to change their diets, but would be asked to double the amount of exercise they do on a weekly basis, as in Group 1. Parents would be asked to keep a food log and record the exercise on a daily basis.

The children in the control group would not be asked to change anything, but parents would be asked to keep a food log and record the exercise on a daily basis.

After the conclusion of the experiment, the health department can compare the weights, cholesterol levels, and fasting blood glucose levels of each group and draw conclusions about the effectiveness of the interventions.

2. d. Katy's experiment involves two types of bread—with preservatives and preservative-free. The experiment uses temperature, moisture, and time as controls in order to discover if the preservative is the true variable in resisting mold growth.

3. c. Mold growth is the responding variable to the presence or absence of preservatives in bread.

4. d. Bread with preservatives is the independent variable.

5. b. Moisture is kept constant, so it is one of the controlled variables.

6. c. By not specifying how she intended to measure mold growth, Katy could prevent others from replicating her findings.

7. The car will travel **26 m** before it stops. First, trace the vertical line from 10 m/s on the *x*-axis until it meets the curve for icy winter conditions. From that point, trace the horizontal line to the *y*-axis and read the braking distance, which is 26 meters.

8. c. There is no curve for wet summer conditions, but these conditions must fall between the curves for wet spring and dry summer. Trace the horizontal line from 60 m on the *y*-axis until it meets the curve for wet spring conditions. This is the minimum speed. From that point, trace the perpendicular line to the *x*-axis and read the initial speed, which is 22 m/s. Repeat the process, but continue the horizontal line until it reaches the dry summer curve. This is the maximum speed. From that point, trace a perpendicular line to the *x*-axis and read the initial speed, which is 27 m/s. The car had to be traveling between 22 m/s and 27 m/s.

9. The initial speed of the car was **18 m/s**. First, trace the horizontal line from 40 m on the *y*-axis until it meets the curve for wet spring conditions. From that point, trace a perpendicular line to the *x*-axis and read the initial speed, which is 18 m/s.

10. a. Sound C had only one negative and was the closest to the reference sound.

11. 0.0105 or 1.05%.

$P(\text{Miami}) = 10\% = 0.1$

$P(\text{Los Angeles}) = 30\% = 0.3$

$P(\text{Seattle}) = 70\% = 0.7$

$P(\text{Chicago}) = 50\% = 0.5$

$P(\text{all 4 cities}) = P(\text{Miami}) \cdot P(\text{Los Angeles})$
  $\cdot P(\text{Seattle}) \cdot P(\text{Chicago})$

$P(\text{all 4 cities}) = 0.1 \cdot 0.3 \cdot 0.7 \cdot 0.5$

$P(\text{all 4 cities}) = 0.0105 = 1.05\%$

12. a. Calculate the mean:

$$\text{mean} = \frac{330 + 335 + 338 + 341 + 341 + 343 + 345}{7}$$

$$\text{mean} = \frac{2{,}373}{7}$$

$$\text{mean} = 339$$

Choice **b** is both the median and the mode of the data set.

13. a. Let *A* represent the outcome of having a male child and *B* represent the outcome of type O+ blood:

$P(A \text{ and } B) = P(A) \times P(B)$

$P(A \text{ and } B) = 0.5 \times 0.374$

$P(A \text{ and } B) = 0.1870 = 18.7\%$

Choice **b** is the difference between the two probabilities. Choice **c** is the sum of the two probabilities. Choice **d** is the probability of having a baby boy.

14. b. The tubes are in the correct order from least color development (Tube C = 1) to most color development (Tube B = 5).

15. d. *Amount* is the independent variable and should be plotted on the *x*-axis. In contrast, *pressure* is the dependent variable and should be plotted on the *y*-axis. Choices **a** and **b** are not student errors because these scales do have even increments. Choice **c** is not an error because a line drawn through the data points is fine.

10 ▶ LIFE SCIENCE

This chapter begins our study of the science topics that are presented on the GED® Science test. Remember, the focus of the exam isn't to assess your science content knowledge; it's to test your science reasoning skills. On the test, you will never encounter a question that asks you to provide your own definition of a specific science term or concept. However, according to the GED® Testing Service, you should be "broadly and generally familiar" with each of the basic science concepts covered in the next three chapters. In other words, to do your best, you should strive to generally understand and recognize all the concepts and terms you'll encounter. Answers and explanations for all practice questions are at the end of this chapter.

What Is Life Science?

Life science explores the nature of living things, from the smallest building blocks of life to the larger principles that unify all living beings. Fundamental questions of life science include:

- What constitutes life?
- What are its building blocks and requirements?

- How are the characteristics of life passed on from generation to generation?
- How did life and different forms of life evolve?
- How do organisms depend on their environment and on one another?
- What kinds of behavior are common to living organisms?

Before Antoni van Leeuwenhoek looked through his homemade microscope more than 300 years ago, people were not aware that there were cells in our bodies and that microorganisms existed. People even believed that fleas, ants, and other insects came from dust or wheat. Leeuwenhoek looked through his microscope and saw blood cells in blood, studied microorganisms in ponds, and showed that pests come from eggs laid by adult pests. It took more than 200 years for Leeuwenhoek's observations to gain wide acceptance and find application in medicine, and yet the questions he asked have led us to learn all that we know now about life science.

Life science questions on the GED® Science test will cover many topics studied in high school biology classes. Reviewing some of the basics of biology will help you to understand passages and find the answers to questions on the GED® Science test.

Cell Theory

Let's start with the cell, which we know today is the building block of life. Every living organism is composed of one or more cells, and all cells come from other cells. Cells are alive—if blood cells, for example, are removed from the body, given the right conditions, they can continue to live independently of the body.

Cells are made up of organized parts, perform chemical reactions, obtain energy from their surroundings, respond to their environments, change over time, reproduce, and share an evolutionary his-

tory. All cells contain a membrane, cytoplasm, and genetic material. More complex cells also contain cell organelles.

The following is a description of cell components and some of the functions they serve, as well as a figure showing the parts of animal and plant cells.

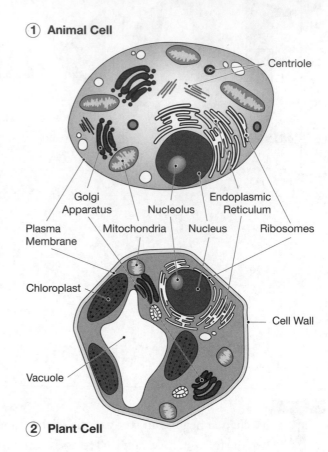

① **Animal Cell**

Centriole
Golgi Apparatus
Plasma Membrane
Nucleolus
Endoplasmic Reticulum
Mitochondria
Nucleus
Ribosomes
Chloroplast
Cell Wall
Vacuole

② **Plant Cell**

Cell Membranes

The **cell**, or **plasma**, **membrane** is the outer membrane of the cell. It carefully regulates the transport of materials in and out of the cell and defines the cell's boundaries. Membranes have selective permeability—meaning that they allow the passage of certain molecules, but not others. A membrane is like a border crossing. Molecules need the molecular equivalent of a valid passport and a visa to get through.

The movement of water and other types of molecules across membranes (including cell membranes) is important to many life functions in living organisms. Movement of these molecules occurs by **diffusion** through semipermeable membranes, which means that the membranes allow small molecules, like water, to pass but block larger molecules, like sugar or glucose. The processes of diffusion and **osmosis** are sometimes called **passive transport** since they do not require any active role for the membrane. The molecules move across the membrane because of osmotic pressure. **Osmotic pressure** forces highly concentrated molecules to move across a membrane into areas of lower concentration until a balance is reached. This balance is called **equilibrium**.

Conversely, sometimes molecules are moved from areas of low concentration to areas of higher concentration. This is the opposite of passive transport, so what do you think it is called?

This process is called **facilitated** or **active transport**. Active transport requires the cell to use energy. You will read more about osmosis and diffusion in the Physical Science chapter.

The **cell wall** is the layer outside of the membrane on plant cells. It is made of cellulose, which surrounds, protects, and supports plant cells. Animal cells do not have a cell wall.

Interior Parts of a Cell

These are parts of a cell that will be useful to review:

- The **nucleus** is a spherical structure, often found near the center of a cell. It is surrounded by a nuclear membrane, and it contains genetic information inscribed along one or more molecules of DNA. The DNA acts as a library of information and a set of instructions for making new cells and cell components. In order to reproduce, every cell must be able to copy its genes to future generations. This is done by exact duplication of the DNA. The **nucleolus** is located inside the nucleus. It is involved in the synthesis of ribosomes, which manufacture proteins.
- **Cytoplasm** is a fluid found within the cell membrane but outside of the nucleus.

- **Ribosomes** are the sites of protein synthesis. They are essential in cell maintenance and cell reproduction.
- **Mitochondria** are the powerhouses of the cell. They are the sites of **cellular respiration** (breakdown of chemical fuels to obtain energy) and production of adenosine triphosphate (ATP), a molecule that provides energy for many essential processes in all organisms. Cells that use a lot of energy, such as the cells of a human heart, have a large number of mitochondria. Mitochondria are unusual because, unlike other cell organelles, they contain their own DNA and make some of their own proteins.
- The **endoplasmic reticulum** is a series of interconnecting membranes associated with the storage, synthesis, and transport of proteins and other materials within the cell.
- The **Golgi complex** is a series of small sacs that synthesizes, packages, and secretes cellular products to the plasma membrane. Its function is directing the transport of material within the cell and exporting material out of the cell.
- **Lysosomes** contain enzymes that help with intracellular digestion. Lysosomes have a large presence in cells that actively engage in phagocytosis—the process by which cells consume large particles of food. White blood cells that often engulf and digest bacteria and cellular debris are abundant in lysosomes.
- **Vacuoles** are found mainly in plants. They participate in digestion and the maintenance of water balance in the cell.
- **Centrioles** are cylindrical structures found in the cytoplasm of animal cells. They participate in cell division.
- **Chloroplasts** exist in the cells of plant leaves and in algae. They contain the green pigment chlorophyll and are the site of photosynthesis—the process of using sunlight to make high-energy sugar molecules. Ultimately, the food supply of most

organisms depends on photosynthesis carried out by plants in the chloroplasts.

Organization of Cells

In a multicellular organism, individual cells specialize in different tasks. For example, red blood cells carry oxygen, white blood cells fight pathogens, and cells in plant leaves collect the energy from sunlight.

This cellular organization enables an organism to lose and replace individual cells and consequently outlive the cells that it is composed of. For example, you can lose dead skin cells and give blood and still go on living. This differentiation or division of labor in multicellular organisms is accomplished by expression of different genes within the cells.

Considering the foregoing passages, let's see if you can pull information from what was presented to answer the following questions.

Practice

1. Match the interior parts of a cell with the correct descriptions. Write the letter next to each statement in the appropriate place in the table.

INTERIOR PARTS OF A CELL	DESCRIPTION
nucleus	
mitochondria	
ribosomes	
plasma membrane	

a. the element that controls the transfer of material into and out of the cell

b. where the DNA of a cell is found

c. the site in the cell where substances are broken down to obtain energy

d. the part of the cell where the synthesis of protein takes place

2. Name the parts of a cell found only in animal cells and those found only in plant cells.
Animal cells _____
Plant cells _____

3. *Facilitated transport* and *passive transport* refer to what? _____

Reproduction and Heredity

Once you've gotten a handle on how to think about cells, let's go a bit deeper into a specific set of cell processes—reproduction and heredity. **Reproduction** is simply the process of an organism creating a new organism and passing along its genetic material. **Heredity** involves what an organism looks like and how it functions, and this is determined by its genetic material. Obviously, these two things are intrinsically related.

Here's a fun fact: the basic principles of heredity were developed by Gregor Mendel, who experimented with pea plants in the nineteenth century. He mathematically analyzed the inherited traits (such as color and size) of a large number of plants over many generations in order to understand how heredity works. The units of heredity are **genes** carried on **chromosomes**. Genetics, which is the study of genes, can usually explain why children look like their parents and why they are, at the same time, not identical to the parents.

Let's look at some of the key terms that will help you to understand questions about reproduction and heredity.

Phenotype and Genotype

The collection of physical and behavioral characteristics of an organism is called a **phenotype**. For example, your eye color, foot size, and ear shape are components of your phenotype. If a puppy is born with brown eyes, what is this an example of? Phenotype!

The genetic makeup of a cell or organism is called the **genotype**. Phenotype (what an organism looks like or how it acts) is determined by the genotype (its genes) and its environment. By environment we don't mean the earth, but the environment surrounding the cell. For example, the hormones in a human mother's body can influence the gene expression in a baby. Essentially, you can think of the genotype as being like a cookbook for the recipe of the phenotype and the environment as being like the kitchen.

Cellular Reproduction

You may have heard the terms *mitosis* and *meiosis*. These are forms of **cellular reproduction**.

Asexual reproduction on the cellular level is called **mitosis**. Because it is asexual, that means it requires only one parent cell, which, after exactly multiplying its genetic material, splits in two. The resulting cells are genetically identical to each other and are clones of the original cell.

Since asexual reproduction requires only one parent cell, **sexual reproduction** requires how many parent cells? Two! Most cells in an organism that reproduces sexually have two copies of each chromosome, called **homologous pairs**—one from each parent. Even though an organism reproduces sexually, these cells reproduce through mitosis to keep all the genetic material.

However, there must be an exception to this rule, right?

Gamete cells (sperm and egg cells) are exceptions to the mitosis rule! They carry only one copy of each chromosome, so there are only half as many chromosomes as in the other cells. For example, human cells normally contain 46 chromosomes, but human sperm and egg cells have 23 chromosomes.

Why would these cells do this? Well, at fertilization, male and female gametes (sperm and egg) come together to form a zygote, the offspring, and the two sets of chromosomes join together to make sure the cell has the normal 46 chromosomes. This is how the genetic information of a zygote is a mixture of genetic information from both parents.

Gamete cells are manufactured through a process called **meiosis** whereby a cell multiplies its genetic material once but divides twice, producing four new cells, each of which contains half the number of chromosomes that were present in the original cell before division. In humans, gametes are produced in testes and ovaries. Meiosis, and how it is used in sexual reproduction, is necessary for **genetic diversity** within a species by generating combinations of genes that are different from those present in the parents. Genetic diversity is super important for healthy populations of any specific species. This is why purebred animals have very well documented genetic lines—to avoid inbreeding and unhealthy animals.

Alleles are alternative versions of the same gene, such as the gene that determines whether a human has blue or brown eyes. An organism with two copies of the same allele is **homozygous**, and one with two different alleles is **heterozygous**. For example, a human with one gene for blue eyes and one gene for brown eyes is heterozygous, while a human with two genes for blue eyes or two genes for brown eyes is homozygous. In a heterozygous organism, whichever of the two genes is expressed (e.g., whether the human is brown-eyed or blue-eyed) is determined by the dominance of the gene. An allele is dominant if it alone determines the phenotype, or expression, of a heterozygote.

If a plant has a gene for making yellow flowers and a gene for making red flowers, and the red flower gene is dominant, what color will the flowers be?

If you said red, you're correct. A plant that has both the dominant gene for red and the gene for yellow will still look red. The gene for yellow flowers in this case is called **recessive**, as it doesn't contribute to the phenotype (appearance) of a heterozygote (a plant containing two different alleles).

What way would this plant make yellow flowers?

The only way this plant would make yellow flowers is if it had two recessive genes—two genes both coding for yellow flowers. For some genes, dominance is only partial and two different alleles can be expressed. In the case of partial dominance, a plant that has a gene that codes for red flowers and a gene that codes for white flowers would produce pink flowers.

Punnett Squares

A **Punnett square** is the visual representation of this type of heredity. It can be used to represent the possible phenotypes that offspring of parents with known genotypes could have. Here's how it works:

- The genes of one parent are listed on the left side of a grid.
- The genes of the other parent are listed on top of the grid.
- The genes are then combined to show offspring in the grid.

Let's look at the example with the yellow and red flowers. Let's label the allele for the dominant red gene as **R** and the allele for yellow flowers as **r**. Cross a plant with yellow flowers (genotype must be **rr**) with a plant with red flowers and genotype **Rr**. A genotype of **RR** or **rr** is considered homozygous. A genotype of **Rr** is considered heterozygous.

What possible genotypes and phenotypes can the offspring have? Remember, in a Punnett square, the genes of one parent are listed on one side of the square and the genes of the other parent on top of the square. They are then combined in the offspring as illustrated here:

Plant (rr)

	r	r
R	**Rr**	**Rr**
r	**rr**	**rr**

Plant (Rr)

Homozygous Yellow Plant Crossed with Heterozygous Red Plant

The possible genotypes of the offspring are listed inside the square. Their genotype will be either **Rr** or

rr, causing them to be either red or yellow, respectively.

50% of the offspring would be homozygous yellow (**rr**)

50% of the offspring would be heterozygous red (**Rr**)

What happens if we breed two of the offspring (heterozygous red—**Rr**)? *What would the percentages be then?*

Then the Punnett square would look like this:

Plant (Rr)

	R	r
R	**RR**	**Rr**
r	**Rr**	**rr**

Plant (Rr)

Heterozygous Red Plant Crossed with Another Heterozygous Red Plant

25% would be homozygous yellow (**rr**)
50% would be heterozygous red (**Rr**)
25% would be homozygous red (**RR**)

Practice

Answer the following questions. Consider using a Punnett square to help you.

4. Angelfish come in a number of different colorations. Black angelfish have the genotype (DD), indicating that the black gene is dominant. If you breed a black angelfish (DD) with a recessive gold (gg) genotype, what will result? *Note:* A Dg genotype will result in a hybrid genotype and produce a hybrid black angelfish that is a milky black coloration.

    black _____%
    hybrid black _____%
    gold _____ %

5. You have your mother's brown eyes. The color of your eyes is an example of

a. genotype.

b. allele.

c. mitosis.

d. phenotype.

Sex Determination

In many organisms, one of the sexes can have a pair of unmatched chromosomes. In humans, the male has an X chromosome and a much smaller Y chromosome, while the female has two X chromosomes. The combination XX (female) or XY (male) determines the sex of humans. In birds, the males have a matched pair of sex chromosomes (WW), while females have an unmatched pair (WZ). In humans, the sex chromosome supplied by the male determines the sex of the offspring. In birds, the sex chromosome supplied by the female determines the sex. Plants, as well as many animals, lack sex chromosomes. The sex of these organisms is determined by other factors, such as plant hormones or temperature.

Identical twins result when a fertilized egg splits in two. Identical twins have identical chromosomes and can be either two girls or two boys. Two children of different sex born at the same time can't be identical twins and are instead fraternal. Fraternal twins can also be of the same sex. They are genetically not any more alike than siblings born at different times. Fraternal twins result when two different eggs are fertilized by two different sperm cells.

Mutation

Changes in DNA (**mutations**) occur randomly and spontaneously at low rates. Mutations occur more frequently when DNA is exposed to mutagens, including ultraviolet light, X-rays, and certain chemicals. Most mutations either are harmful to or don't affect the organism. In rare cases, however, a mutation can be beneficial to an organism and can help it survive or reproduce, like polar bears having a mutation for white fur. Ultimately, genetic diversity depends on mutations, as mutations are the only source of completely new genetic material. Only mutations in germ cells can create the variation that changes an organism's offspring.

Evolution

Evolution is the theory that explains how life developed on earth. It explains the diversity of forms of life, including the vast array of various species across all types of plants and animals.

Through a process of **natural selection**, certain genes or gene combinations give individuals members of a species an edge in surviving in the natural world. Such changes, or adaptations, are passed down to future generations and eventually—over very long periods of time—create variations in species or new species altogether.

Evidence for Evolution

Several factors have led scientists to accept the theory of evolution.

Fossil Record

One of the most convincing forms of evidence is the fossil record. **Fossils** are the remains of past life, often in the form of impressions in mud and debris that has since turned into sedimentary rocks, which form during compression of settling mud, debris, and sand. The order of layers of sedimentary rock is consistent with the proposed sequence in which life on Earth evolved. The simplest organisms are located at the bottom layer, while top layers contain increasingly complex and modern organisms; this reflects a pattern that suggests evolution. The process of **carbon dating**, which is the calculation of the consistent rate of carbon decay over time, has been used to confirm how old the fossils are. It also is used to determine that fossils found in the lower layers of sedimentary rock are indeed older than the ones found in the higher layers. This helps scientists to chart evolutionary history based on time. New fossils are turning up all the time; for example, the fossil called Tiktaalik, which was found in 2004, is believed to mark the transition from fish to land animals.

Biogeography

Another form of evidence comes from the fact that species tend to resemble nearby species in different habitats more than they resemble species that are in similar habitats but far away. For example, there are marsupials in both North America (opossums) and Australia (possums, koalas, kangaroos, wombats, etc.), but the opossums have white and gray fur and look entirely different from the Australian possums and other marsupials.

Comparative Anatomy

Comparative anatomy provides us with another line of evidence. It refers to the fact that the limb bones of different species, for example, are similar. Species that closely resemble one another are considered to be more closely related than species that do not resemble one another. For example, a horse and a donkey are considered to be more closely related than are a horse and a frog. Biological classifications (kingdom, phylum, class, order, family, genus, and species) are based on how organisms are related.

Organisms are classified into a hierarchy of groups and subgroups based on similarities that reflect their evolutionary relationships. The same underlying anatomical structures of groups of bones, nerves, muscles, and organs are found in all animals, even when the functions of these underlying structures differ.

Embryology

Embryology provides another form of evidence for evolution. Embryos go through the developmental stages of their ancestors to some degree. The early embryos of fish, amphibians, reptiles, birds, and mammals all have common features, such as tails.

Comparative Molecular Biology

Comparative molecular biology studies the relatedness of two different species by comparing their DNA. These studies at the molecular level confirm the lines of descent suggested by comparative anatomy and fossil records.

Selection and Adaptation

Darwin also proposed that evolution occurs gradually, through mutations and **natural selection**. He argued that some genes or combinations of genes give an individual a survival or reproductive advantage, increasing the chance that these useful combinations of genes will make it to future generations. Whether a given trait is advantageous depends on the environment of the organism.

One example of natural selection can be seen in antibiotic-resistant bacteria. When a drug is used on a species of bacteria, those that cannot resist die and do not produce offspring. Those bacteria that survive pass on the resistance gene to the next generation. Over time, the population of bacteria will become resistant to the antibiotic.

What other possible forms of natural selection can you think of?

Natural selection is only one of several mechanisms by which gene frequency changes in a population. Other factors include mating patterns and breeding between populations. Mating patterns, as an example, may account for why in certain species of birds, such as cardinals and peacocks, the male birds are very brightly colored while the female birds are less so.

A contrast to natural selection is **artificial selection** (or selective breeding)—the process by which farmers or breeders intentionally select for desirable characteristics or traits (e.g., disease resistance, size, etc.). Only individuals with the desired trait are allowed to breed.

Another way in which organisms change is that over time, living organisms adapt to their environments. **Adaptation** is the process of developing specific advantageous features. An adaptation may also be the feature itself. These features may be anatomical (physical features of the body), such as a certain color wing that provides protection from predators by camouflage or fur that allows a predator to get closer to its prey unseen. An adaptation may also be behavioral, such as a certain way of evading predators. For example, some tiger moths confuse their predators, bats, by emitting ultrasonic clicks that jam the bats' echolocation.

In the context of evolution, individuals with certain adaptive traits tend to be more successful reproductively—meaning that they produce more offspring. And what happens to that trait (if you remember back to reproduction and heredity)? Yes, the offspring will inherit the adaptive traits from their parents. Any time a trait results in a reproductive advantage in a population, **selection pressure** is occurring. Think of selection pressure as an evolutionary push or pressure on the population toward the adaptive trait.

A **species** is defined as a group that can interbreed and produce viable offspring. **Speciation** is the evolutionary process by which a new species emerges. As you can imagine, speciation occurs very slowly.

Practice

6. The fossil record provides evidence for the process of evolution. Another form of evidence for evolution comes from the field of biogeography. Species in different but nearby habitats tend to resemble each other more closely than they resemble species in similar habitats farther away. Which statement explains how this is evidence for evolution?
   a. Neighboring species in different habitats often can share a common ancestor.
   b. Species are less likely to interbreed with their neighbors, and over time they will resemble species farther away.
   c. Species are more likely to interbreed with species farther away, and over time they will resemble species farther away.
   d. Species are not likely to interbreed at all.

7. The peppered moth lives in the United Kingdom and has both light and dark variations. During the Industrial Revolution (1760–1840), many of the trees on which the moths lived became covered with dark soot. Over a period of just 50 years, the population of peppered moths in Manchester, England, changed so that almost the entire local population was made up of dark moths. After the Clean Air Act of 1956, the air quality changed and so did the population of peppered moths; dark moths became rare.
   This information is an example of:
   a. speciation
   b. meiosis
   c. extinction
   d. natural selection

8. Speciation, or cladogenesis, is the formation of new species over time. During allopatric speciation, a species is split geographically into two (or more) isolated populations. Over time new species emerge. This process provides evidence for the theory of _____.

The Human Body and Health

Since we've reviewed some of the basic elements of life, let's take a look close to home at the human body. The human body is made up of cells, as are all living things. These cells take different characteristics, depending on their purpose, and are organized into systems that govern the functions of the human body, such as the skeletal or nervous system.

Organization and Function

The organization of the body is good to keep in mind, and of course goes from smallest part to larger part. In this case cells, the smallest part of the body, are organized into tissues. Muscle tissue, for example, is made up of muscle cells. Tissues then make up organs, and finally organs (e.g., liver, heart, brain, kidneys) make up body systems.

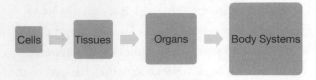

Levels of Biological Organization

The body systems interact with each other to make sure the human body functions properly.

The Nervous System

The nervous system allows us to monitor and interact with the environment around us. It is made up of the central nervous system (the brain and spinal cord) and the peripheral nervous system (the nerves that transport signals to and from the brain). Messages are sent from our sense organs via nerves to other body systems. Our sense organs include the eyes, nose, ears, skin, and tongue.

The nervous system is the boss of the body systems and coordinates all of the systems working with one another to maintain a state of balance or **homeostasis** (function within a normal range). For example, shivering, goose bumps, and sweating are your body's response to being too cold or too hot. If your skin and spinal cord sense cold, they send signals to the muscles to contract and shiver. In contrast, as your temperature rises, the blood vessels in your skin get larger. This process, called vasodilation, allows for cooling of the blood. Sweat glands are also activated when you are hot in an attempt to cool the body and return to homeostasis.

The Musculoskeletal System

The musculoskeletal system includes your bones—all 206 of them—as well as your ligaments, muscles, tendons, and cartilage. The bones meet at joints and are held together by ligaments. Bones are connected to the muscles through the tendons. Cartilage is flexible connective tissue (in the tip of your nose and ears, for instance) and is found in some of your joints, like the knee.

The Circulatory System

The circulatory system moves blood through the body. It includes the heart, blood, and blood vessels. The function of blood is to carry nutrients and oxygen to the cells and to transport waste products from cells. Arteries carry oxygen-rich blood from the heart. Veins carry blood back to the heart. The lymphatic system is also part of the circulatory system. It collects excess tissue fluids. Have you ever had swollen glands? If so, you have felt your lymphatic system at work.

The Respiratory System

The respiratory system helps in breathing and removing waste products from our bodies. Some important parts of the respiratory system are the lungs, the larynx, and the diaphragm, which is a thick muscle that is just beneath the lungs. The diaphragm controls the mechanism of breathing by contracting during inhalation and relaxing during exhalation. Oxygen moves into the blood and carbon dioxide is taken out of the lungs at the alveoli.

The Digestive System

Your digestive system is made up of organs that break down the food you eat into usable molecules that can be absorbed by the blood. These molecules are necessary for life. The breakdown of food starts in the mouth with the enzymes found in saliva. Food then passes through the esophagus to the stomach. Enzymes in the stomach further break down food. The liver produces bile (stored in the gallbladder), which breaks down fat into small droplets. When partially digested food enters the small intestine, the gallbladder releases bile into the intestine to help further break down food.

The pancreas secretes a fluid that helps break down starches, fats, and proteins. The lining of the small intestine has many tiny folds called microvilli, which absorb the products of digestion and transfer them to the circulatory system. The large intestine or colon is the last part of the digestive system. The function of the large intestine is to collect waste products. The waste products of digestion, or feces, are removed through the rectum and anus.

Most of the structures that make up living organisms are made from amino acids, carbohydrates, and lipids (often called fats). **Metabolism** is the process of building amino acids and other molecules needed for life (as during the construction of cells and tissues) or breaking them down and using them as a source of energy, as in the digestion and use of food. Within cells, the **mitochondria** perform this process.

The body needs nutrients to function properly. We get nutrients from the foods we eat. The nutrients that a body needs vary depending on the **calories** that a person burns in a day. A calorie is the way we measure energy in food. For example, a moderately active 30-year-old male of average height and weight needs about 2,600 calories daily to maintain weight. A 30-year-old moderately active female needs approximately 2,200 calories daily to maintain weight.

A calorie is a unit of energy. Technically, a calorie is the energy needed to raise the temperature of 1 gram of water 1°C (usually defined as 4.184 joules). Most of us think of calories in relation to food, as in "This apple has 100 calories." It turns out that the calories stated on a food package are actually **kilocalories** (1,000 calories = 1 kilocalorie). A food calorie contains 4,184 joules. A can of soda containing 200 food calories contains 200,000 regular calories, or 200 kilocalories. A gallon of gasoline contains 31,000 kilocalories.

When you consider this information, how many regular calories does a moderately active 30-year-old male of average height and weight need to maintain weight? The answer is 2,600,000 calories!

The Endocrine System

The endocrine system is made up of glands in different parts of the body. The thyroid, parathyroid, thymus, pancreas, and pituitary are all glands of the endocrine system. Along with helping the digestive system, these glands send out chemical messages via hormones to the rest of the body. Hormones are carried in the blood. Just as the nervous system works to maintain homeostasis in the body, the glands in the endocrine system regulate themselves with a type of feedback system that works to keep things in homeostasis.

An example of how the endocrine system regulates itself, and what happens in a disease state, can be seen in glucose (sugar) regulation in the blood.

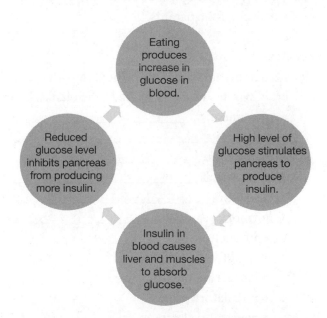

Feedback Mechanism in Glucose Regulation

In diabetes, a metabolic disorder, parts of this system are impaired or do not function. In type 1 diabetes, the body does not produce insulin at all. People with this kind of diabetes have to take insulin throughout their lives. People with type 2 diabetes have difficulty using the insulin that is produced by the pancreas. It often builds up in their blood, which means their cells are not getting the sugar they need. Treatment is necessary for the body to function properly since the endocrine system is unable to create homeostasis itself.

The Reproductive System

Finally, we discuss the reproductive system, as all living organisms reproduce. Some very simple organisms just divide into two. Other organisms, including humans, have developed complex sexual reproduction systems. Sexual reproduction for humans involves the joining of two gametes, an egg (female gamete) and a sperm (male gamete). Each of the gametes carries part of that parent's genetic code (DNA), so the offspring will contain genetic information from each of the parents.

Practice

9. Match the functions in **a** through **g** with the body systems listed by filling in the blanks.
   a. movement _____
   b. breathing _____
   c. metabolism _____
   d. homeostasis _____
   e. blood flow _____
   f. hormone regulation _____
   g. reproduction _____
      ▪ digestive system
      ▪ endocrine system
      ▪ circulatory system
      ▪ musculoskeletal system
      ▪ reproductive system
      ▪ nervous system
      ▪ respiratory system

10. Which answer best represents the levels of organization from simple to complex?
    a. cell, tissue, organ, body system
    b. tissue, cell, organ, body system
    c. organ, tissue, cell, body system
    d. body system, organ, tissue, cell

11. Which is an example of your body trying to maintain homeostasis?
    a. bleeding
    b. urination
    c. sweating
    d. digestion

Disease and Illness

All living things are subject to disease and illness. Disease can be classified as either infectious or noninfectious. However, the symptoms involved in both can be similar.

Infectious Disease

Many diseases are caused by **pathogens** that invade a host body. Pathogens need a host in order to survive and multiply. Some examples of pathogens are bacteria, viruses, and fungi. These pathogens can spread through **direct body contact**, body fluids, and contact with an object that an infected person has touched (some viruses, like the common cold virus, can exist outside the body for a brief period before they get passed on to another host). One way individuals can protect themselves from infection from these pathogens is by hand washing.

Other diseases are transmitted through the air. This kind of disease is called an **airborne** disease. In this case, viruses, bacteria, or fungi can be spread through coughing, sneezing, dust, spraying of liquids, or other activities that create aerosol particles or droplets. Tuberculosis is an example of an airborne disease. Tuberculosis is also an infectious disease. Treatment and vaccines for tuberculosis exist, and this disease has been almost eliminated in some parts of the world. However, the total number of people in the world infected with tuberculosis keeps growing. Individuals can prevent infection from airborne diseases by avoiding close contact with infected persons.

Blood-borne viruses are transmitted through the blood or bodily fluids. HIV is an example of a blood-borne virus; there is no chance of contracting the virus unless one comes in contact with the blood or bodily fluids of an infected person.

Sexually transmitted diseases (STDs) are diseases that are frequently transmitted through sexual contact. HIV is also an example of an STD, as are gonorrhea, chlamydia, syphilis, human papillomavirus (HPV), and herpes. Many STDs, including HIV and herpes, are incurable. There is a vaccine for HPV.

Noninfectious Disease

If a disease cannot spread from person to person, then it is considered noninfectious. Two examples of noninfectious diseases are cancer and heart disease.

Noninfectious diseases can be classified as follows:

- **Hereditary diseases.** Hereditary diseases are caused by genetic disorders that are passed down from previous generations. Since they are inherited, they are more difficult to treat because they are a part of a person's **genetic makeup.**
- **Age-related diseases.** Some diseases start to develop as the body gets older and does not work as efficiently to battle routine diseases and **degenerative diseases** such as Alzheimer's disease. Alzheimer's disease causes mild to severe memory loss or distortion, forgetfulness, anxiety, and sometimes aggressive behavior.

- **Environmentally induced diseases.** An environment that has been polluted with toxins and hazardous waste can affect the population living in or around it. Toxic chemicals in polluted groundwater can cause cancer. Exposure to asbestos can lead to serious lung problems.

Staying healthy by taking care of the body is important in fighting and preventing disease. Diet and lifestyle are major factors that can influence susceptibility to many diseases. Drug abuse, smoking, drinking alcohol, and poor diet, as well as a lack of exercise may increase the risk of developing certain diseases, including type 2 diabetes, heart disease, and some cancers. Recently, scientists and physicians have reported that the numbers of younger people developing diseases (such as type 2 diabetes) are increasing. This is likely related to the increasing rate of obesity among young people. Since 1980, the number of overweight children has doubled and the number of overweight adolescents has tripled.

Looking for Symptoms

Before diagnosing a patient with a disease, a doctor looks for telltale symptoms. Every disease has specific symptoms that cause different reactions in the body. Some common symptoms present in many illnesses are fever, nausea, and pain. A doctor is trained to look for symptoms to give a correct diagnosis and issue proper treatment. Specific blood tests and X-rays are special methods that are used to diagnose some diseases.

Epidemics

An epidemic is a disease outbreak that has infected a considerable portion of the population and that continues to spread rapidly. Epidemics can occur when there is no medicine for the disease, when diseases develop a resistance to medicine and drugs, or when environmental conditions are favorable for a specific type of disease. For example, cancer is rampant in areas with toxic chemicals and high levels of radiation. Autoimmune deficiency syndrome (AIDS), which is caused by the HIV virus, is an epidemic that has killed millions of people worldwide.

Natural and Medical Defenses

Humans and most other living beings have a natural built-in disease-fighting mechanism known as the **immune system**. The immune system is composed of cells, molecules, and organs that defend the body against pathogens. The immune system is responsible for finding the pathogen in the body and killing it, rendering it harmless, or expelling it from the body.

The development and use of vaccines and antibiotics have added to our defenses against diseases. Not only have advances in medicine found ways to fight disease from inside the body, but methods have also been developed to prevent the onset of disease.

Vaccines

Vaccines are usually made from either a dead version of an actual organism known to cause an immune response (such as a virus) or from a weakened or inactive form of the organism. By presenting the body with a weaker or deactivated form of an organism that would normally make a person very ill, the body will produce an immune response without causing any illness. Then if the body ever comes in contact with the strong form of a virus, the **antibodies** that were formed during the immune response to the weaker version will be able to fight off this strong version.

Some people are concerned about the safety of vaccines, but scientists have not found any significant safety concerns related to vaccinations. In the United States, all vaccines must be approved by the U.S. Food and Drug Administration (FDA) and go through extensive testing and trials before they can be used. Some very serious diseases, including smallpox, measles, and polio, have been almost eradicated through vaccination.

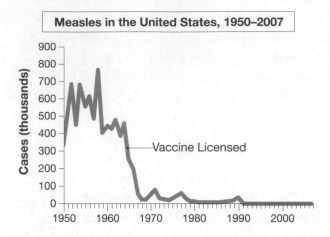

According to the United Nations Children's Fund (UNICEF), vaccines save approximately nine million lives annually around the world.

Antibiotics and Resistance

Antibiotics are chemical compounds that kill bacteria without harming our own cells. Some antibiotics, such as penicillin, kill bacteria by preventing it from synthesizing a cell wall. Other antibiotics interfere with bacterial growth by disrupting their genes or protein production. Bacteria can become resistant to antibiotics—there are strains of bacteria that are resistant to every known antibiotic.

In every population, a small number of bacteria naturally have genes that make them resistant to antibiotics. With increased exposure to antibiotics, a normal population of bacteria, a few of which are resistant, becomes resistant on average. This is a result of natural selection. The bacteria that survive are the ones that are resistant. Their offspring are also resistant, and as a result, the whole population becomes resistant.

Some resistance enables bacteria to survive in the presence of an antibiotic. Another kind of resistance enables the bacteria to actually destroy the antibiotic. This kind of resistance is most dangerous. For example, someone who took antibiotics for treating acne could accumulate bacteria that are capable of destroying the antibiotic. If that same person became infected with a serious disease that is treated with the same antibiotic, the resistant bacteria could destroy the antibiotic before it was able to act on the disease.

Practice

12. Read the following passage and design a controlled experiment that the county health department can use to determine the effectiveness of an intervention. Include descriptions of data collection and how the health department will determine if its hypothesis is correct.

Today about 30% of children in the United States are overweight or obese. This puts them at increased risk for diseases such as diabetes (measured by fasting glucose levels) and heart disease (due to high cholesterol levels). The local county health department wants to improve the health of the young children in the community. Most research indicates that changing diet and exercise is the best way to reduce obesity in children, but the health department suspects that children may not be willing to change both diet and exercise.

The county health department undertakes a new program to encourage children to eat better and exercise. The department enrolls 200 children in a six-month program.

- Intervention 1: diet and exercise
- Intervention 2: diet only
- Intervention 3: exercise only

The county health department hypothesizes that the children in the diet and exercise group will have the best outcomes.

Write your answer on the following lines or on a separate sheet of paper. This task may require approximately ten minutes to complete.

_____

_____

_____

_____

_____

_____

_____

_____

_____

Ecological Networks

Just as the human body has systems, an ecological community also has a network. The many species in a community interact in many ways, competing for space and resources, sometimes as predator and prey, or as host and parasite.

Flow of Energy in Ecosystems

The energy in an ecosystem always flows in a specific direction. Starting with plants and other photosynthesizing organisms, they harness and convert solar energy and supply the rest of the food chain. They are considered **producers**. Herbivores (plant eaters) are next on the energy flow, as they obtain energy directly from plants and are considered **primary consumers**. Carnivores are meat eaters and obtain energy by eating other animals, so they are considered secondary consumers. Omnivores eat both meat and plants (tertiary consumers), while decomposers feed on dead organisms. The flow of energy can then be represented as follows:

Producers → Primary Consumers → Secondary Consumers → Tertiary Consumers → Decomposers

Flow of Energy in Ecosystem Food Chain

Producers are greater in number in most ecosystems than primary, secondary, and tertiary consumers, as shown in the diagram. Think about the number of insects versus the number of foxes in one forest ecosystem, for example. If the foxes were to outnumber the insects or the plants, they would soon starve.

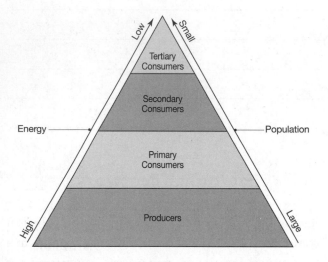

Energy Flow and Population Size in Ecosystems

The food chain is not the only example of the interdependence of organisms. Species often have to compete for food and space, so the increase in population of one can cause the decrease in population of the other. Organisms also may have a symbiotic relationship (live in close association), which could be classified as parasitism, commensalism, or mutualism.

- In a **parasitic** relationship, one organism benefits at the expense of the other.
- **Commensalism** is symbiosis in which one organism benefits and the other is neither harmed nor rewarded.
- In **mutualism**, both organisms benefit.

Under ideal conditions, with ample food and space and no predators, all living organisms have the capacity to reproduce infinitely. However, resources are limited, limiting the population of a species. This is called the **carrying capacity** of the population. The carrying capacity of a population is the maximum population size that the environment can sustain given the necessary resources (food, habitat, water) available in the environment. Expanding beyond that will usually result in the organisms self-limiting by moving away or not procreating or the organisms overwhelming that environment.

Practice

Select from the following three terms to fill in the blanks in questions 13–15.

- mutualism
- parasitism
- commensalism

13. African oxpeckers feed on the insects that are on the backs of zebras and other large African animals. This is an example of _____, a type of symbiotic relationship.

14. Lice feed on the skin and blood of the host. This is an example of _____, a type of symbiotic relationship.

15. Some spiders build their webs on blades of grass. This is an example of _____, a type of symbiotic relationship.

Humans' Influence on the Environment

Humans may be the exception to the carrying capacity rule, as our species probably comes closest to having a seemingly infinite reproductive capacity. The population keeps increasing. When we need more food, we grow more, and when we need more space, we clear some and end up damaging or even destroying other ecosystems. Humans modify ecosystems and destroy habitats through direct harvesting, pollution, atmospheric changes, and other factors. These actions are threatening current global stability and have the potential to cause irreparable damage.

Climate change is one example of the impact humans have on their environment. Scientists now agree that the climate is changing as a result of human activities. Warming of the atmosphere results from increased levels of carbon dioxide and other gases (greenhouse gases), which produce a **greenhouse effect**. The greenhouse effect occurs when the sun's rays, after hitting the earth's crust and bouncing back into space, get trapped in the atmosphere because of the greenhouse gases. What happens when the rays cannot escape the earth's atmosphere? The trapped heat causes a rise in global temperature.

There are other visible examples of how human behavior can disrupt ecosystems.

Invasive species are animal or plant species that are non-native and invade or take over the niche of a native species of an ecosystem. They can have a substantial negative impact on an ecosystem because they use resources such as nutrients, light, physical space, water, or food that the native species need to survive. The relationship to human behavior is that invasive species are sometimes purposely or accidentally introduced by humans into an ecosystem.

An example of an invasive species that you may be familiar with is the kudzu vine, now very common in the southeastern United States.

Desertification is another area of human influence on the environment. This particular situation occurs when an already dry land area becomes increasingly arid and is less able to support plants and animals. Humans contribute to desertification of ecosystems through deforestation (often for fuel or for construction materials), overgrazing, and poor farming practices.

The impact of humans on an environment is often catastrophic. Awareness of the human influence is important for understanding the breaks in some ecological networks.

Life Science Review

1. Answer the question based on the information and graph.

WHAT CAUSES COLONY COLLAPSE DISORDER?

Out of some 100 crop species that provide 90% of food worldwide, 71 of these are pollinated by bees. Over the past six years, colony collapse disorder (CCD) has wiped out an estimated 10 million beehives, worth $2 billion. Scientists have suspected that pesticides, disease-bearing parasites, and poor nutrition may be to blame.

This graph shows the number of honey-producing colonies in the United States since 1945.

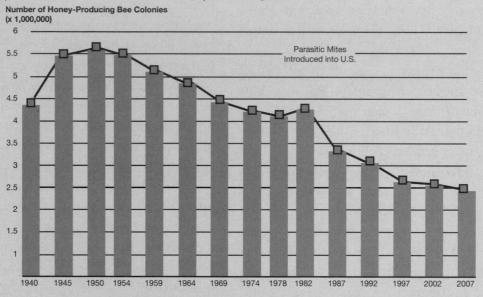

Number of Honey-Producing Bee Colonies (x 1,000,000)

Parasitic Mites Introduced into U.S.

Data source: U.S. Department of Agriculture (USDA)'s National Agricultural Statistics Service (NASS). NB: Data collected for producers with five or more colonies. Honey-producing colonies are the maximum number of colonies from which honey was taken during the year. It is possible to take honey from colonies that did not survive the entire year.

What can you conclude from the information on the graph?

a. Parasitic mites may have contributed to a decline in bee populations.

b. Parasitic mites have caused the decline in bee populations.

c. Bee populations are going to go extinct because of parasitic mites.

d. There was a steady increase in bee populations until the introduction of the parasitic mite.

2. Tapeworms are segmented flatworms that attach themselves to the insides of the intestines of host animals such as cows, pigs, and humans. They survive by eating the host's partly digested food, depriving the host of nutrients. This is an example of which kind of relationship?

a. mutualism

b. commensalism

c. speciation

d. parasitism

Use the following information to answer questions 3–5.

Radiocarbon decays at a measurable rate, called its half-life. The unstable carbon 14 (^{14}C) atom has a half-life of 5,730 years. In 5,730 years, half of the ^{14}C atoms will have decayed into a stable nitrogen atom. Scientists measure the amount of radiocarbon (^{14}C) in the fossil to determine its age.

This graph shows the percentage of radiocarbon remaining over time:

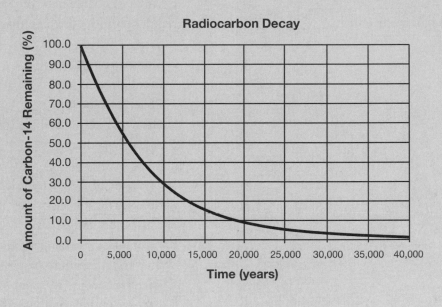

3. After 10,000 years, _____% of the sample remains.

4. After 25,000 years, _____% of the sample remains.

5. A scientist finds a fossilized bone that has about 25% of the natural amount of the ^{14}C remaining. Using the chart, what is the approximate age of the bone?
The bone is roughly _____ years old.

6. Which of the following statements explain(s) how biogeography is evidence for evolution? Check all that apply.
❏ Offspring carry the traits of both parents.
❏ Different species are not likely to interbreed.
❏ The fossil record shows the sequence of evolution in layers of sediment.
❏ Species in different habitats often can share a common ancestor.

7. Cells are the building blocks of life. Which of the following is NOT true about cells?
a. Only some cells contain genetic material.
b. Given the right conditions, cells will remain alive outside of the body.
c. Cells respond to their environments.
d. All cells contain a membrane that controls which molecules enter the cell.

8. The genotype of an organism affects the phenotype of that same organism. Label each of the following as either *genotype* or *phenotype*.

Recessive eye color genes _____

Blue eyes _____

Sex determination _____

Female _____

Curling tongue _____

Dominant hair color genes _____

9. Mitosis and meiosis are both forms of cellular reproduction. Mitosis is the splitting of a cell into two cells, with all the same genetic information being reproduced in both new cells. Meiosis involves splitting of a cell and combining with another cell, with the genetic information being split in half and combined with the other cell. Label each of the following parts of cellular reproduction as either *mitosis* or *meiosis*.

Skin regeneration _____

Blood production _____

Pollen production _____

Growth of a multicellular organism _____

Egg cell production _____

10. What is one of the current dangers of using antibiotics for problems like acne?

a. The acne is not cured.

b. Antibiotics are being used for something they aren't meant to be used for.

c. Bacteria become resistant to that antibiotic.

d. Bacteria end up on the person's face.

11. Place each of the organisms listed into the correct part of the food chain:

PRODUCERS	PRIMARY CONSUMERS	SECONDARY CONSUMERS	OMNIVORES	DECOMPOSERS

- mouse
- cow
- snake
- ant
- grasshopper
- hawk
- mushroom
- fern
- human
- bacteria
- grass
- cougar

Answers and Explanations

Chapter Practice

1.

INTERIOR PARTS OF A CELL	DESCRIPTION
nucleus	**b.** where the DNA of a cell is found
mitochondria	**c.** the site in the cell where substances are broken down to obtain energy
ribosomes	**d.** the part of the cell where the synthesis of protein takes place
plasma membrane	**a.** the element that controls the transfer of material into and out of the cell

2. Animal cells: **centrioles**

Plant cells: **cell walls**; **vacuoles** (found mostly in plant cells)

3. *Facilitated transport* and *passive transport* refer to **the movement of molecules across a cell membrane**.

4. Black: **0%**; hybrid black: **100%**; gold: **0%**

Parent (DD)

		D	D
Parent (gg)	g	Dg	Dg
	g	Dg	Dg

As you can see from the Punnett square, when you cross a black angelfish (DD) with a recessive gold angelfish (gg), all of the offspring (100%) will be hybrid (Dg).

5. d. Phenotype is the physical or behavioral expression of a gene (e.g., eye color, hair color). Choice **a** is incorrect because a genotype is the genetic coding. Choice **b** is incorrect because an allele is an alternative version of the same gene. Choice **c** is also incorrect because mitosis is a process of cell division.

6. a. Choice **a** explains how one species can diverge into two species over time when divided into two separate habitats. A classic example of this is the case of Darwin's finches on the Galapagos Islands, where finch species diverged from a common ancestor to adapt to the unique habitats of each island. Answer choices **b**, **c**, and **d** do not explain how biogeography is evidence for evolution.

7. d. According to natural selection, whether a given trait is advantageous depends on the environment of the organism. In this case the moths that were better camouflaged (those that were the color of the soot-covered trees) survived and reproduced. No new species developed, and therefore this is not an example of speciation (choice **a**). Meiosis (choice **b**) is cell division. This is not an example of extinction (when there are no more individuals of a species left alive); therefore, choice **c** is not correct.

8. This process provides evidence for the theory of evolution. Evolution is the gradual change of inherited characteristics in a population over time.

9. a. movement: **musculoskeletal system**, which provides structure and allows for movement.

b. breathing: **respiratory system**, consisting of the organs that help with inhaling and exhaling.

c. metabolism: **digestive system**, consisting of the organs that aid in breaking down food.

d. homeostasis: **nervous system**, which is primarily responsible for maintaining functioning within a normal range.

e. blood flow: **circulatory system**, which controls blood flow through the body.

f. hormone regulation: **endocrine system**, made up of glands that regulate hormones in the body.

g. reproduction: **reproductive system**, consisting of the organs involved in producing offspring.

10. a. Cells are the smallest and simplest unit in an organism. Tissues are made up of cells (e.g., muscle tissue is made of muscle cells). Organs are made of tissues (a heart is made of heart tissue), and finally, organs are organized into body systems (e.g., the nervous system, the digestive system, etc.).

11. c. Sweating is an example of the body trying to maintain homeostasis through evaporative cooling. Choice **a** is incorrect because bleeding is a result of an injury to the body and does not result in homeostasis. Urination is the excretion of waste products, not the body trying to maintain homeostasis, so choice **b** is incorrect. Choice **d** is incorrect because digestion is the process of breaking down the food we eat so it can be used by our body for fuel. It in itself is not a process for maintaining homeostasis.

12. Read the following scoring guide and the example of a 3-point response.

Scoring Guide for a Short Answer Question (from the GED® Testing Service Assessment Guide for Educators)

3-point responses contain:

- A well-formulated complete controlled experimental design
- A well-formulated data collection method
- A well-formulated complete explanation of the criteria for evaluating the hypothesis

2-point responses contain:

- A logical controlled experimental design
- A logical data collection method
- A logical explanation of the criteria for evaluating the hypothesis

1-point responses contain:

- A minimal experimental design
- A minimal or poorly formulated data collection method
- A minimal or poorly formulated explanation of the criteria for evaluating the hypothesis

0-point responses contain:

- An illogical or no controlled experimental design
- An illogical or no data collection method
- An illogical or no explanation of the criteria for evaluating the hypothesis

Example of a 3-Point Response

The county health department would randomly assign the 200 children to one of three experimental groups or the control group as follows:

- Intervention 1: diet and exercise ($n = 50$)
- Intervention 2: diet only ($n = 50$)
- Intervention 3: exercise only ($n = 50$)
- Control group: no intervention ($n = 50$)

The health department would have to take measurements on all of the children before the intervention begins, at two months, and at six months to measure the change over time. They would take height, weight, cholesterol levels, and fasting blood glucose levels. They would also need to ask questions about the diet of the children and the amount of exercise they do on a daily basis.

The children in group 1 (diet and exercise) would be on a diet lower in fat and sugar (weekly menus provided by the health department) and would be asked to double the amount of exercise they do in a week (e.g., if they normally exercise 20 minutes per week, then they will be asked to exercise 40 minutes per week). (*Note:* If they normally don't exercise at all, then they would be asked to exercise 30 minutes per day three times per week.) Parents would be asked to keep a food log and record the exercise on a daily basis.

The children in group 2 (diet change only) would be on the same reduced-fat and lower-sugar diet as the children in group 1 but would not change their exercise routine. Parents would be asked to keep a food log and record the exercise on a daily basis.

The children in group 3 (exercise change only) would not be asked to change their diet but would be asked to double the amount of exercise they do on a weekly basis, as in group 1. Parents would be asked to keep a food log and record the exercise on a daily basis.

The children in the control group would not be asked to change anything, but parents would be asked to keep a food log and record the exercise on a daily basis.

After the conclusion of the experiment, the health department could compare the weight, cholesterol levels, and fasting blood glucose levels of the groups and draw conclusions about the effectiveness of the interventions.

13. **mutualism.** In this case, both the oxpeckers and zebras are benefiting, which describes a mutualistic relationship. Oxpeckers get food, and the host animals are relieved of the bothersome insects.
14. **parasitism.** The lice are benefiting, and the hosts are being deprived of blood and skin, which is clearly a parasitic relationship.
15. **commensalism.** Spiders are using the grass as a place to build their nest, but there is no impact on the grass, positive or negative.

Life Science Review

1. **a.** The only conclusion you can draw based on the information in the graph is that the parasitic mites *may have contributed* to the decline in bee populations; therefore, choice **a** is the correct answer. The graph does not support a causal relationship. The bee population was generally in decline prior to the introduction in 1983, so we cannot conclude definitively that the mites caused the decline, so choice **b** is incorrect. Although there is a downward trend in the population, there is no way to conclude that the population will go extinct, so choice **c** is incorrect. Choice **d** is incorrect because there was a general decline (not an increase) in the population prior to the introduction of the mite.

2. d. The question states that tapeworms are benefiting and the hosts (cows, pigs, humans) are being deprived of nutrition, which is a parasitic relationship. Parasitism describes a relationship between two organisms where one benefits at the expense of the other. Choice **a** is incorrect because mutualism is a relationship in which both organisms benefit, and the host animals do not benefit from the tapeworms. Commensalism describes a benefit for one organism and no harm or benefit to the other; therefore, choice **b** is incorrect because the hosts are being deprived of food by the tapeworm. Speciation is the development of a new species and is not related to types of symbiotic relationships, so choice **c** is incorrect.

3. After 10,000 years, **30%** of the sample remains.

4. After 25,000 years, **5%** of the sample remains.

5. The bone is roughly **12,500** years old.

6. Only *Species in different habitats often can share a common ancestor* is evidence of evolution. It explains how one species can diverge into two species over time when divided into two separate habitats. A classic example of this is the case of finches on the Galapagos Islands, where finch species diverged from a common ancestor to adapt to the unique habitats of each island.

7. a. *All* cells contain genetic material, so choice **a** is not true. Choice **b**, choice **c**, and choice **d** are all true statements.

8. Recessive eye color genes: **genotype**
Blue eyes: **phenotype**
Sex determination: **genotype**
Female: **phenotype**
Curling tongue: **phenotype**
Dominant hair color genes: **genotype**

9. Skin regeneration: **mitosis**
Blood production: **mitosis**
Pollen production: **meiosis**
Growth of a multicellular organism: **mitosis**
Egg cell production: **meiosis**

10. c. Someone who takes antibiotics for treating acne could accumulate bacteria that are capable of destroying the antibiotic. If that same person becomes infected with a serious disease that is treated with the same antibiotic, the resistant bacteria could destroy the antibiotic before it is able to act on the disease.

11.

PRODUCERS	PRIMARY CONSUMERS	SECONDARY CONSUMERS	OMNIVORES	DECOMPOSERS
grass, fern	grasshopper, ant, cow, mouse	snake, hawk, mouse, cougar	human	ant, mushroom, bacteria

11 ▶ PHYSICAL SCIENCE

Physical science includes the disciplines of physics (the study of energy and how energy affects matter) and chemistry (the study of matter). In this chapter, we review the basic concepts of physical science:

- the structure and properties of matter, including atoms
- chemical properties and reactions
- energy, including conservation of energy, increase in disorder, and interactions of energy and matter
- work, motions, and forces

In reviewing these concepts, you'll be better prepared to solve problems and answer questions on the GED® Science test. There are practice questions throughout. Use them to test your ability to work through solutions. Answers and explanations for all practice questions are at the end of the chapter.

Matter

Matter describes everything that exists. Matter has mass and takes up space. It can interact with other matter and with energy, and these interactions form the basis of physical and chemical reactions. But what actually is matter?

Atoms

You and everything around you are composed of tiny particles called **atoms**. The book you are reading, the neurons in your brain, and the air that you are breathing are all collections of various atoms. Atoms make up matter. Atoms are also the smallest known complete particle. Let's look at the history of the atom.

The term **atom**, which means *indivisible*, was coined by Greek philosopher Democritus (460–370 B.C.). He disagreed with Plato and Aristotle—who believed that matter could be infinitely divided into smaller and smaller pieces—and postulated that matter is composed of tiny indivisible particles.

In spite of Democritus, the belief that matter could be infinitely divided lingered until the early 1800s, when John Dalton formulated a meaningful atomic theory. It stated:

- Matter is composed of atoms.
- All atoms of a given element are identical.
- Atoms of different elements are different and have different properties.
- Atoms are neither created nor destroyed in a chemical reaction.
- Compounds are formed when atoms of more than one element combine.
- A given compound always has the same relative number and kinds of atoms.

These theories are still used today, but there's more to know about atoms.

Protons, Neutrons, and Electrons

An atom is composed of a nucleus surrounded by electrons. The **nucleus** contains positively charged particles called **protons** and uncharged (neutral) particles called **neutrons**. **Electrons** are the negatively charged particles orbiting the nucleus.

Remember that atoms, as the most basic component of matter, have mass. To define that mass, scientists have determined that neutrons and protons have a mass of about 1 atomic mass unit, abbreviated **amu**. An amu is equivalent to about $1.66 \ 10^{-24}$ g. That is a very small mass.

Electrons, in comparison, have a mass that is approximately $\frac{1}{1,836}$ that of a proton.

Electrons are not simply just the orbitals around the nucleus. The ones orbiting in the outermost **electron shell** (the orbit of the electrons) are called **valence electrons**. Valence electrons are most responsible for the properties and reaction patterns of an element to other elements and atoms. In a neutral atom, the number of protons and electrons is equal. A negatively charged atom has more electrons than protons, and a positively charged atom has more protons than electrons. The reason the atom stays together at all is that the negatively charged electrons are attracted to the positively charged nucleus. While this attractive force holds an atom together, the nucleus itself is held together by strong nuclear forces.

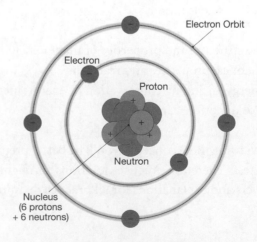

Structure of a Carbon Atom

Periodic Table of Elements

Scientists have been trying to understand the elements of matter through the use of organizational tables since the 1700s. We call the current organizational structure the **Periodic Table of Elements**. As of 2014, the periodic table contains 118 confirmed chemical elements.

The table organizes elements by their properties and helps scientists predict the discovery of new elements. It is a critical tool for understanding how elements react with each other. Each block in the table describes a different element.

1																	18
1 H 1.0079	2											13	14	15	16	17	2 He 4.0026
3 Li 6.941	4 Be 9.0122											5 B 10.811	6 C 12.011	7 N 14.007	8 O 15.999	9 F 18.998	10 Ne 20.180
11 Na 22.990	12 Mg 24.305	3	4	5	6	7	8	9	10	11	12	13 Al 26.982	14 Si 28.086	15 P 30.974	16 S 32.065	17 Cl 35.453	18 Ar 39.948
19 K 39.098	20 Ca 40.078	21 Sc 44.956	22 Ti 47.867	23 V 50.942	24 Cr 51.996	25 Mn 54.938	26 Fe 55.845	27 Co 58.933	28 Ni 58.693	29 Cu 63.546	30 Zn 65.409	31 Ga 69.723	32 Ge 72.64	33 As 74.922	34 Se 78.96	35 Br 79.904	36 Kr 83.798
37 Rb 85.468	38 Sr 87.62	39 Y 88.906	40 Zr 91.224	41 Nb 92.906	42 Mo 95.94	43 Tc (98)	44 Ru 101.07	45 Rh 102.91	46 Pd 106.42	47 Ag 107.87	48 Cd 112.41	49 In 114.82	50 Sn 118.71	51 Sb 121.76	52 Te 127.60	53 I 126.90	54 Xe 131.29
55 Cs 132.91	56 Ba 137.33	57-71 *	72 Hf 178.49	73 Ta 180.95	74 W 183.84	75 Re 186.21	76 Os 190.23	77 Ir 192.22	78 Pt 195.08	79 Au 196.97	80 Hg 200.59	81 Tl 204.38	82 Pb 207.2	83 Bi 208.98	84 Po (209)	85 At (210)	86 Rn (222)
87 Fr (223)	88 Ra (226)	89-103 #	104 Rf (261)	105 Db (262)	106 Sg (266)	107 Bh (264)	108 Hs (270)	109 Mt (268)	110 Ds (281)	111 Rg (272)	112 Uub (285)	113 Uut (284)	114 Uuq (289)	115 Uup (288)	116 Uuh (291)		118 Uuo (294)

* Lanthanide series	57 La 138.91	58 Ce 140.12	59 Pr 140.91	60 Nd 144.24	61 Pm (145)	62 Sm 150.36	63 Eu 151.96	64 Gd 157.25	65 Tb 158.93	66 Dy 162.50	67 Ho 164.93	68 Er 167.26	69 Tm 168.93	70 Yb 173.04	71 Lu 174.97
# Actinide series	89 Ac (227)	90 Th 232.04	91 Pa 231.04	92 U 238.03	93 Np (237)	94 Pu (244)	95 Am (243)	96 Cm (247)	97 Bk (247)	98 Cf (251)	99 Es (252)	100 Fm (257)	101 Md (258)	102 No (259)	103 Lr (262)

Understanding how to read the periodic table is critical to understanding how elements will react with each other. Being able to read a block of the table is useful for the GED® Science test. Look at this example, the block for carbon:

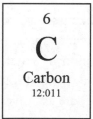

Carbon Entry in the Periodic Table of Elements

- The numeral 6 refers to the atomic number, which is the number of protons in the nucleus.
- C refers to the abbreviation for carbon.
- Carbon is the common name of the element written out under the abbreviation.
- 2:011 is the average weight of the atomic mass in the nucleus of the element's isotopes.

Molecules

Molecules are the next step up in terms of parts of matter. They are composed of two or more atoms held together in molecules by **chemical bonds**. These chemical bonds can be ionic or covalent bonds, which are related to how the valence electrons interact between atoms. Specifically, **ionic bonds** form when one atom donates one or more electrons to another. **Covalent bonds** form when the electrons are shared between atoms. With the atoms bonded together to create a molecule, the **mass** of that molecule can be calculated by adding the masses of its component atoms.

Something that you will most likely see in questions on the GED® Science test is the symbol of an element with a number in a subscript after it. This is shown in a **chemical formula** and is the number of atoms of a given element in a molecule. For example, the glucose (sugar) molecule is represented as $C_6H_{12}O_6$. This formula tells you that the glucose molecule contains 6 carbon atoms (C), 12 hydrogen atoms (H), and 6 oxygen atoms (O). In some cases, you may end up with two chemical formulas interacting and will have to solve what the new formula could be.

States of Matter

Molecules relate to matter, which we've discussed briefly, in that matter itself is held together by **intermolecular forces**—forces *between* different molecules.

A **solid** has a fixed shape and volume. The molecules in a solid have a regular, ordered arrangement and vibrate in place but are unable to move far.

Examples of matter in solid form include

- diamonds (carbon atoms)
- ice (water molecules)
- metal alloys (mixtures of different metals)

Liquids flow, and their **density** (mass per unit volume) is usually lower than the density of solids. Liquids have a fixed volume but take the shape of the container they are in. The molecules in a liquid are not ordered and can move from one region to another through a process called **diffusion**.

Examples of matter in liquid form include

- mercury (mercury atoms)
- vinegar (molecules of acetic acid)
- perfume (a mixture of liquids made of different molecules)

Gases take the shape and volume of the container they are in and can be compressed when pressure is applied. The molecules in gases are disordered and move quickly. The density of gas is much lower than the density of a liquid.

Examples of matter in gaseous form include

- helium gas (helium atoms)
- water vapor (molecules of water)
- air (mixture of different molecules, including nitrogen, oxygen, carbon dioxide, and water vapor)

> Density is calculated by dividing mass by volume:
>
> **Density = mass/volume**

The size and mass of a substance can change, but its density (at a particular temperature) will always remain constant regardless of the size. For example, at 20°C, a very small piece of aluminum will have the same density (2.70 g/cm^3) as a large piece of aluminum.

These may seem like hard rules regarding states of matter, but matter can change its state depending on various factors.

Changes of State

Changes of state, or **phase changes**, involve the transition from one state of matter into another. Freezing water to make ice, condensation of water vapor as morning dew, and sublimation (going directly from a solid to a gas) of dry ice (CO_2) are examples of phase changes.

A phase change is a physical process. No chemical bonds are formed or broken. Only the intermolecular (physical) forces are affected.

- **Freezing** is the process of changing a liquid into a solid by removing heat.

- **Melting** is the opposite process of freezing, whereby heat energy is added to the solid until it changes into a liquid.
- **Boiling** is the change of phase from a liquid to a gas and also requires the input of heat energy.
- **Condensation** is the change from gas to liquid, which often involves removing heat.

Some substances **sublimate**, which means that they change directly from the solid phase to the gas phase, without forming a liquid first. Carbon dioxide is such a substance. Solid carbon dioxide, called dry ice, evaporates into the gas phase when heated. When gas changes directly into a solid, the process is called **deposition**. One example of this is snow formation, which is water vapor in the air turning directly into a solid as ice, also known as snowflakes.

All of these transitions of matter generally involve the addition or removal of heat. This understanding also helps with defining the physical and chemical properties of matter.

Physical and Chemical Properties

The **physical properties** of matter include properties that are observable and measurable without having to alter the chemical structure of a substance. We've already discussed a few of these previously, like mass and density, but there are many more. Some physical properties of matter include:

- **Mass:** a measure of how much matter is in an object, often measured in grams or kilograms
- **Density:** mass per unit of volume (how tightly packed the molecules are)
- **Volume:** how much space is occupied by a substance, measured in liters or milliliters
- **Elasticity:** the ability of a substance to return to its original shape after a deforming (e.g., stretching) force is applied
- **Solubility:** the amount of a substance that will dissolve in another substance (often described in

terms of solubility in water); measured in grams per liter or moles per liter
- **Boiling point:** the temperature at which a substance will boil
- **Hardness:** the measure of how resistant a substance is to shape change when a force is applied (example: resistance to stretching)
- **Viscosity:** the measure of a substance's resistance to flow (example: honey is highly viscous, which is why it is difficult to get out of a jar, while olive oil has low viscosity and is easy to pour)

Chemical properties of matter include properties that cannot be observed; the substance's internal chemical structure must be affected for its chemical properties to be investigated. Some examples of chemical properties of matter include:

- **Heat of combustion:** the energy released when a compound undergoes combustion with oxygen; may be expressed as energy/mole of fuel (kJ/mol)
- **Reactivity:** the rate at which a chemical substance tends to undergo a chemical reaction
- **Flammability:** the measure of how easily a substance burns or combusts

With all of these bits and pieces about matter and the various descriptions of matter, let's look at some sample questions that focus on matter.

Practice
1. Which of the following would NOT be considered a physical property?
   a. flammability
   b. hardness
   c. solubilty
   d. density

2. The smallest unit of matter is the
  a. compound.
  b. atom.
  c. molecule.
  d. proton.

3. Which is an example of a phase change?
  a. oil floating on water
  b. oxygen diffusing in water
  c. paper burning
  d. water freezing

Chemical Reactions

Chemical reactions happen around you (and inside you) every day. Removing stains from clothes, digesting food, and burning wood in a fireplace are all examples of chemical reactions. These types of reactions involve changes in the chemical arrangement of the atoms of a molecule and often show or involve the chemical properties of an element. In a chemical reaction, the atoms of reactants combine, recombine, or dissociate to form new products.

Some of the rules of matter do remain the same. Even as the atoms interact, the number of them in a particular element remains the same after a chemical reaction as before. The total mass is also preserved. Similarly, energy is never created or destroyed by a chemical reaction. If chemical bonds are broken, energy from those bonds can be liberated into the surroundings as heat. However, this liberation of energy does not constitute creation, since the energy only changes form—from chemical energy to heat energy.

Knowing these things about chemical reactions will help with answering questions regarding chemical equations, which is how these reactions are often described.

Chemical Equations

A chemical reaction can be represented by a **chemical equation**, where the reactants are written on the left side and the products on the right side of an arrow, which indicates the direction in which the reaction proceeds.

Let's look at an example. The following chemical equation represents the reaction of glucose ($C_6H_{12}O_6$) with oxygen (O_2) to form carbon dioxide (CO_2) and water (H_2O). This reaction occurs constantly in your body as glucose and oxygen in the blood recombine to obtain energy.

$$(C_6H_{12}O_6) + 6\,(O_2) \rightarrow 6\,(CO_2) + 6\,(H_2O)$$

The numbers in front of the molecular formulas indicate the proportion in which the molecules react. No number in front of the chemical formula means that one molecule of that substance is reacting. In the previous reaction, one molecule of glucose is reacting with six molecules of oxygen to form six molecules of carbon dioxide and six molecules of water.

The number of molecules of each of the substances in the reaction tells you in what proportion the molecules react. So if ten molecules of glucose react with 60 molecules of oxygen, you would obtain 60 molecules of carbon dioxide and 60 molecules of water.

$$10\,(C_6H_{12}O_6) + 60\,(O_2) \rightarrow 60\,(CO_2) + 60\,(H_2O)$$

In many ways, chemical equations are like food recipes.

2 bread + 1 cheese + 2 tomato = sandwich

With two slices of bread, one slice of cheese, and two slices of tomato, you can make one sandwich. If you had six slices of bread, three slices of cheese, and six slices of tomato, you could make three sandwiches. The same principles of proportion apply in chemical reactions.

You'll be able to answer many chemical reaction questions if you think about the proportions of the chemical formulas.

Types of Chemical Reactions

Similar reactions can be classified and categorized into specific types of reactions. For example, chemical reactions can be classified as **synthesis reactions**, **decomposition reactions**, **single-replacement reactions**, and **double-replacement reactions**. Each of these reactions proceeds as you may expect by its name.

> **Synthesis reaction:** two elements merging together to become a new product:
> $$A + B \rightarrow AB$$
> **Decomposition reaction:** a single element splitting into its component parts:
> $$AB \rightarrow A + B$$
> **Single-replacement reaction:** two elements in which a single part moves between one element and the other:
> $$C + AB \rightarrow CB + A$$
> **Double-replacement reaction:** two elements in which two parts flip places:
> $$AB + CD \rightarrow AD + CB$$

You may encounter some of these reactions, but just keep in mind that the description fits what is happening in the reaction. What you're more likely to run into are chemical equations that need to be balanced.

Balancing Chemical Equations

Just as in the sandwich equation previously described, the reactants will always combine in specific ratios to form the product. If two slices of bread are on the left side of the equation, then the sandwich formed on the right side will always have two slices, never one or three. If four slices are on the left side, then you will end up with four slices on the right.

Look at the following synthesis reaction:

$$N_2 + 3H_2 \rightarrow 2NH_3 \; (+ \; \textbf{heat})$$

There are two nitrogen atoms on both sides of the equation. Also, there are six hydrogen atoms on each side of the equation. Matter is conserved. Now look at this synthesis reaction involving ions:

$$2F^- + Ca^{2+} \rightarrow CaF_2$$

In addition to showing the conservation of matter, this example shows the conservation of charge. The two fluoride ions, each with a charge of -1, combine with a calcium ion, which has a charge of $+2$. The product formed is neutral; the two -1 charges and the one $+2$ charge cancel each other out, so charge is conserved.

In fact, all chemical reactions must conserve:

- matter (mass)
- energy
- electric charge

With this in mind, you'll be able to see if an equation balances on both sides or if something is wrong in a question.

Heat of Reaction (Enthalpy)

The heat of a reaction (**enthalpy**) is absolutely related to the type of chemical reaction happening. As chemical reactions involve the breaking of molecular bonds, they require the input of energy to break those bonds. Similarly, the formation of new bonds releases energy. The stronger the bonds, the more energy is released when they are formed, and the more energy is required to break them. Therefore, a chemical reaction will either absorb or give off heat, depending on how many and what kind of bonds are broken and made as a result of that reaction.

These two types of reactions have names. A reaction that absorbs energy is called **endothermic**. A container in which an endothermic reaction takes place gets cold because the heat of the container is absorbed by the reaction. A reaction that gives off energy is called **exothermic**. Burning glucose ($C_6H_{12}O_6$) is a reaction that is exothermic—it gives off energy. Combustion of glucose is exothermic because the energy released by forming the C–O and O–H bonds in CO_2 and H_2O is greater than the energy required to break the chemical bonds in glucose. It's useful to remember that *exo-* means giving off heat, while *endo-* means absorbing.

Catalysts

Often, a reaction needs help getting started. Such help can come from a catalyst. A **catalyst** is a substance that accelerates a reaction, without itself being changed or used up in the reaction. It acts by lowering what is called the **activation energy** of a reaction. This activation energy is often illustrated as a hill separating two valleys, as in the figure here. This hill needs to be crossed in order to get from one valley to the other (one valley representing the reactants, and the other the products). The catalyst acts by making the hill lower and easier to cross.

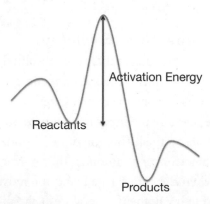

How a Catalyst Works to Activate a Reaction

Being able to read a diagram like this one will be useful to you in answering questions. The line that is drawn between the level of the reactants and the top of the activation energy shows how much energy is needed to create the products that appear on the right side.

Compounds and Mixtures

There are more ways to look at elements and how they interact. When two or more elements combine chemically, the result is a **compound**. Examples of compounds include carbon dioxide (a product of respiration), sucrose (table sugar), serotonin (a human brain chemical), and acetic acid (a component of vinegar). In each of these compounds, there is more than one type of atom chemically bonded to other atoms in a definite proportion. The combination of these atoms also results in a fixed, definite structure. Compounds are chemically bonded.

When two or more elements combine physically, the result is a **mixture**. In a homogeneous mixture, the components can't be visually separated. Homogeneous mixtures also have the same composition (ratio of components) throughout their volume. An example is a mixture of a small amount of salt mixed in water. A uniform mixture is often called a **solution**. In a solution, one substance (solute) is dissolved in another (solvent). In the salt and water mixture, the salt is the solute, and the water is the solvent.

In a heterogeneous mixture, the components can often be visually identified, and the composition may vary from one point of the mixture to another. A collection of dimes and pennies is a heterogeneous mixture. A mixture of sugar and flour is also heterogeneous since sugar has a very different texture than flour.

Saturation is reached when the solution can hold no additional solute. If additional substance continues to be added after saturation has been reached, it will not dissolve (it will either float or sink to the bottom).

Practice

4. This chemical equation represents the combustion (burning) of methane (CH_4). The equation states that 1 mol of methane and 2 mol of oxygen react to produce 1 mol of carbon dioxide and 2 mol of water.

$$CH_4(g) + 2O_2(g) \rightarrow CO_2(g) + 2H_2O(l)$$
$$\Delta H = -890 \text{ kJ}$$

If 890 kJ of heat are released ($\Delta H = -890$ kJ), then this reaction is considered:

a. endothermic

b. exothermic

c. equivalent

d. evaporative

5.

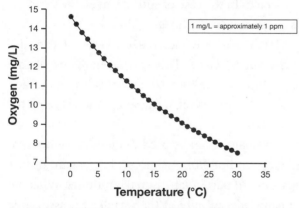

Solubility of Oxygen with Temperature

1 mg/L = approximately 1 ppm

Fish require 5 to 6 ppm of dissolved oxygen and cannot live at levels below 2 ppm.

Which conclusion can you draw based on the data shown in the chart?

a. As temperature increases, oxygen dissolves more quickly.

b. Fish cannot survive in water at 25°C.

c. Warmer water holds less oxygen.

d. If you double the temperature of the water, the amount of dissolved oxygen is decreased by half.

Energy

In science, **energy** is defined as the ability to do work. Similarly to matter and heat in chemical reactions, energy can't be created or destroyed. This is a property called **conservation of energy**. Also, energy can only change form, which is a property called **transformation of energy**. This property is important in considering the forms of energy.

Forms of Energy

Forms of energy include potential energy and kinetic energy. **Potential energy** is energy that is stored. **Kinetic energy** is the energy associated with motion. To understand the difference, look at the following illustration.

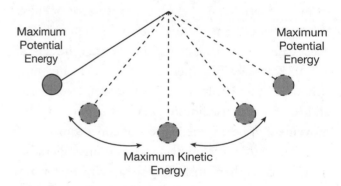

Maximum Potential Energy

Maximum Potential Energy

Maximum Kinetic Energy

As the pendulum swings, the energy is converted from potential to kinetic and back to potential. When the hanging weight is at one of the high points, the gravitational potential energy is at a maximum and kinetic energy is at the minimum. At the low point, the kinetic energy is maximized and gravitational potential energy is minimized.

Examples of potential energy include nuclear energy and chemical energy, where energy is stored in the bonds that hold atoms and molecules together. Heat, hydrodynamic energy, and electromagnetic waves are examples of kinetic energy, where energy is associated with the movement of molecules, water, and electrons or photons (particles of light).

Heat Energy

Heat as energy moves through various forms of matter. It's transferred three ways: by conduction, convection, and radiation.

Conduction is the transfer of heat from one molecule to another through a substance. Not all substances conduct heat at the same speed. Metals are good conductors. Think of how quickly a metal spoon heats up in a cup of coffee or a pot of boiling water. One end starts out cold, the other end is in heat, and the metal spoon eventually warms consistently throughout. Wood, paper, and air are poor heat conductors and are considered **insulators**. You can stir a pot of boiling soup with a wooden spoon, and the spoon will not get hot.

Another way that heat moves through matter is through **convection**, which is the transfer of heat from one place to another by the movement of fluids. When substances are heated, density is reduced. This causes the movement of the fluids (e.g., liquids or gases). For example, when a solution is heated on a stove, the heated water rises (as it becomes less dense) and the more dense liquids sink to the bottom. That movement of heat is the process of convection.

The third way that heat moves is through **radiation**, which is the transfer of energy via one form of electromagnetic waves. This includes the feeling of heat on your face from the sun or from a fire. Electromagnetic waves are one part of energy waves.

Energy Waves

Energy in all its forms can interact with matter. For example, when heat energy interacts with molecules of water, it makes them move faster and boil. Waves—including sound and seismic waves, waves on water, and light waves—have energy and can transfer that energy when they interact with matter. Consider what happens if you are standing by the ocean and a big wave rolls in. Sometimes the energy carried by the wave is large enough to knock you down.

Energy is also carried by electromagnetic waves or light waves. The energy of **electromagnetic waves** is related to their wavelengths. These electromagnetic waves include:

- radio waves (the longest wavelength)
- microwaves
- infrared radiation (radiant heat)
- visible light
- ultraviolet radiation
- X-rays
- gamma rays

The wavelength of the energy waves depends on the amount of energy the wave is carrying. Shorter wavelengths carry more energy than longer wavelengths. When a wave hits a smooth surface, such as a mirror, it is reflected. In the case of sound waves, those reflections come across as echoes.

Matter not only can reflect waves; it can also **refract** or bend waves. This is what happens when a ray of light traveling through air hits a water surface. A part of the wave is reflected, and a part is refracted into the water.

Wavelengths can be used to identify elements as well. Each kind of atom or molecule can gain or lose energy only in particular discrete amounts. When an atom gains energy, light at the wavelength associated with that energy is absorbed. When an atom loses energy, light at the wavelength associated with that energy is emitted. Measuring whether these wavelengths are there or not describes what element is involved.

Parts of Waves

While considering waves and energy, let's look at the four parts that make up a wave:

1. wavelength
2. amplitude

3. crest
4. trough

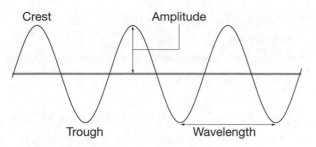

Parts of a Wave

The **crest** is the highest part of the wave, while the **trough** is the lowest part. The **wavelength** is the total distance from trough to trough or crest to crest, and **amplitude** is measured as the height of the wave above neutral. This applies to all types of waves (sound waves as well as ocean waves). In sound waves, the amplitude is equal to the loudness of the sound.

Frequency as it relates to waves is defined as the number of wave cycles that pass in a certain period of time. In sound waves, higher-pitched sounds have a higher frequency. This means that more cycles of waves are compressed into the same period of time. Lower-pitched sounds have lower frequency.

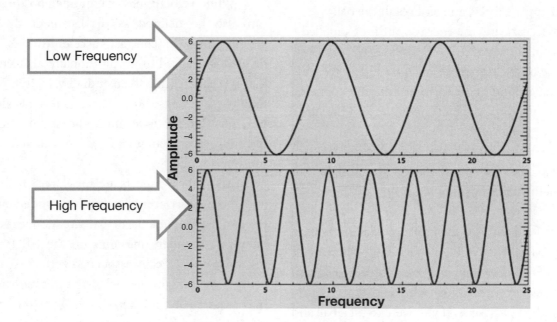

Practice

6. The frequency of the sounds produced by a bottle-nosed dolphin ranges from 20 Hz to 150 kHz. The lower-frequency vocalizations are likely used in social communication. Higher-frequency clicks (40 kHz to 150 kHz) are primarily used for echolocation. The sound waves travel through water at speeds of approximately 1,400 m/s.

Determine the wavelengths of the waves at the lower end of the frequency range used for echolocation. Speed = wavelength × frequency.
a. 35 mm
b. 1,365 m
c. 0.029 m
d. 56 km

Force, Motion, and Work

Energy, which is associated with chemical reactions, also appears in the physical world in familiar ways. A **force** is a push or a pull. Objects move in response to forces acting on them. When you kick a ball, it rolls. A force is also required to stop motion, and in all this, energy is needed to make force happen. It's useful to think about sequential details involved in this action.

1. First your body breaks the chemical bonds in the food you have eaten.
2. This supplies your body with energy.
3. You use up some of that energy to kick the ball.
4. You apply a force, and as a result the ball moves, carrying the energy your foot supplied it with.
5. Some of the energy is transferred from the ball to the ground in the form of heat, due to the frictional force the ball encounters on the surface of the ground.
6. As energy is lost this way, the ball slows down.
7. When all of the energy is used up through friction, the ball stops moving.

This example illustrates the concept of conservation of energy, as well as **Newton's first law—the Law of Inertia**—which is the tendency of an object to remain either at rest or in motion with constant velocity unless acted on by a force. If you were to hit a ball and there was no force working against it (in this case it would be friction), it would continue to move forever.

Measuring Force

Speed, velocity, acceleration, and momentum are all ways or aspects of measuring force. These concepts are used frequently in daily life, but it's a good idea to understand the exact scientific meanings for the GED® Science test.

For example, what is the difference between speed and velocity?

- A **speed**, such as 30 miles per hour, has **magnitude**.
- A velocity has **magnitude** *and* **direction** (e.g., 30 miles per hour north)

A similar distinction can be made between the terms **distance** and **displacement**. If you walk 20 feet to your mailbox and 20 feet back, the *distance* you traveled is 40 feet. Your **displacement** is zero, because displacement compares your ending point to your starting point.

While **velocity** has magnitude and direction, it can also be defined as displacement divided by elapsed time. In contrast, **acceleration** is velocity divided by elapsed time. Additionally, an acceleration that is negative (due to an ending velocity that is less than the starting velocity) is called a **deceleration**. But, for velocity to change, the speed and/or the direction must change and a net or unbalanced force must be applied.

All of these aspects are measurements of force, and these ideas are all needed to understand how force may work in a particular situation, experiment, or question. Often questions on the GED® Science test will be specifically associated with these ideas, so being able to figure out what the question is asking may require you to understand these terms.

When looking at all of these concepts in relation to an object, let's summarize a bit: an object at rest (whose speed is zero) remains at rest unless some force acts on it (e.g., a person pushes it, the wind blows it away, or gravity pulls it down). An object that is moving continues to move at the same speed in the same direction, unless some force is applied to it to slow it down, to speed it up, or to change its direction. The amount of acceleration or deceleration is directly proportional to the force applied. The harder you kick the ball, the faster it will move. The mass of the ball will also determine how much it will accelerate. Kick a soccer ball and then a ball made of lead with the same force (watch your foot!). Which ball moves faster as a result of an equal kick? These observations constitute **Newton's second law—the Law of Acceleration**:

$$\text{Force} = \text{mass} \times \text{acceleration}$$

A related concept is momentum. If an object is in motion, it has **momentum**. The amount of momentum an object has depends on its mass and velocity. Think of a heavy cart rolling downhill fast; it has a lot of momentum (large mass and high velocity). Now think of a textbook sliding down an incline (relatively small mass and low velocity); it has much less momentum than the cart.

$$\text{Momentum} = \text{mass} \times \text{velocity}$$

With momentum, acceleration, velocity, distance, and speed, we can determine a lot about the force these aspects describe.

Types of Forces

Newton's laws specifically relate to the study of how the motion of objects is affected by force. Other types of forces include gravitational, electromagnetic, and contact forces, which are discussed next.

Gravitational Force

Gravitation is an attractive force that each object with mass exerts on any other object with mass. The strength of the gravitational force depends on the masses of the objects and on the distance between them.

When we think of gravity, we usually think of Earth's gravity, which prevents us from jumping infinitely high, keeps objects stuck to the ground, and makes things thrown upward fall down. We, too, exert a gravitational force on the earth, and we exert forces on one another, but these are not very noticeable because our masses are very small in comparison with the mass of our planet.

The greater the masses involved, the greater the gravitational force between them. The sun exerts a force on the earth, and the earth exerts a force on the sun. The moon exerts a force on the earth, and the earth on the moon. The gravitational force of the moon is the reason there are tides. The moon's gravity pulls the water on Earth. The sun also exerts a force on our water, but this is not as apparent because the sun, although more massive than the moon, is very far away. As the distance between two objects doubles, the gravitational force between them decreases four times.

What is the difference between weight and mass? On Earth, the **acceleration due to gravity**, g, is -9.8 m/s^2 (meters per second squared). Your weight (w) is really a force. The formula *Force = mass × acceleration* becomes *Weight = mass × gravitational acceleration*. Since the acceleration, g, is -9.8 m/s^2, the overall force (w) is negative, which just means that its pull is in the downward direction: the earth is pulling you toward its center.

A fun way to think about this is that you have probably heard somebody say: "You'd weigh less on the moon!" This is true because the gravitational force on the moon is less than the earth's gravitational force. Your mass, however, would still be the same, because mass is just a measure of your density and the volume you take up.

Weight is commonly measured in newtons (N), so when you see an N, you'll be dealing with weight and force. Fun fact: 1 N = 0.222 pounds.

Electromagnetic Force

Electricity and magnetism are two aspects of a single **electromagnetic force**, another type of force that you may run into. It is exactly what it sounds like, electricity and magnetism. Moving electric charges produce magnetic forces, and moving magnets produce electric forces. The electromagnetic force exists between any two charged or magnetic objects: for example, a proton and an electron or two electrons.

Opposite charges attract (an electron and a proton), whereas like charges repel (two protons or two electrons). The strength of the force depends on the charges and on the distance between them. The greater the charges, the greater the force. The closer the charges are to each other, the greater the force between them.

Contact Forces

Contact forces, yet another type of force, are those that exist as a result of an interaction between objects physically in contact with one another. They include frictional forces, tensional forces, and normal forces.

The **frictional force** opposes the motion of an object across a surface. For example, if a glass slides across the surface of the dinner table, there exists a friction force in the direction opposite to the motion of the glass. Friction is the result of attractive intermolecular forces between the molecules of the surface of the glass and the surface of the table. Friction depends on the nature of the two surfaces. There would be less friction between the table and the glass if the table was highly polished. The glass would glide across the table more easily. Friction also depends on the degree to which the glass and the table are pressed together. Also, air resistance is a type of frictional force. An example of air resistance is how it affects something like a ball that has been thrown. Both gravitational and frictional force slow it and lead it to land back on the ground.

Tension is the force that is transmitted through a rope or wire when it is pulled tight by forces acting at each end. The tensional force is directed along the rope or wire and pulls on the objects on either end. A kite may use air resistance to catch the wind and rise in the air, while the person holding the end of the kite's line is using tensional force to hold on to and guide the kite and pull it back to the ground.

A last type of contact force is **normal force**, which is exerted on an object in contact with another stable object. For example, the dinner table exerts an upward force on a glass at rest on the surface of the table.

All of these forces are used in everyday objects like simple machines, which use energy and force to do various types of work.

Work and Machines

Machines are built to do work, and at their most basic level, this relates to overcoming the effects of force on an object. A **simple machine** is a device that changes the direction or magnitude of a force. A simple machine can be defined as a mechanism that provides **mechanical advantage** or leverage. In other words, simple machines make it easier to do work.

WORK AND POWER

Work is defined as the product of force and distance:

Work = force × distance

Power is the rate at which work is done:

Power = work/time

The metric unit for power is the watt. One watt equals 1 joule/second. So power is sometimes measured in joules per second. When you see this, remember that it's power related.

There are six basic types of simple machines:

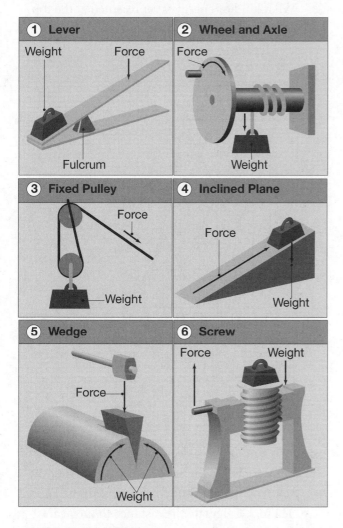

① Lever

Weight   Force

Fulcrum

② Wheel and Axle

Force

Weight

③ Fixed Pulley

Force

Weight

④ Inclined Plane

Force

Weight

⑤ Wedge

Force

Weight

⑥ Screw

Force   Weight

A **lever** produces a mechanical advantage by transferring an applied force over a distance and exerting an output force on an object (example: think of a crowbar).

A **wheel and axle** assembly is formed by two disks, or cylinders, of different diameters that rotate together around the same axis. Forces applied to the edges of the two disks, or cylinders, provide mechanical advantage (example: think of a steering wheel in a car or a doorknob).

A **fixed pulley** can make it easier to lift an object. Although the same amount of force is needed to lift an object with a fixed single pulley as without the pulley, giving it no mechanical advantage, certain

types of pulleys do produce a mechanical advantage. The more pulleys that are added to the system, the less force that is needed to move the object. The mechanical advantage is increased because the force is distributed over the length of the pulley ropes. For example:

- Fixed single pulley: if you wanted to lift a 100-kg object 10 cm, you would need to apply 100 N of force.
- Double pulley system: if you wanted to lift a 100-kg object 10 cm, you would need to apply 50 N of force.
- Triple pulley system: if you wanted to lift a 100-kg object 10 cm, you would need to apply 33.3 N of force.
- Four-pulley system: if you wanted to lift a 100-kg object 10 cm, you would need to apply 25 N of force.

An **inclined plane** produces a mechanical advantage by allowing a smaller force to be applied to increase the vertical distance of an object (for example, think of pushing a cart up a hill versus lifting it straight up).

A **wedge** produces a mechanical advantage by concentrating force on a small area (for example, think of an ax splitting a log).

A **screw**, which is an inclined plane wrapped around a cylinder, produces a mechanical advantage by amplifying the force applied. A small rotational force on the shaft can exert a large force on the load (for example, think of a corkscrew).

Understanding how these various simple machines work is useful for both the GED® Science test and daily life. A question you encounter on the test involving pulleys may include determining from a diagram how much force you would need to apply to lift 100 kg. The diagram might show a single-, double-, and triple-pulley system with all the information previously given here, and the four-pulley system would not tell you how much force you would need. Since each additional pulley reduces the amount of force, this would give you a clue as to how much force you would need. When answering physical science questions, take the information presented and work out the solution with that information and any science knowledge you have learned.

Physical Science Review

1. A blue whale is 30-m long and has a mass of 40,000 kg (400 metric tons). Determine the weight of a blue whale in newtons. _____
   Weight = mass × acceleration due to gravity (g)
   $g = 9.8$ m/s^2

2. Newton's second law of motion is the Law of Acceleration. The calculation can be stated as
   acceleration = force ÷ mass
   If a force of 10 N is applied to a 2-kg object, the object will accelerate at _____ m/s^2.

3. Balance the following equation by writing the correct numbers in the blanks provided.
   ____ NH_3 + ____ O_2 → ____ NO + ____ H_2O

4. Calculate the momentum of a 0.25-kg ball that is moving toward home plate at a velocity of 40 m/s. (*Hint:* Refer to the chapter for any formula you need to solve this problem.) _____

5. This is an image of a section of a roller coaster. What kind of energy is represented at the top of the roller coaster (W)?

   a. kinetic
   b. mechanical
   c. potential
   d. leverage

6. While hiking in a deep canyon, a hiker yells out loud. He hears the echo 0.86 seconds after the yell. The speed of the sound wave in the air is 342 m/s. Calculate the distance to the nearest canyon wall. _____
   Hint: Remember that the echo represents sound traveling to the wall and back. Here are two formulas that will help.
   Velocity = distance/time
   Distance = velocity · time

7. Classify each substance as an **element**, a com-**pound**, or a **mixture**.

water (H_2O): _____

hydrogen (H): _____

salt (NaCl): _____

glucose ($C_6H_{12}O_6$): _____

oxygen (O_2): _____

saltwater: _____

8. Which of the below is NOT a change of state?

a. dew forming

b. gold liquefying

c. boiling water

d. blending fruit

9. Assign each of the following terms to its cor-rect definition.

1. Volume
2. Elasticity
3. Solubility
4. Hardness
5. Viscosity

a. The measure of how much of a substance will dissolve in another substance

b. The measure of how resis-tant a substance is to shape change when a force is applied

c. The ability of a substance to return to its original shape after deforming force is applied

d. The measure of a substance's resistance to flow

e. How much space is occupied by a substance

10. What is the following reaction an example of?

$$AgNO_3 + NaCl \rightarrow AgCl + NaNO_3$$

a. synthesis

b. decomposition

c. single-replacement reaction

d. double-replacement reaction

11. If a person walks forward one mile in 15 min-utes and then back one mile in 15 minutes, what measurement would be described as zero miles: distance or displacement?

_____

Answers and Explanations

Chapter Practice

1. **a.** A physical property is something that is observable and measurable and does not involve a chemical reaction. Flammability is the correct choice as it involves the ability of a substance to burn, a property that cannot be determined without chemically altering the substance. Choices **b**, **c**, and **d** are each observable and measurable properties of substances; therefore, none of them is the correct choice.

2. **b.** The smallest unit of matter is the atom. A compound is a substance made up of multiple different elements, so choice **a** is incorrect. A molecule can be made up of multiple atoms, so choice **c** is incorrect. A proton is a positively charged particle in an atom, but it is not considered a unit of matter, and therefore choice **d** is incorrect.

3. **d.** A phase change is when matter changes from a solid to a liquid, from a liquid to a gas, from a liquid to a solid, or from a gas to a liquid. Choice **d** is the correct answer because water freezing is a phase change from liquid to solid. Choice **a** is incorrect because oil floating represents a difference in density, not a phase change. Choice **b** is incorrect because when oxygen diffuses in water, it stays as a gas in the water and does not change phase. Choice **c** is not correct because there is no change in state when paper burns. This is an example of a chemical reaction, not a phase change.

4. **b.** Because heat is released during the reaction (and indicated by $\Delta H = -890$ kj), the reaction is considered exothermic. Choice **a** is incorrect because a reaction that absorbs energy is called endothermic. Choice **c** is incorrect because it refers to balancing equations, not heat of reaction. Choice **d** is incorrect because it refers to part of the hydrologic cycle, not heat of reaction in chemical reactions.

5. **c.** The graph shows that the amount of oxygen dissolved in water decreases as water temperature increases. Choice **c** is correct because you can conclude that warmer water holds less oxygen based on the information in the graph. Choice **a** is incorrect because the graph does not show the rate at which oxygen dissolves. Choice **b** is incorrect because the caption states that fish can live at 2 ppm and the graph indicates a level of more than 8 ppm at 25°C. Choice **d** is incorrect because the graph does not show this relationship.

6. **a.** The correct answer is 35 mm. You solve this by the following:

   1,400 m/s = wavelength × 40 kHz

   40 kHz = 40,000 Hz = 40,000 s^{-1}

   Divide each side of the equation by 40,000:

   1,400/40,000 = W

   W = 0.035 m = 35 mm

Physical Science Review

1. **392,000 N.** 40,000 kg × **9.8 m/s^2** = 392,000 N
2. The object will accelerate at **5 m/s^2**.

   10 N/2 kg = 5 m/s^2
3. $4NH_3 + 5O_2 \rightarrow 4NO + 6H_2O$

   This equation is balanced because there are 4 atoms of nitrogen (N), 12 atoms of hydrogen (H), and 10 atoms of oxygen (O) on each side of the equation.

4. 10 kg · m/s. The formula for momentum is mass multiplied by velocity. The mass of the ball is 0.25 kg; multiply that by the velocity, 40 m/s, and it's equal to 10 kg · m/s.

5. c. The point (W) at the top of the roller coaster represents high potential energy. The other point (X) shows the point at which the coaster has high energy of movement (kinetic energy).

6. 147.06 m. The velocity of the sound is 342 m/s. The time it takes to hear the sound (the time to travel to the wall and back) is 0.86 s.

$v = 342$ m/s, $t = 0.86$ s (2-way)

If it takes 0.86 seconds to travel to the canyon wall and back, then it takes 0.43 seconds to travel the one-way distance to the wall. Now use $d = v \cdot t$

$d = v \cdot t = (342$ m/s$) \cdot (0.43$ s$) = 147.06$ m

7. water (H_2O): **compound**
hydrogen (H): **element**
salt (NaCl): **compound**
glucose ($C_6H_{12}O_6$): **compound**
oxygen (O_2): **element**
saltwater: **mixture**

8. d. Blending fruit is not a change of state, as this is the chopping of an object until its solid form becomes something only similar to liquid.

9. 1. Volume: **e.** How much space is occupied by a substance.
   2. Elasticity: **c.** The ability of a substance to return to its original shape after deforming force is applied.
   3. Solubility: **a.** The measure of how much of a substance will dissolve in another substance.
   4. Hardness: **b.** The measure of how resistant a substance is to shape change when a force is applied.
   5. Viscosity: **d.** The measure of a substance's resistance to flow.

10. d. This is an example of a double-replacement reaction.

11. Displacement compares the ending point to the starting point. If a person were to walk forward one mile in 15 minutes and then back one mile, the displacement would be zero miles. If a person were to walk one mile forward and one mile back in half an hour, the **distance** traveled would two miles. Final velocity would be zero and speed would be four miles per hour.

12 ▶ EARTH AND SPACE SCIENCE

Earth and space science is concerned with the formation of the earth, the solar system, and the universe; the history of Earth (its mountains, continents, and ocean floors); and the weather and seasons. All of these elements combined have made Earth a very unique planet. The special conditions on Earth, including the distance from the sun, the makeup of the atmosphere, and the presence of freshwater and oceans, allow life to occur.

This chapter reviews areas of earth and space science that will likely appear on the GED® Science test as parts of diagrams or passages. Elements of both physical and life sciences will appear within earth and space science. All of these sciences are interconnected, allowing you to use ideas from one area to interpret questions from another.

Practice exercises are included through the chapter. Use them to help with practicing applying the science knowledge presented to solve problems and questions. Answers and explanations are at the end of the chapter.

Let's start close to home, with Earth's systems.

Earth's Systems

Earth is made up of a series of systems involving the planet's atmosphere, land masses, and oceans. The interdependence of these systems is one of the most important principles involved in earth science and is the basis for how the planet supports life.

Composition of the Earth

Starting with Earth's composition, it is formed from a series of four main layers:

- inner core
- outer core
- rocky mantle
- crust

The **inner core** is a solid mass of iron with a temperature of about 7,000°F. The high heat at the earth's core is a combination of three factors: (1) residual heat from the formation of the earth, (2) frictional heating caused by denser parts of the core moving toward the center and the frictional force that creates, and (3) the decay of radioactive elements such as uranium in the core. The inner core is approximately 1,500 miles in diameter. To give a comparison, the widest point from the East Coast to the West Coast of the United States is more than twice that at 3,400 miles. This inner core is also, as you may guess from its name, the absolute center of the planet.

The **outer core** is the next layer out from the inner core and is a mass of molten iron surrounding the inner core. Electrical currents generated from this area produce the earth's magnetic field. The magnetic field assigns the North and South Poles and protects the earth from the charged particles of solar winds and cosmic rays.

The **rocky mantle**, the next layer, is composed of silicon, oxygen, magnesium, iron, aluminum, and calcium and is about 1,750 miles thick. This mantle accounts for most of the earth's mass. When parts of this layer become hot enough, they turn to slow-moving molten rock or magma. This is what comes out of volcanoes when they erupt; however, volcanoes are on the next layer.

Earth's crust is the outermost non-gaseous layer of the planet. It is from 4 to 25 miles thick and consists of sand and rock. This is the part of the planet that we live on and that is most familiar to us. Since it is called the crust, you could think of it like a pizza or bread crust—the outermost part of a pizza or a loaf of bread.

The following is a diagram of the layers of the planet. You may encounter a question where the layers are not labeled and you are asked to label these parts. One helpful thing about science is that the naming of things usually follows some form of logic. The name of each part of the planet tells you where it is located.

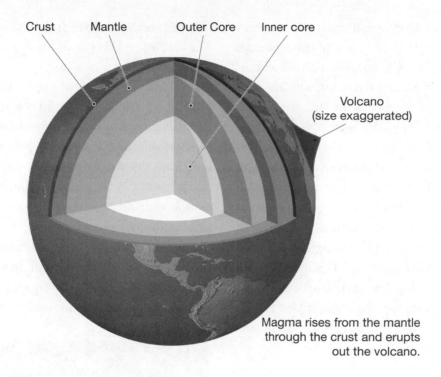

Crust Mantle Outer Core Inner core

Volcano
(size exaggerated)

Magma rises from the mantle
through the crust and erupts
out the volcano.

Next, let's look at the absolute outermost layer of Earth, the atmosphere.

Practice

1. Compared to the earth's crust, the inner core is hotter and contains
   a. more molten iron.
   b. more solid iron.
   c. most of Earth's mass.
   d. mostly sand and rock.

Atmosphere and Water

The atmosphere is a thin layer of gases surrounding the earth. Our atmosphere contains about 78% nitrogen, 21% oxygen, 1% water vapor, and a small amount of other gases. These gases combine to absorb ultraviolet radiation from the sun and warm the planet's surface through heat retention. The atmosphere is divided into four layers:

1. **troposphere**—closest to the earth; up to about 6 miles above. This is the part that we live in and birds fly in.
2. **stratosphere**—second layer, from about 6 to 30 miles above the earth. The lowest part of the stratosphere is as high as planes will fly.
3. **mesosphere**—third layer, from about 30 to 50 miles above the earth
4. **thermosphere**—fourth layer, from about 50 to 300 miles above Earth

When you think of atmosphere, it's easy to assume it's mostly water and oxygen; however, our atmosphere is more nitrogen than oxygen, and it can't hold a lot of water. But living beings need water for both the outside and the inside of their cells. In fact, vertebrates (you included) are about 70% water. Water moves through the atmosphere in a cyclical way. At its simplest, sunlight **evaporates** the water from the oceans, rivers, and lakes. The evaporated water then **condenses** to form clouds that produce rain or snow onto the earth's surface (**precipitation**). This cycle is sometimes called the **water** or **hydrologic cycle** and is critical to sustaining life on Earth. The diagram that follows shows elements of this cycle and is an example of the kind of diagram you might see on the GED® test if you were asked a question about the hydrologic cycle.

Water or Hydrologic Cycle

Carbon Cycle

Another system of Earth is the **carbon cycle**. These systems are characterized by complex patterns of interconnectedness, which are often cyclical in nature. The carbon cycle is one of the most important examples of this.

Carbon is found in the oceans in the form of bicarbonate ions (HCO_3^-); in the atmosphere, in the form of carbon dioxide; in living organisms; and in fossil fuels (such as coal, oil, and natural gas). The bicarbonate ions in the ocean settle to the bottom and form sedimentary rocks, while plants remove the carbon dioxide in the atmosphere and convert it to sugars through photosynthesis. The sugar in plants enters the food chain, first reaching herbivores, then carnivores and omnivores, and finally scavengers and decomposers. All of these organisms release carbon dioxide back into the atmosphere when they breathe.

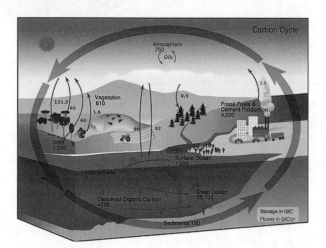

Carbon Cycle
Numbers in black indicate storage of carbon in gigatons (GtC), and numbers in gray alongside arrows indicate annual exchange of carbon (GtC/yr). *Source:* Wikimedia Commons.

Fossil fuels, the last of this list of sources of carbon, represent the largest reserve of carbon on Earth. Fossil fuels come from the carbon of organisms that lived millions of years ago. Burning fossil fuels releases energy, which is why these fuels are used to power machines. When fossil fuels burn, carbon is released into the atmosphere in the form of carbon dioxide (which then is used by the plants, and the cycle continues). However, since the Industrial Revolution, when the consumption of energy began to increase substantially to power machinery, people have increased the concentration of carbon dioxide in the atmosphere by 30% by burning fossil fuels and cutting down forests that would otherwise assist in reducing the higher concentration of carbon dioxide.

Burning fossil fuels and forests also releases nitrogen, and all forms of fixed nitrogen are among the greenhouse gases that cause global warming. In addition, nitric oxide, another gas released when fossil fuels are burned, can convert into nitric acid. This is a main component of acid rain, which destroys habitats. This information is important when considering the health of the planet and the humans and creatures living on it. People are already suffering the consequences of the pollution they have caused. The focus on preventing further damage to the ecosystems and fixing the damage that has been done is another challenge for today's scientists.

With all of these cycles and systems, another part of the earth's composition is the plates in the upper part of the rocky mantle.

Practice

2. What is the role of the ocean in the carbon cycle?
  a. The ocean absorbs carbon from the atmosphere.
  b. The ocean produces carbon dioxide.
  c. The ocean currents transfer heat.
  d. Water evaporates from the ocean surface.

Plate Tectonics

While the earth's upper mantle is rigid and is part of the **lithosphere** (together with the crust), the lower mantle flows slowly, at a rate of a few centimeters per year. The crust is divided into plates that drift slowly (only a few centimeters each year) on the less rigid mantle. This motion of the plates is caused by convection (heat) currents, which carry heat from the hot inner mantle to the cooler outer mantle. This process is called **plate tectonics**. This motion also results in earthquakes and volcanic eruptions.

Evidence suggests that about 200 million years ago, all continents were a part of one landmass, named Pangaea. Over the years, the continents slowly separated in a process called **continental drift**. Oceanic crust is thinner than continental crust, but still affects continental drift. The theory of plate tectonics says that there are now 15 large plates that fit together like a puzzle and yet continue to slowly move on the mantle.

Tectonic plates can slide past each other, separate from each other (**diverge**), or come together (**converge**). The force needed to move billions of tons of rock is unimaginable, and when plates move, some of that energy is released as earthquakes. Faults, or places where the tectonic plates meet, exist all over the world and are often the sites of strong earthquakes. An example of plates sliding past each other is the San Andreas fault in California.

Converging plates often result in the creation of mountains. For example, the Andes Mountains were formed by the Nazca Plate being pushed under the South American Plate. When two oceanic plates meet each other, this often results in the formation of an island arc system. When two plates separate, or diverge, energy is released, earthquakes occur, and magma is released. The Atlantic Ocean was formed by the separation of plates over millions of years.

At some plate boundaries, one plate slides under the other (**subduction**). As the plate slides under the other, the crust melts as it goes deeper into the earth. This creates magma, which rises to the surface and can form volcanoes. Another spot where molten material breaks through to the surface from inside the earth is through the floor of the ocean. It flows from fissures, where it is cooled by the water, resulting in the formation of igneous rocks. As the molten material flows from a fissure, it also forms ridges adjacent to it. One large version of this ridge formation is the Mid-Atlantic Ridge, which is where the Eurasian and North American Plates diverge.

These plates have created the areas where the oceans are contained and also affect the way the oceans behave as a system.

Ocean Currents

Oceanic currents, measured in meters per second or in knots (1 knot = 1.15 miles per hour or 1.85 kilometers per hour), are driven by several factors. One is the rise and fall of the tides, which are affected by the gravitational force of the moon. A second factor that drives ocean currents is wind, which is caused by many things, from high- and low-pressure systems to the rotation of the earth. A third factor that drives currents is density differences in water due to temperature and salinity in different parts of the ocean.

The reasons that ocean currents are so important among the systems of Earth is that they can impact weather globally and locally. For example, the Gulf Stream is an ocean current that runs from the tip of Florida, flowing along the eastern coastline of the United States and to Newfoundland before crossing the Atlantic Ocean. Because it carries warm water, it makes northern Europe warmer than it would be otherwise.

Another example you may have heard of is the weather phenomenon called **El Niño**. El Niño is a band of very warm ocean water that develops off the western coast of South America and can cause climatic changes. Typically, El Niño happens every two to seven years and lasts nine months to two years. Because El Niño's warm waters feed thunderstorms, it creates increased rainfall across the eastern Pacific Ocean. Along the west coast of South America, El Niño reduces the upwelling of cold, nutrient-rich water that sustains large fish populations. This reduction in upwelling has led to lower fish populations off

the shore of Peru. The impact of El Niño, as a weather phenomenon caused by ocean currents, can be felt across the globe. With the tropical thunderstorms fueled by the hot, humid air over the oceans, the atmosphere produces patterns of high and low pressure in response. This can result in higher temperatures in western Canada and the upper plains of the United States and colder temperatures in the southern United States. Additionally, in contrast to the flooding rains experienced in South America, the eastern coast of Africa can experience severe drought during an El Niño event. All this is caused by a band of very warm ocean water.

Natural Hazards

While the earth's systems interact in a way that creates an environment most beneficial to sustaining life, these systems also can lead to natural hazards. Floods, earthquakes, hurricanes, tsunamis, and droughts are all examples of natural hazards, and all of these conditions produce stresses on the environment.

Floods can erode the topsoil; destroy trees, grass, and crops; and even tear down homes. Floods can also contribute to the spread of disease by damaging sewage and waste disposal mechanisms. The results of a flood can take years to undo.

Earthquakes can tear up the land and produce rockslides. They can even cause flooding if a river is redirected. The effects of an earthquake in a big city can be devastating.

Hurricanes are also known as tropical cyclones. A tropical cyclone is a rapidly rotating storm system with a low-pressure center, strong winds, and a spiral arrangement of thunderstorms that produce heavy rain. They form over large bodies of relatively warm water. Hurricanes can wreak havoc along the coasts, destroying plants, trees, buildings, and even highways.

Tsunamis are very large, destructive water waves that are caused by earthquakes, volcanic eruptions, or landslides (not wind). They used to be called tidal waves because they resembled a rising tide, but tsunamis have nothing to do with tides.

Drought occurs when an area receives substantially less precipitation than normal. Droughts can be designated after 15 days with reduced rainfall. Significant and sustained droughts can impact crops and livestock and result in widespread food shortage, malnutrition, and famine.

All of these natural hazards are a part of the cycles of Earth, but they aren't pleasant and they cause damage to habitats and ecosystems.

Practice

3. Earthquakes are caused by
   a. tsunamis.
   b. global warming.
   c. plate tectonics.
   d. ocean currents.

Natural Resources and Energy

While nature may have some major hazards, it also is full of resources that humans depend on to sustain life. A good part of the resources we use every day come directly from the environment. These are called **natural resources**—resources provided by nature.

Resources

Air, water, sunlight, topsoil, plants, and animals are examples of Earth's natural resources. This huge variety of plant and animal life is referred to as **biodiversity**. The effects of human activity on biodiversity are a growing concern of environmental activists and scientists, as habitat destruction has reduced the diversity of life forms in many regions throughout the world.

There are two kinds of natural resources: renewable and nonrenewable.

Renewable resources are resources that can be replaced or replenished over a short period of time. Plants and crops are examples of resources that, with proper agriculture, are replenishable.

Nonrenewable resources are resources that cannot be replaced or that take many years to replenish. Fossil fuels such as oil and coal are examples of nonrenewable resources, as they are formed from organisms that lived millions of years ago.

Oceans

Oceans are a major renewable resource, and even if you live hundreds of miles from the shore, you are still dependent on the ocean. We rely on the ocean for food, jobs, energy, and recreation. At the same time, oceans cover 70% of Earth's surface and contain more than 97% of all water on Earth. About half of the world's population lives near the ocean, and ocean-based businesses contribute more than $500 billion to the world's economy. In fact, there are more than 140 million jobs in fishing, aquaculture, and other related activities. The ocean contains important mineral and energy resources such as oil and gas, and shipping accounts for the transport of 90% of the world's international traded goods. In addition to their economic importance, the oceans contain rich biodiversity. Coral reefs and estuaries (salty or brackish freshwater that runs into the ocean) sustain 75% of all commercial fish and shellfish during some point of their life cycles, and one in six people on Earth depend on ocean fish as their primary source of protein.

Even with all of this, global climate change is having significant negative effects on our oceans. The oceans absorb about one-fourth of the CO_2 emitted from human activities. This is called a **carbon sink**. The oceans contain 500 times more carbon than the atmosphere. When CO_2 is absorbed by the ocean, it interacts with saltwater to form carbonic acid. As the levels of CO_2 in the atmosphere continue to increase, the levels of carbonic acid in the ocean also increase.

This rising acidification of the ocean ends up causing harm to plankton, adversely affecting shellfish larvae, hindering the ability of corals to build new reefs, and causing serious food chain disruptions.

Another result of warmer global temperatures is that the ice sheets in the Arctic are melting. This melting is having negative consequences for many species of marine mammals that live there. With the usually frigid ocean water warming, the results are increased marine diseases and invasive species, changes in weather systems, and the death of coral reefs. This causes larger and more frequent storms that are accelerating shoreline erosion and affecting how the oceans interact with the land. Along with this, sea levels rising will end up causing habitat loss, and people will need to be relocated as their island and coastal homelands are eliminated.

So while the ocean is a huge resource, climate change is altering our relationship to it and the way it acts as a resource.

Energy

Energy as a resource of the earth comes in many varieties. Each type of energy is transferred between the earth's surface and the atmosphere via conduction, convection, and radiation. Radiation specifically comes from the sun and passes through the atmosphere; some is reflected back into space while some is absorbed by clouds or the earth's surface.

Solar Power

Ultimately our energy comes from the sun. The sun's energy reaches our planet in the form of light radiation. Plants use this light to synthesize sugar molecules, which are consumed when the plants are eaten by animals or humans. We obtain energy from the sugar molecules, and our bodies use it. The sun also drives the earth's geochemical cycles.

Along with generally heating the planet, the sun heats the earth's surface and drives convection within the atmosphere and oceans, producing winds and ocean currents. The winds cause waves on the surfaces of oceans and lakes and transfer some of their energy to the water through friction between the air molecules and the water molecules.

Solar power also refers to the conversion of solar energy to another, more useful form. Sunlight can be harnessed and collected in special greenhouses, and photovoltaic cells can produce electricity when sunlight hits them. The energy that strikes the earth's surface from the sun in one hour is nearly as much energy as is used by all of humanity in one year. Considering this, many scientists are convinced that this form of energy will one day replace ordinary fossil fuels.

This all sounds pretty great, but solar-powered cars and houses are not that common yet. One reason is because fossil fuels are cheaper to collect and use. But the solar technology is catching up—solar plants are now being constructed, and in 2012, about 0.14% of all electricity generation was from solar power. This may seem like a small percentage of overall energy production, but it represents a 58% increase over 2011. Along with this, many people are finding employment in the solar industry. In 2012 there were more than 119,000 solar workers in the United States, a 13.2% increase over 2011.

The sun provides energy and jobs to humans. It also helps create wind, which is another big energy resource.

Wind Power

Wind power refers to the conversion of wind energy into a useful form of energy. Large **wind farms** consist of hundreds of individual wind turbines, which are connected to the electric power grid. These farms are established on land and offshore (in the ocean).

Wind power, like solar power, acts as an alternative to fossil fuels. It is plentiful, is renewable, and produces no greenhouse gas emissions. Some countries are far ahead of the United States in harnessing the power of the wind for usable energy. For example,

Denmark generates more than a quarter of its electricity from wind. In 2010 wind energy production was more than 2.5% of total worldwide electricity usage. The cost per unit of energy produced is similar to the cost for new coal and natural gas installations, but in the long term it could be less costly in terms of impact on the environment.

Geothermal Power

Geothermal energy, another energy resource, comes from the heat that is produced in the rocks and fluids beneath Earth's crust. It can be found anywhere from shallow depths to several miles below the surface, and even farther down to the extremely hot molten rock called magma. Deep wells are drilled into the underground reservoirs to tap steam and very hot water that drive turbines linked to electricity generators. This particular type of energy is also renewable simply because the heat of the planet is not cooling that quickly.

Energy from Fossil Fuels

Fossil fuels are a major energy resource, but they are a nonrenewable resource. This energy source includes oil and coal and is used for heat, electricity, and gasoline. Since fossil fuels come from the remains of creatures that died millions of years ago, they are decreasing worldwide as we use them up. Additionally, burning them causes various gases to be released into the atmosphere, as stated earlier.

Carbon dioxide and other gases in the atmosphere can trap solar energy—a process known as the **greenhouse effect**. The greenhouse effect is a naturally occurring process that has been accelerated by human production of so-called greenhouse gases such as CO_2. Increased levels of carbon dioxide and other greenhouse gases can cause **global warming**—an increase of temperatures on Earth. In the past 100 years, the temperatures have increased by 1°C. This doesn't seem like much, but the temperature increase is already creating noticeable climate changes and problems, such as the melting of polar ice caps and the rising of ocean levels. Reducing carbon dioxide concentrations in the atmosphere, either by finding new energy sources or by actively removing the carbon dioxide that forms, is a challenge for today's scientists.

Practice

4. Which of the following is considered a nonrenewable natural resource?
   a. wind
   b. oil
   c. solar
   d. water

5. The greenhouse effect is
   a. when the sun's rays bounce off the earth's surface and are trapped in the atmosphere by greenhouse gases.
   b. when the sun's rays pass through the atmosphere and warm the surface of the earth.
   c. when the sun's rays bounce off the clouds and get absorbed by the greenhouse gases.
   d. when the sun's rays move through the atmosphere and are absorbed by the ocean.

6. Read the following passage and explain how human behavior has indirectly contributed to the destruction of coral reefs across the globe. Include multiple pieces of evidence from the text to support your answer.

CORAL REEFS IN JEOPARDY

Coral reefs are found around the world. They are built by marine invertebrates called coral polyps. The coral polyps that build coral reefs rely on zooxanthellae. Zooxanthellae are a form of photosynthetic algae that live symbiotically in the tissue of corals and provide some of the corals' food supply. For this reason, corals can thrive only in very clear water in a very specific temperature range. They rarely grow deeper than 40 m, and they prefer saltwater. The best temperature for coral reefs is between 25°C and 31°C, and the best salinity is between 34 and 37 parts per 1,000. Also, the pH of ocean water can affect coral growth. Even relatively small increases in ocean acidity can decrease the capacity of corals to build skeletons. Bleaching or whitening of coral reefs occurs when the corals lose their zooxanthallae and can result in the death of the corals.

Coral reefs are important for ecological and economic reasons. They are some of most diverse ecosystems in the world. They occupy less than 0.1% of the world's ocean surface, yet they provide a home for 25% of all marine species. Coral reefs are often referred to as the "rainforests of the sea." Economically, they are important to fishing and tourism industries. The annual global economic value of coral reefs was more than US$350 billion in 2002. Yet, they are being destroyed around the world at alarming rates. About 10% of the world's coral reefs have already been completely destroyed. In parts of the world, the Philippines for example, over 70% of the coral reefs have been destroyed.

Humans have contributed to the destruction of coral reefs both directly and indirectly. Certain fishing practices such as the use of poisons and explosives harm or kill reefs directly. Indirectly, humans have damaged the ocean environment of the corals through warming ocean temperatures, sedimentation, and pollution, including increasing the carbon dioxide in the atmosphere. Because the ocean absorbs carbon dioxide from the atmosphere (and changes it to carbonic acid), an increase in CO_2 in the atmosphere has resulted in a decrease in oceanic pH of 0.1. This change may seem small but has had catastrophic consequences for corals and the coral ecosystem.

Write your answer on the lines or on a separate sheet of paper. You should take approximately 10 minutes to complete this task.

Structure of the Universe

Having gone over the earth in detail, let's take a look at the universe at large. Nobody knows for sure how the universe originated, but a major theory is the **Big Bang theory**. This theory states that the universe started off in a hot, dense state under high pressure between 10 billion and 20 billion years ago, then expanded rapidly, and has been expanding ever since. The universe is still expanding and cooling. Some data suggest that the rate of expansion of the universe is increasing. Whether the universe will continue to expand forever and eventually reach an equilibrium size or shrink back into a small, dense, hot mass is unknown at this point, but it's a mystery that scientists are still looking into.

Stars and Galaxies

Some of the most common objects in the universe are stars. Stars are formed by the gravitational attraction of countless hydrogen and helium molecules. The energy of stars stems from nuclear reactions, mainly the fusion of hydrogen atoms to form helium. These nuclear processes in stars lead to the formation of elements, and the stars become gravitationally bound to other stars, forming galaxies, another major part of the universe.

A galaxy is a system of stars, stellar dust, and dark matter. It is bound together by gravity, and black holes exist in the center of many them. There are billions of galaxies in the known universe (some say over 170 billion!). Our solar system is part of the Milky Way galaxy, which in addition to the sun contains about 200 billion other stars.

When considering the universe, we have a particular perspective on what is out there based on what we can see from Earth. Constellations are a big part of that.

Constellations

If you have seen the Big Dipper in the night sky, then you have seen a constellation, which is a pattern or grouping of stars. Because of the rotation of the earth, certain constellations are visible only at certain times of the year. The reason we even have constellations at all is that organizing these stars into some kind of configuration that looks like something familiar has helped people to remember which stars are which. Also, for centuries people have looked to skies to navigate the seas, to know when to have religious ceremonies, and to know when to plant and reap their crops. All of these things were aided by humans looking into the sky and using the stars to guide their way.

Planets

Earth is a planet, but not all planets are like Earth. A planet is now defined as a celestial body that has enough mass to be spherical, orbits a star, and is not part of a belt (such as an asteroid belt). In our immediate neighborhood, these planets are situated in our solar system.

Solar Systems

Our **solar system** is made up of the sun and all of the objects that orbit around it, including the planets, moons, asteroids, and comets. The sun is very massive, and it has a strong gravitational that pulls on the objects in the solar system.

There are eight **planets** in our solar system. In order (closest to farthest from the sun), they are Mercury, Venus, Earth, Mars, Jupiter, Saturn, Uranus, and Neptune. The first four planets (Mercury, Venus, Earth, and Mars) are called terrestrial planets because they are rocky. The other planets (Jupiter, Saturn, Uranus, and Neptune) are called gas giants because they are made up mainly of gas.

You may have learned that Pluto was one of nine planets in our solar system. In the 1990s, astronomers discovered that Pluto was not a planet in its own orbit but part of a belt of asteroids. This asteroid belt also included several other small planet-like bodies that were around the same size as Pluto. Because of this, in 2006 astronomers voted to change Pluto's designation to that of a dwarf planet. We now recognize only eight true planets.

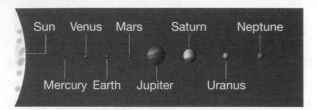

Planets of the Solar System
Compared with each other, the sizes are correct but the distances are not.

A **comet** is a small, icy celestial body that, when passing close to the sun, may display a tail. The tail is caused by solar radiation and the solar wind. Comets range from a few hundred meters to tens of kilometers across and are composed of loose collections of ice, dust, and small, rocky particles. Comets have orbits that range from a few years to several hundred years. Halley's comet, for example, is visible from Earth about every 75 years. Its next appearance should be in 2061. There are over 4,000 known comets, and most are not bright enough to be seen by the naked eye. A very few are extraordinarily bright and are considered "great comets." The Hale-Bopp comet and Halley's comet are examples of great comets.

Some other objects typical of the solar system are asteroids. **Asteroids** are similar to comets but differ in composition. They're made up of metals and rocky materials and have no tail (because they are not composed of ice). There are millions of asteroids, some of which are as small as particles of dust, while others are as large as half a mile in diameter. Most of the known asteroids orbit in the asteroid belt between the orbits of Mars and Jupiter. Astronomers estimate that this belt contains between 1.1 million and 1.9 million asteroids larger than 1 km (0.6 mi) in diameter and millions of smaller ones.

Our solar system is full of a variety of celestial bodies, some of which are occasionally visible in our night sky, and all of which, through studying them, help us learn more about our universe and our planet.

Development of Stars

Understanding how stars are formed helps us to understand how our own sun and solar system were created. Scientists now know that the formation of stars occurs within what are called "stellar nurseries," which are a type of nebula. A **nebula** is a cloud of dust and gas, composed primarily of hydrogen (97%) and helium (3%). Nebulae may be giant, with 1,000 to 100,000 times the mass of the sun, or smaller, with less than a few hundred times the mass of the sun. Also, there are areas within a nebula where gravity causes the dust and gas to clump together. As the clump gains mass, its gravitational attraction increases, which in turn draws more mass to it. This clump is called a protostar at this stage and is the beginning of a star forming.

The protostar keeps drawing in more gas and growing even hotter. Once the protostar gets hot enough, its hydrogen atoms start fusing. If the protostar gathers enough mass, the young star blasts the remaining gas and dust away, stabilizes, and becomes a main sequence star. After a star has formed, it generates thermal energy in its core through the nuclear fusion of hydrogen atoms into helium. This process of stellar (star) development can take millions of years. A star the size of our sun takes about 50 million years to mature to adulthood. Our sun will stay in the mature phase for approximately 10 billion years.

The lifespan of a star is determined by the type of star it is. In some stars, when the core runs out of hydrogen fuel, it contracts under the weight of gravity and heats up. The core's rising temperature heats the upper layers, causing them to expand. As this happens, the radius of the star increases and it becomes a **red giant**. When the helium fuel runs out entirely, the core expands and cools and the upper layers expand and eject material that collect around the dying star to form a **planetary nebula**. Finally, the core cools into a **white dwarf** and then eventually into a **black dwarf**. This entire process takes a few billion years.

In other (more massive) stars, when the core runs out of hydrogen, the stars fuse helium into carbon just like the sun. However, after the helium is gone, their mass is enough to fuse carbon into heavier elements such as oxygen, neon, silicon, magnesium, sulfur, and iron. Once the core has turned to iron, it can no longer burn and the star collapses by its own gravity. The core becomes so tightly packed that protons and electrons merge to form neutrons. In less than a second, the iron core, which is about the size of Earth, shrinks to a neutron core with a radius of about 6 miles (10 kilometers). The core heats to billions of degrees and explodes (**supernova**), releasing large amounts of energy and material into space. The remains of the core can form a **neutron star** or a **black hole**, depending on the mass of the original star.

These are all things that will occur with our own sun and with stars in nearby star systems. Almost all of these ideas are big picture ideas but still applicable to understanding how our universe functions.

Motion of the Earth and Moon

Coming back closer to home, let's look at the motion of the earth and moon and how they intereact. The earth **rotates** (spins) on its axis once every 23 hours and 56 minutes. This causes day and night and makes most extraterrestrial objects seem to move around the sky in about one day. The earth also moves around the sun in an elliptical (nearly circular) orbit. It is moving about 67,000 miles per hour (107,000 km/hr) in its orbit around the sun.

The earth moves around the center of the earth-moon system once a month. In comparison, Earth's **revolution** around the Sun takes much longer than its rotation on its axis. One complete revolution takes 365.24 days, or approximately one year. The earth revolves around the sun because the sun's gravity keeps it in a roughly circular orbit around the sun.

Have you noticed the sun seems to shine a bit differently in the winter sky? It does. The tilt of Earth causes the sun to hit the earth differently at different points in the revolution. Because of this tilt of the earth's axis, we experience spring, summer, fall, and winter. The northern hemisphere experiences summer when Earth is in the part of its orbit where the northern hemisphere is oriented more toward the sun. The sun therefore rises higher in the sky and is above the horizon longer, and the rays of the sun strike the ground more directly. Likewise, during winter in the northern hemisphere, the hemisphere is oriented away from the sun, the sun rises low in the sky and is above the horizon for a shorter period, and the rays of the sun strike the ground more obliquely.

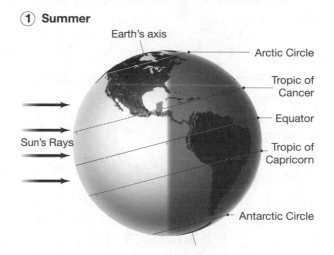

① Summer

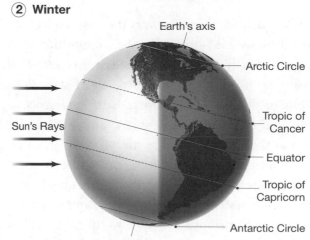

② Winter

Summer and Winter in the Northern Hemisphere

An interesting occurrence that happens regularly for viewers on Earth and gives us information about the movement of the sun, earth, and moon are eclipses. An **eclipse** occurs when an astronomical object is obscured from view either by passing into the shadow of another object or by having another object pass between it and the viewer. A **solar eclipse** is when the moon crosses between the earth and the sun. A **lunar eclipse**, in contrast, is when the moon moves into the earth's shadow.

The **tides**, which are also a major part of the movement of the earth and moon, are the rise and fall of sea levels caused by the gravitational forces of the moon and the sun and the rotation of the earth. Some regions of the world have two high tides and low tides each day, and some experience only one of each.

Practice

7. The length of an Earth day is determined by the time it takes for one
   a. Earth rotation.
   b. Earth revolution.
   c. Sun rotation.
   d. Sun revolution.

Summary

Earth and space science covers the basic concepts of how the universe works, from the composition of the earth to Earth's interacting systems and renewable resources, from the birth and death of stars to the orbits of planets around them. Earth and space are governed by interacting systems, and Earth cycles, such as the hydrologic cycle, are mirrored in cosmic cycles, including the creation of stars and galaxies.

If one of Earth's systems is disrupted, other parts of the system are affected. For example, burning fossil fuels contributes to global warming. It is possible that there are ways in which cosmic systems can

also be disrupted, but these ideas are still being discovered.

After we study Earth's systems and the composition of the universe, it is easier to understand how human actions can affect our world and the universe around us. Earth and space science provides a basis for this understanding.

Earth and Space Science Review

1. What occurs when the moon moves between the earth and the sun?
   a. solar eclipse
   b. lunar eclipse
   c. night
   d. solar flares

2. Which of these statements most accurately explains why the northern hemisphere experiences warming in summer?
   a. The northern hemisphere is closer to the sun in the summer than in the winter.
   b. The northern hemisphere experiences longer days in the summer.
   c. The northern hemisphere is tilted away from the sun in the summer.
   d. The earth's tilt on its axis causes the rays of the sun to hit the northern hemisphere more directly in spring and summer than in fall and winter.

3. Which statement is the primary reason Pluto is no longer considered a planet?
   a. It does not orbit the sun.
   b. It is too small.
   c. It is part of an asteroid belt.
   d. It does not have a moon.

4. Describe two ways that trees and other plants contribute to the carbon cycle.

_____

_____

_____

_____

5. Match each of the natural resources listed with its correct label: renewable or nonrenewable.

RENEWABLE RESOURCE	NONRENEWABLE RESOURCE

- water
- wood
- wind
- gas
- plants
- sun
- coal
- oil

6. Fill in the blanks of the following sentences using the list of words provided.
- mountains
- cliffs
- oceans
- faults

Converging tectonic plates create _____ or island systems. When tectonic plates diverge, _____ are created.

7. What is the correct order of the following steps in the carbon cycle?
- All of these organisms release carbon dioxide back into the atmosphere when they breathe.
- Plants convert carbon dioxide to sugars through photosynthesis.
- Plants remove carbon dioxide from the atmosphere.
- Bicarbonate ions (HCO_3^-) settle on the ocean bottom and form sedimentary rock.
- The sugar in plants enters the food chain, first reaching herbivores, then carnivores and omnivores, and finally scavengers and decomposers.

1._____

2._____

3._____

4._____

5._____

8. Describe what a natural resource is in your own words.

_____

_____

_____

_____

9. The passing of one object in space through the shadow of another object is called an eclipse. The orbits of the moon and Earth in relation to the sun cause both solar and lunar eclipses to occur. During a solar eclipse, the specific alignment of these three objects causes the moon to cast a shadow on the earth. During a lunar eclipse, the alignment causes the earth to cast a shadow on the moon.

The following diagram shows the sun and Earth. Where on the image would the moon need to be for a solar eclipse? Circle the correct place on the diagram.

10. Which of the following is true?
 a. The lithosphere gets thicker as it moves away from a mid-ocean ridge.
 b. The mantle gets thinner as it is subducted beneath a plate.
 c. The mid-ocean ridge is a collision boundary between two plates.
 d. The oceanic crust is thicker than the continental crust.

11. Compared to a planet with a stagnant atmosphere, the Earth's atmospheric circulation causes
 a. the poles to be cooler and the tropics warmer.
 b. the poles to be warmer and the tropics cooler.
 c. the poles to be cooler and the tropics cooler.
 d. the poles to be warmer and the tropics warmer.

12. El Niño is
 a. a current that runs from the tip of Florida and flows along the eastern coastline of the United States.
 b. when the sun's rays bounce off the earth's surface and are trapped in the atmosphere by greenhouse gases.
 c. very large, destructive water waves that are caused by earthquakes, volcanic eruptions, or landslides (not wind).
 d. a band of warm ocean temperatures that develops off the west coast of South America.

Answers and Explanations

Chapter Practice

1. **b.** The inner core is a solid mass of iron with a temperature of about 7,000°F; therefore, answer choice **b** is correct and choices **a** and **d** are incorrect. Most of the mass of the earth is contained in the mantle; therefore, choice **c** is incorrect.

2. **a.** The ocean absorbs carbon dioxide from the atmosphere, rather than producing carbon dioxide; therefore, choice **b** is incorrect. While choices **c** and **d** are factual, they do not answer the question. Regarding choice **d**, evaporation is part of the hydrologic cycle, not the carbon cycle.

3. **c.** Earthquakes are caused by the shifting tectonic plates. Choice **a** is incorrect because tsunamis can result from earthquakes but do not cause them. Choice **b** is incorrect, as global warming causes other natural disasters but not earthquakes. Choice **d** is incorrect because ocean currents do not cause earthquakes.

4. **b.** A nonrenewable natural resource is one that can be depleted. Oil is considered a nonrenewable natural resource because our planet has only a finite amount of it. Choices **a**, **c**, and **d** are all examples of renewable natural resources because they cannot be depleted.

5. **a.** The greenhouse effect is when the sun's rays bounce off the earth's surface and are trapped in the atmosphere by greenhouse gases. This results in increased warming.

6. Read the following scoring guide and the example of a 3-point response.

Scoring Guide for a Short Answer Question (from the GED® Testing Service Assessment Guide for Educators)

3-point responses contain:
- A clear and well-developed explanation of how human behavior has contributed to the destruction of coral reefs across the globe
- Three specific examples of human activities that indirectly affect the health of coral reefs
- Complete support from the passage

2-point responses contain:
- An adequate or partially articulated explanation of how human behavior has contributed to the destruction of coral reefs across the globe
- Partial support from the passage

1-point responses contain:
- Minimal or implied explanation of how human behavior has contributed to the destruction of coral reefs across the globe
- Minimal or implied support from the passage

0-point responses contain:
- No explanation of how human behavior has contributed to the destruction of coral reefs across the globe
- No support from the passage

Example of a 3-Point Response

Coral reefs are important for economic and ecological reasons. Yet human behavior is resulting in their destruction around the globe. Corals and the algae that help them live are very sensitive to changes in salinity, water temperature, and acidity. The effects of global warming and climate change can be seen in the destruction of coral reefs around the world. Increasing water temperatures can negatively affect coral reefs. The best temperature for corals is between 25°C and 31°C. In addition to warming the ocean, increases in greenhouse gases in the atmosphere have made the ocean more acidic (decreased pH by 0.1). Emissions from burning fossil fuels (e.g., cars, industry, coal-burning power plants) contribute to carbon dioxide in the atmosphere. This carbon dioxide is absorbed by the ocean, where it is turned into carbonic acid. This decrease in pH can harm or kill the small symbiotic algae that live in the coral and help it thrive.

7. a. Earth spins (rotates) on its axis once every 23 hours and 56 minutes. This causes day and night and makes most extraterrestrial objects seem to move around the sky in about one day.

Earth and Space Science Review

1. a. A solar eclipse occurs when the moon moves between the earth and the sun. Choice **b** is incorrect because a lunar eclipse occurs when the earth's shadow comes between the sun and the moon. Choice **c** is incorrect because night occurs as the earth rotates every 24 hours. Solar flares are large emissions of energy from the sun; therefore, answer choice **d** is incorrect.

2. d. The seasons are caused by the earth's tilt on its axis. Because the northern hemisphere is tilted toward the sun in summer, the rays of the sun hit that part of the earth more directly. A common misperception is that the seasons are caused by the earth being closer to the sun in summer (choice **a**) and farther away in winter. The days are longer in the summer (choice **b**), but that does not explain why the northern hemisphere experiences warming in summer. Choice **c** is an incorrect statement.

3. c. Pluto is part of the Kuiper (asteroid) belt and shares its orbit around the sun with many other large asteroids; therefore, it is no longer considered a planet. Choice **a** is not true; Pluto does orbit the sun, but it just does so within an asteroid belt. The question asks for the primary reason that Pluto is not a planet, so **b** is not the correct choice. As for choice **d**, some planets have a moon and others do not; this is not a requirement for being considered a planet. In fact, Pluto has five known moons.

4. *Sample answer:*
Plants remove carbon dioxide (CO_2) from the atmosphere and convert it to sugars through photosynthesis. During respiration, plants take O_2 from the atmosphere and replace it with CO_2.

5.

RENEWABLE RESOURCE	NONRENEWABLE RESOURCE
plants	oil
wind	coal
sun	gas
water	
wood	

6. Converging tectonic plates create **mountains** or island systems. When tectonic plates diverge, **oceans** are created.
Tectonic plates can slide past each other, separate from each other (diverge), or come together (converge). At some plate boundaries, one plate slides under the other (subduction). Converging plates create mountains. When two plates diverge, energy is dispersed, earthquakes occur, magma is released, and over the course of ages, oceans can form. The Atlantic Ocean was formed by the separation of plates over millions of years.

7. 1. Plants remove carbon dioxide from the atmosphere.
2. Plants convert carbon dioxide to sugars through photosynthesis.
3. The sugar in plants enters the food chain, first reaching herbivores, then carnivores and omnivores, and finally scavengers and decomposers.
4. All of these organisms release carbon dioxide back into the atmosphere when they breathe.
5. Bicarbonate ions (HCO_3^-) settle on the ocean bottom and form sedimentary rock.

8. *Sample answer:*
Air, water, sunlight, topsoil, and plant and animal life are examples of Earth's natural resources. Natural resources occur and exist in nature in some form and are used by humans for every aspect of survival.

9.

In order for an eclipse to occur, the sun, earth, and moon must be aligned in a particular way. When the moon is positioned between the sun and the earth, the moon will prevent sunlight from reaching a portion of the earth. This is a solar eclipse. When the earth is positioned between the sun and the moon, the earth will prevent sunlight from reaching the moon. This is a lunar eclipse.

10. a. The lithosphere gets thicker as it moves away from a mid-ocean ridge.

11. b. Compared to a planet with a stagnant atmosphere, the Earth's atmospheric circulation causes the poles to be warmer and the tropics cooler.

12. d. El Niño develops in some years as a warm band of ocean water off the west coast of South America. Choice **a** describes the Gulf Stream. Choice **b** describes the greenhouse effect. Choice **c** describes tsunamis.

IV ▶ GED® SOCIAL STUDIES TEST

The GED® Social Studies test measures how well you can apply problem solving, analytical reasoning, and critical thinking skills alongside your understanding of high school–level social studies. Although a good grasp of the core facts, events, and terms commonly taught in social studies classrooms is essential for success on the GED® test and beyond, the test takes it a step further. It measures your ability to analyze key information and apply your knowledge of fundamental social studies concepts in a variety of realistic scenarios. The test also attempts to gauge your level of readiness for success beyond the high school classroom, including college and a career.

This book is designed to get you started on a path to do your best on the GED® Social Studies test. If you're ready to move forward, keep reading!

The new GED® Social Studies test assesses important ideas in two ways:

1. Every question tests a social studies practice skill. These skills measure the critical thinking and reasoning skills that are essential to social studies success.
2. Each question is drawn from one of the four main content areas in social studies—civics and government, U.S. history, economics, and geography and the world.

GED® Social Studies Test Structure

The GED® Social Studies test consists of approximately 35 questions. The questions on the exam are based on relevant social studies materials, including brief texts, maps, graphics, and tables. Many of the brief texts featured will be drawn from materials reflecting "the Great American Conversation," which includes U.S. founding documents, such as the Declaration of Independence, and other documents and speeches from U.S. history that have shaped the country.

Each question on the GED® test is assigned a different point value depending on its difficulty, and a minimum score of 150 is required for passing the test. You'll have 90 minutes to complete the test. Use this time effectively and wisely to ensure you earn your best possible test score.

Multiple-Choice Questions

Multiple-choice questions on the GED® Social Studies test ask you to select the best answer from four choices. To select an answer, click your mouse in the circle next to that answer choice. Your chosen answer will now have a black dot. To change your answer, click the circle of another answer choice.

Fill-in-the-Blank Questions

Fill-in-the-blank questions on the GED® Social Studies test ask you to type information into one or more blank spaces. There are no answer choices given to you—you must come up with what you think is the correct answer and type that word or phrase in the blank.

Drop-Down Questions

Drop-down questions on the GED® Social Studies test ask you to choose an answer from a single drop-down list or a group of drop-down lists within a sentence, paragraph, or equation. To answer the question, click your mouse on the arrow to show all of the answer choices, and then click on your chosen answer to complete the sentence, paragraph, or equation.

Drag-and-Drop Questions

Drag-and-drop questions on the GED® Social Studies test have two areas—one area shows all of the answer choices, and the other area is where you will move the correct answers. You will need to drag one or more answers from the first area to the second area.

To answer a drag-and-drop question, click and hold the mouse on an answer and move it (drag it) to the correct area of the screen. Then let go of the mouse (drop the answer). You can remove an answer and switch it with another answer at any time.

Hot-Spot Questions

Hot-spot questions on the GED® Social Studies test ask you to choose a certain place on an image. To answer the question, click on the correct spot of the image provided. You can change your answer by simply clicking on another area.

Extended Response Question

This question type on the GED® Social Studies test asks you to respond to one question by typing your answer—an essay—into a box. You should feel comfortable typing on a keyboard in order to answer this type of question, since there is a time limit. You will have 45 minutes to construct your response.

Social Studies Practices and Knowledge Chapters

In the next chapter, we will review the social studies practice skills in more detail. These skills, as noted previously, are used in each question to measure the critical thinking and reasoning skills that are essential to social studies success. Reviewing these skills is key to doing well on the GED® Social Studies test. Chapter 14, Social Studies Knowledge, features a basic review of the four social studies areas covered on the GED® test.

13 ▶ SOCIAL STUDIES PRACTICES

This chapter focuses on reviewing and building the skills you need to master for test day. It covers what the GED® Testing Service refers to as social studies practices—the critical thinking and reasoning skills that are essential to social studies success.

These social studies practices are:

- **Reading and Writing in a Social Studies Context:** 30% of the GED® Social Studies test
- **Applying Important Social Studies Concepts:** 40% of the GED® Social Studies test
- **Applying Mathematical Reasoning to Social Studies:** 30% of the GED® Social Studies test

Becoming familiar with these skills and how the GED® test measures them is important for doing your best on test day. In addition to the social studies practices, this chapter provides you with an overview and practice for the extended response question found on the GED® Social Studies test. The answers and explanations for all practice questions are found at the end of the chapter.

Reading and Writing in a Social Studies Context

The GED® Social Studies test addresses reading and writing skills as they relate to the social studies content areas (civics and government, U.S. history, economics, and geography and the world). About 30% of the questions on the test assess these skills. This means that doing well on the GED® Social Studies test requires you to be able to apply reading skills to a broad range of social studies topics.

Your reading skills will be mostly tested through questions related to reading passages. These passages can be as short as a sentence or two, but they are more often one or two paragraphs. Rarely are passages longer than three paragraphs.

The passages used on the GED® Social Studies test include primary source materials, such as speeches, letters, laws, excerpts from the U.S. Constitution, and other documents. Passages may also include secondary source materials in which an author provides an overview of an event, a person, or a geographic region, for example. In addition to reading passages, social studies reading skills may be assessed in written information provided in tables, charts, or other stimuli.

Passages may be paired with just one question, or they may have several questions. The questions are intended to assess your understanding of the passage and related social studies concepts.

Questions related to reading in a social studies context focus on the central ideas, the meaning of words and phrases, the author's point of view, the arguments that are made in the passage, and the evidence that supports those arguments. Sometimes a pair of passages is provided on the same topic, and you will be asked to compare and contrast them.

The best approach for questions related to passages is to look carefully at the clues provided in the passage.

- Read the passage carefully. Think about what the author is saying, the conclusions he or she is drawing, the arguments that are being made, and the details used to support these arguments.
- Read the question and consider your answer options.
- Go back and find specific details in the passage that are related to the question.

Determining Details to Make Logical Inferences or Valid Claims

Making logical inferences sounds complicated, but it's not. In fact, you make inferences every day without thinking about it. When you hear "Happy Birthday" being sung, you infer that it is someone's birthday—even if you know nothing else about this person. If you see a school bus with yellow flashing lights, you would logically infer several things: there is a bus stop nearby. The school bus is about to stop. The traffic going both ways is about to stop. These are all logical inferences—they follow from the evidence provided. Inferences can be illogical, too. If you used what you know about school buses and yellow flashing lights to infer that bus drivers love yellow, this would be an *illogical* inference. It would not be a valid claim.

When taking the GED® test, the inferences and claims you make must be based on the information that is provided. When dealing with reading passages, this is a two-step process.

Step 1: Determine Clearly Stated Details

The first thing you need to do is to focus on the details that the author includes. These may be facts, definitions, examples, or other evidence. This is the information that you will use to make logical inferences or claims. Other than a basic understanding of social studies, you will not need a lot of other technical or factual information outside of what you'll find in the passage.

Step 2: Make Logical Inferences or Valid Claims

This focuses on how you use the information that has been provided in the passage. Some questions will ask you whether you can make a logical inference from the facts, definitions, examples, and other details that have been provided. An **inference** is a conclusion that is drawn from the evidence provided. It is the conclusion that you reach logically from following the author's reasoning. A **claim** is a statement based on this inference. A **valid claim** is a statement that is reasonable or that can be supported by evidence, in this case by the evidence provided in the passage.

INFERENCES VERSUS CLAIMS

- An **inference** is a conclusion that is drawn from the evidence provided. It is the conclusion that you reach logically from following the author's reasoning.
- A **claim** is a statement based on this inference.
- A **valid claim** is a statement that is reasonable or that can be supported by evidence.

The GED® Social Studies test assesses your ability to make inferences in a variety of ways. Questions might ask about the context in which a speech or primary source document was written. Other questions might ask about the opinions or priorities of the author. You might even be asked what likely happened as a result of the speech or document.

Practice

Carefully read the following excerpt from a speech by George Washington and answer the question that follows.

EXCERPT

Friends and Citizens:

The period for a new election of a citizen to administer the executive government of the United States being not far distant, and the time actually arrived when your thoughts must be employed in designating the person who is to be clothed with that important trust, it appears to me proper . . . that I should now apprise you of the resolution I have formed, to decline being considered among the number of those out of whom a choice is to be made.

1. Based on the excerpt, when did George Washington make this speech?
   a. during his tenure as general of the Continental Army
   b. at the Constitutional Convention
   c. prior to his first presidential nomination
   d. during his second term as president

Once you have made your inference, check your answer. Ask yourself: Do the facts and evidence point to this conclusion? In this case, the facts do support the conclusion that Washington made this speech during his second term in office.

As you can see from the example, making inferences may require your knowledge of social studies concepts. You could not determine the context of a speech by George Washington without knowing who Washington was, for instance.

That said, it is important to focus on the evidence provided in the passage without involving your own assumptions or prejudices. Inference questions often ask about how an author—or in the last example, a speaker and a president of the United States—feels about a topic or historical event. When reading an excerpt from a speech by George Washington, how you feel about Washington or the presidency is not important; how Washington feels about his presidency *is*.

Determining Central Ideas

The GED® Social Studies test will also require you to determine the main ideas of excerpts from primary or secondary source documents. A **primary source** is an original piece of writing or art. Some good examples are diary entries, letters, speeches, the texts of laws, and literary passages. A **secondary source** is a document that discusses a primary source. An example is an academic article about a novel. Questions may ask about the main idea of a passage as a whole or a section, paragraph, or other part of the passage.

The **main idea** is a general statement that sums up what the author is saying. To determine the main idea, ask yourself two questions:

1. What is the passage (section/paragraph) mostly about?
2. What is the author trying to tell me?

The main idea is often included in the first sentence, but this is not always the case. An author may include an introductory paragraph to set the scene and then introduce the main idea. Or the author may build up to his or her point, causing the main idea to be found near or at the end of the passage or paragraph.

Have you ever heard the expression that someone "can't see the forest for the trees"? This means that when you are focused on the small stuff (trees), you miss the bigger picture (the forest). This can happen with the main idea as well. To find the main idea, you need to look at the forest—the passage as a whole. This can be somewhat counterintuitive: rather than reading each word carefully, you may be better able to assess the main idea by reading the entire passage as a whole.

Practice

2. Read the following paragraph and underline the sentence that shows the main idea.

When Christopher Columbus landed in the New World, he brought with him horses, cattle, and seeds for planting. Over the next decades, European explorers and settlers brought to the New World other domesticated animals and plants. Wheat and other grains soon became a staple crop in North America. Meanwhile, from the New World to the Old went corn, squash, turkeys, tomatoes, and the ever-important potato. This transfer of plants, animals, and diseases, known as the Columbian Exchange, transformed the diets and lifestyles of people on both sides of the Atlantic.

Figuring Out the Meaning of Words and Phrases

As with any type of study, the social studies disciplines—economics, geography, history, and government—all have words and phrases that are somewhat unique to them. While you should study and learn common social studies terms, you are not expected to know more specific vocabulary terms. What you are expected to be able to do, however, is to figure out the meaning of these words in context.

What does this mean? Basically, you become a detective on the hunt for clues in the rest of the passage. When you come upon an unfamiliar word or phrase, look at the words around that word or phrase. Often, they can unlock the meaning. Then move outward from there, looking for clues in the other parts of the sentence, other sentences, and finally other parts of the passage. In some cases, the word may be defined in a passage. In other cases, its meaning may become clear from the examples that are used. In still others, meaning may be discerned by looking at the greater context—that is, the overall meaning of the sentence, paragraph, and/or passage.

Some words have more than one meaning. You may be expected to figure out how a word with different meanings is used in a sentence or phrase. Take the word *convention*, for example. A convention can mean a formal assembly or gathering, a political meeting at which candidates are selected, an agreed-upon contract, the customary way of doing things, or a familiar or preferred writing style.

Practice

Read each of the following sentences, and then match it to the correct definition of *convention* from the choices listed.

3. The organization will hold its 45th annual *convention* in June.

4. The military government clashed with the *conventions* of the native peoples.

5. One of the reasons it can be difficult to read historical documents is that they follow different *conventions* from those used today.

Definitions:
a. customary way of doing things
b. formal assembly or gathering
c. familiar or preferred writing style

As you can see, you need to think about how a word is used in context to figure out what it means.

Points of View and Purposes

Understanding a text often goes beyond the words in front of you. You must also consider how and why it was written. This involves two things: point of view and the author's purpose (or the purpose of the document).

Point of view is simply the perspective from which someone writes something. A person's point of view is based on his or her background, experiences, and understanding of events and is tied to his or her opinions. For example, the American colonists and the British Parliament clearly had very different points of view regarding the American Revolution and the events leading up to it, and therefore had very different opinions about the Revolution itself. You will often know quite a bit about an author's point of view by knowing who the author is.

Author's purpose is simply the reason that an author is writing something. In some cases, it will help to consider who the intended audience is. Is the document meant for the whole population, or is it written for a certain group, such as the members of Congress? What does the document want to accomplish? Is it trying to document facts to support a proposal? Is it trying to call people to take action?

Ask yourself:

- Why did the author write this?
- Who is the audience?
- What is this document intended to accomplish?

Practice

Read the following excerpt from an 1884 Congressional hearing and then answer the following question.

EXCERPT

They who say that women do not desire the right of suffrage, that they prefer masculine domination to self-government, falsify every page of history, every fact in human experience. It has taken the whole power of the civil and canon law to hold woman in the subordinate position which it is said she willingly accepts.

6. Think about who would have written the passage and why. The purpose of this passage is to

_____.

Fact and Opinion

Just because something is stated in a passage does not mean that it is true. Most written material has some bias. **Bias** is just a preference for one thing or another or one point of view over another. Since almost everyone has personal opinions about everything from food to television shows, bias will probably be a part of anything you read, even if the writer tries very hard to be neutral. A good reader must notice bias and tell the difference between facts and opinions.

A **fact** is a statement that can be verified. Examples typically include the dates in which events took place and the names of the people involved.

An **opinion** is a belief held by one person or a group of people. It cannot be verified or proven. Even if the majority has the same opinion, it does not make it a fact.

To differentiate between facts and opinions, consider the following questions:

- Would everyone agree with this statement?
- Can it be verified by a trustworthy source?

The answer to both of these questions must be "yes" for it to be a fact.

RECOGNIZING OPINIONS	
Be alert to common words that may introduce a statement of opinion:	
likely	believe
possibly	say
probably	charge
should/could	attest
think	feel

Facts and opinions may occur in a wide range of primary and secondary source materials. Editorials by definition include an author's opinion, but they also often include facts that support this opinion. Encyclopedias and social studies textbooks, on the other hand, focus on presenting facts with as little bias as possible.

Differentiating between facts and opinions is not always as easy as it appears. Sometimes this is because we bring our own perspectives and biases to the equation. Consider the following statement.

The American Revolution was a necessary fight for freedom.

You may agree with this statement. Most of the people you know may agree with this statement. There may be many facts and reasons that support this statement. But it is still an opinion. It cannot be verified by any sources.

Sometimes words will be used to emphasize that it is the author's opinion, such as when an author writes "I think . . ." or "we believe." A recommendation for a change is also typically an opinion, although it may be based on very real facts. Look also for comparative or superlative terms (he was the *best* president; there is *too much/not enough* attention paid to this issue).

Practice

Look at the following statements and decide whether each is a fact or an opinion.

7. The United States has a population that exceeds 316 billion. _____

8. The U.S. population is growing too quickly. _____

9. The fastest-growing segment of the U.S. population is adults over the age of 65. _____

Determine the Validity of Hypotheses

A **hypothesis** is a statement that has not been proven to be true or false. Some hypotheses are assumed to be true, but they cannot be proven. In social studies, hypotheses may include what might have happened if an event had not occurred or if someone else had been the leader when an event occurred. People may have many hypotheses about what might have happened had the United States not developed the atomic bomb, for instance. In this case, the hypothesis cannot be proven since this has already happened. People can also have hypotheses about what will happen in the future. For instance, "The threat of terrorism will continue to grow" or "The Republican Party will splinter into two factions" are hypotheses that will prove true or untrue over time.

The GED® Social Studies test assesses your ability to tell whether a hypothesis is based on evidence. What is evidence? **Evidence** is simply the facts and reasons that point to a conclusion. To support the hypothesis that World War II would have dragged on had the United States not developed the atomic bomb, an author might provide evidence about the numbers of casualties prior to the atomic bomb, the readiness plans of Japan and other combatants, letters revealing the impact of the atomic bomb, and so forth.

To decide whether a hypothesis is based on evidence, ask the following questions:

- What is the author saying? What is his or her hypothesis? (This will often be provided as the question.)
- What reasons, facts, and evidence does the author provide?
- Do these reasons, facts, and evidence logically support the author's hypothesis?

Practice

Read the passage and answer the question that follows.

MACHU PICCHU

Machu Picchu is an ancient stone city situated on a mountain ridge high in the Peruvian Andes, above the Sacred Valley. The Incas built the city around 1450, at the height of their empire. The city follows a strict plan in which agricultural and residential areas are separated by a large square. Most archeologists believe that Machu Picchu served as a religious and ceremonial center of the Incan empire.

The Incas chose Machu Picchu for its unique location and features. Getting to Machu Picchu requires a journey up a narrow path. This makes it easily defended, as no one could approach without being spotted.

Machu Picchu was abandoned shortly after Spanish conquistadors vanquished the Incan empire. Over the next several centuries, the jungle reclaimed the site on which Machu Picchu lay. The site was once again discovered by an American historian and explorer in 1911. Since then, archeologists have flocked to the site to see what they can learn about the Incas. Today, Machu Picchu—the Lost City of the Incas—is the most visited site in Peru.

10. Which hypothesis is supported by the evidence in this passage?

a. The Incas would have expanded their empire had Columbus not discovered the Americas.

b. If Machu Picchu had not been discovered in 1911, we would not know anything about the Incas.

c. Machu Picchu would have survived many more years had Columbus not discovered the Americas.

d. If the Incas had built fortified centers on lower ground, they would have been able to beat the conquistadors.

Compare Two Sources on the Same Social Studies Topic

Comparing social studies texts is no different from comparing two movies or two television programs. In some cases, the sources to be compared will express opposite opinions, with one author expressing an opinion *in favor of* a cause and another *against* it, for instance. In other instances, one passage may be a primary source written by an eyewitness or participant in an event, while another might be a secondary source that analyzes that event. In these cases, the differences between the authors' positions might not be as easy to identify.

Regardless of what types of sources are being compared, the approach is the same: comparing and contrasting will require you to look for similarities and differences between them. This will often require you to examine both sources more than once.

For example, you might see pieces of two famous documents from U.S. history, such as a passage from the Declaration of Independence of 1776 and a portion of the Alien and Sedition Acts of 1798.

EXCERPT FROM THE DECLARATION OF INDEPENDENCE, 1776

We hold these truths to be self-evident, that all men are created equal, that they are endowed by their Creator with certain unalienable Rights, that among these are Life, Liberty and the pursuit of Happiness. That to secure these rights, Governments are instituted among Men, deriving their just powers from the consent of the governed, That whenever any Form of Government becomes destructive of these ends, it is the Right of the People to alter or to abolish it, and to institute new Government, laying its foundation on such principles and organizing its powers in such form, as to them shall seem most likely to effect their Safety and Happiness. . . . [W]hen a long train of abuses and usurpations, pursuing invariably the same Object evinces a design to reduce them under absolute Despotism, it is their right, it is their duty, to throw off such Government, and to provide new Guards for their future security.

EXCERPT FROM THE ALIEN AND SEDITION ACTS, 1798

SECTION 1. Be it enacted by the Senate and House of Representatives of the United States of America, in Congress assembled, That if any persons shall unlawfully combine or conspire together, with intent to oppose any measure or measures of the government of the United States, which are or shall be directed by proper authority, or to impede the operation of any law of the United States, or to intimidate or prevent any person holding a place or office in or under the government of the United States, from undertaking, performing or executing his trust or duty, and if any person or persons, with intent as aforesaid, shall counsel, advise or attempt to procure any insurrection, riot, unlawful assembly, or combination, whether such conspiracy, threatening, counsel, advice, or attempt shall have the proposed effect or not, he or they shall be deemed guilty of a high misdemeanor. . . .

SECTION 2. And be it farther enacted, That if any person shall write, print, utter or publish, or shall cause or procure to be written, printed, uttered or published, or shall knowingly and willingly assist or aid in writing, printing, uttering or publishing any false, scandalous and malicious writing or writings against the government of the United States, or either house of the Congress of the United States, or the President of the United States, with intent to defame the said government, or either house of the said Congress, or the said President, or to bring them, or either of them, into contempt or disrepute; or to excite against them, or either or any of them, the hatred of the good people of the United States, or to stir up sedition within the United States, or to excite any unlawful combinations therein, for opposing or resisting any law of the United States, or any act of the President of the United States, done in pursuance of any such law, or of the powers in him vested by the constitution of the United States, or to resist, oppose, or defeat any such law or act, or to aid, encourage or abet any hostile designs of any foreign nation against United States, their people or government, then such person . . . shall be punished by a fine not exceeding two thousand dollars, and by imprisonment not exceeding two years.

In this case, it is helpful to remember some United States history. Thomas Jefferson, who later became the third president of the United States, wrote the Declaration of Independence, which was approved by the Continental Congress in 1776. John Adams, the second president of the United States, signed the Declaration of Independence. Adams was president when the Alien and Sedition Acts were written, and he approved them.

But even if you do not know this context, you would recognize that these two documents emerged during the earliest part of the history of the United States—a period of revolution. Read both carefully and ask yourself: "What do these two passages have in common?" It is clear they are talking about governments and how citizens should behave toward their governments. You don't have to read too far into the Declaration of Independence to know what it is about. In fact, it's clear from the title. Jefferson is arguing that it is the *right* and *duty* of the people to overthrow an unjust government. However, the portion of the Sedition Act above makes it illegal to *com-*

bine or conspire together, with intent to oppose any measure or measures of the government of the United States.

Summary of Reading and Writing in a Social Studies Context

As you can see, the reading skills assessed in the GED® Social Studies test are interrelated. These are the same skills that are needed by a reader in any other discipline. Most social studies passages will be fairly straightforward, but you will need to make inferences based on the passage and an overall understanding of social studies. You may be asked—explicitly or implicitly—to identify the main idea(s) and/or determine the author's point of view and purpose. Other questions may focus on the opinions and claims of the author and whether these are supported by the details.

- **Be a detective.** Look for clues that will help you better understand the text. In addition to the passage itself, look for the title, the date it was written, and the background of the person who wrote it—all of these can provide you with valuable information.
- **Be an active reader.** Ask questions as you read. Stop and reread things that you don't understand.
- **Check your instincts.** In most cases when taking any type of test, your first instinct is correct. But before you submit it, check your answer by looking back at the text to find details that support it.

Applying Important Social Studies Concepts

The GED® Social Studies test asks you to apply reasoning skills to the social studies content areas (civics and government, U.S. history, economics, and geography and the world). About 40% of the questions you'll encounter on the test require these skills.

Success on this part of the test will require you to think logically about arguments, events, and ideas. You may need to look at the evidence and find details that support a claim that is made. You may need to consider the bias or point of view evident in a written excerpt, political cartoon, propaganda poster, or other visual element. Some questions may require you to look at two events and decide whether the first event caused the second or to identify the cause or effect from a list of items.

Let's look in more detail at how more specific reasoning skills may apply to the test.

Use Evidence to Support Inferences or Analyses

The GED® Social Studies test will assess your ability to find evidence in written material to support an inference or a claim. As discussed in the previous section, an **inference** is a conclusion that is drawn from the evidence provided. In addition to making inferences, the GED® Social Studies test will ask you to find the details, facts, or other information to support these inferences.

There are some words and phrases that authors often use to introduce evidence in support of an opinion or main idea. Look for phrases (e.g., *for example, for instance, in particular, a reason is, in one case*) that suggest the author is providing you with a reason or supporting detail.

Charts, graphs, or political cartoons are also sometimes used to assess this skill. For instance, you may be asked to find specific information on a graph that suggests something has happened.

Take a look at the following graph.

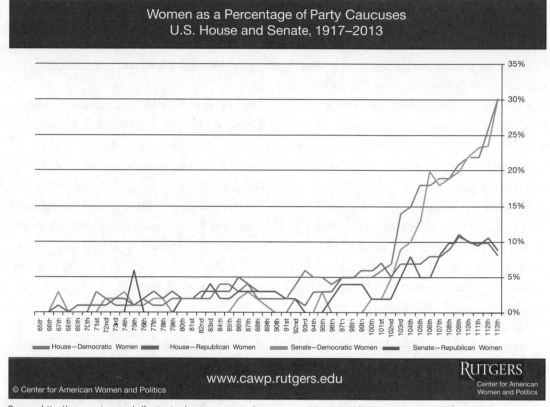

**Women as a Percentage of Party Caucuses
U.S. House and Senate, 1917–2013**

House—Democratic Women   House—Republican Women   Senate—Democratic Women   Senate—Republican Women

RUTGERS
Center for American
Women and Politics
www.cawp.rutgers.edu
© Center for American Women and Politics

Source: http://cawp.rutgers.edu/footnotes/party_caucuses/women-as-percentage-of-party-caucuses-1917-to-2013.

First, let's break this chart down. The *x*-axis—the bottom line—contains a tick mark for each Congress from 1917 to 2013, which are the 65th through the 113th congressional sessions. The *y*-axis—the vertical line—denotes the percentages. The various lines represent women Democrats and women Republicans in the House of Representatives and women Democrats and women Republicans in the Senate.

On the GED® Social Studies test, a graph like this one will often be accompanied by a question like the following. Select the choice that you think is correct, and then we'll analyze each choice to see if there is evidence in the graph to support it.

Which statement about the data presented on this chart is correct?

a. More women run for Congressional seats as Democrats than as Republicans.

b. The number of women Republicans in the Senate has increased steadily since 1917.

c. The percentage of Congressional Democrats who are women has increased sharply since the 102nd Congress.

d. Republicans have tended not to vote for female Congressional candidates since the 102nd Congress.

Choice **c** is the correct answer. To answer this question correctly, you have to consider whether there is evidence in the chart that clearly supports the statement.

Let's start with choice **a**:

a. *More women run for Congressional seats as Democrats than as Republicans.*

This may be an attractive choice because it is clear that female Democrats (the lighter lines in the chart) represent a larger proportion of their party in Congress than Republican women. But we cannot conclude based only on this chart that this is because more Democratic women run for office.

Next, let's look at choice **b**:

b. *The number of women Republicans in the Senate has increased steadily since 1917.*

This might look possible at first glance, but it is important to remember that this is a chart that shows the percentage of Republicans in Congress that are women. It does not show the exact number of women Republicans that were serving in Congress at any given time. Even so, the chart shows that women Republicans as a percentage of all Congressional Republicans has varied widely over time.

Moving on to choice **c**:

c. *The percentage of Congressional Democrats who are women has increased sharply since the 102nd Congress.*

This choice is clearly supported by the chart and is thus correct. Look at the lighter lines in the chart and you can see a sharp upturn in both starting around the 102nd Congress. The percentage of Congressional Democrats who are women increased from around 5% to around 30% in that time span.

Finally, let's examine choice **d**:

d. *Republicans have tended not to vote for female Congressional candidates since the 102nd Congress.*

There is no evidence to support this statement. The chart does not give us any information about the number of women who have run for a Congressional seat on the Republican ticket, and there is no evidence in the chart that would allow us to make speculations about Republican voting preferences. Thus, this choice is incorrect.

Describe Social Studies Concepts and Connections between Them

Some of the questions on the GED® Social Studies test will ask you to describe relationships between or among people, places, environments, processes, or events. Sometimes these questions will stand on their own, but other times there will be a short reading passage or graphic—or both—for you to consider. Being able to sum up or describe quickly what you read is an important skill.

Practice

Read the paragraph and answer the question that follows.

REDUCING CARBON FOOTPRINT

Jim Blanchard is looking for ways to reduce his carbon footprint. He takes his own bags to the grocery store and avoids anything that is packaged in plastic. He also collects recyclables and takes them to the recycling center. Jim does not own a car. He uses mass transit to reach most places he needs to go to. He also owns an electric scooter, so he does not use gasoline.

11. How would you describe Jim Blanchard? Complete the following sentences.

Jim Blanchard is a(n) _____.

He is concerned about _____.

Now try examining the following two charts and describing them as we did previously with the passages.

**Causes of Deforestation in the Amazon
Rain Forest, 2006–2012**

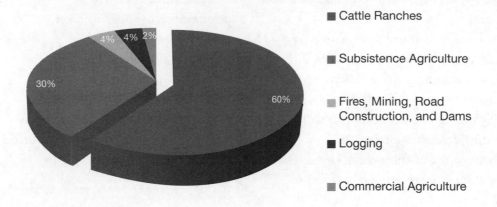

- ■ Cattle Ranches
- ■ Subsistence Agriculture
- ▓ Fires, Mining, Road Construction, and Dams
- ■ Logging
- ▓ Commercial Agriculture

Beef Exports
OECD-FAO Projections, 2006 and 2015

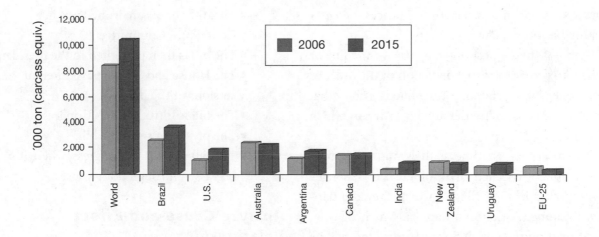

12. Describe, in one sentence, what is depicted in the pie chart.

_____

_____

13. Describe, in one sentence, what is depicted in the bar graph.

_____

_____

Now put it all together and answer the following question.

14. About 60% of the Amazon rain forest is in Brazil. What prediction about the deforestation of the Amazon rain forest can you make based on these charts?

   a. Subsistence agriculture will become an increasing cause of deforestation by 2015.

   b. Commercial agriculture will become an increasing cause of deforestation by 2015.

   c. Brazil's success as a beef exporter will lead to continued deforestation by 2015.

   d. Argentina's lack of success as a beef exporter will lead it to preserve the rain forest in 2015.

Put Events or Steps in Order

Some questions on the GED® Social Studies test will ask you to put historical events in the order in which they occurred. You may also be asked to understand the order of steps in a social studies process, such as how a bill becomes a law.

Some of these questions may use a time line or flowchart to provide a visual depiction of the order of events or steps in a process. A time line is a chart that organizes events or activities in the order in which they occur.

When writers use time as their main organization principle, it is called **chronological order**. They describe events in the order in which they did happen, will happen, or should happen. Much of what you will read on the GED® Social Studies test will be organized in this way, including historical texts, instructions and procedures, and essays about personal experiences.

Passages organized by chronology typically use a lot of transitional words and phrases. The **transitions** help us see when things happened and in what order. They help us follow along when the passage shifts from one period of time to another.

The following is a list of some of the most common chronological transitions:

- *first, second, third, (etc.), before*
- *after, next, now*
- *then, when, as soon as*
- *immediately, suddenly, soon*
- *during, while, meanwhile*
- *later, in the meantime, at last*
- *eventually, finally, afterward*

Practice

15. Put the events listed in the correct order.

   How a Bill Becomes a Law

   1. _____

   2. _____

   3. _____

   4. _____

   5. _____

   6. _____

- The differences are ironed out in a Conference Committee.
- The bill is then presented to the president.
- The House and Senate pass different versions of the bill.
- The bill is introduced to Congress.
- The president signs the bill.
- The bill returns to Congress, where it must be passed through both houses.

Analyze Cause-and-Effect Relationships

The GED® Social Studies test will ask you to identify the relationships between events. Often, historical events are connected to situations that came before them. There are several things to keep in mind when you are considering cause-and-effect relationships:

- There may be multiple causes for an event.
- There may be multiple effects of an event.

- Just because events occur near the same time or in the same place does not mean they are related or that one caused the other.
- Sometimes the question of what is considered a cause can be controversial.

Cause-and-effect questions are often associated with a written excerpt, but they may also ask about data presented in a time line or other chart or graph, or a combination of both.

Practice

Look at the time line, read the excerpt from the declaration made by South Carolina when it seceded from the Union, and then answer the question that follows.

Civil War Time Line, 1860–1865

December 20, 1860	South Carolina is the first to secede from the Union.
April 12, 1861	The first shots of the Civil War are fired at Fort Sumter.
January 1, 1863	Lincoln issues the Emancipation Proclamation.
April 9, 1865	General Robert E. Lee surrenders at Appomattox Courthouse in Virginia.

EXCERPT

The people of the State of South Carolina . . . declared that the frequent violations of the Constitution of the United States, by the Federal Government, and its encroachments upon the reserved rights of the States, fully justified this State in then withdrawing from the Federal Union. . . .

We affirm that these ends for which this Government was instituted have been defeated, and the Government itself has been made destructive of them by the action of the non-slaveholding States. Those States have assumed the right of deciding upon the propriety of our domestic institutions. . . . They have encouraged and assisted thousands of our slaves to leave their homes; and those who remain, have been incited by emissaries, books and pictures to servile insurrection.

16. Based on the time line and excerpt, which is a factor that contributed to South Carolina's decision to secede from the Union?
    a. President Lincoln freed the slaves.
    b. The Union fired upon the Confederacy at Fort Sumter.
    c. Abolitionists were encouraging slaves to rebel.
    d. The Confederacy offered greater protection from foreign aggression.

Compare Sets of Ideas

The GED® test will also assess your ability to compare differing sets of ideas. These ideas might have to do with civics or economics. For instance, you might be asked to compare ideas about how to organize an economy or govern a country.

Practice

The U.S. political landscape is dominated by the Republican and Democratic parties. Review the table and answer the following question.

REPUBLICAN PARTY	DEMOCRATIC PARTY
Free market economy	Minimum wages and labor unions
Limited government	Higher tax rates for wealthy citizens
Strong national defense	Government support for social programs

17. Based on the table, which party would be most likely to cut the food stamp program in order to reduce the deficit?
   a. Republican
   b. Democratic

Identify Bias and Propaganda

The next skill we will look at involves identifying bias and propaganda. Let's first learn about bias.

Bias

Bias is a prejudice in favor of or against one thing, person, or group compared with another, usually in a way considered to be unfair. You can think of bias as a personal preference.

Everyone has personal preferences. Even if writers try not to show these preferences, there is likely to be some bias in what they write. Bias is closely related to an author's point of view. For instance, someone who grew up in a family in which multiple adults served in the military might have a tendency to respect service members and believe them to be honorable and courageous. Someone who grew up in a war-torn area where soldiers behaved violently toward civilians might have a strong bias against members of the armed forces.

To detect bias, watch for words that try to tell the reader how to think or behave. These are called **prescriptive words** and include terms such as *should*

and *must*. Also, watch for strongly worded statements that include terms like *always* or *never*; these often represent strong viewpoints that are prone to bias. Bias can also be shown by using words with positive associations when referring to things the writer agrees with or supports and using words with negative associations when referring to things the writer disagrees with.

Practice

Read the following passage. Then answer the question that follows.

TOUGH TIMES

With the economy lagging, many Americans are out of work. Unemployment benefits should be extended to help citizens weather these tough times. At the same time, the United States cannot afford to turn its back on the elderly, children, and poor families who have always relied on government assistance. Despite the downturn in the economy, the rich continue to get richer. The best way—perhaps the only way—to help the country succeed is to increase revenue by raising taxes for those who can afford to pay higher taxes.

18. What bias is evident in this passage? Write your answer on the following lines.

_____

_____

_____

Propaganda

Propaganda refers to techniques that try to influence opinions, emotions, and attitudes in order to benefit an organization or individual. Propaganda uses language that targets the emotions—fears, beliefs, values, prejudices—instead of appealing to reason or critical thinking. Advertising, media, and political campaigns use propaganda techniques to influence others. To detect propaganda, ask yourself the following questions about the information:

- Whom does it benefit?
- What are its sources?
- What is the purpose of the text?

You should be aware of a number of propaganda techniques:

Bandwagon: The basic message of bandwagon propaganda is: "Everyone else is doing something, so you should do it, too." It appeals to the desire to join the crowd or be on the winning team. Phrases like "Americans buy more of our brand than any other brand" or "the brand that picky parents choose" are examples of the bandwagon technique. To evaluate a message, ask these questions:

- Does this program or policy serve my particular interests?
- What is the evidence for or against it?

Common man: This approach tries to convince you that its message is just plain old common sense. Politicians and advertisers often speak in everyday language and present themselves as one of the people to appeal to their audience. For example, a presidential candidate campaigning in New Hampshire may wear a plaid shirt and chop wood or visit a mill in order to look like an ordinary citizen. To determine if the common-man technique is being used, ask yourself these questions:

- What ideas is the person presenting? Are the ideas presented differently than the person's usual image or language?
- What are the facts?

Euphemisms: Instead of emotionally loaded language that rouses its audience, these terms soften an unpleasant reality. Terms that soften the nature of war are often used. In the 1940s, for example, the U.S. government renamed the War Department the Department of Defense. Stay alert to euphemisms. What facts are being softened or hidden?

Generalities: This approach uses words and phrases that evoke deep emotions. Examples of generalities are *honor*, *peace*, *freedom*, and *home*. These words carry strong associations for most people. By using these terms, a writer can appeal to the emotions so that the reader will accept his or her message without evaluating it. Generalities are vague so that you will supply your own interpretations and not ask further questions. An example might be: "The United States must further restrict immigration in order to preserve freedom and liberty."

Try to challenge what you read and hear. Ask yourself:

- What does the generality really mean?
- Has the author used the generality to sway my emotions?
- If I take the generality out of the sentence, what are the merits of the idea?

Labeling or name-calling: This method links a negative label, name, or phrase to a person, group, belief, or nation. It appeals to hate and fears. Name-calling can be a direct attack, or it can be indirect, using ridicule. Labels can evoke deep emotions, such as *Commie*, *Nazi*, or *terrorist*. They can be negatively charged, depending on the situation: *yuppie*, *hipster*, *slacker*, *liberal*, or *reactionary*. When a written text or speech uses labeling, ask yourself these questions:

- Does the label have any real connection to the idea being presented?

- If I take away the label, what are the merits of the idea?

Testimonials: In advertising, athletes promote a range of products, from cereal to wrist-watches. In politics, celebrities endorse presidential candidates. Both are examples of testimonials. A testimonial uses a public figure, expert, or other respected person to endorse a policy, organization, or product. Because you respect or admire a person, you may be less critical and accept what he or she says more readily. Ask yourself these questions:

- Does the public figure have any expert knowledge about this subject?
- Without the testimonial, what are the merits of the message?

Practice

19. Who was the intended audience for this poster?

_____

20. What was the goal of this poster?

_____

Analyze How Historical Circumstances Shape Point of View

Questions on the GED® Social Studies test may ask you to consider how historical circumstances shape an author's point of view. You may also need to assess how believable an author is based on an understanding of his or her bias.

When you come across information, consider point of view and bias by asking the following questions:

- Who wrote the text?
- Who is the intended audience?
- Under what circumstances was the text written?
- What is the purpose of the text?

In short, the more you know about the text, the more you will understand its point of view and/or bias.

Point of view is how someone looks at an event. A person's point of view is based on his or her background, experiences, and understanding of events. For example, a person who grew up in a family that had little money might think buying an expensive car or jewelry is wasteful. From that person's point of view, spending a lot of money on something that isn't a necessity is bad.

Practice

Read the following excerpt from the speech "Ain't I a Woman?" delivered in 1851 by African-American abolitionist and women's rights activist Sojourner Truth, and then answer the question that follows.

EXCERPT

Well, children, where there is so much racket there must be something out of kilter. I think that 'twixt the Negroes of the South and the women at the North, all talking about rights, the white men will be in a fix pretty soon. But what's all this here talking about?

That man over there says that women need to be helped into carriages, and lifted over ditches, and to have the best place everywhere. Nobody ever helps me into carriages, or over mud-puddles, or gives me any best place! And ain't I a woman? Look at me! Look at my arm! I have ploughed and planted, and gathered into barns, and no man could head me! And ain't I a woman? I could work as much and eat as much as a man, when I could get it, and bear the lash as well! And ain't I a woman? I have borne thirteen children, and seen most all sold off to slavery, and when I cried out with my mother's grief, none but Jesus heard me! And ain't I a woman?

Then they talk about this thing in the head; what's this they call it? [A member of the audience whispers, "Intellect."] That's it, honey. What's that got to do with women's rights or negroes' rights? If my cup won't hold but a pint, and yours holds a quart, wouldn't you be mean not to let me have my little half measure full?

21. In this excerpt, the point of view that Sojourner Truth is expressing when she repeatedly asks "And ain't I a woman?" is
 a. that former female slaves deserve the same courtesies as white women.
 b. that women deserve equal rights because they are as capable as men.
 c. that all men will suffer if they do not offer women equal rights.
 d. that intellect should influence whether a woman deserves equal rights.

Summary of Applying Important Social Studies Concepts

The most important thing when taking the GED® Social Studies test is to think carefully about what the question is asking. You will find that you can answer a lot of the questions by applying simple common sense to a basic understanding of social studies concepts.

Many of the questions will be based on a written excerpt, a graph, a political cartoon, a picture, or a combination of these things. Regardless of the types of passages or graphics you encounter, take the following steps:

- Look at the title or titles (if there are any): What do they tell you about the main idea?
- Look for the date or source of the information: What does this tell you about the context?
- Look at the author: What do you know about his or her background that may influence the point of view?
- Read the passage or visual element carefully: Look for the main idea and supporting details.
- Step back and consider the big picture: What is the author or illustrator trying to tell you?

- Finally, when you are ready to answer the question, look again at the passage or visual stimulus to make sure your initial impulse is correct.

Applying Mathematical Reasoning to Social Studies

The GED® Social Studies test asks you to apply basic mathematical skills to the social studies content areas (civics and government, U.S. history, economics, and geography and the world). About 30% of the questions on the GED® test require these skills.

Success on this part of the test does not require you to be a mathematician. However, you will need to know basic mathematical principles and terms, such as what an *average* means. You will also need to be able to apply basic principles, perhaps by figuring out the average of two or more numbers. Keep in mind that these questions are designed to assess your ability to use math to address *social studies* problems, not such computation skills as adding or multiplying.

Many of these skills are assessed by having you look at information presented in tables, charts, graphs, and maps. You may also be asked to apply mathematical reasoning to a political cartoon, photograph, or short passage. As a basic example, a map or chart may provide statistical data on population growth within individual states, but you may need to use your own knowledge about where the states are located to assess regional trends or how population growth is likely to affect a particular issue.

Let's look in more detail at how mathematical skills are applied to the social studies discipline.

Analyze Information Presented Visually

The GED® Social Studies test will assess your ability to analyze information that is presented visually. This information may be presented in maps, tables, charts, or other stimuli used to organize and present information in a logical manner. You may also be asked to analyze information in a political cartoon, a photograph, an advertisement, or a propaganda poster, for example.

Reading and understanding a map, chart, graph, or other stimulus is very similar to reading a passage. You want to look for clues about the meaning. Ask yourself the same two questions as when trying to understand the main idea of a reading passage:

1. What is this mostly about?
2. What is the author (or illustrator) trying to tell me?

With many types of visual stimuli, the title can provide valuable clues. Often, the year (or years) represented in the map, chart, or graph will be included in the title. If not, look for this information elsewhere.

Tables

Tables organize information in columns and rows. Labels in the first column describe the information contained in the rows to the right of the first column. The labels at the top (column heads) describe the information in the columns below.

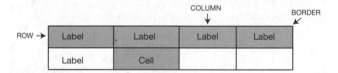

Here is an example of the type of table you will see on the GED® Social Studies test.

World Energy Consumption, 1970–2020	
Year	Quadrillion Btu Consumed
1970	207
1975	243
1980	285
1985	311
1990	346
1995	366
1999	382
2005	439
2010	493
2015	552
2020	612

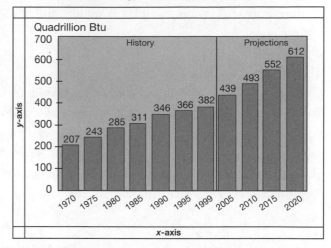

World Energy Consumption, 1970–2020

Bar Graphs

A **bar graph** is one way to present facts visually. A bar graph features a vertical axis (running up and down on the left-hand side of the graph) and a horizontal axis (running along the bottom of the graph).

The horizontal axis is known as the *x*-axis. The vertical axis is known as the *y*-axis. The graph represents quantities in strips or bars. Graphs are especially useful for showing changes over time or comparing two or more quantities or trends.

To construct a bar graph from the table "World Energy Consumption, 1970–2020," mark the five-year increments on the bottom horizontal axis (*x*-axis) and the units of energy consumed (by increments of 100 quadrillion Btu) on the vertical axis (*y*-axis). By representing the table's data in a bar graph, you can visualize the world's energy consumption trend more easily.

Line Graphs

Next, let's look at a **line graph**. It is similar to a bar graph because there is information presented along the *x*-axis and *y*-axis, and you'll need to look at both to understand the graph.

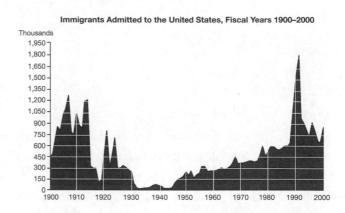

Immigrants Admitted to the United States, Fiscal Years 1900–2000

As you can see, line graphs are good for showing changes over time. In this case, we have a chart that depicts the number of immigrants admitted into the United States between 1900 and 2000. The line is useful because it shows not only an increase in the number of immigrants admitted, but the years in which the numbers increased dramatically or stayed relatively stable. Noticing these kinds of changes will help you interpret line graphs on the GED® Social Studies test because sharp increases and decreases shown on a line graph are usually significant to the question you are facing.

Circle Graphs/Pie Charts

Circle graphs, also called **pie charts**, look nothing like bar and line graphs; they even lack an *x*-axis and a *y*-axis. Circle graphs display information so that you can see relationships between parts and a whole. The information on a circle graph can be presented as percentages or as actual numbers. The circle is divided into parts, or pie slices, that together add up to the whole. To understand a circle graph, first read the title. What does the graph represent? Read all other headings and labels. What does each portion of the circle represent? Now you are ready to see how the parts relate to each other.

The following circle graph illustrates the items making up the entire amount of bakery goods sold by the Grainville Baking Company. Notice that this graph includes a title, labels, and a legend.

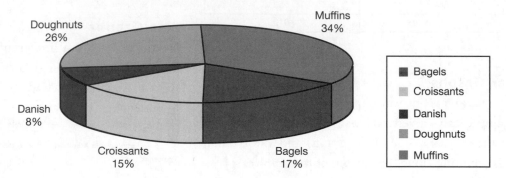

Breakdown of Breakfast Sales

Muffins 34%

Doughnuts 26%

Danish 8%

Croissants 15%

Bagels 17%

Legend:
- Bagels
- Croissants
- Danish
- Doughnuts
- Muffins

Maps

Maps are printed or drawn representations of a geographic area. Social scientists use different types of maps to understand the natural or cultural facts about an area. Maps can visually display many kinds of information, such as the physical features of the land, political boundaries between nations, or population densities.

- **Topographic maps** show the physical features of land, including land elevations and depressions, water depth, rivers, forests, mountains, and human-made cities and roads.
- **Political maps** display political divisions and borders.

- **Special-purpose maps** can depict a wide range of information about an area, from average rainfall, crop distribution, or population density to migration patterns of people.

To read a map, carefully review each of the following:

- **Title** describes what the map represents.
- **Legend or key** is a table or list that explains the symbols used in a map.
- **Latitude and longitude:** Latitude refers to the lines on a map that are parallel to the *equator*; longitude refers to lines parallel to the *prime meridian* that run north and south through

Greenwich, England. These lines help to locate specific areas on a map.

- **Scale** shows the map's proportion in relation to the actual area it represents. For example, on a topographic map, the scale might show the distance on the map that equals a mile or kilometer on land.

Analyze Numerical, Technical, and Written Materials on a Common Topic

Some of the questions on the GED® Social Studies test will include more than one type of stimulus. They might include both a passage and a chart, for example. You may have to figure out whether different types of information go together—in other words, whether the information that is presented in a chart, graph, or other format goes with information in the written material, and vice versa.

These types of questions should be fairly easy; don't overcomplicate them. Look for the main idea of the passage that is provided. What is it mostly about? Then look at the main idea of the chart, graph, or other stimulus that is provided. Is it about the same topic?

Other questions may ask you to point out differences between two types of information on the same topic. For instance, a question might present two sets of information about immigration—from different centuries or focused on different countries. You might then be asked to point out similarities and differences in the information.

Create Tables, Graphs, and Charts

Some questions on the GED® Social Studies test will ask you to take written information and put it into a table or graph. Again, the key here is not to overcomplicate things. Take the following steps:

- Read the excerpt. Look for the numbers and statistics that are included.

- Look at the labels on the table or chart. Note how the information is organized.
- Transfer the numbers and statistics to the table or chart.

Questions may ask you to provide the labels for a chart or graph. The types of labels needed will vary depending on the chart or graph.

- **Line graphs** typically include labels for the x-axis and the y-axis. If the line graph shows a trend over time, the years are typically represented on the x-axis, with the item being measured shown on the y-axis.
- **Bar graphs** typically include a series of bars across the graph. They will need labels for the x-axis and y-axis.
- **Circle graphs** (or **pie charts**) show elements in relation to one another and to the whole. They often use a legend to show what the elements are, but labels may or may not be used to spell out the actual numbers or percentages.

Charts and graphs, like other visual stimuli, will also include titles. Some questions may ask you to add a title to a chart or graph. Again, all you need to do to answer these kinds of questions is to look for the main idea. You may also need to look at the legend to see what years or other categories are included in the graph.

Interpret Graphs and Use Data to Predict Trends

On the GED® Social Studies test, you'll have to do more than understand a chart. You'll need to interpret the data. This just means that you will take the numbers or other information provided and put them into words. It may also require you to relate one number to another, noting that it has decreased, increased, or doubled, for example. Finally, the information may require you to predict trends based on the chart. For example, if a population chart shows that the population of a country has doubled every 50 years, you might be asked what you would expect the population to be 100 years from now.

If you understand what the graph is showing, you should have no trouble with these types of questions. Again, familiarizing yourself with various types of graphs will help.

Practice

The following chart shows the price of SuperSport Sneakers since they were introduced to the U.S. market in 1990. Review the chart and answer the question that follows.

SuperSport Sneakers

22. Based on the information in the chart, you would expect the price of SuperSport Sneakers to
   a. increase steadily.
   b. increase dramatically.
   c. decrease somewhat.
   d. remain the same.

Analyze How Variables, Events, or Actions Are Related

The GED® test will also assess your ability to determine whether different elements, events, or actions are related. Some of these questions will provide a chart or graph and ask you to make a valid conclusion or assess a claim regarding the impact of one variable on another. This will require you to

determine whether they are dependent or independent variables.

- A **variable** is just an object, event, idea, or other category that is being measured. For example, the time at which the sun rises could be a variable.
- A **dependent variable** is a variable that changes if another variable changes—it is dependent upon that variable. If some factor can change a variable, it is a dependent variable. The average life expectancy of a country may be a dependent variable if it is connected to factors such as famine or war.
- An **independent variable** is an element that is not affected by how the values of other variables may change. For example, your age is an independent variable. At a given time, nothing changes the exact number of days you have been on the planet.

Questions on the GED® Social Studies test may present information in a chart along with a written passage. You would then be asked to determine whether one factor has influenced the other. For instance, a question may include a graph that shows a sudden increase in average life expectancy along with a passage that talks about some trends in that country. You could be asked what factor or factors might have contributed to the change in life expectancy. Another question might present a set of data and ask you to assess the validity of one or more claims, requiring you to determine whether one thing relates to another. For instance, there may be a graph showing changes in the federal budget over time coupled with a passage discussing trends in the country. You may be asked to determine whether any connections are supported by the information given.

Closely related to this skill is determining cause and effect. This may involve determining whether one historical event led to another. A tricky part about analyzing cause and effect is that it is tempting to decide something is a cause just because it comes right before some change or effect. Often, so many factors might contribute to a change of some sort that it is impossible to point out a single cause. The key is to think logically about the issue.

Practice

Read the passage and examine the chart that accompanies it, and then answer the question that follows.

A DEADLY WAR

World War I (1914–1918) was one of the deadliest conflicts of the twentieth century. It involved the use of modern weaponry never before used in battle. This allowed combatants to kill each other on a scale that had been impossible in earlier wars. Most of the countries involved in the war were European nations, although the United States and the Ottoman Empire were also involved. Approximately 60 million Europeans fought over the course of the war. About 9 million combatants were killed. At the same time, a global epidemic of a deadly strain of influenza known as the Spanish flu killed some 50 million people around the world.

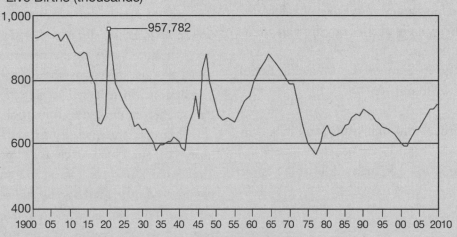

Live Births: England and Wales, 1900–2010

Live Births (thousands)

957,782

Source: Office for National Statistics (ONS), United Kingdom.

23. Which factor was most responsible for the first sharp drop in the birth rate in England and Wales in the early part of the twentieth century?

   a. The Spanish flu epidemic killed most English and Welsh women.

   b. World War I introduced advanced technology.

   c. Millions of English and Welsh men were fighting in World War I.

   d. Women in England and Wales were unable to afford to feed children.

Calculate Mean, Median, Mode, and Range

The final mathematical skill we'll discuss involves mean, median, mode, and range.

Mean

The **mean** is the same as the average. To find the mean, take the values, add them up, and divide by how many values you have.

Here's an example. Find the mean of the following numbers: 9, 14, 22, 11, and 10.

- Add the values. The sum is 66 (9 + 14 + 22 + 11 + 10 = 66).
- Count up how many items or values you have added: 5.
- Divide the sum of the values (66) by the number of values (5), and you get 13.2 (66 ÷ 5 = 13.2).

The mean, or average, is 13.2.

Median

The **median** is the value in the middle of your list of values. To find the mean, reorder the values from lowest to highest. The median will be the number in the middle. If you have an even number of values, the median will be the average of the two numbers in the middle.

Let's find the median of the following list of numbers: 9, 14, 22, 11, and 10.

- First, put in order from smallest to largest: 9, 10, 11, 14, 22.
- Then, find the number in the middle of the list: 11.

Mode

The **mode** refers to the value that occurs most frequently in the list. If you have a list of three numbers and one occurs twice, that will be the mode. In longer lists, it will again help to put the values in order. Then, it's simple! Just look for the number that occurs most often.

Find the mode of the following list of numbers: 18, 12, 10, 2, 9, 6, 18, 42, 18, 2.

- Put in order from smallest to largest: 2, 2, 6, 9, 10, 12, 18, 18, 18, 42.
- Look for the number that occurs most often: there are three 18s, more than any other number.
- The mode is 18.

Range

The **range** is the difference between the largest and the smallest values.

Let's find the range of the previous set of numbers: 18, 12, 10, 2, 9, 6, 18, 42, 18, 2

- The largest number is 42.
- The smallest number is 2.
- The difference between them is 40.

Summary of Applying Mathematical Reasoning to Social Studies

Keep in mind that the GED® Social Studies test is not designed to assess your computational skills, just the mathematical skills directly related to the social studies discipline. You'll have access to a calculator, and social studies questions that require mathematical calculation will usually provide choices, so you will be less likely to make a computational error.

Many of the question formats provide a set of answers from which to choose. Look at each of the answer choices to see if you can figure it out without having to do the math. For instance, a question that asks for the mean or average of a series of numbers may not require you to add up the values and then divide. You may be able to figure out the answer by using common sense.

That said, one of the things that you will need to pay attention to is how numbers work. You should be able to move fairly readily between percentages and fractions, for instance. You should recognize that 1% is equal to $\frac{1}{100}$, meaning that something occurs 1 out of every 100 times. You should know that 50% is the same as one-half of something. Reviewing these basic mathematical principles, as well as the types of graphs you will likely come across, can help you focus on the content of the question that is asked.

The Extended Response Task

The GED® Social Studies test includes an extended response question, also known as an essay question. You will be asked to read a passage (or a pair of passages) that focuses on an enduring issue, meaning a complex topic that has no easy solutions. You will be expected to have some background knowledge to draw on when answering these questions. In order to understand the passage(s) you read, it will be important to understand the historical context in which they were created. About 70% of the time, the focus will be on U.S. history, civics, and government. About 30% of the time, the focus will be on world geography or economics.

You will be asked to write an essay in which you analyze the position taken by the author of each passage. You will support your analysis with evidence from the reading passage, facts, and logical arguments. This kind of essay response is different from what you might have seen on other tests in the past. Often, essay questions ask you to talk about an experience from your own life, respond to a general controversy, or make an argument in support of a general idea. On the GED® Social Studies test, however, the emphasis will be on your ability to analyze passages carefully and then respond to them with a well-reasoned, well-supported argument. The passages you read can be pieces of primary source documents, such as speeches, letters, and journal entries, or secondary source documents, such as parts of articles or books about important social studies events.

To score well, your essay must have a clear structure and be free of grammatical and spelling errors. There is no set minimum or maximum word limit for your essay, but plan on writing about 250 words.

Overview

Most of the prompts—the topics you will be asked to write about in your essay—will ask you to compare or evaluate the ideas, arguments, and effectiveness of a passage or two passages. This means you will have to pull together all the skills you have learned and apply them. You will need to understand the author's purpose, tell the difference between fact and opinion, and identify important parts of the passage.

In general, it is best to write a three- to four-paragraph essay that follows this structure:

- **Paragraph 1:** Introduce your analysis of the passage(s) based on the prompt you are given. This paragraph can be short, but it must clearly summarize, in one or two sentences, what your analysis is.
- **Paragraphs 2 and 3:** Support your analysis in more detail using quotes and evidence from the passage(s). You should also draw on your knowledge of historical events or related issues. However, try not to base your position on your own experience alone. You need to stay focused on the passage(s) and the prompt. You may be able to accomplish these tasks in one long paragraph. If you need two paragraphs, use the first to explain your position and the next to discuss other positions and why you do not agree with them.
- **Paragraph 4:** Conclude your argument. This can be a brief paragraph. Restate your position and very quickly summarize your argument.

When writing an essay response, follow these steps in this order:

1. Read the prompt—the topic you will have to write about. This will help you focus on relevant details as you read the passage or passages.
2. Read the passages carefully, taking note of where each author makes a very strong point or a flawed point.
3. Decide how you will address the prompt.
4. Plan your essay using the basic structure explained earlier. Making an outline will help. Decide in advance what you will say in each paragraph and what details and facts you will use to support your statements.

5. Write your essay.

6. Go back and reread your essay. Make sure you have stayed focused on the topic. If you haven't, cut out material that is off topic. Make sure your argument is easy to follow by using carefully chosen words that make your meaning clear and by organizing your essay logically. Clarify your points as necessary. Make sure your punctuation, spelling, and grammar are all correct; that you use transitional words to make your ideas flow smoothly; and that you change your sentence structure from time to time to make the essay more interesting and easy to follow.

Read the Prompt and Passage(s)

Let's take a look at the following two passages and the sample prompt that follows. Your first two steps in preparing to answer an extended response question are to read the prompt and then read the passages. On test day, you should plan on spending about 25 minutes completing these two steps.

EXCERPT

[T]his [a tax on corn sales] operates then as a tax for the maintenance of the poor.—A very good thing, you will say. But I ask, Why a partial tax? Why laid on us Farmers only?—If it be a good thing, pray, Messrs. the Public, take your share of it, by indemnifying us a little out of your public treasury. In doing a good thing there is both honour and pleasure;—you are welcome to your part of both.

For my own part, I am not so well satisfied of the goodness of this thing. I am for doing good to the poor, but I differ in opinion of the means.—I think the best way of doing good to the poor, is not making them easy in poverty, but leading or driving them out of it. In my youth I traveled much, and I observed in different countries, that the more public provisions were made for the poor, the less they provided for themselves, and of course became poorer. And, on the contrary, the less was done for them, the more they did for themselves, and became richer.

—Benjamin Franklin, 1766

EXCERPT

There are millions of Americans—one fifth of our people—who have not shared in the abundance which has been granted to most of us, and on whom the gates of opportunity have been closed. . . .

The young man or woman who grows up without a decent education, in a broken home, in a hostile and squalid environment, in ill health or in the face of racial injustice—that young man or woman is often trapped in a life of poverty. He does not have the skills demanded by a complex society. He does not know how to acquire those skills. He faces a mounting sense of despair which drains initiative and ambition and energy.

Our tax cut will create millions of new jobs—new exits from poverty. But we must also strike down all the barriers which keep many from using those exits.

The war on poverty is not a struggle simply to support people, to make them dependent on the generosity of others. It is a struggle to give people a chance.

The new program I propose is within our means. Its cost of 970 million dollars is 1 percent of our national budget—and every dollar I am requesting for this program is already included in the budget I sent to Congress in January. But we cannot measure its importance by its cost. For it charts an entirely new course of hope for our people.

—President Lyndon B. Johnson, 1964

PROMPT

In your response, develop an argument about how President Lyndon Johnson's position in his speech reflects the enduring issue in the excerpted letter by Benjamin Franklin. Incorporate relevant and specific information from the letter, the speech, and your own knowledge of the enduring issue and the circumstances surrounding the case to support your analysis.

As you read the excerpts, you should have noted key facts and arguments made by both authors. You need to analyze each excerpt carefully (step 3 of the 6 steps for writing an extended response). Let's practice.

■ Identify the important points and arguments— flawed and strong—made by each author.

■ Think about how you intend to address the prompt. Read it again carefully. Remember to stay focused on it. It is clear now that the enduring issue is what role the government should play in assisting people living in poverty. This is an issue that can produce an emotional response.

■ Stay focused on the prompt and the passages. Your task is to make a well-reasoned, logical argument that is based on facts, not generalities or personal biases.

■ Think of one or two clear sentences that state your position. Everything you write in your essay response should be in support of those one or two sentences. This is your thesis statement—the main idea of your whole essay.

An example of a thesis statement for this prompt might be:

> *President Lyndon Johnson makes a clear argument that while giving money to the poor is not an effective solution to the enduring problem of poverty, the poor can be trapped in a cycle of poverty and the government should do what it can to break that cycle and give the poor better opportunities to succeed. Benjamin Franklin argues that by not helping the poor, the government gives them an incentive to improve their positions in life.*

Plan Your Essay

You have a thesis statement; each individual paragraph should have a main idea, too. Those main ideas should back up and develop your thesis statement with facts and quotes from the passages. After you have decided on the main idea of each paragraph, choose what facts, quotes, and personal knowledge you will use to support your main ideas.

Here are some examples of main ideas for each essay paragraph accompanying the sample thesis, which would represent paragraph 1.

> **Paragraph 2:** *It is possible to be trapped in a cycle of poverty.*
> **Paragraph 3:** *Handouts are still not the answer, but tearing down barriers is.*
> **Paragraph 4:** *Johnson had it mostly right, but Franklin raised a good point about personal responsibility.*

Write Your Essay

Do the main ideas for each paragraph clearly support the thesis statement? Good! Now it's time to write your essay!

PROMPT

In your response, develop an argument about how President Lyndon Johnson's position in his speech reflects the enduring issue in the excerpted letter by Benjamin Franklin. Incorporate relevant and specific information from the letter, the speech, and your own knowledge of the enduring issue and the circumstances surrounding the case to support your analysis.

Here is an example of an excellent response to this prompt:

> *President Lyndon Johnson makes a clear argument that while giving money to the poor is not an effective solution to the enduring problem of poverty, the poor can be trapped in a cycle of poverty and the government should do what it can to break that cycle and give the poor better opportunities to succeed. Benjamin Franklin argues that by not helping the poor, the government gives them an incentive to improve their positions in life.*
>
> *While the United States is a wealthy and powerful nation, a shocking number of its citizens live in poverty and do not share in the general bounty of the nation. In 2010, the U.S. Census showed 15% of Americans lived in poverty. In 1960, the situation was more dire. As Johnson said, "There are millions of Americans—one fifth of our people—who have not shared in the abundance which has been granted to most of us, and on whom the gates of opportunity have been closed." These kinds of statistics did not exist for the U.S. colonies in 1766, when Benjamin Franklin wrote his letter. But it is safe to say that the economy, demographics, and population size of what is now the United States were far different in the 1760s than in the 1960s. Most colonists*

were focused on raising food for their own families. Some, like Benjamin Franklin, had larger farms and were able to sell their produce for profit, which meant they became wealthier. Franklin was not born into a wealthy family and he did indeed become the influential and wealthy person he was through his own ingenuity and hard work. It is easy to see, then, how he might feel that if he could succeed against the odds, so could any other person. That is why he could state that while he believed in helping the poor, he thought "the best way of doing good to the poor, is not making them easy in poverty, but leading or driving them out of it."

What Benjamin Franklin did not see and Johnson did was that not everyone has the same opportunities and tools necessary to succeed. Franklin's parents, though not wealthy, encouraged him in his education. Franklin himself was a man of astonishing intelligence and creativity, whose achievements in everything from publishing to natural science to politics are unmatched. But not everyone can be a Benjamin Franklin, and even Franklin himself could not foresee how much the United States would change over the course of 200 years. The United States had become a world superpower and industrial powerhouse by the 1960s. It was, as Johnson said, "a complex society." In such a society, as Johnson said, a person "without a decent education, in a broken home, in a hostile and squalid environment, in ill health or in the face of racial injustice" could become trapped in poverty. What Johnson wanted to do was offer paths out of poverty, mainly by improving educational opportunities and removing barriers to success, such as racial injustice.

Franklin and Johnson seemed to agree that simply giving handouts to the poor is not a lasting solution to poverty. What might have led Franklin to adopt his position was the fact that giving food and shelter to the poor was the common practice during his day. The cost of charity to the poor was usually borne by city governments or churches. Franklin could certainly make the argument that just giving alms to the poor does little to encourage them to escape poverty. However, as Johnson argued, "The war on poverty is not a struggle simply to support people, to make them dependent on the generosity of others. It is a struggle to give people a chance."

Proofread Your Essay

Once you have a solid first essay draft, reread your essay and make sure it is clear, grammatical, and free of spelling errors. Highlight areas that you feel could be improved based on GED® test guidelines: use of evidence, logical flow of ideas, good grammar and spelling, varied sentence structure, and a sharp focus on the prompt.

Extended Response Scoring

According to the GED® Testing Service, here are the guidelines you should follow when writing your extended response:

- Support your explanation with multiple pieces of evidence, using ideas from both the quotation or excerpt and the passage.
- Incorporate your own knowledge of the topic's background and historical context into your response.
- Answer the prompt directly by staying focused on the passage and the quotation or excerpt throughout your response.
- Build your main points thoroughly.
- Put your main points in logical order and tie your details to your main points.
- Organize your response carefully and consider your audience, message, and purpose.
- Use transitional words and phrases to connect sentences, paragraphs, and ideas.

- Choose words carefully to express your ideas clearly.
- Vary your sentence structure to enhance the flow and clarity of your response.
- Reread and revise your response to correct any errors in grammar, usage, or punctuation.
- You will be given a total score between 0 and 4. Your essay will be evaluated in three different ways, according to three separate traits:
  - Trait 1: Creation of arguments and use of evidence
  - Trait 2: Development of ideas and organizational structure
  - Trait 3: Clarity and command of standard English conventions

You can earn up to 2 points for trait 1, and 1 point each for traits 2 and 3. Then these individual trait scores are combined. Thus, your highest possible total is 4.

Trait 1: Creation of Arguments and Use of Evidence

Trait 1 of the Social Studies Extended Response Rubric focuses on your ability to create an effective argument and use evidence from the text to support that argument.

The official GED® test scorers will use the following guidelines to assign a score in this trait to your response. Knowing what they are looking for can help give you a better idea of what is needed when crafting your response.

SCORING GUIDE FOR TRAIT 1: CREATION OF ARGUMENTS AND USE OF EVIDENCE	
SCORE	DESCRIPTION
2	• Generates a text-based argument that demonstrates a clear understanding of the relationships among ideas, events, and figures as presented in the source text(s) *and* the historical contexts from which they are drawn. • Cites relevant and specific evidence from primary and secondary source text(s) that adequately supports an argument. • Is well connected to both the prompt and the source text(s).
1	• Generates an argument that demonstrates an understanding of the relationships among ideas, events, and figures as presented in the source text(s). • Cites some evidence from primary and secondary source text(s) in support of an argument (may include a mix of relevant and irrelevant textual references). • Is connected to both the prompt and the source text(s).
0	• May attempt to create an argument but demonstrates minimal or no understanding of the ideas, events, and figures presented in the source texts or the contexts from which these texts are drawn. • Cites minimal or no evidence from the primary and secondary source text(s); may or may not demonstrate an attempt to create an argument. • Lacks connection to either the prompt or the source text(s).

Trait 2: Development of Ideas and Organizational Structure

Trait 2 of the Social Studies Extended Response Rubric focuses on how well you organize your response and how effectively you build your response from one idea to the next. It also focuses on the depth of support you provide for your ideas, as well as your understanding of audience and purpose.

The official GED® test scorers will use the following guidelines to assign a score in this trait.

Again, knowing what they are looking for can help give you a better idea of what is needed when crafting your response.

SCORING GUIDE FOR TRAIT 2: DEVELOPMENT OF IDEAS AND ORGANIZATIONAL STRUCTURE

SCORE	DESCRIPTION
1	■ Contains a sensible progression of ideas with understandable connections between details and main ideas. ■ Contains ideas that are developed and generally logical; multiple ideas are elaborated upon. ■ Demonstrates appropriate awareness of the task.
0	■ Contains an unclear or no apparent progression of ideas. ■ Contains ideas that are insufficiently developed or illogical; just one idea is elaborated upon. ■ Demonstrates no awareness of the task.

Trait 3: Clarity and Command of Standard English Conventions

Trait 3 of the Social Studies Extended Response Rubric focuses on how well you adhere to specific conventions of standard English, the sentence structure and variety you use in your response, and the overall fluency you demonstrate with conventions and mechanics. It's important to note, however, that because you will be given only 25 minutes to complete your essay, it is not expected to be totally free of convention or usage errors to receive a score of 1.

SCORING GUIDE FOR TRAIT 3: CLARITY AND COMMAND OF STANDARD ENGLISH CONVENTIONS

SCORE	DESCRIPTION

1	■ Demonstrates adequate applications of conventions with specific regard to the following skills:
	  1. correct use of frequently confused words and homonyms, including contractions
	  2. subject–verb agreement
	  3. pronoun usage, including pronoun antecedent agreement, avoidance of unclear pronoun references, and pronoun case
	  4. placement of modifiers and correct word order
	  5. capitalization (e.g., proper nouns, titles, and beginnings of sentences)
	  6. use of apostrophes with possessive nouns
	  7. use of punctuation (e.g., commas in a series or in nonrestrictive appositives and other nonessential elements, end marks, and appropriate punctuation for clause separation)
	■ Demonstrates largely correct sentence structure with variance from sentence to sentence; generally fluent and clear with specific regard to the following skills:
	  1. correct subordination, coordination, and parallelism
	  2. avoidance of wordiness and awkward sentence structures
	  3. usage of transitional words, conjunctive adverbs, and other words that support logic and clarity
	  4. avoidance of run-on sentences, fused sentences, or sentence fragments
	  5. standard usage at a level of formality appropriate for on-demand draft writing
	■ May contain some errors in mechanics and conventions, but they do not interfere with understanding.

0	■ Demonstrates minimal control of basic conventions with specific regard to skills 1–7 as listed in the first bullet under Trait 3, Score Point 1. ■ Demonstrates consistently flawed sentence structure; minimal or no variance such that meaning may be obscured; demonstrates minimal control over skills 1–5 as listed in the second bullet under Trait 3, Score Point 1. ■ Contains severe and frequent errors in mechanics and conventions that interfere with comprehension. OR ■ Response is insufficient to demonstrate level of mastery over conventions and usage.

Summary of the Extended Response Task

The extended response task you will encounter on your GED® Social Studies test will be challenging, but if you follow the steps outlined in this chapter, you'll be well prepared to earn a great score. Remember:

- Use a three- or four-paragraph structure for your essay with an introduction and thesis statement, a paragraph or two developing your analysis and supporting your thesis statement, and a conclusion.

- Follow the six steps for successful extended response writing.
- Stay formal in your tone, focused on the prompt, and fact-based in supporting your argument.

Social Studies Practices Review

Use the following to answer questions 1–5.

Read the excerpt from a 1940 speech by Winston Churchill and answer the questions that follow.

EXCERPT

I speak to you for the first time as Prime Minister in a solemn hour for the life of our country, of our Empire, of our Allies, and, above all, of the cause of Freedom. A tremendous battle is raging in France and Flanders. The Germans, by a remarkable combination of air bombing and heavily armored tanks, have broken through the French defenses. . . . They have penetrated deeply and spread alarm and confusion in their tracks. . . .

In the air . . . the relative balance of the British and German Air Forces is now considerably more favorable to us than at the beginning of the battle. In cutting down the German bombers, we are fighting our own battle as well as that of France. My confidence in our ability to fight it out to the finish with the German Air Force has been strengthened by the fierce encounters which have taken place and are taking place. At the same time, our heavy bombers are striking nightly at the taproot of German mechanized power. . . .

We must expect that as soon as stability is reached on the Western Front, the bulk of that hideous apparatus of aggression which gashed Holland into ruin and slavery in a few days, will be turned upon us. I am sure I speak for all when I say we are ready to face it; to endure it; and to retaliate against it. . . .

Having received His Majesty's commission, I have found an administration of men and women of every party and of almost every point of view. We have differed and quarreled in the past; but now one bond unites us all—to wage war until victory is won, and never to surrender ourselves to servitude and shame, whatever the cost and the agony may be.

1. Which best explains Winston Churchill's purpose in this speech?
   a. to give an update on the latest battles
   b. to ask for support from other countries
   c. to galvanize popular support for the war
   d. to commemorate the soldiers fighting for freedom

2. Which statement can you infer from this passage?
   a. Germany will win the war at any cost.
   b. Holland has allied itself with Germany.
   c. The German army is advancing toward Britain.
   d. The British counterattack requires support from France.

3. Which of the following expresses the main idea of the second paragraph?

    a. *At the same time, our heavy bombers are striking nightly at the taproot of German mechanized power.*

    b. *My confidence in our ability to fight it out to the finish with the German Air Force has been strengthened by the fierce encounters which have taken place and are taking place.*

    c. *[T]he relative balance of the British and German Air Forces is now considerably more favorable to us than at the beginning of the battle.*

    d. *In cutting down the German bombers, we are fighting our own battle as well as that of France.*

4. During what war was this speech made?

    _____

5. The third paragraph refers to *that hideous apparatus of aggression.* To what does this term refer? _____

Use the following to answer questions 6–8.

AIR POLLUTION IN MEXICO CITY

In 1992, Mexico City topped the United Nations' list of most polluted cities in the world. The air was so toxic that birds dropped in midflight. Air pollution was taking a toll on human health as well. Experts attributed roughly 1,000 deaths and 35,000 hospitalizations a year to the high ozone level.

The city's location has contributed to its air pollution problems. The city is located on a lake basin that was originally drained in the 1600s and is 7,000 feet above sea level. There are lower levels of oxygen at higher altitudes, which causes higher emissions of carbon monoxide and other pollutants. Intense sunlight results in more smog.

Since the mid-1990s, Mexican leaders have attempted to address the problem. The government required that gasoline be reformulated to remove lead. Polluting refineries and factories were encouraged to clean up their emissions and move away from the urban center. Public transportation was expanded to encourage people to drive less.

Change has been gradual, but the steps taken to address Mexico City's pollution problems have paid off. The presence of lead in the air is just one-tenth of what it was in 1990. Dust, soot, chemicals, and other suspended particles have been cut by 70 percent. There are still gains to be made, however, and the government continues to look for ways to reduce pollution. Much of these involve greener solutions to transportation, including the expansion of the low-emissions bus system, the addition of hybrid buses, and a new suburban train system.

6. Based on this excerpt, how does Mexico City's location contribute to its pollution problem?

   a. Its high altitude leads to less oxygen and greater emissions of pollutants.

   b. Its tropical location leads to hotter air temperatures and greater smog.

   c. Its proximity to the United States means that it deals with excess pollution from the north.

   d. Its dry climate leads to more dust particles in the air.

7. According to the passage, which of the follow events occurred first?

   a. Mexico City was named the most polluted city in the world.

   b. The lake basin on which Mexico City is located was drained.

   c. Dust, soot, and chemicals have been reduced in Mexico City's air by 70%.

   d. The Mexican government expanded public transportation to encourage people to drive less.

8. Which of the following best supports the idea that Mexico's policies have made a difference in its pollution levels?

   a. Polluting refineries were encouraged to clean up their emissions.

   b. There are lower levels of oxygen at Mexico City's high altitudes.

   c. The presence of lead in the air dropped to one-tenth of 1990 levels.

   d. The government plans to build a new suburban train system.

Use the following to answer questions 9–11.

In 1904, Udo J. Keppler published the following political cartoon in *Puck* magazine. Look at the cartoon and answer the questions that follow.

9. Based on the cartoon, the artist most likely has a very _____ opinion of Standard Oil.
   a. positive
   b. negative

10. Which of the following is most likely the intended audience for this cartoon?
   a. working-class readers
   b. oil industrialists
   c. politicians
   d. marine biologists

11. Which of the following historical circumstances seems most likely to have informed the artist's point of view in this cartoon?
   a. the expansion of American corporations into foreign markets
   b. the dramatic increase in petroleum extraction and production in the nineteenth century
   c. the spread of powerful corporate monopolies in the late nineteenth century
   d. the territorial disputes between Spain and the United States that led to the Spanish-American War

Use the following to answer question 12.

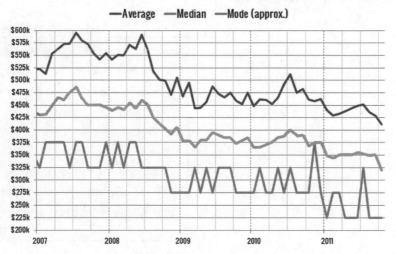

King County (Washington) Single-Family Home Sales

── Average ── Median ── Mode (approx.)

Source: http://seattlebubble.com/blog/2011/11/22/king-co-average-price-30-off-peak-mode-down-40/.

GLOBAL FINANCIAL CRISIS

In 2008, a global financial crisis threatened the stability of countries around the world. Many, including the United States, fell into deep recessions. The crisis was triggered by the bursting of a housing bubble in the United States. In economic terms, a bubble is a rapid increase in the price of some commodity that is not related to the actual change in its value. When a bubble bursts, prices fall rapidly. In the United States, when the housing bubble burst, high real estate prices dropped. Because the mortgages, or home loans, on these pieces of real estate were tied to financial markets around the world, the sharp fall in real estate prices triggered a financial panic and severe strain on banks and government budgets. Though some countries had yet to recover fully from the crisis as of 2014, the United States had recovered substantially from the economic crisis by 2010. Despite this, the real estate markets in many urban areas continue to suffer.

12. Which of the following would be the most accurate indicator of the effects of the global economic crisis on the Seattle, WA, housing market?
   a. average
   b. mode
   c. median
   d. range

Use the following to answer question 13.

Read the Preamble to the U.S. Constitution.

EXCERPT

We the People of the United States, in Order to form a more perfect Union, establish Justice, insure domestic Tranquility, provide for the common defence, promote the general Welfare, and secure the Blessings of Liberty to ourselves and our Posterity, do ordain and establish this Constitution for the United States of America.

13. What is the main purpose of the Preamble?
   a. to tell why the Constitution is needed
   b. to present an outline of the document
   c. to describe the new system of government
   d. to review the reasons for breaking from England

Use the following to answer questions 14–16.

Reasons for Not Voting, 2012

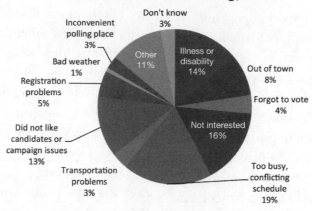

14. What is the biggest reason that people did not vote in 2012?

   a. illness or disability

   b. lack of interest

   c. too busy, conflicting schedule

   d. not liking candidates or campaign issues

15. Which change would likely have the greatest impact on voting rates?

   a. relocating polling places

   b. extending the polling hours or days

   c. sending reminders to registered voters

   d. changing the voter registration process

16. Consider the following opinion.

Americans are apathetic about politics and do not appreciate the right to vote.

What evidence from the chart could be used to support this opinion?

   a. Of Americans who did not vote, 16% said it was because they were not interested.

   b. Of Americans who did not vote, 5% said it was because they had registration problems.

   c. The most often-cited reason for not voting was that people were too busy.

   d. Of those who did not vote, 13% did not like the candidates or campaign issues.

Answers and Explanations

Chapter Practice

1. **a.** This question is asking you to figure out from the details when Washington made this speech. Nothing in the speech says specifically where or when it occurs, so you need to look for clues—the facts or details from which you can make an inference. Return to the passage to explore how the details might give you the clues you need to figure this out. The first clue is that Washington is addressing *Friends and Citizens*. This suggests that it is a speech to a larger group of people than the Continental Army (choice **a**) or Constitutional Convention (choice **b**). From the first sentence, you learn that *The period for a new election . . . [is] not far distant.* You need to apply your knowledge of social studies to understand that Washington is talking about a presidential election. At the end of the paragraph, he says he wants *to decline* the nomination. Only choices **c** and **d** have to do with presidential elections, and as you probably know well, Washington was the first U.S. president. That means he did accept a nomination at some point, but at the time he is giving the speech, he does not want the nomination. So the only answer choice that makes sense by logical inference is choice **d**.

2. When Christopher Columbus landed in the New World, he brought with him horses, cattle, and seeds for planting. Over the next decades, European explorers and settlers brought to the New World other domesticated animals and plants. Wheat and other grains soon became a staple crop in North America. Meanwhile, from the New World to the Old went corn, squash, turkeys, tomatoes, and the ever-important potato. <u>This transfer of plants, animals, and diseases, known as the Columbian Exchange, transformed the diets and lifestyles of people on both sides of the Atlantic.</u>

3. **b.** The organization will hold its 45th annual *convention* in June. The annual convention is a **formal assembly or gathering**.

4. **a.** The military government clashed with the *conventions* of the native peoples. The native conventions are **customary ways of doing things**.

5. **c.** One of the reasons it can be difficult to read historical documents is that they follow different *conventions* from those used today. The historical conventions are **familiar or preferred writing styles of the times**.

6. *Answers will vary:*
   The purpose of this passage is to **convince listeners that women do not want to be dominated by men**.

7. Fact.

8. Opinion.

9. Fact.

10. **c.** This is the only hypothesis that is supported by evidence from the passage. Columbus's discovery led to the Spanish conquest of the New World and the decline of the Incan empire.

11. *Answers will vary:*

Jim Blanchard is an **environmentalist**. He is concerned about **the use of nonrenewable natural resources.**

All the details in the passage describe a person who is mostly likely an environmentalist. The very first sentence of the passage states that Blanchard "is looking for ways to reduce his carbon footprint," and the remaining sentences describe his concern about use of plastic and nonrenewable natural resources such as gasoline.

12. *Answers will vary:*

Cattle ranches are the leading cause of deforestation of the Amazon rain forest. When you look at the pie chart, the biggest slice—cattle ranches—should grab your attention. At 60%, it is twice as large as the next leading cause of deforestation.

13. *Answers will vary:*

Beef exports are projected to significantly increase worldwide by 2015, but especially in Brazil and the United States. Looking at the bar chart, the darker bar (denoting the 2015 projections) is significantly taller than the lighter bar (denoting beef exports in 2006) for overall worldwide beef exports. Of the individual nations, the difference is most stark for Brazil and the United States, indicating that both nations make up a big chunk of that worldwide projection.

14. **c.** We can confidently predict, based on these charts, that a growing beef export industry in Brazil will put increasing pressure on the Amazon rain forest and lead to more deforestation.

15. 1. **The bill is introduced to Congress.**
2. **The House and Senate pass different versions of the bill.**
3. **The differences are ironed out in a Conference Committee.**
4. **The bill returns to Congress, where it must be passed through both houses.**
5. **The bill is then presented to the president.**
6. **The president signs the bill.**

16. **c.** South Carolina complained that the Northern states had encouraged slaves to run away and fueled *servile insurrection*, or slave revolts.

17. **a.** The Republican Party would be most likely to cut the food stamp program in order to reduce the deficit.

18. *Answers will vary:*

The author has expressed a bias in favor of unemployed and poor Americans and believes that helping them should be a responsibility of the wealthy. This bias is evident when the author uses prescriptive words like *should*. When someone says we *should* do something, he or she is usually about to express an idea that reveals bias. The final sentence of the passage also shows clear bias. Strong language such as *The best way—perhaps the only way* is also prescriptive and should alert you that the writer is about to express a strong opinion that will give you a hint about his or her bias.

19. **women.** The depiction of the woman rolling up her sleeves to do work and the "We Can Do It!" in the poster's title indicate that the target audience was women. More specifically, the audience was women in the United States during World War II, while many of the men were overseas fighting in the war.

20. *Answers will vary:*

The goal of the poster was to **keep production up during wartime by boosting the morale of women workers.** This poster was created in 1942 by an artist named J. Howard Miller. It was a part of the Westinghouse Company's War Production Coordinating Committee's series of posters for the war effort.

21. b. In the speech, Truth describes her life, stressing that her strength and abilities are equal to those of men. By asking "Ain't I a woman?" she is calling on the audience to recognize that equality.

22. a. The graph shows a steady increase in the price of SuperSport Sneakers, so you would expect this trend to continue. Note that while there are many variables that could influence this, the question is asking you only to use the information that has been provided.

23. c. The passage states that 60 million soldiers were deployed in the war. Millions of men from each country were deployed. If the men of a country are away from their families or are killed, they clearly cannot father children. Although the question does not ask about this, note that an even deeper dip in the birth rate occurred in the 1930s and early 1940s—the years of the Great Depression and World War II.

Social Studies Practices Review

1. c. The other paragraphs support Churchill's plea for supporting the war *whatever the cost and the agony may be.* Choice **a** is incorrect because although Churchill gives an update on the war, this is not the main reason he gives the speech. Choice **b** is incorrect because Churchill speaks of his allies, but the address is to the people of Britain; this is shown in the first sentence, when he speaks of *our country.* Choice **d** is incorrect because although the tone is indeed solemn and respectful of those fighting for freedom, this is not the purpose of the speech.

2. c. Germany has broken through France's defenses and taken over Holland. Churchill expresses his fears and expectation that Germany will continue its advance toward Britain. Choice **a** is incorrect because Churchill suggests that Germany is a formidable enemy, but he stresses that Britain will be able to defeat it. Choice **b** is incorrect because Holland has indeed been invaded by Germany, but there is nothing that indicates that it has allied itself with Germany; in contrast, Churchill equates Holland's experience with ruin and slavery. Choice **d** is incorrect because although Churchill mentions the alliance with France, he is poised for Britain to act alone.

3. b. Churchill is expressing growing confidence. He admits that fighting has been fierce but states that the British position is much stronger than it used to be. Choices **a, c,** and **d** are incorrect because these sentences support the main idea but do not express the main idea.

4. **World War II.** This can be discerned by the date of the speech—1940. If you did not know the specific dates of the war, you should be able to apply more general knowledge of the war and its battles to be able to correctly identify the context of this speech.

5. **Nazi Germany.** Using context clues should be able to help you discern that this term refers to the German army and tank brigade.

6. **a.** The excerpt points out that the location of Mexico City at a high altitude has contributed to its air pollution problems. Choice **b** incorrect because although the passage mentions smog, it does not claim that the city's tropical location is responsible. Choice **c** is incorrect because the passage does not mention excess pollution from the United States. Choice **d** is incorrect the passage does not mention the dry climate as an important factor in pollution.

7. **b.** The second paragraph states that Mexico City is located on a lake basin that was originally drained in the 1600s. Choice **a** is incorrect because the first paragraph of the passage says that in 1992, Mexico City was named the most polluted city in the world. Choices **c** and **d** are incorrect because they were steps the Mexican government took to reduce pollution in response to the pollution problem.

8. **c.** The drop in lead pollution levels is evidence that the new policies have made a difference. Choice **a** is incorrect because encouraging refineries to clean up their emissions would not be evidence that new policies have been effective. Choice **b** is incorrect because lower levels of oxygen at Mexico City's high altitudes are not the result of antipollution policies. Choice **d** is incorrect because future plans do not indicate evidence that existing policies have made a difference.

9. **b.** Based on the cartoon, the artist most likely has a very **negative** opinion of Standard Oil. The cartoon suggests that Standard Oil is a monster seizing control of the land, the government, and the people.

10. **a.** The cartoon is aimed at working-class readers in an attempt to arouse public sentiments against Standard Oil. Choice **b** in incorrect because the cartoon portrays Standard Oil in a negative light and therefore would not be aimed at oil industrialists. Choice **c** is incorrect because the cartoon suggests that politicians are already under the control of Standard Oil, and therefore politicians would not be swayed by the cartoon's message. Choice **d** is incorrect because although the cartoon depicts Standard Oil as an octopus, its message is not intended for marine biologists.

11. **c.** The cartoon depicts Standard Oil as a corporation that has seized massive power and control, as did several corporate monopolies in the late nineteenth century. Choice **a** is incorrect because the cartoon does not make reference to the expansion of American corporations into foreign markets. Choice **b** is incorrect because although petroleum extraction and production increased in the nineteenth century, the cartoon is aimed specifically at Standard Oil rather than the industry as a whole. Choice **d** is incorrect because the cartoon does not make reference to territorial disputes between the United States and Spain.

12. c. The median is the middle house price at any given time, which gives the clearest picture of a general trend. Choice **a** is incorrect because the mean, or average, housing price could be pulled sharply up or down by an unusually low or high sales price, so it isn't a reliable indicator of the overall state of the housing market. Choice **b** is incorrect because the mode is more or less irrelevant to the question, since it doesn't show an overall trend. Choice **d** is incorrect because the range of housing prices would be not be indicative of a trend.

13. a. The Preamble lists six reasons that a new governing document is needed. Choice **b** is incorrect because although the Preamble is at the beginning of the Constitution, it does not provide an outline of the document. Choice **c** is incorrect because the Constitution describes the new system of government, but the Preamble does not. Choice **d** is incorrect because although the causes for separating from England were very much in the minds of the authors of the Constitution, the Preamble does not review these.

14. c. To find the most common reason given, look for the biggest slice of the pie, or the item with the highest percentage. The most common reason given was being too busy or having a conflicting schedule, which is 19%. The next biggest reasons given were: not interested (16%), illness or disability (14%), and did not like candidates or campaign issues (13%).

15. b. Being too busy was cited by more nonvoters than any other reason. Providing longer polling hours might enable busy people to get to the polls. Choice **a** is incorrect because although this might encourage some people, only 3% of respondents suggested that they had not voted because the polling place was inconvenient. It is not the most influential factor on the list. Choice **c** is incorrect because although some people may benefit from a reminder, only 4% of respondents suggested that they had forgotten to vote; it is not the most influential factor on the list. Choice **d** is incorrect because although people have to register in order to vote, the registration process is not intended to be a barrier. Only 5% of respondents said they had registration problems, so it is not the most influential factor on the list.

16. a. *Apathy* is defined as a lack of interest or enthusiasm. The fact that, according to the chart, 16% of Americans did not vote simply because they were not interested supports this opinion. You cannot assume that a person who is too busy to vote is apathetic about politics or unappreciative of his or her right to vote.

14 ▶ SOCIAL STUDIES KNOWLEDGE

This chapter is designed to serve as a crash course in the four major social studies knowledge areas covered on the GED® Social Studies test:

1. **Civics and government (50% of the exam)**
2. **U.S. history (20% of the exam)**
3. **Economics (15% of the exam)**
4. **Geography and the world (15% of the exam)**

Remember, the focus of the exam isn't to assess your social studies content knowledge; it's to test your critical reasoning and thinking skills in a social studies context. On the test, you will never encounter a question that asks you to provide your own definition of a specific social studies term or concept. However, according to the GED® Testing Service, you should be "broadly and generally familiar" with each of the basic social studies concepts covered in this chapter. In other words, to do your best, you should strive to generally understand all the concepts and terms you'll encounter in the following pages.

There are practice questions throughout the chapter to help test your social studies comprehension skills, much like the questions on the GED® Social Studies test. Answers and explanations for all practice questions are at the end of the chapter.

Civics and Government

The study of civics and government is a core component of social studies literacy. All citizens and residents should understand how local, state, and federal governments affect their lives. This lesson will help build your:

- familiarity with the types of governments throughout history and around the world
- understanding of the historical and philosophical basis of the U.S. government and how it operates
- knowledge of how the U.S. political system functions and shapes policy

Types of Modern and Historical Governments

Government is the overall structure by which nations, states, and cities carry out their political, economic, and social agendas. Many kinds of governments throughout history have shaped the types of governments that exist today.

Democracy

Throughout most of history, political power has been reserved for kings, dictators, and wealthy landowners. The history of democracy is the history of power being transferred from wealthy rulers to everyday people, regardless of social status, gender, race, or creed. Democracy is truly, as Abraham Lincoln stated in his Gettysburg Address, "government of the people, by the people, for the people."

There are four types of democracy.

In a **direct democracy**, or **pure democracy**, power is held directly by the people. In other words, the people vote directly on policies and laws rather than elect representatives to vote for them as in the United States. In 500 B.C., the city-state of Athens became the first direct democracy, although slaves, women, and foreigners could not vote. In modern times, Switzerland is the only example of direct democracy, and then only at the local level. On the national level, the Swiss government is representative.

In a **representative democracy**, or **indirect democracy**, the people elect officials to vote on policy, legislate laws, and appoint other governmental officials, such as judges. Modern democracies, including the United States, United Kingdom, and Germany, are all representative democracies.

Parliamentary democracy is similar to representative democracy because in both forms of government, the people elect officials to represent their interests. However, this system is often also a **constitutional monarchy**, as in the United Kingdom and Japan, where the monarch—a king, queen, or emperor—is a figurehead without true political power. In this case, the head of state (a queen, for example) is different from the head of government (a prime minister, for example).

In a **presidential democracy** or **congressional democracy**, the president is both head of state and head of government, with the power to appoint and nominate government officials. The United States and France are modern examples of this type of democratic government.

Monarchy

There are two types of monarchies. An **absolute monarchy**, or a **despotic monarchy**, is a form of government in which a ruler, or despot, inherits power for life. The despot's power is absolute and not limited by laws or a constitution. For example, ancient Roman despots could put any citizen to death for any reason or for no reason at all. The despot's whim was law.

In a **constitutional monarchy**, the monarch's power is limited by a constitution and the law. As described previously, this kind of government is often associated with parliamentary democracy, in which the king or queen has no real power and only serves as a ceremonial figurehead based on tradition.

Oligarchy

In an oligarchy, a small group of people controls the government. There are four types of oligarchies, each with its own type of ruling class.

1. In an **aristocracy**, political power is in the hands of the nobility, who bear hereditary titles such as baron, duke, or count. Historically, this ruling class has been wealthy landowners entitled to education denied to the lower classes. The American Revolution was a rebellion against the privilege of English aristocracy and the aristocratic system.

2. A **military junta** is government by military leaders. Some South American countries, including Colombia and Brazil, have been governed by juntas, although juntas are not limited to that continent. This type of government is often subject to a military coup d'état, often just called a coup, in which one military force overthrows another to gain power.

3. **Plutocracy** is government by the rich, and the term *plutocrat* is widely used as an insult or warning against the plutocratic state. Many social scientists have described America's Gilded Age (1870–1900) as a plutocratic era because robber-baron industrialists, such as John Jacob Astor and Andrew Carnegie, wielded political power due to the great wealth they had amassed in business.

4. In a **stratocracy**, the government is run by military leaders. It is different from a junta government because in a stratocracy, the military and the government are sanctioned as one by a military constitution. Myanmar (Burma) is the only modern example of this form of oligarchy.

Practice

1. Which of the following is a plutocrat?
   a. duke
   b. robber baron
   c. elected official
   d. military general

2. The American Revolution
   a. was a coup.
   b. opposed oligarchy.
   c. supported oligarchy.
   d. made way for a military constitution.

Authoritarianism

An **authoritarian** government is ruled by a single, absolute dictator or small group of despots whose word is law. Under authoritarianism, the people have no freedom except what is allowed by a supreme ruler. This ruler is often cruel and arbitrary because, as the saying goes, "Power corrupts, and absolute power corrupts absolutely."

One form of authoritarianism is an **autocracy**, in which one person is the absolute ruler of the government. His or her power is unlimited. For example, Kim Jong-un, the dictator of North Korea, has eliminated people he perceives as political enemies by having them sentenced to death and executed without trial.

Despotism and **dictatorship** are two other forms of autocracy. In this type of government, the people are ruled by either a single individual or a small group of despots or dictators. The ancient Egyptian pharaohs were despots and treated their peoples like slaves.

Totalitarianism is similar to autocracy in that power is controlled by a single, absolute ruler or party intolerant of dissent. For example, art is normally an instrument of free expression, but the German Nazis and Soviet Communists dictated that the techniques and subjects of art reflect their politics. They thereby controlled free expression and turned art into political propaganda in favor of their totalitarian goals.

Practice

3. Based on the definitions covered so far in this chapter, _____ government would be the most likely to support freedom of expression.

    a. a democratic

    b. an autocratic

    c. a Nazi

    d. a despotic

Other Types of Government

Political and religious philosophies throughout history have shaped other forms of government besides the types covered previously in this chapter. Each philosophy provides supporting reasons for the existence of the type of government it justifies.

Anarchy is not a form of government but rather the absence of government and laws. Anarchists believe that every form of government is corrupt because people should be free to do as they please without the imposition of any type of authority or rules. Revolutions and civil wars, such as the French Revolution and Russian Civil War, are popularly described as states of lawless anarchy.

In a **meritocracy**, individuals gain power and advance socially based on intellectual ability and talent. For example, civil service exams are used to measure a person's eligibility for employment and promotion. These tests, graded on merit, were first administered by the Chinese during the Han Dynasty in 200 B.C. Today in countries worldwide, civil service exams are taken for jobs ranging from doctor to dog catcher.

A **republic** is similar to a representative democracy in that power is held by the people through their elected officials and not by a monarch such as a king or queen. Rome was the first republican empire in 753 B.C. The United States is the most successful example of a modern republic.

A **theocracy** justifies rule by religious authorities such as priests based on the belief that a god or deity is the supreme ruler of the state. Therefore, the government is controlled by those who interpret and carry out edicts and laws in the deity's name. Vatican City, Iran, and Brunei are modern examples of theocracies.

Finally, the term **puppet government** is an insult directed at any government that lacks the power to control its own destiny. This kind of illegitimate government depends on powers outside the state to support it. For example, during World War II, Germany and Italy controlled puppet governments in Albania, Monaco, and Vichy France.

Practice

4. Which form of government rewards talent?

    a. puppet

    b. republic

    c. theocracy

    d. meritocracy

Principles of American Constitutional Democracy

This section describes the seven key principles that helped establish and shape American democracy.

Natural Rights

The English political philosopher John Locke introduced the concept of natural rights as the right of every human being to life, liberty, and property.

In the United States' Declaration of Independence, Thomas Jefferson put Locke's idea into practice but replaced the word *property* with the phrase *pursuit of happiness*. Jefferson did not explain his reason for this change, but the phrase has been widely interpreted as a call for freedom of opportunity and not just the right to accumulate material goods.

Governments are founded and maintained on the basis of the following three concepts:

1. The concept of **natural rights** is the belief that people are born with inalienable rights that are not to be taken away from them. Therefore, power comes from the people. Most democracies are based on the principle of natural rights.

2. **Divine right** claims that a god or deity bestows the right to rule on an individual. Because this absolute power is god given, the ruler is not accountable to the people but only to that god. Many monarchies and theocracies are based on divine right.

3. **Brute force** is rule by physical power. Dictators, warlords, criminal gangs, and terrorists often depend on brute force and terror to maintain their power.

Constitutionalism

Constitutionalism is the foundation of the government and laws of the United States. It is the set of fundamental principles and established precedents that govern a constitutional government. Constitutions can be written or oral. Great Britain, with a very robust democracy, has only an oral constitution.

The U.S. Constitution is one of the oldest as well as one of the shortest written constitutions in effect today. Whether constitutions are long or short, written or not, they outline the accepted standards to which people and bodies of government must conform.

Practice

Following are some advantages and disadvantages of a written constitution. After each item, write whether it is an **advantage** or a **disadvantage**.

5. It is open to multiple interpretations.

_____

6. It is slow to respond to social, political, and technological changes. _____

7. Laws might not align to standards of justice and human rights. _____

8. The basic structure of the government, as well as the basic responsibilities of each component, is spelled out. _____

9. Individual rights are spelled out and guaranteed. _____

10. The basis of laws is spelled out, providing security and predictability. _____

11. Rule of law protects individuals and organizations. _____

Majority Rule

Majority rule is a fundamental requirement of a functioning democracy. It is implemented through:

- **elections**, in which leaders are elected by a majority of voters
- **representative government** composed of legislators, or lawmakers, answerable to voters

The protection of **minority rights** is equally important. U.S. legislative bodies protect minorities' procedural rights, including the right to campaign to become the majority through the voting process.

Checks and Balances

The U.S. Constitution provides a system of checks and balances that prevents one branch of the government from becoming more powerful than other branches.

The government has three branches, each with its own responsibilities, and each checked, or limited, by the other two branches.

The three branches are:

- the **legislative** branch composed of the United States Congress, which creates laws and the annual budget
- the **executive** branch, headed by the president, who executes the laws enacted by Congress
- the **judicial** branch, or courts, which interpret laws

The idea that government power should be divided among three branches is called separation of powers.

Practice

Describe the checks and balances that are taking place in each question by writing **legislative**, **executive**, or **judicial** in the spaces provided. Each of the three choices can be used more than once.

12. The president nominates judges to the federal court system, including the Court of Appeals and the Supreme Court.
The _____ branch checks the _____ branch.

13. The president has the power to veto laws passed by Congress.
The _____ branch checks the _____ branch.

14. Congress has the power to impeach and remove the president.
The _____ branch checks the _____ branch.

15. The Supreme Court can declare laws unconstitutional.
The _____ branch checks the _____ branch.

16. Congress has the power to impeach and remove federal judges.
The _____ branch checks the _____ branch.

17. Judges who are appointed for life are protected from being controlled by special interests or another branch of government.
The _____ branch checks the _____ branch.

Rule of Law

The *Oxford English Dictionary* has defined *rule of law* as:

> *The authority and influence of law in society, esp. when viewed as a constraint on individual and institutional behaviour; (hence) the principle whereby all members of a society (including those in government) are considered equally subject to publicly disclosed legal codes and processes.*

A democracy cannot function successfully without rule of law. Among other features, rule of law requires:

- clear, publicized laws
- a fair and transparent legislative process
- accountability of officials and leaders to voters
- free, periodic elections
- a free press

Without rule of law, citizens are subject to unwarranted and unauthorized actions by government officials.

Individual Rights

Individual rights include the natural rights of life, liberty, and the pursuit of happiness laid out in the Declaration of Independence and the Bill of Rights.

The Bill of Rights is the first ten amendments to the U.S. Constitution. Unlike the rest of the Constitution, which is primarily concerned with the structure and organization of the government, the Bill of Rights covers rights and protections to individuals, including:

- freedom of expression
- the right to a trial by jury
- freedom from unreasonable searches and seizures
- the right of an individual to practice his or her religion

Federalism

Federalism is a form of government with a central governing authority as well as a more localized government. In the United States, this is comprised of:

- national government, often referred to as the federal government, responsible for issues of national importance
- state and local governments that deal with local issues, such as the funding of public schools and fines for speeding tickets

The line between federal government and state government is not precise and changes over time.

Structure and Design of the U.S. Government

The structure of the U.S. government is based on the system of checks and balances between the executive, judicial, and legislative branches.

Composition of the Three Branches of Government

The **executive branch** is responsible for implementing and enforcing laws. It is composed of the following:

- **president**, the leader of the U.S. government, responsible for the functioning of the government and the health and prosperity of the nation. The president is assisted by a cabinet of advisers.
- **vice president**, with a formal role in two branches. In the executive branch, the vice president takes over for the president if the president becomes incapacitated, resigns, is removed, or dies in office. In the legislative branch, the vice president presides over the Senate, casting a vote only in case of a tie.
- **cabinet**, composed of leaders of the executive agencies, including:
  - **attorney general**, head of the Justice Department

  - **secretary of state**, head of the State Department and responsible for foreign policy
  - **secretary of defense**, head of the Defense Department
  - **secretary of education**, head of the Education Department
  - **secretary of commerce**, head of the Commerce Department

The **legislative branch** creates laws and consists of:
- **Senate:** Each state is represented by two senators, regardless of the state's population, who serve staggered six-year terms. The Senate has the power to consent to treaties before their ratification and to consent to or confirm appointments of Cabinet secretaries, federal judges, federal executive officials, military officers, ambassadors, and other federal uniformed officers.
- **House of Representatives:** Every state has a different number of representatives, based on the state's population. New Jersey is a small state but is densely populated, allowing for 13 representatives. A large, low-population state such as Wyoming has only one representative. There are 435 voting officials in the House of Representatives. The head of the House of Representatives is the Speaker of the House. The House has the ability to impeach officials and start finance and budget bills.

The **judicial branch** is composed of nine Supreme Court justices.

- The head of the judicial branch is the Chief Justice of the Supreme Court. All justices of the Supreme Court are nominated by the president, approved by the Senate, and given lifetime appointments.
- Justices can leave or be removed from office only by resigning or by being impeached by Congress. This also applies to Appeals Court judges, who

are one step lower in power than the Supreme Court.

Federal versus State Government

Some powers and responsibilities are reserved for the federal government, some are reserved for the states, and some are shared by both levels of government, including levying and collecting taxes, issuing bonds, supporting transportation infrastructure, and regulating elections. In addition, the tenth amendment to the Constitution grants all powers not given to the federal government to the states and the people.

Only the federal government can:

- declare war
- regulate interstate commerce
- print money
- set standards of weights and measures
- maintain armed forces
- issue passports and visas
- maintain postal service

Only the state governments can:

- conduct elections
- charter corporations
- regulate intrastate commerce
- control zoning
- establish local governments
- establish state courts

Practice

Write either **federal** or **state** on the line next to each of these scenarios:

18. A family opens a restaurant and wants to incorporate the business to gain tax advantages. The business applies for corporate papers from which level of government? _____

19. A bank with headquarters in New York City has branches in New Jersey, Connecticut, and Massachusetts. The bank is subject to regulation by which level of government?

_____

20. The employees of a post office in rural Mississippi are paid their salaries by what level of government? _____

Individual Rights and Civic Responsibilities

As part of the grand bargain that created the United States, Congress passed, and the states ratified, the first ten amendments to the Constitution known as the Bill of Rights. The amendments and their functions are as follows:

- **The first amendment** protects freedom of speech, press, religion, peaceable assembly, and the right to petition the government.
- **The second amendment** protects the right of the people to keep and bear arms to maintain a well-regulated militia.
- **The third amendment** protects against quartering, or housing, of troops in citizens' homes.
- **The fourth amendment** protects against unreasonable search and seizure.
- **The fifth amendment** protects the right to due process and private property and protects against double jeopardy (being tried twice for the same crime) and self-incrimination.
- **The sixth amendment** protects the right to criminal trial by jury and other rights of the accused.
- **The seventh amendment** protects the right to civil trial by jury.
- **The eighth amendment** prohibits excessive bail and cruel and unusual punishment.
- **The ninth amendment** protects the rights of individuals not described in the Constitution, including the Bill of Rights.

- **The tenth amendment** reserves powers not explicitly granted to the federal government to the states and people.

Political Parties, Campaigns, and Elections in American Politics

Political activity and policy making in the United States are organized around political parties, campaigns, and elections. A political party is made up of individuals who organize to win elections, operate government, and influence public policy. While not described in the Constitution, political parties have played a key role since the beginning of the republic.

Two-Party System: Throughout its history, the United States has had two major political parties, though the two parties in existence today are very different from the two parties of 200 years ago. While there have been attempts to establish third parties, they have not resulted in any lasting electoral impact.

Purpose of Parties: When functioning properly, parties can define and express a group's needs and wants in a way the public and political system can understand. Parties can also help in the formation of alliances of sufficient size and strength to influence and shape policy and political action.

For more than 150 years, the two major political parties have been the Democratic Party and the Republican Party. People can join any political party, including parties other than the major two.

- The **Democratic Party** generally supports government involvement to solve problems. Interest groups that tend to identify with the Democratic Party include organized labor, minorities, women's and gay rights supporters, environmentalists, consumer advocates, immigrants, and liberals.
- The **Republican Party** overall wants to minimize the role of government in most affairs. Interest groups that tend to identify with the Republican Party include corporations, religious fundamentalists, tax opponents, military supporters, and conservatives.

Elections and Voting: Elections and the right to vote are key elements of American democracy. In the United States, citizens who are registered to vote may vote in local, state, and federal elections.

Candidates for offices at the local, state, and federal levels must periodically run for office. The candidate who receives the most votes is elected to office. Many state and local jurisdictions also have votes on ballot questions that relate to public policies and issues, such as education, the environment, and tax/budgeting issues.

Contemporary Public Policy

In order to function, modern governments develop many policies and procedures, in addition to laws. If a policy seems reasonable and is generally accepted, it rarely receives any public attention.

However, many public policies are subject to vigorous public debate. Areas of controversy can arise at any time. Some ongoing topics of dispute are:

- **tax policy**, including simplifying the tax code, whether to raise or to cut revenues, and who should be impacted by these changes
- **budget policy**, including deciding how large a deficit can be tolerated, spending and taxing priorities, and the role and obligations of the government
- **trade policy**, including encouraging or discouraging imports and exports and using trade as a component of foreign policy
- **defense policy**, including the deployment and equipping of armed forces, defining missions, and determining the objectives and exit strategy of military operations
- **environmental policy**, including interventions to address pollution, energy, and development
- **foreign policy**, which affects not only Americans but also people around the world. Every foreign policy decision or action by the president or Congress is open to extensive scrutiny and criticism throughout the country and from abroad. And

because the United States is a democracy that guarantees freedom of speech, foreign policy disputes will continue to be a major component of the national conversation.

Civics and Government Summary

The concepts of self-rule and representative democracy have shaped the United States from its early history. Colonists brought European ideas about government, such as natural rights, to America. The United States' government took shape based on core principles, including constitutionalism, rule of law, checks and balances, and federalism.

The Constitution of the United States of America is the manifestation of those principles. It outlines the relationship between the federal government and the states, the three branches of government, and the method of representative democracy that has shaped public policy from the country's founding to today.

United States History

An understanding of United States history is important to all U.S. citizens and residents. Understanding the historical roots of the country's political system and government, as well as major trends in its history, provides insight into what values have motivated the American people, their government, and businesses. Understanding American history helps shed light on how we got where we are today and helps us make sense of current events and political groups.

Key Historical Documents

American constitutional government, a descendant of the English system of government, has been influenced by ideas set forth in several important documents in the history of Western Europe and the United States.

Magna Carta

The Magna Carta, or Great Charter, was written in 1215 in England. It was the most important document during the medieval period and limited the absolute power and authority of the king of England. Primarily an agreement between the king and the nobility, its key provisions, among others, concerned:

- rights of landholders and tenants
- freedom of the church from the influence of the king
- reform of law, and the fair, nonarbitrary execution of justice

Revised in the centuries that followed, the Magna Carta is considered the foundation of Great Britain's constitutional democracy. As well, it contains the ideals of self-rule and limitation of power that are enshrined in the founding documents of the United States.

Practice

21. In the Magna Carta, *we* refers to

_____.

Mayflower Compact

The Mayflower Compact was the first governmental document written and implemented in a territory that would become part of the United States. The 41 English male colonists on the *Mayflower*, which carried approximately 100 colonists to New England, signed the document on November 11, 1620, and agreed to:

> covenant and combine ourselves together into a civil Body Politick . . . And by Virtue hereof to enact, constitute, and frame, such just and equal Laws, Ordinances, Acts, Constitutions, and Officers, from time to time, as shall be thought most meet and convenient for the general Good of the Colony; unto which we promise all due Submission and Obedience.

Practice

22. Reread the excerpt above and summarize in one or two sentences what the colonists agreed to in the Mayflower Compact.

_____

_____

Declaration of Independence

Probably more than any other document, the Preamble of the Declaration of Independence encapsulates our most idealistic aspirations.

> ## EXCERPT
>
> We hold these truths to be self-evident, that all men are created equal, that they are endowed by their Creator with certain inalienable rights, that among these are life, liberty and the pursuit of happiness.

Most of the Declaration of Independence lists charges of tyranny against the king of Great Britain, which then forced the colonies to declare independence.

Practice

23. What was the purpose of the Declaration of Independence?

a. To allow the United States to become the most powerful nation on Earth.

b. To justify a revolution against the rule of Great Britain.

c. To establish democracy throughout the world.

d. To help create the conditions for the Industrial Revolution.

Constitution of the United States of America

The Constitution describes the structure and nature of the U.S. government. It lays out the duties and responsibilities of the three branches of government and provides for a system of checks and balances.

Written in 1787, the Constitution was the second attempt by the 13 independent colonies to create a United States of America. The first attempt, the Articles of Confederation, created a central government so weak that the new nation was paralyzed. The key problem was that unanimous approval of all the states was required to do almost anything.

The Preamble of the Constitution establishes the purpose of our government.

> ## EXCERPT
>
> We the People of the United States, in Order to form a more perfect Union, establish Justice, insure domestic Tranquility, provide for the common defence, promote the general Welfare, and secure the Blessings of Liberty to ourselves and our Posterity, do ordain and establish this Constitution for the United States of America.

The Constitution then addresses the **legislative** branch, balancing the needs of large and small states by creating a **two-house Congress** composed of:

- **House of Representatives** with membership based on population, giving more power to more populous states
- **Senate**, comprised of two members from each state, giving equal power to less populous states

The intent of this solution was to limit the power of the majority by encouraging compromise and protecting minority rights.

- The legislative article details the lawmaking abilities of the Congress as well as the roles of the president and vice president.

- The impeachment process is also described, with the House of Representatives having the responsibility of impeaching, or charging, a government official and the Senate having the responsibility of conducting the impeachment trial.

This section of the Constitution also stipulates that the Congress has the power to declare war.

Next, the Constitution addresses **executive powers**.

- The first executive section declares that the president is the head of the executive branch.
- It describes the election of the president, with each state appointing electors equal in number to the total of its members of the House and Senate—a system referred to as the **electoral college**.

Each state can decide how its electors are selected. Most states have a system in which the presidential nominee who wins the most votes in the state gets all the electoral votes; however, that is not always the case. Twice in American history, the candidate who lost the popular vote, which is the total vote count, won the electoral vote and became president.

- The remaining executive powers include being commander in chief of the armed forces, appointing executive officials and judges with the advice and consent of the Senate, entering into treaties with the advice and consent of the Senate, and overseeing the executive branch.

The third branch of government is described in the **judicial powers** article of the Constitution.

- It provides for a Supreme Court and gives Congress the power to create lower courts.
- This section also details the scope of the federal judiciary.

The next article describes **state protections**.

- These include the requirement that each state and the federal government respect the laws, records, and judicial proceedings of any other state, the process of admitting new states, and the federal commitment to protect states from attack.

Finally, there are articles that lay out procedures for amending the Constitution and that commit the United States to repay all debts incurred before the ratification of the Constitution. Only nine states were required to sign for the Constitution to go into effect, but all 13 states signed. As part of that agreement, Congress and the states approved the first ten amendments to the Constitution, known collectively as the Bill of Rights. In the more than 200 years since then, there have been only 17 additional amendments.

Emancipation Proclamation and Reconstruction Amendments

The Civil War was the cauldron through which the United States addressed the most pressing issue of its early history—slavery. The **Emancipation Proclamation** and Amendments XIII, XIV, and XV to the U.S. Constitution (known as the **Reconstruction Amendments**) addressed slavery and would begin to heal the injustice of slavery in the United States.

The Emancipation Proclamation, which freed the slaves who lived in the Confederacy, was issued by President Abraham Lincoln on January 1, 1863. It referred to a preliminary version issued in September 1862, which stated:

EXCERPT

That on the first day of January, in the year of our Lord one thousand eight hundred and sixty-three, all persons held as slaves within any State or designated part of a State, the people whereof shall then be in rebellion against the United States, shall be then, thenceforward, and forever free; and the Executive Government of the United States, including the military and naval authority thereof, will recognize and maintain the freedom of such persons, and will do no act or acts to repress such persons, or any of them, in any efforts they may make for their actual freedom.

After listing the states and parts of states still considered to be in rebellion and repeating the announcement of the abolition of slavery in rebellious areas, the Proclamation continued:

EXCERPT

And I hereby enjoin upon the people so declared to be free to abstain from all violence, unless in necessary self-defence; and I recommend to them that, in all cases when allowed, they labor faithfully for reasonable wages.

And I further declare and make known, that such persons of suitable condition, will be received into the armed service of the United States to garrison forts, positions, stations, and other places, and to man vessels of all sorts in said service.

And upon this act, sincerely believed to be an act of justice, warranted by the Constitution, upon military necessity, I invoke the considerate judgment of mankind, and the gracious favor of Almighty God.

At the conclusion of the Civil War, amendments were ratified that resolved the conflict over slavery, including:

- Amendment XIII, abolishing slavery in the United States
- Amendment XIV, guaranteeing the rights of citizens, due process, and equal protection under the law for all people
- Amendment XV, guaranteeing citizens the right to vote, regardless of "race, color, or previous condition of servitude"

Despite their passage, it would take decades before the children of slaves would gain access to equal rights.

Prehistory to Revolutionary and Early Republic Periods

The history of the United States can be traced to the earliest inhabitants of the country, but conflict with early settlers and disease introduced by them decimated Native American populations. By the time the United States was established, colonists faced their own conflicts over freedom and civil liberties with Great Britain, which ruled much of the eastern seaboard of North America. After the American Revolution, the new nation gradually established its political identity and economic independence, fueled largely by the early growth of the Industrial Revolution.

Native Americans

The original inhabitants of North America populated the entire continent before European settlement began. The ancestors of the original inhabitants of the Americas arrived from Asia. Their arrival date has not been exactly determined, but estimates range from about 40,000 to 20,000 years ago. Native American, or Indian, peoples settled North America and formed societies and nations in many regions, including:

- Iroquois and Algonquian in the Northeast
- Creek, Cherokee, and Seminole in the Southeast
- Arapaho, Blackfoot, Sioux, Cheyenne, and Comanche on the Plains
- Hopi, Zuni, and Yuna in the Southwest
- Paiute and Shoshone in the Great Basin
- Hupa, Shasta, and Salina in California
- Chinook, Nez Perce, and Tlingit on the Northwest coast and plateau

These nations and tribes are only a small portion of the many Native American societies settlers encountered after Columbus arrived in the New World in 1492.

The encounters between Native Americans and early colonists shaped the formation of the early United States. Native Americans, who passed on their understanding of the environment and resources to the colonists, numbered approximately 25 million people, according to Howard Zinn in *A People's History of the United States*. These numbers would dwindle as contact with European settlers, disease, and conflict took their toll. In addition, nearly all Native Americans were driven from their lands as Europeans colonized the continent and established control from the Atlantic to the Pacific.

Causes of the American Revolutionary War

While a number of European nations were involved in colonizing the Americas, the area that would become the United States in 1783 was under the control of Great Britain after the end of the French and Indian War, which was part of the larger Seven Years' War fought in Europe from 1754 to 1763. The war left the British government with crushing debt, which it tried to reduce in part by taxing its colonies in North America.

British attempts to assert control and raise money, outlined next, were met by fierce opposition from their colonies.

- The Proclamation of 1763 prohibited settlement west of the Appalachian Mountains.
- The 1764 Currency Act attempted to stop the colonies from printing their own currency.
- The 1764 Sugar Act taxed sugar.
- The 1765 Stamp Act required tax stamps on many documents.
- The 1765 Quartering Act forced homeowners to let British soldiers stay in their homes.
- The 1767 Townshend Revenue Act increased taxes on glass, paper, and tea.
- 1773 Tea Act enforced taxes on tea and the British East India Company's monopoly on its sale.

These measures were fiercely opposed by the Committees of Correspondence, local groups of legislators who began organizing in 1764. By 1772, the Committees had become an established method of coordinated action among colonies when Samuel Adams organized the Boston Committee of Correspondence.

The Boston Tea Party in 1773 was one of the most important protests against the British measures, in which the Sons of Liberty boarded a merchant ship loaded with tea and dumped it into Boston Harbor. In response, the British enacted what came to be known as the 1774 Intolerable Acts, which attempted to punish the colonists by banning town meetings and closing Boston Harbor.

Instead of intimidating the colonists, these actions estranged the colonial leadership from Great Britain and led inexorably to the outbreak of hostilities, which started with the following events:

- the "shot heard round the world" at the Battle of Lexington and Concord on April 19, 1775, between the British and the Massachusetts Minutemen
- the Battle of Bunker Hill on June 17, 1775, considered the beginning of the American War for Independence
- the British evacuation of Boston in March 1776

The Committees of Correspondence had established the Continental Congress to act on behalf of all colonists in 1774.

- The First Continental Congress (1774) consisted of representatives from 12 colonies.
- The Second Continental Congress (1775–1781) comprised representatives from 13 colonies.

The Declaration of Independence, written by Thomas Jefferson and approved by the Continental Congress, was adopted in 1776. The Continental Congress was the government of the United States until the U.S. Constitution was ratified in 1789.

George Washington and Independence

George Washington led the colonists in the War for Independence against Great Britain (1775–1783). Great Britain recognized the independence of the United States in the Peace of Paris Agreement on September 2, 1783.

The first president of the United States, Washington was the rare national leader who, after a period of great service to his nation, voluntarily gave up power.

- Washington voluntarily retired twice, first as commander in chief of the Continental Army after the military victory in the War for Independence, and later after serving two terms as president.
- The tradition that he created was so strong that only one president in U.S. history—Franklin Delano Roosevelt in the twentieth century—has served more than two terms, a limitation that today is formalized as the 22nd amendment to the United States Constitution.

Louisiana Purchase

Spain controlled Louisiana in 1799, but it agreed in 1800 to give it to France, which was ruled by Napoleon Bonaparte. Napoleon was convinced that war with Great Britain was coming and that France could not defend the vast Louisiana Territory from the British who might invade from Canada. The French then offered to sell the entire territory to the United States.

The Louisiana Purchase, completed in 1803, resulted in:

- doubling the size of the United States
- vast expansion of resources under U.S. control
- encouragement of westward expansion

War of 1812

The War of 1812 helped solidify American independence from Great Britain.

- **Leading up to the war**, the British tried to restrict American trade and forced American seamen to join the British Navy. For the British, these were small maneuvers to help in their ongoing war with Napoleon's France. For the United States, these actions were a major attack on its sovereignty.
- **During the war**, the United States unsuccessfully tried to invade Canada. But only after the defeat of Napoleon were the British able to attack the United States, which they did in 1814, burning Washington, D.C. Other British attacks all failed, most memorably the unsuccessful assault on Baltimore, which inspired the national anthem, "The Star-Spangled Banner."
- Because of vast distances and limitations on communications at the time, the **final battle of the war**, the Battle of New Orleans on January 8, 1815, was actually fought after the signing of the peace treaty ending the war.

The War of 1812 was the last armed conflict between the United States and Great Britain or Canada.

The Industrial Revolution

During the Revolutionary War and early republic periods, another revolution was gathering momentum.

The Industrial Revolution, which began in Great Britain, was spreading to the United States by the late 1700s and was beginning to fundamentally change the lives of virtually all Americans. Key to this revolution was a spirit of innovation and experimentation that transformed

- manufacturing
- textiles
- transportation
- power generation
- agriculture

Benjamin Franklin was probably the country's greatest and most versatile eighteenth-century inventor, having invented the Franklin stove, lightning rod, and bifocals. A social innovator as well, Franklin is also credited with creating the first mail-order catalog.

While key inventions such as the power loom and the railroad were developed in Great Britain, the United States was also a center of innovation.

Because early American industrialization focused on water-powered textile factories in the Northeast, early American inventions included the cotton gin, fire hydrant, and steamship.

The list of new processes and products accelerated through the mid-nineteenth century. Morse code and the telegraph transformed communication, while the steamship and the railroad transformed transportation.

By the end of the nineteenth century, many of the components of modern life were already in place, including these inventions:

- telephone
- electric lightbulb
- automobile
- steel
- vacuum cleaner
- escalator
- paper bag
- typewriter

- phonograph
- photography
- skyscraper

And there were thousands of other technological innovations as well.

The era of these material advances in the United States and Western Europe coincided with the development of democratic rule and the capitalist system of production and distribution. While the Industrial Revolution led to the greatest increase in wealth in recorded history, inequality and exploitation of workers were constant challenges.

Civil War and Reconstruction

The greatest challenge and trauma ever to face the United States was the Civil War. It was rooted in slavery and the reliance of Southern states on plantation agriculture. In addition to wrenching the nation apart, the Civil War was also one of the first major wars of the industrial age. The new weapons created for this war, including rifle-barrel shotguns and repeating firearms, in addition to the mass production of war matériel and equipment, introduced an unprecedented level of carnage. The deep-seated animosity between the North and South, the loss of life, and the devastation of land and economic livelihoods would affect the country for decades.

Economic Causes of the Civil War

During the late 1700s and early 1800s, the United States expanded its territory. In 1803, President Thomas Jefferson doubled the size of the country by buying land from France through the Louisiana Purchase. Under President James Monroe, westward expansion continued. Despite this growth and the country's increased wealth, economic and cultural differences between regions developed.

Sectionalism—each section of the country supporting its own self-interests instead of the nation's interests—took root. The Northeast relied on an industrial economy while the South had an agricultural economy supported by slave labor. One major issue concerned whether new states in the Union would become free states or allow slavery.

Slavery and States' Rights

Cotton was a very labor-intensive crop. Southern plantations dealt with their labor needs by using slaves, who were originally from sub-Saharan West Africa. Opposition to slavery came from several sources.

- While the Southern economy depended on slave labor, slavery had become a moral issue in Europe as well as in the United States.
- Slavery was abolished in Great Britain and most of the British Empire in 1833, and by the end of the decade to follow, Britain abolished slavery throughout the rest of its empire.

In the United States, the abolitionist movement against slavery on both moral and practical grounds spread across the Northern states, all of which had abolished slavery by the middle of the nineteenth century. At the end of the previous century, over 90% of slaves in the United States had lived in the South. The Southern states increasingly perceived their influence waning and their way of life threatened. To protect that way of life, states' rights became a focus of the South's opposition to the federal government and the North's rising opposition to slavery. Southern politicians advocated for the right of individual states to overrule federal law or ultimately to secede from the Union.

The Civil War

The Civil War began shortly after Abraham Lincoln, who opposed slavery, was elected president in 1860 even though he was not on the ballot in ten Southern states. Lincoln and his Republican Party were especially against the expansion of slavery into the western territories.

In February 1861, seven states seceded from the United States and formed the Confederate States of America: South Carolina, Georgia, Florida, Alabama, Mississippi, Arkansas, and Tennessee.

On April 12, 1861, Confederate soldiers opened fire on Fort Sumter in Charleston, South Carolina, and the Civil War began. Shortly after, four additional states declared their secession and were admitted to the Confederacy: Virginia, North Carolina, Louisiana, and Texas.

The war ended in 1865 after the surrender of Robert E. Lee, the most important general of the Confederacy. Four million slaves were freed during the period of Reconstruction that followed the war. Five days after the Northern victory, President Lincoln was assassinated by a Confederate sympathizer. Resentment and division between the South and North were not resolved for decades after the war's end.

At least 750,000 people were killed in the Civil War, according to some recent estimates. This was the highest number of Americans ever killed in one conflict and the largest and bloodiest war between the defeat of Napoleon and the beginning of World War I.

Postwar Reconstruction

The Civil War resulted in major destruction of the South. The period after the war, in which the South started the rebuilding process, was called **Reconstruction**.

At first, it appeared that Southern states would adjust to the end of slavery, and former black slaves would be integrated into all aspects of civil and political life, especially once the right to vote was granted to black men through the ratification of the 15th amendment of the Constitution.

By the end of the nineteenth century, Reconstruction had failed. Even though each former Confederate state had been readmitted to the Union, blacks were treated as second-class citizens, without the right to vote and segregated from the white population.

This oppression was legalized by restrictive regulations known as **Jim Crow laws**, which restricted the civil rights of blacks through limitations on voting rights and a "separate but equal" policy regarding education, employment, and other issues.

Southern states oppressed black populations and would not begin to recover economically and repair their fractured social structures for decades to come. Northern states, while less overtly, would continue to restrict the rights of their black citizens as well.

Civil Rights and Women's Rights

While the modern Civil Rights movement is generally considered to have extended from the 1950s to the 1970s, the struggle for equal rights for African Americans stretched back to the abolitionist movement before the Civil War and the passage of the 13th and 14th amendments to the U.S. Constitution after the war.

The history of women's rights in the United States began with the women's suffrage movement, which achieved the vote for women in 1920. Women and supporters of women's rights continue to work for complete parity of women with men—economically, politically, and socially—and while full equality has not been achieved, great strides have been made.

The fight for women's rights stretches back through U.S. history. The struggle for the right to vote, for instance, began to crystallize in the middle of the nineteenth century, and equal pay for equal work is still an issue being fought on many fronts.

Separate but Equal

The heart of the Civil Rights movement was the struggle against segregation, which had been upheld by the Supreme Court at the end of the nineteenth century in *Plessy v. Ferguson*.

In 1892, Homer Plessy sat in a whites-only railroad car in Louisiana, challenging the state's 1890 Separate Car Act, and was arrested when he refused to move to the car reserved for African Americans. Plessy appealed his case to a Louisiana state court, but Justice John Howard Ferguson ruled against him, holding that the state had the right to regulate railroad operations within its state boundaries.

Plessy appealed his case to the U.S. Supreme Court, arguing that separate public accommodations led to unequal treatment in opposition to the 14th amendment of the U.S. Constitution, which guaranteed equal rights and protection under the law for all citizens. In a seven-to-one decision, handed down in 1896, the Supreme Court upheld Louisiana's action, in effect enshrining *separate but equal* for decades to come.

From the beginning, *separate but equal* proved impossible in reality. Throughout the South, public accommodations for blacks were inferior to those reserved for whites. And while more overt in the South, segregation existed in the North and West, as well.

Seeds of the Civil Rights Movement

The Civil Rights movement is rooted in the early twentieth century. At the beginning of the twentieth century, Booker T. Washington tried to convince black leaders to support conciliation toward whites.

In 1905, led by W.E.B. Du Bois, the more militant Niagara movement articulated the goals of the Civil Rights movement and claimed "every single right that belongs to a freeborn American, political, civil and social; and until we get these rights we will never cease to protest and assail the ears of America."

In 1909, Du Bois and other Niagara movement members joined with sympathetic whites to form the National Association for the Advancement of Colored People (NAACP), which for more than a century has been a leader in the Civil Rights movement.

Fighting for Rights

The success of the Civil Rights movement was incremental, but advances gathered steam in the middle of the twentieth century.

In 1947, Jackie Robinson became the first black man in the century to play major league baseball, starting the integration of professional sports.

In 1948, President Truman ended segregation and integrated the U.S. armed forces.

In 1954, NAACP lawyer Thurgood Marshall convinced the U.S. Supreme Court in *Brown v. Board of Education* [*of Topeka, Kansas*] to end separate but equal schools in Topeka. This essentially overturned *Plessy v. Ferguson* and made segregation illegal throughout the United States.

In 1955, Rosa Parks challenged the segregation of buses in Montgomery, Alabama, by refusing to give up her seat to a white man. Her action inspired the Montgomery bus boycott, in which blacks refused to ride the buses unless segregation rules were abolished, and a year later, segregation was abolished.

In 1957, the city school board and supervisor in Little Rock, Arkansas, had a plan to integrate Little Rock High School. However, when the governor of the state resisted, President Eisenhower sent in National Guard troops to enforce the desegregation order.

Five years later, in 1962, when the University of Mississippi was integrated, President Kennedy sent 5,000 troops to maintain order and allow James Meredith to attend classes.

In 1963, leaders of the Civil Rights movement organized the March on Washington for Jobs and Freedom to rally for civil rights. On August 28, civil rights leader Martin Luther King Jr. delivered his "I Have a Dream" speech to 200,000 to 300,000 people gathered on the National Mall in Washington, D.C., in a massive nonviolent political demonstration to end racism.

EXCERPT FROM MARTIN LUTHER KING'S "I HAVE A DREAM" SPEECH

I say to you today, my friends, that in spite of the difficulties and frustrations of the moment, I still have a dream. It is a dream deeply rooted in the American dream.

I have a dream that one day this nation will rise up and live out the true meaning of its creed: "We hold these truths to be self-evident: that all men are created equal."

I have a dream that one day on the red hills of Georgia the sons of former slaves and the sons of former slave owners will be able to sit down together at a table of brotherhood.

I have a dream that one day even the state of Mississippi, a desert state, sweltering with the heat of injustice and oppression, will be transformed into an oasis of freedom and justice.

I have a dream that my four children will one day live in a nation where they will not be judged by the color of their skin but by the content of their character.

Ratified in 1964, the 24th amendment to the Constitution abolished poll taxes in federal elections. These taxes were previously used across the South to disenfranchise black voters.

The Civil Rights Act of 1964 prohibited discrimination of all kinds based on race, color, religion, or national origin and addressed segregation in public accommodations, schools, and the workplace.

The Voting Rights Act of 1965 prohibited all states from instituting qualifications, procedures, and regulations for voting that resulted in discrimination against anyone of any race or color.

Practice

24. As you learned earlier in this chapter, in the 1896 case *Plessy v. Ferguson*, the Supreme Court found that segregation was legal based on the principle of *separate but equal*. Plessy, who was one-eighth black, had been arrested when he refused to leave a whites-only railroad car. The Supreme Court upheld his conviction.

In the 1954 case *Brown v. Board of Education*, the Supreme Court unanimously ruled that "separate but equal" schools were not achievable, and that they were unconstitutional since they violated the equal protection clause of the 14th amendment, adopted in 1868.

The most likely reason for this reversal was:

a. Nearly 60 years' experience showed that separate cannot be equal.

b. Court membership had changed from conservatives to liberals.

c. The 1896 case was about transportation whereas the 1954 case was about education.

d. The equal protection clause of the 14th amendment was not in effect in 1896.

Women's Suffrage

The struggle for women's suffrage began in the middle of the nineteenth century and would stretch into the second decade of the next century.

In 1848, **Elizabeth Cady Stanton** and **Lucretia Mott** organized the first women's rights convention in American history, the **Seneca Falls Convention**, which took place in Seneca Falls, in the Finger Lakes region of Upstate New York.

Written by Elizabeth Cady Stanton and signed by 100 delegates of the convention, the **Declaration of Sentiments** closed with the following remarks:

EXCERPT

Now, in view of this entire disfranchisement of one-half the people of this country, their social and religious degradation—in view of the unjust laws above mentioned, and because women do feel themselves aggrieved, oppressed, and fraudulently deprived of their most sacred rights, we insist that they have immediate admission to all the rights and privileges which belong to them as citizens of these United States.

A few years later, **Susan B. Anthony** emerged as another major leader of the suffrage movement. Anthony joined forces with Stanton and other suffrage leaders in forming the National Women's Suffrage Association (NWSA) in 1869.

In 1890, the NWSA merged with the more moderate American Women Suffrage Association, creating a wider political umbrella that would lead the struggle for voting rights to all states of the union.

By the end of the nineteenth century, some western states, as well as some countries around the world, had given women the right to vote. The pace of the spread of suffrage increased in the early twentieth century.

In the United States, the final triumph of the suffrage movement occurred in 1920 when the 19th amendment guaranteed women the right to vote.

Women's Rights after World War II

Winning the right to vote was only one step in the journey for women to achieve full equality. The modern women's movement has been concerned with issues of health, sexuality, work, and education.

Women first moved into the manufacturing workforce in large numbers during World War II. **Rosie the Riveter** became a cultural icon of the United States, representing the six million women who were employed during the war years. These women took the places of male workers who were away fighting the war. Rosie the Riveter heralded women's economic power to come.

The 1950s are remembered as an era when women retreated to traditional roles, but many women were unhappy in their limited role as house-wives. In 1963, **Betty Friedan's** *The Feminine Mystique* discussed the seeming paradox of women having husbands, children, and material things yet being unhappy and unfulfilled. She made the case that the life of a housewife was not enough and for many women, education and a career were crucial for a complete life.

In 1966, Friedan was one of the founding members of the **National Organization for Women (NOW)**, which became the leader of the women's movement.

In 1960, the release of the **birth control pill** helped give women autonomy and allowed them to plan their reproductive lives in ways that might enhance their economic and social well-being.

In 1973, in *Roe v. Wade*, the Supreme Court legalized abortion, giving women additional control over their choices. However, this decision has stirred up great controversy and opposition, especially among political conservatives and people of certain religious affiliations.

In 1967, women earned 58 cents for every dollar a man earned for the same work. By 2012, that number had grown to 77 cents for each dollar—an improvement, but still a long way from equality.

By the end of the 1970s, for the first time there were more women than men in college. But women are still underrepresented in science, technology, engineering, and mathematics.

One positive development has been the passage of Title IX legislation in 1972, which created equal opportunities for women in college athletics, including more scholarships.

Women have made steady progress in the political arena on local, state, and national levels. Many local and state officials are women, as are judges at all levels, including the Supreme Court, and women continue to win more elections as time goes by.

Immigration

Millions of immigrants from foreign shores have made the journey to the Americas since Columbus's first voyage in 1492. The bulk of these immigrants have been of European origin. In what is now the eastern United States, immigrants came from the British Isles, the Netherlands, France, and other nations of northern Europe. But in recent years, immigrants from Latin America have made up a large portion of the immigrant population. Many have settled in adjacent states, such as California, Arizona, and Texas.

Early Waves of Immigration

Following the settling of the United States by colonists from Great Britain, France, and the Netherlands, other immigrants soon followed, including large groups of Germans, Swedes, and others.

The first great wave of poor immigrants to the United States came from Ireland as a response to the Irish Potato Famine in 1845–1849. Since potatoes were the sole source of food for most poor Irish, many starved in Ireland. Over one million came to the United States.

- Unlike other immigrants, Irish immigrants mostly stayed in the cities, where they were discriminated against and exploited.
- Being the first major group of Roman Catholics to immigrate to the United States, they faced fierce religious discrimination.

In response to their poor treatment, the Irish became involved in politics. Tammany Hall in New York City and the long reign of Mayor James Michael Curley in Boston became synonymous with corruption and patronage. In 1928, Al Smith, the first Roman Catholic of Irish origin to run for U.S. president, was soundly defeated. Thirty-two years later, John F. Kennedy, a descendent of poor Irish immigrants, became president of the United States.

After the end of the Civil War, the United States entered a period of rapid industrial growth. Millions of workers were needed, and the development of steam transport made the voyage across the Atlantic possible for the masses arriving from Europe. Millions of immigrants flooded into America. Many came from southern and eastern Europe and included Italians, Jews, Poles, and other ethnic groups. Chinese immigrants arrived in significant numbers on the West Coast.

Practice

25. In her poem "The New Colossus," which is engraved in the base of the Statue of Liberty, Emma Lazarus wrote: "Give me your tired, your poor, / Your huddled masses yearning to breathe free, / The wretched refuse of your teaming shore. / Send these, the homeless, tempest-tost to me, / I lift my lamp beside the golden door!"

If she were alive today, what immigration policy would Emma Lazarus be most favorable toward?

a. completion of a fence and barrier with motion detectors along the Mexican border

b. increase in the number of work visas for foreign workers with advanced degrees

c. the Dream Act, which provides a path to citizenship to undocumented youth

d. encouragement of potential immigrants to legally apply for permission to enter the United States.

Use the graph to answer questions 26 and 27.

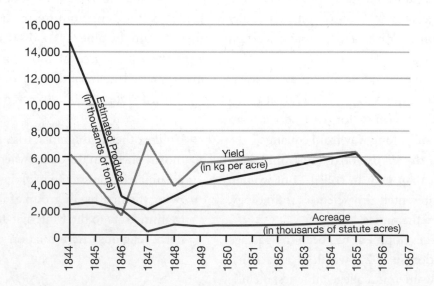

26. Potato production reached a low in Ireland in the year _____.

27. Since the Irish Potato Famine was responsible for mass emigration from Ireland, immigration to the United States was probably highest in the year _____.

The Gilded Age, Labor Movement, and Progressive Era

The era of industrialization following the Civil War is called the Gilded Age, or the age of the robber barons, named after the ruthless group of industrialists and financiers who made great fortunes controlling monopolies in commodities, transportation, and banking.

Rapid industrialization and innovation created so much new wealth that, even with plundering by robber barons and the influx of the new immigrants, the country's wealth grew and the population nearly doubled.

The excesses of the Gilded Age helped spur the development of the labor movement, which was embraced by many new Americans.

- The first truly national labor union, the **Knights of Labor**, formed in 1869 and reached a peak of 700,000 members in 1886, when the group was blamed for deadly riots at the Haymarket in Chicago. The anti-union backlash that followed the event led to the collapse of the Knights of Labor.
- The **American Federation of Labor (AFL)** formed later that year. While the Knights had been a single national union with membership that included craftsmen and unskilled workers, the AFL was a federation of individual craft unions.
- In 1905, the **Industrial Workers of the World (IWW)** was formed and followed a single union model similar to the Knights of Labor model. The IWW tended to be more militant and radical than the AFL. After peaking at 40,000 members in 1923, the IWW declined in numbers and influence.
- The **Congress of Industrial Organizations (CIO)** was formed in 1938, when ten unions left the AFL. The new organization wanted to organize workers by industry rather than by craft.
- The CIO rejoined the AFL to form the **AFL-CIO** in 1955.

Instability in the labor movement has continued. The United Auto Workers left the AFL-CIO in 1968 and returned in 1981. Other unions led by the Teamsters left in 2005 to form the Change to Win Coalition.

The excesses of the robber barons helped provoke calls for reform that became known as the **progressive era**. Progressives believed that, in the face of rampant poverty, education and adequate housing for the poor as well as fair labor practices and safe workplaces were necessary. Political cartoonist Thomas Nast and socially conscious photographer Jacob Riis helped stoke public anger over corruption and the terrible living conditions in American cities with the images they created.

Practice

Use the graph to answer questions 28 and 29.

Historical Overview of Unions

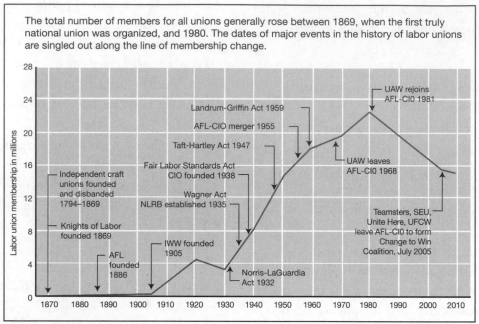

The total number of members for all unions generally rose between 1869, when the first truly national union was organized, and 1980. The dates of major events in the history of labor unions are singled out along the line of membership change.

Source: U.S. Bureau of Labor Statistics, Union Membership, www.bls.gov (accessed April 29, 2010), from *Business,* by William M. Pride, Robert James Hughes, Jack R. Kapoor (Cengage Learning), page 309.

28. According to the graph, which event coincided with the period of greatest union membership?
a. founding of the Knights of Labor
b. founding of the AFL
c. founding of the CIO
d. UAW rejoining the AFL-CIO

29. According to the graph, the event that coincided with the period of highest union growth was
a. founding of the Knights of Labor.
b. founding of the AFL.
c. founding of the CIO.
d. UAW rejoining the AFL-CIO.

World Wars I and II

The United States entered the world arena in the first decades of the twentieth century as a growing economic power. The country's isolationist tendencies gave way to involvement in both World War I and World War II, and this shaped U.S. history in profoundly new ways. Following the second global war, the United States became the most powerful nation in the world, as it emerged relatively unaffected by the carnage and destruction of the war.

World War I

World War I (1914–1918) involved 32 countries, including many European nations, the United States, and other nations around the world. By the war's end, almost 10 million soldiers had been killed and more than 20 million wounded. The assassination of the heir to the Austro-Hungarian throne by a Serbian nationalist was the immediate cause of the war, but conflicts between European nations over territory and economic power were also factors.

Two coalitions of European nations formed. The Central Powers included Austria-Hungary, Germany, Bulgaria, and Turkey. The Allies included Great Britain, France, Serbia, Russia, Belgium, and Italy.

World War I was the most destructive and deadly war the world had seen up to that time:

- 8,528,831 were killed.
- 21,189,154 were wounded.
- An additional 7,750,919 were either prisoners or missing.

Many losses came as a result of trench warfare, when poison gas was used as a weapon.

The **Treaty of Versailles**, signed on June 28, 1919, ended World War I with the complete defeat of Germany and Austria.

- The Austro-Hungarian Empire was dismantled, and Germany was humiliated with the loss of territory, onerous war reparations, and prohibitions against remilitarizing.
- With the stock market crash of 1929, the resulting hyperinflation destroyed the value of German currency, and the worldwide **Great Depression** followed.

The German economy was devastated, leaving the people ready for a radical answer to their problems, so they elected **Adolf Hitler** and his National Socialist Party. The Nazis made sure that the German people never got the opportunity to vote while they were in power.

World War II

In World War II, three ideologies—democracy, fascism, and communism—clashed in a worldwide struggle. Two powerful alliances, the Allies and the Axis, fought to control vast areas of the planet.

- Two dominant democracies, the United Kingdom and France, led the **Allies** in Europe and would later be joined by the Soviet Union and the United States.

- The European fascist nations of Italy and Germany formed the **Axis** alliance, along with Japan in East Asia.

The war began focused on German aggression in Europe and soon spread as Italy and Japan joined forces with Germany, and England and France declared war on Germany.

- The war began in 1939, when Germany invaded Poland.
- In the first two years of the war, the Axis powers swept through Europe and conquered large areas of East Asia and the Pacific.
- During the Battle of Britain in 1940, the United Kingdom stood alone against the Axis powers and withstood brutal aerial bombardment.
- With victory in their sights, Germany and Japan made two major mistakes. Germany attacked the Soviet Union in 1941, and Japan attacked the United States in 1941. Then the world's largest communist state and the world's largest democracy joined the war on the side of the Allies.
- With Soviet victory over the Nazis at Stalingrad in February 1943, the Axis retreated from east Europe.
- The Americans and British had major naval victories in 1943 and 1944 against the Japanese in the Pacific islands.
- After a drawn-out conflict, the Allies took North Africa, driving out the Axis forces in 1943.
- The Allies invaded Europe, first through Italy in 1943, and later through France, notably on June 6, 1944, with the D-Day invasion of northern France.
- The Allies also developed air superiority and bombed areas throughout Germany. The greatest destruction was to the city of Dresden, which was completely destroyed by firebombing in February 1945.
- The Allies accepted the unconditional surrender of the Axis powers on May 8, 1945.

- The Japanese surrendered to Allied forces on August 14, 1945.

The United States developed the most destructive weapon ever created, the atomic bomb, and dropped one on the Japanese city of **Hiroshima** and another one on **Nagasaki**. Although those bombings led to the Japanese surrender, the death and devastation were so extreme that to this day it is debated whether the atomic bombs ever should have been used. While a number of nations currently have nuclear weapons, no atomic bombs have been used since World War II.

World War II was possibly responsible for a greater loss of life than any other event in human history, with total deaths estimated to have been between 60,000,000 and 85,000,000.

One of the most horrific aspects of this carnage was the targeting of innocent civilians by the Nazis. The Nazis imprisoned, tortured, starved, and murdered millions of people, including gypsies and homosexuals, but their main target was Jews. The persecution, enslavement, torture, and murder of millions of Jews is known as the **Holocaust**. The attempt to destroy an entire people was given a name, genocide. After the war, prominent surviving Nazis were put on trial at Nuremberg in Germany and convicted of genocide.

After the war, the United States tried an approach to peace with the defeated Axis powers that was very different from the Treaty of Versailles, which was the punitive peace treaty imposed on Germany after World War I. Instead of assessing reparations and humiliating Germany, the United States implemented the **Marshall Plan**. The plan provided economic assistance to all of Western Europe, including former Axis countries Germany, Italy, and Austria. Economic assistance was provided to Japan as well. The aid given to Western Europe helped the entire region recover and start the process of integration that has led to the formation and development of the

European Union. And nations that once were adversaries of the United States are now among its closest friends and allies.

The Cold War

The end of World War II left the United States and the Soviet Union as the two most powerful nations on Earth. Each nation felt threatened by the other and began a struggle—based on their conflicting ideologies—that involved many regions of the world.

Democracy versus Totalitarianism

The Soviet Union was a totalitarian society run as a one-party state. While the **Communist Party** was supposedly the highest authority, its secretary, **Joseph Stalin**, ruled as an absolute dictator. He was responsible for the deaths of millions of Soviet citizens but was never held accountable for his crimes. Economically, in the communist system all property belonged to the state, including the means of production. In practice, this resulted in a top-down command economy where Soviet bureaucrats decided what would and would not be produced.

The United States is a democracy. Two major parties and other smaller and local parties vie for political influence. The United States embraces capitalism, a system in which a country's trade and industry are controlled by private owners operating in a free market.

International Conflict in the Postwar Era

As World War II ended, Western Europe was occupied by the democratic Allied countries while Eastern Europe was occupied by the Soviet Union, which imposed Communist governments and economies throughout the region.

Winston Churchill, Britain's prime minister during World War II, referred to the ideological boundary between democratic and communist states as the **Iron Curtain**. Feeling threatened by the Soviet

Union, the United States and its allies formed the **North Atlantic Treaty Organization (NATO)**. In response, the Soviet Union created a military alliance called the **Warsaw Pact** with the communist nations of Eastern Europe.

Following the war's end, President Harry S. Truman established the **Truman Doctrine** in 1947. The doctrine set U.S. policy concerning engagement with the rest of the world, promising political, economic, and military support to any country that might come under internal or outside threat from authoritarian forces. Under the doctrine, the United States proclaimed a new interventionist approach, which was a turnaround from its previous isolationist foreign policy.

While the United States and the Soviet Union assembled the most powerful arsenals that had ever existed, with hundreds of lethal missiles pointed at each other, none of these weapons were ever used in direct conflict. As a result, this period was known as the **Cold War**, a war of tension and rivalry but never direct combat.

The two powers were involved in many conflicts across the globe, which often stood as proxies for their own ideological conflict with each other. The United States also openly fought communism in Korea and Vietnam.

In June 1963, President John Kennedy spoke to a crowd of one million people in West Berlin, a city surrounded on all sides by the East German communist state. His most famous statement was *"Ich bin ein Berliner,"* which is German for "I am a Berliner."

Practice

Read the excerpt from the speech and answer the following question.

EXCERPT

Freedom is indivisible, and when one man is enslaved, all are not free.

When all are free, then we can look forward to that day when this city will be joined as one and this country and this great continent of Europe in a peaceful and hopeful globe. When that day finally comes, as it will, the people of West Berlin can take sober satisfaction in the fact that they were in the front lines for almost two decades.

All free men, wherever they may live, are citizens of Berlin, and, therefore, as a free man, I take pride in the words *"Ich bin ein Berliner."*

30. What was the significance of his statement *"Ich bin ein Berliner"*?
   a. Kennedy revealed to the crowd that he had a German ancestor.
   b. Kennedy planned to move to Berlin after his presidency ended.
   c. Kennedy wanted to express his affection and admiration to Berlin.
   d. Kennedy wanted Berliners to know they could trust the United States.

Decolonization

One of the trends that marks the post–World War II era is the gradual process of decolonization in regions of the world once occupied by world powers. Eighty colonies have gained independence since the United Nations (UN) was established in 1945. The progress toward national independence is a project that will be complete only when these former colonies have developed sustainable and productive economies and systems of independent governance.

Colonies and Empires

Since antiquity, powerful empires and nations have controlled and exploited weaker people and nations. When circumstances allowed, colonies would achieve their independence through peaceful or violent means.

- The American Revolution was the violent transformation of 13 colonies into one nation.
- In Latin America, Spain and Portugal's colonies became independent in the early nineteenth century.
- A number of mostly Christian areas in the Balkans in southeast Europe broke away from the declining Islamic Ottoman Empire in the nineteenth century and declared independence.

Prior to World War II, most of Africa, the Middle East, South Asia, and East Asia had been colonized by European nations and Japan. At the end of World War II, most of these countries were still under colonial control.

Achieving Independence

According the United Nations website, "when the United Nations was founded in 1945, some 750 million people, nearly a third of the world's population, lived in territories that were dependent on colonial powers. Today, fewer than 2 million people live under colonial rule in the 16 remaining non-self-governing territories."

The decolonization process gained momentum following the aftermath of World War II and the downgrading of the economic and political capacity of European countries. The devastation of the war weakened the capacity of European colonial powers to suppress the revolts rising within their colonies.

As the process of decolonization continued to advance, in 1960, the United Nations General Assembly adopted its landmark **Declaration on the Granting of Independence to Colonial Countries and Peoples**. The declaration affirmed the right of all people to self-determination and proclaimed that colonialism should be brought to a speedy and unconditional end.

Postwar America

After World War II, the United States became the richest and most powerful nation on Earth, due to the nation's military capacity and innovative economy.

Returning Soldiers

Millions of returning soldiers, known as GIs, needed education and training to fully participate in the new and growing economy post–World War II. In response to that need, Congress passed the **GI Bill**. According to the Veterans Administration, "the law's key provisions were education and training, loan guaranty for homes, farms or businesses, and unemployment pay. Before the war, college and homeownership were, for the most part, unreachable dreams for the average American. Thanks to the GI Bill, millions who would have flooded the job market instead opted for education."

According to the GI Bill's History page on the Department of Veterans Affairs website, "In the peak year of 1947, veterans accounted for 49 percent of college admissions. By the time the original GI Bill ended on July 25, 1956, 7.8 million of 16 million World War II veterans had participated in an education or training program."

Prosperity and Poverty

The 1950s are often thought of as an idyllic time in which an unprecedented number of people joined the middle class and were leading relatively comfortable lives. While there was some evidence supporting this view, millions of Americans were still being left behind, living in extreme poverty.

President Lyndon Johnson believed that the federal government should take on this problem, and in 1964 he declared the **War on Poverty**. In a multipronged approach, a range of programs were established, including:

- Head Start to give a boost to poor children in the preschool years
- food stamps to help the poor pay for food
- Medicare health insurance for the elderly
- Medicaid health insurance for the poor

Unfortunately, poverty persists, as does the debate on the role and responsibility of the government to provide a safety net for the country's neediest and most vulnerable people.

American Foreign Policy since 9/11

On September 11, 2001, the terrorist organization Al-Qaeda hijacked four airplanes and flew two of them into the World Trade Center in New York City and one into the Pentagon in Washington, D.C., and crashed another in a field near Shanksville, PA. The attacks resulted in the deaths of close to 3,000 people, nearly all of them civilians, and the devastation of a large area of lower Manhattan, the site of the World Trade Center.

In the aftermath, the administration of President George W. Bush launched a **War on Terror**, which involved:

- open and covert military operations
- new security legislation
- efforts to block the financing of terrorism
- increased domestic policing and intelligence gathering
- engaging other countries to support the War on Terror

Proponents of the War on Terror point to the fact that, since the attacks of September 11, no attack has occurred on U.S. soil.

Criticism against this strategy is multifold, including these arguments:

- The War on Terror is based on an ideology of fear and repression that creates enemies and promotes violence rather than mitigating acts of terror and strengthening security.
- The worldwide campaign has too often become an excuse for governments to repress opposition groups and disregard international law and civil liberties.
- Governments should address terrorism through international cooperation, using international law and respecting civil liberties and human rights.

Critics also say that governments should address the root causes of terrorism, notably political alienation due to prejudice, state-sponsored violence, and poverty.

United States History Summary

The foundational documents that shaped U.S. history, such as the Declaration of Independence, the Constitution, and the Emancipation Proclamation, contain ideas that determined the country's progress as a society and its response to the rest of the world.

The adoption of the Bill of Rights, the waging of the Civil War, the Civil Rights movement, the struggle for women's suffrage, and the progressive era were all carried out in the quest for freedom and justice.

During the twentieth century, the United States turned outward as its economic power increased and as the world became more interconnected. Today, the United States still leads the world in economic and military power and continues to uphold the founding ideals of the right to life, liberty, and the pursuit of happiness for all.

Economics

It is important to understand how world economies work in general, and especially how the United States developed politically and economically. While some economic concepts are complex and highly technical, the basic building blocks of economic thought are fairly straightforward.

Key Economic Events

The foundation of a healthy economy is trust, and throughout its history, the United States developed institutions such as the **Federal Reserve Board** to help ensure trust by safeguarding financial and economic stability.

Reliable Currency

A crucial component of a stable economy is a reliable currency. This belief was promoted by Alexander Hamilton, the first secretary of the Treasury, who successfully argued that the new government of the United States should pay back all the debts that the Continental Congress had incurred during the American Revolutionary War.

Few believed that the United States would honor its debts, so the debt issued by the Continental Congress and the states was considered worthless. When the debt was repaid, speculators became rich and the financial reliability of the United States was established.

Foundations of the Banking System

Hamilton also argued for a Bank of the United States, which would be able to make loans and have its bills received for payment by the federal government. He believed that such a bank would be helpful for the development of manufacturing in the United States. The Bank of the United States was established and lasted for 40 years.

In the country's early history, opposition to central government's involvement in banking was strong. In 1836, President Andrew Jackson let the Charter of the Second Bank of the United States expire, leaving the nation without a central bank until the Federal Reserve System was created in 1913. Through 1836, state legislatures had the right to charter banks, and they did so.

Despite the Constitution stating that only the federal government had the right to coin money, the Supreme Court ruled in 1837 in *Briscoe v. Bank of Kentucky* that state banks and the notes they issued were also constitutional. Over 700 individual banks had the right to issue paper money. Starting in 1837, the United States passed laws and implemented a free banking system, which did not include any form of government restriction on banking activities, except for the enforcement of legal contracts and prohibitions against fraud.

In practice, the system was unstable. As economic growth began to expand during economic upturns, banks would issue more banknotes, but inflation would result as credit was extended too widely. These business cycles would repeat themselves, leaving the country's economic health subject to wild fluctuations.

The free banking era came to a close with the passage of the National Banking Acts of 1863 and 1864. The laws created a system of national banks and a uniform national currency and helped finance the Civil War.

The banking system still had a problem. A rigid money supply and limited liquidity caused financial panics in 1873, 1884, 1893, and 1907. Each of these panics was followed by a depression and then by renewed prosperity. However, the 1907 panic was so severe that the richest man in the world, J.P. Morgan, loaned money to key banks to keep the entire financial system from collapsing.

The Federal Reserve System

In reaction to the crisis of 1907, the Federal Reserve Act of 1913 created the earliest version of the current Federal Reserve System. Today, the Federal Reserve System consists of

- 12 regional banks
- a board of governors
- a board chairman

The system is responsible for maintaining the financial security and well-being of the United States. In all actions that it takes, the goals of the Fed are to encourage employment and control inflation (a general increase in prices). The Federal Reserve System accomplishes what Hamilton had hoped the Bank of the United States would do.

Modern Fiscal Policy

Fiscal policy—how government raises revenue and budgets its expenditures—became more important in shaping the economy in the first half of the twentieth century, especially as the Great Depression devastated livelihoods and destroyed wealth.

Milestones in the development of fiscal policy include:

The **16th amendment to the Constitution** was ratified in 1913, the same year as the Federal Reserve System, making it possible for Congress to authorize a graduated income tax.

The Federal Reserve System and enhanced government fiscal powers were not strong enough to enable the country to avoid the **stock market crash of 1929**, which was preceded by extensive uncontrolled speculation in real estate and stock markets in the earlier part of the decade.

Following the crash of 1929, the economy headed into a long downward spiral known as the **Great Depression**. Businesses closed, people withdrew their savings in runs on banks, and millions lost their jobs. Many scholars suggest that the economy didn't fully recover from the Depression until fiscal spending on defense increased substantially during World War II.

The election of Franklin Delano Roosevelt in 1932 was the beginning of a new era of governmental involvement in the national economy and the personal welfare of millions of Americans. Roosevelt proposed and the Congress approved an unprecedented series of federal programs called the **New Deal** to help the country recover from the Depression. The New Deal included the creation of the following:

- **Tennessee Valley Authority**, which built dams and electric power lines
- **National Industrial Recovery Act**, which enabled the president to regulate industry
- **Glass-Steagall Banking Bill**, which instituted safe banking policies
- **Works Progress Administration (WPA)**, which provided jobs for the unemployed
- **National Labor Relations Act**, which created the National Labor Relations Board
- **Social Security Act**, which guaranteed pensions to millions, as well as assistance to dependent children and the disabled

Types of Energy

Wind and water power allowed parts of northern Europe to become the first countries in world history not dependent on animals and people for the bulk of their energy needs. After 1600, thousands of windmills were built, with the greatest concentration in Holland. About 500,000 water mills and 200,000 windmills in Europe helped create economies totally based on renewable energy.

At the beginning of the industrial age, **steam engines** powered mainly by coal, the first widely used fossil fuel, became the most important source of power. In the nineteenth and twentieth centuries, **electric motors and internal combustion engines** powered by oil and gas fossil fuels became key components of the energy needs of the United States and other industrialized economies.

Since the first **commercial oil well** was drilled in 1859, and through most of the twentieth century, the United States was the world's leading oil producer. But by the 1970s, the United States and other industrialized nations were importing a substantial amount of oil from the Middle East.

1970s Energy Crisis

Fossil fuels, including oil, coal, and gas, have powered much of the economic development of the modern era. In the 1970s, the price of oil, one of the main energy sources, skyrocketed and had serious effects on the economic health of the country and subsequent debates about energy policy in the United States and around the world. Energy is an important part of any nation's economy.

The **Energy Crisis in the 1970s** was an international event. It arose from the manipulation of oil prices by the **Organization of Petroleum Exporting Countries (OPEC)**, an organization of Middle Eastern countries that control most of the world's oil production. In 1973 and 1974, led by Saudi Arabia, OPEC restricted the supply of oil in response to the Yom Kippur War between Israel and Arab nations, resulting in oil prices more than tripling.

In 1979, there was a second energy crisis set off by the Iranian Revolution, which resulted in decreases in the amount of oil being produced. Since the United States had price controls on oil, supplies of oil dropped, resulting in shortages.

Since the 1970s, the United States and many other countries have been encouraging the development of alternative forms of energy to offset reliance on fossil fuels.

Practice

The following table shows world crude oil prices from 1965 to 2004. For each year, two prices are given, the actual price of oil that year and the price adjusted for inflation in U.S. dollars in 2004. Use this table to answer questions 31 and 32.

World Crude Oil Prices (U.S. dollars per barrel)

Year	Actual Price	2004 Dollars	Year	Actual Price	2004 Dollars
1965	1.80	8.64	1985	27.53	42.74
1966	1.80	8.41	1986	14.38	21.84
1967	1.80	8.15	1987	18.42	27.24
1968	1.80	7.82	1988	14.96	21.39
1969	1.80	7.45	1989	18.20	25.08
1970	1.80	7.80	1990	23.81	31.59
1971	2.24	8.39	1991	20.05	25.70
1972	2.48	8.90	1992	19.37	24.27
1973	3.29	11.18	1993	17.07	20.91
1974	11.58	36.09	1994	15.98	19.16
1975	11.53	32.84	1995	17.18	20.19
1976	12.38	33.34	1996	20.81	24.00
1977	13.30	33.67	1997	19.30	21.89
1978	13.60	32.17	1998	13.11	14.71
1979	30.03	65.60	1999	18.25	20.18
1980	35.69	71.48	2000	28.26	30.59
1981	34.28	62.76	2001	22.95	24.26
1982	31.76	54.81	2002	24.10	25.06
1983	28.77	47.76	2003	28.50	29.10
1984	28.06	44.89	2004	36.20	36.20

Source: U.S. Energy Information Administration, U.S. Departments of Commerce and Labor. Nominal prices are not adjusted for the effects of inflation. www.econlib.org/library/End/OPEC.htm.

31. Adjusted for inflation, the cost of oil was the highest in the year _____.

32. Adjusted for inflation, the cost of oil was the lowest in the year _____.

Relationship between Political and Economic Freedoms

Many have argued that an intimate link exists between political and economic freedoms. Ideas about that relationship have been instrumental throughout American economic and political history.

Milton Friedman and Economic Freedom

In his 1962 book *Capitalism and Freedom*, economist Milton Friedman argued that economic freedom and political freedom are linked, claiming:

- It is no accident that modern capitalism and democracy arose at the same time in the same nations.
- Civil liberties, political freedom, and the existence of free markets are all necessary as a whole for each to exist.

Friedman took a strict view of free markets, for example, claiming that Social Security is an attack on economic freedom.

Alternative Views

As nations evolve and adapt, the relationship between political and economic freedom has been, and will be, tested. In **Russia**, following the breakdown of the Soviet Union in 1991, an experiment in increasing personal freedom did not lead to economic freedom, and the country has even seen an erosion of individual rights, as a corrupt and coercive economic system developed. In **China**, the growth of the economy has been proceeding in concert with an improvement in economic freedom. But even though China seems to be on track to become the world's largest economy, it is unclear whether political freedoms are on the rise. It is an open question whether in coming years economic prosperity will lead to political freedom or the lack of political freedom will undermine the thriving economy.

Many economists and development experts have linked the level of inequality in a society with negative economic, as well as social, results. For instance, Daron Acemoglu and James Robinson argue in *Why Nations Fail* (Crown, 2012) that a country's economic health and success rise the more individuals across the spectrum share in a country's wealth. If the wealthy elite of a nation successfully control a disproportionate amount of its resources and production, they conclude, that nation is in danger of falling into a downward spiral of authoritarianism and corruption.

Fundamental Economic Concepts

A knowledge of key concepts in economics is critical to understanding how societies operate. The operation of **capitalism**—the economic system in place in the United States and throughout much of the world—revolves around several basic ideas.

Markets and Competition

A **market** is a place where buyers and sellers engage in transactions involving the exchange of goods and services for money. A market can be a physical place, a virtual place, or a combination of the two. For example, the New York Stock Exchange is a physical place that is located on Wall Street in New York City. However, many investors participate in this market electronically from their computers, never actually visiting the stock exchange.

A **free market** is a market that, theoretically, has little or no government intervention, such as taxes, subsidies, or regulation. In reality, in free-market economies such as in the United States, the government intervenes in the market to a lesser or greater extent to ensure its smooth operation.

Competition is the situation in which two or more sellers create the same types of goods and services to sell. Free markets depend on competition.

A **monopoly** exists when a single company or group dominates all or nearly all of the market for a given type of product or service.

Competition and monopoly are often seen as opposites. While for the most part the U.S. financial system encourages competition, there are a few instances where monopolies are allowed and even encouraged. For example, public utilities, such as supplying of water to homes, stores, and factories, are often set up as monopolies.

Economic Production

Economic production is the capacity to produce goods. Inputs of economic production include labor and capital.

- **Labor** is the work of people that provides goods and services.
- **Capital** is money and assets for the production of goods and services. Examples of assets include tools, such as an electric drill; infrastructure, such as a road or the Internet; and buildings, such as a factory.

A **capitalist economy** is a system based on the existence of the private ownership of capital.

When people engage in a business, they usually expect to make a **profit**. Profit is the return a business receives after all operating expenses have been met. Profit is usually measured in terms of money.

A key element of a capitalist economy is its ability to develop new businesses that produce new products and services. **Entrepreneurship** is the capacity and willingness to develop, organize, and manage a business venture while taking on the possible risks.

An entrepreneur takes on **risk** for the potential to make profit. Entrepreneurship combined with land, labor, natural resources, capital, expertise, and ideas can produce profit. For example, Bill Gates started his company Microsoft with little more than his understanding of computer programming and capacity to develop a computer operating system. He built it into one of the most successful and influential companies in the world.

While entrepreneurs start companies and come up with innovations, investors provide a company with money that can be spent to grow and run the business. The money that an investor gives to help finance a company in return for partial ownership is called an **investment**. Sometimes an entrepreneur provides investment to start his or her own company. Investments can consist of time as well as money.

Practice

The following is an excerpt from a campaign speech by Elizabeth Warren when she ran for the U.S. Senate seat from Massachusetts.

EXCERPT

There is nobody in this country who got rich on his own. Nobody. You built a factory out there? Good for you. But I want to be clear: you moved your goods to market on the roads the rest of us paid for; you hired workers the rest of us paid to educate; you were safe in your factory because of police forces and fire forces that the rest of us paid for. You didn't have to worry that marauding bands would come and seize everything at your factory, and hire someone to protect against this, because of the work the rest of us did.

Now look, you built a factory and it turned into something terrific, or a great idea? God bless. Keep a big hunk of it. But part of the underlying social contract is you take a hunk of that and pay forward for the next kid who comes along.

33. Based on the views expressed in this excerpt, Elizabeth Warren would most likely support which of the following policies?

    a. a tax cut for small businesses so that they have a better chance to succeed and hire more workers

    b. higher taxes on corporate profits so that successful companies help support infrastructure

    c. cutting the federal deficit so that future generations are not saddled by the debts we incurred

    d. privatization of much of our infrastructure, including major roads, water supply, police, and firefighters

Division of Labor

People and companies have discovered that it is often more profitable and efficient to focus on what each does best to increase production.

Specialization is the situation in which each person or company in the production effort creates what each is best at creating. For example, expert welders would probably buy their safety shoes rather than make them themselves. They specialize in welding and use earnings from plying their specialty to pay for their other needs.

Productivity is a measure of output in relation to the inputs of raw materials, labor, and capital. Usually, companies that are more productive, producing quality products for less cost than their competition, will survive best in a free market.

American society has a high degree of **division of labor**, where people depend on each other to produce most of the goods and services required to sustain life. Economic interdependence exists even in remote areas. People depend on each other for protection, keeping roads open, and for information, such as weather reports.

Microeconomics and Macroeconomics

The study of how economies work is commonly divided into microeconomics and macroeconomics. Both deal with important concepts, such as supply and demand and the price and cost of production. But each branch of study comes at these concepts from a different perspective.

Small Details and the Larger Picture

Microeconomics deals with how factors such as price feed into the decisions of buyers and sellers in a marketplace. It looks at the smaller picture and focuses on:

- basic theories of supply and demand
- how businesses decide how much of something to produce
- how businesses decide what to charge for a commodity

Macroeconomics considers the national economy as a whole, looking at the factors that influence aggregate supply and demand. Since macroeconomics is associated with national economies, it deals with, among other variables:

- unemployment rates
- gross domestic product (GDP)
- overall price levels, including inflation

To understand the difference between microeconomics and macroeconomics, consider the price of a smartphone. Microeconomics looks at the demand for a smartphone at different price points and with different amounts of supply. Macroeconomics looks at the current state of prices in general as measured by the consumer price index, which is based on data collected nationwide.

Supply and Demand

The laws of supply and demand are key components in economic activity.

Supply is the amount of a good or service available at a given place and time. **Demand** is how much people desire to acquire a good or service at that same place and time. **Price** is the amount charged for a good or service at a given place and time.

In a free market, prices vary for a good or service until there is a balance between supply and demand.

Practice

The following graph shows the relationship between supply and demand. Equilibrium is the point where the two lines cross and represents a balance of supply and demand.

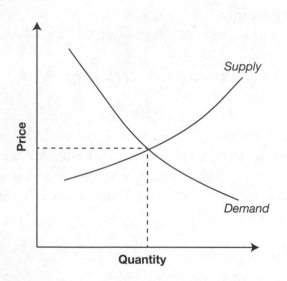

34. After the introduction of the new model, the price and quantity of the current model truck would likely _____.

35. When a new model truck is introduced, demand for the current model would likely _____.

National and International Institutions

On the national level, the key institution is the **Federal Reserve System**. It is the central bank of the United States supporting its mandates for maximum employment, stable prices, and moderate long-term interest rates.

At the international level, two major institutions are the **International Monetary Fund (IMF)** and the **World Bank**. In addition to promoting economic growth, these institutions also act to protect and stabilize the world economy.

- The **IMF**'s main objectives are to help facilitate international financial stability in the global banking system and monetary cooperation. It also works to promote trade and economic growth around the globe.
- The **World Bank** provides loans to developing countries for the purpose of promoting foreign investment and international trade and for facilitating capital investment.

Key Components in Economic Policy

Fiscal policy is the use of governmental taxation and spending to influence the economy. **Monetary policy** is the control of the supply of money and interest rates by the monetary authority of a country.

Inflation is a rise in the general level of prices of goods and services in an economy over a period of time, whereas **deflation** is a drop in the general level of prices of goods and services. While excessive inflation is commonly seen as a threat to the economy by eroding the purchasing power of individuals, deflation can be a problem as well. If prices are generally perceived as falling, an incentive exists to delay purchases until a later time when they will cost less, depressing economic activity.

The **gross domestic product (GDP)** is the monetary value of all finished goods and services produced within a country's borders in a specific time period, usually a year. The size of a nation's GDP as well as changes to the GDP from year to year are strong macroeconomic indicators of an economy's overall health.

Unemployment occurs when people are looking for work and cannot find a job. The best known measure of unemployment is the unemployment rate, which is a macroeconomic measure of economic health.

A **tariff** is a tax imposed on imported goods and services. In addition to raising revenue, tariffs on imported products give an advantage to domestically produced competitors.

Keynesian versus Supply-Side Economics

Two opposing views of monetary and fiscal policy are Keynesian and supply-side economics.

Keynesian economic theory is named after its founder, John Maynard Keynes. His model contends that:

- Monetary policy and fiscal policy should be managed by the public sector, or government.
- Centralized policies are needed to smooth out the recurring boom-or-bust periods of the business cycle.

First proposed during the Great Depression, it was the dominant economic theory until the stagflation period of the 1970s, in which the U.S. economy suffered from high inflation coupled with poor job and economic growth.

Supply-side economics was proposed in the 1970s as a conservative alternative to Keynesian economics. It claims that:

- Prosperity is promoted through increased production or supply.
- Supply generates demand for products and other related products.
- Focus on economic producers leads to a more robust economy and greater capacity to generate jobs.

The theory promoted limiting or eliminating restraints on production by lowering income and capital gains tax rates and restricting regulation.

In the **Great Recession** that began in 2008, Keynesians advocated for government stimulus spending to jump-start the economy, even if it resulted in high federal budget deficits. Supply-siders advocated for tax cuts and severe cuts in government spending. In general, Keynesian proposals have come from Democrats while supply-side proposals have come from Republicans. A combination of the two was implemented to alleviate the recession.

Practice

36. A _____ economist would be more likely to support a very high sugar tariff.
   a. supply-side
   b. Keynesian

Consumer Economics

All of us are consumers. Nearly all activities we engage in have an economic component. Going out to dinner, buying a home, and attending college are all decisions that have economic aspects and outcomes.

Savings and Banks

For an individual or family, savings is the difference between the amount of money spent in a time period and the amount of money earned. Savings can either be set aside for future use or be invested.

Most people save their money in a **bank**, a financial institution that accepts deposits and makes loans. Its customers include individuals, nonprofit organizations, and businesses. Banks offer their customers savings and checking accounts, certificates of deposit, credit cards, automobile and student loans, mortgages, and lines of credit.

Sometimes we obtain a good or service and enter into an agreement to pay for it later, usually with interest. That agreement is a request for credit. Consumers use various types of credit. We use a **credit card** to obtain many goods and services; we then receive a statement at the end of the month and pay interest on balances left unpaid at the due date.

The largest credit commitment that most people enter into is a **mortgage** for a home. The home buyer pays a down payment to the seller while the bank or other lender pays the balance. The home buyer agrees to pay the bank back, with interest, in payments that can last as long as 30 years.

Student loans now comprise the second largest form of consumer debt after home mortgages. The national government helps students finance their education because it is considered an investment in the productive capacity of the nation. However, the rising debt burden faced by students is considered by some to threaten the economic health of future workers and the country.

When consumers buy goods or services on credit, they may be victimized by theft or fraud. Consumer credit laws protect buyers and limit their liability in situations such as identity theft, especially if the fraud or abuse is reported quickly. Other consumer credit laws are written to protect companies.

Economics Summary

Economic and political freedoms are closely linked in capitalist systems, which are based on free markets and the ability of consumers and producers to engage in economic activity of their own choosing without much government regulation. In practice, however, governments regulate economic activity to ensure safe financial practices and healthy levels of competition.

Markets and competition, supply and demand, and division of labor are among the cornerstones of the U.S. capitalist system. Just about everyone participates in this system, both as suppliers of capital, labor, or investment and as consumers and producers of goods and services.

Given the high level of freedom allowed, entrepreneurship is a hallmark of the U.S. economy. This spirit of economic freedom fuels the growth of new products and services, and government involvement,

limited as it is, aims to protect the consumer and business from excesses and abuses of this very freedom.

Geography and the World

Understanding the world around you (its history, environmental processes, and cultures) is critical to living as an informed citizen.

Development of Classical Civilizations

Until about 12,000 years ago, the most advanced humans were hunter-gatherers, taking what they needed to live from the surrounding environment. Starting at about 10,000 B.C. in the Middle East, agriculture began, initiating a process of development that has continued ever since. Innovations in the Neolithic period included the first villages and towns, domestication of plants and animals, and the development of pottery. The oldest structure found from this period is a wall and tower in Jericho that are at least 11,000 years old.

Early Civilizations

As agriculture advanced and food surpluses could be accumulated, larger population centers could be supported. By 3500 B.C., this led to the development of the early civilizations we are familiar with today.

First among these early civilizations were the **Sumerians**, who settled in the valley between the Tigris and Euphrates rivers in what is today called Iraq and is also known as Mesopotamia. This civilization developed characteristics common to those that followed it, including a large population center, art and monumental architecture, a system of government, division of labor and social classes, and written language.

With the invention of written language, humanity moved from prehistory to history. In the eastern hemisphere, ancient civilizations developed in a number of river valleys, including:

- the Nile in Egypt, where civilization remained stable for centuries
- the Huang Ho or Yellow River in China, wherein another civilization also lasted for centuries
- the Indus in India, where the civilization vanished around 1500 B.C.E. until archeologists rediscovered it

In the western hemisphere, civilization developed independently a few thousand years later. None of these ancient civilizations developed an alphabet for written language like we use today.

The first written language was **Phoenician**, developed in what is today called Lebanon. The oldest surviving alphabetic written language still in use today is Hebrew, developed in what is now called Israel, which is south of Lebanon. For the most part, pictographic written languages, such as Egyptian hieroglyphics, which could contain thousands of different symbols, have disappeared. Chinese and Japanese are the only two surviving pictographic written languages.

Rising Populations, Technology, and Warfare

At the beginning of the Neolithic period, roughly from 10,000 B.C.E. to 2000 B.C.E., there might have been as few as five million people on Earth. By the time of the Roman Empire (which began in 27 B.C.E.), that number had probably increased to about 200 million people.

While warfare became one destructive way to deal with rising populations in limited territory, a more constructive approach was the development of **tools** that allowed the creation of more wealth and increased the capacity of the planet to support more people. The development of metals such as bronze and iron resulted in more durable and effective farm-

ing tools that could increase crop yields. However, these new technologies were also used to make more lethal weapons to kill more adversaries.

While today we know about the rise and fall of many ancient civilizations, we are still not sure why warfare developed as a way of settling disputes. A number of factors were most likely involved, including the pressure of expanding populations, greed and ambition of the most powerful, and temptation of great wealth generated in the large cities.

Greece and Rome

The last of the major Mesopotamian empires was the Persian Empire, centered in what is now Iran. The failure of the Persians to defeat the Greek city-states, followed by the Greek conquest of the Persian Empire in 334 B.C.E., led to a major cultural change throughout the Middle East. But the most important legacies of the Greeks were cultural, not military.

- The earliest form of limited democracy was developed in the Greek city-state of Athens.
- Theater and philosophy flourished in Athens.
- Art and science were taken to a higher level of development.

The Greek states were eventually defeated by the **Roman Empire**, which had overthrown the Roman Republic (established around 500 B.C.E.). During the republican period, Rome introduced a new form of government, including an important role for the Roman Senate, which performed a pivotal advisory role in the republic's governance.

Unfortunately, by the time it collapsed, the Roman Empire had high levels of corruption and dysfunction. At the same time, it developed great public works such as aqueducts and roads and constructed the most complete and just law code of the ancient world.

The Environment and Societal Development

For much of human history, societal development did not appear to have major consequences on the environment. The earth is so huge and its resources so vast, human impact seemed negligible. However, even in prehistory, humans have had significant impact on the environment. For example, humans probably played a role in the extinction of large Ice Age mammals, such as the mammoth, the mastodon, and the saber-toothed cat.

Environmental Issues and Sustainability

Ongoing societal impacts have placed increasing pressure on the environment. These impacts include population growth, economic activities, and consumption patterns. Humanity has reached a point where environmental degradation threatens sustainable development as well as human health and well-being.

WHAT IS SUSTAINABILITY?

According to the Merriam-Webster dictionary, sustainable means:

> of, relating to, or being a method of harvesting or using a resource so that the resource is not depleted or permanently damaged

While the developed worlds of Europe and North America have contributed the most to environmental degradation, rapidly industrializing countries such as China, India, and Brazil are starting to take a larger role. Issues include the following:

- **Climate change**, resulting from emissions of carbon into the atmosphere from industrial processes, is a major worldwide concern.

- **Air pollution** due to industrial processes and auto emissions is a threat to health and the environment. In China, for instance, air quality in major cities is one of the biggest concerns.
- **Deforestation** due to commercial development is a threat to biodiversity and is one of the major factors in climate change.

Practice

37. Which of the following actions would most support sustainable development?

    a. Encourage workers to telecommute when possible and work from home.

    b. Use recently developed fracking technology to get oil from shale.

    c. Pump more water from underground aquifers in arid areas of the world.

    d. Encourage industrial development in developing economies.

Population Growth and Urban Development

Human population has been exploding since the beginning of the Industrial Age, when it was less than one billion. Population has increased massively since then, but growth has begun to slow.

- Population is now more than seven billion.
- Population growth peaked at 2.2% in 1963, and by 2012 had declined below 1.1%.
- Some nations, such as Japan and Russia, are already experiencing an aging of the total population as birth rates remain below replacement rates.

Early civilizations were marked by the development of **urban centers**. However, since the beginning of the Industrial Revolution, urban settlement has dramatically increased, first in the developed world and now in regions of the developing world as well.

To support growing cities and populations, rural areas have had to adapt. While a much smaller percentage of the population lives in **rural areas**, these areas must still produce sufficient food for a growing population while maintaining an environ-ment that protects biodiversity and mitigates the impact of climate change.

Practice

38. According to the information given in the table, what do you think will be the most pressing issue in Russia in 2025?

#	Top Ten Most Populous Countries	World Population (millions)			
		1980	1990	2008	2025*
1	China	981	1,141	1,333	1,458
2	India	687	849	1,140	1,398
3	United States	228	250	304	352
4	Indonesia	151	178	228	273
5	Brazil	122	150	192	223
6	Pakistan	81	108	166	226
7	Bangladesh	81	116	160	198
8	Nigeria	76	94	151	208
9	Russia	n/a	148	142	137
10	Japan	117	124	128	126

*2025 projections based on 2008 figures.

Source: Based on data from the International Energy Agency.

a. food supply
b. housing
c. aging population
d. unemployment

Peoples and Nations

Place, region, and nation, along with culture, are critical concepts in geography and help us analyze variations across physical and political boundaries. Recognizing these variations in human society allows for increased understanding between peoples around the globe. The ways physical and cultural life is organized form some of the key concepts in geographic study.

Places and Regions

In geography, it is important to understand the difference between a place and a region.

A **place** is a location that has some meaning to an individual or group of individuals. That meaning can have a physical and/or a human dimension. A **region** is an area that is distinct for either physical or social reasons. Regions are bounded by homogeneous characteristics.

- Regions can be climate based, such as the Sahara desert region.
- Regions can be politically based, such as the Communist bloc region in the middle of the twentieth century.
- The boundaries of a region are determined by the extent of the area of homogeneity sharing the distinct characteristic(s).

Types of regions include:

- continental
- geographical
- historical
- paleogeographic (or historical geographic)
- natural resource
- religious
- political
- administrative
- regions controlled by military force

A **nation** is a group of people who are bound together through history, culture, language, religion, customs, and values.

A **state** is a portion of land with a sovereign government and laws. (*State* can be applied to the subnational areas in the United States and other countries, but the term also applies to completely separate countries as well.) The difference between *nation* and *state* can be considered the difference between ethnicity and citizenship, though the terms are often used interchangeably.

Culture

Culture, the set of beliefs and social practices shared by a group of people, is one factor that helps to define regions, nations, and states. According to the **Declaration on Cultural Diversity** issued by the **United Nations Educational, Scientific, and Cultural Organization (UNESCO),**

Culture should be regarded as the set of distinctive spiritual, material, intellectual and emotional features of society or a social group, and . . . it encompasses, in addition to art and literature, lifestyles, ways of living together, value systems, traditions and beliefs.

Article 1 goes on to say:

EXCERPT

Culture takes diverse forms across time and space. This diversity is embodied in the uniqueness and plurality of the identities of the groups and societies making up humankind. As a source of exchange, innovation and creativity, cultural diversity is as necessary for humankind as biodiversity is for nature. In this sense, it is the common heritage of humanity and should be recognized and affirmed for the benefit of present and future generations.

Cultural diffusion or exchange occurs between groups of people as they spread their products or ideas to one another. This phenomenon has increased greatly in the past few decades as globalizing forces, including the Internet, have taken hold in all regions of the world.

Assimilation occurs when a minority group, or individuals, adopts the customs and ideas of the dominant culture. Assimilation is an issue of considerable debate as populations have become more mobile and immigration across national borders has escalated during the current era of globalization.

Human Migration

Human migration has been a constant throughout history. People migrate for a wide range of reasons, including the need for food and livelihood, greater economic opportunity, and freedom from oppression. Few regions of the world today are not the products of wide-ranging human migration and cultural exchanges that result from migration.

Out of Africa and Early Migrations

From their origins in Africa, humans have spread to every continent on Earth.

Human migration has continued throughout historical times. One example was the migration of the Germanic peoples into Europe, which helped bring an end to the Roman Empire. Another was the migration of Turks from Central Asia to what is now Turkey.

The following map illustrates human migration routes out of Africa and Asia.

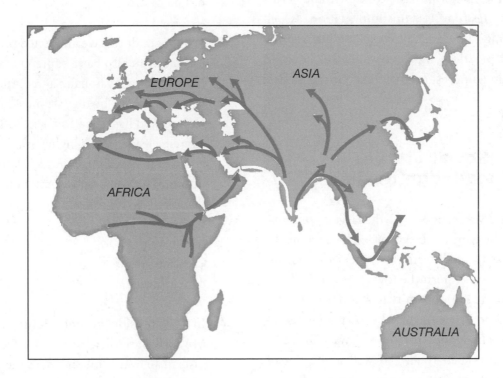

Practice

39. Based on the map, humans first entered Western Europe from what direction?

    a. north

    b. south

    c. east

    d. west

Migration in the Modern Era

Human migration continues today and is aided by modern technology. Immigrants from all over the world have been moving to the Americas, especially to the United States. People from Africa and the

Middle East have been immigrating to Europe. The benefits and costs of immigration are a topic of debate around the world.

    Migrations can also occur within a country.

- In nineteenth-century America, many pioneers migrated from the east to the west.
- In the twentieth century, Southern rural African Americans moved to Northern cities, while many whites of varying ethnicities moved from urban areas to the suburbs.

Migration is an ongoing feature of human history. It began when our ancient ancestors migrated from Africa and peopled the continents. It continues today as the increasing interconnectedness across the world allows people to seek new opportunities and better lives in other countries.

Social Studies Knowledge Summary

You should now have a broad familiarity with the core social studies knowledge, concepts, and terms you'll need for test day. Use this information, as well as your existing knowledge of social studies and the other helpful practices and reviews in this book, to get ready to do your best on the GED® Social Studies test!

Social Studies Knowledge Review

1. Andover, MA, claims to be the largest community in the world to be governed by an annual town meeting. All registered voters are eligible to attend and vote at the town meeting. Citizens have the opportunity to stand up and be counted on issues such as the town and school budgets, changes in the zoning laws, and special projects such as new sidewalks. The type of government in Andover is best described as
   a. anarchy.
   b. oligarchy.
   c. dictatorship.
   d. democracy.

2. The notion that a legitimate government can function only with the consent of the governed is known as *popular sovereignty*. Which of the following slogans from the American Revolutionary period most directly supports the notion of popular sovereignty?
   a. Don't tread on me.
   b. A man's house is his castle.
   c. No taxation without representation.
   d. Join or die.

3. While Iran does have an elected president and legislature, it also has a supreme leader, the Islamic cleric, Ayatollah Sayyed Ali Khamenei, who was elected by the Islamic Assembly of Experts and has ruled Iran since 1989. The supreme leader is the highest-ranking political and religious authority in the Islamic Republic of Iran. The type of government in Iran is best described as
   a. theocracy.
   b. oligarchy.
   c. dictatorship.
   d. democracy.

4. In 1770, outside the State House in Boston, MA, British soldiers shot and killed five colonists in an event still known as the Boston Massacre. When the soldiers were brought to trial, their lawyer was the colonist patriot John Adams. Which of the following foundational principles was most likely the key reason Adams took on this case?
   a. defending the underdog
   b. individual rights
   c. right to bear arms
   d. rule of law

5. In 1734, the governor of New York, William Cosby, had the printer Peter Zenger arrested and tried for libel for accusing Cosby of corruption in the newspaper the *New York Weekly Journal.* The governor ordered copies of the newspaper burned. At the trial, the judge, who owed his job to the governor, instructed the jury that they must determine only whether the criticism was printed and that it did not matter whether it was true. The jury disagreed and found Zenger not guilty. This case was a landmark in the development of

a. governmental corruption.

b. freedom of the press.

c. book burning.

d. separation of powers.

6. In the early 1960s, an independence movement swept across Africa. In just a few years, colonies of European nations, such as France, the United Kingdom, and Belgium, became independent nations with constitutions and free elections. This movement was a clear expression of the philosophy of

a. natural rights.

b. divine rights.

7.

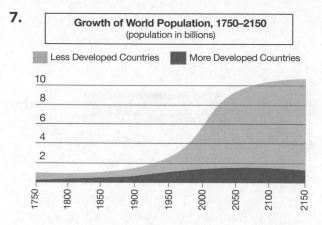

Growth of World Population, 1750–2150
(population in billions)

☐ Less Developed Countries   ■ More Developed Countries

Which of the following predictions is best supported by the world population growth data in the chart?

a. The world population growth rate will begin declining by 2050.

b. The less developed countries will continue to grow rapidly for the next 150 years.

c. The developed countries will experience a population collapse in the next century.

d. Within the next century, world population will level off and begin to decline.

8. In order to finance the American Revolution, the Continental Congress issued paper money that became known as continentals. During the war, this currency was referred to by colonists in the popular phrase *not worth a continental*, which meant which of the following?

a. They considered continentals to be priceless.

b. They could not use continentals as money.

c. Continentals would regain their value at the end of the war.

d. Continentals would become a sought-after collectible.

9. On September 22, 1862, what was President Lincoln's motivation when he declared the following?

EXCERPT

That on the first day of January, in the year of our Lord one thousand eight hundred and sixty-three, all persons held as slaves within any State or designated part of a State, the people whereof shall then be in rebellion against the United States, shall be then, thenceforward, and forever free; and the Executive Government of the United States, including the military and naval authority thereof, will recognize and maintain the freedom of such persons, and will do no act or acts to repress such persons, or any of them, in any efforts they may make for their actual freedom.

    a. moral outrage at the dehumanization of slavery

    b. to increase the chances of the Union winning the Civil War

    c. to confirm his legacy as one of the greatest presidents

    d. the need to recruit former slaves into armed forces

10. What is the main idea of this passage?

EXCERPT

At the heart of the U.S. Civil Rights movement in the 1950s and 1960s was the use of nonviolent direct-action protest, including student sit-ins at lunch counters. Inspired by the example of Jesus, and the teachings of Mahatma Gandhi during India's struggle for independence, black church and community leaders in the United States began advocating the use of non-violence in their own struggle. Beyond spontaneous and planned student sit-ins, several organizations were formed to fight for civil rights using Gandhi's model of nonviolent dissent and action. Three of the most influential groups—the Congress of Racial Equality (CORE), the Southern Christian Leadership Conference (SCLC), and the Student Nonviolent Coordinating Committee (SNCC)—were pivotal in bringing about social change in America.

Source: www.pbs.org/independentlens/februaryone/civilrights.html.

    a. The use of nonviolent direct-action protest was at the heart of the Civil Rights movement.

    b. Nonviolent protest, as developed by Mahatma Gandhi, is a powerful instrument for gaining rights.

    c. Black church and community leaders supported the use of nonviolence in the struggle for civil rights.

    d. CORE, SCLC, and SNCC were civil rights organizations that provided leadership for the movement.

11. The cartoonist who drew this image is most likely hoping to elicit which of the following reactions?

Source: College Debt #106133, by Bob Englehart, *The Hartford Courant*, February 10, 2012.

   a. If you can't manage your money, you need to suffer the consequences.
   b. People who can't afford to go to college should not have incurred the debt in the first place.
   c. Families need to spend on more practical things than a college education.
   d. We need to help our college graduates who are drowning in debt.

12. One of the powers that is shared by the federal and state governments is the power to raise revenue. What was the most likely reason that led to this power being shared?
   a. The federal and state governments both need money to operate effectively.
   b. The federal government would be too weak without the power to raise revenue.
   c. The federal government would be too strong with the power to raise revenue.
   d. It helps maintain the balance of power between the two levels of government.

13. The amendment process to the U.S. Constitution requires that three-quarters of the states approve a proposed amendment for it to go into effect. Which of the following conclusions regarding the number of states needed to ratify an amendment is correct?
   a. All the original 13 states were needed to ratify the first ten amendments since they were proposed with the Constitution and were part of a grand bargain between Federalists and Anti-Federalists.
   b. Twenty-seven states were needed to ratify the 13th amendment, which abolished slavery, since there were 36 states at the end of the Civil War.
   c. The reason that 36 states were needed to repeal the 18th amendment in 1933 was that 36 states were needed to ratify the 18th amendment creating Prohibition in 1919.
   d. Because the United States now has 50 states, 37 states will have to be on record ratifying the 16th Amendment—which was passed in 1909 and authorized the income tax—even though only 36 states were needed then.

Answers and Explanations

Chapter Practice

1. **b.** A *plutocrat* is an individual whose power is based on wealth. Although a duke (choice **a**) is part of the privileged class in an aristocracy, the term *plutocrat* refers to wealthy individuals without aristocratic titles. An elected official (choice **c**) is selected by a democratic process, ideally unrelated to wealth or social status. A military general (choice **d**) does not usually rule government except in the case of a military junta or in a stratocracy, although military leaders can also run for elected office.

2. **b.** The American Revolution was a rebellion against the privilege of English aristocracy and the aristocratic system. Although it was won by militia, the battle was against the British king and his aristocracy, not one junta against another.

3. **a.** In a democratic society, power rests in the free thought and expression of individuals. Authoritarian forms of government suppress personal freedoms and expression.

4. **d.** A meritocracy is based on merit, intelligence, and talent, and civil testing leads to social promotion.

5. **disadvantage**

6. **disadvantage**

7. **disadvantage**

8. **advantage**

9. **advantage**

10. **advantage**

11. **advantage**

12. The **executive** branch checks the **judicial** branch.

13. The **executive** branch checks the **legislative** branch.

14. The **legislative** branch checks the **executive** branch.

15. The **judicial** branch checks the **legislative** branch.

16. The **legislative** branch checks the **judicial** branch.

17. The **judicial** branch checks the **executive** branch.

18. **state.** State governments have the power to grant corporate status to businesses.

19. **federal.** The federal government regulates interstate commerce, including banks that have headquarters and branches in different states.

20. **federal.** The federal government runs the U.S. Postal Service and therefore pays local post office employees, even in rural areas.

21. **the king.** In the Magna Carta, *we* refers to the king, also known as the *royal we*. The Magna Carta cites barons and freemen, and common people are not referred to at all.

22. *Answers will vary:*
The colonists agreed to form a government that would make laws. They also agreed to obey the laws and listen to officials appointed by the government.

23. **b.** The Declaration of Independence laid out the justification for a revolution against the rule of Great Britain. In declaring independence, the authors and signers of the declaration were revolting against the current government.

24. a. The reason for the reversal between the 1896 and 1954 cases is that nearly 60 years of experience showed that "separate but equal" was a fallacy. By 1954, the evidence was overwhelming that segregation was very damaging for black people. Although the court membership had more liberals in 1954 than in 1896 (choice **b**), the decision was unanimous, so that could not have been the most important reason. While the 1954 case was about education (choice **c**), it was also influential in ending segregation in transportation and public accommodations. The equal protection clause (choice **d**) had been in effect since 1868.

25. c. Emma Lazarus would be most favorable toward the Dream Act if she were alive today. She expresses support in her poem for immigration of the least fortunate and the idea of the United States as a country that welcomes needy individuals hoping for a better life. Completion of a fence and barrier with motion detectors along the Mexican border (choice **a**) is opposite to the greeting of poor immigrants that Lazarus supports in her poem. She would be less concerned with immigrants complying with bureaucratic details in order to gain entry to the United States (choices **b** and **d**).

26. 1847.

27. 1847.

28. d. Union membership was close to its all-time peak of approximately 23 million when the UAW rejoined the AFL-CIO in 1981.

29. c. At the time of the founding of the CIO, the slope of the membership line was steeper than it was at the other times.

30. d. President Kennedy used metaphorical language to let Berliners know they could trust the United States. By identifying with Berliners, he was saying that he and the United States would protect West Berlin. Kennedy and Berliners did have a special rapport, but it was the unspoken security guarantee that was most important.

31. **1980.** Adjusted for inflation, the cost of oil was the highest in the year 1980, when it was $71.48 a barrel in year 2004 dollars.

32. **1969.** Adjusted for inflation, the cost of oil was the lowest in the year 1969, when it was $7.45 a barrel in year 2004 dollars.

33. b. Elizabeth Warren would most likely support higher taxes on corporate profits so that successful companies help support infrastructure. She makes it clear that the existing infrastructure helped these companies succeed.

34. After the introduction of the new model, the price and quantity of the current model truck would likely **decrease**. When demand drops, the price drops. With fewer sales, the quantity of unsold cars would likely increase until a new equilibrium is established.

35. When a new model truck is introduced, demand for the current model would likely **decrease**.

36. a. Tariffs give an advantage to domestic supply, so they would more likely be supported by a supply-side economist.

37. a. Encouraging workers to telecommute—working from home—would most support sustainable development, since energy from fossil fuels is saved when workers do not have to commute. Using recently developed fracking technology to get oil from oil shale (choice **b**) would result in more CO_2 in the atmosphere, worsening global warming, and it is not sustainable. Pumping more water from underground aquifers in arid areas of the world (choice **c**) is not sustainable because, without other measures, the underground water will be depleted. Industrial development (choice **d**) uses a great deal of resources and may not be sustainable.

38. c. With a steadily declining population involving fewer new births, Russia's population will be older; that will most likely be the most pressing of the listed issues. Russia will have fewer people than it has today, which means it will need less food (choice **a**). Since housing (choice **b**) requires maintenance, it will need some attention, but not as much as dealing with the needs of the aging population.

39. c. According to the map, humans first entered Western Europe from the east. There are no immigration routes from any other direction entering Western Europe.

Social Studies Knowledge Review

1. d. Town meeting, in which every registered voter can participate, is considered to be direct democracy.

2. c. **No taxation without representation** most directly expresses the notion of popular sovereignty. The colonists claimed that the right to collect taxes depended on the consent of the people. *Don't tread on me* (choice **a**) was a defiant warning to the British but did not address the notion of popular sovereignty. *A man's house is his castle* (choice **b**) was said by James Otis, who was objecting to British soldiers living in private homes in Boston. *Join or die* (choice **d**) was a demand that the colonies and the colonists all join the Revolution coupled with a threat of what would happen if they did not.

3. a. While having an elected Parliament and president is considered to be evidence of democracy (choice **d**), in Iran all democratically elected individuals can be overruled by a religious authority. A government in which the final say is given to a religious leader is a theocracy. An oligarchy (choice **b**) is rule by a small group of people, and even though the Assembly of Experts is a small group and does vote the supreme leader into power—and technically can vote the supreme leader out of power, although since it was created in 1979, it has not done so—the supreme leader has ultimate power. He gets his legitimacy from his religious stature, not his military power, which is often how a dictator (choice **c**) attains power.

4. d. The rule of law would dictate that every accused person is entitled to a competent defense and a fair trial.

5. b. The case was a landmark in the freedom of the press because the jury ignored the corrupt judge and ruled that the printer had the right to print criticism of the governor. Even though the case was a struggle against governmental corruption (choice **a**), the more important issue was its place in the development of freedom of the press. While book burning (choice **c**) continues to be an instrument of intimidation, the positive outcome of Zenger's acquittal was the more important legacy. With Governor Cosby controlling the judge, though not the jury, the separation of powers (choice **d**) was not the focal point of this trial.

6. a. This movement was a clear expression of the philosophy of natural rights, which claims that the right to rule comes from the people. Transferring political power from a foreign colonial power to an elected local government would be a real-life example of the philosophy of natural rights. Divine rights is a philosophy proposing that the right to rule comes from a connection with God, a divine power.

7. a. That the world population growth rate will begin declining by 2050 is the prediction best supported by the graph. While the total population will continue to increase, the slope of the line, or rate of growth, will be decreasing. The graph shows that the population growth of the less developed countries is expected to slow down after 2050, not grow rapidly (choice **b**). The graph shows that the population of the developed countries will remain stable, not collapse (choice **c**). While the graph does show world population leveling off, it does not predict a decline (choice **d**).

8. b. People expected that they could not use continentals as money or for anything else.

9. b. Lincoln's motivation, according to most analysis, was to increase the chances of the Union winning the Civil War, since slaves would be freed in those areas in armed rebellion. Lincoln was morally outraged (choice **a**) and the abolition of slavery did help establish his legacy (choice **c**), but there is no evidence that these were motivations for his actions. While the proclamation helped to recruit former slaves into the Union's armed forces (choice **d**), that was only one advantage leading to attainment of the main goal, preserving the Union.

10. a. That the use of nonviolent direct-action protest was at the heart of the Civil Rights movement is the main idea of the passage. While the writer of the passage would probably agree that nonviolence, as developed by Mahatma Gandhi, is a powerful instrument for gaining rights, this statement is too broad to be the main idea of this passage.

11. d. The cartoonist hopes that the reaction would be sympathy for the college grad and a desire to help; he urges sympathy in the viewer through a depiction of the just-graduated college student as being pulled under water by the heavy responsibility of student loan debt.

12. d. Sharing the power to raise revenue helps keep both levels of government strong and independent and maintains a balance of power. While it is true that the federal and state governments both need money to operate effectively (choice **a**), one level could grant money to the other. While it is true that the federal government would be too weak without the power to raise revenue (choice **b**), this option does not address the relationship between the federal and state governments. Simply giving it the power to raise revenue does not make the federal government too strong (choice **c**).

13. b. Three-quarters of 36 states, the number of states at the end of the Civil War, is 27 states. Choice **a** is incorrect because not all of the states had to ratify the first ten amendments or Bill of Rights; they were subject to the three-quarters rule. Choice **c** is incorrect because while 36 states were needed to repeal the 18th amendment, it was because of the three-quarters rule, not because of the number of states originally needed to ratify the amendment. Choice **d** is incorrect because once an amendment reaches the three-quarters threshold and goes into effect, no further action is needed if additional states subsequently join the Union.

Try to take the tests in this book under the same conditions you'll have on the actual test day. The beginning of each test tells you how long you have. Sit down in a quiet spot, set your timer, and try to take the exam without any interruptions.

After you finish each section, you will find detailed answer explanations for every question. Not only will these explanations tell you why the correct answer is right, but they will also explain why each of the choices is wrong.

You will also find scoring information for the short-response and essay questions, along with sample essays to compare your to.

Scoring Your Best

Practicing with GED®-test-like questions is the best way to prepare for the exam. This section is filled with questions that mirror the ones you will see on the test day. Taking these practice tests, especially under the same timing conditions as the real GED® test, will help you get used to pacing yourself. You can see in which subjects you excel and in which you need a bit more study. Use the practice tests as part of your study toolkit, and you will be well on your way to succeeding on the exam!

15 ▶ MATHEMATICAL REASONING PRACTICE TEST

This practice test is modeled on the format, content, and timing of the official GED® Mathematical Reasoning test. Like the official test, the questions focus on your quantitative and algebraic problem-solving skills.

You may refer to the formula sheet in the Appendix on page 577 as you take this exam. Answer questions 1–5 *without* using a calculator. You may use a scientific calculator (or a calculator of any kind) for the remaining exam questions.

Before you begin, it's important to know that you should work carefully but not spend too much time on any one question. Be sure you answer every question.

Set a timer for 115 minutes (1 hour and 55 minutes), and try to take this test uninterrupted, under quiet conditions.

Complete answer explanations for all of the test questions follow the exam. Good luck!

45 Questions
115 Minutes

1. Joseph owns v video games. Harry owns 10 fewer than two times the number of video games that Joseph owns. Which expression represents the number of video games that Harry owns in terms of v?
   a. $10v - 2$
   b. $2v - 10$
   c. $2(v - 10)$
   d. $10(v - 2)$

2. Which of the following is equivalent to $\frac{\sqrt[3]{9} \times \sqrt[3]{18}}{3}$?
   a. $\sqrt[3]{2}$
   b. $3\sqrt[3]{2}$
   c. $\sqrt[3]{6}$
   d. $\sqrt[3]{18}$

3. Write your answer on the line below. You may use numbers, symbols, and/or text in your response.

   An expression is shown below. Simplify the expression completely. Be sure to leave your answer in radical form.

   $$\frac{\sqrt{72}}{\sqrt{36}}$$

4. Draw a dot on the grid below to plot the point indicated by the ordered pair $(-2,1)$.

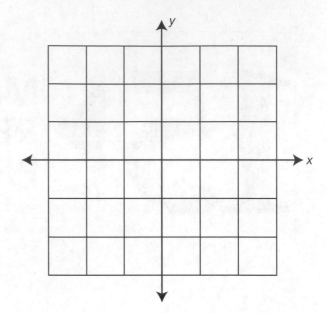

5. As part of a game, Gilbert must take a number and use a special procedure to come up with a new number. To come up with his new number, Gilbert takes the original number, cubes it, adds 5 to it, and finally multiplies it by 2. If the original number is represented by x, which of the following represents Gilbert's new number?
   a. $2(3x + 5)$
   b. $2(x^3 + 5)$
   c. $2x^3 + 5$
   d. $x^6 + 5$

6. The sum of a number n and 4 is less than 5 times the number m. If m is 6, which of the following is true?
   a. n is greater than 6
   b. $n + 4$ is less than 26
   c. n is less than 26
   d. n is equal to 26

7. A company pays its sales employees a base rate of $450 a week plus a 4% commission on any sales the employee makes. If an employee makes $1,020 in sales one week, what will be his total paycheck for that week? Write your answer in the box below.

> [   ]

8. The diameter of a circle is 10 meters. In meters, which of the following is the circumference of this circle?

  a. 5π

  b. 10π

  c. 25π

  d. 100π

9. Which of the following is equivalent to $\left(\frac{3}{4}\right)^3$?

  a. $\frac{3^3}{4^3}$

  b. $\frac{3 \times 3}{4 \times 3}$

  c. $\frac{3^3}{4}$

  d. $\frac{3}{4 \times 3}$

10. The line n is parallel to the line $y = 3x - 7$ and passes through the point $(5,1)$. At what point does the line n cross the y-axis? Write your answer in the box below.

> [   ]

11. A line passes through the point $(4,0)$ and has a slope of $-\frac{1}{2}$. What is the equation of this line?

  a. $y = -\frac{1}{2}x + 2$

  b. $y = -\frac{1}{2}x - 2$

  c. $y = -\frac{1}{2}x + 4$

  d. $y = -\frac{1}{2}x - 4$

12. What is the value of $f(-1)$ if $f(x) = 3(x - 1)^2 + 5$?

  a. 8

  b. 11

  c. 15

  d. 17

13. What is the equation of the line that passes through the points $(-2,1)$ and $(4,5)$ in the Cartesian coordinate plane?

  a. $y = \frac{2}{3}x - \frac{4}{3}$

  b. $y = \frac{2}{3}x - \frac{1}{3}$

  c. $y = \frac{2}{3}x + \frac{7}{3}$

  d. $y = \frac{2}{3}x + 4$

14. A 9-foot-long ladder is placed against the side of a building such that the top of the ladder reaches a window that is 6 feet above the ground. To the nearest 10th of a foot, what is the distance from the bottom of the ladder to the building?

  a. 1.7

  b. 2.4

  c. 6.7

  d. 10.8

15. The figure below represents the rate of cooling for a particular material after it was placed in a super-cooled bath.

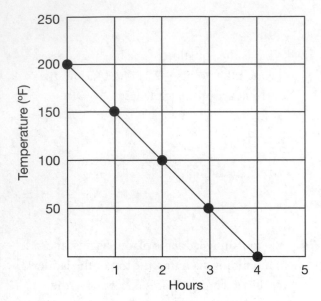

If the temperature, in Fahrenheit, is represented by T and the number of hours elapsed is represented by H, then which of the following would represent a situation where the rate of cooling was faster than the rate indicated in the graph?

a. $T = -25H + 150$
b. $T = -60H + 300$
c. $T = -10H + 200$
d. $T = -50H + 250$

16. In a study of its employees, a company found that about 50% spent more than 2 hours a day composing or reading emails. The overall distribution of time employees spent on these activities was skewed right with a mean time of about 2.5 hours. Complete the box plot below so that is matches the given information.

Draw as many vertical lines as needed on the graph to represent the data.

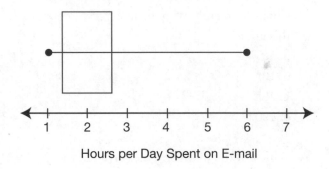

Hours per Day Spent on E-mail

17. What is the equation of the line graphed in the figure below?

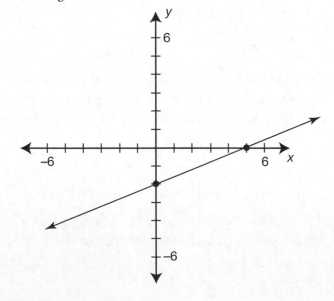

a. $y = \frac{2}{5}x - 2$
b. $y = -\frac{2}{5}x - 2$
c. $y = \frac{2}{5}x + 5$
d. $y = -\frac{2}{5}x - 5$

18. What is a positive solution to the equation $x^2 - 5x = 14$?

   a. 2

   b. 7

   c. 5

   d. 9

19. What is the slope of the line represented by the equation $10x - y = 2$?

   a. 1

   b. 2

   c. 5

   d. 10

20. Which of the following is equivalent to $5^{\frac{1}{2}} \times 5^2$?

   a. $5^{-\frac{3}{2}}$

   b. 5

   c. $5^{\frac{5}{2}}$

   d. $5^{\frac{1}{4}}$

21. A specialized part for a manufacturing process has a thickness of 1.2×10^{-3} inches. To the ten-thousandth of an inch, what would be the thickness of a stack of 10 of these parts?

   a. 0.0001

   b. 0.0012

   c. 0.0120

   d. 0.1200

22. A line is perpendicular to the line $y = \frac{5}{6}x + 1$ and has a y-intercept of $(0,-4)$. What is the equation of this line?

   a. $y = -4x + 1$

   b. $y = \frac{5}{6}x - 4$

   c. $y = -\frac{6}{5}x + 1$

   d. $y = -\frac{6}{5}x - 4$

23. Which of the following expressions is equivalent to $\frac{3}{x} \div \frac{5x}{2}$ for all nonzero x?

   a. $\frac{6}{5x^2}$

   b. $\frac{15x^2}{2}$

   c. $\frac{3}{2}$

   d. $\frac{15}{2}$

24. A factory is able to produce at least 16 items, but no more than 20 items, for every hour the factory is open. If the factory is open for 8 hours a day, which of the following are possibly the numbers of items produced by the factory over a 7-day work period?

Select all of the correct possibilities from the list and write them in the box below.

   128

   150

   850

   910

   1,115

   ┌─────────────────────────┐
   │   │
   └─────────────────────────┘

25. A 32-ounce bag of potato chips has a retail cost of $3.45. To the nearest 10th of a cent, what is the price per ounce of this item (in cents)?

   a. 9.3

   b. 10.8

   c. 28.5

   d. 35.45

26.

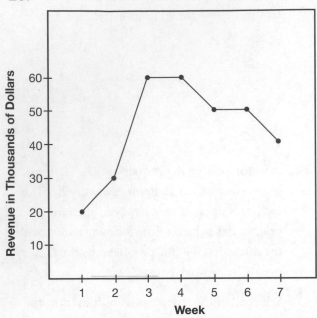

The graph shown here represents the total weekly revenue of a company over several weeks. For which of the following periods has the weekly revenue increased?
a. between weeks 2 and 3
b. between weeks 3 and 4
c. between weeks 4 and 5
d. between weeks 6 and 7

27. Circle the line in the coordinate plane below that represents the graph of the equation $3x - 2y = 1$.

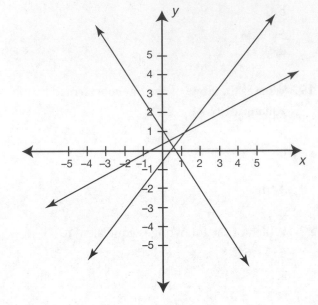

28. A line z is perpendicular to the line $y = -x + 5$. If z passes through the points $(0,-2)$ and $(x,5)$, what is the value of x?
a. 0
b. 3
c. 7
d. 10

29. Which of the following is equivalent to the numerical expression $\sqrt{2}(\sqrt{18} - \sqrt{6})$?
a. $4\sqrt{3}$
b. $5\sqrt{6}$
c. $6 - \sqrt{3}$
d. $6 - \sqrt{6}$

30. A beauty-product manufacturer has been researching the way that people use various beauty products. After several surveys, it has collected the data shown in the scatterplot below, which shows the time that participants spent on their beauty routines on a typical morning versus the amount of money the participants spent per month on beauty products.

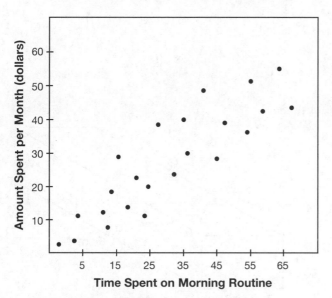

Given this plot, which of the following best describes the relationship between the amount of time spent and the amount of money spent?

a. In general, the longer people spent on their morning beauty routine, the more money they spent per month on beauty products.

b. In general, the longer people spent on their morning beauty routine, the less money they spent per month on beauty products.

c. In general, the amount of time people spent on their morning beauty routine was about the same as the amount of money they spent in dollars on beauty products.

d. In general, there is no clear relationship between the amount of time people spent on their beauty routine and the amount of money they spent per month on beauty products.

31. A walking trail is 11,088 feet long. If a mile is 5,280 feet, how many miles long is the walking trail?

a. 0.2

b. 0.5

c. 1.6

d. 2.1

32. The product of $x^2 - 6$ and x^4 is

a. $x^8 - 6$

b. $x^6 - 6$

c. $x^6 - 6x^4$

d. $x^8 - 6x^4$

33. The table below indicates the behavior of the price of one share of a given stock over several weeks.

END OF	CHANGE
Week 1	Increased by $5.00
Week 2	Decreased by 10%
Week 3	Decreased by $1.10
Week 4	Doubled in value

If the stock was worth $10.15 a share at the beginning of week 1, what was the value of one share of this stock at the end of week 4?

a. $25.07

b. $29.46

c. $32.20

d. $50.12

34. What is the mode of the data set 9, 4, −1, 12, 4, 8, 7?

a. −1

b. 4

c. 7

d. 13

35. There are 48 total applicants for a job. Of these applicants, 20 have a college degree, 15 have five years of work experience, and 8 have a college degree and five years of work experience. If an applicant is randomly selected, what is the probability, to the nearest tenth of a percent, that he or she has a college degree or has 5 years of work experience?
a. 41.7%
b. 56.3%
c. 72.9%
d. 89.6%

36. A customer uses two coupons to purchase a product at a grocery store, where the original price of the product was $8.30. If the final price paid by the customer was $7.00 and each coupon gave the same discount, what was the value of the discount provided by a single coupon?
a. $0.65
b. $0.90
c. $1.30
d. $2.60

37. Lee is planning to buy a new television and has been watching the price of a particular model for the past month. Last month, the price was $309.99, while this month, the price is $334.99. To the nearest tenth of a percent, by what percent has the price increased over the past month? Write your answer in the box below.

 %

38. Which of the following are the two solutions to the equation $x^2 - 2x - 3 = 0$?
a. 3 and −1
b. −3 and 1
c. −3 and −2
d. 2 and 2

39. Which of the following represents the solution set of the inequality $x + 2 > 5$?
a. $\{x: x > 10\}$
b. $\{x: x > 7\}$
c. $\{x: x > 3\}$
d. $\{x: x > 2.5\}$

40. What is the value of $\frac{x-5}{x^2-1}$ when $x = \frac{1}{2}$?
a. −10
b. $\frac{3}{2}$
c. 6
d. 0

41.

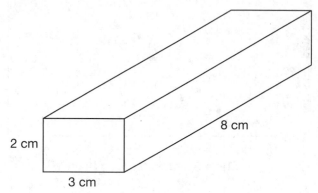

What is the volume of the figure above?
a. 6
b. 24
c. 48
d. 108

42. The bar chart represents the total dollar value of sales for four product versions in July.

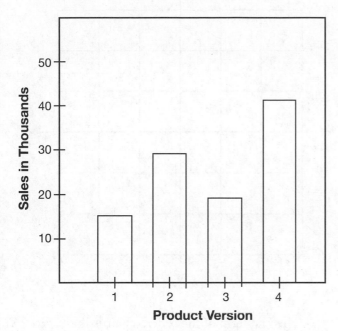

Which two products have combined sales of more than $50,000 in July?
a. Products 1 and 2
b. Products 2 and 3
c. Products 2 and 4
d. Products 1 and 3

43. The surface area of a sphere is 36π cubic meters. To the nearest meter, what is the diameter of this sphere?
a. 3
b. 6
c. 12
d. 24

44. What value of x satisfies the system of equations $x - 2y = 8$ and $x + 2y = 14$?
a. –6
b. 11
c. There are infinitely many values of x that satisfy this system.
d. There are no values of x that satisfy this system.

45. $(x^2 + 5) - (x^2 - x) =$
a. $5 + x$
b. $5 - x$
c. $2x^2 - 5x$
d. $2x^2 + x + 5$

Answers and Explanations

1. **Choice b is correct.** "10 fewer than" implies that 10 should be subtracted from the next stated term. That term is "2 times the number of video games that Joseph owns," or $2v$.

   Choice **a** is incorrect. This expression represents 2 fewer than 10 times the number of video games Joseph owns.

   Choice **c** is incorrect. This expression represents 2 times 10 fewer than the number of video games Joseph owns.

   Choice **d** is incorrect. This expression represents 10 times 2 fewer than the number of video games Joseph owns.

2. **Choice c is correct.** The product in the numerator can be written as $\sqrt[3]{3 \times 3 \times 3 \times 6}$ $= 3\sqrt[3]{6}$. The 3 in the denominator cancels out the 3 in front of the root.

   Choice **a** is incorrect. The numerator is made up of a product. The denominator can only cancel one factor of the numerator.

   Choice **b** is incorrect. The denominator cannot cancel out a factor within a cube root.

   Choice **d** is incorrect. The cube root of 9 is not 3.

3. **Correct answer:** $\sqrt{2}$

   Two factors of 72 are 2 and 36. Further, $\frac{\sqrt{a}}{\sqrt{b}} = \sqrt{\frac{a}{b}}$ for positive numbers a and b.
   Using these properties, $\frac{\sqrt{72}}{\sqrt{36}} = \frac{\sqrt{2 \times 36}}{36} = \sqrt{2}$.

4.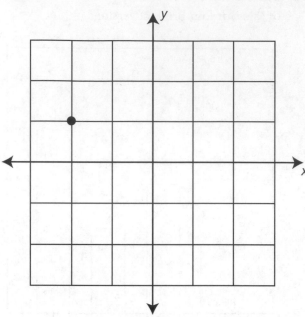

   The first term of the ordered pair is the x-coordinate. Since this is negative, the point will be on the left-hand side of the y-axis. The second term is the y-coordinate. This indicates how many units above the x-axis the point is located.

5. **Choice b is correct.** To cube means to take the number to the third power. Adding 5 to this yields the expression $x^3 + 5$. Finally, multiplying this by 2 yields $2(x^3 + 5)$.

   Choice **a** is incorrect. This represents multiplying the number by 3 as the first step. To cube means to take the number to the third power.

   Choice **c** is incorrect. This represents multiplying by 2 before adding 5.

   Choice **d** is incorrect. Two times x cubed is not equivalent to x to the 6th power.

6. **Choice c is correct.** The original statement can be written as $n + 4 < 5m$. Given the value of m, $5m = 5 \times 6 = 30$, therefore $n + 4 < 30$. This can be simplified further, to $n < 26$.

Choice **a** is incorrect. The original statement can be written as $n + 4 < 5m$. This statement can be used to show what n is less than, but it can't indicate what n is greater than.

Choice **b** is incorrect. The original statement can be written as $n + 4 < 5m$. Given the value of m, $5m = 5 \times 6 = 30$, therefore $n + 4 < 30$. While $n < 26$, it is not necessarily true that $n + 4 < 26$.

Choice **d** is incorrect. The original statement can be written as $n + 4 < 5m$. This statement can be used to show what n is less than, but it can't indicate what n is equal to.

7. **Correct answer: $490.80.** The employee is paid a 4% commission on his sales of $1,020. Therefore, he will be paid $0.04 \times \$1,020 = \$40.80$ for the sales. This is on top of his regular pay of $450. Therefore, his total paycheck will be $450 + \$40.80 = \$490.80$.

8. **Choice b is correct.** The radius of the circle is 5, and the circumference is $2 \times \pi \times (\text{radius})$, or 10π. This can also be found simply by multiplying the diameter and π.

Choice **a** is incorrect. The radius of the circle is 5 and must be doubled in order to find the circumference.

Choice **c** is incorrect. This is the area of the circle, which is found by squaring the radius and multiplying by π.

Choice **d** is incorrect. The diameter does not need to be squared in order to find the circumference.

9. **Choice a is correct.** Applying an exponent to a fraction is equivalent to applying that exponent to the numerator and denominator.

Choice **b** is incorrect. An exponent of 3 is not equivalent to multiplication by 3.

Choice **c** is incorrect. The exponent must be applied to both the numerator and the denominator.

Choice **d** is incorrect. An exponent of 3 is not equivalent to multiplication by 3 and would be applied to both the numerator and the denominator.

10. **Correct answer: (0,–14)**

Since n is parallel to the given line, it must have the same slope, 3. Given this and the point that n passes through, we can use the point-slope formula to determine the equation for n.

$$y - 1 = 3(x - 5)$$
$$y - 1 = 3x - 15$$
$$y = 3x - 14$$

Now that the equation is in the form $y = mx + b$, we can see that the y-intercept is –14. By definition, this means that the line passes over the y-axis at the point (0,–14).

11. **Choice a is correct.** The answer choices are in the form $y = mx + b$. Using the given information, when $x = 4$, $y = 0$, and the slope is $m = -\frac{1}{2}$, this gives the equation $0 = -\frac{1}{2}(4) + b$, which has a solution of $b = 2$.

Choice **b** is incorrect. When solving for the y-intercept b, the –2 must be added to both sides of the equation.

Choice **c** is incorrect. The given point (4,0) is not a y-intercept; it's an x-intercept. The equation $y = mx + b$ uses a y-intercept.

Choice **d** is incorrect. If the x-intercept is (4,0) as given, the y-intercept will be –4 only if the slope is 1. Here the slope is $-\frac{1}{2}$.

12. Choice d is correct. Substituting -1 for the x, $f(-1) = 3(-1-1)^2 + 5 = 3(-2)^2 + 5 = 3(4) + 5 = 12 + 5 = 17$.

Choice **a** is incorrect. When substituting -1 for x, $x - 1$ represents $-1 - 1 = -2$, not multiplication.

Choice **b** is incorrect. It is not true that $(x-1)^2 = x^2 + 1$.

Choice **c** is incorrect. By the order of operations, the subtraction within the parentheses as well as the squaring operation must be performed before the multiplication by 3.

13. Choice c is correct. Using the slope formula first, $m = \frac{5x-1}{4-(-2)} = \frac{4}{6} = \frac{2}{3}$. Now, applying the point-slope formula, we have:

$$y - 1 = \tfrac{2}{3}(x - (-2))$$

$$y - 1 = \tfrac{2}{3}(x + 2)$$

$$y - 1 = \tfrac{2}{3}x + \tfrac{4}{3}$$

$$y = \tfrac{2}{3}x + \tfrac{4}{3} + 1 = \tfrac{2}{3}x + \tfrac{7}{3}$$

Choice **a** is incorrect. In the point-slope formula, the x_1 and y_1 must come from the same point.

Choice **b** is incorrect. When the point $(-2,1)$ is used in the point-slope formula, the result is $y - 1 = m(x - (-2))$. On the right-hand side of this equation, the 2 ends up being positive.

Choice **d** is incorrect. The slope is found using the change in y on the numerator: $\frac{5-1}{4-(-2)} = \frac{4}{6} = \frac{2}{3}$.

14. Choice c is correct. Using the Pythagorean theorem, the hypotenuse of the right triangle formed by the ladder and the building is 9, while the length of one leg is 6. This yields the equation $6^2 + b^2 = 9^2$ or $b^2 = 81 - 36 = 45$. Therefore, $b = \sqrt{45} \approx 6.7$.

Choice **a** is incorrect. The terms in the Pythagorean theorem are squared.

Choice **b** is incorrect. Applying the Pythagorean theorem to this problem yields the equation $6^2 + b^2 = 9^2$. The exponent of 2 indicates to multiply the term by itself twice, not multiply by 2.

Choice **d** is incorrect. The length of the ladder represents the hypotenuse, or c, in the Pythagorean theorem.

15. Choice b is correct. The rate of cooling indicated in the graph is the slope of the line passing through the points $(0,200)$ and $(4,0)$. This slope is -50, which implies the material is losing 50 degrees every hour. The slope of the equation in this answer choice is -60, which implies the material is losing 60 degrees every hour, a faster rate of cooling.

Choice **a** is incorrect. This slope would imply that the material is losing 25 degrees every hour, which is a slower rate of cooling.

Choice **c** is incorrect. This slope would imply that the material is losing 10 degrees every hour, which is a slower rate of cooling.

Choice **d** is incorrect. This slope would indicate the material is losing 50 degrees every hour, which is the same rate of cooling that is given in the graph.

16.

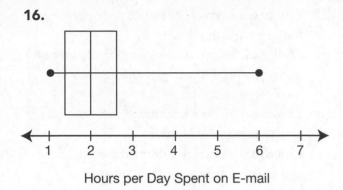

Hours per Day Spent on E-mail

The statement "50% spent more than 2 hours a day composing or reading emails" indicates that the median of this data set is 2. This is typically indicated on a box plot by a vertical line in the center of the box.

17. Choice a is correct. Using the two given points, whenever y increases by 2 units, x increases by 5 units. This means the slope must be $m = \frac{2}{5}$ (the change in y divided by the change in x). Further, the y-intercept is $b = -2$. Using the equation $y = mx + b$, we have $y = \frac{2}{5}x - 2$.

Choice **b** is incorrect. The line rises from left to right; therefore, the slope must be positive.

Choice **c** is incorrect. The x-intercept is not used when writing the equation as $y = mx + b$. In fact, b represents the y-intercept.

Choice **d** is incorrect. The line rises from left to right; therefore, the slope must be positive. Additionally, the y-intercept is -2 and not 5.

18. Choice b is correct. Rewriting the equation by subtracting 14 from both sides yields the quadratic equation $x^2 - 5x - 14 = 0$. The left-hand side of this equation can be factored into $(x - 7)(x + 2)$, indicating that the solutions are 7 and -2.

Choice **a** is incorrect. Once the quadratic equation is rewritten and factored, the zero product rule states that $x - 7 = 0$ or $x + 2 = 0$. Therefore one of the solutions is -2 instead of 2.

Choices **c** and **d** are incorrect. To factor the rewritten quadratic equation, find factors of 14 that sum to -5 instead of numbers that sum to -14.

19. Choice d is correct. To find the slope of the line with this equation, move the y-variable to one side on its own to put the equation in the form $y = mx + b$, where m is the slope. Adding y to both sides and subtracting 2 from both sides gives the equation $y = 10x - 2$, so the slope is 10.

Choice **a** is incorrect. The coefficient of x, not the coefficient of y, represents the slope when the equation is written in the form $y = mx + b$.

Choice **b** is incorrect. The slope cannot be read from the equation in the form it is currently written.

Choice **c** is incorrect. When solving for y to find the slope, 10 will be divided by 1 and not by 2.

20. Choice c is correct. When multiplying terms with the same base, the exponents are added. Therefore $5^{\frac{1}{2}} \times 5^2 = 5^{\frac{1}{2} + 2} = 5^{\frac{1}{2} + \frac{4}{2}} = 5^{\frac{5}{2}}$.

Choice **a** is incorrect. When multiplying terms with the same base, the exponents are added, not subtracted.

Choice **b** is incorrect. When multiplying terms with the same base, the exponents are added, not multiplied.

Choice **d** is incorrect. When multiplying terms with the same base, the exponents are added, not divided.

21. Choice c is correct. $1.2 \times 10^{-3} = 0.0012$ and $10 \times 0.0012 = 0.0120$.

Choice **a** is incorrect. It is not possible for the thickness of ten parts to be smaller than the thickness of one part.

Choice **b** is incorrect. This is the thickness of a single part.

Choice **d** is incorrect. This is the thickness of a stack of 100 such parts.

22. Choice d is correct. The slope will be the negative reciprocal of the given slope, and b in the equation $y = mx + b$ is -4.

Choice **a** is incorrect. The slope of a perpendicular line will be the negative reciprocal of the slope of the original line.

Choice **b** is incorrect. Parallel lines have the same slope, while perpendicular lines have negative reciprocal slopes.

Choice **c** is incorrect. The term added to the x-term will be the y-intercept, which is not -1.

23. Choice a is correct. The division is equivalent to $\frac{3}{x} \times \frac{2}{5x} = \frac{6}{5x^2}$.

Choice **b** is incorrect. The division of two fractions is equivalent to multiplying the first fraction by the reciprocal of the second fraction.

Choice **c** is incorrect. This is the result of multiplying and not dividing the fractions if the 5 cancelled out. There are no terms that would cancel with the 5.

Choice **d** is incorrect. This is the result of multiplying the two fractions.

24. Correct answers: 910 and 1,115. The minimum number of items the factory could produce in this time frame is $16 \times 8 \times 7 = 896$ items, while the maximum is $20 \times 8 \times 7 = 1,120$. Any whole number value in between these numbers is a possible number of items the factory could produce over the given time frame.

25. Choice b is correct. The price per ounce is found by dividing 3.45 by 32.

Choice **a** is incorrect. Dividing the number of ounces by the cost will give the number of ounces per cent.

Choice **c** is incorrect. Subtracting terms will not give an interpretable value.

Choice **d** is incorrect. Adding these two terms will not give an interpretable value.

26. Choice a is correct. The revenue is increasing whenever the graph is rising from left to right. This occurs between weeks 2 and 3.

Choice **b** is incorrect. The revenue is increasing whenever the graph is rising from left to right. This does not occur between weeks 3 and 4.

Choice **c** is incorrect. The revenue is increasing whenever the graph is rising from left to right. This does not occur between weeks 4 and 5.

Choice **d** is incorrect. The revenue is increasing whenever the graph is rising from left to right. This does not occur between weeks 6 and 7.

27.

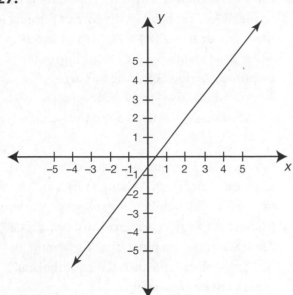

Each of the given lines has a different y-intercept. Solving for y in the given equation will put the equation in $y = mx + b$ form, where b is the y-intercept. In this case, that equation is $y = -\frac{1}{2} + \frac{3}{2}x$. The line given in the image above is the only line with a y-intercept of $-\frac{1}{2}$.

28. Choice c is correct. Since z is perpendicular to $y = -x + 5$, it must have a slope of 1. The given point $(0, -2)$ is a y-intercept since the x-value is 0, so the equation of z must be $y = x - 2$. Plugging in the given y-value of 5 in the point $(x, 5)$ yields the equation $5 = x - 2$, which has the solution $x = 7$.

Choice **a** is incorrect. The y-intercept of the line is -2 and not 5. A perpendicular line does not necessarily have the same y-intercept. Further, the 5 in the point $(x, 5)$ is a y-value and not an x-value.

Choice **b** is incorrect. The 5 in the point $(x, 5)$ is a y-value and not an x-value.

Choice **d** is incorrect. The y-intercept of the line is -2 and not 5. Two perpendicular lines do not necessarily have the same y-intercept.

29. Choice c is correct. Distributing the square root of 2 and simplifying:

$$\sqrt{2}(\sqrt{18} - \sqrt{6}) = \sqrt{36} - \sqrt{12} = 6 - \sqrt{4 \times 3}$$
$$= 6 - 2\sqrt{3}.$$

Choice **a** is incorrect. Radicals and whole numbers are not like terms and therefore cannot be combined.

Choice **b** is incorrect. The square root of 2 must be distributed to both terms. Additionally, the radical and the remaining whole number are not like terms.

Choice **d** is incorrect. The square root of 2 must be distributed to both terms in the parentheses.

30. Choice a is correct. The pattern in the scatterplot has a general upward trend from left to right. This indicates a positive relationship. As one variable increases, the other variable also increases.

Choice **b** is incorrect. A negative relationship would be indicated by a pattern that is generally falling from left to right.

Choice **c** is incorrect. This would be true if, for each point, the x- and y-coordinates were the same. But there are many points where this is not the case.

Choice **d** is incorrect. A general sloping pattern indicates a relationship between the two variables.

31. Choice d is correct. The conversion given can be written as a ratio, 1 mile : 5,280 feet. Using this to cancel out units: $11,088 \text{ ft} \times \frac{1}{5,280} = \frac{11,088}{5,280} = 2.1$.

Choice **a** is incorrect. There is no need to divide by 12 since the units are not in inches.

Choice **b** is incorrect. Dividing 5,280 by 11,088 leaves the units in terms of $\frac{1}{\text{miles}}$, which doesn't make sense.

Choice **c** is incorrect. Subtracting the two values will not give an interpretable value.

32. Choice c is correct. The two steps are to distribute and add exponents. $x^4(x^2 - 6) = x^{4+2} - 6x^4 = x^6 - 6x^4$.

Choice **a** is incorrect. When two terms with the same base are multiplied, their exponents are added. Further, the term x^4 must be distributed to every term in the given binomial $x^2 - 6$.

Choice **b** is incorrect. The term x^4 must be distributed to every term in the given binomial $x^2 - 6$.

Choice **d** is incorrect. When two terms with the same base are multiplied, their exponents are added.

33. Choice a is correct. After increasing by $5.00, the share was worth $15.15. It then decreased in value by 10%, or by $0.1 \times 15.15 = 1.515$. Therefore, at the end of week 2, it was worth $15.15 - $1.515 = $13.635 a share. At the end of week 3, it was worth $13.635 - $1.10 = $12.535. Finally, it doubled in value and was worth $2 \times $12.535 = $25.07 per share.

Choice **b** is incorrect. The stock decreased in value by $1.10 at the end of week 3. This represents subtraction in the problem.

Choice **c** is incorrect. A 10% decrease can be found by multiplying 0.9 and the current value. This answer comes from using 1% or 0.01 as the decrease.

Choice **d** is incorrect. To double means to multiply by 2 and not 4.

34. Choice b is correct. The mode is the most commonly observed value. In this case, 4 occurs the most number of times.

Choice **a** is incorrect. This is the minimum value of the data set.

Choice **c** is incorrect. This is the median of the data set.

Choice **d** is incorrect. This is the range of the data set.

35. Choice b is correct. Given the final question is about an "or" probability, the correct formula to use is $P(A \text{ or } B) = P(A) + P(B) - P(A \text{ and } B)$, where $P(A)$ stands for the probability of the event A occurring. Applying this here:

$P(\text{degree or five years}) = P(\text{degree}) + P(\text{five years}) - P(\text{degree and five years}) = \frac{20}{48} + \frac{15}{48} - \frac{8}{48} = \frac{27}{48} = 0.5625$

Finally, 0.5625 is equivalent to 56.3%.

Choice **a** is incorrect. Although this is an "or" probability, the numbers for college degree and five years of work experience must be included.

Choices **c** and **d** are incorrect. When finding "or" probabilities, the probability of the "and" event must be subtracted.

36. Choice a is correct. If x represents the discount provided by a single coupon, then $2x$ represents the combined discount provided by both. Given the prices before and after, the following equation can be written and solved:

$8.3 - 2x = 7$
$-2x = -1.3$
$x = 0.65$

Choice **b** is incorrect. If each coupon gave a 90-cent discount, the final price would have been $8.30 - $1.80 = $6.50.

Choice **c** is incorrect. This is the value of both coupons together.

Choice **d** is incorrect. The coupons provide a discount of $1.30 together, so it is not possible that one coupon by itself has a larger discount value.

37. The correct answer is 8.1%.

The percent increase can be found by finding the difference between the two prices and then dividing by the original price:

$\frac{334.99 - 309.99}{309.99} = 0.0806$.

Multiplying by 100 to convert this to a percentage yields 8.06%. Rounded, this is 8.1%.

38. Choice a is correct. The equation can be factored and rewritten as $(x - 3)(x + 1) = 0$. Using the zero product rule, this results in the equations $x - 3 = 0$ and $x + 1 = 0$. The solutions to these equations are 3 and –1, respectively.
Choice **b** is incorrect. After factoring, the zero product rule must be applied. This will result in the equations $x - 3 = 0$ and $x + 1 = 0$.
Choices **c** and **d** are incorrect. The solutions can't be read off the coefficients. Instead, factoring, the quadratic formula, or completing the square should be used to solve a quadratic equation like this.

39. Choice c is correct. Subtracting 2 from both sides yields the solution $x > 3$.
Choice **a** is incorrect. In this inequality, the 2 is added to the variable. Therefore, when attempting to isolate the x, both sides should not be multiplied by 2. Instead, 2 should be subtracted from both sides.
Choice **b** is incorrect. In this inequality, the 2 is added to the variable. Therefore when attempting to isolate the x, 2 should be subtracted from both sides instead of being added.
Choice **d** is incorrect. In this inequality, the 2 is added to the variable. Therefore, when attempting to isolate the x, both sides should not be divided by 2. Instead, 2 should be subtracted from both sides.

40. Choice c is correct. After plugging in the given value of x, we must simplify the result using basic operations with fractions:
$$\frac{\frac{1}{2} - 5}{\frac{1}{4} - 1} = \frac{\frac{1}{2} - \frac{10}{2}}{\frac{1}{4} - \frac{4}{4}} = \frac{-\frac{9}{2}}{-\frac{3}{4}} = \frac{9}{2} \times \frac{4}{3} = \frac{36}{6} = 6$$
Choice **a** is incorrect. When plugging in the given value of x, the 5 is subtracted, not multiplied.
Choice **b** is incorrect. When simplifying a fraction over a fraction, the fraction in the numerator is multiplied by the reciprocal of the fraction in the denominator. Dividing the fractions piece by piece is not a valid method.
Choice **d** is incorrect. Taking a value to the power of two is not the same as multiplying it by two. Furthermore, a fraction with a denominator of zero is undefined, not equal to zero.

41. Choice c is correct. The area of the base is $2 \times 3 = 6$ square centimeters. Multiplying this by the height of 8 cm gives us the volume in cubic centimeters: $6 \times 8 = 48$.
Choice **a** is incorrect. This is the area of one of the smaller faces.
Choice **b** is incorrect. This is the area of one of the larger faces.
Choice **d** is incorrect. This is the surface area of the given shape.

42. Choice c is correct. Since product 2 had almost $30,000 in sales and product 4 had over $40,000 in sales, the total must be more than $50,000.
Choice **a** is incorrect. The total sales in July for these two products was about $45,000.
Choice **b** is incorrect. The total sales in July for these two products was slightly less than $50,000.
Choice **d** is incorrect. The total sales in July for these two products was about $35,000.

43. Choice b is correct. Using the surface area formula:
$$36\pi = 4\pi r^2$$
$$9 = r^2$$
$$r = 3$$
Since the radius is 3, the diameter is $3 \times 2 = 6$.
Choice **a** is incorrect. This is the radius of the sphere. The diameter is twice as large as the radius.
Choice **c** is incorrect. When solving the equation $36\pi = 4\pi r^2$, divide, do not multiply, both sides by 4. Additionally, the diameter will be two times as large as the radius.
Choice **d** is incorrect. When solving the equation $36\pi = 4\pi r^2$, divide, do not multiply, both sides by 4.

44. Choice b is correct. Using the addition method, adding the two equations yields the equation $2x = 22$, which has a solution of $x = 11$.
Choice **a** is incorrect. Subtracting the two equations will eliminate the x from both equations, making it where y must be found first.
Choice **c** is incorrect. If there were infinitely many solutions, the equations would be multiples of each other.
Choice **d** is incorrect. If there was no solution, the equation would yield an incorrect statement such as $0 = 1$ or $-5 = 3$.

45. Choice a is correct. Distributing the negative and combining like terms yields $(x^2 + 5) - (x^2 - x) = x^2 + 5 - x^2 - (-x) = 5 + x$.
Choice **b** is incorrect. The negative must be distributed to every term in the parentheses.
Choice **c** is incorrect. Since the second term is being subtracted, the x^2 terms will cancel out. Further, the 5 and the x are not being multiplied.
Choice **d** is incorrect. Since the second term is being subtracted, the x^2 terms will cancel out.

This practice test is modeled on the format, content, and timing of the official GED® Reasoning through Language Arts test.

Part I

Like the official exam, this section presents a series of questions that assess your ability to read, write, edit, and understand standard written English. You'll be asked to answer questions based on informational and literary reading passages. Refer to the passages as often as necessary when answering the questions.

Work carefully, but do not spend too much time on any one question. Be sure you answer every question.

Set a timer for 95 minutes (1 hour and 35 minutes), and try to take this test uninterrupted, under quiet conditions.

Part II

The official GED® Reasoning through Language Arts test also includes an essay question, called the Extended Response. Set a timer for 45 minutes, and try to read the given passage and then brainstorm, write, and proofread your essay without interruption, under quiet conditions.

Complete answer explanations for every test question and sample essays at different scoring levels follow the exam. Good luck!

Part I

48 Questions
95 Minutes

Please use the following to answer questions 1–6.

Remarks by the First Lady on a visit to thank USDA employees.

May 3, 2013

1   Thank you for supporting our farmers and our ranchers and working tirelessly to market their products across the globe, which, by the way, helps to create jobs right here at home. Thank you for protecting our environment by promoting renewable energy sources that will power our country for generations to come. So that's an impact on not just us but our children and our grandchildren and their children. Thank you for that work. Thank you for lifting up rural communities. And thank you for keeping our food safe. And I think this is something most of the country doesn't realize—the work that you do here to protect the environment, you keep our food safe, working to end hunger, improve nutrition for families across this country.

2   And the nutrition issue, as Tom mentioned, as you all know, is something near and dear to my heart, not just as First Lady but as a mother. In fact, one of the first things that I did as, you know, as First Lady, was to plant the garden at the White House. And it's really pretty. [*Laughter.*] I hope you guys get a chance to see it—it's beautiful now. It rained a couple of days. Thank you. [*Laughter.*] And the idea with planting the garden wasn't just to encourage kids to eat more vegetables. I also wanted to teach them about where their food comes from.

3   I think you've known this—we see this as we traveled around the country—some kids have never seen what a real tomato looks like off the vine. They don't know where a cucumber comes from. And that really affects the way they view food. So a garden helps them really get their hands dirty, literally, and understand the whole process of where their food comes from. And I wanted them to see just how challenging and rewarding it is to grow your own food, so that they would better understand what our farmers are doing every single day across this country and have an appreciation for that work, that tradition—that American tradition of growing our own food and feeding ourselves.

4   And the garden helped spark a conversation in this country about healthy eating that led us to create Let's Move. As you know, it's a nationwide initiative to end childhood obesity in this country in a generation, so that all of our kids can grow up healthy. And all of you all at USDA, let me just tell you, have been such a critical part of this effort right from the very start. This would not happen—all the conversation, all the movement around health—that's all because of so many of you right here in this room and throughout this building, and in agencies and facilities all over this country. You helped to launch our new MyPlate icon, which is changing the way families serve their meals and gives them a really easy way to understand what a healthy plate looks like.

1. What is the likely overall purpose or intent of the passage?
   a. to discuss the programs Mrs. Obama began with the goal of inspiring kids to eat healthier
   b. to thank farmers for their work
   c. to introduce Mrs. Obama's nutrition initiative
   d. to emphasize the important role of USDA employees in creating good nutrition in the United States

2. Write your response in the box below.

   According to Mrs. Obama, [   ] mentioned that the nutrition issue is something near and dear to her heart.

3. Based on the passage, Mrs. Obama would most likely
   a. take her children to watch a professional basketball game.
   b. spend an evening teaching her children how to cook dinner.
   c. organize a family game night.
   d. spend an afternoon playing soccer with her husband, the president.

4. Which statement is NOT supporting evidence that the health of United States citizens is important to the First Lady?
   a. "Thank you for protecting our environment by promoting renewable energy sources that will power our country for generations to come."
   b. "And thank you for keeping our food safe."
   c. "And the nutrition issue, as Tom mentioned, as you all know, is something near and dear to my heart not just as a First Lady but as a mother."
   d. "You helped to launch our new MyPlate icon, which is changing the way families serve their meals and gives them a really easy way to understand what a healthy plate looks like."

5. Which of the following is a synonym of the word **initiative** as it's used in this sentence: "It's a nationwide initiative to end childhood obesity in this country in a generation, so that all our kids can grow up healthy"?
   a. program
   b. enthusiasm
   c. disinterest
   d. involvement

6. How does the inclusion of Paragraph 3 affect the overall theme of the passage?
   a. It damages Mrs. Obama's claim.
   b. It strengthens Mrs. Obama's position.
   c. It has no effect on the overall theme.
   d. It intentionally confuses the reader.

Please use the following to answer questions 7–11.

Excerpt from "The Cask of Amontillado," by Edgar Allan Poe

1 He had a weak point—this Fortunato—although in other regards he was a man to be respected and even feared. He prided himself on his connoisseurship in wine. Few Italians have the true virtuoso spirit. For the most part their enthusiasm is adopted to suit the time and opportunity, to practice imposture upon the British and Austrian millionaires. In painting and gemmary, Fortunato, like his countrymen, was a quack, but in the matter of old wines he was sincere. In this respect I did not differ from him materially—I was skillful in the Italian vintages myself, and bought largely whenever I could.

2 It was about dusk, one evening during the supreme madness of the carnival season, that I encountered my friend. He accosted me with excessive warmth, for he had been drinking much. The man wore motley. He had on a tight-fitting parti-striped dress, and his head was surmounted by the conical cap and bells. I was so pleased to see him that I thought I should never have done wringing his hand.

3 I said to him—"My dear Fortunato, you are luckily met. How remarkably well you are looking today. But I have received a pipe of what passes for Amontillado, and I have my doubts."

4 "How?" said he. "Amontillado, a pipe? Impossible! And in the middle of the carnival!"

5 "I have my doubts," I replied, "and I was silly enough to pay the full Amontillado price without consulting you in the matter. You were not to be found, and I was fearful of losing a bargain."

6 "Amontillado!"

7 "I have my doubts."

8 "Amontillado!"

9 "And I must satisfy them."

10 "Amontillado!"

11 "As you are engaged, I am on my way to Luchresi. If anyone has a critical turn it is he. He will tell me—"

12 "Luchresi cannot tell Amontillado from Sherry."

13 "And yet some fools will have it that his taste is a match for your own.

14 "Come, let us go."

15 "Whither?"

16 "To your vaults."

17 "My friend, no; I will not impose upon your good nature. I perceive you have an engagement. Luchresi—"

18 "I have no engagement—come."

19 "My friend, no. It is not the engagement but the severe cold with which I perceive you are afflicted. The vaults are insufferably damp. They are encrusted with nitre."

20 "Let us go, nevertheless. The cold is merely nothing. Amontillado! You have been imposed upon. And as for Luchresi, he cannot distinguish Sherry from Amontillado."

21 Thus speaking, Fortunato possessed himself of my arm; and putting on a mask of black silk and drawing a roquelaire closely about my person, I suffered him to hurry me to my palazzo.

7. Who are Fortunato's "countrymen"?
- **a.** Italians
- **b.** Britons
- **c.** Austrians
- **d.** Spaniards

8. What do Fortunato and the narrator have in common?
- **a.** an interest in Italian history
- **b.** they are wearing the same clothing
- **c.** a passion for wine
- **d.** a love of the carnival season

9. Which statement, in context, is NOT supporting evidence that Fortunato has a passion for wine?
- **a.** "But in the matter of old wines he was sincere."
- **b.** "I was so pleased to see him that I thought I should never have done wringing his hand."
- **c.** "Luchresi cannot tell Amontillado from Sherry."
- **d.** "The cold is merely nothing. Amontillado!"

10. In the context of the story, which of the following is an example of irony?
- **a.** "He prided himself on his connoisseurship in wine."
- **b.** "For most part their enthusiasm is adopted to suit the time and opportunity. . . ."
- **c.** "My dear Fortunato, you are luckily met."
- **d.** "The vaults are insufferably damp."

11. Why does the narrator first insist that he will ask Luchresi's opinion of the Amontillado?
- **a.** because Luchresi has more expertise in wine than Fortunato does
- **b.** because Fortunato and the narrator are known enemies
- **c.** to gain the trust of Fortunato
- **d.** to prey on Fortunato's pride

Please use the following to answer questions 12–16.

Excerpt from "My First Lie, and How I Got Out of It," by Mark Twain

1 I do not remember my first lie, it is too far back; but I remember my second one very well. I was nine days old at the time, and had noticed that if a pin was sticking in me and I advertised it in the usual fashion, I was lovingly petted and coddled and pitied in a most agreeable way and got a ration between meals besides.

2 It was human nature to want to get these riches, and I fell. I lied about the pin—advertising one when there wasn't any. You would have done it; George Washington did it, anybody would have done it. During the first half of my life I never knew a child that was able to raise above that temptation and keep from telling that lie. Up to 1867 all the civilized children that were ever born into the world were liars—including George. Then the safety pin came in and blocked the game. But is that reform worth anything? No; for it is reform by force and has no virtue in it; it merely stops that form of lying, it doesn't impair the disposition to lie, by a shade. It is the cradle application of conversion by fire and sword, or of the temperance principle through prohibition.

3 To return to that early lie. They found no pin and they realized that another liar had been added to the world's supply. For by grace of a rare inspiration a quite commonplace but seldom noticed

(continues)

fact was borne in upon their understandings—that almost all lies are acts, and speech has no part in them. Then, if they examined a little further they recognized that all people are liars from the cradle onward, without exception, and that they begin to lie as soon as they wake in the morning, and keep it up without rest or refreshment until they go to sleep at night. If they arrived at that truth it probably grieved them—did, if they had been heedlessly and ignorantly educated by their books and teachers; for why should a person grieve over a thing which by the eternal law of his make he cannot help? He didn't invent the law; it is merely his business to obey it and keep it still; join the universal conspiracy and keep so still that he shall deceive his fellow-conspirators into imagining that he doesn't know that the law exists. It is what we all do—we that know. I am speaking of *the lie of silent assertion*; we can tell it without saying a word, and we all do it—we that know. In the magnitude of its territorial spread it is one of the most majestic lies that the civilizations make it their sacred and anxious care to guard and watch and propagate.

4 For instance. It would not be possible for a humane and intelligent person to invent a rational excuse for slavery; yet you will remember that in the early days of the emancipation agitation in the North the agitators got but small help or countenance from anyone. Argue and plead and pray as they might, they could not break the universal stillness that reigned, from pulpit and press all the way down to the bottom of society—the clammy stillness created and maintained by the lie of silent assertion—the silent assertion that there wasn't anything going on in which humane and intelligent people were interested.

12. Which of the following can be inferred from the first two paragraphs?
   a. The author grew up in the same state as George Washington.
   b. Before 1867, parents punished infants by poking them with pins.
   c. Before 1867, infants wore diapers fastened with straight pins.
   d. Safety pins were critical to eliminating a child's disposition to lie.

13. In the first two paragraphs, which of the following does the author present as evidence that humans are born liars?
   a. scientific data
   b. personal experience
   c. physical evidence
   d. historical documentation

14. Which of the following best expresses the author's position on lying?
   a. It should be forbidden.
   b. It should be forgiven, but only for children.
   c. It should be studied so that its cause can be found and eliminated.
   d. It should be accepted as a fundamental part of human nature.

15. Based on the fourth paragraph, why does the author think that slavery was allowed to continue for so long?
   a. because people acted as though it was not an important issue
   b. because people understood the economic importance of slaves to the South
   c. because slave owners lied to everyone else about how they treated their slaves
   d. because agitators in the North didn't state their case

16. Which of the following details does NOT support the main idea of the passage?
   a. Even babies have a disposition to lie.
   b. The introduction of the safety pin occurred in 1867.
   c. People often lie through acts rather than words.
   d. Early opponents of slavery faced indifference from society.

Please use the following to answer questions 17–20.

Rebecca Garcia, Executive Director
Abacus Childcare
2404 Bellevue Ave
Baton Rouge, LA 70810

(1) I would like to submit an application for the childcare position that was recently posted on your website. I've (2) with children in varying capacities for almost four years, and absolutely love kids of all ages. I have a high energy level and infinite amount of patience that blends well with successfully managing a group of children.

(3), I nannied two preschool-aged twins before they entered kindergarten. During that time, I learned to effectively develop entertaining and educational activities, manage disputes and disruptive behavior in a caring yet firm manner, and maintain a safe environment in the home. I also helped teach the children proper manners, personal cleanliness, and appropriate social skills. I believe the time I spent working with the family allowed me to develop excellent communication skills and management capabilities.

Outside of my work experience, I'm detail-oriented and very organized. I pride myself in (4) problem-solving abilities and love working hard to provide value to my work environment. I am dependable, always on time, and keep the promises that I make.

I would love to speak with you regarding the position if you feel like I would be a good fit on your team. I have attached my resume with contact information and have three references available upon request.

Thank you for your time,

Mallory Holloway

17. Which is the correct choice for (1)?
   a. Dear Ms. Dyer,
   b. dear ms. dyer,
   c. dear ms. Dyer,
   d. Dear ms. dyer,

18. What is the correct form of the verb "to work" in (2)?
   a. to work
   b. works
   c. worked
   d. work

19. Which transitional word fits best in the beginning of (3)?
   a. Recently
   b. Currently
   c. However
   d. In addition

20. Which of the following is a correct fit for (4)?
   a. your
   b. me
   c. my
   d. mine

Please use the following to answer questions 21–24.

John F. Kennedy's Inaugural Address, 1961

1 Vice President Johnson, Mr. Speaker, Mr. Chief Justice, President Eisenhower, Vice President Nixon, President Truman, Reverend Clergy, fellow citizens:

2 We observe today not a victory of party but a celebration of freedom—symbolizing an end as well as a beginning—signifying renewal as well as change. For I have sworn before you the same solemn oath our forebears prescribed nearly a century and three quarters ago.

3 The world is very different now. For man holds in his mortal hands the power to abolish all forms of human poverty and all forms of human life. And yet the same revolutionary beliefs for which our forebears fought are still at issue around the globe.

4 We dare not forget today that we are the heirs of that first revolution. Let the word go forth from this time and place, to friend and foe alike, that the torch has been passed to a new generation of Americans—born in this century, tempered by war, disciplined by a hard and bitter peace, proud of our ancient heritage—and unwilling to witness or permit the slow undoing of those human rights to which this nation has always been committed, and to which we are committed today at home and around the world.

5 Let every nation know, whether it wishes us well or ill, that we shall pay any price, bear any burden, meet any hardship, support any friend, oppose any foe, to assure the survival and the success of liberty.

6 This much we pledge—and more.

7 To those old allies whose cultural and spiritual origins we share, we pledge the loyalty of faithful friends. United, there is little we cannot do in a host of cooperative ventures. Divided, there is little we can do—for we dare not meet a powerful challenge at odds and split asunder.

8 To those new states whom we welcome to the ranks of the free, we pledge our word that one form of colonial control shall not have passed away merely to be replaced by a far more iron tyranny. We shall not always expect to find them supporting our view. But we shall always hope to find them strongly supporting their own freedom—and to remember that, in the past, those who foolishly sought power by riding the back of the tiger ended up inside.

9 To those peoples in the villages of half the globe struggling to break the bonds of mass misery, we pledge our best efforts to help them help themselves, for whatever period is required—not because the communists may be doing it, not because we seek their votes, but because it is right. If a free society cannot help the many who are poor, it cannot save the few who are rich.

10 To our sister republics south of our border, we offer a special pledge—to convert our good words into good deeds—in a new alliance for progress—to assist free men and free governments in casting off the chains of poverty. But this peaceful revolution of hope cannot become the prey of hostile powers. Let all our neighbors know that we shall join with them to oppose aggression or subversion anywhere in the Americas. And let every other power know that this hemisphere intends to remain the master of its own house.

11 To that world assembly of sovereign states, the United Nations, our last best hope in an age where the instruments of war have far outpaced the instruments of peace, we renew our pledge of support—to prevent it from becoming merely a forum for invective—to strengthen its shield of the new and the weak—and to enlarge the area in which its writ may run.

12 Finally, to those nations who would make themselves our adversary, we offer not a pledge but a request: that both sides begin anew the quest for peace, before the dark powers of destruction unleashed by science engulf all humanity in planned or accidental self-destruction.

21. Which sentence best represents the theme of the speech?
   a. "We observe today not a victory of party but a celebration of freedom—symbolizing an end as well as a beginning—signifying renewal as well as change."
   b. "We dare not forget today that we are the heirs of that first revolution."
   c. "But this peaceful revolution of hope cannot become the prey of hostile powers."
   d. "Let all our neighbors know that we shall join with them to oppose aggression or subversion anywhere in the Americas."

22. What word or phrase signifies to the reader the meaning of the word **tyranny** in the following sentence? "To those new states whom we welcome to the ranks of the free, we pledge our word that one form of colonial control shall not have passed away merely to be replaced by a far more iron tyranny."
   a. new states
   b. ranks of the free
   c. colonial control
   d. iron

23. What is the purpose of repeating "little we cannot do" and "little we can do" in the following sentence? "United, there is little we cannot do in a host of cooperative ventures. Divided, there is little we can do—for we dare not meet a powerful challenge at odds and split asunder."

a. to contrast the difference between being united and being divided

b. to highlight the similarity of being united and being divided

c. to stress the United States' role in foreign politics

d. to promise what Kennedy wants to accomplish during his presidency

24. From the list of 5 choices below, circle *all* of the characteristics that Kennedy displays in this speech.

1. fear
2. a strong will
3. compassion
4. morality
5. aggression

Please use the following to answer questions 25–30.

Franklin Delano Roosevelt's Pearl Harbor Address to the Nation, 1941

> 1 Mr. Vice President, Mr. Speaker, Members of the Senate, and of the House of Representatives:
>
> 2 Yesterday, December 7, 1941—a date which will live in infamy—the United States of America was suddenly and deliberately attacked by naval and air forces of the Empire of Japan.
>
> 3 The United States was at peace with that nation and, at the solicitation of Japan, was still in conversation with its government and its emperor looking toward the maintenance of peace in the Pacific.
>
> 4 Indeed, one hour after Japanese air squadrons had commenced bombing in the American island of Oahu, the Japanese ambassador to the United States and his colleague delivered to our Secretary of State a formal reply to a recent American message. And while this reply stated that it seemed useless to continue the existing diplomatic negotiations, it contained no threat or hint of war or of armed attack.
>
> 5 It will be recorded that the distance of Hawaii from Japan makes it obvious that the attack was deliberately planned many days or even weeks ago. During the intervening time, the Japanese government has deliberately sought to deceive the United States by false statements and expressions of hope for continued peace.
>
> 6 The attack yesterday on the Hawaiian Islands has caused severe damage to American naval and military forces. I regret to tell you that very many American lives have been lost. In addition, American ships have been reported torpedoed on the high seas between San Francisco and Honolulu.
>
> 7 Yesterday, the Japanese government also launched an attack against Malaya.

(continues)

8 Last night, Japanese forces attacked Hong Kong.

9 Last night, Japanese forces attacked Guam.

10 Last night, Japanese forces attacked the Philippine Islands.

11 Last night, the Japanese attacked Wake Island.

12 And this morning, the Japanese attacked Midway Island.

13 Japan has, therefore, undertaken a surprise offensive extending throughout the Pacific area. The facts of yesterday and today speak for themselves. The people of the United States have already formed their opinions and well understand the implications to the very life and safety of our nation.

14 As Commander in Chief of the Army and Navy, I have directed that all measures be taken for our defense. But always will our whole nation remember the character of the onslaught against us.

15 No matter how long it may take us to overcome this premeditated invasion, the American people in their righteous might will win through to absolute victory.

16 I believe that I interpret the will of the Congress and of the people when I assert that we will not only defend ourselves to the uttermost but will make it very certain that this form of treachery shall never again endanger us.

17 Hostilities exist. There is no blinking at the fact that our people, our territory, and our interests are in grave danger.

18 With confidence in our armed forces, with the unbounding determination of our people, we will gain the inevitable triumph.

19 I ask that the Congress declare that since the unprovoked and dastardly attack by Japan on Sunday, December 7, 1941, a state of war has existed between the United States and the Japanese empire.

25. What is the tone of the address?
   a. shocked but assertive
   b. timid and fearful
   c. surprised and scared
   d. insecure yet aggressive

26. What purpose does the word **indeed** serve in the third paragraph?
   A. to conclude his former idea
   B. to alert the audience of a new premise
   c. to emphasize the surprise of the attack
   d. to introduce a new theme in the speech

27. What can be inferred from the first sentence in paragraph 5?
   a. Japan is close to Hawaii.
   b. Japan and Hawaii are a significant distance apart.
   c. The United States mainland is as close to Hawaii as Japan is.
   d. Japan announced that it was going to attack.

28. What is the purpose of repeating the phrase "Last night, Japanese forces attacked"?
 a. to show that Japanese forces were disorganized
 b. to emphasize that it is cowardly to attack at night
 c. to show how other countries are united against Japan
 d. to emphasize the extent of Japan's attack

29. Which of the following describes "the character of the onslaught against us"?
 a. expected
 b. aggressive
 c. regretful
 d. unintentional

30. Which of the following is NOT evidence that the attack came as a surprise?
 a. "The United States was at peace with that nation."
 b. "One hour after Japanese squadrons had commenced bombing in the American island of Oahu, the Japanese Ambassador to the United States and his colleague delivered to our Secretary of State a formal reply to a recent American message."
 c. "During the intervening time, the Japanese government has deliberately sought to deceive the United States by false statements and expressions of hope for continued peace."
 d. "Hostilities exist."

Please use the following to answer questions 31–34.

Memo to: All Employees
From: Alexandra Chandler
Subject: Work Hours

Hello all!

(1) Beginning next week, we will poll the office in order to receive everyone's input as we modify work hours.

The company (2) they want to change the schedule in order to better fit the needs of the employees. We will have three options to choose from. The first option is to keep the work schedule as it is currently: 9 to 5, Monday through Friday. The second option is to work one more hour per day on Monday through Thursday, but work only half a day on Friday. The third option is to work two extra hours on Monday through Thursday, and have Fridays off.

Although (3) completely open to all three options, the members of the executive board feel that the second option may fit the goals of the company and employees the best. Many of us already stay to work late at the beginning of the week, and the extra hour would not feel unnatural. We have also noticed that on (4). We understand this to be normal behavior and want to alter hours so that we can better serve you.

We think that the second option would fit well with the patterns we have already observed; however, we still want your opinions. We will be sending questionnaires via email for you to fill out within the week. Please take some time to think about your responses before completing the survey as we want the possible change to best reflect the needs of the office.

Please keep a lookout for the questionnaire and return it to us by the end of next week.

Thank you for your time,

Alexandra Chandler

31. Which choice fits correctly in (1)?
   a. We are announcing some really big changes that might really affect us in the next few months.
   b. We would like to announce some potential changes affecting our team in the next few months.
   c. FYI, stuff might be different soon.
   d. PS: Thank you for your cooperation.

32. Choose the correct form of **decide** for (2).
   a. will decide
   b. has decided
   c. decides
   d. decide

33. Which choice fits correctly in (3)?
   a. there
   b. their
   c. they is
   d. they are

34. Which choice fits correctly in (4)?
   a. Friday, afternoons employee activity drops
   b. Friday afternoons employee, activity drops
   c. Friday afternoons, employee activity drops
   d. Friday afternoons employee activity, drops

Please use the following to answer questions 35–42.

Excerpt from Barack Obama's First Inaugural Address, January 20, 2009

1 In reaffirming the greatness of our nation we understand that greatness is never a given. It must be earned. Our journey has never been one of short cuts or settling for less. It has not been the path for the faint-hearted, for those that prefer leisure over work, or seek only the pleasures of riches and fame. Rather, it has been the risk-takers, the doers, the makers of things—some celebrated, but more often men and women obscure in their labor—who have carried us up the long rugged path towards prosperity and freedom.

2 For us, they packed up their few worldly possessions and traveled across oceans in search of a new life. For us, they toiled in sweatshops, and settled the West, endured the lash of the whip, and plowed the hard earth. For us, they fought and died in places like Concord and Gettysburg, Normandy and Khe Sahn.

3 Time and again these men and women struggled and sacrificed and worked till their hands were raw so that we might live a better life. They saw America as bigger than the sum of our individual ambitions, greater than all the differences of birth or wealth or faction.

4 This is the journey we continue today. We remain the most prosperous, powerful nation on Earth. Our workers are no less productive than when this crisis began. Our minds are no less inventive, our goods and services no less needed than they were last week, or last month, or last year. Our capacity remains undiminished. But our time of standing pat, of protecting narrow interests and putting off unpleasant decisions—that time has surely passed. Starting today, we must pick ourselves up, dust ourselves off, and begin again the work of remaking America.

5 For everywhere we look, there is work to be done. The state of our economy calls for action, bold and swift. And we will act, not only to create new jobs but to lay a new foundation for growth. We

(continues)

will build the roads and bridges, the electric grids and digital lines that feed our commerce and bind us together. We'll restore science to its rightful place and wield technology's wonders to raise health care's quality and lower its cost. We will harness the sun and the winds and the soil to fuel our cars and run our factories. And we will transform our schools and colleges and universities to meet the demands of a new age. All this we can do. All this we will do.

6   Now, there are some who question the scale of our ambitions, who suggest that our system cannot tolerate too many big plans. Their memories are short, for they have forgotten what this country has already done, what free men and women can achieve when imagination is joined to common purpose and necessity to courage. What the cynics fail to understand is that the ground has shifted beneath them, that the stale political arguments that have consumed us for so long no longer apply.

7   The question we ask today is not whether our government is too big or too small, but whether it works—whether it helps families find jobs at a decent wage, care they can afford, a retirement that is dignified. Where the answer is yes, we intend to move forward. Where the answer is no, programs will end. And those of us who manage the public's dollars will be held to account, to spend wisely, reform bad habits, and do our business in the light of day, because only then can we restore the vital trust between a people and their government.

Excerpt from Barack Obama's Second Inaugural Address, January 21, 2013

1   We, the people, still believe that every citizen deserves a basic measure of security and dignity. We must make the hard choices to reduce the cost of health care and the size of our deficit. But we reject the belief that America must choose between caring for the generation that built this country and investing in the generation that will build its future. For we remember the lessons of our past, when twilight years were spent in poverty, and parents of a child with a disability had nowhere to turn. We do not believe that in this country, freedom is reserved for the lucky, or happiness for the few. We recognize that no matter how responsibly we live our lives, any one of us, at any time, may face a job loss, or a sudden illness, or a home swept away in a terrible storm. The commitments we make to each other—through Medicare, and Medicaid, and Social Security—these things do not sap our initiative; they strengthen us. They do not make us a nation of takers; they free us to take the risks that make this country great.

2   We, the people, still believe that our obligations as Americans are not just to ourselves, but to all posterity. We will respond to the threat of climate change, knowing that the failure to do so would betray our children and future generations. Some may still deny the overwhelming judgment of science, but none can avoid the devastating impact of raging fires, and crippling drought, and more powerful storms. The path towards sustainable energy sources will be long and sometimes difficult. But America cannot resist this transition; we must lead it. We cannot cede to other nations the technology that will power new jobs and new industries—we must claim its promise.

(continues)

That's how we will maintain our economic vitality and our national treasure—our forests and waterways; our croplands and snowcapped peaks. That is how we will preserve our planet, commanded to our care by God. That's what will lend meaning to the creed our fathers once declared.

3　We, the people, still believe that enduring security and lasting peace do not require perpetual war. Our brave men and women in uniform, tempered by the flames of battle, are unmatched in skill and courage. Our citizens, seared by the memory of those we have lost, know too well the price that is paid for liberty. The knowledge of their sacrifice will keep us forever vigilant against those who would do us harm. But we are also heirs to those who won the peace and not just the war, who turned sworn enemies into the surest of friends, and we must carry those lessons into this time as well.

4　We will defend our people and uphold our values through strength of arms and rule of law. We will show the courage to try and resolve our differences with other nations peacefully—not because we are naïve about the dangers we face, but because engagement can more durably lift suspicion and fear. America will remain the anchor of strong alliances in every corner of the globe; and we will renew those institutions that extend our capacity to manage crisis abroad, for no one has a greater stake in a peaceful world than its most powerful nation. We will support democracy from Asia to Africa; from the Americas to the Middle East, because our interests and our conscience compel us to act on behalf of those who long for freedom. And we must be a source of hope to the poor, the sick, the marginalized, the victims of prejudice—not out of mere charity, but because peace in our time requires the constant advance of those principles that our common creed describes: tolerance and opportunity; human dignity and justice.

35. Which best summarizes the main idea expressed in the first paragraph of Obama's First Inaugural Address?
  a. Luck made the United States a successful and great nation.
  b. Those who worked hard and took risks shaped America.
  c. The United States is a great nation, and hard work will keep it so.
  d. Obama feels very fortunate to have been elected president.

36. Which sentence's meaning is strengthened by the "men and women [who] sacrificed and struggled" mentioned in the first three paragraphs of Obama's First Inaugural Address?
  a. "Our capacity remains undiminished."
  b. "For everywhere we look, there is work to be done."
  c. "We'll restore science to its rightful place, and wield technology's wonders to raise healthcare's quality and lower its cost."
  d. "Their memories are short, for they have forgotten what this country has already done, what free men and women can achieve when imagination is joined to a common purpose, and necessity to courage."

37. From the list of five choices below, circle *all* of the phrases that support the main idea of Obama's First Inaugural Address.

1. "Our journey has never been one of shortcuts or settling for less."
2. "This is the journey we continue today."
3. "All this we can do. All this we will do."
4. "We will harness the sun and the winds and the soil to fuel our cars and run our factories."
5. "What the cynics fail to understand is that the ground has shifted beneath them, that the stale political arguments that have consumed us for so long no longer apply."

38. What is Obama's purpose in beginning each of the first three paragraphs of his second inaugural address with "We, the people"?

a. to show American pride
b. to stress past successes in order to prove the country does not need to change
c. to quote the Preamble
d. to emphasize the theme of betterment in the United States of America

39. What is the effect of repeating the words **generation** and **build** to compare "the generation that built this country" with the "generation that will build the future?"

a. to emphasize that he is talking about the same people
b. to create a connection between the past and the future
c. to show that he thinks the next generation will be better than the last
d. to emphasize that both generations still have work to do

40. Which of the following does not support Obama's claim in his Second Inaugural Address that Americans feel an obligation to future generations?

a. "For we remember the lessons of our past, when twilight years were spent in poverty, and parents of a child with a disability had nowhere to turn."
b. "We will respond to the threat of climate change, knowing that the failure to do so would betray our children and future generations."
c. "Time and again these men and women struggled and sacrificed and worked till their hands were raw so that we might live a better life."
d. "We will defend our people and uphold our values through strength of arms and rule of law."

41. Where will Obama support democracy, according to his Second Inaugural Address?

a. in the Americas
b. worldwide
c. in Europe
d. in the Middle East

42. Which of the following sentences from the Second Inaugural Address best fits into the theme of the First Inaugural Address?

a. "They do not make us a nation of takers; they free us to take the risks that make this country great."
b. "That's what will lend meaning to the creed our fathers once declared."
c. "We, the people, still believe that enduring security and a lasting peace do not require perpetual war."
d. "We must make the hard choices to reduce the cost of health care and the size of our deficit."

Please use the following to answer questions 43–48.

Remarks upon Signing the Civil Rights Bill (July 2, 1964), Lyndon Baines Johnson

1 My fellow Americans:

2 I am about to sign into law the Civil Rights Act of 1964. I want to take this occasion to talk to you about what that law means to every American.

3 One hundred and eighty-eight years ago this week a small band of valiant men began a long struggle for freedom. They pledged their lives, their fortunes, and their sacred honor not only to found a nation, but to forge an ideal of freedom—not only for political independence, but for personal liberty—not only to eliminate foreign rule, but to establish the rule of justice in the affairs of men.

4 That struggle was a turning point in our history. Today in far corners of distant continents, the ideals of those American patriots still shape the struggles of men who hunger for freedom.

5 This is a proud triumph. Yet those who founded our country knew that freedom would be secure only if each generation fought to renew and enlarge its meaning. From the minutemen at Concord to the soldiers in Viet-Nam, each generation has been equal to that trust.

6 Americans of every race and color have died in battle to protect our freedom. Americans of every race and color have worked to build a nation of widening opportunities. Now our generation of Americans has been called on to continue the unending search for justice within our own borders.

7 We believe that all men are created equal. Yet many are denied equal treatment.

8 We believe that all men have certain unalienable rights. Yet many Americans do not enjoy those rights.

9 We believe that all men are entitled to the blessings of liberty. Yet millions are being deprived of those blessings—not because of their own failures, but because of the color of their skin.

10 The reasons are deeply imbedded in history and tradition and the nature of man. We can understand—without rancor or hatred—how this all happened.

11 But it cannot continue. Our Constitution, the foundation of our Republic, forbids it. The principles of our freedom forbid it. Morality forbids it. And the law I will sign tonight forbids it.

43. Which sentence is NOT an example of an American ideal?

   a. "We believe that all men are created equal."

   b. "The principles of our freedom forbid it."

   c. "Not only for political independence, but for personal liberty."

   d. "Yet many are denied equal treatment."

44. Which sentence expresses the same idea as "Yet many are denied equal treatment"?

   a. Yet many Americans do not enjoy those rights.

   b. We believe that all men are entitled to the blessings of liberty.

   c. We can understand—without rancor or hatred—how this all happened.

   d. Americans of every race and color have died in battle to protect our freedom.

45. Based on Johnson's remarks, which is the best example of the United States' "unending search for justice within our own borders"?

   a. Civil War

   b. The Grand Canyon

   c. Civil Rights Act of 1964

   d. Vietnam War

46. Which answer best summarizes the main idea expressed in the paragraph that begins "One hundred and eighty-eight years ago"?

   a. The United States was formed a long time ago.

   b. The founding fathers worked hard to create a just nation.

   c. The country has always treated everyone fairly.

   d. Men of all races fought for freedom 188 years ago.

47. Which sentence best expresses the theme of President Johnson's remarks?

   a. American ideals include fair treatment for everyone.

   b. The United States is a great country.

   c. Everyone is treated the same in the United States.

   d. Lyndon B. Johnson was one of the best presidents.

48. Which of the following does NOT support Lyndon B. Johnson's stance that the Civil Rights Bill is in line with American values?

   a. "They pledged their lives, their fortunes, and their sacred honor not only to found a nation, but to forge an ideal of freedom."

   b. "Today in far corners of distant continents, the ideals of those American patriots still shape the struggles of men who hunger for freedom."

   c. "Americans of every race and color have died in battle to protect our freedom."

   d. "The reasons are deeply imbedded in history and tradition and the nature of man."

Part II

1 question
45 minutes

This practice allows you to compose your response to the given task and then compare it with examples of responses at the different score levels. You will also get a scoring guide that includes a detailed explanation of how official GED® test graders will score your response. You may use this scoring guide to score your own response.

Before you begin, it is important to note that on the official test this task must be completed in no more than 45 minutes. But don't rush to complete your response; take time to carefully read the passage(s) and the question prompt. Then think about how you would like to respond.

As you write your essay, be sure to:

- Decide which position presented in the passages is better supported by evidence.
- Explain why your chosen position has better support.
- Recognize that the position with better support may not be the position you agree with.
- Present multiple pieces of evidence from the passage to defend your assertions.

- Thoroughly construct your main points, organizing them logically, with strong supporting details.
- Connect your sentences, paragraphs, and ideas with transitional words and phrases.
- Express your ideas clearly and choose your words carefully.
- Use varied sentence structures to increase the clarity of your response.
- Reread and revise your response.

Good luck!

Please use the following to answer the essay question.

An Analysis of Nuclear Energy

1   America runs on energy. As a matter of fact, the United States is the second largest energy consumer in the world, behind China. In recent years, it can be argued that we need to ease our dependence on foreign countries that supply us with oil and develop energy at home. But where can we get the energy we need?

Benefits of Nuclear Energy

2   The U.S. Department of Energy (DOE) promotes the development of safe, domestic nuclear power, and there are many who support the idea that nuclear power is the answer. Compared to fossil fuels such as gas, coal, and oil, nuclear energy is the most efficient way to make electricity. For example, the Idaho National Laboratory reports that "one uranium fuel pellet—roughly the size of the tip of an adult's little finger—contains the same amount of energy as 17,000 cubic feet of natural gas, 1,780 pounds of coal, or 149 gallons of oil."

3   Supporters of nuclear energy cite that nuclear generators don't create the great amounts of poisonous carbon dioxide, nitrogen oxides, and sulfur dioxide like the burning of fossil fuels does. The DOE reports that a nuclear generator produces 30 tons of spent fuel a year compared to the 300,000 tons of coal ash produced by a coal-powered electrical plant.

4   In terms of safety, the Nuclear Regulatory Commission ensures that each and every nuclear reactor maintains strict safety standards. Radioactive waste is contained deep underground behind steel-reinforced, 1.2-meter-thick concrete walls. The DOE also points out that "ash from burning coal at a power plant emits 100 times more radiation into the surrounding environment than a nuclear power plant."

(continues)

Arguments against Nuclear Energy

5   Opponents of nuclear energy argue that nuclear reactors endanger all life on Earth for three basic reasons. First, nuclear radioactivity is deadly and must be contained for thousands of years. Second, no matter how many safety measures are in place, accidents happen, and nuclear meltdowns are global environmental catastrophes. Finally, nuclear fuel used to generate electricity can also be used to build atomic bombs.

6   Nuclear generators used radioactive plutonium and uranium for fuel. Scientists say that exposure to a millionth of an ounce of pluntonium causes cancer. Even nuclear energy proponents agree that life-threatening nuclear waste must be contained for half a million years before it becomes safe to be around. Radioactive dumps last generations.

7   Opponents of nuclear energy also cite the ever-present threat of meltdowns. Widespread radioactive contamination and death caused by the nuclear accidents at Three Mile Island, Chernobyl, and Fukushima are cautionary lessons. Researchers disagree on how possible it is to safely contain radioactivity, but it's undeniable that nuclear meltdown causes widespread contamination of the air, water, and land with deadly radioactivity. It is also verifiable that nuclear accidents have caused environmental catastrophes that continue to this day.

8   Perhaps even more disturbing than the threat of toxic waste and meltdown is the use of uranium for sinister purposes. On December 7, 2013, Reuters reported that ". . . in news that may concern world powers . . . Iran is moving ahead with testing more efficient uranium enrichment technology. . . ." Indeed, the United Nations and the entire world are worried about Iran's enhancement of uranium for use in nuclear power plants because the same enhanced uranium can be used to build atomic weaponry.

9   Opponents argue that in the same way we learned that fossil fuels are limited and destroy the environment, so must we learn from nuclear disasters. Opponents say the answer is to develop safe, clean, and renewable sources of alternative energy, such as solar, wind, tidal, and geothermal power. Why gamble? The future of the world is at stake.

QUESTION:

Nuclear energy proponents argue that it is safe and efficient, while opponents make the case for alternative energy sources, citing the deadly consequences of nuclear disaster.

In your response, analyze both positions presented in the article to determine which one is best supported. Use relevant and specific evidence from both articles to support your response.

You should expect to spend up to 45 minutes planning, drafting, and editing your response.

_____

_____

_____

_____

_____

_____

_____

_____

_____

_____

_____

_____

_____

_____

_____

Answers and Explanations

Part I

1. **Choice d is correct.** This is the only answer that encompasses everything Mrs. Obama speaks about, from thanking the USDA employees to explaining how the healthy initiatives could not succeed without them.
Choice **a** is incorrect. Although Mrs. Obama discusses different programs she has created with that goal, she uses those examples to demonstrate the greater theme.
Choice **b** is incorrect. Mrs. Obama shows her appreciation for farmers, but this answer ignores many other ideas and information brought up throughout the passage.
Choice **c** is incorrect. Mrs. Obama mentions the *Let's Move* initiative, but it is clear from her comments that the initiative is already underway; therefore, the purpose of Mrs. Obama's remarks is not to introduce *Let's Move*.

2. According to Mrs. Obama, a man named **Tom** mentioned that the nutrition issue is something near and dear to her heart. In the second paragraph, Mrs. Obama states: ". . . the nutrition issue, as *Tom* mentioned, as you all know, is something near and dear to my heart . . ."

3. **Choice b is correct.** Selecting this answer choice shows that the reader comprehends the importance Mrs. Obama places on family and healthy habits.
Choice **a** is incorrect. This answer ignores the main topics of the passage, which include an emphasis on participating in an active lifestyle, not watching one.
Choice **c** is incorrect. This answer choice only identifies one theme and ignores the focus on nutrition.
Choice **d** is incorrect. Although this answer incorporates both the themes of family and having healthy habits, it disregards Mrs. Obama's emphasis on teaching children healthy habits.

4. **Choice a is correct.** Even though Mrs. Obama is stating another of the USDA's contributions, this answer does not focus on health or food, but rather on renewable resources. Also, the other three answer choices clearly support the question's conclusion.
Choice **b** is incorrect. This sentence demonstrates Mrs. Obama's concern through her gratitude.
Choice **c** is incorrect. This statement explicitly states Mrs. Obama's personal interest in health in the United States.
Choice **d** is incorrect. In this sentence, Mrs. Obama gives a specific example of the ways in which she, along with the USDA, has worked to teach citizens healthy habits.

5. **Choice a is correct.** If you replace the word "initiative" with the word "program," the sentence would retain its meaning.
Choice **b** is incorrect. The word "enthusiasm" does not fit the context.
Choice **c** is incorrect. "Disinterest" is an antonym of "initiative."
Choice **d** is incorrect. Replacing "initiative" with "involvement" loses the meaning of the sentence.

6. Choice b is correct. It demonstrates the necessity of garden programs by highlighting the fact that some children don't know how food is grown or where their food comes from. Choice **a** is incorrect. This response neglects Mrs. Obama's emphasis on why nutritional programs are important. Choice **c** is incorrect. The paragraph supports the theme of the speech by providing information about why the programs and worker involvement are necessary. Choice **d** is incorrect. Mrs. Obama is very clear and explicitly states that children not only do not know about nutrition, but do not know where their food comes from. This ties into the overall theme of health and demonstrates why Mrs. Obama believes these programs are needed.

7. Choice a is correct. Two sentences before "countrymen," the narrator says, "Few Italians have the true virtuoso spirit." The next few sentences, including the one that uses "countrymen," are descriptions of traits that Italians do or do not have, according to the narrator. Choice **b** is incorrect. Two sentences before "countrymen," the narrator says "Few Italians have the true virtuoso spirit." The next few sentences discuss how the enthusiasm of many Italians is often a deception to take advantage of the British or Austrians, according to the narrator. Choice **c** is incorrect. Two sentences before "countrymen," the narrator says "Few Italians have the true virtuoso spirit." The next few sentences discuss how the enthusiasm of many Italians is often a deception to take advantage of the British or Austrians, according to the narrator. Choice **d** is incorrect. There is no mention or indication in the passage that Fortunato is a Spaniard.

8. Choice c is correct. The narrator states that Fortunato is "sincere" in his knowledge of "old wines," and that in "This respect I did not differ from him materially." Choice **a** is incorrect. At no point does the narrator say anything about Italian history. Choice **b** is incorrect. The narrator describes Fortunato's "parti-striped dress," but does not describe his own clothing. Choice **d** is incorrect. The narrator states the events happened "one evening during the supreme madness of the carnival season," but makes no declarations about his feelings at the time.

9. Choice b is correct. This describes the narrator's reaction to finding Fortunato, not Fortunato's feelings about wine. Choice **a** is incorrect. The narrator is clearly stating Fortunato knows about wine. Choice **c** is incorrect. Fortunato is attempting to prove that he knows about wines and convince the narrator to take him to the cask of Amontillado instead of to their friend Luchresi. Choice **d** is incorrect. After the narrator warns Fortunato that his health would be in danger if they went to find the vault because of the cold, Fortunato dismisses the concern in favor of the wine.

10. Choice c is correct. Fortunato is actually quite unlucky as he has just stumbled across a man who wants to, and later does, kill him. Choice **a** is incorrect. The narrator is being sincere. Choice **b** is incorrect. This is a follow-up statement used to explain the narrator's claim that "few Italians have the true virtuoso spirit." Choice **d** is incorrect. Although the narrator does not actually mean to deter Fortunato from the journey to his death, there is no text-based reason to believe that the vaults are not cold and wet.

11. Choice d is correct. Early in the text, the narrator states that Fortunato "had a weak point—this Fortunato—although in other regards he was a man to be respected and even feared. He prided himself on his connoisseurship in wine."

Choice **a** is incorrect. There is nothing in the text that indicates Luchresi has more expertise in wine than Fortunato. As a matter of fact, the narrator himself states that "in the matter of old wines [Fortunato] was sincere."

Choice **b** is incorrect. On the contrary, if the narrator and Fortunato were known enemies, Fortunato would not trust him and follow him down to the vault.

Choice **c** is incorrect. The two men already know and trust each other, which is evidenced in their interactions and dialogue.

12. Choice c is correct. The author suggests that before 1867 many babies were poked by pins, and then the safety pin came along and eliminated the problem. It can be inferred that the reason the earlier babies were being poked was because their diapers were fastened with straight pins.

Choice **a** is incorrect. The only connection the author makes between himself and George Washington is that he, like Washington, was born into the world a liar.

Choice **b** is incorrect. Although the author suggests that before 1867 infants were often poked by pins, he does not imply that pin-poking was a form of parental punishment.

Choice **d** is incorrect. Although the author states that safety pins made children unable to "lie" by crying as if they had been poked by a pin, the author also states that this "doesn't impair the disposition to lie."

13. Choice b is correct. The author states, "During the first half of my life I never knew a child that was able to raise above that temptation and keep from telling that lie."

Choice **a** is incorrect. The author offers no scientific data to support his claim.

Choice **c** is incorrect. The author does not present any physical evidence to support his claim.

Choice **d** is incorrect. Although the author states that George Washington lied as a child, he offers no historical documentation to support this statement.

14. Choice d is correct. The author states that "all people are liars from the cradle onward" and also asks, "[W]hy should a person grieve over a thing which by the eternal law of his make he cannot help?"

Choice **a** is incorrect. The author does not suggest that lying should be forbidden and, in fact, argues that stopping a person from lying does not remove a person's disposition to lie.

Choice **b** is incorrect. The author does not suggest that different rules should be applied to adults and children.

Choice **c** is incorrect. The author does not suggest that eliminating lying is a goal toward which people should strive.

15. Choice a is correct. The author argues that those who didn't speak up about slavery implied "that there wasn't anything going on in which humane and intelligent people were interested," which was a quiet way of countering anti-slavery activists.

Choice **b** is incorrect. The author does not mention economics as an issue related to slavery.

Choice **c** is incorrect. The author does not suggest that slave owners lied to others; the main idea of the paragraph is that people lied to themselves about slavery.

Choice **d** is incorrect. The author says that anti-slavery agitators in the North would "argue and plead and pray," but they didn't get enough support in response.

16. Choice b is correct. While this detail is mentioned in the passage, it does not reflect the main idea of the passage, which is that lying is a part of human nature.

Choices **a**, **b**, and **c** are incorrect. These details support the main idea of the passage, which is that lying is a part of human nature.

17. Choice a is correct. All three words need to be capitalized. Beginning letters of sentences are always capitalized, and people's names and titles are capitalized.

Choice **b** is incorrect. This answer lacks all necessary capitalization. All three words need to be capitalized. Beginning letters of sentences are always capitalized, and people's names and titles are capitalized.

Choices **c** and **d** are incorrect. All three words must be capitalized.

18. Choice c is correct. This is the correct past tense for a singular subject.

Choice **a** is incorrect. "I have to work with children" does not make sense within the context. The author is explaining what she has done in the past.

Choices **b** and **d** are incorrect. These answer choices do not make sense in context.

19. Choice a is correct. This word correctly matches the past-tense verb "nannied."

Choice **b** is incorrect. This does not fit in context with the past-tense verb "nannied."

Choice **c** is incorrect. The word "however" indicates contrast with a previous statement. The ideas in the sentence compliment previous sentences and do not offer contrast.

Choice **d** is incorrect. This answer choice does not make sense in context. In order to keep with form, "recently" is a better answer.

20. Choice c is correct. "My" is the correct possessive pronoun.

Choice **a** is incorrect. This is not the correct possessive pronoun. The speaker is talking about her abilities.

Choice **b** is incorrect. "Me" is not a possessive pronoun. It is clear that the abilities belong to someone.

Choice **d** is incorrect. Although "mine" is possessive, one uses it to indicate objects that belong to them, and it would be awkward to say "mine abilities."

21. Choice a is correct. This choice summarizes the passage in totality, identifying Kennedy's emphasis on the past and the present as he accepts the presidency.

Choice **b** is incorrect. This choice neglects Kennedy's focus on the future of the nation and the world.

Choice **c** is incorrect. Kennedy stresses hope and good things to come throughout the text; however, this is just a small slice of everything he says and is not the main theme.

Choice **d** is incorrect. Although Kennedy speaks about the United States' and its allies' role in furthering peace and democracy, this choice ignores the weight Kennedy puts on how the past shaped the country.

22. Choice c is correct. The use of "replaced" and "more" signifies that "colonial control" and "tyranny" mean similar things.

Choice **a** is incorrect. The sentence is addressed "to the new states"; this is who the promise of a guard against more tyranny is made.

Choice **b** is incorrect. This phrase represents the opposite of tyranny, the state to which the countries have been "welcomed" to. The second half of the sentence is a promise to protect them and guard against tyranny.

Choice **d** is incorrect. "Iron" is an adjective used to describe tyranny.

23. Choice a is correct. Kennedy is contrasting being united with being divided in order to make a point about why countries should cooperate (because they can accomplish anything "in a host of cooperative ventures").

Choice **b** is incorrect. This is the opposite of Kennedy's intention.

Choice **c** is incorrect. Kennedy is focusing on everyone working together and not on foreign policy.

Choice **d** is incorrect. Although Kennedy says that he is committed to peace and cooperation, this speech focuses on discussing the perils of not working together.

24. Choice 2 is correct. Many times Kennedy emphasizes doing what is necessary to help those in need and that the United States will "pay any price."

Choice 3 is correct. Kennedy stresses that he is committed to showing people who are "struggling" how to "help themselves" and wants to "assist free men and free governments in casting off the chains of poverty."

Choice 4 is correct. Kennedy states he pledges the United States' "best efforts" not for political reasons "but because it is right." He also says he wants to "convert our good words into good deeds."

Choice **1** is incorrect. Kennedy makes a point of saying that the United States will "pay any price, bear any burden, meet any hardship, support any friend, oppose any foe, in order to assure the survival and the success of liberty." This does not show fear.

Choice **5** is incorrect. In the last paragraph, Kennedy explicitly asks "that both sides begin anew the quest for peace." He does not threaten his opponents but rather warns against the consequences of not working together.

25. **Choice a is correct.** Roosevelt emphasizes that the attack was a complete surprise because the two nations were not warring, yet states that he has "directed that all measures be taken for our defense." Even though he was not expecting the event, he knows that "hostilities exist" and has handled the situation.

    Choice **b** is incorrect. Roosevelt says the United States has "confidence in our armed forces" and "determination of our people" and will "gain the inevitable triumph." These are not words of a timid or fearful person.

    Choice **c** is incorrect. Although he asserts many times that the attack came as a surprise, he does not show fear through his words. Rather, he shows confidence in the country.

    Choice **d** is incorrect. Some of what Roosevelt says is aggressive, like asking Congress to declare war, but he seems confident in the abilities of the nation rather than insecure.

26. **Choice c is correct.** Roosevelt is effectively stressing how "the United States was at peace with that nation" by emphatically pointing out that the Japanese ambassador responded to the American message.

    Choice **a** is incorrect. The third paragraph is an example that there were "existing diplomatic negotiations," an example of how Japan was "still in conversation," as stated in the previous paragraph.

    Choice **b** is incorrect. The third paragraph supports the premise of the second paragraph.

    Choice **d** is incorrect. The third paragraph supports the theme of the previous paragraphs.

27. **Choice b is correct.** Roosevelt is implying that the two islands are far enough apart that the attack had to have been "deliberately planned." Choice **a** is incorrect. The attack wouldn't have had to have been planned "days or even weeks ago" if the island was close and easy for the Japanese to attack.

    Choice **c** is incorrect. The United States mainland is not mentioned and is irrelevant in this context.

    Choice **d** is incorrect. There is no evidence in the speech to support this answer choice. The opposite is true.

28. **Choice d is correct.** The drumbeat rhythm of repetition emphasizes the great number of attacks on one country after another.

    Choice **a** is incorrect. There is no evidence in the speech that Japan is disorganized. In fact, evidence in the speech supports the conclusion that the opposite is true.

    Choice **b** is incorrect. There is no evidence in the speech to support this conclusion.

    Choice **c** is incorrect. There is no mention of how the other countries handled or will handle the attack.

29. **Choice b is correct.** Roosevelt states many times that the attack was an intentional move that put "our interests . . . in grave danger."

    Choice **a** is incorrect. Contrary to this answer choice, evidence in the speech supports the conclusion that Japan launched a surprise attack on the United States.

    Choice **c** is incorrect. There is no evidence in the speech to support this conclusion.

    Choice **d** is incorrect. It is clear from the speech that the attack was planned.

30. Choice d is correct. This sentence comes after describing how the surprise attack was carried out, acknowledging resulting clear and present danger.

Choice **a** is incorrect. An attack is not expected from a nation in peaceful accord with the United States.

Choice **b** is incorrect. This sentence shows that the nations were working together to find a solution prior to the attack.

Choice **c** is incorrect. This sentence describes how Japan worked to make sure the attack was a surprise by deceiving the United States.

31. Choice b is correct. The tone is appropriate for a work email.

Choice **a** is incorrect. The phrases "some really big" and "that might really affect" are informal and awkward.

Choice **c** is incorrect. The tone is too informal for a work email.

Choice **d** is incorrect. A postscript (PS) comes at the end of a letter, not at the beginning.

32. Choice b is correct. This is the past participle verb. The decision "has" already been made.

Choice **a** is incorrect. This is the future tense, and the decision has already been made.

Choice **c** is incorrect. This is the present tense, and the action is not happening now.

Choice **d** is incorrect. This is the present tense of the verb.

33. Choice d is correct. The plural pronoun matches the plural form of the verb. The contraction of these two words is "they're" and is a homophone of "there" and "they're."

Choice **a** is incorrect. The word "there" refers to location.

Choice **b** is incorrect. "Their" is a possessive pronoun.

Choice **c** is incorrect. Although this has the correct plural pronoun, "is" is for singular subjects.

34. Choice c is correct. This answer correctly closes off the thought from the first part of the sentence before introducing the second part of the sentence. It shows a natural pause.

Choice **a** is incorrect. "Friday" modifies "afternoons," so they cannot be broken up by a comma.

Choice **b** is incorrect. "Employee" serves as an adjective for "activity." They cannot be separated.

Choice **d** is incorrect. "Activity" is the noun and "drops" is the verb. They should not be separated.

35. Choice b is correct. Obama remarks that greatness is not a given and must be earned, implying that the United States is not great by luck, but by work and determination.

Choice **a** is incorrect. The future of our great nation is assured.

Choice **c** is incorrect. The future is not mentioned in the first paragraph.

Choice **d** is incorrect. Obama does not discuss his personal feelings about being president in the address.

36. Choice d is correct. The sentence later in the passage recalls the men and women mentioned earlier to stress that the cynics are wrong in thinking great things cannot be accomplished.

Choice **a** is incorrect. Although this answer recognizes the theme of the sentence, that the United States has a large and historical "capacity" for greatness, it does not explicitly call on the image of the people working or modify that idea.

Choice **b** is incorrect. This choice neglects the connection Obama makes between the people who worked hard to shape America and the cynics who are ignoring their struggles by doubting change.

Choice **c** is incorrect. This phrase in the question has nothing to do with the cost of healthcare or technology.

37. Choice 1 is correct. The main idea in the Address is that America was formed by hard work and that that attitude needs to and will be continued throughout this presidency. This phrase supports the main idea by firmly stating that taking the easy way out is not what "our journey" has been about.
Choice 2 is correct. This phrase supports the theme of the future of the United States.
Choice 3 is correct. This phrase supports the idea that citizens and the government must work hard and will work hard.
Choice **4** is incorrect. This phrase is about renewable energy, which is used as a detail of what Obama wants to focus on and is not the main focus.
Choice **5** is incorrect. This phrase stresses the negative and opposition to progress; it does not support the idea of ambition.

38. Choice d is correct. Obama draws on the history of the United States, like "the creed our fathers once declared," to stress that citizens have an "obligation" to help "all posterity."
Choice **a** is incorrect. Although Obama docs carefully praise the country throughout, the point of the passage is to discuss the future challenges and how past successes enable us to face those challenges.
Choice **b** is incorrect. This answer shows that the reader does not comprehend that the main focus of the text is what Obama believes needs to change.
Choice **c** is incorrect. This is the tool Obama is utilizing, not the effect of utilizing that tool.

39. Choice b is correct. Obama uses words, or rhetoric, to show that he thinks the two are connected and that their interests both matter.
Choice **a** is incorrect. This choice neglects the verb tense change of "built" to "will build." This shows he is talking about past people/actions and future people/actions.
Choice **c** is incorrect. This sentence makes no value judgment on either party and does not state one is better than the other.
Choice **d** is incorrect. One generation's actions are in the past, as "built" is the past tense verb; their work is done.

40. Choice b is correct. Obama is looking to the future, arguing that failure to act to halt climate change would "betray our children and future generations."
Choice **a** is incorrect. In this sentence, Obama looks to the past for solutions to today's problems.
Choice **c** is incorrect. Here, Obama draws on the past as a reason United States citizens must fight for the future.
Choicc **d** is incorrect. Obama is stressing American might and willingness to use its power, not speaking of obligations to future generations.

41. Choice b is correct. Specifically, Obama says, "We will support democracy from Asia to Africa; from the Americas to the Middle East. . . ."
Choices **a**, **b**, and **c** are incorrect. Obama says, "We will support democracy from Asia to Africa; from the Americas to the Middle East. . . ."

42. Choice b is correct. This sentence supports the first address's theme of continuing the hard work of the past in order to secure prosperity and freedom for tomorrow.
Choice **a** is incorrect. This sentence refers to healthcare and taking care of the country's citizens; this is mentioned in the first address, but it is not the theme.
Choice **c** is incorrect. Obama's First Inaugural Address did not focus on war.
Choice **d** is incorrect. These details are not the theme of the first address.

43. Choice d is correct. It is not an American ideal to deny freedom. The opposite is true. Freedom is the theme of American ideals.
Choice **a** is incorrect. This American ideal is cited in paragraph 7.
Choice **b** is incorrect. This American ideal is cited in the last paragraph.
Choice **c** is incorrect. This American ideal is cited in paragraph 3.

44. Choice a is correct. People not having the same rights as others means roughly the same thing as the denial of equal treatment.
Choice **b** is incorrect. This means the opposite of the quotation in question.
Choice **c** is incorrect. In this sentence, Johnson is explaining that there were reasons for what happened rather than restating the problem of people being treated differently.
Choice **d** is incorrect. Johnson is affirming that Americans of all races have contributed to their country.

45. Choice c is correct. This is the best answer because one of the main points of the remarks is to explain that the Civil Rights Act will bring the United States closer to achieving its goals and values.
Choice **a** is incorrect. Johnson does not mention the Civil War in the passage.
Choice **b** is incorrect. The Grand Canyon is one of America's natural wonders, unrelated to America's unending search for justice domestically.
Choice **d** is incorrect. Johnson alludes to the Vietnam War in the text and uses it as an example of how American values are spanning the globe, but this is a small detail in the passage rather than a main idea. As well, Vietnam is outside of "our own borders."

46. Choice b is correct. Johnson talks about the values that the forefathers focused on when forming the nation in this paragraph.
Choice **a** is incorrect. This is a detail of the passage, but not the main theme.
Choice **c** is incorrect. This idea is not stated in the paragraph, and it also runs counter to the entire point of the speech.
Choice **d** is incorrect. There is no evidence to support this conclusion in the remarks.

47. Choice a is correct. Johnson expresses many times and in a variety of ways that equality is one of the cornerstones of American values.
Choice **b** is incorrect. Johnson talks about how he believes America is a great country, but this is not the main idea of his remarks.
Choice **c** is incorrect. Johnson's remarks are about America's ideal of ensuring equality, yet to be achieved.
Choice **d** is incorrect. Johnson makes no value judgment about himself.

48. **Choice d is correct.** This is Johnson's brief explanation of how inequality happened, rather than an explanation of how the law aligns with American values.

Choice **a** is incorrect. Johnson uses history and the vision of the forefathers to illustrate that freedom is a core American value and that freedom includes equality.

Choice **b** is incorrect. Johnson says that because American values are shaping foreign struggles, the United States must continue to make sure that it upholds its own values.

Choice **c** is incorrect. Johnson uses this sentence to say that all kinds of people, regardless of race, have fought for the country.

Part II

Your Extended Response will be scored based on three traits, or elements:

Trait 1: Analysis of arguments and use of evidence

Trait 2: Development of ideas and structure

Trait 3: Clarity and command of standard English conventions

Your essay will be scored on a 6-point scale—each trait is worth up to 2 points. The final score is counted twice, so the maximum number of points you can earn is 12.

Trait 1 tests your ability to write an essay that takes a stance based on the information in the reading passages. To earn the highest score possible, you must carefully read the information and express a clear opinion on what you have read. You will be scored on how well you use the information from the passages to support your argument.

Your response will also be scored on how well you analyze the author's arguments in the passages. To earn the highest score possible, you should discuss whether you think the author is making a good argument, and why or why not.

For your reference, here is a table that readers will use when scoring your essay with a 2, 1, or 0.

TRAIT 1: CREATION OF ARGUMENTS AND USE OF EVIDENCE	
2	• Makes text-based argument(s) and establishes an intent connected to the prompt • Presents specific and related evidence from source text(s) to support argument (may include a few unrelated pieces of evidence or unsupported claims) • Analyzes the topic and/or the strength of the argument within the source text(s) (e.g., distinguishes between supported and unsupported claims, makes valid inferences about underlying assumptions, identifies false reasoning, evaluates the credibility of sources)
1	• Makes an argument with some connection to the prompt • Presents some evidence from source text(s) to support argument (may include a mix of related and unrelated evidence that may or may not cite the text) • Partly analyzes the topic and/or the strength of the argument within the source text(s); may be limited, oversimplified, or inaccurate
0	• May attempt to make an argument OR lacks an intent or connection to the prompt OR attempts neither • Presents little or no evidence from source text(s) (sections of text may be copied from source directly) • Minimally analyzes the topic and/or the strength of the argument within the source text(s); may present no analysis, or little or no understanding of the given argument
Non-scorable	• Response consists only of text copied from the prompt or source text(s) • Response shows that test-taker has not read the prompt or is entirely off-topic • Response is incomprehensible • Response is not in English • No response has been attempted (has been left blank)

Trait 2 tests whether you respond to the writing prompt with a well-structured essay. Support of your thesis must come from evidence in the passages, as well as personal opinions and experiences that build on your central idea. Your ideas must be fully explained and include specific details. Your essay should use words and phrases that allow your details and ideas to flow naturally. Here is a table that outlines what is involved in earning a score of 2, 1, or 0.

TRAIT 2: DEVELOPMENT OF IDEAS AND ORGANIZATIONAL STRUCTURE	
2	• Contains ideas that are generally logical and well-developed; most ideas are expanded upon • Contains a logical sequence of ideas with clear connections between specific details and main ideas • Develops an organizational structure that conveys the message and goal of the response; appropriately uses transitional devices • Develops and maintains an appropriate style and tone that signal awareness of the audience and purpose of the task • Uses appropriate words to express ideas clearly
1	• Contains ideas that are partially developed and/or may demonstrate vague or simplistic logic; only some ideas are expanded upon • Contains some evidence of a sequence of ideas, but specific details may be unconnected to main ideas • Develops an organizational structure that may partially group ideas or is partially effective at conveying the message of the response; inconsistently uses transitional devices • May inconsistently maintain an appropriate style and tone to signal an awareness of the audience and purpose of the task • May contain misused words and/or words that do not express ideas clearly
0	• Contains ideas that are ineffectively or illogically developed, with little or no elaboration of main ideas • Contains an unclear or no sequence of ideas; specific details may be absent or unrelated to main ideas • Develops an ineffective or no organizational structure; inappropriately uses transitional devices, or does not use them at all • Uses an inappropriate style and tone that signals limited or no awareness of audience and purpose • May contain many misused words, overuse of slang, and/or express ideas in an unclear or repetitious manner
Non-scorable	• Response consists only of text copied from the prompt or source text(s) • Response shows that test-taker has not read the prompt or is entirely off-topic • Response is incomprehensible • Response is not in English • No response has been attempted (has been left blank)

Trait 3 tests how you create the sentences that make up your essay. To earn a high score, you will need to write sentences with variety—some short, some long, some simple, some complex. You will also need to prove that you have a good handle on standard English, including correct word choice, grammar, and sentence structure.

Here is a table that outlines what is involved in attaining a score of 2, 1, or 0.

TRAIT 3: CLARITY AND COMMAND OF STANDARD ENGLISH CONVENTIONS	
2	• Demonstrates generally correct sentence structure and an overall fluency that enhances clarity with regard to the following skills: 1) Diverse sentence structure within a paragraph or paragraphs 2) Correct use of subordination, coordination, and parallelism 3) Avoidance of awkward sentence structures and wordiness 4) Use of transitional words, conjunctive adverbs, and other words that enhance clarity and logic 5) Avoidance of run-on sentences, sentence fragments, and fused sentences • Demonstrates proficient use of conventions with regard to the following skills: 1) Subject-verb agreement 2) Placement of modifiers and correct word order 3) Pronoun usage, including pronoun antecedent agreement, unclear pronoun references, and pronoun case 4) Frequently confused words and homonyms, including contractions 5) Use of apostrophes with possessive nouns 6) Use of punctuation (e.g., commas in a series or in appositives and other non-essential elements, end marks, and punctuation for clause separation) 7) Capitalization (e.g., beginnings of sentences, proper nouns, and titles) • May contain some errors in mechanics and conventions that do not impede comprehension; overall usage is at a level suitable for on-demand draft writing
1	• Demonstrates inconsistent sentence structure; may contain some choppy, repetitive, awkward, or run-on sentences that may limit clarity; demonstrates inconsistent use of skills 1–5 as listed under Trait 3, Score Point 2 • Demonstrates inconsistent use of basic conventions with regard to skills 1–7 as listed under Trait 3, Score Point 2 • May contain many errors in mechanics and conventions that occasionally impede comprehension; overall usage is at the minimum level acceptable for on-demand draft writing
0	• Demonstrates improper sentence structure to the extent that meaning may be unclear; demonstrates minimal use of skills 1–5 as listed under Trait 3, Score Point 2 • Demonstrates minimal use of basic conventions with regard to skills 1–7 as listed under Trait 3, Score Point 2 • Contains numerous significant errors in mechanics and conventions that impede comprehension; overall usage is at an unacceptable level for on-demand draft writing OR • Response is insufficient to show level of proficiency involving conventions and usage
Non-scorable	• Response consists only of text copied from the prompt or source text(s) • Response shows that test-taker has not read the prompt or is entirely off-topic • Response is incomprehensible • Response is not in English • No response has been attempted (has been left blank)

Sample Score 6 Essay

Weighing the pro and con arguments presented in the article, I conclude that the case against nuclear energy is more compelling than the case for nuclear energy. While both positions are well reasoned, organized and supported with authoritative quotes and examples, the unimpeachable evidence against nuclear energy, upon reflection, is greater.

Both sides agree that fossil fuels are not healthy for the environment and people. Opponents and proponents also agree that radioactivity is deadly, although the proponents whitewash this fact by only describing the need to keep radioactivity contained by stating in paragraph 4 that "Radioactive waste is contained deep underground behind steel-reinforced, 1.2 meter thick concrete walls." On the other hand, the second essay speaks more plainly, "First, nuclear radioactivity is deadly and must be contained for thousands of years." In fact, the second essay uses evidence found in the first essay to support its premise.

The pro-nuclear position also avoids the topics of meltdown and the construction of atomic weapons from radioactive materials used in nuclear power plants. To not address and gloss over these topics makes the first essay seem more like an advertisement for the nuclear industry rather than an objective assessment of well-known and troubling facts. In paragraph 7, the writer points out what we all know, that "Widespread radioactive contamination and death caused by the nuclear accidents at Three Mile Island, Chernobyl and Fukushima are cautionary lessons." and that "it's undeniable that nuclear meltdown causes widespread contamination of the air, water and land with deadly radioactivity. It is also verifiable that nuclear accidents have caused environmental catastrophes that continue to this day." For me, nothing more needs to be said about the absolute truth about the real danger of nuclear energy, but the author of the second essay indeed provides up-to-date evidence from Reuters regarding international fears of Iran developing atomic weaponry under the guise of building nuclear power plants.

In the end, the opponent position offers a safe and sane solution to fossil fuels and nuclear power.

About this essay:

This essay has earned the maximum number of points in each trait for a total of 6 points.

Trait 1: Creation of Arguments and Use of Evidence

This response evaluates the arguments in the source text, develops an effective position supported by the text, and fulfills the criteria to earn 2 points for Trait 1.

This response establishes its stance in the first sentence (*I conclude that the case against nuclear energy is more compelling than the case for nuclear energy*) and provides a summary of support for that stance (*While both essays are well reasoned, organized and supported with authoritative quotes and examples, the unimpeachable evidence against nuclear energy, upon reflection, is greater*).

It also weighs the validity of evidence (*although the proponents whitewash this fact by only describing the need to keep radioactivity contained*) and critiques omissions (*To not address and gloss over these topics makes the first essay seem more like an advertisement for the nuclear industry rather than an objective assessment of well-known and troubling facts*).

Trait 2: Development of Ideas and Organizational Structure

This response is well developed and fulfills the criteria to earn 2 points for Trait 2. It is well organized, from the writer's clear point of view in the first paragraph to the step-by-step comparison of the pros and cons presented in the source material.

The writer's vocabulary and sentence structures are sophisticated, and the tone shows an urgency of purpose.

Trait 3: Clarity and Command of Standard English Conventions

This response fulfills the criteria for draft writing and earns 2 points for Trait 3. Besides employing sophisticated sentence structure (*Both sides agree that fossil fuels are not healthy for the environment and people. Opponents and proponents also agree that radioactivity is deadly, although the proponents whitewash this fact by only describing the need to keep radioactivity contained by stating in paragraph 4 that. . . .*) this response uses clear transitions in its compare and contrast construction (*On the other hand, the second essay speaks more plainly. . . .*)

In addition, the writer adheres to proper grammar and usage.

Sample Score 4 Essay

The supporters of nuclear energy best show how it is superior to other forms of energy. We have only begun to use nuclear energy, and while the opposing position only describes the danger of radioactivity, it is true from another point of view that scientists learn more everyday about how to contain these types of materials. We have only just begun to fulfill the promise of nuclear energy.

In the first paragraph the author states that "The U.S. Department of Energy (DOE) promotes the development of safe, domestic nuclear power…" The United States government and its agencies are powerful and highly-regarded authorities, so if the DOE says that nuclear energy is the way to go, I don't have an argument with that.

The opposing position to nuclear power states that radioactivity is dangerous, that containing the danger is difficult and that evil-doers can create atomic bombs from enriched uranium are scare tactics. First of all, the "Nuclear Regulatory Commission ensures that each and every nuclear reactor maintains strict safety standards." Nuclear accidents are a thing of the past as scientists work hard to be able to control nuclear power plants. Not to mention that so far, there no one has built a bomb from plutonium stolen used in a nuclear power plant.

All in all, a strong case against nuclear energy was not made and the case for nuclear energy continues to build on the authority of science.

About this essay:

This essay earned 1 point each for Trait 1 and Trait 2 and 2 points for Trait 3.

Trait 1: Creation of Arguments and Use of Evidence

This response makes an argument, supports it with some evidence from the source text, and offers a partial analysis of the opposing argument, earning it 1 point for Trait 1.

The writer makes an issue-based statement of position in the first sentence: *The supporters of nuclear energy best show how it is superior to other forms of energy.* The essay goes on to cite textual evidence in the second paragraph for support (*The U.S. Department of Energy (DOE) promotes the development of safe, domestic nuclear power. . . .*) but then relies on the fallacy of authority to validate this position (*The United States government and its agencies are powerful and highly-regarded authorities, so if the DOE says that nuclear energy is the way to go, I don't have an argument with that*).

The summary of opposing arguments in paragraph 4 is superficial and simplistic: *The opposing position to nuclear power states that radioactivity is dangerous, that containing the danger is difficult and that evil-doers can create atomic bombs from enriched uranium are scare tactics.*

Trait 2: Development of Ideas and Organizational Structure

The response's general conclusion has no support, and in general it displays only adequate skill of word choice, although the tone is audience appropriate. The response is fairly organized, but the ideas rely on authority, earning this response 1 point for Trait 2.

The writer establishes a stance in the beginning of the response and roughly organizes material in a compare-and-contrast structure loosely based on speculation not found in the source text: *We have only begun to use nuclear energy, and while the opposing position only describes the danger of radioactivity, it is true from another point of view that scientists learn more everyday about how to contain these types of materials.*

Trait 3: Clarity and Command of Standard English Conventions

Because the response fulfills level criteria for draft writing on demand, it earns the full 2 points for Trait 3.

Overall, this response displays proper sentence structure and appropriate use of transitional words: *We have only begun to use nuclear energy, and while the opposing position only describes the danger of radioactivity, it is true from another point of view that scientists learn more everyday about how to contain these types of materials.*

In general, the response demonstrates proper use of conventions, including subject-verb agreement, pronoun, and punctuation use.

Sample Score 3 Essay

The benefits of nuclear energy are by far more beneficial to supply America's need for power than fossil, solar or any other kind of alternative energy source. As the introduction states, "it has become clear that we need to ease our dependence on foreign countries that supply us with oil and develop energy at home." That's common sense and pretty much proves the point.

The supporters show how nuclear energy is safe and efficient and gives statistics about how much waste comes from nuclear energy and how much comes from fossil fuels. The opposers suppose nuclear power plants will have meltdowns and contaminate the environment. They also worries about irresponsible people making atom bombs.

After reading both sides though I was convinced that compared to fossil fuels such as gas, coal, and oil nuclear energy is the most efficient way to make electricity, Nuclear energy leaves less waste too.

In conclusion, I agree with the first opinion and hope disasters like Three Mile Island, Chernobyl and Fukishima are a thing of the past.

About this essay:

This essay earned 1 point each for Trait 1, Trait 2, and Trait 3.

Trait 1: Creation of Arguments and Use of Evidence

This draft fulfills the criteria for Trait 1 by generating an argument in the opening sentence that demonstrates a connection to the prompt: *The benefits of nuclear energy are by far more beneficial to supply America's need for power than fossil, solar or any other kind of alternative energy source.*

The argument is then supported by source text (*it has become clear that we need to ease our dependence on foreign countries that supply us with oil and develop energy at home*), but the writer's analysis of the source text is simplistic and limited: *That's common sense and pretty much proves the point.*

Trait 2: Development of Ideas and Organizational Structure

Overall, the writer demonstrates awareness of audience and purpose, earning this response 1 point for Trait 2.

The writer simply summarizes the pro and con arguments without quotation (*The supporters show how nuclear energy is safe and efficient and gives statistics about how much waste comes from nuclear energy and how much comes from fossil fuels. The opposers suppose nuclear power plants will have meltdowns and contaminate the environment. They also worries about irresponsible people making atom bombs*), but demonstrates a logical flow of ideas.

The conclusion in favor of the supporting position is abrupt and unsupported, although the writer's final clause shows attention to the source material and genuine consideration of both sides of the issue: *In conclusion, I agree with the first opinion and hope disasters like Three Mile Island, Chernobyl and Fukushima are a thing of the past.*

Word choice is adequate throughout, and although ideas progress and develop somewhat, thoughts are not fully executed to a supported conclusion.

Trait 3: Clarity and Command of Standard English Conventions

This sample response is comprehensible and maintains an acceptable level of appropriateness to earn it 1 point for Trait 3.

The writer's short response lacks a variety of sentence structures, and although most sentences are grammatically correct, there are usage and punctuation errors in the text. For example: *The supporters show how nuclear energy is safe and efficient and gives statistics* and *They also worries about. . . .*

Additionally, source text is cited without quotation marks: *After reading both essays though I was convinced that ["]compared to fossil fuels such as gas, coal and oil, nuclear energy is the most efficient way to make electricity,["] Nuclear energy leaves less waste too.*

Sample Score 0 Essay

The best way to think if solar energy is better then nuclear energy or if fossil fuels is better then wind power are to look at the facts not just listen to opinions of people who don't know what they're talking about or are not scientists which know about energy in the broadest sense of the term... These facts. Most folks got no idea that nuclear power is so much stronger than fossil fuel power because just a tiny bit of uranium can make more energy than barrels of oil or tons of coal. You can take that to the bank.

If you want to know the dangers about nuclear energy, read the second part of the story. People can make bombs from uranium and thereve been lots of accidents too. Some say we should throw the dice with nuclear power though because we have to be independent.

Why we don't want to blow up the Earth. But we need electricity and gas to live our everyday lives. That's why the United States needs to grab the bull by the horn and get scientists to make nuclear energy. Better for future generations.

About this essay:

This essay earned 0 points in Trait 1, Trait 2, and Trait 3.

Trait 1: Creation of Arguments and Use of Evidence

In general, this response provides minimal summary of the source text and lacks insight and topic analysis, earning this response 0 points for Trait 1.

The writer fails to summarize source text in a coherent and organized structure. Although this response addresses the source material, the writer fails to cite evidence to support any arguments.

Trait 2: Development of Ideas and Organizational Structure

Overall, the response is poorly developed, is disorganized, and lacks any clear progression of ideas, earning it 0 points for Trait 2.

The writer uses informal and colloquial language (*You can take that to the bank*) and fails to demonstrate awareness of audience and purpose. The response lacks organizational structure and a clear progression of ideas.

Trait 3: Clarity and Command of Standard English Conventions

Many sentences lack sense and fluency and are incorrect and awkward. The writer misuses and confuses words, punctuation, and usage as well as the conventions of English in general, making the response almost incomprehensible and earning it 0 points for Trait 3.

This short response shows flawed sentence structure, including run-on sentences (*The best way to think if solar energy is better then nuclear energy or if fossil fuels is better then wind power are to look at the facts not just listen to opinions of people who don't know what they're talking about or are not scientists which know about energy in the broadest sense of the term. . . .*) and fragments (*These facts* and *Better for future generations*).

This practice test is modeled on the format, content, and timing of the official GED® Science test and, like the official exam, presents a series of questions that focus on the fundamentals of scientific reasoning.

Work carefully, but do not spend too much time on any one question. Be sure you answer every question.

Set a timer for 90 minutes (1 hour and 30 minutes), and try to take this test uninterrupted, under quiet conditions.

Complete answer explanations for every test question follow the exam. Good luck!

PART I

35 total questions
90 minutes to complete

Please use the following to answer questions 1–3.

A non-predatory relationship between two organisms that benefits at least one of the organisms is called a *symbiotic relationship*. These relationships can be categorized further based on the effect of the relationship on the second organism. The table shows the three types of symbiotic relationships and their effects on each organism.

SYMBIOTIC RELATIONSHIP	SPECIES 1	SPECIES 2	KEY
Mutualism	+	+	+ benefits
Commensalism	+	0	– harmed
Parasitism	+	–	0 no effect

Veterinary clinics often treat pets with illnesses resulting from parasitism. Three common parasites diagnosed in dogs are the dog flea, the deer tick, and *Cheyletiella* mites.

Dog fleas and deer ticks both feed on the host animal's (dog's) blood and can transmit diseases to the host animal through their bites. Dog fleas lay their eggs on the host animal's body and can survive on the host animal or on surfaces the animal comes in contact with, such as bedding. Deer ticks lay their eggs on the ground and attach to the host animal only while feeding.

Cheyletiella mites live within and feed on the keratin layer of the host animal's skin. *Cheyletiella* mites reproduce on the host animal and can survive away from the host animal only for short periods of time.

1. Read the two descriptions of symbiotic relationships below, and select the correct term for each relationship from the following list. Write the correct answer in the box after each description.
   commensalism
   mutualism
   parasitism

Mistletoe attaches to spruce trees. Using specialized structures, mistletoe penetrates into and extracts water and nutrients from the tree's branches.

[ ]

E. coli bacteria live within the intestinal tract of humans, obtaining nutrients from the food particles that pass through the intestines. Vitamin K produced by the E. coli is absorbed through the intestinal walls for use in the human body.

[ ]

2. According to the passage, all of the dog parasites gain which benefit from their symbiotic relationships with the host dogs?
   a. a habitat for living
   b. a vector for disease
   c. a source of nutrients
   d. a site for reproduction

3. A veterinary technician is preparing to examine a dog suspected of having *Cheyletiella* mites. Based on the information in the passage, which precaution would most effectively prevent the transmission of mites to other animals in the clinic?
   a. administering a vaccine to the infected dog
   b. wearing disposable gloves while examining the dog
   c. avoiding contact with open wounds on the dog
   d. sterilizing the exam room before examining the dog

4. The passing of one object in space through the shadow of another object is called an eclipse. The orbits of the moon and Earth in relation to the sun cause both solar and lunar eclipses to occur. During a solar eclipse, the specific alignment of these three objects causes the moon to cast a shadow on the Earth. During a lunar eclipse, the alignment causes the Earth to cast a shadow on the moon.

The following diagram shows the alignment of the sun, Earth, and moon during a lunar eclipse. Draw an "X" in the correct spot to identify the location of the moon necessary to produce a solar eclipse.

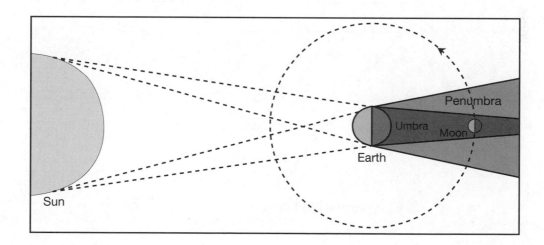

5. The table below compares characteristics for four different groups of plants. A "1" indicates that the characteristic is present, and a "0" indicates that the characteristic is absent.

Plant Type	Vascular Tissue	Seeds	Flowers
Confers	1	1	0
Ferns	1	0	0
Flowering Plants	1	1	1
Mosses	0	0	0

A cladogram illustrates the relatedness of organisms based on shared characteristics. Branches below a given characteristic represent organisms that do not exhibit that characteristic. Branches above a given characteristic represent organisms that do exhibit that characteristic. Each branch represents one plant type.

Use the information in the table to organize the four plant types onto the appropriate branches in the cladogram.

Write the correct plant type into each box. Select from the choices below.

conifers
ferns
flowering plants
mosses

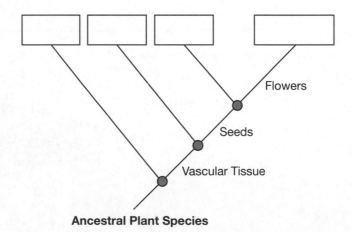

Please use the following to answer questions 6 and 7.

The amount of oxygen gas dissolved in a body of water can provide information about the health of the aquatic ecosystem. In general, the closer the dissolved oxygen level to the maximum level, the more productive and less polluted the ecosystem can be assumed to be.

The table below shows the maximum amount of oxygen gas that can be dissolved in water at various temperatures.

WATER TEMPERATURE (°C)	MAXIMUM OXYGEN SOLUBILITY (MG/L)
0	14.6
10	11.3
20	9.2
30	7.6
40	6.4
100	0

6. The data in the table support which of the following statements about the relationship between water temperature and oxygen solubility?

a. Bodies of water with a lower average temperature can support a higher concentration of dissolved oxygen.

b. Bodies of water with an average temperature higher than 40°C contain no dissolved oxygen.

c. A 10°C increase in water temperature results in an approximately 3-mg/L change in oxygen solubility.

d. The oxygen solubility of a body of water is affected by many variables, including water temperature.

7. Researchers find that a body of fresh water with an average temperature of 21°C has a dissolved oxygen concentration of 7.2 mg/L. What is a reasonable prediction of the water's dissolved oxygen concentration after the population size of freshwater grasses doubles?
a. 6.3 mg/L
b. 7.2 mg/L
c. 8.5 mg/L
d. 14.4 mg/L

8. The chart below shows that the color of the light emitted by a star is dependent on the star's temperature.

CLASS	COLOR	SURFACE TEMP. (K)
O	Blue	>25,000 K
B	Blue-white	11,000–25,000 K
A	White	7,500–11,000 K
F	White	6,000–7,500 K
G	Yellow	5,000–6,000 K
K	Orange	3,500–5,000 K
M	Red	<3,500 K

Which of the following statements is supported by the data in the table?

a. In general, white stars are hotter than blue-white stars.

b. A star with a surface temperature of 3,700 K produces red light.

c. Yellow light is produced by stars within the narrowest temperature range.

d. The highest known surface temperature of a star is 25,000 K.

9. The diagram below illustrates the structure of an ocean wave.

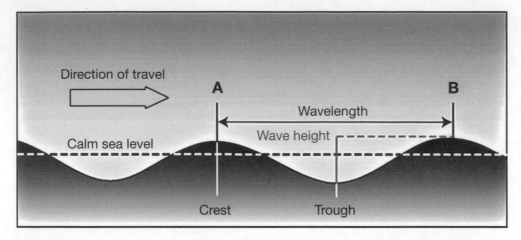

The *period* of a wave is the time required for the wave crest at point A to reach point B. The wave period can also be described as the amount of time required for a wave to do which of the following?

a. reach the shoreline

b. travel one wavelength

c. return to calm sea level

d. travel from crest to trough

Please use the following to answer questions 10 and 11.

The U.S. Geological Survey (USGS) tracks the annual occurrence and effects of natural hazards in the United States. Based on its data, the USGS has calculated the probability of a natural hazard occurring in any given year that would cause 10 or more fatalities. The table below lists the probabilities for the four most commonly occurring natural hazards.

EVENT	PROBABILITY OF AN ANNUAL EVENT WITH ≥10 FATALITIES IN THE UNITED STATES
Earthquake	0.11
Hurricane	0.39
Flood	0.86
Tornado	0.96

0 = no chance of occurring / 1 = 100% chance of occurring

10. What is the probability of a hurricane and a tornado, each with 10 or more fatalities, both occurring in the same year?

a. 0

b. 0.37

c. 0.96

d. 1.35

11. Write the appropriate natural hazard from the table in the box below.

A boundary between the Pacific and North American tectonic plates lies along the west coast of the continental United States. The probability of a(n) [ ] with 10 or more fatalities is much higher in this region than the probability for the United States as a whole.

12. A marathon runner consumes foods with a high carbohydrate content before and during a race to prevent muscle fatigue. This practice, called carb loading, supports which of the following energy transformations within the runner's body?
   a. chemical to thermal
   b. thermal to kinetic
   c. kinetic to thermal
   d. chemical to kinetic

Please use the following to answer questions 13–15.

Consumers in an ecosystem are classified by feeding level. Primary consumers feed on producers. Secondary consumers feed on primary consumers, and tertiary consumers feed on secondary consumers. Consumers in a food web are classified according to their highest feeding level.

A consumer's population size is determined largely by the complex relationships that exist within the ecosystem's food web. Population size is most obviously limited by the population size of the consumer's food source(s). An increase or decrease in a food source population often leads to a similar change in the consumer population. The availability of a food source may be limited by other consumer populations competing for the same food source. An increase in a competitor population may lead to a decreased availability of the shared food source. Population size is also limited by the population size of the consumer's predator(s). Predation by higher-level consumers keeps the lower consumer population from growing out of control and upsetting the ecosystem's balance.

The food web for a woodland ecosystem bordering an area of farmland is shown below.

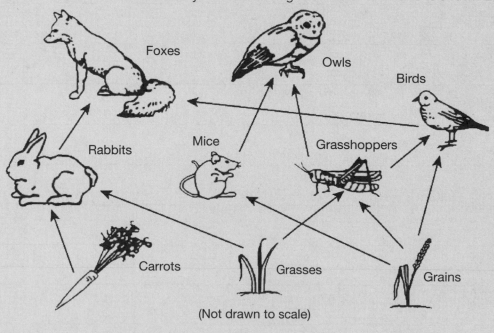

(Not drawn to scale)

13. According to the passage, rabbits are considered primary consumers because they
a. feed on grasses and carrots
b. are consumed by foxes only
c. compete with grasshoppers only
d. are the only consumer of carrots

14. Which three organisms in the food web obtain energy directly or indirectly from grasshoppers?
a. owls, birds, and mice
b. owls, birds, and grains
c. foxes, rabbits, and mice
d. foxes, owls, and birds

15. A bacterial disease has destroyed most of the farm's carrot crop for the past two seasons. As a result, the rabbit population has been forced to rely more heavily on grasses for a food source.

Explain how this disruption is likely to affect the rest of the ecosystem's food web. Include multiple pieces of evidence from the text and discuss specific populations (other than carrots and rabbits) as examples to support your answer.

Write your response on the lines below. This task may take approximately 10 minutes to complete.

16. The table below illustrates the range of normal body temperatures in Fahrenheit for different age groups.

NORMAL BODY TEMPERATURE	
AGE GROUP	TEMPERATURE (IN °FAHRENHEIT)
Newborn	97.7°F–99.5°F
Infants (1 year or less)	97.0°F–99.0°F
Children (1–17 years)	97.5°F–98.6°F
Adults (above 18 years)	97.6°F–99°F
Elders (above 70 years)	96.8°F–97.5°F

The formula for converting Fahrenheit to Celsius is shown below.

$$(°F - 32) \times \frac{5}{9} = °C$$

The normal body temperature range of a newborn baby is ⬚ °C to ⬚ °C. (You may use a calculator to answer this question.)

17. The process of meiosis is depicted in the diagram below.

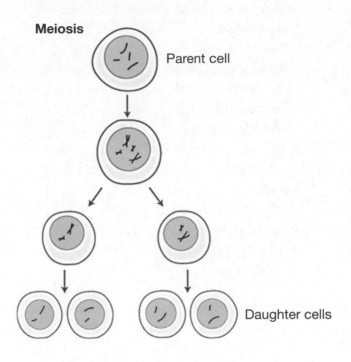

Meiosis

Parent cell

Daughter cells

The daughter cells produced during meiosis are used for what purpose?

a. growth

b. tissue repair

c. differentiation

d. reproduction

18. A highway patrol officer is monitoring the speed of vehicles along a stretch of highway with a speed limit of 55 mph. The results are shown below.

Vehicle 1: 61 mph

Vehicle 2: 48 mph

Vehicle 3: 61 mph

Vehicle 4: 51 mph

Vehicle 5: 59 mph

What is the average speed of the five vehicles? (You may use a calculator to answer this question.)

a. 55 miles per hour

b. 56 miles per hour

c. 59 miles per hour

d. 61 miles per hour

19. Meiosis produces cells containing one chromosome from each chromosome pair. The diagram below shows the chromosome combinations that can be produced from a cell containing two pairs of chromosomes.

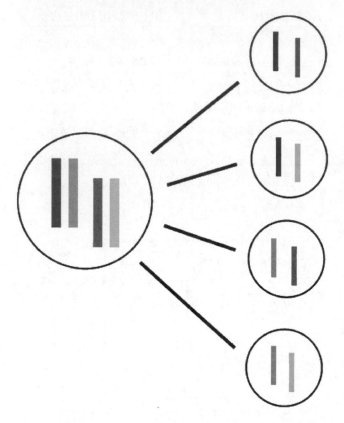

A barley plant has seven pairs of chromosomes. How many unique combinations of chromosomes can result from meiosis in barley?

a. 7

b. 14

c. 49

d. 128

Please use the following to answer questions 20–22.

Respiration is the cellular process used by living things to convert the chemical energy in food to a form that can be used by cells. Adenosine triphosphate (ATP) is the high-energy molecule that all living things use to fuel cellular processes. During respiration, a molecule of glucose is converted to molecules of ATP to be used by the cell.

Depending on the conditions, respiration occurs by two different pathways: aerobic and anaerobic. When a cell has a sufficient supply of oxygen, aerobic respiration occurs. This pathway uses oxygen as a reactant, along with glucose, to produce 36 to 38 molecules of ATP from each molecule of glucose. Aerobic respiration is the preferred pathway in most cells. The general equation for aerobic respiration is shown below.

$$C_6H_{12}O_6 + 6O_2 \rightarrow energy + 6CO_2 + 6H_2O$$

When sufficient oxygen is not available, anaerobic respiration occurs. This pathway produces two molecules of ATP from each molecule of glucose. Anaerobic respiration sometimes occurs in human muscle cells. During exercise, muscle cells use energy faster than the oxygen supply can be replenished, causing the cells to switch temporarily to anaerobic respiration.

20. A student draws the model below to represent the process of aerobic respiration.

Which change would improve the accuracy of the student's model?
a. connecting all of the circles to each other to show bonds
b. moving the energy symbol to the left side of the equation
c. adding five triangles to balance the right side of the equation
d. making the rectangles smaller to show relative molecular sizes

21. The energy produced by respiration is in what form?
a. ATP
b. oxygen
c. glucose
d. carbon dioxide

22. Explain the benefit of having two pathways for respiration in the human body.

Include multiple pieces of evidence from the text to support your answer.

Write your response on the lines on the following page. This task may take approximately 10 minutes to complete.

Please use the following to answer questions 23 and 24.

Matter exists in solid, liquid, and gas states. A substance may change between these three states. State changes can alter the physical properties of a substance, as depicted in the models below.

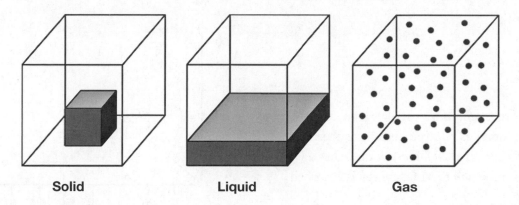

| Solid | Liquid | Gas |

23. Which summary best explains the model of the states of matter?

   a. Liquids have a fixed shape like solids but assume the volume of the container as gases do.

   b. Liquids have a fixed volume and shape like solids. Gases assume the volume and shape of the container.

   c. Liquids have a fixed volume like solids but assume the shape of the container as gases do.

   d. Liquids assume the volume and shape of the container as gases do. Solids have a fixed volume and shape.

24. Based on the model, which state change increases the density of a substance?

   a. gas to liquid

   b. solid to gas

   c. liquid to gas

   d. solid to liquid

Please use the following to answer questions 25–26.

Information about five different fuel sources is listed in the table below.

	ENERGY CONTENT (KJ/G)	CO_2 RELEASED (MOL/10^3KJ)
Hydrogen	120	------
Natural gas	51.6	1.2
Petroleum	43.6	1.6
Coal	39.3	2.0
Ethanol	27.3	1.6

25. Which statement represents a fact supported by the data in the table?

   a. All cars will be fueled by hydrogen cells in the future.

   b. Petroleum is a better fuel source for cars than ethanol is.

   c. Natural gas is too expensive to use as a fuel source for cars.

   d. Ethanol fuel provides a car with less energy per gram than petroleum does.

26. Natural gas, petroleum, and coal are fossil fuels. Ethanol is derived from biomass.

Based on the data in the table, what is the best estimate of the energy content of fossil fuels?
a. 40 kJ/g
b. 42 kJ/g
c. 45 kJ/g
d. 50 kJ/g

27. The term *exothermic* describes a process in which energy is released, usually as thermal energy. The term *endothermic* describes a process in which thermal energy is absorbed.

Which of the following is an example of an exothermic process?
a. a candle burning
b. a snow bank melting
c. a loaf of bread baking
d. a plant making sugar

28. The graph below represents the motion of a remote-controlled car. The car's acceleration, or change in velocity, is indicated by the slope of the graph.

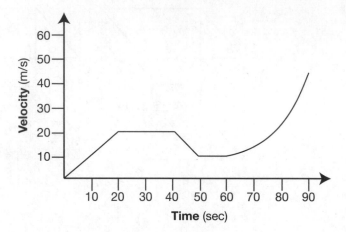

During which period did the car experience a constant positive acceleration?
a. between 0 and 20 seconds
b. between 20 and 40 seconds
c. between 40 and 50 seconds
d. between 50 and 90 seconds

Please use the following to answer questions 29 and 30.

The mechanical advantage (MA) of a machine is a measure of how much the machine multiplies the input force applied to it.

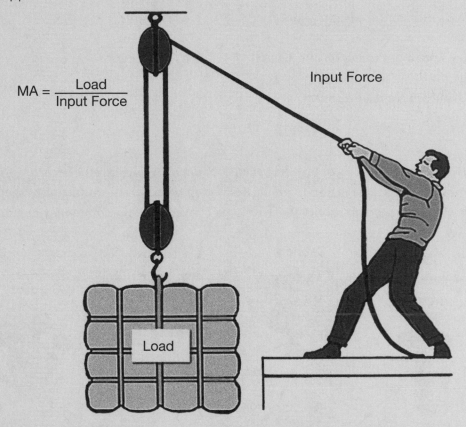

$$MA = \frac{\text{Load}}{\text{Input Force}}$$

Input Force

Load

The table below shows the input force required to lift different loads using the pulley system shown above.

LOAD (N)	INPUT FORCE (N)
30	10
60	20
90	30
150	50

29. Based on the data in the table, what happens to the mechanical advantage of the pulley system as the load size increases?
   a. The mechanical advantage increases at a constant rate.
   b. The system's mechanical advantage does not change.
   c. The pulley system multiplies the mechanical advantage.
   d. The mechanical advantage decreases at a constant rate.

30. A 1-Newton load has a mass of 10 grams. According to the table, what is the maximum mass that can be lifted by the pulley system using an input force of 50 Newtons?
   a. 15 grams
   b. 50 grams
   c. 150 grams
   d. 1,500 grams

31. Artificial selection is the process of breeding plants or animals to increase the occurrence of desired traits. Farmers use artificial selection to produce new crop species from existing plant species. The diagram below illustrates six crop species that have been derived from the common wild mustard plant.

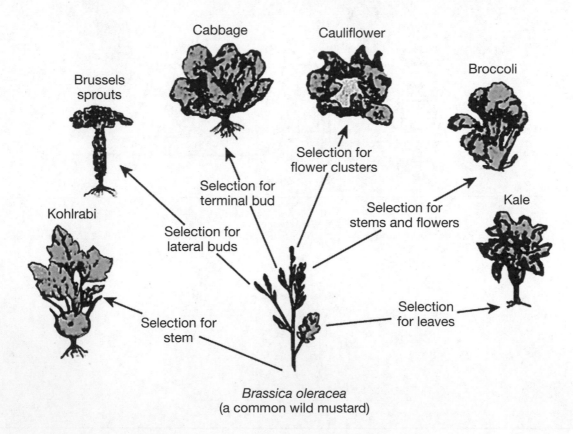

Based on the information in the passage, how did farmers produce kale?
   a. Farmers removed the stems and flowers from mustard plants as they grew.
   b. Farmers allowed only wild mustard plants with large leaves to reproduce.
   c. Farmers bred small-leafed plants with large-leafed plants to increase leaf size.
   d. Farmers prevented wild mustard plants with large leaves from reproducing.

32.

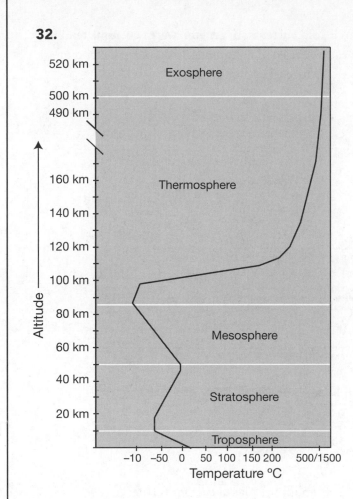

According to the graph, in which atmospheric layers does temperature decrease as altitude increases?

a. mesosphere and exosphere

b. troposphere and thermosphere

c. stratosphere and thermosphere

d. troposphere and mesosphere

33. Surface currents in the ocean are classified as warm or cold currents. In general, warm currents tend to travel from the equator toward the poles along the eastern coast of continents. Cold currents tend to travel from the poles toward the equator along the western coast of continents.

The map below shows the major surface ocean currents of the world.

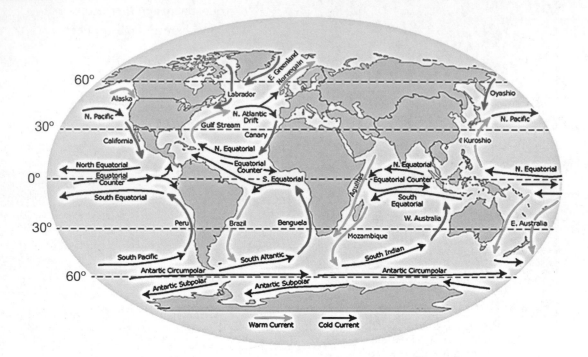

Based on the passage, which of the following statements about the Alaska current is true?

a. The Alaska current is a typical cold current because it travels along the western coast of the continent.

b. The Alaska current is not a true surface current because it does not follow the general pattern of surface currents.

c. The Alaska current is an exception to the general pattern because warm currents typically travel along the eastern coast of continents.

d. The Alaska current transports water from the north pole toward the equator because it travels along the western coast of the continent.

34. Every person has two copies, or alleles, of the ABO blood type gene. A person's ABO blood type is determined by his or her specific combination of alleles. The table below shows the allele combinations that cause the four different ABO blood types.

BLOOD TYPE	GENOTYPE
A	I^AI^A or I^Ai
B	I^BI^B or I^Bi
AB	I^AI^B
O	ii

Suppose that a mother's allele combination is I^Ai, and a father's allele combination is I^AI^B. Which of the following statements is true about the blood type of their first child?

a. The child will have the same blood type as the mother.

b. The child cannot have the father's blood type.

c. The child will have a blood type different from both parents'.

d. The child cannot have blood type O.

35. Blood glucose levels are tightly regulated in the human body by the hormones insulin and glucagon. When glucose levels become too high or low, the pancreas produces the appropriate hormone to return the body to homeostasis. The diagram below shows the feedback mechanism for regulating blood glucose levels.

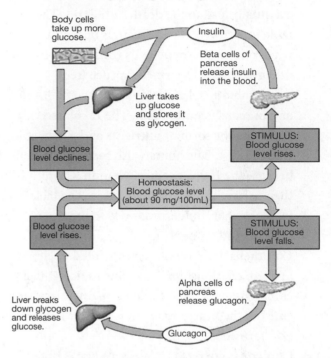

Diabetes mellitus is a disease in which the pancreas is unable to produce the insulin needed to regulate blood glucose levels. What result would occur from providing an insulin injection to a diabetic person with high blood sugar?

a. The insulin travels to the liver, where it binds to and destroys excess glucose in the bloodstream.

b. The insulin signals the pancreas to produce glucagon, which increases the level of glucose in the bloodstream.

c. The insulin causes the liver to convert glucose to glycogen, removing excess glucose from the bloodstream.

d. The insulin breaks down glycogen into glucose, releasing stored glucose into the bloodstream.

Answers and Explanations

1. The symbiotic relationship exhibited by mistletoe and spruce trees is **parasitism**. The mistletoe receives a benefit in the form of a source of nutrients and water. The spruce tree is harmed because it loses nutrients and water, which can eventually lead to the death of the tree. The table indicates that parasitism is occurring when one organism benefits (mistletoe) and the other organism is harmed (spruce tree).

   The symbiotic relationship exhibited by *E. coli* and humans is **mutualism**. The *E. coli* receive a benefit in the form of nutrients and a habitat in which to live. The human also receives a benefit because the *E. coli* produce vitamin K, which is then used within the human body. The table indicates that mutualism is occurring when both organisms benefit.

   Commensalism is not demonstrated in either of these relationships. The table indicates that commensalism occurs when one organism benefits but the other organism is neither helped nor harmed.

2. **Choice c is correct.** The fleas and ticks obtain nutrients from the host animal's blood, and the mites obtain nutrients from the host animal's skin.

   Choice **a** is incorrect. Although the fleas and mites may live on the host animal's body, the ticks do not.

   Choice **b** is incorrect. Parasites can transmit diseases to the host animal, but this does not provide a benefit to the parasite.

   Choice **d** is incorrect. Although the fleas and mites reproduce on the host animal's body, the ticks do not.

3. **Choice b is correct.** The passage states that *Cheyletiella* mites live within the outermost layer of the dog's skin and have difficulty surviving away from the host animal's body. A technician wearing gloves during examination of the dog and disposing of them afterward helps to prevent mites that may be on the technician's hands from being transmitted to other animals in the clinic.

   Choice **a** is incorrect. Vaccines can be administered to uninfected individuals to prevent the transmission of diseases caused by viruses. Mites are arthropods that live on the host animal's body and cannot be eliminated with a vaccine.

   Choice **c** is incorrect. Avoiding contact with open wounds would help prevent the transmission of blood-borne pathogens, such as those transmitted by fleas and ticks.

   Choice **d** is incorrect. Sterilizing the exam room after, not before, examination of the infected dog could help prevent the transmission of mites to other animals in the clinic.

4. In order for an eclipse to occur, the sun, earth, and moon must be aligned in a particular way. When the earth is positioned between the sun and the moon, the earth will prevent sunlight from reaching the moon. This is a lunar eclipse. When the moon is positioned between the sun and the earth, the moon will prevent sunlight from reaching a portion of the earth. This is a solar eclipse.

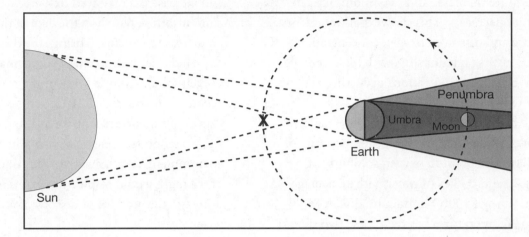

On the diagram, the moon has reached the position in its orbit that is in Earth's shadow, resulting in a lunar eclipse. From its current position on the diagram, the moon would need to travel 180° (or halfway) around its orbit to produce a solar eclipse. In this new position, the moon would cast a shadow on the earth.

5. In a cladogram, the group that exhibits the fewest characteristics is listed on the bottom left branch and the group exhibiting the most characteristics is listed on the top right branch.

Mosses are placed on the first (lower left) branch because they exhibited none of the characteristics listed in the table. Ferns contain vascular tissue, so they are listed on the second branch. Confers are the third branch because they contain vascular tissue and produce seeds. Flowering plants exhibit all three characteristics listed in the table, so they are the fourth (highest) branch.

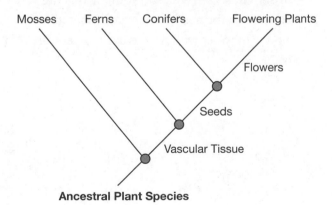

6. **Choice a is correct.** Describing the pattern in the data allows for the relationship between water temperature and oxygen solubility to be identified. As you look down the table, water temperature increases and maximum oxygen solubility decreases. This shows that water temperature and dissolved oxygen concentration have an inverse relationship, with highest dissolved oxygen concentrations occurring at the lowest temperatures.

   Choice **b** is incorrect. According to the table, bodies of water with an average temperature of 40°C have a maximum oxygen solubility of 6.4 mg/L, and bodies of water with an average temperature of 100°C contain no dissolved oxygen. Temperatures between these two should support oxygen concentrations between 6.4 and 0 mg/L.

   Choice **c** is incorrect. Although an increase from 0 to 10°C results in a 3 mg/L increase in oxygen solubility, oxygen solubility does not continue to increase by the same increment with each additional 10°C increase in temperature.

   Choice **d** is incorrect. Although many variables can affect oxygen solubility, the table focuses only on the relationship between oxygen solubility and water temperature.

7. **Choice c is correct.** Grasses release oxygen into the environment as a byproduct of photosynthesis. Using this reasoning, it can be predicted that an increase in freshwater grasses will increase the dissolved oxygen concentration. Based on the data in the table, an increase to 8.5 mg/L brings the dissolved oxygen concentration closer to the maximum oxygen solubility for a body of water with an average temperature of 21°C.

   Choice **a** is incorrect. Aquatic plants like freshwater grasses release oxygen into the environment. A dissolved oxygen concentration of 6.3 mg/L would result from an event that decreases the amount of dissolved oxygen in the water.

   Choice **b** is incorrect. A dissolved oxygen concentration of 7.2 mg/L would indicate no change in the ecosystem. A change in the freshwater grass population would alter the amount of dissolved oxygen in the water.

   Choice **d** is incorrect. A doubling of the freshwater grass population would cause an increase in dissolved oxygen concentration but not a doubling. According to the table, a dissolved oxygen concentration of 14.4 mg/L far exceeds the maximum oxygen solubility for a body of water with an average temperature of 21°C.

8. **Choice c is correct.** Range can be determined by calculating the difference between the lowest and highest values in a data set. The table shows that the temperature of a yellow star is between 5,000 K and 6,000 K. This is a range of 1,000 K, which is the smallest (or narrowest) range listed in the table.

Choice **a** is incorrect. White stars have a maximum temperature of 11,000 K. The minimum temperature of blue-white stars is 11,000 K.

Choice **b** is incorrect. Red stars have a maximum temperature of 3,500 K. A star with a temperature of 3,700 K would be within the range of an orange star.

Choice **d** is incorrect. The table does not provide information about the highest surface temperature recorded for a star. The minimum temperature of a blue star is shown to be 25,000 K. This indicates that blue stars can have temperatures higher than 25,000 K.

9. **Choice b is correct.** In the context of this ocean wave diagram, a wavelength is the horizontal distance between two crests (*A* and *B*). Using the given definition of wave period, it can be determined that the wave period is the amount of time required to travel one wavelength.

Choice **a** is incorrect. A shoreline is not shown or mentioned in the diagram.

Choice **c** is incorrect. Wave period relates to the horizontal movement of a wave, while calm sea level is a reference point used to measure the vertical movement of a wave.

Choice **d** is incorrect. In the diagram, points *A* and *B* used to measure wave period are both crests. The time required to travel from crest to trough would be half of a wave period.

10. **Choice b is correct.** A hurricane and tornado occurring in the same year would be considered a compound event because two events are occurring together. The probability of a compound event can be determined by multiplying the probabilities of each event occurring individually. The probability of a hurricane (0.39) multiplied by the probability of a tornado (0.96) provides a compound probability of 0.3744.

Choice **a** is incorrect. A probability of 0 indicates that there is no chance of an event occurring. Since there is a possibility of a hurricane and a possibility of a tornado occurring individually, there is also a possibility of both events occurring in the same year.

Choice **c** is incorrect. This is the probability of a tornado alone occurring during any given year. The probability of both a tornado and a hurricane occurring in the same year would be much lower because the probability of a hurricane is much lower (0.39) than the probability of a tornado (0.96).

Choice **d** is incorrect. A probability greater than 1 indicates that an event is guaranteed to occur. Since the individual probabilities of a hurricane or tornado occurring are both less than 1, the probability of both events occurring in the same year would also be less than 1.

11. The natural hazard that best completes this statement is **earthquake**. The Earth's crust is made up of tectonic plates. The location where two or more tectonic plates meet is called a plate boundary. When the pressure built up at a plate boundary becomes too great, energy is released in the form of an earthquake. Earthquakes can be expected to occur most frequently along plate boundaries. Since the west coast of the continental United States lies on a plate boundary, the probability of an earthquake occurring in this region can be predicted to be much higher than the probability for the United States as a whole, most of which does not lie on plate boundaries.

The occurrence of hurricanes, floods, and tornadoes is not specifically tied to the activity of tectonic plates. An increase in the probability of any of these natural hazards along a plate boundary as compared to the United States as a whole is not a reasonable prediction.

12. Choice d is correct. The runner takes in chemical energy in the form of carbohydrates. This chemical energy is transformed into kinetic energy as the runner's muscles contract and relax, causing the runner to move. Runners carb load to ensure that their bodies have enough chemical energy to be transformed into the kinetic energy required to run a marathon. Choice **a** is incorrect. The runner does take in chemical energy in the form of carbohydrates. Though some of this chemical energy is transformed into thermal energy in the form of body heat, the purpose of carb loading is to improve muscle performance, not increase body heat.

Choice **b** is incorrect. The purpose of carb loading is to increase the amount of energy available for transformation into kinetic energy (motion). Carb loading increases the availability of chemical energy, though, not thermal energy. Carbohydrates contain energy stored in their chemical bonds, not as heat.

Choice **c** is incorrect. The goal of carb loading is to improve muscle performance (motion), not increase body heat. Muscle performance is improved by increasing the chemical energy available for transformation into kinetic energy.

13. Choice a is correct. A primary-level consumer feeds on producers. Producers, such as plants, make their own food using energy from sunlight. Rabbits feed on two producers, carrots and grasses, making rabbits a primary-level consumer.

Choice **b** is incorrect. An organism's feeding level is determined by how it obtains its food, not by the organisms that it provides food for. Though the rabbits in the food web are consumed by foxes, this does not determine the rabbits' feeding level.

Choice **c** is incorrect. Competition with other organisms does not affect how an organism's feeding level is classified.

Choice **d** is incorrect. The presence of other organisms that consume the same food source does not affect how an organism's feeding level is classified.

14. Choice d is correct. An organism provides energy to all organisms above it in the food web. In this food web, the grasshoppers provide energy to the birds, owls, and foxes. The birds and owls obtain energy directly when they consume the grasshoppers. The foxes obtain energy indirectly when they consume birds that previously consumed grasshoppers.

Choice **a** is incorrect. Although owls and birds obtain energy from grasshoppers, mice do not obtain energy from grasshoppers.

Choice **b** is incorrect. Grains provide energy to grasshoppers but do not obtain energy from grasshoppers.

Choice **c** is incorrect. Rabbits and mice do not obtain energy from grasshoppers either directly or indirectly.

15. Answers will vary.

The highest number of points you can earn on this short-response essay is 3.

A **3-point essay** contains:

- a clear and well-developed explanation of how a change in one population effects change in other populations within the food web
- well-developed examples from the given food web describing the likely effects of change in the rabbit population on other specific populations
- complete support from the passage

Sample 3-point response:

The interrelatedness of populations in the food web makes it likely that all populations will be affected in some way by the shift in the rabbits' feeding habits. The rabbits' increased reliance on grasses will cause a domino effect on the availability of food for all primary consumers. Since grasshoppers directly compete with rabbits for grasses, the availability of grasses for grasshoppers may be limited. As a result, grasshoppers would likely increase their dependence on grains, decreasing the availability of this food source for birds and mice. The overall increase in competition among primary consumers may cause some decreases in population sizes, which would also limit the population sizes of higher-level consumers.

A **2-point essay** contains:

- an adequate or partially articulated explanation of how a change in one population effects change in other populations within the food web
- partial examples from the given food web describing the likely effects of change in the rabbit population on other specific populations
- partial support from the passage

Sample 2-point response:

When the rabbits start eating more grasses, the grasshoppers will have less food because they eat grasses too. This means that the grasshopper population might get smaller, so the owls and birds would have less food. Foxes eat birds, so they would have less food too.

A **1-point essay** contains:

- a minimal or implied explanation of how a change in one population effects change in other populations within the food web
- one or incomplete examples from the given food web describing the likely effects of change in the rabbit population on other specific populations
- minimal or implied support from the passage

Sample 1-point response:

The rabbits will eat more grass. Grasshoppers will not have as much grass to eat. Some grasshoppers will die because they don't have enough food.

A **0-point essay** contains:

- no explanation of how a change in one population effects change in other populations within the food web
- no examples from the given food web describing the likely effects of change in the rabbit population on other specific populations
- no support from the passage

16. **Blank 1:** The appropriate value to complete this statement is **36.5**.
The formula for converting temperature from Fahrenheit to Celsius is given as $(°F - 32) \times \frac{5}{9} = °C$. Replacing the lower variable $°F$ with 97.7 and solving gives $(97.7 - 32) \times \frac{5}{9} = 36.5$.
Blank 2: The appropriate value to complete this statement is **37.5**.
The formula for converting temperature from Fahrenheit to Celsius is given as $(°F - 32) \times \frac{5}{9} = °C$. Replacing the lower variable $°F$ with 99.5 and solving gives $(99.5 - 32) \times \frac{5}{9} = 37.5$.

17. **Choice d is correct.** As indicated in the diagram, the daughter cells produced during meiosis each have half the total number of chromosomes as the parent cell does. These daughter cells, called gametes, are used for reproduction. When reproduction occurs, two gametes (egg and sperm) unite to create a cell with a full set of chromosomes.
Choice **a** is incorrect. To allow an organism to grow larger, the daughter cells produced must be identical to the parent cell. Cells used for growth are produced by the process of mitosis.
Choice **b** is incorrect. To allow an organism to repair tissues, the daughter cells produced must be identical to the parent cell. The cells used for tissue repair are produced by the process of mitosis.
Choice **c** is incorrect. Cell differentiation occurs when a single, non-specialized cell is converted to a specialized cell type, like a blood cell or skin cell. No daughter cells are produced during the differentiation process.

18. Choice b is correct. The average speed can be determined by adding the individual vehicle speeds and dividing by the total number of vehicles. This is calculated as $\frac{61 + 48 + 61 + 51 + 59}{5} = 56$ mph.

Choice **a** is incorrect. This is the speed limit for the highway, not the average speed of the five vehicles listed.

Choice **c** is incorrect. This is the median speed of the five vehicles, not the average (mean) speed.

Choice **d** is incorrect. This is the mode for the speed of the five vehicles, not the average (mean) speed.

19. Choice d is correct. Each new cell created by meiosis must contain one chromosome from each of the seven chromosome pairs. As illustrated in the diagram, these single chromosomes can be combined in multiple ways. To determine the total number of unique chromosome combinations, the number of chromosomes in each set (pair) must be multiplied. Seven sets of two chromosomes each means that seven 2's must be multiplied ($2 \times 2 \times 2 \times 2 \times 2 \times 2 \times 2 = 128$) to determine the total number of unique chromosome combinations possible.

Choice **a** is incorrect. There are seven total chromosomes in a cell produced by meiosis, but the specific chromosome present from each chromosome pair can vary.

Choice **b** is incorrect. Two chromosomes in each of seven pairs provides a total of 14 chromosomes, but the specific chromosome present from each pair can vary.

Choice **c** is incorrect. Multiplying 7×7 does not provide the total number of chromosome combinations possible. To determine this, the number of chromosomes in each pair must be multiplied by the number of chromosomes in each other pair.

20. Choice c is correct. The products of respiration are six molecules of carbon dioxide, six molecules of water, and energy. On the right side of the model, six rectangles are present but only one triangle. To accurately represent a balanced equation, all molecules must be represented in the model.

Choice **a** is incorrect. The circles represent the six molecules of the reactant oxygen. Connecting the circles would not improve the model's accuracy because separate molecules are not bound to each other.

Choice **b** is incorrect. Energy is a product of the respiration reaction and is therefore appropriately placed on the right side of the equation. Moving the energy symbol to the left side of the equation would indicate that energy is a reactant.

Choice **d** is incorrect. Reducing the size of the rectangles is not the most needed change, since the other molecules are not represented to scale.

21. Choice a is correct. The purpose of respiration is to convert energy into a form that is useable by cells. Respiration produces ATP, a high-energy molecule, which the cell can use to carry out cellular functions.

Choice **b** is incorrect. Oxygen is a reactant—not a product—of aerobic respiration and does not provide energy for the cell.

Choice **c** is incorrect. Respiration uses the glucose in food to produce ATP. Respiration does not produce glucose.

Choice **d** is incorrect. Although respiration does produce carbon dioxide, this molecule does not provide energy for the cell.

22. The highest number of points you can earn on this short-response essay is 3.

A **3-point essay** contains:
- a clear and well-developed explanation of the benefits of the aerobic respiration pathway in the human body
- a clear and well-developed explanation of the benefits of the anaerobic respiration pathway in the human body
- complete support from the passage

Sample 3-point response:
The human body may use two different pathways to carry out respiration. The presence of two different pathways is valuable because it allows a cell to choose the pathway that best meets its current energy needs. Aerobic respiration produces the greatest amount of ATP per glucose molecule. Under normal conditions with adequate oxygen, this pathway provides the greatest possible amount of energy to the cell. Anaerobic respiration produces much less ATP per glucose molecule but does not require oxygen. Under strenuous conditions when the cell demands energy faster than the oxygen supply can be replenished, this pathway provides enough energy to maintain cell functions. The ability to switch between aerobic and anaerobic pathways allows the human body to function properly under varying conditions.

A **2-point essay** contains:
- an adequate or partially articulated explanation of the benefits of the aerobic respiration pathway in the human body
- an adequate or partially articulated explanation of the benefits of the anaerobic respiration pathway in the human body
- partial support from the passage

Sample 2-point response:
Aerobic respiration produces the most ATP, but requires oxygen. Anaerobic respiration produces much less ATP, but does not require oxygen. Having two pathways is important because sometimes oxygen is available, and sometimes it is not.

A **1-point essay** contains:
- a minimal or implied explanation of the benefits of the aerobic respiration pathway in the human body
- a minimal or implied explanation of the benefits of the anaerobic respiration pathway in the human body
- minimal or implied support from the passage

Sample 1-point response:
Cells use aerobic respiration most of the time. Muscle cells use anaerobic respiration when a person is exercising. Both types of respiration are important.

A **0-point essay** contains:
- no explanation of the benefits of the aerobic respiration pathway in the human body
- no explanation of the benefits of the anaerobic respiration pathway in the human body
- no support from the passage

23. Choice c is correct. As shown in the model, a solid has a fixed volume and shape. A liquid has a fixed volume but assumes the shape of the container. A gas assumes the volume and shape of the container. A liquid has one property in common with solids and one property in common with gases.

Choice **a** is incorrect. In this summary, the properties of a liquid are reversed. Liquids have a fixed volume and assume the shape of the container.

Choice **b** is incorrect. Liquids have a fixed volume, as solids do, but not a fixed shape.

Choice **d** is incorrect. Liquids assume the shape of the container, as gases do, but not the volume.

24. Choice a is correct. The density of a substance describes how tightly packed the substance's molecules are. As shown in the model, a substance's molecules are most spread out when in the gas state. This means that a substance's density is lowest when in the gas state. The substance's density increases when going from gas to liquid state because the molecules become more tightly packed.

Choice **b** is incorrect. A substance's molecules become more spread out when changing from solid to gas state. This causes the substance's density to decrease.

Choice **c** is incorrect. A substance's molecules become more spread out when changing from liquid to gas state. This causes the substance's density to decrease.

Choice **d** is incorrect. A substance's molecules may become slightly more spread out, or less dense, when changing from solid to liquid state. However, the density of a substance does not change much during this state change.

25. Choice d is correct. Based on the data in the table, this statement can be identified as a fact. The energy content of ethanol is 27.3 kJ/g, about 16 kJ/g less than the energy content of petroleum (43.6 kJ/g).

Choice **a** is incorrect. This statement is speculation based on data from the table. According to the table, hydrogen has the greatest energy content and releases no carbon dioxide. Although this data supports the speculation that cars may be fueled by hydrogen cells in the future, this statement is no guarantee.

Choice **b** is incorrect. This statement is a judgment based on data from the table. According to the table, petroleum has a higher energy content than ethanol. Although this data can be used to support the judgment that petroleum is the better fuel source, this statement is an opinion rather than a fact.

Choice **c** is incorrect. This statement is speculation based on data from the table. Although the data in the table suggests that natural gas is a relatively efficient and clean fuel source, the statement is speculation because no information is provided about the cost of natural gas.

26. Choice c is correct. The passage identifies natural gas, petroleum, and coal as fossil fuels, because each is derived from the fossil remains of organisms. The energy content of each fossil fuel can be approximated to 50 kJ/g, 45 kJ/g, and 40 kJ/g, respectively. This provides an estimated average energy content of 45 kJ/g.
Choice **a** is incorrect. This would be an appropriate estimate for the energy content of coal, not for the energy content of all three fossil fuels.
Choice **b** is incorrect. This would be an appropriate estimate for the energy content of petroleum and coal, but natural gas is also a fossil fuel.
Choice **d** is incorrect. This would be an appropriate estimate for the energy content of natural gas, not for the energy content of all three fossil fuels.

27. Choice a is correct. Burning a candle is an exothermic process because thermal energy, or heat, is released as a result of the process.
Choice **b** is incorrect. Melting a snow bank is an endothermic process because the input of heat is required to melt the snow. This means that thermal energy is absorbed during the process, not released.
Choice **c** is incorrect. Baking a loaf of bread is an endothermic process because the input of heat is required to convert the ingredients to bread. This means that thermal energy is absorbed during the process, not released.
Choice **d** is incorrect. Photosynthesis is an endothermic process because the input of energy (sunlight) is required for plants to make sugar. This means that energy is absorbed during the process, not released.

28. Choice a is correct. The car has a constant positive acceleration when the car's velocity is increasing at a steady, or constant, rate. Between 0 and 20 seconds, the graph moves upward in a straight diagonal line, indicating that the velocity is increasing at a constant rate.
Choice **b** is incorrect. Between 20 and 40 seconds, the car is maintaining a constant velocity of 20 m/s. Since the velocity is constant within this time period, the car is not accelerating (has an acceleration of 0 m/s^2).
Choice **c** is incorrect. Between 40 and 50 seconds, the car's velocity is decreasing at a constant rate. This indicates a constant negative acceleration.
Choice **d** is incorrect. Between 50 and 90 seconds, the car's velocity is increasing, but not at a constant rate. The graph moves upward in a curved line within this time period, indicating that the velocity is increasing at a variable rate.

29. Choice b is correct. The mechanical advantage of a pulley system does not change with the load. Mechanical advantage is calculated as load divided by input force. In the data table, dividing each load by its corresponding input force produces a mechanical advantage of three.
Choice **a** is incorrect. As the load size increases, the input force required to lift the load increases at a constant rate. The mechanical advantage of the pulley system does not change.
Choice **c** is incorrect. A pulley system multiplies the input force, not the mechanical advantage, applied to a load.
Choice **d** is incorrect. No decrease in mechanical advantage occurs with an increase in load. The mechanical advantage of a pulley system is constant regardless of the size of the load.

30. Choice d is correct. According to the table, an input force of 50 N can lift a 150-N load. If a 1-N load has a mass of 10 grams, the mass of a load can be determined by multiplying the force of the load by 10. A 150-N load therefore has a mass of 1,500 grams.
Choice **a** is incorrect. This value is the result of dividing the force of the load (150 N) by 10. The mass of the load is determined by multiplying, not dividing, the force of the load by 10.
Choice **b** is incorrect. This is the value of the input force, not the mass of the load.
Choice **c** is incorrect. This is the value of the force of the load in Newtons, not the mass of the load in grams.

31. Choice b is correct. Kale is a leafy crop species. According to the diagram, wild mustard plants were selected for leaves to produce kale. This means that wild mustard plants that had large leaves were specifically bred together to increase leaf size. This selective breeding over multiple generations led to a new species (kale) characterized by large leaves.
Choice **a** is incorrect. Plants with desired characteristics (large leaves for kale) must be bred together to produce offspring plants with those characteristics. Removing stems and flowers from existing mustard plants will not increase leaf size in subsequent generations.
Choice **c** is incorrect. Breeding small-leafed plants and large-leafed plants allows the possibility that offspring will have either small or large leaves. To ensure offspring have the best chances of large leaves, large-leafed plants should be bred together.
Choice **d** is incorrect. Preventing plants with large leaves from growing works to remove the large-leaf trait from subsequent generations rather than increase its appearance.

32. Choice d is correct. In the graph, temperature increases to the right and altitude increases upward. Any portion of the graph that has a negative slope, or slopes to the left, indicates a decrease in temperature. The graph has a negative slope in the troposphere and mesosphere layers.
Choice **a** is incorrect. The graph has a negative slope within the mesosphere but a slight positive slope in the exosphere. This means that temperature decreases as altitude increases in the mesosphere but increases with altitude in the exosphere.
Choice **b** is incorrect. The graph has a negative slope within the troposphere but a positive slope in the thermosphere. Even though the slope is not constant within the thermosphere, the slope remains positive within this layer. This means that temperature decreases in the troposphere but increases in the thermosphere.
Choice **c** is incorrect. The graph has a positive slope within both the stratosphere and the thermosphere. This means that temperature increases with altitude in both layers.

33. Choice c is correct. The Alaska current is a warm current. The passage states that warm currents typically travel along the eastern coast of continents, but the Alaska current travels along the western coast of North America.
Choice **a** is incorrect. Although the Alaska current does travel along the western coast of the continent, the map key indicates that it is a warm current.
Choice **b** is incorrect. The Alaska current does not follow the typical pattern for a warm current but is identified as a surface current on the map.
Choice **d** is incorrect. The map key identifies the Alaska current as a warm current. Warm currents transport warm water originating near the equator toward the poles.

34. Choice d is correct. The blood type O can be produced only by the allele combination ii. A child receives one allele from each parent. Since the mother has an i but the father does not, the allele combination ii is not possible for their children.

Choice **a** is incorrect. Based on the table, the mother's blood type is A. The child can receive I^A or i from the mother and I^A from the father, resulting in type A blood caused by the possible allele combinations I^AI^A or I^Ai. However, the child could receive I^B from the father, which would result in a blood type different from the mother's.

Choice **b** is incorrect. Based on the table, the father has blood type AB. The child can receive I^A from the mother and I^B from the father, resulting in the possible allele combination I^AI^B. This allele combination will produce the same blood type as the father's.

Choice **c** is incorrect. Based on the table, the mother's blood type is A and the father's is AB. The child can receive I^A or i from the mother and I^A from the father, resulting in type A blood caused by the possible allele combinations I^AI^A or I^Ai. The child can receive I^A from the mother and I^B from the father, resulting in the blood type AB caused by the possible allele combination I^AI^B. This means it is possible for the child to have the same blood type as one of the parents.

35. Choice c is correct. According to the diagram, when a person's blood glucose level rises, the pancreas secretes insulin. The insulin signals body cells to absorb glucose from the blood and signals the liver to convert excess glucose into the storage molecule glycogen. These processes remove excess glucose from the blood, returning the blood glucose level to homeostasis. Insulin injected into a diabetic person initiates the same pathway as insulin produced in the pancreas of a healthy person.

Choice **a** is incorrect. Insulin signals the liver to convert and store excess glucose to glycogen, not to destroy the glucose.

Choice **b** is incorrect. Insulin and glucagon do not signal each other but perform opposite functions. Insulin works to decrease blood glucose levels, while glucagon works to increase these levels.

Choice **d** is incorrect. Glucagon signals the breakdown of glycogen into glucose when blood glucose levels are low. Insulin signals the conversion of glucose to glycogen when blood glucose levels are high.

18 ▶ SOCIAL STUDIES PRACTICE TEST

This practice test is modeled on the format, content, and timing of the official GED® Social Studies test and, like the official exam, presents a series of questions that focus on the fundamentals of social studies reasoning.

Part I

You'll be asked to answer questions based on brief texts, maps, graphics, and tables. Refer to the information provided as often as necessary when answering the questions.

Work carefully, but do not spend too much time on any one question. Be sure to answer every question.

Set a timer for 65 minutes (1 hour and 5 minutes), and try to take this test uninterrupted, under quiet conditions.

Part II

The official GED® Social Studies test also includes an Extended Response question—an essay question. Set a timer for 25 minutes and try to read the given passage, brainstorm, write, and proofread your essay uninterrupted, under quiet conditions.

Complete answer explanations for every test question and sample essays at different scoring levels follow the exam. Good luck!

Part I

35 total questions
65 minutes to complete

Please use the following passage to answer questions 1–3.

This excerpt is from a speech by George W. Bush given on March 19, 2008.

Operation Iraqi Freedom was a remarkable display of military effectiveness. Forces from the U.K., Australia, Poland, and other allies joined our troops in the initial operations. As they advanced, our troops fought their way through sandstorms so intense that they blackened the daytime sky. Our troops engaged in pitched battles with Fedayeen Saddam, death squads acting on the orders of Saddam Hussein that obeyed neither the conventions of war nor the dictates of conscience. These death squads hid in schools, and they hid in hospitals, hoping to draw fire against Iraqi civilians. They used women and children as human shields. They stopped at nothing in their efforts to prevent us from prevailing, but they couldn't stop the coalition advance.

Aided by the most effective and precise air campaign in history, coalition forces raced across 350 miles of enemy territory, destroying Republican Guard divisions, pushing through the Karbala Gap, capturing Saddam International Airport, and liberating Baghdad in less than one month.

Because we acted, Saddam Hussein no longer fills fields with the remains of innocent men, women, and children. . . . Because we acted, Saddam's regime is no longer invading its neighbors or attacking them with chemical weapons and ballistic missiles.

---

1. Based on the primary-source excerpt concerning a central idea of American foreign policy since 9/11, what was President Bush's purpose for launching Operation Iraqi Freedom?
   a. to liberate Baghdad in less than one month by destroying Republican Guard divisions
   b. to liberate Iraqi people from a brutal regime and remove Saddam Hussein from power
   c. to stop Saddam Hussein from invading other nations
   d. to join countries in aiding Saddam Hussein's control of the Iraqi people's natural rights

2. Which of the following statements is an opinion, NOT a fact?
   a. "coalition forces raced across 350 miles of enemy territory, . . . liberating Baghdad in less than one month"
   b. "Forces from the U.K., Australia, Poland, and other allies joined our troops in the initial operations."
   c. "Our troops engaged in pitched battles with Fedayeen Saddam, death squads acting on the orders of Saddam Hussein."
   d. "Operation Iraqi Freedom was a remarkable display of military effectiveness."

3. Based on the primary-source excerpt, what can be concluded about the credibility of Bush's choice to launch Operation Iraqi Freedom?
   a. The operation was not justified, and Bush makes this clear in his speech.
   b. Bush feels that the operation was justified, but the realities of Saddam's regime discredit any justification.
   c. The operation was justified in trying to bring down a detrimental and brutal regime.
   d. The actions of Saddam's regime justify the operation, but Bush expresses his concern that the operation may not have been justified in his speech.

Please use the following to answer questions 4–6.

This excerpt is from the U.S. Constitution.

> The President shall be Commander in Chief of the Army and Navy of the United States, and of the Militia of the several States, when called into the actual Service of the United States. . . . He shall have Power, by and with the Advice and Consent of the Senate, to make Treaties, provided two thirds of the Senators present concur.

4. In this portion of the U.S. Constitution, which branch of the government checks the power of which other branch of government by a two-thirds agreement?
   a. the executive checks the power of the legislative
   b. the judicial checks the power of the executive
   c. the legislative checks the power of the executive
   d. the legislative checks the power of the judicial

5. Why is it important for the U.S. Constitution to include rules, such as the one in the excerpt, that allow for power checking between the different branches of government?
   a. to ensure that the legislative branch has power over the executive and judicial branches
   b. to ensure a separation of power that balances the powers of the three branches in order to prevent any one person or group from holding too much or all power
   c. to ensure that the president has the ability to check the power of all other branches
   d. to ensure that the president does not have the power to make treaties without some say from the Senate

6. Based on the excerpt from the U.S. Constitution, what can you infer would be the effect of a failure to receive a two-thirds agreement from the Senate in this instance?
   a. the Senate could not make a treaty but the president could make a treaty
   b. the Senate could make a treaty
   c. the president could not make a treaty because the Senate does not agree
   d. the president could make a treaty

7. What is the difference between a government ruled by popular sovereignty and a government ruled by a dictatorship?

   a. a government ruled by popular sovereignty means that the authority has the consent of the governed to rule, and a government ruled by a dictatorship means that the authority is held by one individual

   b. a government ruled by a dictatorship means that the authority has the consent of the governed to rule, and a government ruled by popular sovereignty does not have consent

   c. popular sovereignty means that the government is ruled by the most popular individual, and a dictatorship means that the government is ruled by the least popular individual

   d. a dictatorship means that the government is ruled by the most popular individual, and popular sovereignty means that the government is ruled by the least popular individual

8. Determine whether each aspect of the federal government listed below is associated with the executive, legislative, or judicial branch of government. Write your answers in the boxes below.

   The Supreme Court
   The House of Representatives
   The Senate
   The president's Cabinet
   The president

Executive Branch	Legislative Branch	Judicial Branch

Please use the following passage to answer questions 9 and 10.

This excerpt is from a speech by Bill Clinton given on July 19, 1995.

The purpose of affirmative action is to give our Nation a way to finally address the systemic exclusion of individuals of talent on the basis of their gender or race from opportunities to develop, perform, achieve, and contribute. Affirmative action is an effort to develop a systematic approach to open the doors of education, employment, and business development opportunities to qualified individuals who happen to be members of groups that have experienced longstanding and persistent discrimination.

It is a policy that grew out of many years of trying to navigate between two unacceptable pasts. One was to say simply that we declared discrimination illegal and that's enough. We saw that that way still relegated blacks with college degrees to jobs as railroad porters and kept women with degrees under a glass ceiling with a lower paycheck.

The other path was simply to try to impose change by leveling draconian penalties on employers who didn't meet certain imposed, ultimately arbitrary, and sometimes unachievable quotas. That, too, was rejected out of a sense of fairness.

So a middle ground was developed that would change an inequitable status quo gradually but firmly, by building the pool of qualified applicants for college, for contracts, for jobs, and giving more people the chance to learn, work, and earn. When affirmative action is done right, it is flexible, it is fair, and it works.

9. According to the excerpt from Clinton's speech, affirmative action is a partial solution to which long-standing societal problem that has affected history?
   a. slavery
   b. discrimination
   c. unemployment
   d. poverty

10. According to the excerpt, what changes would affirmative action cause to come about for minority groups that suffer from discrimination?

a. It will give more people in these minority groups the chance to work, learn, and earn a living by increasing the number of qualified applicants from these groups who are accepted for job positions and places in college.

b. It will give fewer people in these minority groups the chance to work, learn, and earn a living by decreasing the number of qualified applicants from these groups who are accepted for job positions and places in college.

c. It will change nothing for minority groups and will instead only reduce penalties on employers who do not meet a certain quota of minority workers in their workplaces.

d. It will reduce the pay of women in the workplace and decrease the number of minority groups in universities.

Please use the following two documents to answer questions 11 and 12.

This excerpt is from the Declaration of Independence.

We hold these truths to be self-evident, that all men are created equal, that they are endowed by their Creator with certain unalienable Rights that among these are Life, Liberty and the pursuit of Happiness. That to secure these rights, Governments are instituted among Men, deriving their just powers from the consent of the governed. That whenever any Form of Government becomes destructive of these ends, it is the Right of the People to alter or to abolish it, and to institute new Government, laying its foundation on such principles and organizing its powers in such form, as to them shall seem most likely to effect their Safety and Happiness.

This excerpt is from the U.S. Constitution.

We the People of the United States, in Order to form a more perfect Union, establish Justice, insure domestic Tranquility, provide for the common defence, promote the general Welfare, and secure the Blessings of Liberty to ourselves and our Posterity, do ordain and establish this Constitution for the United States of America.

11. Analyze the two excerpts taken from key historical documents that have shaped American constitutional government. Based on these excerpts, which of the following ideas is incorporated into both documents?
   a. the equality of men
   b. the right to abolish destructive government
   c. the abolition of slavery
   d. the right to liberty

12. In the excerpt from the Declaration of Independence, what concept is being described in the following sentences?

"That to secure these rights, Governments are instituted among Men, deriving their just powers from the consent of the governed. That whenever any Form of Government becomes destructive of these ends, it is the Right of the People to alter or to abolish it, and to institute new Government, laying its foundation on such principles and organizing its powers in such form, as to them shall seem most likely to effect their Safety and Happiness."
   a. federalism
   b. popular sovereignty
   c. popular socialism
   d. capitalism

13. The table below displays the number of men killed, wounded, and captured during two battles of the Revolutionary War on both the American and British sides.

Date	Engagement	Commander	Troops	Killed	Wounded	Captured
Apr. 19, 1775	Lexington/Concord	American: Capt. John Parker, et al.	3,763	49	41	0
		British: Lt. Col. Francis Smith	1,800	73	174	7
June 17, 1775	Bunker (Breed's) Hill	American: Gens. Putnam & Ward	2,000	140	271	30
		British: General William Howe	2,400	226	826	0

Based on this information, what was the mean value of men killed in both engagements? Write your answer in the box below. (You may use a calculator to answer this question.)

14. The graph shows the changes in unemployment rates for nonfarm workers between 1926 and 1947.

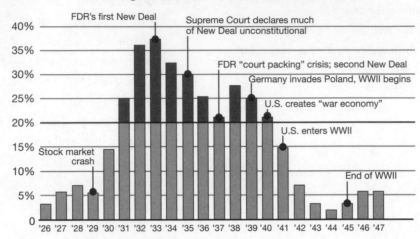

Unemployment Rate During the New Deal

Percentage of Jobless Nonfarm Workers, 1926–1947

Based on the information shown, select the event that led to the greatest drop in the unemployment rate the following year for nonfarm workers.

a. FDR's first New Deal

b. the United States enters World War II

c. the stock market crash

d. Germany invades Poland, World War II begins

15. Read the following definition of capitalism.

Capitalism is an economic and political system that allows a country's trade and industry to be controlled by private owners for profit.

Based on this definition, write the appropriate word in the box that makes the following statement true.

Capitalism gives [ ] owners the freedom to make a profit from control of the country's trade and industry.

16. The graph shows the percentage of citizens affiliated with each U.S. political party.

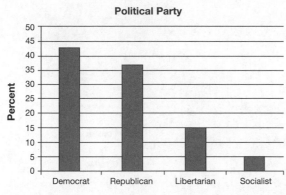

Political Party

Which political party has the most members, and how does the graph show that?

a. The Democratic Party has the most members. Political parties are labeled on the *x*-axis, and the percent of members in those parties is labeled on the *y*-axis. The bar for percentage of Democrats is highest.

b. The Democratic Party has the most members. Political parties are labeled on the *y*-axis, and the percent of members in those parties is labeled on the *x*-axis. The bar for percentage of Democrats is highest.

c. The Libertarian Party has the most members. Political parties are labeled on the *x*-axis, and the percent of members in those parties is labeled on the *y*-axis. The bar for percentage of Libertarians is highest.

d. The Libertarian Party has the most members. Political parties are labeled on the *y*-axis, and the percent of members in those parties is labeled on the *x*-axis. The bar for percentage of Libertarians is highest.

17.

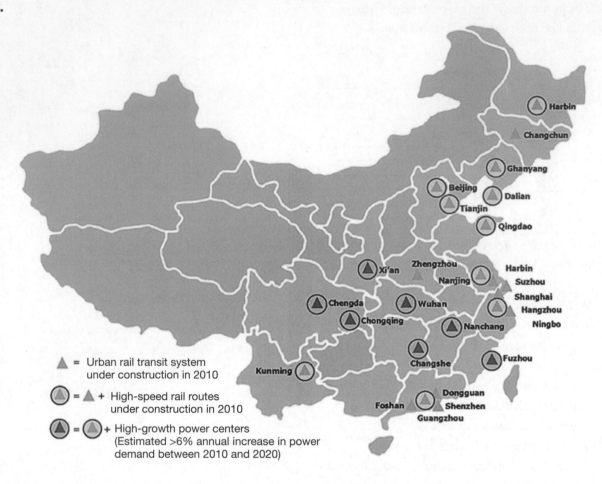

Based on this map of China, select the answer that correlates to a gray triangle surrounded by a circle.

a. urban rail transit system under construction in 2010

b. urban rail transit system and high-speed rail routes under construction in 2010

c. high-speed rail routes under construction in 2010

d. high-growth power centers

18. The graph shows the total campaign expenditures by candidates for the California State Legislature between 1975 and 1998.

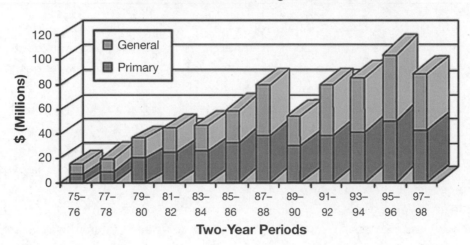

Total Campaign Expenditures by Candidates for the California State Legislature: 1975–1998

What was the trend in expenditures by candidates for the California State Legislature from 1983 to 1988?
a. decreasing
b. increasing then decreasing
c. decreasing then increasing
d. increasing

Please use the following passage to answer questions 19 and 20.

This excerpt is from a speech by Barack Obama announcing his candidacy for president in Springfield, Illinois, in 2007.

All of us know what those challenges are today—a war with no end, a dependence on oil that threatens our future, schools where too many children aren't learning, and families struggling paycheck to paycheck despite working as hard as they can. We know the challenges. We've heard them. We've talked about them for years.

What's stopped us from meeting these challenges is not the absence of sound policies and sensible plans. What's stopped us is the failure of leadership, the smallness of our politics—the ease with which we're distracted by the petty and trivial, our chronic avoidance of tough decisions, our preference for scoring cheap political points instead of rolling up our sleeves and building a working consensus to tackle big problems.

For the last six years we've been told that our mounting debts don't matter, we've been told that the anxiety Americans feel about rising health care costs and stagnant wages are an illusion, we've been told that climate change is a hoax, and that tough talk and an ill-conceived war can replace diplomacy, and strategy, and foresight. And when all else fails, when Katrina happens, or the death toll in Iraq mounts, we've been told that our crises are somebody else's fault. We're distracted from our real failures, and told to blame the other party, or gay people, or immigrants.

And as people have looked away in disillusionment and frustration, we know what's filled the void. The cynics, and the lobbyists, and the special interests who've turned our government into a game only they can afford to play. They write the checks and you get stuck with the bills, they get the access while you get to write a letter, they think they own this government, but we're here today to take it back. The time for that politics is over. It's time to turn the page.

19. Based on the excerpt from Obama's speech announcing his candidacy for president, which of the following pairs of words represents instances of loaded language?
- **a.** hoax, frustration
- **b.** today, decisions
- **c.** void, lobbyists
- **d.** page, diplomacy

20. The paragraph starting with "For the last six years. . . ." could be viewed as an example of which of the following?
- **a.** economic chart
- **b.** campaign speech
- **c.** statistical data
- **d.** campaign promise

Please use the following passage to answer questions 21 and 22.

This is an excerpt from a speech about health care delivered to Congress by President Obama on September 9, 2009.

Then there's the problem of rising cost. We spend one and a half times more per person on health care than any other country, but we aren't any healthier for it. This is one of the reasons that insurance premiums have gone up three times faster than wages. It's why so many employers, especially small businesses, are forcing their employees to pay more for insurance or are dropping their coverage entirely. It's why so many aspiring entrepreneurs cannot afford to open a business in the first place and why American businesses that compete internationally, like our automakers, are at a huge disadvantage. And it's why those of us with health insurance are also paying a hidden and growing tax for those without it, about $1,000 per year that pays for somebody else's emergency room and charitable care.

Finally, our health care system is placing an unsustainable burden on taxpayers. When health care costs grow at the rate they have, it puts greater pressure on programs like Medicare and Medicaid. If we do nothing to slow these skyrocketing costs, we will eventually be spending more on Medicare and Medicaid than every other government program combined. Put simply, our health care problem is our deficit problem. Nothing else even comes close. Nothing else.

21. In the excerpt from Obama's speech on health care, what type of statement is "we aren't any healthier for it"?
  a. supported fact
  b. statistic
  c. warning
  d. opinion

22. According to the excerpt from Obama's speech on health care, what does he think will be the eventual effect of unchecked added pressure being put on Medicare and Medicaid from rapidly increasing health-care costs?
  a. the government spending less on Medicare and Medicaid than every other program combined
  b. the government spending more on Medicare and Medicaid than every other program combined
  c. the shutdown of Medicare and Medicaid instead of other programs
  d. the government no longer spending any money on Medicare and Medicaid

23. Why did Christopher Columbus set sail in 1492 in an expedition that would eventually bring him into contact with the Americas for the first time?

a. He was attempting to claim new territory in the Americas for Spain.

b. He was going to the Americas to trade with the native peoples.

c. He was attempting to find a new route to Asia for trade purposes.

d. He was going to the Americas in order to start a settlement.

24. Based on the pie chart showing the number of women working in the U.S. military during World War II, fill in the box in the following statement to make it correct.

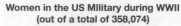

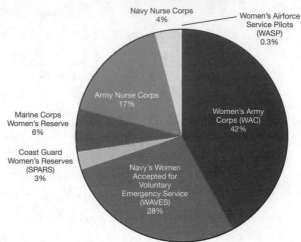

During World War II, the number of women who joined [   ] was almost equal to the combined number of women who joined WASP, the Army and Navy Nurse Corps, SPARS, and the Marine Corps Women's Reserve.

25. The map shows the division of European countries according to political alignment during most of the Cold War.

According to the map, how was Turkey aligned in this division?
   a. with the Western Bloc
   b. with the Eastern Bloc
   c. with the Iron Curtain
   d. with the United States

26. This excerpt is from a speech by George W. Bush given on March 19, 2008.

> To ensure that military progress in Iraq is quickly followed up with real improvements in daily life, we have doubled the number of Provincial Reconstruction Teams in Iraq. These teams of civilian experts are serving all Iraqi—18 Iraqi Provinces, and they're helping to strengthen responsible leaders and build up local economies and bring Iraqis together, so that reconciliation can happen from the ground up. They're very effective. They're helping give ordinary Iraqis confidence that by rejecting the extremists and reconciling with one another, they can claim their place in a free Iraq and build better lives for their families.

Based on the excerpt, you can infer which of the following is NOT a reason that it was important to have civilian expert teams in Iraq after the military action in the area?
- **a.** to strengthen the local leadership and economy
- **b.** to take control of the local leadership and economy
- **c.** to help give confidence to the people of Iraq
- **d.** to help the Iraqi people build a free Iraq

27. If a company purchases a product for $1 and sells it to consumers for $2.35, the $1.35 that the company receives is an example of what economic concept?
- **a.** monopoly
- **b.** expense
- **c.** profit
- **d.** loss

28. Write the word in the box that completes the following definition.

A ☐ is a tax or duty a government places upon imported or exported goods.

29. This excerpt describes the eligibility requirements for a Stateside Union Bank College Credit Card.

> To qualify for a Stateside Union Bank College Credit Card, a student must be at the age of majority in the state of residence and show proof of enrollment in an accredited college or university.
>
> Applicants must have a minimum income greater than $4,000. Applicants who do not meet this criterion will need a co-applicant with an ability to repay the debt.

Based on the excerpt, in which of the following situations would someone NOT qualify for the card?
- **a.** aged 20, student at the University of Texas, income of $5,000
- **b.** aged 14, high-school student, no income
- **c.** aged 24, graduate student at Rice University, income of $11,000
- **d.** aged 18, student at Baylor University, income of $4,250

30.

> Government spending during war that is associated with wartime expenses has short-term positive economic benefits because high levels of spending associated with conflict increase economic growth. However, after the war is over, unintended residual effects of that heightened wartime spending, which is no longer taking place, tend to cause long-term impediments to economic prosperity.

Based on the information above, choose the best description of the economic effects of war.

a. short-term negative effects followed by positive long-term effects

b. wars produce neither positive nor negative economic effects

c. short-term positive effects followed by negative long-term effects

d. wars produce short-term and long-term negative effects

31. The graph below shows the correlation between metal exploration budgets in the United States and the prices of metals between 1989 and 2008.

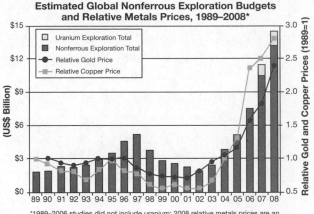

Estimated Global Nonferrous Exploration Budgets and Relative Metals Prices, 1989–2008*

*1989–2006 studies did not include uranium; 2008 relative metals prices are an average through September.

Based on the graph, how did the price of gold and copper correlate to U.S. exploration spending from 2006 to 2008?

a. as the price of gold and copper increased, the amount that the U.S. spent on exploration increased

b. as the price of gold and copper increased, the amount that the U.S. spent on exploration decreased

c. as the price of gold and copper decreased, the amount that the U.S. spent on exploration increased

d. as the price of gold and copper decreased, the amount that the U.S. spent on exploration decreased

32. The following two excerpts are taken from separate sources about the Industrial Revolution.

> The era known as the Industrial Revolution was a period in which fundamental changes occurred in agriculture, textile and metal manufacture, transportation, economic policies and the social structure in England. . . . The year 1760 is generally accepted as the "eve" of the Industrial Revolution. In reality, this eve began more than two centuries before this date. The late 18th century and the early 19th century brought to fruition the ideas and discoveries of those who had long passed on, such as, Galileo, Bacon, Descartes, and others.

> Industrial Revolution, in modern history, is the process of change from an agrarian, handicraft economy to one dominated by industry and machine manufacture. This process began in England in the 18th century and from there spread to other parts of the world.

What is the discrepancy between what is stated in these two passages?
  a. the date of the 18th century as the time period
  b. defining the time period as a time of fundamental change
  c. the real start beginning two centuries before the 18th century
  d. the revolution starting and growing in England

33. The map below shows the major ethnic regions of Pacific Asia.

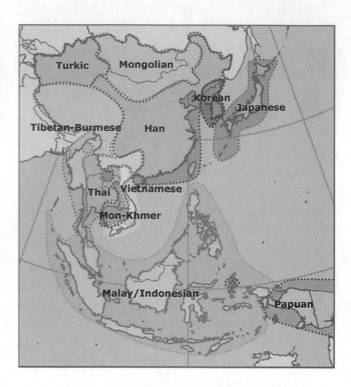

What is the label for the region on the map that covers one island that borders the Korean ethnic region and is located north of the Malay/Indonesian and Papuan ethnic regions?
  a. Turkic
  b. Thai
  c. Han
  d. Japanese

Please use the following maps to answer questions 34 and 35.

These maps are based on information from the U.S. Census Bureau.

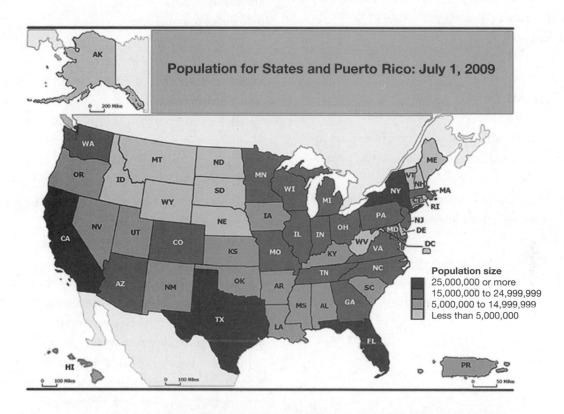

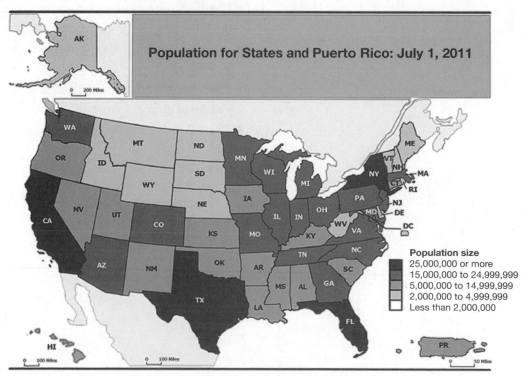

34. Based on the maps showing the population of American states in 2009 and 2011, what has been the population trend between those years for the state of Texas?

    a. increased

    b. stayed the same

    c. decreased

    d. increased then decreased

35. Based on the 2011 Census map, how does the population of California relate to the population of Texas?

    a. population two categories larger than Texas

    b. in the same population category as Tennessee

    c. population two categories smaller than Texas

    d. in the same population category as Texas

Part II

1 question

25 minutes to complete

This practice test will familiarize you with the Extended Response question found on the GED® Social Studies test.

Before you begin, it is important to note that on the official test, this task must be completed in no more than 25 minutes. But don't rush to complete your response; take time to carefully read the passages and the prompt. Then think about how you would like to respond to the prompt.

As you write your essay, be sure to:

- Develop an argument about how the ideas expressed by President Kennedy are related to the quotation from the Declaration of Independence
- Thoroughly construct your main points, organizing them logically, with strong supporting details
- Present multiple pieces of evidence, using ideas from the quotation and the excerpt
- Connect your sentences, paragraphs, and ideas with transitional words and phrases
- Express your ideas clearly and choose your words carefully
- Use varied sentence structures to increase the clarity of your response
- Reread and revise your response

Good luck!

Please use the following passages to answer the essay question.

This excerpt is from the Declaration of Independence.

> We hold these truths to be self-evident, that all men are created equal, that they are endowed by their Creator with certain unalienable Rights, that among these are Life, Liberty, and the pursuit of Happiness.

This excerpt is from a speech on civil rights given by President John F. Kennedy on June 11, 1963.

> This Nation was founded by men of many nations and backgrounds. It was founded on the principle that all men are created equal, and that the rights of every man are diminished when the rights of one man are threatened. Today we are committed to a worldwide struggle to promote and protect the rights of all who wish to be free. And when Americans are sent to Viet-Nam or West Berlin, we do not ask for whites only. It ought to be possible, therefore, for American students of any color to attend any public institution they select without having to be backed up by troops. It ought to be possible for American consumers of any color to receive equal service in places of public accommodation, such as hotels and restaurants and theaters and retail stores, without being forced to resort to demonstrations in the street, and it ought to be possible for American citizens of any color to register and to vote in a free election without interference or fear of reprisal. It ought to be possible, in short, for every American to enjoy the privileges of being American without regard to his race or his color. In short, every American ought to have the right to be treated as he would wish to be treated, as one would wish his children to be treated. But this is not the case. The Negro baby born in America today, regardless of the section of the Nation in which he is born, has about one-half as much chance of completing a high school as a white baby born in the same place on the same day, one-third as much chance of completing college, one-third as much chance of becoming a professional man, twice as much chance of becoming unemployed, about one-seventh as much chance of earning $10,000 a year, a life expectancy which is 7 years shorter, and the prospects of earning only half as much. This is not a sectional issue. Difficulties over segregation and discrimination exist in every city, in every State of the Union, producing in many cities a rising tide of discontent that threatens the public safety. Nor is this a partisan issue. In a time of domestic crisis men of good will and generosity should be able to unite regardless of party or politics. This is not even a legal or legislative issue alone. It is better to settle these matters in the courts than on the streets, and new laws are needed at every level, but law alone cannot make men see right. We are confronted primarily with a moral issue. It is as old as the scriptures and is as clear as the American Constitution.

QUESTION:

In your response, develop an argument about how President Kennedy's stance on the civil rights issues of the time reflected beliefs that were already built into the section of the Declaration of Independence quoted here, even though the Declaration of Independence was written centuries before civil rights for African Americans became a national focus. Incorporate relevant and specific evidence from the two excerpts and your knowledge of the enduring issue and circumstances surrounding the Civil Rights movement to support your analysis.

_____

_____

_____

_____

_____

_____

_____

_____

_____

_____

_____

_____

_____

_____

_____

_____

_____

_____

_____

Answers and Explanations

Part I

1. **Choice b is correct.** The liberation of the Iraqi people from a brutal ruling regime and the removal of Hussein from power are both goals that would have the ability to bring about all of the changes for Iraq that President Bush mentions came about after the success of the operation. Therefore, it is safe to say that this choice represents the main purpose of the launching of the operation by President Bush.

   Choice **a** is incorrect. While the liberation of Baghdad led to Operation Iraqi Freedom's success, it alone was not the purpose of the operation. The capture of this one city would not have been enough to bring about the other changes and freedoms for the Iraqi people that Bush mentions, such as those in the excerpt's final paragraph.

   Choice **c** is incorrect. Stopping Hussein from invading nations was an outcome of the operation's success in removing Hussein from power, not the actual purpose of the operation. That purpose would be to remove Hussein, which would result in this beneficial outcome.

   Choice **d** is incorrect. These nations joined forces for the common cause of the operation to stop Saddam Hussein's control of the Iraqi people's natural rights.

2. **Choice d is correct.** This statement is an opinion held and expressed by Bush. He uses the term "remarkable," which is inherently a term of opinion. Bush may feel that the operation "was a remarkable display of military effectiveness," but this is an opinion, not a fact.

   Choice **a** is incorrect. All of these events are facts that are confirmed by the actions and technicalities of the operation. All of these actions were actually carried out during the operation.

   Choice **b** is incorrect. This is a fact. These forces did all join with the U.S. in the beginning of the operation.

   Choice **c** is incorrect. This is a fact of the actions carried out during the operation when troops actually did battle Saddam's death squads.

3. **Choice c is correct.** All of the atrocities carried out by Saddam that Bush mentions in his speech serve to show the justification for the operation and show just how brutal Saddam's regime was and how detrimental it was to the citizens of that regime who were exposed to atrocities. Bush mentions in the end all the negative things that have been stopped due to the operation, once again bolstering its justification.

Choice **a** is incorrect. Everything that Bush says about the operation in this part of his speech implies that the operation was justified and successful. He mentions on many occasions the brutality of Saddam's regime and gives examples. He then goes on to list atrocities that have been stopped due to the operation.

Choice **b** is incorrect. Everything that Bush says would imply that he feels the operation was justified. However, the realities of Saddam's regime that Bush mentions only lend credit to this justification. Instead of discrediting the operation, the atrocities that Saddam imposed on his people only bolster the idea that it was justified.

Choice **d** is incorrect. While the atrocities of Saddam's regime that Bush mentions justify the operation, Bush does not disagree with that justification. The fact that he mentions all of said atrocities implies that he agrees that the operation was justified, and in the last paragraph he goes on to mention all of the atrocities that have been stopped due to the operation. He never expresses any doubts about the operation's justification.

4. **Choice c is correct.** The legislative branch involves the Senate and the House of Representatives, and the executive branch consists of the president and his administration. The fact that the Senate must have a two-thirds agreement in order to allow the president to make a treaty means that the legislative branch is checking the power of the executive branch so that the president does not have full and unopposed power to make treaties.

Choice **a** is incorrect. The president is part of the executive branch, and that branch is not checking the powers of any other branches but actually having its own powers checked.

Choice **b** is incorrect. The judicial branch involves the courts, and this branch is not even mentioned in this section of the Constitution.

Choice **d** is incorrect. The judicial branch does not even factor into this section of the Constitution.

5. Choice b is correct. The system of checks and balances in the U.S. government is meant to separate the powers of the branches of government and provide a balance to those powers so that one person or group does not hold all power, which could then be abused and exploited.

Choice **a** is incorrect. The idea behind checks and balances between the branches of government is to keep a balance of power, not to allow the legislative branch to have power over the executive or judicial branches. In the excerpt, this check on the power of the president does not imply that the Senate has power over the president or courts, but rather it is a balance of power.

Choice **c** is incorrect. If the president had the ability to check the power of all the other branches, his power would be more like a dictatorship than a presidency. The system of checks and balances is meant to prevent this. Also, the excerpt shows that the president does not have this power due to the fact that the Senate is actually checking the president's power in this example.

Choice **d** is incorrect. While the example in the excerpt does refer to this check on the power of the president, this is only an example of one instance of checks and balances in the U.S. government and not the actual point of this system. There are many other examples of checks and balances written into the U.S. Constitution.

6. Choice c is correct. Without a two-thirds agreement in the Senate, the president cannot make a treaty. This is part of the system of checks and balances in the U.S. government. It is a check on the power of the executive branch. Choice **a** is incorrect. The president is the one who makes treaties with the consent of the Senate. Therefore, failure to receive a two-thirds agreement would make a treaty impossible, not just in the Senate but for the president as well. Choice **b** is incorrect. The Senate does not make the treaties; the president does. The Senate consults with the president and must agree with the treaty in order for it to be made. Choice **d** is incorrect. Without a two-thirds agreement in the Senate, the president cannot make a treaty. This is part of the system of checks and balances in the U.S. government. It is a check on the power of the executive branch.

7. Choice a is correct. The concept of popular sovereignty implies that the government holds authority through the consent of the governed, and if the governed fails to approve of said authority, the people can change it. A dictatorship does not take the consent of the governed into account, and one individual rules without consent.

Choice **b** is incorrect. The concept of popular sovereignty implies that the government holds authority through the consent of the governed and if the governed fails to approve of said authority, the government can change it. A dictatorship does not take the consent of the governed into account, and one individual rules without consent.

Choice **c** is incorrect. The concept of popular sovereignty does not necessarily mean that the government is run by the most popular person, but rather that the leader of the government has consent of the governed. A dictatorship does not necessarily mean that the government is run by the least popular person, but rather that said person does not take the consent of the governed into account.

Choice **d** is incorrect. A dictatorship does not mean that the government is run by the most popular person, but rather that the leader of the government does not take the consent of the government into account. The concept of popular sovereignty does not mean that the government is run by the least popular person, but rather that said person has the consent of the governed.

8. The executive branch is made up of the **president** and the **president's Cabinet**.

The legislative branch is made up of the **Senate** and the **House of Representatives**, collectively known as Congress.

The judicial branch is made up of the **Supreme Court**.

9. Choice b is correct. At the beginning of the excerpt, Clinton references the problems of discrimination from the past and says that it continues to plague the country. He makes it apparent that affirmative action is a way to lessen this discrimination and hopefully solve many problems that it creates for minority groups.

Choice **a** is incorrect. Slavery was a problem that has been abolished by law since the Civil War and Reconstruction. Affirmative action is not addressing slavery or a solution.

Choice **c** is incorrect. While unemployment can be caused by discrimination, affirmative action addresses discrimination, which could then inadvertently help with unemployment as a side effect. Affirmative action is not directly addressing unemployment or providing a direct solution to it.

Choice **d** is incorrect. While poverty can be caused by discrimination, affirmative action addresses discrimination, which could then inadvertently help with unemployment and poverty as a side effect. Affirmative action is not directly addressing poverty or providing a direct solution to it.

10. Choice a is correct. According to Clinton, affirmative action will benefit minority groups "by building the pool of qualified applicants for college, for contracts, for jobs, and giving more people the chance to learn, work, and earn. When affirmative action is done right, it is flexible, it is fair, and it works."

Choice **b** is incorrect. This change is the opposite of the purpose of affirmative action and is the opposite of the correct answer. According to Clinton, affirmative action will benefit minority groups "by building the pool of qualified applicants for college, for contracts, for jobs, and giving more people the chance to learn, work, and earn. When affirmative action is done right, it is flexible, it is fair, and it works."

Choice **c** is incorrect. Clinton mentions that the idea to have penalties for employers who fail to meet high quotas was actually rejected and affirmative action helps to keep this from happening. However, affirmative action has as its main goal the improvement of conditions for minority groups. Therefore, the idea that it would not change anything for minority groups is wrong.

Choice **d** is incorrect. Both of these statements represent things that affirmative action is trying to fix. Affirmative action would increase the amount of minority groups in college, not decrease their numbers. According to Clinton, affirmative action will benefit minority groups "by building the pool of qualified applicants for college, for contracts, for jobs, and giving more people the chance to learn, work, and earn. When affirmative action is done right, it is flexible, it is fair, and it works."

11. Choice d is correct. Both excerpts mention the importance of liberty for all citizens. The Declaration of Independence says all men have the right to liberty, and the Constitution says that the government must "secure the Blessings of Liberty to ourselves and our Posterity."

Choice **a** is incorrect. The concept of all men being equal is mentioned only in the excerpt from the Declaration of Independence.

Choice **b** is incorrect. This idea is mentioned only in the excerpt from the Declaration of Independence.

Choice **c** is incorrect. Neither excerpt mentions anything about slavery or the need to abolish it. Furthermore, the Declaration of Independence was made during a time when slavery was still very prominent.

12. Choice b is correct. Popular sovereignty refers to a government run by the people, where the people have the ability to affect, change, and replace their government as they see fit. This is what the excerpt is essentially describing.

Choice **a** is incorrect. Federalism refers to the concept of a federal government. This excerpt references the ability to replace the government; it doesn't describe a federal system of government.

Choice **c** is incorrect. Socialism deals with a centralized control of wealth in order to make the spread of wealth more equal. This has nothing to do with the ability to replace the government. The term *socialism* is not preceded by the word *popular*.

Choice **d** is incorrect. Capitalism deals with the idea of free markets and private ownership in the economy. This is an economic system, not a system of replacing a destructive form of government.

13. **The correct answer is 122.**
The mean is the average. Therefore, add up all of the numbers in the column listing the number of men killed: 49 + 73 + 140 + 226 = 488.
Then divide the answer by the number of values given: $\frac{488}{4} = 122$.

14. **Choice b is correct.** The United States entering World War II took the rate from 14.5% in 1941 to 7% in 1942, or a 7.5% decrease.
Choice **a** is incorrect. FDR's first New Deal took the rate from 37% in 1933 to 33% in 1934, or a 4% drop. This was not the largest decrease.
Choice **c** is incorrect. The stock market crash *increased* the unemployment rate by 9%, from 5.5% in 1929 to 14.5% in 1930.
Choice **d** is incorrect. In the year following the German invasion of Poland, the unemployment rate dropped from 25% to 21%, or a 4% drop. This was not the largest decrease.

15. The answer is **private**, based on an understanding and comprehension of the definition and logical reasoning to understand how it can fit into the statement.

16. **Choice a is correct.** The Democrat bar is the highest and is shown on the graph with political parties being labeled on the *x*-axis (horizontally) and the percentage of members labeled along the *y*-axis (vertically). This allows a viewer to see that the Democratic Party has the highest percentage of members.
Choice **b** is incorrect. While the Democratic Party does have the most members based on the percentages, the political parties are labeled on the *x*-axis, not the *y*-axis. Also, percentages are labeled on the *y*-axis, not the *x*-axis.
Choice **c** is incorrect. While the political parties are labeled on the *x*-axis and percentages are labeled on the *y*-axis, which shows, through the use of bars, which party has the most members, the Libertarian Party does not have the highest bar. Therefore, it does not have the most members.
Choice **d** is incorrect. The Libertarian Party does not have the highest bar representing percentage of members and consequently does not have the most members. Also, political parties are labeled on the *x*-axis, not the *y*-axis, and percentages are labeled on the *y*-axis, not the *x*.

17. **Choice b is correct.** The key indicates that a circle surrounding a gray triangle includes **both** "urban rail transit system under construction in 2010" and "high-speed rail routes under construction in 2010."
Choice **a** is incorrect. The symbol for "urban rail transit system under construction in 2010" is a simple gray triangle.
Choice **c** is incorrect. The key indicates that a circle surrounding a gray triangle includes both "urban rail transit system under construction in 2010" and "high-speed rail routes under construction in 2010."
Choice **d** is incorrect. High-growth power centers are designated by a circle surrounding a black triangle.

18. Choice d is correct. The bars indicating expenditures for that time period are increasing. They increase from around $40 million to $80 million based on the dollar amount labeled on the y-axis (vertical) and years labeled on the x-axis (horizontal). Choice **a** is incorrect. The bars indicating expenditures for that time period are not decreasing. They increase from around $40 million to $80 million based on the dollar amount labeled on the y-axis (vertical) and years labeled on the x-axis (horizontal). Choice **b** is incorrect. The bars indicating expenditures for that time period are increasing, but they never decrease during that time. They increase from around $40 million to $80 million based on the dollar amount labeled on the y-axis (vertical) and years labeled on the x-axis (horizontal). Choice **c** is incorrect. The bars indicating expenditures for that time period are increasing, and they never decrease during that time. They increase from around $40 million to $80 million based on the dollar amount labeled on the y-axis (vertical) and years labeled on the x-axis (horizontal).

19. Choice a is correct. Loaded language means language that is highly emotive and used to gain support, sway emotions, degrade others, or push an agenda. *Hoax* and *frustration* are words that are being used by Obama to sway voters against the previous political administration in order to win the presidency in the coming election. Choice **b** is incorrect. Loaded language means language that is highly emotive and used to gain support, sway emotions, degrade others, or push an agenda. *Today* and *decisions* are not words that serve this purpose in this excerpt. Choice **c** is incorrect. Loaded language means language that is highly emotive and used to gain support, sway emotions, degrade others, or push an agenda. *Void* and *lobbyists* are not words that serve this purpose in this excerpt. Choice **d** is incorrect. Loaded language means language that is highly emotive and used to gain support, sway emotions, degrade others, or push an agenda. *Page* and *diplomacy* are not words that serve this purpose in this excerpt.

20. Choice b is correct. Obama is publicizing a point of view or political cause. He does not acknowledge who has been telling Americans this but implies that it is coming from members of the government. Obama wants to replace these members by hopefully winning the presidency. This speech announces his political campaign for president. Choice **a** is incorrect. Obama is stating his opinions. Obama wants the people hearing him to feel he is right about these issues. He does not present an economic chart. Choice **c** is incorrect. Obama is stating his opinions. Obama wants the people hearing him to feel he is right about these issues. He does not present statistical facts. Choice **d** is incorrect. The third paragraph of Obama's speech does not mention anything that he promises to do when he becomes president.

21. Choice d is correct. In the excerpt, Obama does not give any factual evidence to support this statement. Therefore it falls into the category of an opinion or unsupported claim.

Choice **a** is incorrect. In the excerpt, Obama does not give any factual evidence to support this statement.

Choice **b** is incorrect. A statistic is a piece of data that typically comes from a study involving a large amount of numerical data. Obama does not mention any numbers in this statement.

Choice **c** is incorrect. Obama's statement is not a warning that something will happen.

22. Choice b is correct. If Medicare and Medicaid are struggling, then the government would have to spend more on them in order to help the programs. Obama explicitly says, "we will eventually be spending more on Medicare and Medicaid than every other government program combined."

Choice **a** is incorrect. If Medicare and Medicaid are struggling, then the government would have to spend more on them in order to help the programs, not less. Obama explicitly says, "we will eventually be spending more on Medicare and Medicaid than every other government program combined."

Choice **c** is incorrect. While Obama mentions that Medicare and Medicaid are struggling due to rapidly increasing health care costs, he never mentions that this would lead to the shutdown of these programs. It is more likely that the government would spend more money on them instead of shutting them down. Also, due to the fact that so many people rely on these programs, it would take a lot more to actually shut them down.

Choice **d** is incorrect. This is the opposite of what Obama implies will happen. The government would more likely spend more money on them to help them when they are struggling. If the government stopped spending money on them, their struggles would increase to the point where they could no longer function. Also, Obama explicitly says, "we will eventually be spending more on Medicare and Medicaid than every other government program combined."

23. Choice c is correct. This was the goal of his expedition in 1492. The spice trade was very lucrative at the time, and Columbus had the idea that he could sail in the direction of the Americas and eventually reach Asia, thereby avoiding overland trade routes in the other direction. He did not realize that there was a large landmass in the way, and this is how he discovered the Americas.

Choice **a** is incorrect. Columbus' first expedition in 1492 had nothing to do with finding new territory. He did not know that the Americas existed since this expedition brought him into contact with the land for the first time. While he did eventually make future expeditions to the Americas on behalf of Spain, this was after he knew it existed.

Choice **b** is incorrect. He did not know that the Americas existed since this expedition brought him into contact with the land for the first time. While he did eventually make future expeditions to the Americas for goods on behalf of Spain, he could not be planning an expedition to trade with native peoples who he did not know existed.

Choice **d** is incorrect. Columbus' first expedition in 1492 had nothing to do with creating a new settlement for Spain in the Americas. He did not know that the Americas existed since this expedition brought him into contact with the land for the first time, and he could not be looking to make a settlement in a place he didn't know existed. While he did eventually make future expeditions to the Americas on behalf of Spain, this was after he knew it existed.

24. The correct answer is **Navy's Women Accepted for Voluntary Emergency Service**, or **WAVES**. Based on the pie chart, 0.3% of the women joining the military during World War II were Women's Airforce Service Pilots or WASPs, 4% were Navy Nurse Corps, 17% were American Nurse Corps, 6% were Marine Corps Women's Reserves, and 3% were Coast Guard Women's Reserves or SPARS. The combination of all of those percentages comes out to 30.3% of women joining the military. This is closest to the 28% of the Navy's Women Accepted for Voluntary Emergency Service rather than the 42% that was the Women's Army Corps.

25. Choice a is correct. The map shows countries in the Eastern Bloc in darker gray and the Western Bloc in lighter gray. Turkey is colored lighter gray and is, therefore, part of the Western Bloc.

Choice **b** is incorrect. The map shows countries in the Eastern Bloc in darker gray and the Western Bloc in lighter gray. Turkey is colored lighter gray and is, therefore, part of the Western Bloc.

Choice **c** is incorrect. The Iron Curtain is a dividing line. Therefore, it is not one of the divisions that countries could be put into during the Cold War. It is shown as a white line, which Turkey only barely touches.

Choice **d** is incorrect. This map does not give any information about Turkey's relationship with the United States. The United States is not depicted on the map.

26. Choice b is correct. Bush never mentions that the goal is to control the local leadership and economy in Iraq, but rather the goal is to help the Iraqi people eventually be able to completely control their own government. Therefore, this is not a reason that it was important to have civilian experts in Iraq. Choice **a** is incorrect. Bush explicitly states, "they're helping to strengthen responsible leaders and build up local economies." Therefore, this choice is a reason that it was important to have civilian experts in Iraq. Choice **c** is incorrect. Bush explicitly states, "they're helping give ordinary Iraqis confidence." Therefore, this choice is a reason that it was important to have civilian experts in Iraq. Choice **d** is incorrect. Bush explicitly states, "they can claim their place in a free Iraq." Therefore, this choice is a reason that it was important to have civilian experts in Iraq.

27. Choice c is correct. A profit is a financial gain. Since the company only spent $1 on the product and then sold it for $2.35 to consumers, the company makes a financial gain of $1.35 every time a consumer purchases the product. The company makes a profit of $1.35. Choice **a** is incorrect. A monopoly is an entity that has exclusive control over a product or service. A dollar amount cannot be an example of something that has complete control over a product or service. Also, the example gives no indication that the company has exclusive control of the product.
Choice **b** is incorrect. The $1.35 would only be a part of the expense for the consumer, not an expense for the company. The company's only expense was the $1 that it spent on the product before selling it.
Choice **d** is incorrect. Since the company only spent $1 on the product and then sold it for $2.35 to consumers, the company makes a financial gain of $1.35 every time that a consumer purchases the product. The company makes a profit of $1.35, not a loss.

28. The correct answer is tariff.
A tariff is a tax or duty placed on imports or exports.

29. Choice b is correct. The person in this situation would not qualify for the card. He or she is not old enough, is a high school student, and does not have an income greater than $4,000.
Choices **a**, **b**, and **c** are incorrect. The people in these situations would qualify for the card. They are old enough, are students of an accredited university, and have an income greater than $4,000.

30. Choice c is correct. The excerpt mentions that the economy benefits in the short term from substantial spending increase during the conflict; however, this leads to negative residual effects that hurt the economy in the long term after the war is over and there is no longer a spending boom related to the conflict.

Choice **a** is incorrect. The excerpt mentions that the economy benefits in the short term from substantial spending increase during the conflict; however, this leads to negative residual effects that hurt the economy in the long term after the war is over and there is no longer a spending boom related to the conflict.

Choice **b** is incorrect. The excerpt mentions that the economy benefits in the short term from substantial spending increase during the conflict; however, this leads to negative residual effects that hurt the economy in the long term after the war is over and there is no longer a spending boom related to the conflict. Therefore, wars definitely have economic effects.

Choice **d** is incorrect. The excerpt mentions that the economy benefits in the short term from substantial spending increase during the conflict; however, this leads to negative residual effects that hurt the economy in the long term after the war is over and there is no longer a spending boom related to the conflict. The effects are not all negative due to the positive short-term effects.

31. Choice a is correct. Dark gray bars represent the amount that the U.S. spent on metal exploration. The two lines represent the price of gold and copper. Based on this information, between the years 2006 and 2008, the prices of gold and copper along with U.S. spending on metal exploration all increased.

Choices **b**, **c**, and **d** are incorrect. Dark gray bars represent the amount that the U.S. spent on metal exploration. The two lines represent the price of gold and copper. Based on this information, between the years 2006 and 2008, the prices of gold and copper along with U.S. spending on metal exploration all increased.

32. Choice c is correct. The quote from the first source says, "in reality, this eve began more than two centuries before this date," while the quote from the second source does not mention this idea.

Choice **a** is incorrect. Both quotes mention that the time period of the Industrial Revolution was in the 18th century.

Choice **b** is incorrect. Both quotes define the Industrial revolution as a time of great change. "The era known as the Industrial Revolution was a period in which fundamental changes occurred" and "Industrial Revolution, in modern history, is the process of change from an agrarian, handicraft economy to one dominated by industry and machine manufacture."

Choice **d** is incorrect. Both sources mention that England is where the Industrial Revolution began and grew. "The era known as the Industrial Revolution was a period in which fundamental changes occurred in agriculture, textile and metal manufacture, transportation, economic policies and the social structure in England" and "This process began in England in the 18th century and from there spread to other parts of the world."

33. Choice d is correct. The Japanese region covers an island, borders the Korean region, and is north of the Malay/Indonesian and Papuan regions.

Choice **a** is incorrect. The Turkic region is above the Malay/Indonesian and Papuan regions, but it is not covering an island and does not border the Korean region.

Choice **b** is incorrect. The Thai region is above the Malay/Indonesian and Papuan regions, but it is not covering an island and does not border the Korean region.

Choice **c** is incorrect. The Han region is above the Malay/Indonesian and Papuan regions and borders the Korean region, but it is not covering an island.

34. Choice a is correct. The map key shows that states labeled with the darkest gray have a population size of 25,000,000 or more, and the states labeled with one shade lighter have a population size of 15,000,000 to 24,999,999. In the 2009 map, Texas is colored the second to darkest shade, and in the 2011 map, it is colored the darkest shade. Therefore, its population increased from the 15,000,000–24,999,999 range to the 25,000,000 or more range.

35. Choice d is correct. Texas and California are both colored the darkest shade of gray, representing a population of 25,000,000 or more. Therefore, the population of California is in the same category as the population of Texas according to the information given in the map.

Choice **a** is incorrect. California does not have a larger population than Texas. Both are colored the darkest shade of gray, representing a population of 25,000,000 or more. Therefore, the population of California is in the same category as the population of Texas according to the information given in the map. The map does not show exact population numbers, so there is no way to determine which one actually has a slightly larger or smaller population.

Choice **b** is incorrect. Texas and California are both colored the darkest shade of gray, representing a population of 25,000,000 or more. Tennessee has a smaller population than either Texas or California.

Choice **c** is incorrect. Texas and California are both colored the darkest shade of gray, representing a population of 25,000,000 or more. Therefore, the population of California is in the same category as the population of Texas according to the information given in the map. The map does not show exact population numbers, so there is no way to determine which one actually has a slightly larger or smaller population.

Part II

Your Extended Response will be scored based on three traits, or elements:

Trait 1: Creation of arguments and use of evidence

Trait 2: Development of ideas and organizational structure

Trait 3: Clarity and command of standard English conventions

Your essay will be scored on a 4-point scale—Trait 1 is worth 0–2 points, and Traits 2 and 3 are worth 0–1 point.

Trait 1 tests your ability to write an essay that takes a stance and makes an argument based on the information in the passages. To earn the highest score possible, you must carefully read the information and express a clear opinion on what you have read. You will be scored on how well you use the information from the passages to support your argument. Your response will also be scored on how well you analyze the information in the passages.

For your reference, here is a table that readers will use when scoring your essay with a 2, 1, or 0.

	TRAIT 1: CREATION OF ARGUMENTS AND USE OF EVIDENCE
2	• Makes a text-based argument that demonstrates a clear understanding of the connections between ideas, figures, and events as presented in the source text(s) and the historical contexts from which they are drawn • Presents specific and related evidence from primary and secondary source text(s) that sufficiently supports an argument • Demonstrates a good connection to both the source text(s) and the prompt
1	• Makes an argument that demonstrates an understanding of the connections between ideas, figures, and events as presented in the source text(s) • Presents some evidence from primary and secondary source texts in support of an argument (may include a mix of related and unrelated textual references) • Demonstrates a connection to both the source text(s) and the prompt
0	• May attempt to make an argument, but demonstrates little or no understanding of the ideas, figures, and events presented in the source text(s) or the contexts from which they are drawn • Presents little or no evidence from the primary and secondary source text(s); may or may not demonstrate an attempt to create an argument • Lacks a connection to either the source text(s) or the prompt
Non-scorable	• Response consists only of text copied from the prompt or source text(s) • Response shows that test taker has not read the prompt or is entirely off-topic • Response is incomprehensible • Response is not in English • No response has been attempted (has been left blank)

Trait 2 tests whether you respond to the writing prompt with a well-structured essay. Support of your thesis must come from evidence in the passages, as well as personal opinions and experiences that build on your central idea. Your ideas must be fully explained and include specific details. Your essay should use words and phrases that allow your details and ideas to flow naturally. Here is a table that outlines what is involved in earning a score of 1 or 0.

TRAIT 2: DEVELOPMENT OF IDEAS AND ORGANIZATIONAL STRUCTURE	
1	• Contains a logical sequence of ideas with clear connections between specific details and main ideas • Contains ideas that are developed and generally logical; multiple ideas are expanded upon • Demonstrates an appropriate understanding of the task
0	• Contains an unclear or indiscernible sequence of ideas • Contains ideas that are inadequately developed or illogical; only one idea is expanded upon • Does not demonstrate an understanding of the task
Non-scorable	• Response consists only of text copied from the prompt or source text(s) • Response shows that test taker has not read the prompt or is entirely off-topic • Response is incomprehensible • Response is not in English • No response has been attempted (has been left blank)

Trait 3 tests how you create the sentences that make up your essay. To earn a high score, you will need to write sentences with variety—some short, some long, some simple, some complex. You will also need to prove that you have a good handle on standard English, including correct word choice, grammar, and sentence structure. Here is a table that outlines what is involved in attaining a score of a 1 or 0.

TRAIT 3: CLARITY AND COMMAND OF STANDARD ENGLISH CONVENTIONS	
1	• Demonstrates adequate use of conventions with regard to the following skills: 1) subject-verb agreement 2) placement of modifiers and correct word order 3) pronoun usage, including pronoun antecedent agreement, unclear pronoun references, and pronoun case 4) frequently confused words and homonyms, including contractions 5) use of apostrophes with possessive nouns 6) use of punctuation (e.g., commas in a series or in appositives and other non-essential elements, end marks, and punctuation for clause separation) 7) capitalization (e.g., beginnings of sentences, proper nouns, and titles) • Demonstrates generally correct sentence structure and sentence variation; demonstrates overall fluency and clarity with regard to the following skills: 1) correct use of subordination, coordination, and parallelism 2) avoidance of awkward sentence structures and wordiness 3) usage of transitional words, conjunctive adverbs, and other words that enhance clarity and logic 4) avoidance of run-on sentences, sentence fragments, and fused sentences 5) standard usage at a level appropriate for on-demand draft writing • May contain some errors in mechanics and conventions that do not impede comprehension
0	• Demonstrates minimal use of basic conventions with regard to skills 1–7 as listed under Trait 3, Score Point 1 • Demonstrates consistently improper sentence structure; little or no variation to the extent that meaning may be unclear; demonstrates minimal use of skills 1–5 as listed under Trait 3, Score Point 1 • Contains numerous significant errors in mechanics and conventions that impede comprehension OR • Response is insufficient to show level of proficiency involving conventions and usage
Non-scorable	• Response consists only of text copied from the prompt or source text(s) • Response shows that test taker has not read the prompt or is entirely off-topic • Response is incomprehensible • Response is not in English • No response has been attempted (has been left blank)

Sample Score 4 Essay

Although equal civil rights for all Americans, regardless of race, were not guaranteed by law until the 1960s, the same ideals that inspired the civil rights movement were part of the basic structure of American government from its creation, nearly two centuries before. While cultural, economic, and political factors may have interfered with the achievement of this goal for many years, its inclusion in the founding documents of the nation underlines the enduring nature of this issue.

The Declaration of Independence is widely regarded as the first formal expression of American democracy. The document states that "all men are created equal," and refers to "certain unalienable rights," meaning that these basic rights cannot be taken away. While the United States was not the first nation to suggest that citizens should be given basic rights, it was undoubtedly one of the first to support the notion of equal rights for all citizens. This extended basic protections to even the lowest classes of society, and also held the higher classes accountable to the same laws as everyone else.

At the time the Declaration of Independence was written, the idea that "all men are created equal" was, in many ways, difficult to implement in its purest form. Slaves were not considered as equals, and were in fact treated by the law as property; women were also excluded from many of the basic protections and rights that men enjoyed. Even among free white men, the application of equality was inconsistent at best. For example, in the nation's first elections, only wealthy, land-owning men were allowed to vote.

The history of the United States is a history of edging ever closer to the ideals expressed in the Declaration of Independence and the U.S. Constitution. The obstacles that have impeded this progress have been economic and social factors such as slavery and prejudice. When slavery ended in the mid-nineteenth century, the U.S. Congress passed constitutional amendments intended to protect the voting rights and citizenship of former slaves. However, as Kennedy stated, "law alone cannot make men see right." These laws, despite their

intent, proved ineffective at preserving the rights of African Americans in many situations. For example, many parts of the country established separate facilities for blacks such as schools, bathrooms, and even drinking fountains. However, these facilities rarely met the same standards as those for whites. This sort of fundamental racial discrimination led to conditions like the ones Kennedy lists in his speech: African Americans were likely to be poorer, less educated, and to die sooner than white Americans. This is why Kennedy supported new civil rights legislation intended to strengthen protections of the rights of all people, regardless of race— bring the United States one step closer to the dream of a nation where, indeed, all men are created equal.

About this essay:

This essay has earned the maximum number of points in each trait for a total of 4 points.

Trait 1: Creation of Arguments and Use of Evidence

The sample response presents an argument about the role of equality in the Civil Rights movement and how it relates to the very beginnings of the founding of the United States, even though the founding fathers did not yet realize that the idea of equality would be used in this way. The test taker's argument cites multiple ideas from the source texts that bolster his or her position. Additionally, the writer incorporates into the response background knowledge about the importance of equality throughout U.S. history in general, and the role of equality in the Civil Rights movement in particular. Taken as a whole, the response offers an argument that is closely aligned to what is directed by the prompt and is well supported by the source texts.

Trait 2: Development of Ideas and Organizational Structure

This response earns one point in Trait 2 because it makes clear and understandable connections between ideas and establishes a progression in which one idea logically leads into the next, starting from the very beginning: *Although equal civil rights for all Americans, regardless of race, were not guaranteed by law until the 1960s, the same ideals that inspired the civil rights movement were part of the basic structure of American government from its creation, nearly two centuries before.*

The main points are fully developed, with multiple details given in support of each. Additionally, this response applies a level of formality appropriate for communicating in workplace and academic settings, while also keeping in mind the purpose of the task, which is to present a well-supported argument.

Trait 3: Clarity and Command of Standard English Conventions

This response earns one point on Trait 3 because it effectively applies standard English language usage and conventions to convey ideas with clarity. In general, the response contains minimal mechanical errors, and the errors that do exist do not impede readers' understanding. The response contains language appropriate for expressing its ideas and thoughtfully composed sentences that generally avoid wordiness and awkwardness. Additionally, clarity and flow of the response are enhanced with varied sentence structure and appropriate application of transitional words and phrases to connect sentences, paragraphs, and ideas.

Remember, however, that because the Extended Response question on the GED® Social Studies test asks for a draft written in approximately 25 minutes, there is no expectation that your response be completely free of convention and usage crrors.

Sample Score 2 Essay

In Kennedy's speech, he states that "every American ought to have the right to be treated as he would wish to be treated, as one would wish his children to be treated." This idea directly reflects the beliefs held by the Founding Fathers, as evidenced in the statement "all men are created equal" found in the declaration of independence.

For a number or reasons at the time of the signing of the declaration of independence "all men" did not include slaves and women. At the time of Kennedy's speech, Africans Americans still weren't being treated as equals in America, especially in the south. I know this is true because my grandmother lived in Mississippi during that time. Kennedy also states in his speech how African Americans were poorer and did not live as long as white people.

Kennedy argued that the issue of equality is a moral one that goes all the way back to the Constitution. Actually, it goes back to the declaration of independence, which came first and says "all men are created equal." So he supported new laws to make sure that people all other races were all treated fairly. This was exactly what the Founding Fathers argued in favor of, even though they couldn't really do it themselves at the time.

About this essay:

This essay has earned 1 of 2 possible points in Trait 1, 0 points in Trait 2, and 1 point in trait 3, for a total of 2 out of the 4 maximum points.

Trait 1: Creation of Arguments and Use of Evidence

This somewhat brief response offers an argument that demonstrates an understanding of how the enduring issue of equality for all men is presented in both of the excerpts: *[Kennedy's] idea directly reflects the beliefs held by the Founding Fathers, as evidenced in the statement "all men are created equal" found in the declaration of independence.*

The writer also provides some evidence from both excerpts; for example, in the third paragraph: *He argues that the issue of equality is a moral one that goes all the way back to the Constitution. Actually, it goes back to the declaration of independence, which came first and says "all men are created equal."* However, the writer also interjects a personal aside about his or her grandmother that is unrelated to the excerpts.

Though this brief sample response is connected to the prompt and the excerpts, it does not offer much information beyond what is presented in the excerpts about the enduring issue of equality or the Civil Rights movement in the 1960s, so it earns only one point in this trait.

Trait 2: Development of Ideas and Organizational Structure

This response does not earn a point in Trait 2. Although it does demonstrate an understanding of the task, the sequence of ideas is unclear and only limited ideas are developed. For example, the writer begins the second paragraph with: *For a number or reasons at the time of the signing of the declaration of independence "all men" did not include slaves and women.* But he or she does elaborate upon those reasons other than at the closing of the essay: *even though* [the Founding Fathers] *couldn't really do it themselves at the time.*

Trait 3: Clarity and Command of Standard English Conventions

This response earns one point on Trait 3. In general, the response contains minimal mechanical errors (though, glaringly, the writer does not capitalize *Declaration of Independence* throughout); however, these errors do not impede readers' understanding. The response contains appropriate language for expressing its ideas and thoughtfully composed sentences that generally avoid wordiness and awkwardness.

Sample Score 0 Essay

The foundling fathers beleived that all man were created equal and we all have rights. I beleive this too and so does JFK.

JFK said we are committed to a worldwide struggle to promote and protect the rights of all who wish to be free. Laws needed to be passed JFK he passed them and the world is better today.

Difficulties over segregation and discrimination exist in every city, in every State of the Union, producing in many cities a rising tide of discontent that threatens the public safety. Nor is this a partisan issue. In a time of domestic crisis men of good will and generosity should be able to unite regardless of party or politics. This is not even a legal or legislative issue alone.

About this essay:

This essay earns a score of 0 in each of the three traits.

Trait 1: Creation of Arguments and Use of Evidence

This sample response earns a score of 0 in Trait 1. It is extremely brief, is composed mostly of direct quotations or paraphrases from the excerpts, and attempts an argument that is barely connected to the ideas in the excerpts: *The foundling fathers beleived that all man were created equal and we all have rights. I beleive this too and so does JFK.* Therefore, it is not sufficiently connected to the prompt.

Trait 2: Development of Ideas and Organizational Structure

This sample response earns a score of 0 in Trait 2. The organizational structure is scattered, and the progression of the one idea (Kennedy recognized the need to pass laws for equality) is barely discernible.

Trait 3: Clarity and Command of Standard English Conventions

This sample response earns a score of 0 in Trait 2. The bulk of the response is composed of text lifted directly from the excerpts, with the exceptions of the first paragraph and *Laws needed to be passed JFK he passed them and the world is better today.* This lack of original writing by the writer demonstrates an insufficient level of mastery of conventions and usage. In addition, the original writing does not employ the proper punctuation to mark quotations from the excerpts and contains numerous errors in sentence construction.

APPENDIX: MATHEMATICAL REASONING FORMULAS SHEET ▶

The following are the formulas you will be supplied with on the GED® Mathematical Reasoning Test.

Area

Parallelogram: $A = bh$

Trapezoid: $A = \frac{1}{2}h(b_1 + b_2)$

Surface Area and Volume

Rectangular/right prism:	$SA = ph + 2B$	$V = Bh$
Cylinder:	$SA = 2\pi rh + 2\pi r^2$	$V = \pi r^2 h$
Pyramid:	$SA = \frac{1}{2}ps + B$	$V = \frac{1}{3}Bh$
Cone:	$SA = \pi rs + \pi r^2$	$V = \frac{1}{3}\pi r^2 h$
Sphere:	$SA = 4\pi r^2$	$V = \frac{4}{3}\pi r^3$

(p = perimeter of base B; $\pi \approx 3.14$)

Algebra

Slope of a line: $m = \dfrac{y_2 - y_1}{x_2 - x_1}$

Slope-intercept form of the equation of a line: $y = mx + b$

Point-slope form of the equation of a line: $y - y_1 = m(x - x_1)$

Standard form of a quadratic equation: $y = ax^2 + bx + c$

Quadratic formula: $x = \dfrac{-b \pm \sqrt{b^2 - 4ac}}{2a}$

Pythagorean theorem: $a^2 + b^2 = c^2$

Simple interest: $I = prt$

(I = interest, p = principal, r = rate, t = time)

Using the codes below, you'll be able to log in and access additional online practice materials!

Your free online practice access codes are:
FVEIH6EDMLEEW1604L54
FVEWGS11RG7X07D62VCO
FVEHV24WLBSRO1W3GQP4
FVEWX5D44IJEN28L1R11

Follow these simple steps to redeem your codes:

- Go to **www.learningexpresshub.com/affiliate** and have your access codes handy.

If you're a new user:
- Click the **New user? Register here** button and complete the registration form to create your account and access your products.
- Be sure to enter your unique access codes only once. If you have multiple access codes, you can enter them all—just use a comma to separate each code.
- The next time you visit, simply click the **Returning user? Sign in** button and enter your username and password.
- Do not re-enter previously redeemed access codes. Any products you previously accessed are saved in the **My Account** section on the site. Entering a previously redeemed access code will result in an error message.

If you're a returning user:
- Click the **Returning user? Sign in** button, enter your username and password, and click **Sign In**.
- You will automatically be brought to the **My Account** page to access your products.
- Do not re-enter previously redeemed access codes. Any products you previously accessed are saved in the **My Account** section on the site. Entering a previously redeemed access code will result in an error message.

If you're a returning user with new access codes:
- Click the **Returning user? Sign in** button, enter your username, password, and new access codes, and click **Sign In**.
- If you have multiple access codes, you can enter them all—just use a comma to separate each code.
- Do not re-enter previously redeemed access codes. Any products you previously accessed are saved in the **My Account** section on the site. Entering a previously redeemed access code will result in an error message.

If you have any questions, please contact LearningExpress Customer Support at LXHub@LearningExpressHub.com. All inquiries will be responded to within a 24-hour period during our normal business hours: 9:00 A.M.–5:00 P.M. Eastern Time. Thank you!

NOTES

NOTES

NOTES

NOTES